Dead Wrong

Dead Wrong

A Death Row Lawyer Speaks Out
Against Capital Punishment

Michael A. Mello

With a Foreword
by David Von Drehle

THE UNIVERSITY OF WISCONSIN PRESS

The University of Wisconsin Press
2537 Daniels Street
Madison, Wisconsin 53718

3 Henrietta Street
London, WC2E 8LU, England

Printed in the United States of America

Library of Congress Cataloging-in-Publication Data
Mello, Michael.
Dead wrong: a death row lawyer speaks out against capital punishment /
Michael A. Mello.
410 pp.   cm.
Includes bibliographical references and index.
ISBN 0-299-15340-1 (cloth: alk. paper).
1. Capital punishment—United States.   I. Title.
KF9227.C2M383   1997
345.73'0773—dc21   97-6427

For Deanna

Contents

Foreword

I have on my shelf three and a half feet of books about the death penalty in America, and it is the tip of an iceberg. I've read down below the waterline, nowhere near the bottom, but far enough to know that this book is unlike any other. There are books that describe the process, books that attack it, and books that defend it; there are documentary books and analytical books; critiques and indictments and collections of anecdotes. This is the first real report from inside.

Oh yes: there have been memoirs of death row prisoners, and of their jailers and spiritual counselors. My seven years studying the death penalty taught me, however, that the guts of our American death penalty are not to be found in prison. Death row—with its prisoners and wardens and pastors—is a dull, slow hell of waiting and despair. The real death penalty enterprise is a bustling, frantic mill of investigation, litigation, brief drafting, strategy, oral and written argument, a Rube Goldberg contraption kept clanking perpetually by the fuel of caffeinated lawyers and their cousins, the poll-driven politicians. It is a madhouse.

Start by picturing some 20,000 Americans killed every year by homicide. Imagine, next, a few paragraphs of legalese, bartered into being by legislators, by which the thousand shades of evil coloring these cases will be translated into black and white, life or death. Picture prosecutors with their myriad personal views and public pressures, lawyers of varied gifts and dedication and resources, vast ranks of untrained jurors, making their way through arcane laws to choose 300 killers each year for the death house. This is only the beginning.

Now envision each case sifted by state appellate judges, sifted again by federal district judges, federal appeals court judges, and justices of the U.S. Supreme Court. Imagine a system so complicated that nearly half the cases are found to be flawed on appeal. Picture 1,000 people on death row in America in 1980, and 2,000 in 1988, and 3,000 in 1996.

The average case will involve about eight years of litigation after the death sentence. Eight years in the lives of a small constellation of lawyers, judges, clerks, and paralegals. It will cost $2 million, $3 million—who knows? It will last so long that the law will change and change again while it creeps toward its conclusion, which is death for some but not for many: the executioner is busier in America than he has been in 40-some years, but only two or three in every hundred death row prisoners will reach the death chamber this year or next or ever. Consider this state of affairs: The appeals process could be ended tomorrow, and the rate of executions reach the highest in U.S. history, and still America's death rows would grow.

Former Justice Harry Blackmun of the U.S. Supreme Court called it "the machinery of death," and it's a clunker. What else can be said of a system that costs millions per shot and succeeds 2 or 3 percent of the time? Years ago, the death penalty may have been a liberal-vs.-conservative issue. Now the difference is between those who understand it and those who don't. Alex Kozinski, the bright conservative star of the Ninth Circuit Court of Appeals in California, touted for the Supreme Court, wrote an essay not long ago on the sorry burden that capital punishment has become for the justice system. It could have come from the ACLU.

In this machine a James Card can come before the Florida Supreme Court having robbed a store, abducted the clerk, driven eight miles to a secluded spot, and cut her throat, and he can have his death sentence upheld. And Robert Preston can come before the same court having robbed a store, abducted the clerk, driven to a remote spot, and cut her throat, and he can have his sentence overturned. Theodore Robert Bundy, America's quintessential serial killer, can spend nearly 10 years reaching the electric chair, and this is the express track to death. In this machine a James "Doug" McCray can spend 17 years on death row without seeing his case even reach the federal courts. Joseph Spaziano can spend 20 years on death row and have his case argued to courts hither and yon; then, on the eve of execution, a newspaper can come along and demolish the case against him in a couple of weeks of vigorous reporting.

Michael Mello was Spaziano's lawyer. As you will read in these pages, that experience—in which the death penalty mill spluttered for two decades over a case that couldn't stand up to a week or two of fresh-eyed scrutiny—drove him from the madhouse. After nearly 15 years inside the machine, he tossed a wrench into the works and came out screaming as the gears groaned and seized.

Plenty of people who watched this spectacle concluded that Mello is reckless and maybe nuts. I can report, after dozens of hours of interviews, that his problem (if that's what it is) is that he sees the whole thing too clearly.

So now death row inmates have lost one brilliant, tireless, quirky, creative, passionate defender. Most of us are hard-pressed to care much about death row inmates, who are mostly depraved, conniving, hurtful people. We do care, though—and deeply—about our justice system, which is disfigured and mocked by an arbitrary, costly, inefficient, and demoralizing death penalty. In this book, Michael Mello, advocate, becomes Mello the scourge. A witness from inside the machine.

DAVID VON DREHLE

Acknowledgments

This, like most long-term projects, has been a collaborative enterprise. The many students, friends, neighbors, and colleagues from a wide variety of disciplines who have discussed its ideas with me, suggested articles and other resources, commented on earlier versions, shared personal experiences, or allowed me to glimpse their own fears and angers have collaborated with me on this project and have made its development possible, whether they knew it or not. Deanna Peterson, my partners Paul Perkins, Emily Kucer, Nell Joslin Medlin, Dawn Seibert, Lydia Bottome, Martha Colburn, Bob Brannan, Kevin Barber, Dawn Poland, Ian Ridlon, Chris Hamb, Erik FitzPatrick, Leslie Stout, Diane Campbell, Paul Cavanaugh, Sharyn Grobman, Margaret Feinstein, Peter Hecht, James Hanson, and Carmela Miragula have my deep gratitude for providing indispensable research and other assistance when they were students.

I owe a large debt to the students of my capital punishment seminar, whose honest and articulate feelings I have drawn on in these pages and whose work often pushed forward my own: to Laura Gillen (without whom there would be no book and no author), Beth Curnow, Judy Hilts, Eloise Williams, Barbara Thomas, Lisa Eberly, Leann Cushman, and Virginia Fifield, who typed the manuscript in its various incarnations; to the people who read some version of the manuscript and/or commented helpfully on the thoughts expressed in it, including Nell Joslin Medlin, Nancy Skove, Virginia Blackert, Mark Evans, Jane Rocamora, Margaret Vandiver, Chris Vasil, Joseph Spaziano (whose case is discussed throughout), Ruthann Robson, Leslie Silberberg, Karen Schmidt, Mitzi McCrory, Tina Buehler, Ken Driggs, Marc Bressler, Vivian Berger, Karin Sheldon, James Coleman, Sandy D'Alemberte, Karen Gottlieb, David Reiser, Carl Shultz, Eva Ansley, Scharlette Holdman, Richard Jorandby, George Kendall, Jan Elvin, Robert Spangenberg, Tom Seligson, Sidney Stowe, Shabaka Waglini (Joseph Green Brown, whose case is discussed in Chapter 5), Seth Waxman, Lissa Gardner, Leslie Bender, Louis Bilionis, Faith and Larry

Acknowledgments

Spalding, Marie Deans, Donna Duffy, Ron Tabak, Gil Kujovich, Stephen Dycus, Rebecca French, Joseph Giarratano, Barbara Junge, Nancy Levit, Heather McArn, Rick Melberth, Alice Miller, Anthony Paredes, Kimberly J. Cook, Jeffrey Robinson, Richard Rosen, Elliot Scherker, Pamela Stephens, Esther Lardent, Virginia Tomasich, Leigh Dingerson, David Baldus, William Bowers, Judge Paul Michel, Elizabeth Morgan, Bob Trebilcock, Stephanie Willbanks, the passengers and crew of the S.S. *Hanley Hazelden,* the folks at the Beachmere Inn in Ogunquit (Room 24), and the folks at the Four Aces Diner in Lebanon, N.H. ("We serve breakfast till we drop"; "We serve breakfast and lunch, not brunch"; etc.), where sizable chunks of this book were written, mercilessly reality-tested and dissected, purged of unnecessary legalese, and rewritten.

I am also deeply grateful to David Von Drehle, who wrote the Foreword—on extremely short notice and for a manuscript that was still undergoing major revisions until five minutes before I got it into Fed Ex to send to the publisher. David has little patience for polemics but endless patience for a good story well told. He can listen backwards.

This project owes a special debt to Rosalie Robertson and Jane Barry of the University of Wisconsin Press, Professor Ronald Farrell, University of Nevada at Las Vegas, Department of Criminal Justice, and Professor James Acker, State University of New York at Albany, Department of Criminal Justice. The central ideas of this book were first articulated at a 1990 symposium in Albany set up by Jim Acker, and his thoughts and suggestions are reflected in virtually every page of this book. Ronald Farrell wrote a superb review of the manuscript. And Ro brought it all together and kept it fun.

I am especially thankful to *pro bono* paralegals (and criminologists) Michael Radelet and Margaret Vandiver for sharing with me their notes and sometimes painful recollections of our conversations and other events during the final days of Theodore Bundy's life; to Watt Espy for opening up his extraordinary Headland, Alabama, archive documenting the how and who and where and when of executions in America; to Rick Halperin of Dallas (formerly of Alabama) for his indispensable newspaper clipping files on capital punishment; to Margaret Vandiver (again) for turning me on to the gold mine of information in Albany on New York executions; to Victor Streib for documenting executions of children and women; to Michael Radelet (again) for graciously sharing with me his data on Florida's jury override; and to William Geimer and Jonathan Amsterdam for sharing with me the raw interview data behind their superb Florida jury study. George Couture, Marty McClain, Tim Ford, and Jeffrey Robinson generously shared with me the fruits of their archival research into the Thurgood Marshall papers. David Von Drehle and Ray Jenkins provided me with prepublication manuscripts of their superb books on, respectively, Florida's culture of the condemned and a judge who affected it greatly, Robert S. Vance. Several social science boffins, including David Baldus, Bill Bowers, Michael Radelet, Kimberly Cook, Margaret Vandiver, and Rick Melberth, helped make their world comprehensible to my quantitatively challenged self; they saved me from several embarrassing gaffes, and the ones remaining are solely my own. Don West and William Styron taught me more about clinical depression than I ever wanted to know.

In addition to the specific sources and references listed in the endnotes, I owe enormous intellectual (and spiritual) debts to the wisdom of Mark Evan Olive, Scharlette Holdman, Henry Schwartzschild, Anthony Amsterdam, Charles Black, Emily Kucer, Samuel Hazo, Faye Resnick, Susan Cary, Craig Barnard, Rosemary Barkett, Tim O'Brien, Irvin Yalom, Phillip Caputo, Wilfred Owen, Fred Roddell, Robert Cover, Siegfried Sassoon, Harper Lee, Anthony Lewis, Richard Kluger, Robert Musil, Thurgood Marshall, William Brennan, Harry Blackmun, Paul Monette, Molly Ivins, John Leonard, Sylvia Plath, Roger Rosenblatt, Andrew Kopkind, Christopher Hitchins, Jeffrey Rosen, Bella English, Donella Meadows, Larkin Mello, Curtis Wilkie, Katha Pollitt, H. L. Mencken, Harold Bloom, Bernard Knox, Mary Chapin Carpenter, Joan Baez, Nanci Griffith, Brenda Kahn, Christine Lavin, Anne Sexton, Primo Levi, Jean Améry, William Faulkner, Thomas Wolfe, Hunter S. Thompson, Karen Nelson Moore, and David Bruck.

My personal debts begin with my mother, Ida Goldberg Mello (and her circle of strong, smart, supportive, hard-dancing, irreverent women friends like Ellen Brugger, Yat Nai Kchao, Lee Leon, Bonnie Tarrant, Edith Cohen, Marie Tolley, Beryl Esserman, Sylvia Cymes, Gloria Norris, and Estella Swindells); with my aunt Harriet Anne Goldberg, who formed the habits of my heart and who taught me never to forget that I am (present tense) of the working class; and with my father, Everett Mello, who taught me to show no fear. I'm not sure whether Freud was right that no man who is secure in the love of his mother can ever be a failure, but I am certain that Ida Mello has been the emotional center of gravity in my life. Everett Mello, Pashe Goldberg, and Robert Vance taught me more about how things work than they can ever possibly know; I've proven to be fairly uneducable, but not for want of great teachers. My own weave of (sometimes long-distance) friends has never failed to see me through the rough spots: Deanna, Emily, Tina, Pam and Rick, Chris V., Dr. Don, Laura and Cam, and Mary, Lisa E., Mark ("like the fruit"), Diane, Jeff and Donna and Joshua and Michelle, Margaret V., Jane R., Michael and Sally and Matthew (and Bandit), Karen and Elliot, Lissa, Michael and Lisa and Jake.

Acknowledgments

Brennan and Marshall and Marshall and Brennan keep me sane. Larkin is my life; this, like all of my writings, is for him.

A number of years ago I resolved never to do two things for money, and one of them was to make profits from the stories of my clients, many of whom are (or were) also my friends. All royalties from the sale of this book will be donated to charity.

Dead Wrong

1

Deathwatch
A Sort of Introduction

"Whatever does not kill me strengthens me."
Yes, but . . . And how painful it is to dream of happiness. The crushing weight of it all.
Better to say nothing and pay attention to everything else.
—Albert Camus, *Notebooks, 1942–1951*
(apparently quoting Friedrich Nietzsche)

I am incapable of more knowledge.
—Sylvia Plath, "Elm"

Capital punishment is here to stay. Important battles remain, but the war is over. We lost.

For the first 14 years of my professional life as a lawyer, I worked within the legal system to prevent the state from executing some of its citizens. In 1995, I decided that I could no longer in good conscience participate in the legal machinery of death. This book describes the terminus of that 14-year journey; it also sets out why I chose to spend my professional life in the service of society's most hated members, and it attempts to explain why I decided to stop. I'm content that I've spent my time as an attorney leading a life of death, and, if I had it to do over again, there isn't much about my professional life I would change. I'd try not to let my work life consume my personal life, but I tried that during my first time around. I failed then, and I would probably fail again, even if I could rewind the tape of my life back to 1982, the year I graduated from law school.

Since 1983 I have argued that lawyers should represent death row prisoners in postconviction proceedings. I tried to practice what I preached. I represented condemned prisoners; I encouraged attorneys to do the same;[1] I worked for the creation of a Florida public defender office to do postconviction deathwork. When the Florida legislature created such an office in 1985 (the office of the Capital Collateral Representative, or "CCR"), I

3

went to work there. Over the past few years CCR has devolved into a hack public defender office. I didn't see that devolution because I didn't want to see it. But now that I *do* see it, I must write about it, even though criticizing CCR is painful and goes against the grain. "As writers we are guilty of treason in the eyes of history if we do not denounce what deserves to be denounced. The conspiracy of silence is our condemnation in the eyes of those who come after us."[2]

So I walked out on this mess of a legal system.[3] The Supreme Court's deregulation of death has marginalized the role of capital postconviction defense lawyers in today's system of capital punishment. Since the departure of Justices Brennan and Marshall,[4] the Supreme Court is bored with these cases and more bored with the lawyers who bring them. The Court seems to be saying: "We've said capital punishment is constitutional. States have wide latitude in crafting a capital punishment regime. Now *stop bothering us.* Go away and leave us alone."

This political and legal topography is forcing defense lawyers to think about whether we can, in good conscience, continue to participate in a legalistic crap game that is so stacked against our clients. On the one hand, there is today a desperate (albeit difficult to quantify) shortage of competent capital postconviction defense lawyers.[5] Virtually all death row convicts are too poor to hire lawyers on their own.[6] In California as of April 1996, 128 men and 6 women awaiting their first appeals had no lawyers.[7] In Pennsylvania, according to Professor Shelley Stark of the University of Pittsburgh Law School, "There are about 190 people on death row, and almost none are represented after the direct appeal stage."[8]

And things will get worse—much worse. In 1996 Congress gutted habeas corpus[9] and completed the dismantling of the death penalty resource centers in 21 states.[10] In the coming years, the number of executions will depend less on lawyers' efforts than on the demographics of the death rows in the various states: As more and more prisoners' cases clear the federal circuit courts of appeals (which will happen regardless of what we attorneys do), more and more people will be put to death. Such inexorable math is impervious to constitutional challenges raised by postconviction lawyers like me.

Representing death row prisoners in capital postconviction litigation is among the most satisfying jobs a lawyer can have. The work is hard, intellectually gratifying, and important. You honest-to-god make a difference in concrete and identifiable ways. And while doing good you'll have fun. It's a hell of a ride.

But taking that ride has consequences. How should defense lawyers of conscience and honor respond to a capital punishment system that is, by any fair measure, hideously, lawlessly unjust? For a long time, this was for me an easy question: the place for honorable defense attorneys to be was in the thick of the fight in court, representing death row prisoners in postconviction proceedings. Deciding to do deathwork and deciding to keep doing it were easy decisions for me.

Deciding to quit was the hard part. In 1995, a client of mine, "Crazy Joe" Spaziano—co-founder of the Orlando chapter of the Outlaws Motorcycle Brotherhood, 20 years on death row, five death warrants—came very close to being executed for a crime he did not commit; he was saved not by me or by any other attorney or by the courts, but rather by the *Miami Herald*.

Mr. Spaziano's case and, more precisely, the ways in which that case was treated by the courts and CCR, were the final push that led to my personal decision no longer to participate directly in the American system of capital punishment. Over 13 years, a total of 26 judges read my legal arguments concerning Mr. Spaziano's innocence. With rare exceptions, those judges invoked procedural technicalities to avoid even considering the new evidence of innocence. But for the *Miami Herald* and ABC's *World News Tonight,* Mr. Spaziano would have been executed on schedule, at 7:00 A.M. on June 27, 1995. The systemic failure in *Spaziano* was not limited to the courts; my former employer and Florida's death row representation agency, CCR, performed as abysmally as did the judges.

Although I see how naive I was to think it, I didn't really believe, in my bone marrow, that these judges and prosecutors and governors would kill an innocent man like Joe Spaziano. I didn't really believe they would willfully misrepresent the truth about the case or that they would fob off their responsibility on this innocent man's *pro bono* lawyer or that they would manufacture a subterfuge to fire that lawyer and replace him with a lapdog law firm run by a bureaucrat appointed by the governor who signs the death warrants on the agency's clients. I didn't believe these things because I didn't want to.

But now that the justices have rubbed my nose in it, I believe. Of course I've always known how howlingly unjust the capital punishment system is. Still, I didn't think they'd kill an *innocent* man. But they will; they almost did; they may yet; they probably already have.[11] That realization was for me transformative.

Where does a lawyer turn when he gives up on the law and its courts? I took Joe's case to the media, violating Florida's ethics rules.[12] When the governor's general counsel lied to the press, I called him on it—publicly, in the press.[13] In a letter to Governor Chiles, I wrote that in killing this innocent man he was nothing less (and nothing more) than an accomplice to murder.[14] I suppose that all of these actions might fairly be characterized as civil disobedience,[15] although I prefer Andrew McThenia's term "civic resistance," or Robert Cover's "radical reinterpretation" of the law.[16] I was intentionally disobeying an order of the Florida Supreme Court, as well as the positive black-letter requirements of Florida's rules of professional ethics. The last thing I did before my final oral argument in the Florida Supreme Court in *Spaziano* was to arrange for a bail bondsman to be standing by. My client and I both thought it likely that the court would order me to act in a way I knew was unethical. I knew I would refuse. I expected the justices would hold me in civil contempt until I complied. We both would have been in for a very, very long wait. After taking Mr. Spaziano's case to the media, I was fully prepared to go to the Leon County jail for willful defiance of the state's highest court—a court before which I had practiced, respectfully, for more than a decade. The justices are honorable people, but the system of capital punishment impelled them to kill an innocent man. If the system could cause *them* to act so badly, what was the system forcing *me* to do? If those judges were not immune, how could I think I could be immune?

My actions were deliberate and taken with full (albeit quite painful and disorienting) awareness of the risks to my license to practice law and to my freedom. All of this was unnatural in the extreme for me. This is so partly for reasons of professional ethics and partly for reasons of tactical and strategic prudence. I have long followed Millard Farmer's dictum that "if you're trying to smuggle somebody across the border, why would you shine a floodlight on him?" Media attention was the *last* thing you wanted; you wanted to work behind the scenes quietly, leaving no fingerprints. Judges don't like it when the media put *them* on trial; if they think you're the reason for the media spotlight being focused on them, they'll resent it and take it out on your condemned client.

This isn't the way I practiced law, and it isn't the way I've ever wanted to practice law. I don't try my cases in the media. I obey court orders. I play by the rules. I have tremendous respect for movement lawyers like William Kunstler and Michael Tigar who practice "law against order," to use Charles Morgan's phrase,[17] but I'm not one. I've always tried to remain civil toward and respectful of the judges, politicians, and prosecutors who are my opponents. Joe's case was different because he was innocent. I fight hard for all my clients. I didn't think innocence would matter. But it did with an intensity that surprised the hell out of me.

The Armageddonesque approach I took in Joe Spaziano's case does not really fit comfortably under the rubric of "legal advocacy"; by deliberately flouting the legal rules and professional ethical constraints, I was actually acting antithetically to legal advocacy. I have come to think of what I did in Joe's case as "moral advocacy." Moral advocacy is legal advocacy carried out through other means. Looking back on it now, I see that it is a search for truth in ways that legal advocacy is not. At the time I was running on instinct and adrenalin, making it up as I went along.

By the mid-1990s, when it was becoming clear to me that postconviction attorneys were being marginalized to the vanishing point, two nonlawyers showed us another way. Sister Helen Prejean's *Dead Man Walking* and Jesse Jackson's *Legal Lynching* made more people think about capital punishment than has 30 years of collateral litigation and 40 years of academic scholarship by people like me.[18] One organizing theme of this book is that the era of the attorneys and legal academics as the important actors in our system of capital punishment is over. For years now, the lawyers have controlled the conversation about legal homicide, marginalizing other voices. Now we need to reverse this. I mean no disrespect to traditional legal scholars. All I mean is that doctrinal analysis isn't what we need now. What we need are poets and historians and anthropologists and criminologists and sociologists and philosophers. In short, storytellers with experience.

What we need most are storytellers who have spent time—a lot of time—living within the culture of the condemned. Lawyers at their best are storytellers (and some of our best storytellers have been lawyers). The fact that Sister Helen was a nun didn't make it impossible for her to tell stories about what she had seen and heard and smelled in Louisiana. Quite the opposite. Her life with the church gave her the conceptual framework, the syntax, and the grammar to make sense of the living death she had come to know in Angola State Prison.

I have come to know a fair number of people whom various states were trying to kill—and also the families and loved ones who were victims of my clients' crimes (except for the surprising—to my mind at least—number who were factually innocent of the crimes for which they are condemned to die; i.e., they didn't do it, period). The only generalization I can make about the killers I have known is that no generalizations really work. They're a surprisingly random slice of American culture, with the only clear unifying characteristic being that virtually all of them came from backgrounds of extreme poverty and family dysfunction. And they couldn't afford to hire the lawyers who might well have kept them from death row. So they got the best defense no money can buy. They got what they paid for.

Not that that explains away or justifies their hideous crimes. And, as often as not, they are ashamed of their backgrounds and reluctant to let me raise their histories as legal issues, even when raising such claims would get them off death row. They'd rather die in the electric chair than let their lawyers tell the world about how they were raped by their parents or about how their family lived in a tar-paper shanty and subsisted on dog food.

The fact is that prisoners, on and off death row, are more like us "normal" people than we often want to admit or acknowledge. Sometimes they are too recognizable for our comfort. "Ted" Bundy, for instance, remains our culture's leading metaphor of incomprehensible evil and horror, even half a decade after his execution. If you were to meet Bundy in your local bar, you'd never know he had allegedly confessed to many, many murders. You'd think he was just like you, and for the most part you'd be right. That's the scariest part for many of us: not that he's so different from us, but rather that he's so similar. As we are similar to him.

There is no "us" and "them." We're all part of "us."

This introductory chapter outlines where the book is going, why a Florida focus is appropriate, and how Florida's modern capital statute is situated within the litigation effort to achieve abolition by use of the courts and constitutional law. One narrative theme of the book is the need for lawyers at every stage of the capital postconviction process. The best of these lawyers—Mark Olive, David Bruck, Millard Farmer—turn death into a fighting chance to live. For myself, I'm glad I tried to be one of these lawyers. If I hadn't tried, the cost would have been my soul.

In this book I use the device of storytelling. "Crazy Joe" Spaziano and Theodore Bundy are the twin polarities of my life as a lawyer; that is why their stories are the two most detailed in this book. But Bundy and Spaziano also emblemize the twin polarities of capital punishment today: the hated serial killer and the innocent man; the metaphors for the person whom we most want to execute and the person whom we are most afraid of killing under color of law. Along the temporal cord linking Bundy and Spaziano hang the politics, the events, and the personalities of one long, cold season of legal homicide—a backsliding in the evolving standards of decency that mark the progress of a maturing society. The legal system that let us kill Ted Bundy also let us come perilously close to killing "Crazy Joe" Spaziano.

Ted Bundy makes some capital punishment abolitionists squeamish, and he should. If you think executions are wrong or immoral or indecent or unconstitutional, then you must deal with Bundy. It is too easy to oppose capital punishment for an innocent or sympathetic man. We abolitionists must deal with Bundy precisely *because,* at least on the surface, he is such a hard case for us. We have a duty to listen to the Bundy case.

Conversely, capital punishment supporters must confront the Joe Spaziano case. Given human fallibility, any legal system that allows you to kill the Bundys also creates the risk of executing the Spazianos. Perhaps it is worth the risk of killing the Spazianos to get the Bundys. But only someone hopelessly naive could deny that the risk is there, that it is real, and that limiting the capital appeals process will, as inexorably as the law of averages, increase that risk.

Chapters 2 and 3 describe how I came to deathwork in Florida and what that work is like. Chapter 2 briefly describes my year as "death clerk" to a hanging judge who personally loathed capital punishment. Chapter 3 tries to capture the kaleidoscopic surrealism of my four years as a capital public defender in Florida in the 1980s, when Florida was the 'buckle of the deathbelt.' This chapter (including The Paragraph; trust me, you'll know it when you see it) is chaotic, random and sharp—just like my law practice (which is to say my life) was in those days.

Chapter 4—the Bundy chapter—is my first extended treatment of one of this book's *operandi;* constitutional storytelling. I have more than a little squeamishness about telling the stories of my former clients— particularly those who have been executed. I hope I succeed in not ro- manticizing or sentimentalizing my clients or their crimes. The latter point is crucial to me. Some of my clients have committed crimes of breathtaking horror. They have degraded women and children. They have destroyed lives for no good reason. I know these things, and I try to get my clients to know them too. Thus, while I try hard not to sugarcoat the crimes of my clients, I also try to remain respectful. But my prime goal is to be truthful. To the living we owe respect, to the dead we owe the truth, someone wrote.

In Chapter 4 I use Theodore Bundy's cases as illustrative of the *actual* functioning of the capital postconviction process in a case widely perceived to have received extraordinarily careful judicial scrutiny. In reality, it did not, far from it, and there are lessons to be drawn both from the public misperception and the gritty reality of how the legal and political systems dealt with Theodore Bundy's attempt to prove that his death sentence was unlawful. Substantively, Chapter 4 attempts to debunk two pervasive myths about the case: (1) that Bundy received "super due process,"[19] delib- erate, painstaking, individualized judicial review of the legality of his con- victions and sentences, and that such process identified, and corrected, any serious constitutional defect in Bundy's cases; and (2) that Bundy and his lawyers caused a 10-year "delay" between imposition and execution of sentence by manipulating the legal system, and in particular by failing to initiate collateral litigation in a timely manner.

The remainder of Chapter 4 seeks to understand the disparity between public perception and legal reality in Bundy's cases, and it employs femi- nist theory to suggest that the distance between perception and reality can be bridged, and partially explained, by metaphor: Bundy is seen as having received heightened due process, although he actually received minimal postconviction process of any sort, because he became a symbol—and he became an enduring emblem of evil because his recognizability by the domi- nant culture made him a mirror of the deepest fears of the people of the United States. White race; male gender; comparatively affluent social class; good formal education, including, as the media reports on the case never failed to remind us, a year of law school (during which Bundy did *badly,* but that information made the Bundy-the-law-student factoid less sexy, so it did not get equal air time)—he was of the dominant culture. He was one of us.

9

Chapter 4 suggests that Bundy exists for us on at least two levels. The first is the historical Bundy—a flesh and blood person who did (or did not do) certain actions our law defines as capital murder. This Bundy biography has been told and retold endlessly in the media, and is not the subject of Chapter 4. This chapter attempts to explore the cultural *story* of Theodore Bundy, an intensely collective phenomenon, but only because we identify him (not to say identify *with* him) on a personal level at which many citizens of a certain age and background find the threads of their own stories intertwined with, at times knotted with, his. *Story* is the heart of the matter. The language of culture—and of law—is too narrow and simplistic to open up the mythic aspects of Theodore Bundy's meaning for us, for better or worse. Without forgetting that Bundy was a human being, it is instructive to think of him as the central figure in a great work of public imagination, of which we have all been co-authors; Bundy is the protagonist of his generation's legal novel about capital punishment.

The materials in Chapters 5 and 6 are sort of difficult to describe. At their most descriptive level, they discuss the archeology of capital punishment's impact on judges and lawyers. In these two chapters I attempt to set out why I did deathwork for 14 years and why matters of conscience required that I quit.

Chapter 6 of this book tells the story of Joseph Robert ("Crazy Joe") Spaziano. Mr. Spaziano has been my client on and off for the past 13 years. (A few years ago, when I applied to become a member of the District of Columbia bar, the bar asked for references from "typical clients" I had represented. Mr. Spaziano wrote me a reference; the bar's letter to Mr. Spaziano requesting the reference hangs on the wall of my office.) I am convinced that Joseph Spaziano is totally innocent and that his jury recommended life imprisonment, rather than death, because they also were worried that he was innocent; we know the latter from a juror affidavit obtained through the postconviction process. Further, and perhaps not coincidentally, in 1984 Joseph Spaziano's case was the vehicle chosen by the U.S. Supreme Court to test the federal constitutionality of certain aspects of the jury override; I helped write the losing portion of his brief addressing the override issue.

The book concludes with an attempt to identify the duties of law-abiding attorneys who practice in a system they know to be evil. Ought the lawyer of conscience to participate in the system—to do his or her bit to ameliorate its harshness, because if they weren't there someone else, and possibly someone worse, would be there in their stead? Ought such a lawyer to play by the legal system's rules, or ought she also to engage in the litigation equivalent of guerrilla warfare, raising every conceivable procedural obstacle to execution, and trying to make executions as costly as possible? Or ought honorable lawyers to conscientiously abstain from participation in the legal machinery of death? These questions are not rhetorical for me. They are deadly real and immediate. My 14 years in the capital punishment free-fire zone have moved me from the first position to the second to the third. For now.

My 1995 decision to become a conscientious objector in the capital punishment wars had been a long time coming. Still, two series of events transformed my increasing angst into an imperative for personal action. The first was the near-execution of "Crazy Joe" Spaziano, my very first client and, as it turned out, also my last. The second was my re-reading of Hannah Arendt's haunting 1964 book *Eichmann in Jerusalem: A Report on the Banality of Evil.* If ever a cultural, political, and legal regime was evil, it was the Third Reich. Yet most of the functionaries in Hitler's killing machine were average Joes, regular folks suddenly given the opportunity to revert to barbarism. An appalling number jumped at the chance. Recent scholarship[20] reinforces the idea that the perpetrators of the Final Solution were, by and large, ordinary men and women, workers, merchants, doctors, attorneys, and so on, who, millions strong, ravaged the ghettos, brutally supervised the death camps, and enthusiastically carried out Hitler's plan to obliterate world Jewry in all its manifestations—its people, of course, but also its culture, its history, and its memory. The inescapable, fundamental truth is that for the Shoah to have occurred, an enormous number of ordinary, law-abiding Germans and sympathizers—including lawyers and judges, some well intentioned—had to become Hitler's willing executioners. (Of course, I am not in any manner equating capital punishment in the United States with the Shoah; any such comparison would be a monstrosity.)

"How much would be the price for your soul?" asks a terrifying old gospel song. Even the most armor-plated death penalty supporters ought to shudder at that lyric when adding up the real costs of capital punishment. I am not at all comfortable with the ideas set out in the final chapters of this book, nor am I convinced that they do not sink under the weight of self-indulgence and self-referentiality, although they may seem at times to be fever charts of anger and sadness. In these chapters, I attempt to explain why I'm "on the side of the criminals," and why I plan to stay there. "For me, the honor in the world is found among the oppressed, not those who hold power," Camus wrote. The final chapters also attempt to explain why, for me, "staying there" means no longer continuing to represent people on death row. The last chapter sets out, inadequately, why I have chosen to abstain from participating in the "legal" system of capital punishment. "You cannot use the master's tools to dismantle the master's house." I read Audre Lorde's words 15 years ago. I should have heeded them sooner.

A few years ago[21] I argued that Theodore Bundy was not so different

11

from the rest of us; he was in many ways an "ordinary" middle-class white man. My point was not to diminish the horror of what Bundy confessed to doing; my point was that many, many white men in contemporary American culture have more in common with Bundy than we might want to admit. The subject of my critique wasn't Ted Bundy. It was the culture that made Bundy possible if not inevitable.

Similarly, my point here is not that capital punishment judges and capital punishment lawyers are ogres. They are the operators in what Justice Blackmun called "the machinery of death,"[22] but they are not monsters. They are your fathers and sisters and uncles and sons. They are the judges for whom you clerk. They are your supervisors on the job. In a few years they may be you.

Like the books by Sister Helen and the Reverend Jackson, this book views capital punishment from the cultural and political world of experience rather than from the realm of abstract moral philosophy disengaged from the messy reality of choosing who among us have lost their moral entitlement to live. Much excellent scholarship has been done by Hugo Bedau, Walter Berns, Ernest Van den Haag, Michael Radelet, William Bowers, Robert Bohm, Margaret Vandiver and others on the philosophical, utilitarian, and empirical arguments for and against capital punishment.[23]

If the death penalty is ultimately to be abolished in this country, it will most likely be abolished not because of these kinds of abstract arguments, but rather because (1) people will come to admit that, no matter how hard the legal system tries, factually innocent people will continue to be sentenced to death and executed, and (2) the practicalities and costs (social as well as fiscal) of implementing the *system* of capital punishment will become prohibitive. Eventually the system will collapse under the weight of its accumulated baggage. Or perhaps capital punishment's stories—its *true* stories, combined with its true poetry and music—will lead to its abolition.

This is a book I never wanted to write, and I am squeamish about the thought that strangers will read it. This book is angry and bitter in places, rife with exhausted sadness. Sadness for our dead. Sadness for those killed by my clients. Sadness for the waste beyond measure. Sadness, most of all, for the manifold ways capital punishment has deformed our law and the people who practice it, and sadness that our criminal justice system and the law itself, so noble in theory, are so shabby and seedy in practice. Because I'm a lawyer, and because this is the aspect of capital punishment I have experienced most intimately, all I can see, at the end of the day, is how the death penalty is eating away at the moral foundations of law with the lethal tenacity of a cancer.

Certain readers will dismiss this as too passionate to be scholarship, or too scholarly to be passionate: too simple, too Southern, too New England, too legalistic, too narrow-ranged, too lightweight, or just too straightforwardly comprehensible to pass muster. Oh, well. I try to write in a language that my mother could read, and in a voice she would recognize as my own.

It seems to me that one's beliefs about capital punishment seldom are explicable in terms of logic. I know of no convincing, much less irrefutable, argument against capital punishment as an instrument of social policy— from ethics, moral philosophy, empirical philosophy, legal doctrine, or jurisprudence. But I also know of no such argument against rape or other forms of torture as an instrument of state policy.[24] Since 1976, for 20 years, for as long as Joe Spaziano has lived on death row for a crime he didn't commit, the Supreme Court has said, again and again, that capital punishment is constitutional. Capital punishment is constitutional: That fact damns the Constitution and diminishes the Court; it does not legitimize the punishment or the Court that validated it.

I do know that for myself the arguments grounded in logic, philosophy, and public policy provide useful tools for discourse and for bringing some conceptual order to the chaotic universe of capital punishment as a legal system and as a cultural and political phenomenon. But at bottom nothing intellectual explains my belief that the American machinery of death is indecent and atavistic and obscene; the source of my abolitionism is in my stomach and in my heart, not in my head. I do have reasons for opposing capital punishment. But the reasons came later, as *post hoc* explanations for my intuition that legal homicide is simply wrong. I knew it when I saw it, and I knew it for certain when I saw it up close and personal.

A few years ago, Amnesty International created a documentary film called *14 Days in May*. The movie traced the two weeks leading up to the Mississippi gassing of a black death row prisoner. Shortly after the killing, the prison officials held a press conference. The bureaucrats provided the banal details of the execution. Then the reporters wanted to hear from the man's lawyer, who happened to be Clive Stafford-Smith, one of the most brilliant and generous capital postconviction attorneys in the nation. Mr. Stafford-Smith began by saying: "Everyone here has been very cool and collected. Where, I'm not cool and collected." He reminded me of Mario Savio's 1964 Sproul Plaza speech. "There is a time," Savio said, "when the operation of the machine becomes so odious, makes you so sick at heart, that you can't take part; and you've got to put your bodies upon the gears and upon the wheels, and upon the levers, upon all the apparatus; and you've got to make it stop. And you've got to indicate to the people who run it, to the people who own it, that unless you're free, the machine will be prevented from working at all." Our bodies won't stop this particular ma-

13

chine. But telling the stories of those lives destroyed by this machine—the stories of the ghosts in the machine—might in time cause the thing to slow, seize, and stop.

Table Talk at the Restaurant of the Absurd: Capital Punishment as a Legal System, Where the Mad Are Cured so They Can Be Driven Mad Again

> Some days you do have to rob the dead.
> —Susan Montez, "Eking Out a Living in the
> Third Poorest County in Virginia"

First the numbers. Camus warned against engaging in the "algebra of blood." Every condemned person is an individual, each prisoner's legal case reflects that individualization at the core, and, as all college students learn, statistics apply to populations, not people. Still, more people live under sentence of death today than at any other time in the nation's history: 3,009 people (virtually all men)[25] on death row in 38 states and federal custody (in 1994 Kansas became the first state since 1982 to reenact a death penalty statute; in 1995 New York became the second, and Massachusetts came close to following). The United States also imprisons more people than ever before, and it locks up a higher percentage of its population than any other nation—and that includes Russia, China, and the Third World.[26] Approximately 300 new arrivals reach America's death row in a typical year.

Three hundred sixty-six men and one woman have been put to death by the state (as of February 26, 1997) since 1977 (108 in Texas alone[27]). When Florida's death row inmate Jerry White let out a muffled scream during his electrocution on December 4, 1995, he became the fiftieth person to be executed in the United States that year.[28] Since 1976, when the U.S. Supreme Court allowed states to resume executions after a decade-long moratorium,[29] the most executions in a single year had been 31, in 1993.[30] Meanwhile, clemency has ceased to exist in capital cases; while state governors commuted 10 death sentences in 1991, that number fell to one in 1994, zero in 1995, and two in 1996.[31]

In 1995, there were 56 executions, the most since 1957.[32] The post-conviction demographics of death row—the increasing numbers of condemned prisoners whose cases have reached the federal courts of appeals stage—suggest that these numbers will rise in years to come.[33] The first person executed in 1996 was Walter Correll, a borderline retarded man (IQ: 68) electrocuted on January 5, 1996, in my home commonwealth of Virginia; between 1984 and 1996, 30 individuals with mental retardation were executed in America.[34] January 1996 was billed as "the month for the strange and the bizarre. There is the firing squad in Utah, a hanging in Delaware, and in Illinois, there is Guinevere Garcia, only the second woman to be executed since 1976."[35] The Utah firing squad and the Delaware gallows were used as scheduled. The woman got clemency.

In 1994 Arkansas executed three men in rapid succession on the same day; Arkansas did it again in January 1997. Describing the 1994 triple execution, the *New York Times* reported laconically:

> Arkansas prison officials argue that the multiple executions were more efficient and produced less strain on prison workers than individual executions. "Nobody wants to get up in the morning and go kill somebody," said Alan Ables, a spokesman for the Corrections Department.
>
> For the previous week, guards had rehearsed the process in 15 steps. The lethal injections began at 7 P.M. and were repeated at about one-hour intervals in a small concrete-block room at the Cummins Unit of the state prison system. The order of the executions was originally scheduled according to prisoner numbers. That plan had to be abandoned when a Federal court temporarily stayed the execution of the man who was supposed to die second. . . .
>
> Mr. Ables, the Corrections Department spokesman, countered [critics]: "It's nice to be criticized for being efficient. The people that are involved in this are very concerned that what they do is proper, done professionally and with decorum. They want this to go well."[36]

In 1994 Nebraska held its first execution in 35 years, since Charles Starkweather died in the same electric chair.

In Joliet, Illinois, 47-year-old child-killer and rapist George Del Vecchio was executed on November 22, 1995, less than three weeks after undergoing an angioplasty in the wake of a heart attack.[37] Robert Brecheen was a model prisoner during his 12 years on Oklahoma's death row. But a few hours before he was scheduled to be killed by lethal injection he attempted suicide by taking an overdose of sedatives. Doctors had to pump his stomach at a local hospital and make sure he was mentally fit. Then prison officials brought him back to the prison. Forty minutes later, the execution squad strapped him to a gurney and executed him.[38]

Some Dallas television viewers got an unexpected dose of ugliness one Wednesday night when, without warning, KTVT-TV aired graphic scenes from a video documentary called *Executions;* the video features 21 actual executions, several of which were shown on the newscast.[39] *Harper's* May 1995 issue reprinted an excerpt from a proposal for a half-hour television show about prisoners on death row, distributed at a convention for television executives in Las Vegas. According to the proposal, each episode of "Death Row: True Stories" will feature someone "currently on Death Row or executed in the past" and will use "dramatic reenactments, personal interviews and news clips [to] present a fresh, unbiased, informative, and ultimately revealing look from both sides of the bars." The pitch:

WHY WILL AMERICA TUNE IN TO *DEATH ROW: TRUE STORIES*

It's timely!
Every day, the death penalty is a topic in newspapers, magazines, TV talk shows, novels, and movies. Witness best-selling novelist John Grisham's latest novel, *The Chamber* —about death row. Or Sharon Stone's next movie, *Last Dance* —about a woman on death row.
It's provocative!
Do you know anyone who doesn't have an opinion on the death penalty? No matter which side they're on, it's something people are passionate about.
It looks great!
Every episode will be made with the care and quality demonstrated in our pilot, "Special Edition: Women on Death Row."
Martin Milner's a *great host!*
Audiences remember Milner fondly from *Adam 12* and *Route 66.*
It's focused!
From the name of the show alone, audiences know just what they're going to get.
It's life or death!
Unlike those cop shows that deal with all kinds of cases, our shows are linked by the ultimate penalty for a crime—death![40]

And: More than a few citizens wish executions to be more interactive experiences. When word got out in Utah in early 1996 that the state was preparing to execute child-killer John Albert Taylor by firing squad, the telephone of the prison spokesman started to ring off the hook with a flood of volunteer sharpshooters. "For two days, all I did was answer the phone. Finally, I had a form letter printed up. We are not taking volunteers." The Utah prison officials thus could focus on more prosaic matters, such as commissioning carpenters to start customizing a firing squad execution chair for the nineties: "Blood-borne pathogens are a big issue now," Utah's prison spokesman said. "There will be a pan underneath the chair to catch the blood." AIDS, and all that.[41]

In July 1995, a Philadelphia newspaper ran a public service announcement on page 6, section 5, nestled near the bottom of the paper like a chicken dinner announcement. It began: "The State Department of Corrections is seeking applications from Pennsylvanians who want to serve as witnesses to executions."[42] The ad invited respondents to specify whether they are interested in witnessing any particular executions.

We have a president who, when he was governor of Arkansas and in the midst of his presidential campaign, denied clemency to Ricky Ray Rector, a man who was lobotomized as a result of a self-inflicted bullet wound. (Rector was destroyed on January 24, 1992, the same weekend Bill and Hillary Clinton appeared on *60 Minutes* to stave off rumors that Bill had had an affair with one Gennifer Flowers, prompting one commentator to conclude that "the element of low calculation in the Rector decision is so evident and so naked that it makes one gasp.")[43] Not everyone, of course.

One *county* in Texas (Harris County, which includes Houston, the nation's fourth-largest city) has sent more convicts to their death than any *state* (except Texas of course); as of February 26, 1997, Harris County, Texas, had executed 40 people, as opposed to 39 in Virginia, 38 in Florida, 24 in Missouri, 23 in Louisiana, 22 in Georgia, 15 in Arkansas, 14 in Alabama, 11 in South Carolina and 8 in Delaware. More than 10 percent of all inmates executed since executions resumed in 1977 have come from Harris County, Texas. The county had 21 death penalty trials in 1992, 18 in 1993, and 25 in 1994, making it "the country's busiest capital murder trial jurisdiction per capita," and causing the administrative judge for the county's criminal courts to observe that they were "probably trying more capital cases this week in Harris County than 36 of the other *states* will try in a year." (The administrative judge compiled figures showing that each Texas capital trial costs Harris County an average of $2 million from arrest to execution.) The popular chief prosecutor for Harris County, who has sole discretion over whether to seek the death penalty in any capital case, "take[s] no great pride in the fact that we are No. 1 in death penalty cases. I don't like being called a killer. But I have a job to do."[44] On January 4, 1995, Texas executed Jesse Dewane Jacobs for the 1986 killing of a grocer that prosecutors first attributed to him but later—after he had been convicted and sentenced to die—ascribed to his sister; the execution of Jacobs, despite the prosecutor's changed account as to who fired the gunshot that had killed the victim, drew an unusual rebuke from the Vatican, which called it "monstrous" and attacked the U.S. Supreme Court for letting it proceed. Twenty-six days later, in Texas' first multiple execution in 44 years, two condemned men—Clifton Russell, followed by Willie Williams—were put to death 88 minutes apart. Texas also executed a former lawyer convicted of killing two prosecutors in a courthouse rampage. There is a 1 in 13 chance that an execution performed at a U.S. prison will not succeed on the first try.

According to rankings by Morgan Quitno Press, a publisher of state and city statistical reference books, these were the 10 most dangerous states as of March 1995, in descending order of dangerousness: Louisiana, Maryland, Nevada, Florida, Illinois, Texas, Arizona, California, New

Mexico, South Carolina. Louisiana remained number 1 for 1994 and 1995, notwithstanding an active death penalty; Maryland remained at number 2 for 1994 and 1995, notwithstanding a virtual moratorium on executions; Florida moved from fifth to fourth from 1994 to 1995, notwithstanding an active death penalty; Texas moved from number 3 in 1994 to number 6 in 1995. Miami and Houston have two of the highest homicide rates in the nation.

Texas is where Dr. James Grigson, "Dr. Death," made his rounds in a gleaming white Cadillac, sporting a golden cigarette holder. The legendary circuit-riding forensic psychiatrist, as of a few years ago, had testified against 124 murderers, and, acting on his advice, juries have sentenced 115 of them to death (including Randall Dale Adams of the *Thin Blue Line* case. Grigson had predicted that Adams would "kill again," and he *still* believes the now-absolved Adams was guilty and "will kill again.") In April 1995, the Texas state senate approved by unanimous voice vote legislation that would combine the direct appeal and the state postconviction stages into one proceeding in which death row prisoners would be required to raise simultaneously all issues they want to address, rather than allowing them to raise different categories of issues in different categories of postconviction proceedings; the bill would also put time limits and other restrictions on appeals by death row inmates. (Had these timelines been in place at the time of Randall Dale Adams' case, he would have been dead years before the proof of his innocence came to light.)

In September 1995, Texas began holding executions in the evenings; previously, they had been held between midnight and daybreak. A Texas Department of Criminal Justice official was quoted as explaining: "It'll be a matter of prime time. We'll have a live-at-five type of thing. . . . We've also got a parking problem to deal with."[45] For generations, executions in Texas have been held after midnight to avoid disturbances among inmates and the public.

The operational mechanics of the death penalty as a system forces some fairly grotesque issues to the center stage of constitutional adjudication; this is not the way legislators who enacted the current death penalty statutes planned it, but it is the inevitable product of a legal *system* designed to cull out and then kill those who deserve to die. There was the Texas judge who accompanied his signature with a smiling "happy face" when setting execution dates.[46]

Or take the case of Mitchell Rupe:

> Rupe, 39, who was convicted of murdering two women during a bank robbery in 1981, claims the state cannot force him to face the gallows because at 409 pounds he is too heavy. Under the force of his own weight he

18

would risk decapitation—deemed a cruel and unusual punishment in the last century and therefore illegal under the Eighth Amendment.

His case, heard by a federal judge last month, has divided the state of Washington over how to handle the death penalty. Prisoners who are sentenced to death there get to choose between hanging and lethal injection. But if they cannot decide which way to go, they automatically will hang.

Since Rupe would not choose, he is among those facing the hangman's noose.

But his lawyer claims that if he is beheaded in the process, the state will violate the Eighth Amendment. "This case focuses in a very grisly and graphic way what capital punishment is all about," said Todd Maybrown, Rupe's attorney.

"To some degree we are in completely new territory here. It is a case where they are intending to hang someone, but medical evidence suggests it's going to be a beheading. It's one of a kind."[47]

In September 1994 a federal district court judge concluded that hanging Rupe would offend "basic human dignity" and go against "public perceptions of standards of decency."

Equally important, the cultural *idea* of the death penalty is ascendant in the United States, particularly in the nine states of the old Confederacy that make up the Death Belt and that have accounted for 90 percent of the nation's executions since 1976: Texas, Florida, Louisiana, Georgia, Virginia, Alabama, Mississippi, North Carolina, and South Carolina.

We live in punitive times; perhaps it does not exaggerate to label this a golden age of postmodern punitiveness. One might ask, along with Joe Hallinan, "who do you want sitting next to you or your family on public transportation: somebody that we just unchained from a wall? Or do you want somebody who we have tried to provide an opportunity for them to make changes while they're in prison?" Few people *do* ask these questions, and the answer would no longer matter to those who make public policy. The answer now seems to be: "We just don't *ever* want to unchain them. Ever." Alabama, in 1995, brought back the chain gang, immortalized in movies like *Cool Hand Luke:* convicts, shackled together by leg irons, laboring by the roadside. Finally, after six weeks of practice runs inside the prison grounds, 320 men, shackled at the ankle in three-pound leg irons (the warden advises prisoners to wear two pairs of socks) and bound together by eight-foot lengths of chain, took to the fields with swing blades, shovels, and plastic garbage bags. More than 60 percent of them are black, reflecting Alabama's prison population. (When the warden extended the chain gang idea to women prisoners, Alabama's governor fired him.)

In May 1995, Florida, not to be outdone, signed on. The Florida Senate and House overwhelmingly passed a bill saying: "The Department of Corrections shall implement a plan by Dec. 1, 1995, to require selected inmates to perform labor wearing leg irons in chain gang work groups."[48] But before Florida's chain gangs were in place, Alabama again upped the ante. On July 29, 1995, the *New York Times* reported that the once-common sight of felons in chains breaking rocks under a searing sun was about to be a reality again. The commissioner of state prisons was preparing to "have rocks trucked to at least three state penitentiaries so that chained inmates can break the stones into pea-sized pellets. The only goal of the program is to increase the level of punishment for prisoners, since state highway officials say they have no use for the crushed rock."[49] And in December 1995, Arizona began shackling its 109 condemned prisoners (hand and foot) and marching them out to a prison garden, where they will be forced to work 40 hours a week.[50] In spring 1997 Wisconsin joined the number of states instituting chain gangs.

Our complex crime problem has inspired some creative solutions. One fellow, for instance, created an organization called Dead Serious, Inc., a club offering $5,000 to any member who kills someone committing a crime against a family member, home, business, or other personal property. The group's founder, a Fort Worth, Texas, resident, combs local newspapers and watches television news for names of crime victims throughout the Metroplex to contact with his message. He distributes leaflets for the organization in high-crime neighborhoods, urging people to take back their streets. The organization claims as many as 800 members in Texas and 12 other states who pay $10 annually to join the group. I wrote to Dead Serious, Inc., asking for materials. They mailed me a flier:

DEAD SERIOUS, INC.

We are tired of being afraid

We are tired of seeing our streets controlled by gangs

We are tired of supporting criminals in prison at a higher standard of living than 15% of our law abiding population

We are tired of a legal system that treats murderers and rapists with more consideration and dignity than their victims

So we are doing something about it.

We are Dead Serious Inc., an organization intent on taking back our streets, school yards, and neighborhoods. Through our program of giving $5000.00 to any dead serious member forced to kill a criminal (in accordance with Texas penal code chapter 9), we are serving notice that we are through being afraid.

We are fighting back and we will win. Deadly force is a serious matter, traumatic to all involved. The money offered by dead serious is *not* a bounty. It is given to help ease the way back to normal living.

One thing is however obvious, deadly force is the only thing today's criminals understand and fear. *Fear is the best crime deterrent there is.* We must make criminals afraid to come to our homes, our businesses. They must be made afraid to approach us in parking lots. They must be made fearful of doing all the things that used to make us afraid.

We must also remember, if you only wound someone that same criminal could *sue you,* come back and *kill you,* or commit other crimes which, when he is caught, would cost tax payers to prosecute. As a result, wounding someone does not qualify for the $5000.00 cash payment.

Law enforcement is doing all it can but with their hands tied by the "bleeding hearts" they just can't keep up.

Come join us. Be a part of the solution.

David Bruck has argued eloquently that the decisive moment of the 1988 presidential election was a reporter's question to Michael Dukakis about capital punishment, an issue that has almost nothing to do with being president, but that President Bush had managed to put at the center of the campaign. The assault was continued by Bush's son Jeb, a candidate for governor of Florida. Jeb Bush criticized the incumbent, Governor Lawton Chiles (who, in his three and one-half years in office, presided over 10 executions), for not enforcing the death penalty aggressively enough. One writer called Jeb Bush's charge "an early start on what has become a grisly rite of fall: the executioner's song as a central theme in political campaigns. The death penalty once again is emerging as a critical, even dominant, issue in several high-profile campaigns, particularly gubernatorial elections in some of the largest states." Capital punishment became an "issue" (once again) in gubernatorial elections in Florida, Texas, New York, Massachusetts, and California.[51] In the 1990 Texas Democratic primary, two gubernatorial candidates, former Governor Mark White and former Attorney General Jim Maddox, bragged in their respective campaign ads about how many criminals they had executed. (White's campaign ad: "These hardened criminals will never again murder, rape, or deal drugs. As governor, I made sure they received the ultimate punishment—death. And Texas is a safer place for it." Maddox's campaign ad: "Mark White carried out the death penalty one time. I carried it out 32 times.")

In Congress, pressure for more executions carried out more quickly is now bursting the seams of the system of federal habeas corpus. Although even the states most committed to capital punishment execute only a handful of prisoners annually, political consultants say that support for the death penalty has become virtually a threshold question for voters assessing candidates' attitudes toward crime. "Voters understand the death penalty isn't the end-all or be-all, but it says to them: 'We know where a candidate stands, whose side he is on,' " said one media consultant. "Are you on the side of the victims or, for lack of a better way of putting it: 'Are you an ACLU liberal on the side of the criminals?' "

Few politicians and fewer lawyers who want to be nominated for judge-ships by Clinton or to be confirmed by this Senate can afford to be "on the side of the criminals" in this black and white landscape. For a political candidate, opposing the death penalty during an election campaign can become painfully unattractive: Just ask New York gubernatorial candidate Mario Cuomo, who said in 1982, during his first campaign for governor, "I don't want to fool you: If the electric chair is what you want more than anything else, vote for someone else." His simple "no" on this issue that is so crucial to a society's moral self-definition was the height of eloquence, but in the 1994 election cycle he muted his longstanding, steadfast, and principled abolitionist position by reaching for the easy way out, urging a nonbinding referendum on executions (he lost anyway). Or ask Vermont U.S. senatorial candidate Jan Backus, who did not back off,[52] but who nonetheless won the endorsement of primary voters, 58–42 percent, de-spite having been outspent 10-to-1 by an opponent with national promi-nence.[53] During her campaign, Backus emphatically said she would have voted against the federal crime bill because she opposed its death penalty extension, and "I'm advocating an agenda, like it or leave it."[54] With a handful of exceptions, such opposition has disappeared from electoral politics without a trace. Now politicians play "can-you-top-this" with each other, proclaiming how passionately they themselves "believe in" the death penalty or how recent was their opponent's conversion.

The competition can become intense: A Georgia candidate for the House of Representatives said he "favors the death penalty even for small-time drug offenses. 'I'd shoot 'em myself in the public square if they'd let me,' he said, sounding disappointed that they wouldn't."[55] A special ses-sion of the Mississippi legislature convened in the summer of 1994 to, according to the Jackson *Clarion-Ledger,* hear the governor call for "an overhaul [that] would put Mississippi back on the execution map. I would like for the killers, across the country and here at home, to consider Missis-sippi the capital of capital punishment."[56] One state legislator taunted his colleagues to "go home and tell the voters you're really tough on crime. Let's burn 'em and hang 'em and fry 'em."[57]

After six hours of debate, the Mississippi house of representatives re-portedly passed, by a vote of 102 to 16, a statute to ban state inmates from having televisions or radios, forbid them to use body building equipment in prison, and make them wear traditional striped uniforms.[58] " 'We want a prisoner to look like a prisoner, to smell like a prisoner and, who's ever going to do it, to taste like a prisoner,' Rep. Mack McInnis, D-Lucedale, told the House. 'When you see one of these boogers a'loose, you'll say "I didn't know we had zebras in Mississippi." ' "[59] And so on.

The Devil in Those Details

COFFEE MADE HER INSANE
—Headline, St. Paul, Minnesota,
Pioneer Press, July 9, 1895

The devil is in the details, however.[60] Although the central policy issue of whether the state should be in the business of taking the lives of some of its citizens is settled for this moment in the Republic's history, a plethora of ancillary but critically important questions of public policy and decency remain unresolved: Should executions be televised,[61] or, if not, should members of the victim's family have a right to witness the execution?[62] Should the sentencing judge and jury be *required* to witness the execution?[63] Are lethal injections less cruel (and therefore more constitutional?) than old-fashioned electrocutions, hangings, gassings, or firing squads?[64] (Executions by gassing are performed by lowering one pound of sodium cyanide pellets wrapped in cheesecloth into a mixture of sulfuric acid and distilled water. The chemical reaction produces hydrogen cyanide gas, the same gas—known by its trade name, Zyklon B—used by the Nazis at Auschwitz-Birkenau;[65] and, speaking of the mechanics of executions, "the strongest link between blood atonement and mainstream Mormondom exists in the simple fact that to this day the states of Utah and Idaho, unlike the other fourty-eight [*sic*], provide a condemned prisoner the option of dying by firing squad rather than by lethal injection in order that his or her blood might mix with the soil and become that 'smoking incense' that will atone for their sins.")[66] Should we execute juveniles,[67] the mentally retarded,[68] the floridly insane, or the less-than-floridly crazy?[69] If it is inhumane (and therefore unconstitutional?) to execute the presently insane, then may a condemned prisoner who *is* insane be forcibly medicated in order to render him competent enough to be executed "in his lucid interval"?[70] (As a Mississippi prosecutor argued, "We could put him in [the mental hospital], and if found to be competent, come to this court and execute him in his lucid interval. [The law] does not say this court can vacate his death sentence. It only says we can come back and try again.")[71] And apart from the legalities, what are the medical ethics of restoring insane prisoners to sanity so that the "patient" becomes sufficiently mentally competent to be put to death?[72] Does lethal injection degrade the medical profession in a more intimate way than the use of more traditional methods of state killing? And in any event what are the professional ethics of participation in lethal injection[73] by doctors, nurses, medical technicians, and members of the healing professions enjoined by the Hippocratic Oath to "give no deadly medicine" and to "abstain from whatever is deleterious and mischievous,"[74] or, as this injunction is commonly understood, "First, do no harm"?[75] (The prison director of Texas' death row calls it medicine,

23

and a former attorney general observed, "It's not a lot different from putting a dog to sleep.")[76] Should condemned prisoners be permitted to "volunteer" for execution by waiving their appeals, and, if so, should their lawyers fight to enforce their condemned clients' decisions?[77] Now that more than 50 federal offenses are capital, how will the *federal* death penalty be applied in states (such as the District of Columbia,[78] Vermont, and, as of this writing, Massachusetts) that have rejected capital punishment for state crimes? How, if at all, ought international law and norms and customs limit the domestic scope of capital punishment in the United States?[79] Who should decide who deserves to die: judges, juries, or, as in Florida and three other states, a combination? Should states provide postconviction lawyers[80] for condemned prisoners beyond the trial and first appeal, for the sometimes protracted, and often bitterly controversial, "collateral" postconviction litigation[81] that can last for more than a decade? Does a condemned person lose his right to write and publish a book if he kills a cop?[82] After spending a long time on death row—17 years, say—may a condemned prisoner argue that the very delay in his execution was a form of "cruel and unusual punishment"?[83] What about race?[84] As the endnotes attached to these questions will attest, the queries are neither rhetorical nor hypothetical.

I've given these questions some thought, and when invitations came my way, I leaped to produce my own manifestoes. But to my surprise, when I sat down to write (in order to discover, as E. M. Forster once said, what I really think),[85] I found that I agreed with all sides in the debate at once.

This book is a view from the ground. Richard Posner wrote recently that legal scholarship must become "more empirical,"[86] and I think he is right. To borrow Jack Greenberg's term, it explores capital punishment as an administrative and bureaucratic and legal *system* through the experience of lawyers, judges, and juries, combining constitutional analysis and history with storytelling.

Why storytelling? Not, as I said above, to romanticize the condemned. But storytelling does bridge distance. Joan Howarth is right that "the power of storytelling" is to "remove distance between the decisionmaker and the object of her decision."[87] Howarth writes that the "appellate judges who determine that a defendant deserves death are the epitome of distanced, clean, bureaucratic, executioners. This is sentencing by paperwork. The real-life defendant never makes an appearance."[88] The rhetoric of the appellate court "pushes the flesh and blood defendant into the distance in several ways, from the general willingness to transform a death penalty trial into a metaphor for fighting crime, to the failure to include the defendant's story in the opinion, even the choice to hide the actual connection behind rhetorical distance."[89] Appellate court opinions thus are lousy history. If our dead are to be remembered truthfully, *we* must do the remem-

24

bering; it is the only way to counter the judges' war against memory. We must write our own history. "It is difficult / to get the news from poems / yet men die miserably every day / for lack / of what is found there," William Carlos Williams wrote.

In the meantime, the nation has entrusted its legal system with the responsibility of meting out death as a punishment. Robert Cover had this in mind when he wrote that "legal interpretation takes place in a field of pain and death."[90] Politicians and the people who elect them seldom face what capital punishment really means; how it works or doesn't work; and what it says about our society if we insist upon extending rather than abolishing it.

Capital punishment grants the state—an entity currently at an all-time level of public mistrust—the right to take a life; not the right to tax, or draft, or run the health care system, but to take a life. It is more than passing strange that an electorate whose distrust of government seems at times paranoiac, and which more than sometimes borders on the rabid, *does* trust its government to decide who dies. But, curiouser and curiouser, that appears to be the case. Something is amiss when a government that does not adequately deliver the mail delivers death sentences to some of its citizens.

Devil's Advocates, Devil's Justices, and Devil's Justice

As I've said more than once, it's been exceedingly depressing assembling the selections for this new edition, rereading all I've said for so long. It's actually made me physically ill to my stomach. I want to throw up or fart or shit or something physical to void my insides of all this bile that gets spewed up in order to keep my sanity in a world run by people far crazier than I. This task, of rereading and selecting and editing and writing these connecting passages, has taken far longer than it should have. I can't bring myself to the computer each day without depression and physical discomfort. "And here's another one that didn't work."

Larry Kramer, *Reports From the Holocaust*

This being the United States, capital punishment the public policy issue has become capital punishment the legal/constitutional issue. Capital punishment starkly frames the question: *What* is law all about?

The U.S. Supreme Court Justices, whom Max Lerner called those "nine scorpions in a bottle,"[91] have struggled with mapping out the federal constitutional borders of capital punishment for some time now. A few years ago Justice Sandra Day O'Connor, one of the Court's important constitutional cartographers in this area, began a capital opinion with breezy, lawyerly detachment: "This is a case about federalism."[92]

In striking rhetorical contrast, Justice Harry Blackmun's impassioned dissent on February 22, 1994,[93] against the execution of Bruce Edwins

25

Callins in Texas was in large part a revolt against such pronouncements; to him the delicate constitutional balance invoked by O'Connor is a jurists' self-justifying illusion. Blackmun's understanding, articulated shortly before he announced his retirement from the Court, came from two decades of grappling with capital cases as a Supreme Court Justice and followed years of struggling with them as an intermediate appellate court judge.[94] "I feel morally and intellectually obliged simply to concede that the death penalty experiment has failed. . . . The death penalty remains fraught with arbitrariness, discrimination, caprice, and mistake. . . . From this date forward, I no longer shall tinker with the machinery of death."[95] (Former Justice Lewis Powell's reported postjudicial conversion to the abolitionist position is worth a footnote.)[96]

David Von Drehle wickedly described Blackmun's *Callins* dissent as revealing a "Purloined Letter" sort of "secret":

> For years, the American government—lawmakers, executives and courts—has been keeping a secret from the public. Supreme Court Justice Harry Blackmun recently raised the veil. "I feel morally and intellectually obliged simply to concede that the death penalty experiment has failed," he announced.
>
> More than 20 years ago, the U.S. Supreme Court swept away existing death penalty laws and invited the states to begin anew. They were instructed to draft new laws that would consistently and reliably identify only the very worst arch-demons among America's vast criminal population, cull them and kill them. The effort has turned out to be as taxing and fruitless as the medieval exercise of counting angels on the head of a pin. The soul of a villain is very hard to plumb, we have discovered, and the nature of evil impossible to corral.
>
> Hundreds of millions of dollars have been spent. The death penalty, affecting a minuscule slice of the criminal population, has come to consume time and energy beyond belief: Nearly half the working hours of the Florida Supreme Court, for example; a third or more of the resources of the Eleventh Circuit Court of Appeals. The results? Last year, the number of executions climbed steeply, reaching the highest level in 30 years. Yet for every execution, there were roughly six new death sentences. Death rows continue to expand rapidly—the main force containing them is the number of death sentences reversed on appeal. These far outnumber the executions, owing to a permanent confusion as to the standards governing capital punishment. The population of America's condemned is approaching 3,000.
>
> Here is the truth: If the United States suddenly outlawed all death row appeals, and began executing prisoners at the swiftest rate in history—200 per year—death row would keep growing. What should a man on death row fear most: electrocution, gassing or lethal injection?
>
> Try: Old age.
>
> Anyone who wants to take the time to dig can unearth the secret. This

isn't some gentle whim of Blackmun's; it has been bubbling through the legal community for more than a decade.

* * *

Philosophy is not the problem. The problem resides in the essential enterprise—trying to define shades of evil on a consistent basis. Chief Justice William Rehnquist, one of the great conservative jurists of the century, has conceded that the death penalty requires "especially careful review of the fairness of the trial, the accuracy of the fact-finding process and the fairness of the sentencing." When you look at death row in America— nearly 3,000 strong, including men who have been there nearly 20 years— you discover the real reason applying the death penalty has been so problematic. "Especially careful review" has crushed the system. Between the day of his *Callins* dissent and his retirement from the Court two months later, Justice Blackmun dissented from the imposition of capital punishment in every single one of the sixty-plus death cases to reach the Court, usually with a boilerplate reiteration of his *Callins* statement that capital punishment violates the Constitution.[97]

Unlike Justices William Brennan and Thurgood Marshall, who dissented from the death penalty at the outset—and then relentlessly, in each and every capital case to reach the Court—on federal constitutional grounds,[98] Blackmun, as an intermediate federal court of appeals judge and, later, as a Supreme Court Justice, voted to enforce the death penalty; in 1976 he was among the majority voting to uphold the abstract federal constitutionality of capital punishment.[99] With Marshall and Brennan no longer on the Court, Blackmun had more experience with death penalty cases than any other sitting justice. His *Callins* dissent came at the end of 20 years of capital punishment that his votes on the Court helped make possible. The evidence of capital punishment's intrinsic unfairness has not really changed much since 1976. And yet, incremental though his journey has been, Blackmun had been moving toward his *Callins* dissent for some years, and his judicial language about capital punishment had grown progressively more urgent. "Perilously close to simple murder"[100] was how he described the death sentence of Leonel Herrera, who was executed by the State of Texas shortly thereafter. In time his words may resonate even in the ears of those Justices today absorbed with fine-tuning judicial balancing acts.

That capital punishment law has become labyrinthian and complexified is evidence of its intellectual vacuity. There is no logical requirement that the solution to a complex problem itself be complex. Quite the reverse. The philosophical rule known as Ockham's Razor decrees that a simple answer is to be preferred to a complex one if both explain the same phenomenon. The complex Ptolemaic astronomical system (which held that the sun went around the earth) predicted eclipses quite as accurately as the

Copernican system (which holds that the earth goes around the sun). In order to get these correct predictions, however, it needed to add a host of exceptions and qualifications to the basic theory—that is, the theory had to be complex because it was wrong.

I oppose capital punishment as it exists *as a legal system* in the United States today. From my personal experience with that legal system, I am convinced that the death penalty is imposed mostly on the basis of arbitrariness and capriciousness. Capital punishment is a lottery, but it is a rigged lottery, skewed by matters of politics, class, race, geography and, most importantly, the quality and resources of the defense lawyer at trial.

Even apart from my personal experience with capital punishment as a legal system, I would probably oppose the death penalty on visceral grounds. Of course, I readily concede that reasonable minds can disagree about the abstract morality, wisdom, or constitutionality of capital punishment. Valid reasons exist in favor of the death penalty.

It seems to me that there are four legitimate goals for punishment in general, and capital punishment in particular. The first is specific deterrence or incapacitation (we punish *A* to prevent *A* from repeating his crime); execution would surely accomplish that (assuming *A* is in fact guilty), but so would incarceration until the prisoner is too aged to pose a danger to anyone, and a lot more inexpensively. The second goal of punishment is general deterrence (we punish *A* to scare *B, C, D,* etc., out of committing crimes); 40 years of social science has shown that the threat of capital punishment deters no more effectively than does the threat of lengthy imprisonment; indeed, criminologists like William Bowers have suggested that, far from deterring future crime, executions actually have a "brutalizing effect" that *increases* crime levels by cheapening the value of human life. The third goal of punishment is rehabilitation; this has never been a goal the United States has taken seriously enough to fund in any meaningful way, and in any event you can't rehabilitate someone you've executed—and why bother trying to rehabilitate someone you plan to electrocute or gas or hang or shoot or inject in the end anyway? The fourth aim of punishment is retribution: the community's expression of anger and outrage at especially offensive behavior. Capital punishment *does* serve this goal, and, if public opinion data are to be believed, it serves this goal better than does life imprisonment without possibility of parole (a sentencing option in many states). Whether this sense of community expiation, catharsis, and revenge is worth the cost of our system of capital punishment is an open question in my own mind.

Capital punishment does have benefits, some of them important. Killing Theodore Bundy was cathartic for many Americans. Collective expiation is more than gratuitous revenge; when people feel that their sense of righteous outrage is validated in the form of execution, then those people may resist the temptation to engage in self-help vigilante justice, and they may be more likely to trust the law to deal with the bad guys. This is a form of revenge utilitarianism, and its benefits, while unquantifiable, are, I think, real.

Capital punishment has other benefits as well, it seems to me. It gets private, civil, non-criminal-defense lawyers ("uptown lawyers") involved in a criminal justice system *their* typical corporate clients would never encounter (*Bonfire of the Vanities* notwithstanding). Bundy's big-firm *pro bono* lawyers followed a pattern I saw again and again when I was a Florida public defender: hotshot civil litigator takes on *pro bono* capital client out of an inchoate professional sense that "every scumbag needs a lawyer"; then, after being battered about the capital postconviction system for four or five years, after judges and prosecutors treat them like worm slime and don't give "their guy" even a shadow of the due process they're used to getting as a matter of course in their civil cases, "their guy" is electrocuted or gassed or injected, and there's not a goddamn thing they can do about it. It is good for the uptown lawyers to experience the poor person's criminal justice system up close. And systemic problems of race and class that pervade the criminal justice system as a whole are a little harder to ignore when the stakes are life and death for *your* guy.

So capital punishment does have societal benefits. But it also has fiscal and social costs: Innocent people will continue to be convicted and executed; race and poverty will warp any such system in this country; retarded people and crazy people will be sentenced to die and will be executed; courts will become swamped with capital cases, diverting already scarce resources from all other types of cases, particularly civil cases. And study after credible study has confirmed what any lawyer or judge with a lot of capital experience will tell you: Across the whole system, it costs more money—a lot more money—to run a constitutional capital punishment system than it does to run a noncapital system; trials are longer, more complex, and more likely to require expensive expert witnesses; the appellate and postconviction process is seemingly endless, mainly because most judges want to be extra careful not to make fatal errors.

The average cost per execution is $3 million. Reduce those costs and you increase the risk of executing people who are innocent or who otherwise do not deserve to die. According to a study published by the *Stanford Law Review* in 1987, 350 people were mistakenly convicted of potentially capital crimes from 1900 to 1985; since 1978, the researchers' inventory of miscarriages of justice has grown to more than 400. Does the name Joseph Green Brown (Florida) ring a bell? How about Freddie Lee Pitts (ditto) and Wilbert Lee (ditto)? How about Joe Giarratano (Virginia) or Roger Coleman (ditto)? How about Clarence Brantly (Texas, again) or Randall Dale Adams, of *Thin Blue Line* fame (ditto)? Of these innocent people, 139 were sentenced to death, and 23 were actually executed. One may think those risks are worth taking, but one ought to acknowledge that those risks exist.

It's easy to be a nation of blowhards about executions at a distance. Capital punishment as an abstract political belief is one thing; seeing it up close and personal is quite another. The prosecutors of O. J. Simpson didn't even *seek* the death penalty; those prosecutors knew that it's hard to execute someone you know. The prosecutors of Susan Smith learned this lesson late in the day. Public sentiment in favor of Smith's execution ran high soon after the crime occurred, but, by the time of the trial, the community's picture of her had become considerably more ambiguous. Tom Teepen noted that the difference was that people around Union County knew Smith, and while they could not forgive her act, they could realize she was a troubled woman. None of that excused her crime. You can't excuse the inexcusable. But the knowledge did provide a context in which the thoughtful and caring—and that is most of us, after all—could sense a skein of cause and effect, something more explicable than random evil. Easily supported in theory, execution loses its allure up close, where the troubling details of our humanity are more distinct.

Florida: The "Buckle of the Death Belt"

> You do what you do best, not what's best to do.
> —Martin Amis, *Time's Arrow*

This book focuses on Florida more than any other single state. Partly because of Ted Bundy and Paul Hill,[101] Florida is, in public consciousness, virtually synonymous with the death penalty; more importantly, for the purposes of this book's overarching themes, Florida is typical, representative, and just plain interesting. When it comes to capital punishment, Florida is a bellwether state. Wherever the rest of the nation is headed on capital punishment, Florida seems to get there first. Florida was the first of the United States to enact a "modern" capital punishment statute in the wake of *Furman v. Georgia*'s invalidation of all extant capital statutes in 1972.[102] Florida has led the nation in the implementation of the death penalty since then. Florida was the first state to commit a nonconsensual[103] execution in a decade.[104] Florida is third in the number of persons on death row (378 as of March 24, 1997, according to Florida Criminologist Michael Radelet), and until 1986 Florida led in the number of executions since the modern resumption of capital punishment. And, as of February 1997, Florida had executed more people (38) than only two other states, Virginia (39), and Texas (108).[105]

Equally important for the purposes of this book, the demographics of

Florida's condemned population in the mid-1980s made it one of the first states where the lack of postconviction counsel for the condemned became a recognizable crisis of epidemic proportions. Moreover, Florida became a pioneer of sorts by crafting a legislative solution to its counsel crisis through setting up a publicly funded state agency to provide direct representation for the state's condemned. Before that, Florida experimented with the creation of a resource center to provide litigation support for members of the private bar who represented death row inmates *pro bono;*[106] as of August 1995, 20 states had created resource centers[107] (the most recent being the Pennsylvania Capital Case Resource Center, which opened its doors in spring 1994; at that time Pennsylvania had 186 people on death row), although Congress zero-funded the resource centers, effective October 1, 1995. In addition, Florida's jury override system invites unique comparison between how judges and juries understand the same evidence and apply the same sentencing criteria.[108]

The state and federal courts in Florida take capital punishment—and the constitutional conundra raised by capital punishment—seriously; these judges, for the most part, really struggle with these cases. Eleventh Circuit Judge Frank Johnson said in 1990, "We're overwhelmed with death cases."[109] So is the U.S. Supreme Court; I did not really appreciate the massive amount of time the Supreme Court Justices and their staff devote to death penalty cases before I worked through the 567 cartons of raw materials in the Thurgood Marshall papers, made public in 1993.[110]

In part because the state courts treat death cases so seriously, Florida has one of the most fully developed bodies of capital punishment jurisprudence in the nation. Between January 1, 1973, the effective date of Florida's current death penalty statute, and August 31, 1996, 917 death sentences were imposed in Florida; 624 people have been condemned (many condemned prisoners have more than one death sentence, due to either multiple charging counts or multiple sentencing proceedings). By August 1996, the Florida Supreme Court had rendered more than 1,611 capital decisions, usually issuing one or more each week.[111] The U.S. Supreme Court regularly uses Florida cases as vehicles for fine-tuning its constitutional jurisprudence of death; in recent years the high Court usually has granted plenary review to at least one Florida case each term.[112]

Other states look to Florida's capital sentencing system as a model. Three other states, two with large death rows (Alabama and Indiana), also permit judges to impose death sentences notwithstanding a jury recommendation of life imprisonment. Mississippi may soon follow suit. In the August 1994 special legislative session discussed earlier, Mississippi's Governor Kirk Fordice took on issues of crime generally and the death penalty specifically. At the close of the special session, the Jackson *Clarion-Ledger* observed that Governor Fordice was "optimistic that he eventually will get judge-only sentencing in death-penalty cases. The provision died in the Senate Judiciary committee. 'It passed the House and 27 senators signed on to a jury-advised, judge-only sentencing law. So I feel sure it's not over,' Fordice said."[113] Indeed.

And Florida is . . . well . . . *Florida.* For reasons not really clear to me, the Sunshine State generates compelling death row characters who have fascinating stories. Perhaps more telling than the numbers cited above is the raw, visceral enthusiasm with which many Floridians, at least many Florida politicians, embrace capital punishment. When Atlanta capital defense attorney Millard Farmer referred to Florida as the "buckle of the death belt,"[114] he was not talking about statistics. The Bundy execution in January 1989 resembled a tailgate party in its revelry. Margaret Vandiver witnessed the events outside Florida State Prison and described them as "terrible and entirely banal at the same time."[115] The festivities did not begin in the 1980s. Historian Richard Kluger described the scene of a 1952 Florida capital trial:

> [Thurgood] Marshall and Jack Greenberg were greeted by a Saturday night torchlight parade of the KKK upon their arrival in Orlando, to defend a young black originally charged with beating up a white man and raping his wife near the town of Groveland. Marshall stayed at the home of a black resident and Greenberg at a white hotel, out of deference to local custom. Klan members circled Greenberg's hotel with trucks and torches throughout the night. . . . Though Marshall gave one of his finest courtroom performances, the all-white, all-male jury found the defendant guilty and doomed him to the electric chair. Marshall, stunned, came out of the courtroom fighting back tears, and promised the convicted man's mother, "Don't worry, darling, we're going to stick by you. We're going to keep on fighting for you." And he did. Twice he appealed the Groveland case to the Supreme Court. Eventually, the Governor, LeRoy Collins, commuted the death sentences.[116]

Tax-paying Floridians appear willing to foot the bill for their death penalty despite economic recession. A 1988 *Miami Herald* study done by David Von Drehle, relying on the most conservative estimates available, calculated that Florida had spent at least $57 million on a capital punishment system that had executed 18 people—an average cost of $3.2 million per execution (this did not include the millions spent by volunteer defense lawyers, described in Chapter 5); this is six *times* more than the average cost of keeping a person in prison until his natural death.[117] Special cases can cost extra. A Florida prosecutor estimated that it cost the state $6 million to execute Theodore Bundy; Bundy's law firm estimated that it spent $1.4 million in the first two years the firm handled Bundy's postconviction case. In late 1992 Florida inaugurated what one journalist described as a "state-of-the-art death row." State officials "ordered a new death row built to accommodate more condemned prisoners and to isolate them from other inmates." The "new $15 million building is solely for those sentenced to death. Death row will have its own medical and dental area, its own basketball courts and its own room for inmates to receive visitors on Sundays."[118] Visiting clients scheduled to be killed in this high-tech theme park can become surreal.

Passionate Witness, Passionate Scholarship:
Our War Against Memory

What we have lost! I try not to remember people. There are too many to remember and I get confused. Confused that all their faces are fading. Confused there are so many of them. I can no longer hold onto all their names. Confused why there should be so many of them. Confused that so many have been allowed to die.
                              —Larry Kramer, *Reports from the Holocaust*

Possess your soul; that you alone can save.
                              —Siegfried Sassoon, "To My Son"

As the foregoing pages suggest, this project is not a piece of traditional legal scholarship. Although there is a lot of law in these pages, the intended audience is far broader than legal scholars or lawyers. In the tradition of Charles Black's work *Capital Punishment: The Inevitability of Caprice and Mistake*, this is a book also for the "laity" (to borrow Black's term).

Lawyers for condemned inmates sometimes take the view that we are litigating for the anthropologists, the sociologists, and the historians, in addition to litigating for the courts. This perspective helps to sustain one's soul when the chances of legal success are small. Even though the person who has entrusted his life to you loses in the courts and the execution occurs, the litigation has still made a record for the future. Taken as a whole, these cases form a historical corpus of information about whom the state is killing and under what circumstances. And that corpus will survive.

And maybe we're litigating for the poets, building a record for them to mine. Poets serve us by putting names on the nameless powers of the dark. To paraphrase the terrifying poet Paul Monette's searing words about the AIDS plague, I would rather have this volume filed under Civil Rights (legal homicide seems to me the ultimate civil rights violation), or Death Studies, or Capital Punishment than Law, "because if these words speak to anyone they are for those mad with loss, to let them know they are not alone."[119] Wilfred Owen wrote in the "Preface" to the poems he wrote in 1917 and 1918, "Above all I am not concerned with poetry. / My subject is War, and the pity of War. / The Poetry is in the pity."[120] Monette called this "Preface" "the best caution I know against beauty and eloquence. [Owen] begs us not to read his anthem for the doomed youth of his generation as a decorous celebration of heroes. Decorum is the contemptible pose of the politicians and preachers, the hypocrite slime whose grinning hatred slicks this dying land like rotten dew." Monette did "not presume on the nightmare of Owen's war—may the boys of Flanders be spared all comparison—and I don't pretend to have written the anthem of my people." God knows, neither do I.

I do, however, hope through this book to bear witness in some way. Writing may be either the record of a deed or a deed, Thoreau wrote (the ominous-looking, black-bordered death warrants signed by the governor and secretary of state, and embossed with the state seal, might be an example of both). Kate Millett: "The French, who have a word for this kind of writing, call it *témoignage,* the literature of the witness; the one who has been there, seen it, knows. It crosses genres, can be autobiography, reportage, even narrative fiction. But its basis is factual, fact passionately lived and put into writing by a moral imperative rooted like a flower amid carnage with an imperishable optimism, a hope that those who hear will care, will even take action." [121]

The feminist historian Barbara Du Bois coined a term that aptly describes this book's intent: "passionate scholarship." By passionate scholarship Du Bois meant scholarship that integrates experience with logic, subjectivity with objectivity, substance with process, passion with responsibility, and the knower with the known. Passionate scholarship *is* real scholarship; here, as elsewhere in our academic community, the task of learning is criticism; our tradition comes to us from the French Enlightenment, and the German tradition of objective science (*Wissenschaft*), and the English tradition of pragmatism and insistence on "hard" (i.e., verifiable) data. It should go without saying that passionate scholarship tries to be fair, particularly in its recognition of and engagement with opposing views and its uses of legal, historical, empirical, and jurisprudential sources (so does good appellate advocacy and traditional legal scholarship, in my view); partly for this reason, and at the consciously assumed risk of putting some readers off, I err on the side of overcitation. (As readers familiar with law review style know, one quickly learns to read straight through the seemingly endless footnotes; most law journal articles are as likely to stir an appetite for law as a visit to the slaughterhouse is to stir an appetite for meat.) [122]

"I talk a lot, but some things I can't say." [123] Many, many people can tell these stories far better than I can. They know more; they've seen more; they're smarter; they're better writers: Scharlette Holdman, Patsy Morris, Marie Deans, Mark Olive, Steve Bright, Millard Farmer, Joe Nursey, Tim Ford, George Kendall. I've been waiting and hoping that one of *them* would do this, but they're too busy representing their condemned clients. If my doomed and flawed and failed writing project inspires any of *them* to write their own stories—even if out of anger or a sense of betrayal or a desire for vengeance—then this thing will have been worthwhile to me.[124]

"What a fine balance between too much fear / and too much forgetting."[125] This project is, partly, about my ongoing attempts to keep promises to—or, perhaps better, contracts with, covenants with—Edward ("Sonny") Kennedy and Ronald ("Frog") Straight, two men, one black and one white, who were former clients of mine, and who were friends, and who were executed for committing heinous crimes. They asked me to keep on telling the true war stories from Florida's machinery of death. "Stories held in common make and remake the world we inhabit," wrote Marina Warner.

Every deathworker has his or her Ronnie Straights and Ed Kennedys. No one involved in fighting the death penalty does so without the constantly insistent, haunting, painful memories of many too many friends who aren't here in body anymore. They, more than anyone or anything else, have provided all the fuel my energy requires.

In recent years the concepts of lawyering as storytelling and client voice as narrative have come into vogue.[126] As a practical matter, lawyers have always seen their work as in part "storytelling,"[127] but only recently has legal scholarship framed lawyering in these terms.[128]

Even when I was writing legal briefs and petitions and stay applications, when the main audiences were the judges and their law clerks, I remained fairly conscious of the fact that our litigation work products were also making a record for future students of state-sanctioned killings. The idea of using litigation as a means of leaving footprints in the historical sand reminds me that the best-known single sentence to come out of America's part in World War II was not from a general's dispatch or a politician's speech. It was three words from the common soldier whose name stood for every soldier: "Kilroy was here." Nobody knows for sure if there was a Kilroy, but it doesn't matter; he was the universal American soldier, and the *here* where he declared himself to have been was any place where Americans fought, or waited to fight. Kilroy's self-commemorating inscription, written on any flat surface available, was his response to an impulse that other GIs satisfied by scratching their initials on foreign monuments, or by having their pictures taken with helmet and rifle in some war zone; he was placing himself in history, recording that once in his life he had been present where great public events were happening.

My war is personal. Judges like Lewis Powell and Ed Carnes—capital prosecutors who are cross-dressing as life-tenured federal judges—would tell you, and would tell my clients, that nothing they did was personal. They would say that they were just doing their jobs; they were just following orders—the orders of the positive law and the doctrine of precedents, *stare decisis* —even though they might *personally* disagree with the "law" it was their sworn duty to uphold and enforce.

No. It's personal as hell. When those black-robed gods judged, men died. Those men were strangers to their judges/executioners, but they were not strangers to me. Their lives mattered. Yes, they were murderers, but they also were human beings with parents and brothers and sisters and children and friends. Some of them were *my* friends. They were flawed human beings, to be sure, just like the rest of us. Powell and Carnes and their fellow travelers would say they *were* different from the people whose killings they ordered: Powell and Carnes never killed anyone. But they *do* kill people, and not just a few. Powell and Carnes would say they never killed *innocent* people. But neither did Joseph Spaziano.[129] And none of the judges were inflamed by the heat of passion or crack cocaine. Powell and Carnes killed in ice cold blood, the coldest in my experience. I've never had a client who premeditated his killing for 20 years. Twenty years—that's how long Joseph Spaziano has lived under sentence of death.[130]

Twenty years is a long time. Twenty years ago I was in high school. And time in prison is different from time in the world. Prison time is slow time. Death row time is the slowest, at least until a death warrant comes. In the world of prison, death row is a separate country. People there share a time reference that is unique, a calendar that disobeys the rule of nature. Imagine knowing the precise day, hour, minute you are scheduled to die. If you get lucky in court, you'll be permitted to live a little while longer, until another date and time is set for you. Joe Spaziano has had five dates set. Five dates; five stays, over a period of 20 years. Twenty years is a long time.

So it's *very* personal. On April 14, 1992, I received a handwritten letter from Edward Kennedy. Ed—that's how he signed his paintings. Mr. Kennedy had been my client. He was a black man. His crime was bad. While serving a sentence for murder, he had escaped from Florida's maximum security prison ("The Rock"), and he had killed two white peace officers, Floyd Cone and Florida Highway Patrol Trooper Robert McDermon, with their own weapons, and he had done it in Union County, only a few miles away from the building that houses Florida's electric chair. His case never had any real constitutional issues to speak of, and he wrote to me a few days before he knew he was to be electrocuted. He was executed on schedule. Mr. Kennedy's letter arrived while he was on Phase II of Deathwatch, which means that he mailed it from the very lip of the grave. This is what he wrote:

Dear Mr. Mello
    I received your letter the other day and it was very nice to hear from you again.

I appreciate your concern very much and I know that you can see what the Federal Courts are doing with my appeal.

I know that you are angry about this but the best way that you can use that anger is to use it in a way that will turn it into a positive force rather than a negative one.

I would like to see you teach your law students what they are doing to me and others like myself, I believe the best thing that you can do is make people aware of just what these Courts are doing, this is the best thing that I believe that you can do to fight this thing.

Take Care
Your Friend
Ed

To try to speak, or write, or to remain silent. "I wanted most of all . . . to tell you—with what words, with what silence?—that you must not believe words like yours can remain unheard," wrote Paul Celan. "With what words, with what silence": The phrase sharply divides in half, with the second element almost, but never entirely, undoing the first. There is all the difference in the world between being silent and being silenced. That is why I do this work.

I Am the Shadow

you write as if you believe in love
—T. Owen, *Fireweed*

I can no longer tolerate being part of this system of injustice that requires me to represent a client in a superficial and ineffective way and to have my name and reputation attached to a miscarriage of justice.
—Charles Ogletree, "Gideon v. Wainwright"

It was T. S. Eliot who wrote, in "The Hollow Men": "Between the idea / and the reality / falls the shadow." I am the shadow. I don't have answers. I'm not even so sure anymore that I'm asking the right questions. What I do know is that I possess a great deal of sadness about the futility I've seen, the wasted lives (including my own professional life, in my more honest moments). Capital punishment is all for nothing. It's all for nothing. So if you are looking for certitude, you won't find it here. Certainly not about capital punishment. Anyway, this isn't a book about "capital punishment." It's certainly not about the law of capital punishment; in my experience, there is surprisingly little law *in* capital punishment, although there are legal doctrines and lawyers who argue them and judges who interpret them. This is a book about people whose lives are affected, in large or small ways, directly or indirectly, by capital punishment as a legal system. Mostly, it turns out, it's about people.

Four things gave me the nerve to write this book as I have, and to write it *now*. The first is the gift of solitude in Vermont, a place of extraordinary physical beauty and nurturing peace. To be able to live, write, and teach here is a gift from the gods.

The second impetus was Justice Blackmun's dissent in *Callins v. Collins,* discussed earlier. (Passionate judging? Hmmmm . . .) One of Justice Blackmun's former law clerks observed that Blackmun "frequently alluded to the conversation with [Justice] Hugo Black, in which Black told him, 'never show the agony.' Probably, every one of [Blackmun's] famous opinions has some statement in it about how hard the issue is or the personal costs involved."[131] The same person commented that the "thing that makes you a good law professor is that you're clever and you can manipulate doctrine. The thing that makes you a good justice is that you're wise. Justice Blackmun is not a flashy, clever person. He is a wise, good person. And goodness and wisdom are not always the sorts of things that people who admire cleverness admire. . . . [It] has something to do with head and heart. There is some feeling among legal scholars that you can't let your heart get into it. The willingness to show his agony shows that he worried about cases, both because they were intellectually and doctrinally difficult, but also because they were personally painful. Other judges recognized this as well and tried to put personal pain away or be less candid about what they were doing."[132]

The third experience was reading Tim O'Brien's stories about the Vietnam War, beginning with *The Things They Carried* and soon the rest of his books. To paraphrase Dylan's remark about Elvis Presley, the first time I read O'Brien was like breaking out of jail. I have never been in the military, much less been at war (had I been of age during Vietnam, I do not think I would have had the courage to dodge the draft and go to jail or to Canada; I am afraid that I would have done what men in my family did: I would have gone to war), but in his stories I felt a shock of recognition that helped me organize what I had been doing for the past 10 years: not why I had been litigating (that I've known all along), but why I had been trying to write about it. "What stories can do, I guess, is make things present." The "war occurred half a lifetime ago, and yet the remembering makes it now. And sometimes the remembering will lead to a story, which makes it forever. That's what stories are for. . . . Stories are for eternity, when memory is erased, when there is nothing to remember except the story." And: "In ordinary conversation I never spoke much about the war, certainly not in detail, and yet since my return I had been thinking about it virtually nonstop through my writing."[133]

Our own deathwork stories are mostly told only within the community; there is much that I cannot tell, and much that I would not tell even if I could, out of respect for the human dignity of our dead, and out of reverence for their stories. I hope that the stories told in this book and elsewhere remain faithful to the texture of those memories. My goal is not to "educate" people about the death penalty or to win converts to the abolitionist cause, and you should not think you understand what life is like in the trenches of this war because you read this book or any other book describing it.

You don't; you can't. It's like trying to describe the color blue or the taste of Cabernet and chocolate. There is a selfish interest at play here, or at least a self-referential one, since "by this act of remembrance, by putting the facts down on paper, I'm hoping to relieve at least some of the pressure on my dreams." I have never seen my writing as therapy; I do not now. But, as O'Brien wrote, "the act of writing had led me through a swirl of memories that might otherwise have ended in paralysis or worse. By telling stories, you objectify your own experience. You separate it from yourself. You pin down certain truths." And, most importantly: "And as a writer now, I wanted to save Linda's life. Not her body—her life."

Since leaving Florida and its culture of the condemned, I find myself drawn more and more to memoirs of war, never of much interest to me previously. Laurie Lee, in his memoirs of the Spanish Civil War, wrote: "There was a fragmented madness about our group, but it seemed to be necessary." And: "We spend most of our days now just watching and waiting; watching each other and waiting for the war to move. It was a festering time, drenched in doubt and suspicion. The Republic was in peril, and one took no risks with its enemies. . . . One hoped, yet doubted, that they had a purpose, but as in most wars they were bungled and malevolent jokes."[134]

I'm not fascinated by war itself, but rather by the Vietnam War and World War I: those examples of *pointless* slaughter. Dalton Trumbo's *Johnny Got His Gun;* Pat Barker's World War I trilogy, for example. The Vietnam memoirs of Philip Caputo, Tim O'Brien, and Tobias Wolff and Michael Herr resonate with me; so do the accounts, and the poetry, of nurses and doctors, like Ronald Glasser's *365 Days.*

"Capital punishment is warfare writ small," Yale professor Robert Burt has written.[135] Well, no. Unless it is writ *very* small. Of course, capital litigation is not a war, and I'm no warrior. We were playing a cultural role game that Walter Truett Anderson, in *Reality Isn't What It Used To Be,* described as "camp": living between quotation marks. The idea of camping is to do something, but do it with an understanding that it is only semireal. If the game works at all well, you get some of the fun of participating in it that people got when they took it more seriously, and you always have extra added advantages, like the ability to change games from time to time and the opportunity to make fun of people who *did* take it seriously. If you are attracted to the glamour of war, for instance, you can participate in a structured war game during which you wear a uniform and carry a weapon that shoots harmless but noisy charges at your enemies. If you always wanted to be a cowboy, you can go off to a dude ranch where you get not only the standard trail rides and barbecues, but—in "working" dude ranches—the opportunity to ride off with the cowboys and herd real cattle. Sort of.

Law as war; war as chess. The masters of our game, people like Millard Farmer and Joe Nursy and Mark Olive, are pros at waiting, at patience. You have to *watch* your opponent and learn what he is going to do before *he* knows what he is going to do, and long before he actually does it. You have to recognize, and be willing to wait for, that one moment in a fight when either you win or you lose. The trickiest part is being patient and waiting for it. And you must be willing to risk everything, not to risk your own life—that would be comparatively easy—but rather the life of some-one else you have come to know. Self-sacrifice is easy; it's sacrificing some-one you love that puts your convictions to the test. On some existential level, therefore, you must not care whether your charge lives or dies on the field. If you fear death, you may move forward when you should move rearward. The hardest thing to do is to do nothing, when your world is exploding with activity and when all other voices are calling upon you to *do* something, to do anything. It's not hard to know where the danger lies if you are looking for it.

The metaphor of war typically sees the law as the battleground, the medium through which the warfare rages and in which the antagonists fight. I have come to believe, however, that the law itself is more than the field of battle; the law is one of the sides, and it is not the side that is winning. Much of the scholarly doctrinal analysis of capital punishment can be seen as describing the warping effect of the death penalty *upon* the law. Capital punishment poisons all it touches, but perhaps its most endur-ing victim is the law itself. The law has lost.

There was a fourth impetus to this book, which I would prefer not to mention but which formed the atmosphere through which I appreciated the first four. Twice in 1994 I came fairly close to dying myself when, late at night, my car hit patches of black ice. Then, in the first three months of 1995, I had cancer surgery and developed pneumonia. So, on four separate occasions over a period of 18 months, I thought I was going to die.

When it came to my condemned clients, I've had some success in cheat-ing death, in tricking it, and then I've patted myself on the back for clever-ness and ingenuity. Yet, until my own body revolted against me, I've never *faced* death. I thought I had, vicariously, through my clients. I was wrong, frighteningly wrong.

My recent adventures in postmodern health care jolted a lot of things into clearer focus. They gave me a fierce desire to live life (I have learned from my condemned clients that proximity to death *does* bring with it a corresponding proximity to life). It also made me determined to write it down, to make whatever record I can of . . . of what? I am not quite sure, yet. I am working on it. Stay tuned, if you want.

Writing in the face of my own (perceived) death sentence meant I was writing on deadline. I learned as a public defender in Florida that daily deadline pressure is the best training for writers, who need to learn the bank robber's rule: "Get in. Get the money. Get out."

But my proximity to my own death has had the effect of vaporizing my tolerance for polite euphemisms and dissemblings about the legal machinery of death and the functionaries whose participation makes it possible for the machine to keep chugging along. In particular it has vaporized my tolerance for those defense lawyers who grease the machinery of death. In this book I simply attempt to tell the truth as I see it, without much bullshit.

I'm painfully aware that my writing ability is not up for the job at hand. For this reason I use the language of others. Part of this has to do with emotional and psychic distancing, which is a nicer-sounding word than simple cowardice. When I read a passage of Hunter Thompson's, say, and his language resonates with my own experiences, even though he is talking about an entirely different subject than my own, co-opting his words allows me to tell my own (or my clients') stories while maintaining enough personal detachment to remain reasonably sane. The distance itself remains fairly short—it may not exist at all, but I can't allow myself to believe that, at least not quite yet—but the distance (or the illusion) is necessary.

Finally, this book is about the failure of the word. I'd hoped and hoped and hoped that my words might make a difference, that anybody who is telling the truth would and could make a difference. I've learned otherwise. I've learned that judges do leave innocent people to die, quite intentionally, in this country of ours. Many different kinds of people. I've learned that "equal justice under the law" does not protect one and all. I have learned that the phrase "death penalty law" is an oxymoron in all but the most aridly positivistic sense. I have learned that democracy and its legalistic superstructure protect only the white man with the money and the power to demand that he be protected. I have learned that everybody else is pretty much left to die.

41

2

Judge Robert S. Vance
The Hanging Judge Who Hated
Capital Punishment

They challenge, warn and witness.
—W. H. Auden,
"New Year Letter (Jan. 1, 1940)"

Hold on to your self
For this is going to hurt like hell
—Sarah McLaughlan, "Hold On"

My father always wanted me to become a doctor and to try to save lives. I
guess I got it half right.

Nanci Griffith has a song: "I am a child of the sixties / where dreams
could be held on TV / with Disney and Cronkite and Martin Luther / and I
believed, I believed, I *believed*." My childhood was filled with funerals. I
was building a plastic model of a Chris-Craft pleasure boat when JFK was
murdered; my babysitter burst into tears, and, later, my father held me
aloft on that cold November day as the cortege wended its way down
Pennsylvania Avenue. When Martin Luther King was shot, Washington
burned; I watched from my neighborhood field in Arlington, Virginia, as
the smoke billowed above the nation's capital, and, later, I watched the
Chinook helicopters take off and land at Haynes Point Golf Course. When
RFK was killed in Los Angeles, my mother woke me up with the words,
"It's happened again"; from the hillside beside my elementary school, we
waited for him to die. But, for some reason, the televised funerals of the
Apollo astronauts Grissom, White, and Chaffee hit me the hardest. I had
nightmares about their funerals for years.

I grew up in northern Virginia, in Fairlington, when it was Fairlington
Apartments (my mother and I had to move when the development "went

condo" and became Fairlington Villages): Fairlington Elementary School; Gunston Junior High School; Wakefield High School, '75, barely. Besides lacking any academic credentials to speak of, my family couldn't afford to "send me" to college; money was tight (except for books; we always managed to find money for books). My mother was a secretary at the Pentagon ("always treat your secretary as you would your mother [or father] because she might well be *somebody's* mother, and there but for the grace of God go you . . . "); my father was a baggage handler for Amtrak (Alexandria Station, in fact); and they could barely make ends meet as it was. But I applied to a few schools, and to our pleasant surprise I got into Mary Washington College. I started at MWC two years after the college went coed, and they were pretty much admitting any male Virginians who applied; given my modest (to put it politely) high school grades and SAT scores, clearly I was part of the school's gender-based affirmative action program.

My real college education came in spending four years at a woman-centered school; we males constituted about 5 percent of the student body, and a good number of the other 95 percent were none too thrilled that we were there—often with good reason. The law degree came from UVA, or The University, or, better, Mr. Jefferson's Academical Village, as it likes to call itself: but please don't hold the ugly fact of my Charlottesville past against me. When I was growing up in Arlington, I *swore* I'd never go to that pretentious relic of white male privilege, a tradition-encrusted university that admitted African Americans only after having the hell sued out of it by the NAACP. Purely pragmatic considerations landed me at UVA. For a resident of the Commonwealth, the tuition was dirt cheap. I thought I wanted to be a civil rights lawyer (I basically think of myself *as* a civil rights lawyer), so racking up student loans of $80,000 (the average debt load of my students at the Vermont Law School) was out of the question. And the area around Charlottesville *is* spectacularly beautiful; the Blue Ridge Parkway and a lot of Wild Turkey kept me sane, for the most part. So I've been lucky enough to be formally well educated.

I can't recall a time when I didn't think capital punishment was wrong. For me it began as a matter of gas. I opposed capital punishment instinctively from the moment in high school when I read that some American states (including the People's Republic of California) still executed by the use of Zyklon B, the same gas, chemically, used at Auschwitz-Birkenau. This was not a rational connection to make, I know (and knew). I find *any* comparison of capital punishment with the Holocaust deeply offensive; the United States isn't Nazi Germany, the people we're killing aren't innocent Jews, and, anyway, most states don't kill by gas.[1] But, still, two of the most powerful documents for abolition are a pair of pamphlets, one published in August 1944 by the Polish Labor Group and entitled "Nazi Justice," and the other published in 1940 by J. Walter Jones and entitled "The Nazi Conception of Law." Perhaps the emotional parallel was an inevitable one, since, according to family lore, portions of my family tree ended in the Warsaw Ghetto and Treblinka. So maybe abolition is imprinted somewhere in my genetic makeup.

My response to capital punishment was visceral. But, as John Leonard argued, "mitigate the circumstances though we might, extenuations of passion or psychosis notwithstanding, when we murder we do not create. When the state murders, it assumes an authority I refuse to cede: the authority of perfect knowledge in final things."[2] When people die because we didn't, at the time, have the facts straight, we participate not in a perplexity but in a murder. And we will never have the facts entirely straight.

The Judge's Rules

> It is better to allow our lives to speak for us than our words.
> —Mohandas Gandhi, *All Men Are Brothers*

> Ce n'est qu'un début,
> Continons le combat.
> —Paris '68 slogan

The play *Inherit the Wind* suggested a pair of potential career paths to me when I was a high school student in Virginia. I was fascinated by the Clarence Darrow and H. L. Mencken characters and fantasized about having the option of pursuing law or journalism. I ultimately decided I wasn't a good enough writer to be a working journalist. So I went to law school.

I came to full-time death penalty work more or less by accident, if one believes in accidents. After graduating from law school in Virginia, I spent a year in Birmingham, Alabama, working as a judicial clerk for Judge Robert Vance of the U.S. Court of Appeals for the Eleventh Circuit, the court that hears all manner of appeals, including capital habeas corpus appeals, from Florida, Georgia, and Alabama. I do not recall whether our use of the term originated with Judge Vance or with me, but in conversation we sometimes referred tongue-in-cheek to the Eleventh Circuit as the "death court." All three states that make up the Eleventh Circuit remain at the leading edge of capital punishment and its resultant constitutional challenges. Judge John Godbold, former Chief Judge of the Eleventh Circuit, wrote that "we are sort of experts on habeas death penalty cases. The Eleventh Circuit, geographically a small circuit of only three states, has approximately as much death penalty litigation as all the other circuits in the country combined. On any one day, our court will have at least 50 pending death cases."[3] I have already set out the importance of Florida in the capital punishment cosmos. Georgia cases provided the principal vehicles for testing the constitutionality of the death penalty, theoretically and as applied systemically: *Furman v. Georgia* in 1972, *Gregg v. Georgia* in 1976, and *McCleskey v. Kemp*[4] in 1987. Alabama got off to a slow start, but is making up for lost time. The "death court" moniker fits, with the qualification that the Eleventh Circuit is now one of a growing number of death courts. As capital punishment becomes a truly national phenomenon, other circuits have become, or will soon become, death courts as well. These circuits are now experiencing what the Eleventh Circuit first encountered in the 1980s.

Eleventh Circuit Judge Frank Johnson told Jack Bass at the end of January 1990, "We're overwhelmed with death penalty cases. I spent eight hours on one that was filed last week. I didn't do anything else all day. My clerks haven't seen it yet. And that's before the briefs are filed. This was a two hundred and something page petition, at least twenty five substantial issues raised."[5] Bass wrote:

> The Judge picked up a court document that had just come in from the circuit executive's office in Atlanta, giving the status of fifty pending death penalty cases. Pointing with his finger as he went down the pages, Johnson explained the report.
>
> "Here's where they start. That's the District Judge they come from. The judges on the panel, their initials. There's three I'm on. That's a stay, pending cert. We've already written that opinion. Cert pending in this case. We've written that one. That one's awaiting rehearing. Here's another one. That's four. That one's on a stay. Here's two more. Appellant's brief due. This one's waiting calendaring. The briefs are already due. We've set it for oral argument for sometime in March. Here's two more I'm on. Briefs due on both of those—means about ready for argument. Here's two more. Appellant's brief got an extension. Reply brief is due. That one's ready. We agreed today to a sitting on that one, oral argument."

Judge Johnson estimated, "I guess I spent four hundred hours of work on the *Bundy* case. That's the most I've ever spent in one case."[6] This last comment is significant, coming from a legendary civil rights judge who, when he was on the district court bench, sat on the Rosa Parks Montgomery Bus Boycott case, the Selma-to-Montgomery march case, the Viola Liuzzo case, and more, a judge who heard some of the most significant civil rights cases and prisoner's rights cases of the 1960s and 1970s.

Early in my clerkship, Judge Vance explained that he followed two rules when he reviewed the federal constitutionality of state-imposed death sentences. The first rule was that Judge Vance personally did not believe in capital punishment; if he were a legislator he would vote against it; if he were an executive he would commute death sentences; and if he were a

Supreme Court Justice, he might well vote to hold it unconstitutional. Robert Vance's *personal* opposition to capital punishment was genuine and heartfelt. The judge's son has written that "my father often made decisions with which he personally disagreed. He did not believe that the death penalty was a proper form of punishment, and he considered death penalty cases to be almost unbearable. During his tenure, however, he affirmed a great number of death penalty convictions because they were found to be the result of proper administration of our justice system, and he knew that it was not his role to change that system to suit his personal preferences."[7] Ironically, as of August 1994, Alabama state prosecutors were planning to try Walter Leroy Moody, Jr., for the capital murder of Judge Vance, even though Moody had been sentenced in federal court to life imprisonment, and even though Judge Vance's widow, Helen Vance, did not want a capital trial for Moody.[8] (In November 1996 a state jury convicted him of capital murder and recommended that he be given the death penalty.)

Vance's second rule was that the first rule did not matter, that he was *not* a legislator, nor was he a governor or Supreme Court Justice. Circuit Judge Vance's range of action and discretion, his legitimate power to do justice as he saw it, was severely constrained by the institutional structure of federalism as well as by his place on an intermediate court of appeals. These two rules coalesced into an underlying rough-justice approach informed by pragmatic intuition, which I believe animated Vance's judging although he never articulated it to me. If states must have the death penalty, then they had best apply it fairly.

During the time when the Supreme Court was deregulating death—accelerating its deference to states in the capital punishment and habeas areas—Judge Vance was in the trenches deciding cases. By my count, his name appears as author of 25 published capital habeas opinions. Judge Vance would have granted interim or permanent relief (such as retrials, resentencings, evidentiary hearings or stays of execution) in 11 cases, slightly less than half, and he would have denied relief in 14 cases. Judge Vance also voted in 81 capital habeas cases in which he did not write opinions, voting to grant some form of relief in 34 cases and to deny it in 47.[9]

A longitudinal evaluation of Vance's capital habeas jurisprudence defies neat categorization because the individual cases are so intensely fact-specific. His judging in capital cases evolved in stages, or at least involved three narrative themes. First, at the beginning of his judicial tenure, Judge Vance was willing to recognize constitutional principles even though such recognition would by implication have had the effect of removing classes (and potentially large numbers) of people from death row. This theme is implicit in the Court's opinion in John Evans' case, and it ended when the Supreme Court reversed that case.[10] Judge Vance was on the *Evans* panel, of which one member dissented. Had the panel's opinion stood, it would by implication have invalidated all convictions and death sentences imposed under Alabama's 1975 capital statute.[11]

The second decisional theme mirrored the first. Following the Supreme Court's resounding reversal of *Evans,* Judge Vance never again voted in favor of constitutional claims that would have had wide-ranging impact on death row. He had at least two opportunities to do so. While I was clerking for him, Judge Vance cast the deciding vote in Alvin Ford's case, and later wrote a brief concurrence in Warren McCleskey's case.[12] *Ford* involved a broad-based challenge to Florida's capital sentencing process, and *McCleskey* presented an attack upon Georgia's death penalty system. The Eleventh Circuit rebuffed both assaults, and the Supreme Court approved.

The third decisional theme was Judge Vance's commitment to maintaining the integrity of the judicial process from before the trial through the conclusion of federal habeas corpus review. His opinion for the *en banc* court in David Leroy Washington's case,[13] which articulated the standards that should govern the Sixth Amendment right to the effective assistance of counsel at trial (in capital and noncapital cases), illustrated Judge Vance's prowess as a judicial pragmatist on matters of consummate practical importance. The delicate doctrinal balance struck in his *Washington* opinion makes more sense than the vacuous constitutional standard subsequently devised by the Supreme Court when it reversed him.[14] Further, though Judge Vance's predisposition (based on his understanding of Supreme Court commands) was to deny habeas relief in all but the clear cases, he remained committed to the process of habeas unless and until Congress amended the habeas statute to the contrary (as it did when it dismantled habeas in 1996). This commitment was illustrated by his insistence that even Theodore Bundy, the nation's most hated death row inmate and the focus of Chapter 4, receive his day in federal habeas court.[15]

To call a judicial approach characterized as rough justice or common sense a jurisprudence may seem oxymoronic. Jurisprudence, the theory of the law at its broadest and most abstract, is usually thought of as an overarching theory. But pragmatism can be the theory in jurisprudence, as it has emerged as the United States' singular contribution to philosophy. Richard Posner defined pragmatism in this way: "It means looking at problems concretely, experimentally, without illusions, with full awareness of the limitations of human reason, with a sense of the 'localness' of human knowledge, the difficulty of translations between cultures, the unattainability of 'truth,' the consequent importance of keeping diverse paths of inquiry open, the dependence of inquiry on cultural and social institutions, and above all the insistence that social thought and action be evaluated as instruments to valued human goals rather than as ends in themselves."[16]

"Common sense," as a method of reasoning and as a foundational basis of a theory of judging, may lack the analytical rigor that keeps law reviews in business and legal academics in tenure. Common sense reasoning is "one of the intellectually weakest methods of analysis. Common sense is dependent on cultural fabric, on social, ethnic, and geographic variations, and on historical traditions."[17] Still, the core of pragmatism/common sense reasoning resonates. The concept of *usefulness* is at least as important as the concept of truth. "Pragmatism" I define fairly narrowly, as the idea that concepts and theories ought to be judged for their practical value as well as for their success or failure in representing the world. Maybe the message of Judge Vance's capital habeas cases is that in this area of the law there can be no grand theories; no unified field theory works. There can only be common sense, rough justice. This is arguably an anti-jurisprudence. But then perhaps anti-jurisprudence is the jurisprudence of the nineties.

Judge Vance was short on unified field theories and long on practicalities and on *action*. One way to view Vance's central jurisprudential identity is through the philosophical method of "phenomenology." This clunky term translates into the relatively simple idea that one can come to understand the truth of something not simply by reference to the authority of science, or ideology, but by "moving around" it, experiencing it from different perspectives and letting the reflections of each perspective communicate the truth of the object. The central metaphor of such philosophy is "walking around," in the world, to remain *of* the world, even from the rarified perch of the federal appellate court.

Applied to the law and to the art of judging, these ideas have their roots in "Aristotle's idea of phronesis or practical wisdom. For Aristotle, the exercise of good judgment required experience and reflection, and it was comprised of qualities of character and experience and methods of deliberation."[18] As Nancy Levit puts it, Aristotle's solution to the conundrum of judicial legitimacy was to "select judges who possessed a constellation of appropriate character traits."[19] But Aristotle's judges were not sitting on intermediate appellate courts, and they were not straitjacketed by formalistic notions of *stare decisis*. Whether Judge Vance intended his actions as a federal judge to mirror the philosophy of pragmatism, or was even aware that they did, is unimportant. The point is that as a person and as a judge he personified the defining elements of pragmatism. It came naturally to him.

Capital habeas corpus is an area of the law imbued with endless controversy and legalese. Still, at bottom each capital habeas case presents concrete problems that mean life or death to the condemned person. These cases require a practical decision reached through a practical process of inquiry. They demand that the forms of doctrine and confusion be stripped away so that a common sense solution can be reached and justice served, albeit roughly. As Posner phrases it, the tools of inquiry generally available to the courts are of such limited power that "the highest realistic aspiration of a judge faced with a difficult case is to make a 'reasonable' (practical, sensible) decision."[20] Capital habeas appeals are among the most difficult cases, and Judge Vance believed his first priority was to reach sensible decisions and to create workable standards for decisionmaking in this conundrum of an area. "Often the judge will have no choice but to reason to the outcome by nonlegal methods from nonlegal materials and sometimes she will have to set inarticulable intuition against legal arguments." In Posner's evaluation of pragmatism he states a truth that I think Judge Vance's capital habeas opinions illustrate quite well: "Law is functional, not expressive or symbolic either in aspiration or—so far as yet appears—in effect."[21]

Judge Vance appreciated that as a federal circuit judge he had a set of ever-shifting parameters within which to work, but he realized as well that the jurisprudential bottom line in distinguishing a good decision from a poor one is its functional and practical implication for the real world. He also appreciated that the personal bottom line was the ability to look at oneself in the bathroom mirror at the end of the day. Or, as Lord Denning explained his reasons for dissent: "I was reluctant to dissent. But in the last resort I did so. It was for my own peace of mind. So long as I did what I thought was just, I was content. I could sleep at night."[22]

At the end of the day, Judge Vance was humble and clear-eyed about both bottom lines. He never got too caught up in the solemn self-importance that permeates the Law and separates it from the real world within which the law (small *l*) lives and with which the law interacts. Again, Posner: "Law . . . has its high priests, its sacred texts and sacred cows, its hermeneutic mysteries, its robes and temples, rituals and ceremonies."[23] Although Judge Vance recognized their existence, he never became lost in participating in their perpetuation. Instead he tried to make a practical connection between the world and this lofty institution we call the judicial system, while at the same time retaining his sense of decency, sense of distance, sense of irony, and sense of humor. (*Always* his sense of humor.) The spirit of rough justice and common sense that embodied Judge Vance's capital habeas jurisprudence cannot be quantified and is difficult even to identify with precision. What does emerge vaguely from his cases is a determination to humanize the law as he understood it. When he was called upon to articulate rules of general application, as in *Washington*,[24] he did so with experience firmly rooted in the real world where such rules would operate.

Ivon Ray Stanley: Why I Am Going to Hell
(An Incomplete Explanation)

> I live, out there, in washing-line and mailbox America, innocuous America, ineffable, melting pot, primary color, you're-okay-I'm-okay *America*. My name, of course, is Tod Friendly. Tod T. Friendly.
>
> —Martin Amis, *Time's Arrow*

As you might suspect, the judge's rough-justice approach to capital cases caused some tension between the judge and myself in these cases. Before clerking for Judge Vance, I had a visceral-liberal-knee-jerk aversion to the death penalty; the truth was, I had never given the issue much thought. I gave it a great deal of thought during my year in Birmingham, and the more I learned about it the less I liked it. Capital cases consumed about half of my clerkship workload, and this experience became the engine that has driven my work in the years since. I knew that when I was working for Judge Vance, I was living the fundamental experience of my life. I was 25 years old.

It soon became clear that my tender sense of fairness was more easily offended than was Judge Vance's; to be more precise, I found at least one (and usually more than one) reason that every death sentence that came before the court was "unfair" and thus, in my naive view, unconstitutional. Sometimes the judge agreed; usually he did not, and we spent long afternoons deconstructing concepts like "fundamental unfairness," as opposed to garden-variety unfairness; error of federal constitutional magnitude, as opposed to garden-variety error that was benignly harmless. The Constitution does not require a perfect trial, the judge told me more than once; it only requires a fundamentally fair one, or at least one not fundamentally *un*fair. For a long time I jokingly (well, mostly jokingly) referred to my role in these cases as the reason I was going to go to hell.

Judge Vance enjoyed a good argument, and we argued a lot; this reached its zenith when I was assigned the task of drafting an opinion affirming the denial of resentencing relief in the case of Ivon Ray Stanley,[25] a retarded African American from rural Georgia who followed along while the mastermind and main mover committed the murder for which both men were sentenced to die in Georgia's electric chair. In his federal habeas corpus case, Stanley's counsel argued that the defense lawyer at trial had been ineffective in failing to investigate evidence in mitigation. This was an uphill battle, because some mitigating evidence did trickle in before the jury. First, there was evidence that Stanley had at least a learning disability; he was a slow learner, and he had been placed in an educable mentally retarded class in school. A state sheriff read into the record the results of a psychological evaluation conducted on the man when he was 14 years old. That evaluation had concluded that (1) the man had an IQ of 62 (counsel had previously informed the jury that "imbecile" was defined as a person with an IQ of 0 to 65); (2) the man's test scores "suggest[ed] a history of culture deprivation. . . . The test results and observation indicated he was an educatable mentally retarded youngster"; (3) it was "therefore recommended that he be placed in the exceptional child class designed for educatably mentally retarded youngsters as soon as possible to avoid any further experience that he has undoubtedly incurred throughout his school history." Similarly, a psychologist testified for the state as to Stanley's mentality and psychiatric makeup. The psychologist testified that his examination revealed that Stanley had an IQ of 81, which he defined as not "too significant" in deciding whether "this particular man is mentally retarded." He did concede during cross-examination by Stanley's trial attorney that the IQ placed him in "the upper range of borderline mental retardation." Finally, Stanley's mother read into evidence, during the penalty phase of the trial, a letter written to her by her son (reading the letter was the totality of the mother's trial testimony):

THE WITNESS: It says, "Dear Mother, I just sending a letter to let you know I am going to hope," I think it is—I don't know whether it is—it is R-O-O-K, room that is room, July 6, 1976. "Hay Mother, I having" let me see. "Hay Momma, I have seen the lawyer, mother, and he say this carries the chair and, mother, I don't know—don't know, what to go to—what now, I don't know what to do now about it, Momma. I didn't murder no one and rob no one and kidnap no one. To mother, and mother, I not lying to you. God knows it, but no one believes me, Momma. I don't know what to do. I don't know, I want—want to go to no chair for nothing I didn't do. Tell me what to do, say, hay Momma, are you coming to see me when I go, Momma, hay, Momma, you have told me, told us to be good and you will, we won't have to go to jail. I been good," I think way, he got this W.A.Y., it say, "Momma." It is the same thing he got down there. W.A.Y.
No, it says, "Momma, don't worry. I sorry, Momma. I didn't do it, believe me, and Mary, and Cat, you good to Momma and Senator, too, be a sweet baby for me, Cat, Sheriff, pray for me, I didn't do it because no one believes me, Momma."
"I want to come home and, Momma, he told them I robbed him and I—won't make them believe it. Id didn't do it. Tell me what to do."
"Hay, tell T.C. to come and I go to Court and tell him I say hay and come, too."[26]

So some mitigating evidence came in at trial, but that was only a small fraction of what was available had Stanley's trial attorney bothered to look for it. Postconviction counsel produced the testimony of five members of the Stanley family and a family friend to the effect that if called they would have testified that he had never been in trouble, was obedient, helpful, and cooperative, and was not violent. His mother stated that he had difficulty in school and indicated that he was a slow learner. Stanley himself testified at the habeas hearing on his own behalf. He stated that his lawyer had once asked him about people who could testify about his character, that he had given the lawyer names of some people, but it never came up again. He also introduced into evidence a letter from the pastor of his church that noted his good character, as well as a high school report that indicated that his character was thought to be excellent in every respect.

Judge Richard Arnold, of Little Rock, Arkansas, was sitting on the Eleventh Circuit as a visitor and dissented in *Stanley*. At that time, I believe, Judge Arnold's Eighth Circuit had not yet encountered any capital cases first-hand, which made his *Stanley* dissent all the more impressive. Anyway, the oral argument was held shortly before I started working for Judge Vance, but I listened to the audio tape about two dozen times while I was drafting Judge Vance's *Stanley* opinion. ("Drafting" is exactly what it was; the judge wrote his own opinions, and our job as law clerks was to translate his analysis into drafts, which he then virtually rewrote; that's why his opinions had such similar analytical and writing styles down through the years.) The *Stanley* oral argument tapes were painful to listen to because Stanley's habeas lawyer's palpable condescension toward these benighted judges from the Bad Old South obscured, in my opinion, Stanley's quite powerful challenges to the legality of his death sentence. Stanley's trial *was* atrociously unfair. By contrast, Stanley's co-perpetrator in the murder, a fellow named Joseph Thomas, was represented on his habeas case by Millard Farmer and Joe Nursey, two of the best capital habeas litigators in the country, then and now. From the trial transcripts it seemed to me that Thomas' culpability was far greater than Stanley's: the record did not indicate that Thomas was retarded, as Stanley was; Thomas was the planner and leader of the murder for which Thomas and Stanley were condemned to die. Thomas' trial lawyer, like Stanley's, put on virtually no mitigating evidence, but Stanley lost in the Eleventh Circuit, and he was executed in 1984, about a year after I drafted his opinion.

I also drafted Judge Vance's opinion in *Thomas,* remanding his case for an evidentiary hearing on his claim of ineffective assistance of trial counsel. During that remand, and during Thomas' subsequent appeal back to the Eleventh Circuit after the district court held the evidentiary hearing and again ruled against Thomas, the U.S. Supreme Court rendered an opinion in *Francis v. Franklin,* another Georgia death case. The Supreme Court held in *Franklin* that the reasonable doubt instruction given routinely in Georgia capital cases unconstitutionally shifted the burden of proof from the prosecution to the defense. So Robert Franklin gets a whole new trial, say the Supremes, a new guilt/innocence trial as well as a new penalty phase trial. This was good news to Georgia's condemned population—

those who were still alive when *Franklin* was decided, that is. In particular, it was good news for Joseph Thomas, whose case was still bouncing around between the Eleventh Circuit and the district court because of the then-still-unresolved ineffective assistance issue. Because Thomas was still alive and litigating at the time the Supreme Court issued its *Franklin* decision, he was able to raise a challenge to his *conviction* based on *Franklin*. And he won, as he should have, because Mr. Thomas' and Mr. Franklin's juries were given virtually identical reasonable doubt instructions.

The problem is that Ivon Ray Stanley's jury *also* got a reasonable doubt instruction functionally identical to the ones given in *Thomas* and *Franklin*. But by the time the U.S. Supreme Court decided *Franklin,* Ivon Stanley had been dead for several years. So, with the benefit of 20–20 hindsight, we can see that the critical time frame in *Thomas* and *Stanley* was 1982–83, when the Eleventh Circuit sent Mr. Thomas' case back down the judicial ladder for an evidentiary hearing on ineffective assistance of trial counsel, and sent Mr. Stanley's case along to the next level of the capital punishment assembly line that ended for Stanley with his execution in 1984. The question then becomes: Why was Mr. Thomas, the *really* bad actor in the Thomas/Stanley joint venture of capital murder, sent back for an evidentiary hearing in district court, while Stanley, the retarded follower, was not? Part of the answer, I suggested earlier, was simply that Mr. Thomas had a better habeas lawyer. But the *legal* difference between Joseph Thomas' and Stanley's cases in the Eleventh Circuit was a technicality of habeas: Stanley had already received an evidentiary hearing in Georgia *State* Court, on his ineffective assistance claim, and Thomas had not. Never mind that the "hearing" in *Stanley* was presided over by a state judge whose boredom with the hearing shone through even in a cold appellate record. The fact was that Stanley had received some sort of hearing in state court, and Thomas hadn't. That lethal procedural technicality, in the end, was what decided that Ivon Ray Stanley would die and Joseph Thomas would live.

But I'm getting ahead of the story. On my first day as Judge Vance's law clerk, he handed me, for my maiden voyage into the waters of opinion drafting, the case files for *Thomas* and *Stanley*. I knew bean dip about capital punishment at that moment—I don't think it ever came up during my education at Mr. Jefferson's University—but it seemed pretty straightforward: Stanley had gotten an evidentiary hearing in state court, and Thomas had not. Judge Vance warned me that his opinion in *Thomas* would likely be unanimously accepted, but that a Judge Arnold, a visiting judge from Arkansas, would likely write a dissenting opinion in *Stanley*. Arkansas? Does Arkansas even *have* a death penalty? All I knew from Arkansas was the Little Rock abomination and Governor Faubus.

It ended up taking me three months to draft the opinions in *Thomas* and *Stanley*. I highlighted, in electric yellow, the place in the *Stanley* record where his mother read the letter written by her son. (The first time I read that portion of the letter, I went home and poured myself a stiff shot of Wild Turkey.) I tried to recast *Stanley* as a civil rights case, since he is— was—an African American. Robert Vance, before Jimmy Carter made him "Judge Vance" in 1977, had been leader of the non-George-Wallace wing of the Alabama Democratic Party, back in the '60's, and the architect of the "Freedom Democrat" challenge at the 1964 Democratic National Convention. Frank Johnson was Vance's hero. Judge Vance and I were arguing over *Stanley* in the Birmingham courthouse; I ate my lunch in Kelly Ingram Park, site of some of the most brutal atrocities of Birmingham Sheriff "Bull" Connor's fire hoses and police dogs. Judge Vance always worked with Jack Bass's book *Unlikely Heroes* within easy reach: not for reference purposes, because he had lived through so many of those civil rights wars as a ferocious combatant, but rather for purposes of memory and perhaps inspiration. During my year as Judge Vance's clerk, my sanctimoniousness about *Stanley* could not have made his life easier. He always listened patiently to my petulant tirades, and he didn't fire me even when I once stormed out of his office in tears over the case.

Eventually, my draft opinions were done. Judge Vance reworked them from the bottom up, and then he circulated them to the other two judges on the *Stanley/Thomas* panel. Word filtered back that Judge Arnold would, after all, circulate a dissent in *Stanley*. I was delighted.

And when Judge Arnold's dissent arrived, I was ecstatic. It was magnificent, all the more so because it was (I think) his first opinion in a capital case, ever. His dissent, eloquently and efficiently, decimated the draft opinion I had written for Judge Vance. There seemed to be more than the usual likelihood that a majority of the complete complement of Eleventh Circuit judges would vote to take *Stanley en banc*, automatically vacating Judge Vance's opinion for the 2–1 panel majority. The court, then only a year old, rarely took cases *en banc*. And the last time the court *had* given *en banc* consideration to a capital case raising a claim of ineffective assistance of trial counsel had been in *Washington v. Strickland*, decided by the court shortly before the *Stanley* panel opinions were circulated. *Washington* had resulted in a bitterly divided Eleventh Circuit *en banc* court, with several concurring and dissenting opinions. Judge Vance had written the opinion for the *en banc* majority in *Washington*, a carefully principled and practical treatment of how the court ought to go about analyzing ineffective assistance claims. That made Vance in some sense the court's "expert" on such claims, which did not seem to bode well for Mr. Stanley's chances of persuading the *en banc* Eleventh Circuit to give plenary consideration to his case. Ineffective assistance of trial counsel is raised, routinely, in virtually *every* capital case, and the Eleventh Circuit judges were frankly sick of the issue. Besides, the future of Judge Vance's handiwork in *Washington* was in doubt (the U.S. Supreme Court ended up granting plenary review and then reversing *Washington*). And, as though that wasn't enough, the *en banc* request filed by Mr. Stanley's habeas lawyer was nothing to write home about. His chances of getting *en banc* consideration seemed slim to nil.

We "death clerks," in our respective judge's chambers, spoke among ourselves and commiserated fairly regularly, an informal practice tolerated to a greater or lesser extent by our bosses (Judge Vance, as a product of the rough-and-tumble world of Alabama politics, was especially indulgent, because when I was whining to other judges' law clerks, I wasn't whining to *him*). Those informal clerk-to-clerk chats left me more fearful than ever that the full *en banc* court might not agree to take up Ivon Ray Stanley's case.

What I *hadn't* counted on was the power of Judge Arnold's *Stanley* dissent. It moved Eleventh Circuit Judge Frank Johnson to ask for a poll of the full Eleventh Circuit, the first step toward *en banc* consideration of a case. The written votes trickled into Judge Vance's chambers, one or two a day, over the next few weeks. I kept a tally in my personal journal. And when all the votes were in, it was a tie vote: 6 to 6. The outcome: The panel opinion by Judge Vance would stand, since a majority was required to displace a panel opinion and take a case *en banc*. Judge Arnold's dissent gathered the votes of six Eleventh Circuit judges, exactly half of the court. Since Judge Arnold was sitting as a visitor in the Eleventh Circuit in *Stanley*, he didn't get a vote.

As I hope this book makes clear, I have tremendous and unalloyed respect for Judge Arnold and for his craft, but also for his decency. I've followed his capital opinions over the years, as the Eighth Circuit has, of necessity, become as expert as the Eleventh Circuit was by 1983 in deciding who dies. I've wanted to thank him for a long time. Now, at least, I have tried.

Ivon Ray Stanley lost in the Eleventh Circuit, two votes to one, because, according to binding precedent, his trial lawyer did a good enough job. Judge Vance was absolutely right on the law, but a piece of me died when the *Stanley* opinion was sent to the court's printer for publication under the judge's name. Another piece of me died when Ivon Ray Stanley was executed, about a year later. And, yet again, when Judge Vance himself was assassinated by a mail bomb sent to his home a few days before Christmas 1989. Joseph Thomas is still alive.

I had seen too much. I knew too much to walk away. By knowing and walking away I would become the evil thing itself. By knowing and staying to fight—a fight I knew I could not possibly win—I would become the evil thing itself. "The people should fight for their law as for a wall," Heraclitus wrote.

So I headed for Florida. I went because I couldn't *not* go.

Florida Fragments
A Montage of a Lawyer's Life of Death

As my allotted year as Judge Vance's death clerk ended, I found myself thinking a lot about death and his lawyers. Robert Vance was a fine and heroic man, and he was a scrupulously fair and impartial judge; had he not been on the bench, things would have been much, much worse; had I not been his clerk, maybe the job would have been occupied by someone worse. Part of me at the time must have rebelled at such a self-justifying rationalization—I had, after all, read in high school the full transcripts of the Nuremberg trials of the major war criminals, and Hannah Arendt's *Eichmann in Jerusalem* was one of my favorite books. But this wasn't Nazi Germany.

Anyway, I thought it might be interesting (and purging) to go to work representing death row inmates in one of the three southern states that make up the Eleventh Circuit, Georgia, Alabama, or Florida. Part of me wished I had never seen the constitutional horror show of capital cases that paraded before the Eleventh Circuit during my year clerking with Judge Vance. But you can't unring a bell. I found that the knowledge about capital punishment I'd acquired as Judge Vance's clerk just wouldn't let me rest; it kept nagging at me to try to do something about it.

I loaded all my worldly possessions into my 1972 VW bug and relocated to South Florida, where I hoped to find deathwork. I settled in West Palm Beach. Soon after I arrived in West Palm, somebody sent me Hunter Thompson's *Rolling Stone* piece on the Roxanne Pulitzer divorce trial in Palm Beach. Let me explain. The trial ran from July 21 to August 4, 1983, and I was living in Miami at the time. But I was studying for the Bar, and I missed the whole thing. Thompson's third paragraph got my attention:

This chapter originated as a letter to my wife.

"There are no jails or hospitals in Palm Beach. It is the ultimate residential community, a lush sandbar lined with palm trees and mansions on the gold coast of Florida—millionaires and old people, an elaborately protected colony for the seriously rich, a very small island and a very small world. The rules are different here, or at least they seem to be, and the people like it that way." In the two years I lived in South Florida, I never made it over the bridge into Palm Beach. Parents and visiting friends brought me word about Worth Avenue, but that wasn't the world of my clients. It wasn't my world, either.

Never confuse Palm Beach with *West* Palm Beach. I lived at the wrong end of the bridge. The Capital Appeals Division of Richard Jorandby's Public Defender's Office in West Palm Beach, Florida, had a position open (starting salary $16,500, to be increased to $18,000 when applicant passed the bar exam; Judge Vance, and most of my friends and all of my family, thought I should accept a job with the corporate law department of the Wall Street firm of Cravath, Swaine & Moore). I pestered Jorandby and Craig Barnard (Jorandby's chief assistant) with letters and writing samples and references and visits until they hired me (most likely so I'd let them alone and give them some peace) in the summer of 1983; they took me on notwithstanding my past work for Judge Vance, who was regarded as a "hanging judge" by some folks in the death penalty defense community. I remember doing a lot of explaining during the job interview about how I could have drafted the opinion in Ivon Ray Stanley's case. I went to West Palm Beach, as I vividly recall, in part because I'd been told *not* to go.

What I did not anticipate when I began this work was how hard it would be to *stop* doing it, to leave behind clients and their families whom I'd come to know, even though I'd be leaving them in very capable hands. So a year became two, with Florida's counsel crisis becoming ever more volatile. Then in mid-1985 the Florida legislature created the office of the Capital Collateral Representative, and it seemed to me a logical place to work. For a little while, at least. I went to CCR for the same reason that Willie Sutton found himself inside bank vaults: That's where the money is. CCR is where the cases are.

Thus a year became two, became three, became four. In 1987 I took a job with the private law firm of Wilmer, Cutler & Pickering, representing corporations like Amtrak (in an insurance indemnity action against Conrail) and individuals like Elizabeth Morgan (who was jailed for her refusal to produce her daughter for visitations with the child's father, who Dr. Morgan believed had raped the child) and Stephen Booker and Roy Harich, Florida death row prisoners and *pro bono* clients of the law firm; a couple of years later I went into full-time law teaching, carting my capital caseload with me, first to D.C. and then to Vermont.

Since the U.S. Supreme Court upheld the constitutionality of capital punishment in 1976, Florida has carried out 38 executions, all by the electric chair. Thirty-seven of these executions have occurred since fall 1983, when I began working as a capital public defender in West Palm Beach, Florida: Bob Sullivan (November 30, 1983), Anthony Antone (January 26, 1984), Freddie Goode (April 5, 1984), James Adams (May 10, 1984), Carl Shriner (June 20, 1984), David Leroy Washington (July 13, 1984), Ernest Dobbert (September 7, 1984), James Dupree Henry (September 20, 1984), Tim Palmes (November 8, 1984), J.D. Raulerson (January 30, 1985), Johnny Paul Witt (March 6, 1985), Marvin Francois (May 29, 1985), Daniel Thomas (April 15, 1986), David Funchess (April 29, 1986), Ronald Straight (May 20, 1986), Buford White (August 28, 1987), Willie Jasper Darden (March 15, 1988), Jeffrey Daugherty (November 7, 1988), Theodore Bundy (January 24, 1989), Dennis Adams (May 4, 1989), Jesse Tafero (May 4, 1990), Anthony Bertolotti (July 27, 1990), James Hamlin (September 21, 1990), Ray Clark (November 11, 1990), Roy Harich (May 29, 1991), Bobby Francis (June 26, 1991), Nollie Lee Martin (May 12, 1992), Ed Kennedy (July 27, 1992), Robert Henderson (April 21, 1993), Larry Joe Johnson (May 5, 1993), Michael Durocher (August 25, 1993). . . . Enough.

The frenetic pace of deathwork has its narcotic charms, and those charms are more apparent in hindsight than they perhaps were at the time, although the pieces of memory don't fit snugly together, they're chaotic and conflicting, they collide with one another and crowd each other out, they mutate and they subdivide like cells, they mix like my metaphors, with the full view looking more like a kaleidoscope-on-acid than like a completed jigsaw puzzle: the high velocity gonzo litigation, racing against a ticking clock that came to possess mythic qualities; the sinking feeling when a man who is scheduled to be killed in 72 hours hatches a hideous bones-for-time scam in which he will identify the locations of his victims' bodies in exchange for a stay, when he really wants to confess and close the unsolved cases, but you know his case contains a powerful constitutional claim, which will self-destruct if the saturation publicity about the bones-for-time offer leaks to the press, so you tell him in no uncertain terms to "shut up, shut the fuck up, and shut the fuck up right now," but he doesn't shut up, and the news of the bones proposal hits the media like an atomic bomb—but even with the case's notoriety, and even with the bones-for-time scam, he still loses in the Rehnquist Court, 5–4, one vote shy of a stay, and the man is executed on time, while outside the prison, crowds of people cheer and set off fireworks; or the rush that comes with not giving an inch of intellectual ground to a life-tenured federal judge who despises you and your client and who will seize on *any* reed as a basis of a ruling against you (often the prosecutors are not ratbags, but they are non-factors, bless their hearts; the *judges* are your real adversaries; on occasion, your colleagues have raised legal jujitsu to a form of high art); or the giddy satisfaction of fighting to maintain your professional cool and composure when you put your hands on that one critical piece of exculpatory evidence that the prosecutors have been telling you for 10 years doesn't exist, but that your investigator found in the dusty attic of the deceased chief detective on your client's case; or the raw, mind-clearing panic when, in the days before fax machines, you learn that the stay papers you've been working on for the last 36 straight hours did make it onto the plane in Tallahassee, that the plane departed on time but was in a holding pattern above the Atlanta Hartsfield Airport (with that dreamy, computer-generated, stoned-sounding voice repeating, repeating, "Hellooooo. You have entered . . . [pause for a beat] . . . the transportation maaaallll . . . "), because the airport was about to close because of snow, not *much* snow, but this was Atlanta, a city that prides itself on its inability to deal with "northern" weather, and you dread telling this news to the court death clerk, who is a friend and who personally drove to the airport in the middle of the night to pick up your stay papers during the *last* emergency, which had been only a month before . . . ; and then there was the time Governor "Bob" (that's how he signed death warrants) Graham, doubtless thinking himself clever, signed two warrants on two prisoners, both with the last name of Thomas, Dan Thomas and Ed Thomas, scheduled to be killed on the same day, and Dan Thomas was executed, and Ed Thomas was not, and you thought Governor Graham was just being his cute self, sophomoric but harmless, until you got a call from Ed Thomas' sister, who was in tears because she'd heard on the radio that a "Thomas" had been executed in Florida, and she had thought that *her* Thomas had won a reprieve, and you assure her that, yes, *her* Thomas was safe (for now), it was the *other* Thomas who was electrocuted; or the sometimes delicious sensation of playing chicken with a cranky, creaky judiciary that dearly wishes our clients (and their lawyers; *especially* their lawyers) would just shut up and go away and die quietly; the adrenalin blast of a 3:00 A.M. stay of execution in a case you had no rightful *business* getting a stay in; and your mission for the next 72 hours is to find the co-perpetrator of your client's crime, and you can't find her through DMV or VA or medical records, but you find out the county where she lives, and it's one of the big, sprawling counties in the Panhandle, the region that a prosecutor referred to as "one of those Klan counties," so now you've narrowed your field of search to one county, but the witness you're looking for doesn't have a phone, but she *does* have a daughter, and you calculate that the daughter is of junior high school age, so you follow school bus after school bus, but you still can't find them, and so you go door to door, apartment by apartment, but no dice, so you report back to your boss, whom years later someone describes as "a cat," and tell him you just can't find the witness, and he gives you a level stare and says softly, "No, no, that's not the right answer," and finally, finally you find a neighbor who used to date the mail carrier of your witness, and you feel flushed with excitement when you knock on her door, but she refuses even to talk with you, and your client is executed on schedule; or the time your public defender office is interviewing psychologists who will conduct confidential interviews with and evaluations of your clients, and one candidate shows up in a gray skirt and power jacket, gray hair in a bun, and she tours the office, and sees the roll-out beds from the night before and the night before that, the appellate attorney, who is wearing a *Cohen v. California* t-shirt and who is stretched out on the back office couch, because he has a vicious head cold, and he's surrounded by piles of Puffs unscented facial tissues and boxes of voir dire transcripts, and the music and the phones and the photocopier, and at the end of the interview day she says, "You couldn't *pay* me enough to work for you people. But I *would* give the office's employees a group rate, because you people don't know how messed *up* you all are"; or the peaceful, easy experience of sipping iced tea, on a flawless Orlando afternoon, on the front porch of a grandmotherly woman straight out of central casting, who has slate gray *eyes* that demand italics, eyes that tell you that this woman has experienced things, who a decade earlier had been a juror in your client's case, who had been one juror of 10 whose verdict of life imprisonment was overridden by the trial judge; whose eyes narrow to slits and flash with anger as her voice becomes low and hard, a whispering hiss that you *must* pay attention to, when you ask her about the override, because "we thought long and hard about our verdict, and if *that* Judge McGregor (always he was "*that* Judge McGregor") was going to ignore it, why on earth did he ask us for our opinion in the first place?" and you feel like a boob for having asked her whether she remembered the case, because of *course* she still remembers the capital case in which the judge disregarded her verdict against death for that defendant (and that's what she called it: "my verdict," not "our" verdict; she took it personally), she remembers it "like it was yesterday," because she is still pissed off about it, even now, now more than ever; your juror who, when you broach the most sensitive topic of the discussion, the *reason* behind the jury's life verdict, tells you something better than your wildest fantasy: the jury voted for life because they had lingering, nagging doubt about whether your client was guilty *at all,* of *anything,* much less of capital murder; who tells you that, of *course* she would swear in writing to what she's just told you, she'd be glad to sign a notarized affidavit, but it's Sunday on a holiday weekend and the banks are all closed, but she has a friend who works in the local bank and who would be happy to notarize the affidavit; but, you sheepishly explain to your juror, there *is* no affidavit to notarize, because when you got into your VW bug in Tallahassee to make the drive to Orlando, you couldn't have brought an affidavit, because you didn't know that your client's trial jury wasn't certain your client did the crime, until this wonderful old lady told you so, there, face to face on her porch, and you haven't slept much recently and you forgot it was Sunday, and you forgot to bring a typewriter, which you don't know how to use anyway; your juror gives you an understanding smile (you can just *hear* her thinking "such a nice young person, but if only he'd get his suit pressed, and that *tie* . . ."), and she tells you it's not a problem, because her bank friend can also type the affidavit, so you get your affidavit signed and sealed (and, oh, yes, your juror tells you as you hug her goodby, she'd be *delighted* to testify in the Florida legislature about how judges shouldn't be permitted to reject jury verdicts of life) and you leave Orlando with your affidavit, at one point pulling over to the side of I-10 to make sure that the affidavit really is as good as you think, and, yup, it is (the juror's affidavit says: "During our jury deliberations at the sentence portion of the Spaziano trial, I voted for a life sentence rather than the death penalty. Nine or ten jurors felt as I did: that we did not want to see this man die. One of the major reasons for most of us favoring a life sentence was our doubts about whether Mr. Spaziano was guilty of the crime as charged. I distinctly remember this being expressed as a factor in many of the jurors' minds. One of our major concerns was the testimony of the 16-year-old boy, Tony Dilisio, which we didn't entirely believe at the time of the trial. Had we known his testimony was prompted by hypnosis, I believe it would have made a difference"), and you think: Yes! This case is over; they won't kill an innocent person, but then over the next decade you try to persuade some court somewhere, any court anywhere, to *look at* the affidavit, to consider it, and they all refuse, at every step down the line, first every state court you go to and then every federal court you go to, and now your client is running out of appeals and the governor is a decent man but he's in a tough reelection campaign against Jeb Bush (the meaner and more rabidly right-wing of the Shrub's two political sons, Jeb and George the Younger, both of whom are smarter than brother Neil), and the governor is making dangerous-sounding rumblings about signing your client's death warrant, and you still can't convince a court that your client ought not be electrocuted because even his bloody *jury* thought that maybe he didn't do it, and you're not a religious person, but you *pray* that your client won't be killed, and you resolve never again to work on a case involving an innocent person, you'll just take your share of the clearly guilty, and even as you make the resolution you know you won't keep it; or the not-quite-real experience of going through an execution with the man who, as a child, played Dennis The Menace on the TV show, who'd become close with a man on death row, and who simply *couldn't* believe that they were really going to kill his friend, even after they did, and his pain is real, and he's sobbing in your arms, and you feel terribly guilty, because the thought keeps going through your mind, *This is Dennis The Menace;* and the dynamics of participating in a meeting of the senior attorneys in your office, to decide who among you would be the designated witness to the killing of the office's clients: Should it be one of the front-line litigators, who know the clients best and who might be rendered dysfunctional by the experience of witnessing the executions, or the politically appointed director of the office, who, of all of you, could most afford to take a week or so off from work after witnessing the killing to deal with her own posttraumatic stress; or the time you called every private attorney in your Rolodex (favorite line from a lifetime friend: "You are not your Rolodex") to beg them to take on a death case (or to take on *another* death case) because your caseload is bursting the rivets of your capacity, and it's an interesting, and therefore potentially marketable, case—a 1980 Mariel Boatlift Cuban, and a not-so-bad crime, a home break-in that went bad, and the client was caught attempting to flee the scene on his getaway bicycle (this was the runner-up for your most-creative-but-doomed-getaway-scheme, the clear winner being the fellow who tried to time his robbery so he could catch the local uptown bus and make good his escape), and the client had been steeped in Cuba's criminal justice system, where one's "defense lawyer" is really working with the prosecutor, and at the Florida capital murder trial, the translator was pretty incompetent and so your client was unable even to follow the court proceedings, much less to participate in his own defense in any meaningful way, and you find a brilliant Columbia Law School professor, a superstar scholar and a former prosecutor to boot, who is willing to take the case over, but only if the Florida Supreme Court will extend the due date for the brief by two weeks, because the record is massive and because she'd need to come up to speed on the applicable Florida law, but the court refuses to do that, so you're stuck with the case, and you send one of your lawyers to Cuba, which is of course illegal, but you work it out through the Cuban Interests Section in D.C., with an assist from the Congressional Black Caucus, and the lawyer flies to Cuba (indirectly, via a third country) and he finds *dynamite* information for the case, and he brings you back a box of Cuban cigars, and eventually you win the case; or the time your office represents the first Vietnam war veteran to be put to death, even though his evidence of posttraumatic stress disorder was overwhelming and his craziness was not subtle, but it wasn't diagnosed until he was already on death row for murder, the manifestations of his mental illness were florid and flamboyant, and it was painful to even read the medical reports: digging tunnels underneath his house, setting up trip wires and spring-guns on his property, episodic dyscontrol, followed by blackouts and night sweats and panic attacks; during the 72 hours leading up to the execution, when there are respites in the litigation frenzy ("lucid intervals," you call them without humor), you leave your law office in the

Independent Life Insurance Building and join the vigil being kept by the Vietnam vets, at Tallahassee's memorial to their service, and after your client is killed, on schedule, he's buried on land owned by your co-counsel in the case, a man who also was a Vietnam veteran, but you don't attend the funeral, because you don't do funerals, and the death warrants just keep on coming; or the time your client is a man whose mind is being ripped apart by a treatable mental illness, but you know that if you permit the prison to treat the illness and ease the pains of the disease, he might become sufficiently sane so that the state could, constitutionally, execute him; or the weight of showing up in court to argue a stay of execution, in front of a bored judge, and realizing that your client's *entire* extended family, parents, uncles, aunts, sisters, brothers, cousins, second cousins, nieces, and nephews, are there in the courtroom, all fidgeting nervously and uncomfortably in the Sunday-Going-to-Meeting clothes they're not used to wearing during the week; or the warm interior glow when, after the stay comes through from "your court," the Florida Supreme Court, your client's mother asks what you're doing for Thanksgiving—and when she hears that *your* mother is in Virginia and that you're not married or otherwise attached, she *demands* that you join them (*all* of them, minus one, of course) for "a real Italian turkey dinner with all the trimmin's, and then some"; the epiphany that you might as well concede to reality and just bring a sleeping bag into the office; the disorienting feeling of dreaming the telephone is ringing, realizing that it really *is* ringing, it's morning, and it's your daily wake-up call from your friend the clerk in the federal courthouse ("What? You're *sleeping?* Sleep? You?"); or the futility of explaining to your mother why you're doing this zany work, for the equivalent of subminimum wage (one night when you have too much free time on your hands, you divide the money you've made by the number of hours you've spent on capital cases, and discover that you could have done better pumping gas or flipping burgers at McDonald's), but knowing that she loves you anyway, even if she silently (well, *usually* silently) prays that this is "just a phase," and that you'll grow out of it and get a real lawyer's job, and she can never read this, not because of the profanity or the stories, but rather because here you confess to smoking cigarettes; or the Christmas Eve when, at 2:00 A.M. the computer crashed, erasing the federal appellate court brief that had to be filed in Atlanta not later than December 26, a brief you'd been working on nonstop for a month, a brief in the first case to claim in any federal court anywhere that states ought not be permitted to execute people who were younger than age 18 at the time they committed their capital crimes (the "killing kids" constitutional claim, you call it in shorthand around the office), and your secretary, who is awesomely dedicated but also awesomely exhausted, looks as if he might be on the verge of having a psychotic episode, and you call your other support staff at their respective homes, and some of them are pretty well into the holiday spirits, this being the one day of the year that they don't have to worry about being called into the office, because even the governor doesn't schedule executions between Christmas and New Year, but, yes, of *course* they'd come in, and they do, they *all* do, and by dawn the brief and its multi-volume appendices look *beautiful,* and they're filed on time, and later you win the case in the federal court of appeals, which sends the case down for a resentencing, and at the resentencing your client's mother insists that you stay at her home, a hotel is simply out of the question, and after she cooks you a dinner of meatloaf and mashed potatoes ("comfort food," she explains, "and food for good luck"), and she turns in to bed early, since tomorrow a Florida jury will decide whether her youngest boy will die or not, and you work at the dining room table for a while, but eventually the caffeine loses its effect, and you trundle off to your designated bedroom, and only then does it hit you that you're going to be sleeping in your *client's* old room, in your client's own bed, a room that has remained unchanged since his arrest for murder at age 16, and the room is a lot like *your* bedroom at age 16, with posters and books and a turntable and records, and then another thing hits you, that you and your client are *exactly the same age,* that while you've been going to college and law school and clerkship and public defending and teaching and writing, he's been living on death row all that time, and while you've always known, intellectually, how long he's been imprisoned (ciphering isn't your strong suit, but you are able to count up days and hours and months and decades), you didn't really *know* it until you spent the sleepless night (and the next three nights) in that room, that room which was such a vivid snapshot of arrested development, of a boy's life interrupted, frozen in time because of the things that that "boy" had done to a girl, who was about his age when he kidnapped, raped, and murdered her, his life was interrupted because he had interrupted hers, and you wonder whether *her* room, in *her* parents' nearby home, has also been frozen in a state of suspended animation for the past 10 years, then over the next few days, while the case is being presented to the resentencing jury, your client's momma has been knitting a maroon and white afghan, and after the jury returns a verdict of life imprisonment, she gives you the afghan as your fee, and it still graces your couch at home; or your first meeting, when you are still a baby lawyer, with your client's father-from-hell, a belt-brandishing beast who used his children as punching bags and prostitutes, a mean drunk if ever there was one, a man who wouldn't even let you in the door if he knew how much you *know* about him, how much you've documented through family members and neighbors and doctors and cops and VA reports and divorce records, some information that you had to extract from people who are, as they say in the recovery industry, "into deep denial," so you've come to hate this man vicariously, and when he meets you at the door of his beachside condo, he's an old man who walks with a cane, and he offers you coffee "or something stronger," and you have to keep telling yourself that Adolph Eichmann also looked like a harmless old codger when he went on trial in Jerusalem for *his* crimes, and this bastard got off scot-free for the carnage he caused, including the carnage who is your client; or the case of Ed Kennedy, an African American man who escaped an Inferno of a prison, and who during a gunfight shot two white peace officers, and who was sentenced to death for it, but who was such a gentle soul, and a good man, a man who, of the death row prisoners you've gotten to know over the years, would be a finalist for inmate-you'd-most-welcome-as-your-neighbor, but whose case never really possessed much in the way of constitutional issues, because being a nice guy and a talented painter (peaceful landscapes, mostly; Ed had been in prison for a long time, but he had a good memory) and an aficionado of New Orleans jazz were good qualities to have, but they don't form a legal basis for invalidating a death sentence, although we sure tried, and all you can do after his inevitable execution, after you've screamed and pounded your walls, and rent your garment, all you can really do for *him* and for his family is dedicate one of your law journal articles to him, remembering his last request to you ("Remember me when you see the clouds"), and that last request was his gift to you, after you had been able to do so little to keep the state from killing him, but it's a gift so *typical* of that gentle man, and whenever you see clouds you think of Ed and you remember Ed, and in our age where just about everything is analyzed by experts down to the subatomic level, no expert can explain the way those clouds move you, since each person gazing at them will be free to draw her own conclusions, and all theories can be right, and no one will laugh; Ed Kennedy, whose last words were "peace be with you all, Allah Akbar," and you learn this from an October 25, 1994, Florida newspaper story, at the height of an election battle royal over capital punishment, entitled "The Last Word," featuring the obligatory photo of Bundy, captioned he "had few words, in the end"; Ed Kennedy, about whose killing it's hard to talk, even today, years later, and even among your close-knit family of deathworkers, until you read somewhere about your friend Susan Cary, and about something that happened at Florida State Prison, in Starke, soon after Ed Kennedy was put to death: The rare phenomenon of a Florida rainbow was the last thing that Susan expected to see as she stepped out of the prison; just moments earlier she had been present at the death of Ed Kennedy, a man she had grown to love, a man who made peace with himself and the world before going to the electric chair; too downcast in the grief of the moment to notice the brilliance of the morning, friends gently drew Susan's attention to the vivid spectrum of color arching over the prison, so close it could almost be touched; and today, with the healing of time, Susan Cary views that unexpected rainbow as symbolic of the power of redemption and renewal, a power that fuels her whole life and her struggle against the death penalty; and as an attorney and prisoners' counsellor, Susan is all too familiar with the terrible acts that take men to death row, and the sorrow and pain of the victims' families; it is not for us to forget either, but she knows too of the other side: the damaged lives of many prisoners, often more damaged than even we could understand; their struggle for self-worth in a world that offers them none; their capacity for change; and in the case of a man like Edward Kennedy, their painful honesty with themselves and their search for atonement; "We grieve for the story that isn't told," says Susan; and about the scores of prisoners for whom she has worked, Susan has no doubts: "Each one of them has given me something; has been my teacher in some way; that's not to romanticize—but there are still daily miracles that happen"; and Susan often recalls a poem that defines love as contraband in hell: "You see, love is an acid that melts away bars—that's why it is contraband," she said; the importance of human care and warmth for those living in total sensory deprivation—"there is nothing beautiful, gentle or nurturing in a cold concrete and steel environment"—could not be overstated; "those of us who fight the death penalty mentality are a small group of people, but you will never find better people anywhere, and I am honoured to be part of this"; . . . and then there was the time . . . and the mild edge of danger you feel when visiting your client's motorcycle brothers in their clubhouse, and for a moment you're devoting all your mental energy to sphincter control, and thinking, "For this I went to law school?" to try to unearth information on who really did the crime for which your client is scheduled to die, from chaps named "Wildman" and "Tall Paul," who sure as shootin' *look* like Outlaws, or at least outlaws—and Wildman looks at you kind of funny when you *don't* have a Second Amendment–protected handgun to declare before entering the clubhouse, and you can *see* your stock of credibility dropping with these guys, because you're unarmed, so you make a mental note to borrow a 9 millimeter Glock for your next visit, and to carry one bullet, in your suit pocket, Barney Fife–like, which is silly, if you think about it, as you later do, because you got along just fine with the brothers, the clubhouse was rather pleasant, actually, a rambling ranch house alongside the river, a cozy home, almost, with fake wood paneling and a threadbare carpet and overstuffed chairs and a couch, with women passing through like ghosts, trying to remain invisible and never making eye contact, and you worry about them, but they appear healthy, and your job is to meet with the brothers, and once you all had Budweisers, and once you got settled in the couch and y'all started chatting about the local judges and the like (the brothers know the judges much better than you do), and of *course* you get along, you're their president's attorney, and their president is innocent, and they're certain you'll find some legal loophole or technicality, because that's what lawyers do, yet, still, the brotherhood's clubhouse *is* 20 miles away from the nearest neighboring house, and you breathe just a tad more freely when you get on the road; or the mindless nausea when you walk up to the podium in the ornate ceremonial courtroom of the federal court of appeals in Atlanta, in your first case before the full (*en banc*) court, in a case with potentially far-reaching consequences for scores of Florida death row prisoners, but that's not what makes your stomach constrict to the density of lead; rather it is because this is your first argument, as a lawyer, in front of the judge for whom you clerked, and after the argument your co-counsel thinks he knows why there's a spring in your step, but really it's because your judge didn't ask any questions during the 30-minute oral argument; or the selfish there-but-for-the-grace-of-God-go-I gratitude you can't help but feel when you meet your client's family in a tarpaper shack that has never known electricity or running water, even though this is the go-go 1980s, when it is supposed to be Morning Again in America; or the time you "do *Nightline*," which you had never heard of because you've never owned a TV, and you're in the middle of a "real" death warrant (i.e., one most likely to be carried out, although in that case the Supreme Court stays the execution), and you change from your blue jeans and your *Cohen v. California* ("Fuck the Draft") t-shirt into a suit, and as the camera crews start to set up, you flee to your office, with the piles of paper that are taller than you are, and the "I Have A Dream" poster, and the paintings by Joe Spaziano and Ed Kennedy, and you start drinking, bourbon, straight, and the interviewer comes to your office to fetch you and stops short and exclaims, "There! we have to have the interview here!"—not in your boss's office, which is the only one that looks like a real law office (you call it "the presentable office"), with bookshelves full of law books (all blissfully unread by the office's occupant, but the bookcases were pretty nonetheless), tasteful furnishings, and artwork, and you tell the interviewer, in what sounds to you like a deferential tone of voice, "No, we do our interviews in the front office," and he sort of steps back and asks if he can at least shoot some footage of you, sitting at your desk, surrounded by transcripts and briefs and the rest, and you agree, so they film you, reading something (which in fact was a trashy novel), and then you do the interview, in the front office, and it goes well, because these people really did their homework and ask smart questions; or the private humor ("private" until you get back to your office, anyway) of being advised, in funereal tones, by an associate with a large law firm representing a prisoner *pro bono,* that you could talk to the partner on the case if you really want to, but that it would be more appropriate and proper, and *he* wouldn't get into trouble with the partner, don't you see, if you just deal with the junior associate, or, better yet, the associate's paralegal; or the first time a man the same age as you is executed; or the vaguely superior feeling when you see a lawyer with a big corporate law firm, who is accustomed to being treated with deference, or at least with civility, by judges and opponents, who starts out on his *pro bono* death case personally in favor of capital punishment but wanting to do his public service by representing "his guy," metamorphose, over the years of trying to use the courts and the law and the promises of the criminal justice system to save "his guy's" life, transformed into a flaming abolitionist who will never again look at the law or its judges the same way he did at the beginning (a process that occurs with such thudding predictability that one of your office's investigators makes up a ditty about this suit-to-firebrand conversion phenomenon, to be sung to the tune of "My Guy"); or the incandescent joy of telling a mother that her son *won't* be killed tomorrow morning at 7:00, as scheduled, at least not this time; or the foxhole camaraderie and the cast of brilliant and insane characters you meet along the road, and the complex geometry of relationships among them, people who pour out their souls, and who put their own personal lives on hold, who would rather work nights and weekends and Christmas and Thanksgiving and New Year's Day because the phones don't ring as often then, people who work tirelessly, mostly behind the scenes, to keep Florida from killing certain of its citizens, people with names you most likely won't recognize, like Scharlette Holdman ("Hold*person*," to the politically-correctness-challenged; Scharlette is a woman whose brilliance and audacity defy any metaphor, but who can be described as a transitive verb with a southern accent) and Laura Gillen and Lisa Eberly and Lissa Gardner and Eloise Williams (your guardian angel) and Barbara Thomas (your other guardian angel) and Ginny Schubert and David Bruck (your poet and flautist) and Millard Farmer (your Ezekiel) and Anthony Amsterdam (your Socrates) and Patsy Morris (your saint) and Marie Deans (your other saint, because you're greedy) and George Kendall and Tanya Coke and Bill Bowers and Hugo Bedau and Ron Tabak and Debbie Fins and Sonny Goldenfarb and Margaret Good and Charlene Carres and Greg Thomas and Sara Blakely and Joe Giarratano and Tom McCoun and Gail Rowland and Jimmy Lohman and Judy Doherty and Jack Boger and Joel Berger and Tim Ford and Esther Lardent and Leigh Dingerson and Eric Cumfer and Karen Gottlieb and Elliot Scherker and Jeff and Donna Robinson and Michael and Sally Millemann (so are they *both* Millemanns? Millepeople? You've always been afraid to ask) and Henry Schwartzschild and Leigh Bienan and Lee Norton and Mandy Welch and Bob Morin and Russ Canan and Matthew Lawry and Chris Cox and Steve Goldstein and Pat Doherty and Bob Mahler and Rich Rosen and Lou Bilionis and David Reiser and Ali Miller and Faith Blake and Larry Spalding and Craig Barnard and Jerry Justine and Leon Wright and Lee Currie and Richard Jorandby and Richard Greene and Richard Burr (respectively known as "Big Dick, Little Dick, and No Dick") and Steve Malone and Mark Evans and Margaret Vandiver and Michael and Lisa Radelet and Mark Olive ("Olive, like the fruit"), your ferociously brilliant peerless peer, your boss, who was the Joe DiMaggio of deathwork, moving gracefully, never overdoing it, making everything look easy, moving with a precision and a patience that made those qualities seem to be tactile objects, and whatever happened, he never blinked (the word "cat" fits him like a skin: silky, jumpy, contemptuously independent, poised for fight or flight, sensual and vain; cats make things look easy, and have an exquisite sense of balance) (or, as Baudelaire wrote of Delacroix, he "was passionately in love with passion, but coldly determined to express passion as clearly as possible") (Polly Nelson, in her book *Defending the Devil: My Story as Ted Bundy's Last Lawyer,* describes her first meeting with Olive at that well-known den of steamy eroticism, the Tallahassee Airport: "Mark Olive did not look like the lawyers at Wilmer Cutler & Pickering, . . . the wise teacher with the voice like simmering molasses, brown hair that fell to his shoulders, wire rim eyeglasses and skin tight beat up blue jeans. . . . With his deep, velvety southern drawl, Mark Olive put the purr in persuasion. Not that I offered much resistance, allowing Mark Olive's smooth, insinuating voice to slither over me like a warm snake" and so on); and the seemingly endless number of funerals, for Bob Sullivan and James Adams and James Dupree Henry and David Washington and Anthony Antone and Ernest Dobbert and Freddie Goode and Tim Palmes and Ronald Straight and Dan Thomas and David Funchess and Marvin Francois and Ed Kennedy and Nollie Lee Martin and Ted Bundy and Buford White and Jim Hamlin and Larry Joe Johnson, and the fathers and sons of our clients *and* of their crime victims; and after one particular execution, you go to the funeral, even though you don't do funerals, but this time you go because you promised Ronald Straight you would, and it's on a flawless May day in Gainesville, and his momma won't leave your side, she clings to you like Velcro, like a terrorized child, not saying much in words, but saying more about the nature of agony by the configuration of the lines in her face, the way her hair is pulled back from her face, reminding you of Jacqueline Kennedy's furious, and equally silent, refusal to change her suit after the assassination, "to let them see what they've done," not saying who the "they" are, but that doesn't matter, let it alone . . . ; and exactly one year after your client's execution (*exactly* one year, one year to the fucking *day*), you learn that the Supreme Court has decided unanimously, 9–0, in another Florida death case, that the constitutional issue you had hung your client's mortal hat on was meritorious after all, and you're happy for the prisoner who won, because he had been your client, too, but you wonder: Why did the Supreme Court let my other client die, where in that case I had raised the selfsame constitutional issue, exactly the same issue in almost exactly the same language . . . and you ask *why,*

why was I unable to persuade them in this case, when it was so clear to them in that other case, why not *my* guy; for eight years you ask why, until you discover the answer, by luck, buried among the 576 cartons of Thurgood Marshall papers at the Library of Congress: the Supreme Court, 5–4, let your client die because the Justice who cast the outcome-determinative fifth vote was under a delusion that the prisoner's lawyer (i.e., you) had "sandbagged" the Court by waiting until the last minute to raise the issue, and so as punishment for the sins of the lawyer, the lawyer's client must pay with his life . . . and you read the Court's papers over and over, you can't not read them, even though it's making you physically ill, and you leave them to go throw up into the toilet, and then you go back to read them some more, even though by now you have them memorized, you can't put them down, it's like watching a slow-motion car wreck, the wish to avert your gaze is just overcome by the horrified need to see what happens next, but it is worse than observing a wreck, because *you* helped cause the wreck and because someone you'd come to care about, a deeply flawed human being, but a friend nonetheless, died in the wreck that was at least partly your fault; or the time when your lover of several years (who gave birth to your child, Larkin, the night before, an unplanned home birth with a dozen paramedics from Jupiter [Florida] Fire and Rescue Station Number 2 in attendance) is asleep in the maternity room and your child is in the nursery, and you quietly spread your papers out over the adjoining bed, because your first U.S. Supreme Court brief is due to be filed in a week, and you look over and see that your lover is awake and gazing at you with an expression of bottomless anger, tempered by pity, and you know, *right then,* that the relationship is doomed; or burying your dead, not only clients, but also colleagues and teachers and friends and unindicted co-conspirators who died way, way too young (Joan Baez: "idols are best when they're made of stone / savior's a nuisance to live with at home / stars often fall, heroes go unsung / And martyrs most certainly die too young"): Craig Barnard, the serene, unflappable, pipe-smoking architect, the grand chess master of the litigation campaign to outlaw capital punishment in Florida, who hired you into the public defender's office (because, you are convinced to this day, you could recite from memory, during the job interview, the entire lyrics of Monty Python's "Philosophers' Song." Kind of scary: Some of your brain cells are taken up remembering that), Craig Barnard, who personified the qualities most admired by H. L. Mencken: "a serene spirit; a steady freedom from moral indignation, and all embracing tolerance. Such a man is not to be mistaken for one who shirks the hard knocks of life. On the contrary, he is frequently an eager gladiator, vastly enjoying the opposition. But when he fights he fights in the manner of a gentleman fighting a duel, not in that of a longshoreman cleaning out a waterfront saloon. That is to say, he carefully guards his armor proper by

assuming that his opponent is as decent a man as he is, and just as honest—
and perhaps, after all, right"—and what Craig Barnard always understood was that the world's work gets done, and always will get done, in the
space between the laws' pieties and human possibilities; Craig Barnard
was not a saint, he was a litigator fluent in the language of the laws' promises; Craig Barnard, the likes of whom we have not seen since his death, but
anyone who looked at the rows of wounded compatriots' faces that lined
the memorial service celebrating his life knew what might have been—the
stone is once again at the bottom of the hill, and we are alone; Craig Barnard, from whom you learned how to do deathwork, who drowned in his
bathtub in an inch of water, after an epileptic seizure, at age 39—and you
hear about it when you're in Atlanta, preparing to argue the next morning
a capital case in the federal court of appeals, and you put your oral argument notes aside, by that time you either know the case or you don't, you
can't cram for these things, call a friend, and spend most of the night drinking Wild Turkey and listening to tapes by Mary Chapin Carpenter and
Joan Armatrading and the Cowboy Junkies and Brenda Kahn and Patty
Larkin, and at 9:00 A.M. next morning you give the best oral argument of
your life, for once you have control of the courtroom like you never have
before, and you can't quite explain it or account for it, because your issues
were pretty lame, and later, as your're walking down Forsythe Street to the
Tip Top Diner, you realize the answer, even though it seems sappy and
uncool—*Craig* was there in court with you, he was *with* you—and you
think that maybe it's time that you and God got back on speaking terms,
maybe She can explain the Holocaust and the death of Harriet Goldberg so
young, and maybe it's time to start going to synagogue regularly; and your
judge, Judge Robert S. Vance, who survived the sixties even though he was
in the thick of the civil rights combat, only to be blown apart in the newly
remodeled kitchen of his home in Mountain Brook, just outside Birmingham, by a letter bomb disguised as materials about breeding horses, because whoever sent the bomb must have known that Judge Vance loved his
horses; or Steve Goldstein, a Florida State University law professor who
moonlighted as counsel for the Florida Resource Center, dead of a heart
attack the day before Thanksgiving, dead in his jogging shorts, not long
before he was supposed to celebrate his fiftieth birthday; or Mark Evans,
your co-counsel in Bennie Demps and Davidson James and Joe Spaziano,
who had the physique of a body builder and who died of a heart attack, one
of the original Monkey Wrench Gang, who went from Harvard Law
School to Hollywood to make his fortune as a drug lawyer to the starlets,
retired at age 45 and bought a piece of desert in Utah, but learned later that
there was an Indian artifact goldmine on his land, which he wanted to
preserve but which kept getting looted by poachers, so Evans struck back,
got into firefights and fistfights, but that wasn't adventuresome enough, so

he came to Florida to represent the condemned and write his memoirs about the Utah Indian artifact wars, and every spring, religiously, he came to Vermont to go to the Five College Book Sale and visit and drink shots of Jose Cuervo and smoke Dominican cigars and plot strategy for our death cases and for the overthrow of the Trilateral Commission (Evans was paranoid, and more than a little insane, as he would cheerfully tell you, with a malicious smile that left no doubt that *he* believed it, and so did you), but he finally pried himself loose from his litigation commitments and from his condemned clients, and moved into a friend's cabin in upstate New York to *finally* finish his Utah book, and one night he died in his sleep, of a massive heart attack, at age 55 (the third time he'd died, in fact, because twice his heart had stopped beating during surgery, after Evans had been beaten and jailed by the bad guys in Utah—that extraordinary porcelain heart, that heart that could be as generous to friends as it could be fearsomely deadly to enemies); so Evans' people gathered at Bryce Canyon, Utah, Evans' favorite spot on earth (he'd never been to Paris) to celebrate his life, and most everyone was there, death penalty lawyers and investigators, dope lawyers, Hollywood starlets—all of whom appear, from the photo you received, to be anorexic—but you don't go because still you don't do funerals, except the one, and that was different, that was keeping a promise to a client whose life you hadn't been able to save, even though you had the silver bullet issue (as it turned out, later, years later, eons later, too late, for every purpose and in every way, too late), so you don't go to Evans' funeral, but folks send you pictures of the event, including a photo of the cardboard, bigger-than-life blown-up photo of Evans that his sister had made, and it's odd that you always referred to him as "Evans," and he called you "Mello," oh, well, another mystery of our faith; so you do what you do to show love for someone who dies long before their time, you hunt until you find a poem that fits, and that Evans might appreciate, because he, too, admired William Carlos Williams, and you dedicate a law review article to him: "This article is dedicated to the indestructible spirit of Mark Evans who was constitutionally allergic to bullshit and who journeyed to Vermont every spring for the Five College Book Sale with the regularity of a pilgrim." To borrow from Faulkner's *The Unvanquished*, "I don't reckon that [Mark] or anyone who ever knew [him] has to be told where [he] has gone. And I don't reckon that anybody who ever knew [him] would want to insult [him] by telling him to *rest* anywhere in peace." Peace, yes; but *rest*? Not likely. And no *funeral* service, thank you very much. Evans would

> teach you my townspeople
> how to perform a funeral
> for you have it over a troop

of artists—
unless one should scour the world—
you have the ground sense necessary.
See! the hearse leads.
I begin with a design for a hearse.
For Christ's sake not black—
nor white either—and not polished!
Let it be weathered—like a farm wagon—
with gilt wheels (this could be
applied fresh at small expense)
or no wheels at all:
a rough dray to drag over the ground.
Knock the glass out!
My God—glass, my townspeople!
For what purpose? Is it for the dead
to look out or for us to see
how well he is housed or to see
the flowers or the lack of them—
or what?
To keep the rain and snow from him?
He will have a heavier rain soon:
pebbles and dirt and what not.
Let there be no glass—
and no upholster, phew!
and no little brass rollers
and small easy wheels on the bottom—
my townspeople what are you thinking of?
A rough plain hearse then with gilt wheels and no top at all.
On this the coffin lies
by its own weight.
  No wreaths please—
especially no hot house flowers.
Some common memento is better,
something he prized and is known by:
his old clothes—a few books perhaps—
God knows what! You realize
how we are about these things
my townspeople—
something will be found—anything
even flowers if he had come to that.
So much for the hearse.
For heaven's sake though see to the driver!
Take off the silk hat! In fact
that's no place at all for him—
up there unceremoniously
dragging our friend out to his own dignity!

Bring him down—bring him down!
Low and inconspicuous! I'd not have him ride
on the wagon at all—damn him—
the undertaker's understrapper!
Let him hold the reins
and walk at the side
and inconspicuously too!
Then briefly as to yourselves:
Walk behind—as they do in France,
seventh class, or if you ride
Hell take curtains! Go with some show
of inconvenience; sit openly—
to the weather as to grief.
Or do you think you can shut grief in?
What—from us? We who have perhaps
nothing to lose? Share with us
share with us—it will be money
in your pockets.
Go now
I think you are ready.

—William Carlos Williams, "Tract"

I think I bought this collection during our 1991 book buying binge; so you're leaving Florida and front-line deathwork to go into private practice with a large D.C. firm, and this is your last oral argument in the Florida Supreme Court, for the foreseeable future, and the justices are *nice* to you, expansive, almost friendly, and that makes you *very* squeamish, because you think of the Florida Supreme Court as "your court," because for the past few months you've been orally arguing before them at least once a week, and one justice, a fellow whose judicial demeanor personifies the phrase "crusty but lovable," and whose only questions to you at oral argument are variations on the inquiry "did he *do* it? Counsel, that's what I want to know, did your client *do* it?" but who this morning seems to be trying to engage you in a general *conversation* about the morality of capital punishment, and you keep trying to shift the dialogue back to the specifics of your client's particular case, but there he goes again, asking you about deterrence and retribution, and the other justices are sitting by quietly, and you think, "This is not going well: they don't appear to even want to *talk* about the constitutional claims I've raised in this case," and yet you're kind of having fun with this, and it is as though you and the justice are the only two people in the grand chamber of the Supreme Court of Florida, it's as though the two of you are sitting on stools at the Tallahassee Hilton bar, where you encountered one of the justice's brethren a few weeks earlier, and had a down and dirty chat about what the death penalty really *is* and what it really means, but here you are at the lectern, just you and a justice whose nickname was "Stormin' Norman," but then they grant the stay, and you wonder if perhaps the stay was a little going-away present from the justices, but you'll never know; and your last oral argument in the federal court of appeals, too, and the judges begin by wishing you well in D.C. and commenting about the beard you're trying to grow, and you make a bad joke ("I'm trying to change my appearance, your honor, so the next time I come before you, maybe you won't recognize me"), and the judges chuckle politely, and, *mirabile dictu,* they rule in your client's favor; so now you're in D.C., and you end up on the Elizabeth Morgan child custody/child rape case, and your client, not a death row prisoner, but rather a mother who has just been sent to jail for contempt of court, indefinitely, for refusing to produce her young daughter for unsupervised visits with the father, and even though it's a civil case, being litigated in our nation's capital, the case's atmospherics are much like those of a death case: a media blitz that portrays your client as a lunatic who bears no visible comparison to this soft-spoken-but-steel-willed woman in an orange jail jumpsuit, sitting across the table from you in a visiting room of the D.C. lockup, and you just *know* that she's serious about staying in jail until her daughter turns 18, the age that would divest the ratbag judge of jurisdiction over the case; and you have priceless and unforgettable *Morgan* skull sessions with the partner on the case, a noble man who has been a lifelong prosecutor, the attorney general of Maryland for eight years, the lawyer who argued (and won) the seminal case upholding the constitutionality of Maryland's death penalty statute, a man who now would join his client in the D.C. jail if he had to, because he believes in her, but finally, after an act of Congress and a signature by President Bush, Dr. Morgan is released from jail, and she is too poised to celebrate publicly, and the story has a happy ending, with Dr. Morgan joining her daughter in Christchurch, New Zealand, and settling there, and sending Christmas letters and recent photos to her friends and supporters; and so you're working for "Lloyd Cutler's law firm," which you will always think of as John Pickering's law firm, because while Cutler provides the glitz, Pickering provides the soul of the place, and you are still remembered there for two things: setting a record for accounted-for hours (billable hours plus *pro bono* hours), something like 3,500 in one year, and the 575 dollar lunch for three people you held at La Pavillion; and you come to realize that being in D.C. means getting calls from lawyers all over the country, but especially from states that seem particularly maniacal about executions, asking, at the last minute, *please* would you throw together a bare-bones stay application to file in the U.S. Supreme Court—yes, yes, the execution is set for one minute past midnight tonight, and it's noon now, but . . . well . . . ; so you admit that "you can take the lawyer out of Florida, but you can't take Florida out of the lawyer," and you *know* that's a tired cliche, but it's a true cliche, but maybe that's *why* it's a cliche, just because it's true and because all cliches were true at one time, that's how they *became* cliches, and, anyway, you're tired yourself sometimes, but you resolve that rather than trying to repress memories of your time in combat in the Sunshine State, you let them loose, let them wash over you, knowing that "let" falsely implies you have more power over them than you in fact have, because they'd wash over you anyway, uninvited and unwelcome, whether you "let" them or not; or the time that a .52 (this is not a typo, sadly) blood alcohol level—moderation never having been your strong suit—earned you an ambulance ride, with all the trimmings, and a night in the ICU, on suicide watch, in a room that included an elderly woman, a candy striper, sitting in a chair beside your bed to make sure you don't rip out the IV tubes, and she's not supposed to talk to you, she's just supposed to read her book, but you get her to tell you her life story anyway, and you wind up having a delightful chat about Florida and Virginia and North Carolina, and you explain to her, and later to a doctor who does all he can to ape the appearance of Sigmund Freud, down to the unlit cigar, which you can't help but notice is a pretty cheap one, so you conclude that he must still be an intern or resident, and he asks you the "suicide questions," and his eyebrows arch when you tell him that, yes, you often think about death, because that's your job, and you tell him that you were *not* suicidal, that you're a lot of things, but incompetent isn't among them, and that if you wanted to kill yourself you have a 9mm Glock, and one bullet to the heart (it would have to be to the heart, wouldn't it; anywhere else would be the wrong metaphor altogether), so let's quit talking about suicide, shall we, and it's clear that this baby doc must have flunked Bedside Manner 101 in Dartmouth Medical School, because he's doing all the things you implore your law students to avoid when dealing with their future clients: playing the Great White Doctor, talking in the code of medical jargon, telling you what you feel and think and making you feel guilty if you don't, condescending to answer your stupid questions about your own health by talking in opaque medical terminology that, if you wrote it out and diagrammed its paragraphs, would read like a bad Hegel translation; but it does seem wise and prudent to quit drinking hard booze, and you do, and doing so has proven surprisingly easy, and even the night in lockdown gave you good insights into how your clients live 24 hours a day, although you wouldn't recommend the experience, and plan never to risk repeating it; so you give up full-time law practice altogether and move to Vermont to write and teach, but the ghosts come along, and so do the *pro bono* cases and the legal issues they raise; a Texas case, an Arkansas case, a Virginia case, a Georgia case; U.S. Supreme Court briefs for the ABA, the ACLU, your Florida public defender office, the American Jewish Congress, the American Jewish Committee, the National Legal Aid and Defender Association, the National Association of Criminal Defense Lawyers; testifying before the U.S. Senate Judiciary Committee and the ABA on the proposed federal death penalty legislation (now law); and all that's OK, up to a point, because it animates your teaching and lets law students get real-world experience, and you write about capital punishment, at first just in scholarly law reviews, because it's fun and because it is necessary for academic tenure, but after *getting* tenure, you feel liberated to write more about the people and less about the law, and the law reviews keep on publishing you, but only after long conversations about, for example, whether you may use the word "fuck" three times in a law review article, and the editors want to spell it "f_ _ _," or "f * * *," and you say, no, the word is "fuck," thank you very much, and they relent, because they really like the article, and you have to smile, because your only enduring contribution to your own school's law review, when you were a student and articles editor of the journal, was to make Fred Rodell's 1937 classic "Goodbye to Law Reviews," the best piece your law review has published in its 85-year history, required reading for new editors; or the case when you stood up to argue in front of the state trial court judge, to find the courtroom filled with uniformed state troopers, and the judge himself peering down at you from the bench with a nasty smile, as he fondled brass knuckles in one hand and a .44 magnum in the other; or when Stephen Bright collected, all in one place and all scrupulously footnoted and cite-checked, and published in 1994 in the prestigious *Yale Law Journal*, a parade of horribles in capital cases, demonstrating just how pitiful are the lawyers who are often assigned to represent people on trial for their lives: a lawyer in one Georgia case conceded his client's guilt and argued for a life sentence at the guilt phase; he continued to plead for mercy even after he was admonished by the trial judge to save his argument on punishment for the sentencing phase; a judge in a Florida case took a defense lawyer into his chambers during the penalty phase to explain what it was about; the lawyer responded: "I'm at a loss. I really don't know what to do in this type of proceeding. If I'd been through one, I would, but I've never handled one except this time"; an Alabama defense lawyer asked for time between the guilt and penalty phases so that he could read the state's death penalty statute; the lawyer in a Pennsylvania case tailored his presentation of evidence and argument around a death penalty statute that had been declared unconstitutional three years earlier because it limited the arguments on which the defense could rely in presenting mitigating circumstances; the Georgia Supreme Court affirmed a death sentence after receiving a brief that contained only five pages of argument and was filed only in response to the threat of sanctions against the lawyer (the dissent noted that the court-appointed counsel raised a single point of error and the substantive portion of the brief was 150 words); or other cases: one page of argument, raising a single issue and citing one case; six pages of poorly written argument, citing only nine cases, which failed to raise issues regarding the mental incompetence of the defendant, lack of counsel at the preliminary hearing, mental competency of the state's two key witnesses, vagueness of the aggravating circumstance on which the death sentence rested, and other issues which were later raised in a brief of 70 pages which cited 96 cases in the postconviction appeal of the case to the Eleventh Circuit; an African American facing the death penalty in Walker County, Georgia, represented by a white defense attorney whose attitudes on race were described as follows by a federal district court before concluding that the lawyer had *not* rendered ineffective assistance:

> Dobbs' trial attorney was outspoken about his views. He said that many blacks are uneducated and would not make good teachers, but do make good basketball players. He opined that blacks are less educated and less intelligent than whites either because of their nature or because "my grand-daddy had slaves." He said that integration has led to deteriorating neighborhoods and schools, and referred to the black community in Chattanooga as "black boy jungle." He strongly implied that blacks have inferior morals by relating a story about sex in a classroom. He also said that when he was young, a maid was hired with the understanding that she would steal some items. He said that blacks in Chattanooga are more troublesome than blacks in Walker County [Georgia].

Or the time when you were arguing for a stay of execution in the U.S. Court of Appeals in Atlanta, and you heard behind you a sloshing sound, apparently originating from the defense counsel's chair, and when you turned from the podium to turn the argument over to your co-counsel, you were almost overcome with feelings of both horror and hilarity, because the sloshing sound you heard was just as you thought it was, your co-counsel, in an attempt to water his parched throat, had poured half a pitcher of water into his lap, but what could you do?—and he strode up to the podium, trying not to laugh, as you were trying not to laugh, as the judges were trying not to laugh, as the prosecutor was trying hard not to laugh, as the reporters were scribbling down notes, and you thought that perhaps at least this bit of levity might incline the judges to rule in your client's favor, but it didn't, and your client was executed on schedule anyway; and for a while you drink to forget, to squelch memory, but you soon learn that it doesn't work, because alcohol affects only short-term memory, leaving long-term memory painfully intact, and so you can't remember the conversation you had with your secretary yesterday, but you can remember, all too vividly, life among Florida's culture of the condemned; or Governor "Bob" Graham, a blow-dried southern politician, a liberal Democrat "wimp," who parlayed a political career as governor for four years, U.S. senator for six years, so far, by being "tough on crime" and signing lots of death warrants; and then there was the courtly north Florida trial judge, a fellow whose accent was captured indelibly in a 1991 column lampooning Strom Thurmond's performance during the Anita Hill–Clarence Thomas hearings: "Soam-whoan ben cudrin's mheah widm tan' bfust drang," which translates as "Somebody has colored my hair with what appears to be Tang breakfast drink"; or Ricky Ray Rector, an Arkansas death row prisoner who gave his life in service of the political career of Bill Clinton; Rector, who had been lobotomized as a result of a self-inflicted bullet wound at the time of his arrest for murder; Rector, whom Clinton had destroyed by lethal injection on January 24, 1992, the governor's big *60 Minutes* weekend, and you can well imagine that the last thing he felt he needed was idle talk about his softness on crime, tempting Christopher Hitchens to be pontifical about this moral contrast—a temptress on one side and an executioner on another, and the mob turning from the medicalized gibbet to the exposed love nest, but actually concluding, correctly, that the Rector case tells us nothing that we do not already know all too well about the death penalty, that it is cruel and unusual, that, especially in the South, it is applied in a racist manner, that humane and defensible alternatives to it are within easy reach, and that Bill Clinton is a calculating opportunist, none of this is news, and yet, discussing with partisans of Governor Clinton the decision to license the lethal injection by denying clemency, Hitchens found himself more powerfully nauseated than in past arguments with rednecks and racists who really don't know any better, while the strategic and tactical thinking displayed by Clinton's supporters convicted him of a base and hungry cunning—the last two executions he authorized (of John Swindler in June 1990 and Ronald Gene Simmons later in the same month) were both of white men, so it was argued that staying the execution of Ricky Ray Rector would have opened Clinton to a charge of affirmative action, but Hitchens could not offhand think of a more contemptible reason, and neither can I, because the mentally devastated Rector had to die because two men of different shade had already been put to death? In other words, never act justly now, for fear that you may have to act justly later, because, after all, justice can set that frightful thing, a *precedent,* and it is also impossible to acquit Clinton of the charge of having people snuffed to suit his own political and career needs, since in the candidates' debate on January 19, 1992, the governor bragged of his firmness in dispatching Swindler and Simmons, as if to preempt any Hortonizing of his future ambitions, and when he briefly lost the Arkansas state house to a neolithic Republican named Frank White in 1980, Clinton was considered "vulnerable" to White's demagogic charge that he was weak on law and order, thus proving Hitchens' point that the element of low calculation in the Rector decision is so evident and so naked that it makes one gasp; or the least controversial major innovation of the bitterly fought 1994 federal crime bill being the bill's expansion of the death penalty to cover more than 50 crimes (until the 1994 change, the death penalty could have been imposed for two federal crimes: aircraft hijacking that results in loss of life, and murder committed by "drug kingpins," whatever those are, except they invariably seem to be racial minorities, as do people condemned pursuant to the military death penalty); or the time you are sharing a bottle of good red wine with a prosecutor, a woman with whom you have become friends over the years, even though you are always on the opposite sides of capital cases, who makes you an offer: because she likes you and she trusts you and she thinks you are an honorable person, she is willing to arrange things so that one of your clients—but only one—will be permitted to escape the death penalty by operation of a plea bargain that she would arrange, and you know, or you fervently believe, that one of your present clients is absolutely, totally innocent of the offense for which he is sentenced to die, so maybe he should be the one that you choose, but then there is the profoundly retarded client, who committed the act of murder, but has the mind of a toddler, and, anyway, both of those cases have fairly strong legal issues, so there is a better than usual likelihood that you will be able to win them some relief in the courts at some point, either resentencing, or retrial, or commutation of sentence to something less than the death penalty, so perhaps you should exercise your option in a way that would benefit your worst client, who has committed the most heinous crimes, who has the fewest mitigating circumstances, who has the fewest legal issues likely to win any judicial relief in the future, maybe that's the one you should choose in exercise of your Sophie's choice, but then it occurs to you that you do *all* of your clients a disservice by even going through this thought process, and that if you give one name to your friend the prosecutor, then, sure, that one person gets off death row, but what about the rest of them, your other clients, the ones that you didn't choose, because in essence you have told the prosecutor that these other clients are less worthy of life than the one whom you do select, so maybe you shouldn't select anyone, but how can you make *that* decision, because you now have it *within your power* to save the life of a human being whom you represent, except that you represent many human beings, and so you take another sip of wine, and ask your friend the prosecutor where the hell she came up with that crazy offer? and she replies that the other night she was reading a biography of Chief Justice Earl Warren, the great liberal hero of the criminal procedure revolution on the U.S. Supreme Court, and that was one thing that Warren did when he was attorney general of California, and so if it was good enough for Warren, it was good enough for her . . . ; and you keep remembering—keep *hemorrhaging* memories, sometimes,

80

like a hemophiliac—as if you had any choice about whether to remember; and you resolve to commit to paper nothing more, and nothing less, than a fair reflection of the honest and long-settled convictions of your heart, approaching your subject with humble awe and with fear and trembling, but also aware of Murray Kempton's statement that "a man's spirit can be marked most clearly in its passage from the reform to the revolutionary· impulse at the moment he decides that his enemy will not write his history," and seeing the sometimes ferocious heroics your colleagues and your co-conspirators, and clients, grow out of such moments of self-determination; OK, fine, but there's no rush, you're young, 37, and you can write at your leisure, but then things happen to remind you—as your clients *never* need reminding, even though they're men engendered in this culture, too, and even though once they did feel immortal; living on death row beats that feeling out of one—that you're mortal and fragile, that young people die: two car wrecks, due to Vermont's black ice and the late hour, in both you were driving to your office in the middle of the night to work on an ABA brief, and in one your car rolled over thrice and ended up at the bottom of an embankment, you've never been so happy to see a state trooper in your life (you chat in his car, watching the snow come down, and end up inviting him to talk to your criminal law students); and then clinical depression hits you like a fist, and you reread the novels of Evelyn Waugh and shave with a fork, and Doris Lessing was right that sometimes when people fly apart it's a way of self-healing, of the inner self dismissing false dichotomies and divisions; and you're a little amazed that you're still among the sentient ("All. I. Know. Is. I'm. Still. Standing." as your favorite singer said), you're living proof of Nietzsche's dictum that "whatever does not kill me outright makes me stronger," and your vicarious proximity to death, through your clients' intimacy with the ultimate punishment, turns out to be *very* different from your own, personal encounter with the End; but you resolve to live realistically—which is to say, to live as though you might die tomorrow—and to take care of unfinished business, like spending more time with your angelic son (who is a combination of Calvin *and* Hobbes), and like making a will, something you exhort your law students to do, and like reconciling with your father, who was there for you when you needed his support, such as when you worked as a volunteer EMT at Alexandria Hospital's ER, back when the ER was in Old Town, where you learned from the Nine-and-I victims to *always* wear seat belts; or when you cut nine weeks of high school one semester because you wanted to be a pilot and you'd hang out in the control tower of DCA (Washington National Airport); or when you lied about your age to enroll in the first EMT class at Northern Virginia Community College, and then a few weeks later a high-rise building near your high school collapsed, and you bolted from science class to help look for survivors in the wreckage, only there weren't any, and it became a search for bodies, and then a search for body parts; or the years you were in the Northern Virginia Wing of the Civil Air Patrol, learning how to fly Cessnas and how to set up a communications network for a search and rescue mission and how to run a ground rescue team, and it was all a swell game until a real mission turned ugly, and you spent a solid week on the radio directing air and ground rescue teams through Elizabeth's Furnace, Virginia, and finally you learned, against your will and against every instinct in your being, how to rappel down (and up, but up was easy) the face of mountains; and who was there throughout your stupid youth, who told you to ignore the Neanderthal high school guidance counsellor who'd concluded that you just weren't smart enough for college, but had you thought about taking auto shop?; or when you and 400 other people occupied the administration building at Kent State University in 1978, to protest the school's decision to build a gymnasium over part of the site of the May 4, 1970, shootings, or when you were a medic for the Yippies at the Democratic and Republican conventions in 1976, sleeping in tents in Central Park and Kemper Square Park, respectively, treating everything from knife wounds to heroin-induced cardiac arrest; like writing this book as a robust and wide-open treatment of the subject, without self-censorship; like getting back into Joe Spaziano's case and just kicking *ass,* treating it like Armageddon, sparing no expense, because what else are credit cards for?—and for him it *is* Armageddon, a silent, miniaturized violence far removed from public view, Joe's Armageddon, and Mello's, too; or the resentencing, a case in which you were lucky enough to persuade a federal court to mandate that your client receive a new sentencing proceeding before a new jury, and your co-counsel, miracle of miracles, has managed to convince the prosecutor to accept a negotiated plea of life imprisonment, because "it's never too late to talk settlement," but your client, who is as guilty as he is cocky, was absolutely *wired* and convinced that you can get him off completely, free jail delivery, do not pass go, and you won't need the $200, and so in one of the jail visiting rooms you try to convince him, browbeat him, that he really does need to take the negotiated plea of life imprisonment, because at the end of the resentencing he might well end up back on death row, back where he started, back where we all started, and this time in his trip through the federal courts he might not be so lucky as to win a resentencing, but the client is so wired that you aren't able to convince him, and you tell him that he must calm down, how can you help him calm down? and he raises an eyebrow, looks at you, and says, "I could relax much more effectively if you could just arrange for me to look at the crime scene photographs in the privacy of my cell or of this room," and you feel your stomach turn, because you know that as an attorney you have access to the photographs, and you can bring the photographs into the visiting room with you, but you can't leave them with your client, and so you do that, you bring in the photographs, and your client excitedly looks at them, his breathing rate increases, his pupils begin to dilate, and the next thing you hear is a slight zipping sound, and, as you stare into the middle distance, there is your client, masturbating over the photographs of the crime scene, and he ejaculates, he does it again, he does it until the photographs are covered with a punky, milky sheen, and all you can do is think to yourself, "For this I went to law school?"—but it works, it does calm your client down, it calms him down enough so that he agrees to take the plea bargain, and the case has a happy ending, of sorts: life imprisonment, with a mandatory 25 years before parole eligibility; and so your life begins to feel as though it is bursting the rivets of your control, and a combination of exhaustion, stress, overwork, and depression caused by the end of a long-term relationship results in seizures, which, even after the MRIs and the EEGs and the CAT scans, are still unexplainable, because, as you know from your litigation experience, medical science really knows next to nothing about the way the brain works, so you go on disability from your teaching job for a month, and are in the hospital for six weeks, and you get some great stories from the experience and meet some fascinating people, and you get a great gift idea: to give your significant other (who has always loved you for your mind) a framed four-color MRI photograph of your brain, and you pester the hospital staff until they give you your own access code into their fax and photocopying machines, and still no one really knows why you were having seizures, and so you decide, what the hell, you'll start smoking cigarettes at age 37, just when Robert Reich and his band of merry trolls at the Occupational Safety and Health Administration propose by ukase to purge the workplace of every last filthy weed, and city councils in half the nation's top six dump sites vote to shut down mild-mannered restaurants, even bars, where once upon a time our Bogeys and Bacalls gazed at each other through a pall of smoke, and the frightwig who just sat herself down next to you in an otherwise empty *smoking* section at the local coffee shop, wearing the pelt of a dead marsupial, smelling like the guts of a sperm whale, complains immediately about the cigarette you'd already stubbed out, because you've been browbeaten into feeling ashamed of your pariah self in a shameless *republic* of moralizing busy-body bullies, professional crybabies, post-therapeutic vegetarian hysterics, and Rogaine-abusing health nazi joggers; and you have a client named Bennie, and whenever you work on his case, you can't help but hum "B B B B B Bennie and the Jets," and whenever your secretary word-processes a brief in *Bennie* her computer crashes, and it's sort of cute until you lose the case in the federal court of appeals, and then you lose it in the Supreme Court, and then you wait for a death warrant . . . ; or when you travel the back roads of Florida, to interview witnesses, or to appear in court, you're always struck by the frontier quality of the place, particularly the Florida Everglades, which a hundred years ago was a lawless frontier, a labyrinth of mangroves and shell mounds where renegades and desperadoes played out their lives beside fishermen and hunters, where Judah Benjamin and other Confederate leaders escaped after Appomattox, and you keep returning to Faulkner and Thomas Wolfe and Robert Penn Warren, and especially Peter Matthiessen's *Killing Mister Watson* and the time when "there was no law down there, men settled their differences amongst themselves, and the killing was not what you might call uncommon. . . . Them kind I'm talking about don't want no part of them damned paper-wavers from the city, trying to tell a man where he could take a shit"; or: " 'They won't lynch you in Fort Meyers.' 'No? How about a legal lynching like that stranger got, a couple of years ago, where self defense against some local mean mouth who picked a fight with him? That feller was as good as lynched, my Cary tells me, not because he deserved to die but because that's what the local people howled for. And nobody had to dirty their hands expecting you.' He puts his watch back, then waves his hand to quiet me, as if reminded by the hard night wind that the world is closing in on him too fast. 'I know, I know, the law's the law, it was your duty.' 'You know that feller?' 'Nobody knew him. That's why he was hung' "; and of all the pain and the gore you've seen as the collateral damage of capital punishment, what's branded in your brain isn't the charred corpse of Jesse Tafero, whose head burst into flames when the prison officials used an inferior grade of sponge, which is a necessary detail of the execution ritual minutiae, because the sponge is soaked in a saline solution and placed between the electrode and your client's shaved head, which has been shaved especially for this occasion, and if the saline-soaked sponge is cheap, then it doesn't conduct the electricity into your client's head, the sponge will just ignite, and if the members of the execution detail aren't paying attention, your client's head will ignite too, which is what happened when they electrocuted Mr. Tafero, and the crime scene and autopsy photographs *are* horrifying beyond description, but they're not the worst, no, the most spine-chilling document you encounter during your travels among the condemned is a piece of bureaucratese, which has been typed on a government-issue standard manual typewriter, which is on three-hole paper, which has "confidential" stamped all over it, and which is called "Execution Guidelines for Active Death Warrant," the manual of protocols used by the Florida State Prison, which doesn't deal with the blood but rather with the bureaucracy: The best way to approach the horror of this war is the way Hannah Arendt approached the horror of Eichmann, through the banality of the *small* things, the casual human expedients, hitched to a killing technology and distant and abstracted purposes like deterrence, retribution, whatever; that capital punishment is a local-level manifestation of the fact that global bipolarity has given way to universal anarchy, to civil wars from South Central L.A. to Bosnia to Rwanda—and a historically unprecedented nihilism has gripped our great urban centers, where the young revolutionaries of this epoch are fighting civil wars about nothing at all, their conflicts completely divorced from ideology, without substantive content or conviction, with death and destruction as the ends, and not the means, of these wars, it's hard to survey the battlefields of these modern molecular civil wars and not see marauding bands haunting the globe, with no need of a Führer, destroying themselves as much as others, acting out a patricide of sorts, and these modern civil wars ignite spontaneously from inside, and they are as much about hatred of the self as hatred of the other, and somewhere there is a *Gewalt* linkage between neo-nazi attacks on immigrants and Florida's killing of Ronald Straight or Ted Bundy, the *Gewalt* is the same, the German word for violence that includes the sense of helplessness that accompanies it; though you would not avert your gaze, neither would you stare directly; and, oddly, the scariest, like sending that thank you letter you've been trying to write to Faye Resnick, now, today, before you lose your nerve, and you look at the letter and think about William Carlos Williams' lines "Go now / I think you are ready," but you're *not* ready, not quite yet, just a few more edits . . . ; and in the end, even though you never say this out loud because it would sound arrogant, you're settled and secure and quietly serene in the absolute *conviction* that you're *right* about this nation's system of state-sponsored death, a conviction grounded not in smug self-righteousness, but rather born anew each day by your own experience, relearning time and time again that you're not just making legalistic arguments, but that this system of capital punishment really *is* as hopelessly bad as you say it is in your briefs; that it really *is* warped by race and class; that the people who end up on death row didn't necessarily commit the worst crimes, but they often did get the worst defense lawyers at trial; that the whole sputtering system of state sponsored death in this Republic is *lawless,* simply neither tameable by, nor containable within, the rule of law, it's a machine concocted by Rube Goldberg, a pinball machine that never goes "tilt," even when it's turned upside down.

But I'm getting too old for that shit. Maybe I always have been. Writing in fragments. Beginning sentences with prepositions. Not good. There is also the matter of nerve, failure thereof. When you're no longer willing to go to jail for contempt of court, or to be disbarred, for demanding that the law keep its promises of fairness and equality and due process to your clients who are litigating for their lives—then it's time to quit. When you start to minimize the crimes of your clients, or to sentimentalize them, it's time to go on home. When I quit hard alcohol a while ago, and gave up illicit substances a millennium ago (still working on cigars and cigarettes and pipes, but, obviously, not very seriously; full disclosure: I'm also a hopeless caffeine addict; like Brenda Kahn, I don't sleep: I drink coffee instead), I was a little worried that the scribbling might suffer; but surprise, surprise, the opposite happened. Now music is what transports me. "Scottie, beam me aboard. There's no intelligent life on this planet."

As I've said, this chapter is about memory. We are what we remember (and forget). It's interesting that Holocaust historians are turning to memory as the locus, and the subject, of their inquiries, and that memory has become something of a cultural obsession for Americans, in our *fin de siècle,* much as it was for Europeans a century ago. I have some spooky closets in the mansion of my mind, and many of those closets are wallpapered with Florida scenes. What Florida has splintered may remain fragmented, or, if pieced together, the whole may prove unlovely—and unlovable, threatening to collapse, as if the best one can do is jury-rig with duct tape, which is man's *real* best friend.

The more I think about this, digging through the archeological levels of memory, like the archeologist Yigal Yadin, poking around in the sands soon after Israel's 1948 War of Independence, the more I appreciate Tim O'Brien's meditations on the Vietnam War. For those of us who did not serve in Vietnam, O'Brien's *The Things They Carried* could be our Dead Sea Scrolls. As O'Brien wrote of soldiers at war: We used a hard vocabulary to contain and mask a terrible softness. *Fried,* we'd say. We'd say *burned, zapped, greased, offed.* It wasn't cruelty, just stage presence. We were actors. When someone died, a client or a colleague, it wasn't quite dying, because in a curious way it seemed scripted, and because we all had our lines mostly memorized, irony mixed with tragedy, and because we called it by other names, as if to encyst and destroy the reality of death itself. Deathwork brought out the best, and the worst, in us; our public defender office was a place where all tendencies became obsessions, and a place of extremes, a landscape of stark blacks and whites. The memory of my days in Florida is like a nail in the eye. The pain goes away but the wound stays forever. The scar never quite heals over, and whenever it seems that it is going to, you pick at it.

My first assignment during my first week as a public defender was a certiorari petition for Joseph Spaziano. Now, more than a dozen years later, I see a narrative thread from the Ivon Ray Stanley decision to my work on behalf of Joe Spaziano to my decision now to walk away from my work as a lawyer in death row postconviction litigation.

"It is all in how we die," Kate Millett wrote in *A.D.* Everything I learned I learned from people who are waiting to die or to be killed. I learned what I know about class and poverty from all of my clients. I learned what I know about Vietnam, and about a thing called posttraumatic stress disorder, from David Funchess, who was electrocuted in 1986. In May 1995 I visited, for the first time, The Wall. I looked for the name of

David Funchess, and, of course, it wasn't there. Mr. Funchess was the first Vietnam veteran suffering from posttraumatic stress disorder to be executed in the United States; he was destroyed in Florida in the spring of 1986. Vets from all over Florida, and beyond, stood silent vigil at the Tallahassee Memorial to our Vietnam War dead, as the days, and then the hours, wound down toward Mr. Funchess' killing. He is buried in Quincy, Florida, on the land of a fellow Vietnam veteran. I learned what I know about racism from James Adams, Class of '84. And so on.

In the following two chapters I want to tell two stories. The first is Ted Bundy's. The second is Joe Spaziano's. What I learned from Theodore Bundy's case was how little I understand the public psyche of capital punishment, at least in Florida. The more I try to understand the cultural archeology of the law of capital punishment, the more arbitrary and random it becomes to me. The more I try to demystify it, the more random and mysterious it becomes. The more I try to understand the case—and what the case *means,* what it teaches us about Mr. Bundy or about ourselves—the less I understand, the greater the mystery. All I can say for sure is that Mr. Bundy and his killing mean a lot. If Cleopatra's nose had been shorter, wrote Blaise Pascal, the face of the earth would have been changed. Had Bundy looked different, or acted differently or *been* different, the history of capital punishment, and not just in Florida, would have been different.

4

On Metaphors, Mirrors, and Murders

Theodore Bundy and the Rule of Law

Some 230 people lived on Florida's death row by 1986, including several men who had been there a dozen years. And newly condemned prisoners arrived at the rate of almost one per week. The little town of Starke—a plain vanilla town no different from a thousand other American hamlets: one main drag featuring a McDonald's, a Western Sizzlin' steakhouse, a convenience store, a Best Western and a Denny's—little Starke had seen more executions in the previous two years than any place in the whole Western world. Hardly a day dawned in Florida that a life-or-death drama was not playing out in one courthouse or another. Florida's death penalty soaked up millions of dollars and thousands of hours; it was the state's most compelling political issue. And yet the whole vast, clamorous, chaotic enterprise boiled down in the public mind to a single man.

Bundy.

Bear in mind: you can hardly shake the sand out of your beach blanket in Florida without getting a few grains in the chest hair of one criminal or another. What Manhattan is to fashions, what Hollywood is to glitz, what Nashville is to sad songs, Florida is to crime—the source, the acme, the vault. Land sharking, telephone fraud, cocaine cowboys waging machine-gun shoot-'em-ups . . . Florida invented or perfected them all. It is a place where the street scum are crooked, and so, very often, is the guy from the Chamber of Commerce. Year in and year out, Florida has one of the highest crime rates in America, which means one of the highest crime rates in the world. Even amidst this great flood of iniquity, Ted Bundy stood out, he was by far the most infamous criminal in Florida. During his 1979 murder trial, one poll found that his statewide name-recognition was second only to the governor's. His notoriety spread beyond the state lines, too; if he was not, in 1986, the best-known killer in all America, he soon would be, for NBC was preparing to devote four hours of prime time to dramatize his bloody career. Five books had been written about him, countless magazine and newspaper articles. Ted Bundy could, if he wished, command an interview with any television network; even the staid New York Times sought an audience with him. In his infamy, he became an archetype—not one condemned man among hundreds in Starke, but the essence of death row itself. Bundy's enigmatic face became the very face of evil; his undistinguished flesh the embodiment of America's spreading dread.

—David Von Drehle, *Among the Lowest of the Dead: The Culture of Death Row*

88

"Ted" Bundy: Just Can't Seem to Get Him out of Our Minds

> This is not the way the legislators who passed our current death penalty laws planned it. The death penalty was supposed to be about getting even with Ted Bundy, not executing teenagers and the retarded, or wrestling condemned schizophrenics to the gurney for forced doses of Haldol.
> —David Bruck, "Does the Death Penalty Matter?"

> Send lawyers, guns, and money,
> Dad, the shit has hit the fan.
> —Warren Zevon, "Lawyers, Guns, and Money"

During my time in Florida deathwork, Theodore Bundy served as a kind of background radiation—a legalistic version of the vestigial heat from the Big Bang, 2.7 degrees Kelvin, which bathes the cosmos. I first encountered the Bundy phenomenon up close, in a professional capacity, in 1986, when I was an attorney in Florida's new state agency, CCR.

Making a record, or setting the record straight, is one task of this chapter. It tells my version of a story that you probably think you know already: the history of Theodore Robert Bundy's efforts to ward off the Florida executioner.[1] These thoughts were recorded soon after Bundy was executed in January 1989, when the memories were fresh. This chapter's principal source is my memory as recorded at the time, supplemented where possible by public documents and secondary materials.

Our Bundy Fascination

> Dying
> Is an art, like everything else
> I do it exceptionally well.
> —Sylvia Plath, "Lady Lazarus"

> Dying's the best
> Of all the arts men learn in a dead place.
> —James Wright, "Three Poems by Lise Goett"

The trials of Theodore Bundy exerted a hold on the American imagination of the day somewhat as Charles Manson did not long ago. Still, I write reluctantly. Too much has already been said about Theodore ("Ted," to the media) Bundy, the serial sexual murderer[2] suspected of raping and then killing dozens of young women during the 1970s; in a February 1978 announcement adding him to the Federal Bureau of Investigation's list of the 10 most wanted fugitives, the FBI reportedly stated that Bundy was wanted for questioning in connection with 36 sexual slayings that began in California in 1969 and extended through the Pacific Northwest and into Utah and Colorado.[3] Theodore Bundy continues to preoccupy. The cottage industry of commentary on him has generated at least seven nonfiction books (the most recent being published in 1994, five years after Bundy's execution),[4] two fiction books (the most recent, published three years after Bundy's execution, was entitled *The Stranger Returns* and was described in bold-face red and black letters on the book's cover as "The Terrifying Novel of Serial Killer Ted Bundy and His Second Rampage of Death"; Bundy's 1989 electrocution was dismissed with the phrase, "Now Bundy has the perfect alibi"),[5] and countless in-depth magazine and newspaper articles,[6] as well as a television miniseries (starring Mark Harmon as Bundy),[7] a dance drama,[8] and media preoccupation at times comparable to coverage of the space program.[9] Articles in national newspapers that discuss serial killers frequently mention Theodore Bundy;[10] Wendy Lesser's thoughtful meditation on the subject of murder, *Pictures at an Execution,* returned to the Bundy theme again and again.[11] From the Buffalo Bill character in the top-grossing film *Silence of the Lambs* to fictional murder mysteries with serial killer plots (or only passing references), Bundy is ubiquitous.[12] A 1991 nonfiction book about the Elizabeth Morgan child sexual abuse/child custody case quoted a lawyer's reference to Bundy.[13] A psychiatrist noted in September 1990, a year and a half after Bundy was executed: "[D]uring the last annual meeting of the American Academy of Psychiatry and the Law, a panel on the topic of Ted Bundy clearly captured the most attention. An extra loudspeaker was hauled into the hotel corridor so that folks could listen to the proceedings." He went on: "I was among them, straining to hear about the man who murdered so many coeds in Florida. I was a little embarrassed by my morbid interest, and most of us avoided glancing at one another, preferring to appear professional, detached and intent on the dialogue. One woman peacefully knit as she listened, Madame DeFarge-like."[14] Robert Martinez, the Florida governor who signed Bundy's final death warrant, used him in his unsuccessful 1990 reelection campaign. The *National Law Journal* provided the most detailed description of the former governor's campaign ad:

> A guard opens a prison door, walks through and slams it shut behind him. Cut to Florida's Republican Gov. Bob Martinez sitting at his desk, looking severe.
>
> "One of the most serious things that I have to address every day is the whole issue of the death penalty," Martinez says stiffly into the camera. The flag frames him in red, white and blue. A family photo is on the mantel. "I now have signed some 90 death warrants in the state of Florida," he proclaims. "Each one of those committed a heinous crime that I don't choose to describe to you."
>
> [The ad then switches to] footage of . . . Bundy, electrocuted in 1989 as a mob outside the prison gates chanted, "Burn, Bundy, Burn." A vague

smirk crosses Bundy's face. "I believe in the death penalty," Martinez says over Bundy's freeze-framed image.

The camera moves in for a tight closeup of the governor at his desk. "I believe it's the proper penalty for one who has taken someone else's life," Martinez somberly concludes.[15]

Judges and (other) politicians use Bundy as well, even though presumably they know better. U.S. Supreme Court Chief Justice William Rehnquist cited the "Ted Bundy" case as an example of judicial chaos in his February 1989 speech at the American Bar Association's midyear meeting:

> In the case of Ted Bundy, the so-called "serial killer" executed in Florida last month, the Supreme Court of the United States received three separate applications for a stay on the day before the date scheduled for execution. The first sought review of a refusal by the federal district court in Florida to grant a stay, and raised four separate federal issues. The second sought a stay of execution pending review of a denial by the Supreme Court of Florida for state postconviction relief. The third sought a stay pending review of an original action brought in the Supreme Court of Florida on the same day. All three of these actions were being prosecuted in these courts simultaneously on the day before the execution of a prisoner who had been on death row for nine years. Surely it would be a bold person to say that this system could not be improved. . . . To my mind the flaw in the present system is not that capital sentences are set aside by federal courts, but that litigation ultimately resolved in favor of the state takes literally years and years and years.[16.]

Two of the most strident and irresponsible purveyors of public misconceptions about Bundy's postconviction litigation efforts are Judge G. Kendall Sharp (a federal district judge who heard his habeas cases and who once characterized Bundy's efforts to challenge the legality of his death sentence as "a waste of time") and Robert Graham (former Florida governor and now U.S. senator). Judge Sharp, testifying before a congressional subcommittee studying habeas corpus reform, said that he "would like to concentrate on the case of Ted Bundy, which is one that points up the problems that we have in the Federal court."[17] After a lengthy recitation of the procedural history of Bundy's cases—in Judge Sharp's courtroom and elsewhere—Sharp's written statement to the subcommittee quoted himself as having commented "that if every death-row inmate 'milked the system' as Bundy has done, then it would shut down the civil side of the courthouse."[18] This testimony followed Judge Sharp's denial of Bundy's first habeas petition, but the judge must have been aware that the case would most likely be before him again soon, as in fact it was.

Governor "Bob" Graham similarly used Bundy to illustrate perceived flaws in the habeas statute. As governor, he reportedly accused Bundy of trying to " 'endlessly manipulate' the legal system to delay his execution."[19] The day after Bundy received a federal court stay in 1986, Governor Graham was quoted as stating, "Again, we've seen a situation where people who have been on death row for many years wait until the last hour to raise claims."[20] His proposed solution was reform of habeas: "I think that we've got to demand some changes at the federal level that say a person only has a reasonable number of years after his trial to bring these claims of constitutional deprivation. . . . It's an abuse of justice to be questioning competency of counsel eight, 10, 12 years after the trial."[21] When he was elected to the U.S. Senate, Graham proposed just such an amendment to the habeas statute, again reportedly characterizing Bundy's litigation as a "typical abuse of the system."[22]

The Bundy Books

> There is nothing more intimate than sharing someone's dying with them. When you've got to do that with someone and give that person, at the age of nineteen, a chance to say the last thing they are ever going to get to say, that act of helping someone die is more intimate than sex, it is more intimate than childbirth, and once you have done that you can never be ordinary again.
>
> —Dusty, army nurse, 1967

The nonfiction books on the Bundy case itself possess varying indicia of reliability. Here, as with other aspects of Florida's culture of the condemned, David Von Drehle's *Among the Lowest of the Dead* is the most faithful to my own understanding of the truth.[23] Stephen Michaud and Hugh Aynesworth, both journalists, conducted extensive tape-recorded interviews with Bundy; I consider their works relatively reliable, mainly because they often quote Bundy in what they purport to be his own words. The books by Richard Larsen and Ann Rule have, like Michaud and Aynesworth's first work, been updated to include narratives of the final acts of Bundy's collateral litigation. Winn and Merrill's *Ted Bundy: The Killer Next Door,* now 15 years old, has not been updated, and it does not discuss many of the legal developments in Bundy's Florida cases relevant here. "Elizabeth Kendall," a pseudonym for a person claiming to have been Bundy's "girlfriend" for six years, did not address his Florida legal proceedings and is therefore not illuminating for my purposes. Interestingly (and, to me, oddly), Kendall's book has the ring of truth to it.

I cite these secondary sources from the trade presses with some skepticism. None of the books provides source notes or other verifiable documentation. Rule and Larsen, both self-styled Bundy "friends," were reporters who covered his Florida legal proceedings for their respective news organizations. Further, the Rule book has several obvious errors. For example, "Bob" Graham did not lose the 1986 Florida gubernatorial election;[24] indeed, he did not run. He did, however, *win* his race to become United States senator. The Florida attorney general's office did not formally estimate that it cost $6 million to execute Bundy.[25] The Supreme Court did not deny certiorari review 30 days after the district court denied Bundy's first federal habeas corpus petition in 1987.[26] Such errors, though relatively minor, do not inspire confidence. However, most of Rule's narrative does coincide with events as I understand them.

In any case, these various secondary sources typically are, with one exception, cited only when they confirm my understanding or recorded recollections of the events described. The exception is Polly Nelson's 1994 book *Defending the Devil,* which is in a class of its own. Nelson worked on the Bundy case for three years, beginning when she was a first-year associate with the District of Columbia law firm of Wilmer, Cutler & Pickering. One can only wonder how the law firm's other death row clients might feel reading Nelson's book. I judge her book with a little squeamishness. To paraphrase Murray Kempton, the closer one draws to one's own appointment with the Recording Angel,[27] the stronger swell the pleadings of one's sister sinners; on some level her effort suggests an affirmative response to a question posed by Camus: "Is there a tragic dilettantism?"[28] As Michael Radelet wrote me soon after reading Nelson's book, "Throughout her association with the case, I took your advice and treated Polly simply as Jim Coleman's secretary. This book confirms her incompetence."[29]

I am harsh about Nelson because, as her book describes more or less accurately, and as I will discuss below, her law firm took on Bundy's case largely at my behest. Thus, I bear a good measure of responsibility for Nelson's handling of Bundy's case—and for the book based on her view of that representation.

Actually, it does more than just confirm Nelson's lack of judgment or taste. The book slams the Wilmer firm as well as its present and former lawyers (particularly Coleman and Jeffrey Robinson); especially revolting is Nelson's view of the firm's attitude toward *pro bono* clients, one of singular and inspirational generosity. I experienced it first-hand when I worked there as an associate during part of the time Nelson and James Coleman were representing Bundy. It was the *firm* that represented Bundy *pro bono*—not Polly Nelson, who throughout "her" representation of him drew her usual salary. (This, she tells us, started at $80,000 per year when she began working there; it is typical of the inflated salaries paid by major national law firms to people fresh out of law school, which Nelson more or less was. She had clerked for a federal judge for a year before joining Wilmer, a prestigious job that Nelson, with characteristic generosity, describes simply as "tedious.") During the entire time she represented Bundy, then, the firm paid her eighty-plus thousand dollars per annum to spend most of her time doing cutting-edge, state-of-the-art constitutional litigation in one of the most interesting, significant, and high-profile capital cases of this generation, with the full litigation support of a great law firm (her complaints to the contrary are simply not true).

Most frightening to me, however, because Nelson's law firm took on Bundy's case at my pleading, is the possibility that her account of her representation of Mr. Bundy is accurate. From the book's subtitle to its closing vignettes, the picture that emerges of Polly Nelson, self-described as the lawyer having principal decisionmaking authority in the case ("He was my baby now," etc.), is one of an inexperienced, incompetent new lawyer (her terms: "wet behind the ears," "neophyte," etc.), working alone in a virtual supervisory vacuum despite her repeated bleats for help, who after her client's execution felt free to exploit harmful confidential information for personal financial gain. His execution liberated Ms. Nelson to describe Mr. Bundy (in her terms and with her capitalization) as, "without a doubt, the Devil Incarnate, a killing machine set loose on society, to do the will of a diabolical power";[30] to describe his confessions—of factual guilt to murders, to her, in the midst of their attorney-client relationship—as the killer of 35 people[31] (the book's index conveniently lists twelve entries under "Bundy, Theodore Robert 'Ted': admission of guilt by," and the author's descriptions of these "admissions" are at times brutally graphic);[32] to describe her own wish that Bundy's first victim had killed him. (After watching the made-for-TV movie about the killings, Nelson recalled, "As each woman was approached, I rooted for her, I willed the story to turn out differently than I knew it had. I willed her to kill Ted instead of being harmed herself. To kill him over and over, to tear him apart, to rip him to shreds.").[33] Nelson's contempt for her client oozes out of her memoir on every page, but perhaps her disdain is expressed best in the headline of an *L.A. Times* "Bookmark" excerpt from her book: "Ted Bundy and Earthworms: Compassion for the Lower Orders of Life."[34] If things were as she described them, it is a miracle that Bundy received high-quality representation. Because, as detailed below, Bundy *did* receive high-quality representation, if not from Polly Nelson.

It seems odd that a licensed attorney would risk disciplinary sanctions from the bar by writing such a book. Nelson explained that once her client was dead, "I didn't have to pretend any longer that Ted was not a murderer. That was over. And I didn't have to put a spin on everything to make sure it didn't harm Ted's case. That was over, the play. The curtain had fallen on the last act at 7:06 that morning. I was no longer Bundy's lawyer."[35] This apologia is puzzling, because it misstates Florida law and because Nelson seemed aware of that fact at least five years before her book was published.[36]

The flaws in her book are all the more disappointing because, as his lawyer, Nelson had a unique opportunity to explode in a credible and responsible way two pervasive public misunderstandings about Bundy's cases. Because of his central place in America's capital punishment imagination, these false notions also perpetuate myths about the legal machinery of capital punishment generally. First, a great many people believe that Bundy received what Margaret Jane Radin termed in another context "super due process for death"[37] (deliberate, painstaking, individualized judicial review of the legality of his convictions and sentences), and that such process identified and corrected any errors of constitutional magnitude in Bundy's cases. Second, there is a pervasive Rehnquistian view that Bundy and his lawyers caused a 10-year execution "delay" following imposition of sentence in 1979 by manipulating the legal system, and in particular by failing to initiate collateral litigation in a timely manner.

Both perceptions are false. The next part of this chapter, in describing the actual course of Bundy's postconviction litigation, shows that in fact his postconviction cases were shoved through the legal system at a speed that can most charitably be characterized as unseemly and that can most accurately be described as periodically frenzied. Further, all of the much-vaunted "delay" in Bundy's cases occurred while litigation was pending and proceeding in at least one court. Indeed, there was no "delay," as the word is commonly understood. There was a 10-year temporal gap between imposition and execution of sentence in the cases, but that gap was caused by the courts rather than by Bundy or his lawyers. No time was lost by his failure to initiate and pursue litigation in a timely fashion.

The disparity between public perception and legal reality in Bundy's cases raises a separate constellation of intriguing inquiries. The distance between perception and reality can be bridged, and perhaps partially explained, by metaphor.[38] Bundy is seen as having received heightened due process, although he actually received minimal postconviction process of any meaningful kind, because he became a symbol—an emblem for evil and a mirror of Americans' deepest fears and desires. The third part of this chapter explores why Bundy's notoriety warped the legal system's standards and procedures to an extraordinary extent. The judicial process created a series of "Bundy exceptions" to the rule of law. Despite the outward appearance of hyper due process (a decade of repetitive review; lawyers at trial and beyond), in reality the legal system failed.

This narrative is as much about cultural perception as it is about legalistic reality. The text certainly is not an attempt to discover the "real" Theodore Bundy or to explain the man or his actions, real or perceived—the historical person is not significant for my purposes. The inquiry focuses, rather, on Bundy as a symbol constructed by U.S. culture to represent death row and on the legal system's response to and interaction with that symbol/litigant. It is a symbol with which we, as members of that culture, ought to be profoundly uncomfortable, for reasons examined in the chapter's third part.

Where Did the Time Go? Bundy's Interaction with the Capital Punishment System

> I can't understand your behavior. This [Bundy] case is going to be reversed and sent down there [to federal district court] because of a stupid error.
> —Eleventh Circuit Judge Robert Vance, addressing an attorney representing the state of Florida during oral argument in *Bundy v. Wainwright*

> In Vietnam, the only measure of victory was one of the most hideous, morally corrupting ideas ever conceived by the military mind—the body count. We fought over the same ground again and again, month after month, our only object to kill more of them than they did of us. When we did, the official logic went, that week at least we had won the war—even if the contested area was still controlled by the enemy, even if we hadn't won any "hearts and minds" in the countryside. Commanders liked good body counts, even when they were fudged, which was not uncommon. They liked high kill ratios; it meant they were doing something right.
> —Philip Caputo

Given the amount of work and soul and emotional energy that capital postconviction litigation requires, CCR's caseload was staggering. I have never worked so hard in my life, and I never will again. The office's lawyers, support staff, and investigators routinely worked 80-hour weeks and 15-hour days, and longer hours were required in (frequent) crises. During an especially frenetic five weeks in 1986, one CCR lawyer seldom left the office except to shower. Three people represented by CCR were put to death during this period: Daniel Thomas (executed April 15, 1986), David Funchess (executed April 22, 1986), and Ronald Straight (executed May 20, 1986).[39] Maniacal commitment to the clients, and not nearly enough time in the day or night to fulfill that commitment, was the essence of the job.[40] If after reading this description one has the feeling of being in a madhouse, it is the right feeling.

Extensive posttrial reinvestigation must be undertaken in every capital postconviction case. At the time CCR commenced operations on October 1, 1985, approximately 200 people lived on Florida's death row. About half of these had not reached the state postconviction litigation stage, and therefore they were not yet represented by CCR. Of the approximately 100 cases that were in the postconviction stages of litigation, 30 or so inmates were represented by volunteer, *pro bono* counsel. CCR was not directly responsible for those prisoners, although the agency did what it could to help the *pro bono* attorneys. That left about 70 inmates, divided among three comparatively experienced and several less experienced CCR lawyers.

At any given time, execution dates were scheduled for two to four of these prisoners. In Florida, the governor signs a death warrant to trigger an execution date.[41] Unless a stay is obtained prior to the specified execution date, the subject of the warrant will be put to death, even though his conviction may rest upon error of constitutional magnitude.

Into this madness called a law office clanked the Bundy cases, with only four weeks until the scheduled execution date. Bundy was the defendant in two capital cases, and his death warrant had been signed by the governor on February 5, 1986. The killing was scheduled for 7:00 A.M. on March 4, 1986. It quickly became clear that Bundy's cases would overwhelm CCR's paper-thin resources.

In retrospect, I see that what I did was to sell one CCR client, Bundy, down the river in order to give CCR's other clients a shot at effective post-conviction representation. I thought I was leaving Bundy in Jim Coleman's hands; instead he ended up in the care of Polly Nelson. Sending Bundy's case from CCR was one of the worst decisions I've made as a deathworker. I still sometimes wake up in the middle of the night drenched with sweat and weighted down by a recurring nightmare, and there they are at every turn: Theodore Bundy's wife and child. We're in a Tallahassee Howard Johnson's, and I'm telling them that CCR isn't abandoning Ted. That was my first lie to them.

Bundy had been convicted by two different Florida juries of first-degree murder. They had returned nonbinding sentencing "recommendations" that capital punishment be imposed, and the trial judges in both cases had agreed with the jury recommendations and sentenced Bundy to the electric chair. The Florida Supreme Court had affirmed the convictions and sentences on direct appeal. Bundy had fired his appellate lawyer and filed a *pro se,* out-of-time certiorari petition in the case that was the subject of the death warrant. He was also sparring publicly with the governor about executive clemency.[42]

Like most Floridians, I knew about the Bundy cases—or thought I did. There were really two Bundy cases, each proceeding on a different litigation track. In one, Bundy was on death row for bludgeoning to death two Tallahassee sorority women, Lisa Levy and Margaret Bowman, in the Chi Omega chapter house at Florida State University. Ironically, the scene of the murders was about two blocks from the Independent Life Insurance Building, the site of CCR's first office. Several other women were beaten severely in the sorority house that night.[43] The crime occurred in 1978; Bundy was convicted and condemned in 1979. The direct appeal had been orally argued in the Florida Supreme Court in 1982, and the court affirmed the convictions and sentences in 1984—five years after their imposition.[44]

It was for these two murders that Bundy was scheduled to die on March 4, 1986.

In addition to the Chi Omega case, Bundy had been condemned for killing 12-year-old Kimberly Leach in Lake City, Florida, in 1978; he was convicted and sentenced in 1980. This case had been affirmed on direct appeal in 1985 by the Florida Supreme Court,[45] though the time for seeking U.S. Supreme Court review had not yet expired when the death warrant was signed on the Chi Omega case. Bundy was also suspected of dozens of West Coast crimes, but he had been convicted of only one; the kidnapping in Utah of Carol DeRonch.[46] At the time of the Florida murders, Bundy was an escapee from a jail in Aspen, Colorado, where he had been scheduled to stand trial for the kidnapping and murder of Caryn Campbell (for which he was eventually sentenced to one to 15 years).

Bundy's was the largest and most complicated criminal case in the history of the Florida Supreme Court; the trial records alone comprised more than 28,000 pages, "roughly the expanse of the *Encyclopaedia Britannica*."[47] CCR designated a "Bundy room" in which to organize the massive amounts of paper generated by his cases. Mark Olive was Bundy's lead counsel; my peripheral job was to assist Olive. I read the transcripts of the Kimberly Leach (Lake City) trial, summaries of the Chi Omega (Tallahassee) trial, and other documents in the cases.

I learned from my reading that reporters covering the Chi Omega trial thought that the odds of conviction, based on the evidence presented to the jury, were 50–50. "[M]oving into final arguments," Ann Rule wrote, "the press was still wagering even odds on the outcome of the trial"; as the jury deliberated Bundy's guilt, the "odds were still even. Fifty-fifty. Acquittal or conviction."[48] Richard Larsen agreed, writing that when the trial court ruled that Bundy's statements made during custodial interrogation must be suppressed because they had been obtained in violation of his constitutional rights, "suddenly, Ted Bundy's defense had a winnable case."[49] During jury deliberations, some reporters predicted acquittal and others conviction: "[O]bviously there was 'reasonable doubt' in the state's mostly circumstantial case."[50] Two *Miami Herald* reporters covering the trial wrote that it took the jury "five [separate] votes to reach the decision" of guilty.[51] The sentencing jury initially deadlocked 6–6 on whether Bundy should die, notwithstanding that (1) the community from which the jury was selected had been saturated for months before the trial with publicity about Bundy as serial rapist-murderer, and (2) the process by which capital juries are death-qualified[52] culled all immovable opponents of the death penalty from Bundy's jury. Apparently following interviews with at least one juror in the Chi Omega case, two *Miami Herald* staff writers reported:

It took [the jury] an hour and 40 minutes to decide [Bundy's sentence]. They voted three times. They split 6–6 twice. They prayed.

"I requested that 10 minutes meditation be taken," said jury foreman Rudolph Tremi, 38, a projects engineer for Texaco.

The tie was broken.[53]

Ann Rule wrote (without citing sources), "The jury would say later that they had been split at one point with a six-six deadlock, a deadlock that had been broken after ten minutes of 'prayer and meditation.' "[54]

The initial tie vote is significant, and troubling. Florida jury recommendations of life or death sentences need not be unanimous.[55] But although the capital statute speaks in terms of a recommendation by a "majority" of the jury, the Florida Supreme Court has held (subsequent to Bundy's sentencing) that a split vote of six-six is to be treated as a recommendation of life imprisonment; under Florida law, a life recommendation in Bundy's case would almost certainly have meant a life sentence, given the amount of mitigating evidence presented to the jury.[56] The problem is that Bundy's jury was never told that a jury life recommendation would most likely mean a life sentence. More importantly, they were not told that a six-six vote would have been sufficient for a life recommendation.

Then there was the problem of saturation pretrial publicity. Even after the trial's venue was changed from Tallahassee to Miami, 450 miles to the south, Rule thought it "extremely doubtful that Ted Bundy could ever have received an impartial trial in the state of Florida. He was becoming better known than Disney World, the Everglades, and the heretofore all-time media pleaser: Murph the Surf [sic]."[57] According to Michaud and Aynesworth, the Chi Omega prosecutors "were working with a jury sensitized by seventeen months of publicity since the sorority house murders. The men and women selected to judge Ted Bundy might honestly tell the court their verdict would be based upon the evidence, but the overwhelming bulk of what they had been exposed to in the media was suggestive of guilt. Never was Ted Bundy mentioned except in connection with murder and mayhem."[58]

Surprisingly, the evidence of guilt presented to Bundy's Chi Omega jury was "not overwhelming," as Larsen put it.[59] The jury reportedly needed to take five separate votes "before the jurors were unanimous on guilt."[60] The "scientific evidence was at times equivocal and produced sharply differing opinions among the experts called to testify. No fingerprints were found."[61] Both Florida cases against Bundy relied upon the testimony of eyewitnesses, yet they had undergone police hypnosis before testifying. Bundy's lawyers challenged the reliability of such hypnotically "refreshed" or "created" testimony. The Florida Supreme Court agreed that hypnosis destroys the reliability of memory and its resulting testimony, and it held in Bundy's cases that such testimony would henceforth be per se inadmissible in the state.[62] The court managed, however, to affirm Bundy's convictions and sentences.[63] This was my first encounter with what some have come to call the "Bundy exception to the rule of law." Hypnotically "refreshed" testimony was per se unreliable and thus inadmissible as evidence . . . *except* in Bundy's cases and in cases decided prior to the court's 1985 *Bundy* decision.

The surprises kept coming. Prosecutors in both Florida cases had offered Bundy negotiated pleas of life imprisonment in exchange for his agreement to plead guilty to the charges,[64] most likely because of the weakness of the evidence against him. Convinced that he could prove his innocence at trial,[65] Bundy rejected the plea bargains, acting against the strident advice of his family and his lawyers. Bundy's trial attorneys wondered whether he was even mentally competent to stand trial. This concern resulted in a competency hearing scripted by Kafka, with Bundy and two psychiatrists (asserting that he was competent) pitted against his senior trial lawyer and a third psychiatrist (who questioned whether Bundy was competent).[66] The judge found Bundy competent because of his demand that he be deemed competent and because he looked and sounded competent.[67]

At trial, Bundy had been denied his defense lawyer of choice, Atlanta attorney Millard Farmer,[68] one of the best capital defense attorneys in the United States. Because he was a Georgia lawyer and not a member of the Florida bar, Farmer was required to seek permission to appear *pro hac vice* in the Florida courts as Bundy's counsel. Although such requests are routinely granted, in this case it was denied, in general because Farmer had a reputation for being "disruptive," and in particular because he had a contempt of court citation outstanding in Georgia. That citation[69] was based on Farmer's unrelenting insistence that the prosecutor in a 1978 Georgia capital trial refer to the African American defendant, George Street, as "Mr. Street" rather than "George," since the prosecutor referred to all other participants in the case (including prospective jurors) as "Mr.," "Miss," or "Mrs." The prosecutor refused, instead referring to the defendant by his first name (as did Farmer). The trial judge ruled that this behavior by the prosecutor was fine. Farmer's refusal to permit the trial to proceed under these circumstances (to further make his point, he insisted upon calling the judge by his first name) earned him the contempt citation that disqualified him from appearing as Bundy's trial lawyer. The trial attorneys who did represent Bundy were zealous but inexperienced,[70] and they also clashed with him over trial tactics.[71] Bundy understandably felt set up; in any event, he never got over his anger at being denied the counsel of his choice for the trial of his life.[72] Farmer's consummate lawyering skills and experience could well have made the difference between life and death in the case.

As CCR delved more deeply into the Bundy cases, it became evident that they would involve massive investigation and litigation. Representing him would have been the equivalent of adding 10 cases to its already savage workload.

However, a more immediate problem confronted CCR. Jurisdictionally, the office could not represent Bundy in seeking plenary U.S. Supreme Court review of the Florida Supreme Court's direct appeal decision; CCR could represent him only in the postconviction stages. To undertake his immediate representation would have required bypassing certiorari and going directly into state postconviction litigation. That avenue appeared unattractive, since at least one direct appeal issue (the hypnotism claim) was ripe for plenary Supreme Court consideration.[73] The posture was further confused because, as noted above, Bundy had fired his direct appeal lawyer and was representing himself in the U.S. Supreme Court. He had filed a *pro se*, out-of-time certiorari petition and a handwritten stay application.

CCR began to explore quietly the possibility of placing Bundy's case with a private law firm willing to represent him *pro bono,* at least for the immediate certiorari petition. In the past I had consulted on another Florida death case, that of Stephen Todd Booker, with the firm of Wilmer, Cutler & Pickering in Washington, D.C. The firm had done a superb job on Booker's case; someday I hope Jeff Robinson writes the full story of his, Coleman's, and Marian Lindberg's commando-like drop into the Gainesville Airport at the time of that first Booker death warrant. Anyway, through a mutual friend I asked James Coleman, a partner in the firm, to consider taking on, without pay, the Bundy out-of-time certiorari petition. After much free-form negotiation and soul-searching, Coleman agreed on February 19 (16 days before the scheduled execution date). Initially, the firm made a commitment *only* to represent Bundy in the U.S. Supreme Court on the out-of-time certiorari petition and stay application. Gradually, however, Coleman was persuaded to take over more and more of the Bundy cases, and eventually the firm became Bundy's sole counsel.

At this point recall that plenary review of the Chi Omega case—the one with the scheduled March 4 execution date—had been sought only through Bundy's *pro se*, out-of-time petition for review, which he had supplemented with a handwritten stay application filed soon after the death warrant had been signed. Lewis Powell, circuit justice for the Eleventh Circuit (which includes Florida), denied the stay without prejudice and instructed Bundy to obtain proper legal counsel to file an application complying with the rules of the court.[74] This was an oblique hint that Bundy should seek a stay from the Florida Supreme Court before going to the U.S.

Supreme Court. Thus encouraged, his lawyers filed for a stay in the state supreme court, which was summarily denied. They next filed a stay application in the U.S. Supreme Court, along with a request to file an amended out-of-time petition for review. The Court granted both on February 26, nine days before the scheduled execution date.[75] The execution was, therefore, stayed until such time as the amended petition for review could be filed and decided by the Supreme Court.

When Bundy got a stay, it seemed as though the whole attorney general's office was left stunned and shuddering. Since the mid-1960s, no Florida condemned prisoner had been executed on a first death warrant, but the *Bundy* prosecutors thought—and so did I, actually—that if any death row prisoner was likely to be killed on a first warrant, it was Bundy. They were grinning like wolves as Bundy's case was blasted from one court after another. The stay seemed to take Assistant Attorney General Mark Menser by surprise (Menser had once explained to a horrified U.S. Supreme Court that Joseph Spaziano, whose case is discussed in the next chapter, ought to have been happy that he was tried by an Orange County jury and "not by one of the juries in Klan County" in North Florida). Menser was *off balance*. His points of order were not working.

The immediate crisis was over, as was my role as a direct participant in the cases. Henceforth, Coleman would be Bundy's chief attorney, and I would be one tangential advisor among many. CCR could turn its attention to other clients with other execution dates, secure that Bundy's case was safe in Coleman's hands.

In May 1986 the Supreme Court denied plenary review in the Chi Omega case, simultaneously dissolving the stay.[76] To Ann Rule the timing of the denial was "all show-biz perfection. The Court's answer [denying certiorari] was announced during a break in a two-part mini-series about Ted. Mark Harmon (*People* magazine's 'Sexiest Man Alive') played Ted . . . as a young Kennedy clone."[77] The Supreme Court's decision was front-page news in Florida. Ordinarily, Bundy's lawyers would have been granted some time to react before a new execution date was set.[78] But this was Bundy, and Bundy was different. Seventeen days after the Supreme Court declined review, the governor signed a second death warrant on Bundy in the Chi Omega case. The warrant was signed on May 22, and the execution was scheduled for July 2.

All manner of big-bore hell broke loose in the next few days. Words cannot adequately capture the frenetic activity of the month leading up to the scheduled execution. Coleman wrote that he and Nelson "worked feverishly to complete our review of the Chi Omega record and to prepare the state and federal papers for collateral relief."[79] Rule described that period as "wild. Polly Nelson and Jim Coleman had spent consecutive nights without sleep, racing the clock set by Ted's pending death warrant."[80] Between June 19 and June 31, Bundy's lawyers unsuccessfully sought postconviction relief (and stay of execution) from the state trial court,[81] the Florida Supreme Court,[82] and the federal district court.[83] The district court denied an indefinite stay without bothering to obtain, much less read, the 15,000-page state court record in the case upon which Bundy's constitutional claims were based. The state court record was in the trunk of the prosecutor's car during the short time that the district court had the case under consideration.[84] The district judge granted a 24-hour stay to permit Bundy to live long enough to appeal his rulings. The U.S. Court of Appeals for the Eleventh Circuit stayed the execution indefinitely, less than 15 hours before the rescheduled date.[85] The court put the case on an expedited briefing and oral argument timetable.[86]

By the time your death case reaches the U.S. Court of Appeals for the Eleventh Circuit, things are usually out of hand, no matter which side you're on. Win or lose, the die is almost cast by the time you hit the Eleventh Circuit. The glue has hardened and you are fixed in it—and the only thing left is waiting for the Rehnquist Court.

Meanwhile, Bundy's lawyers had filed, during the summer of 1986, a timely petition for plenary review asking the U.S. Supreme Court to hear the Kimberly Leach case. On October 14, 1986, the Court refused.[87] Seven days later, on October 21, the governor signed a death warrant in that case, setting the execution for 7:00 A.M. on November 18, 1986.[88]

Coleman repeated the same drill as in the Chi Omega case. This time it was, if anything, even more frantic. Bundy was denied stays by three courts (the state trial court, the Florida Supreme Court, and federal district judge G. Kendall Sharp) in one day.[89] Margaret Vandiver recalled: "We were denied in [state trial] court about 11 in the morning on November 17th. Polly and Jim went on to Tallahassee, and I drove the [federal district court] papers to Orlando. The [Florida Supreme Court denied a stay] sometime in the early afternoon, and I filed the [district court] papers around 2:30. The [district] judge denied the stay at about 10:30 P.M. on the 17th."

The Eleventh Circuit stayed the execution the next day.[90] The prosecutors applied unsuccessfully to the Supreme Court to dissolve the stay,[91] which the Court upheld less than seven hours before Bundy was to have been electrocuted.[92] ("Bundy already had been fitted for his funeral suit from Jim Tatum's Fashion Showroom in Jacksonville [$69.95].")[93] So, by late 1986, both Bundy cases were in the Eleventh Circuit, on chillingly expedited briefing and oral argument schedules.

The road off of Florida's death row has always been tricky and dangerous, but in the mid-1980s a truly awesome new hazard was added: the expedited appeal; and some weeks it was working overtime. The fast lane, such as it was, was littered with lumps of clotting blood.

The Eleventh Circuit oral argument in the Chi Omega case sizzled. The judges seemed dumbfounded (1) that the district court could have denied habeas relief (and a stay) without even a pretense of looking at the 15,000-page record of the state court proceedings upon which Bundy's constitutional claims were based, and (2) that the prosecutors could have led the district court into such a glaring error. The late Judge Robert S. Vance, no bleeding-heart opponent of death row by any stretch of the imagination,[94] reportedly blistered the prosecutor: "I can't understand your behavior. This case is going to be reversed and sent down there [to district court] because of a stupid error. If you had called it to the attention of the [district] judge at the time, it could have been corrected in four days. It's wrong. It's clearly wrong, counsel. It's not arguable by an attorney of integrity."[95] Later in the argument, Judge Vance allowed that "maybe the Court has been a little too harsh on you personally, counsel."[96] Still, the handwriting was on the wall: The Eleventh Circuit intended to remand the Chi Omega case. In fact, the court planned to send the Kimberly Leach case back as well.

In 1987 the Eleventh Circuit remanded both Bundy cases to the respective federal district courts for evidentiary hearings on Bundy's mental competency to stand trial.[97] Again, the proceedings were to be truncated. The district judge in the Chi Omega habeas case, who was new to the federal bench[98] (and whose error reportedly had been termed "stupid" by Judge Vance in the appellate oral argument), appeared determined to proceed with extreme deliberation. By contrast, the district judge in the Kimberly Leach habeas case, Judge G. Kendall Sharp, moved with extreme speed. He held the evidentiary hearing on Bundy's competency to stand trial[99] and ruled against him.[100] Rule described Judge Sharp's actions as "swift, impatient and firm."[101] According to Coleman, Judge Sharp was "quoted by a reporter as saying that he thought the proceeding was a waste of time."[102] The Leach case therefore returned to the Eleventh Circuit, while the Chi Omega litigation languished in district court limbo until after the end of Bundy's life.[103]

The Eleventh Circuit accelerated briefing and oral argument in the Leach case. In mid-1988 the court affirmed the district court's denial of habeas relief.[104] In December 1988 Bundy's lawyers filed a certiorari petition asking the Supreme Court to review the decision of the Eleventh Circuit. The justices conferenced on Friday, the 13th of January, 1989—not a good sign. Shortly after 10:00 A.M. on Tuesday, January 17, 1989, the Court released its order denying review in the Leach case.[105] Within minutes,[106] Florida's Governor Martinez signed a seven-day death warrant, and the execution was scheduled for Tuesday, January 24, 1989, at 7:00 A.M.

The Supreme Court's decision denying plenary review had been predictable, and Bundy's lawyers were as ready as could have been expected. The day after the warrant was signed, Coleman traveled south from Washington to seek a stay from the state trial court in Lake City, in central Florida. The stay application was filed on the morning of January 18 and was denied the next day.[107] Minutes after the stay was denied, the Florida Supreme Court announced that it would hear oral argument the following morning in Tallahassee. Coleman drove from Lake City to Tallahassee and spent the night preparing a brief for the state supreme court. The brief was filed in the early morning hours of January 20, and oral argument began at 9:00 A.M. The Florida Supreme Court unanimously denied the stay shortly after noon, less than an hour after the conclusion of oral arguments scheduled for the day.[108]

The topography of contemporary capital punishment jurisprudence in this strangely suspended epic is strewn with the skeletons of abandoned arguments, lowered visions, dying dreams. Soon after the stay was denied, Coleman and I happened to have a lengthy and wide-ranging telephone conversation.[109] The initial thrust of the discussion was to explore what he and his associates ought to do next: Should they go to the U.S. Supreme Court to seek a stay, or should they go directly to the federal district court? In the course of the conversation, however, it became clear that Bundy's case contained a previously unexplored constitutional issue, that of diminished sentencing responsibility.[110] It was an issue that had formed the basis of stays in several Florida cases before his.[111]

The constitutional issue turned on whether Bundy's jury had been misled as to its central role in Florida's trifurcated capital-sentencing scheme. The backdrop was Florida's hybrid judge-jury sentencing structure. This structure created the danger that no one at the trial stage in Bundy's case, judge or jury, would feel that they had the real responsibility for making the decision that Bundy had lost his moral entitlement to live. The jury did not have full responsibility for the decision, since in Florida sentencing juries are—and are told *repeatedly* that they are—"advisory" only. The jury renders a nonbinding "recommendation" of life or death, which the judge theoretically may follow or disregard. But the judge also does not have complete sentencing responsibility. The jury's recommendation of life carries tremendous weight, and it may be overridden by the judge only in those rare instances where "virtually no reasonable person"[112] could disagree that death should be imposed in the case. As a result of this division of sentencing responsibility, both jury and judge could look to the other as the real authority responsible for making this hard moral choice, with neither ever doing so.[113]

The avoidance-of-responsibility problem could be pervasive. According to early results from the most comprehensive study of capital jurors to date, jurors in capital murder trials misunderstand sentencing instructions, their role, and their guided responsibility in choosing life or death for a

105

convicted murderer. After analyzing data collected in seven states, William Bowers, Margaret Vandiver, and other researchers with Northeastern University's Capital Jury Project concluded that jurors frequently did not feel personally responsible for choosing the defendant's sentence: only 21.6 percent rated themselves largely responsible for the sentence; the others held the defendants or "the law" itself responsible.[114]

When responsibility for a death sentence is divided, there exists the danger that no one bears the ultimate responsibility for this awesome life-or-death decision (identified by the Supreme Court in *Caldwell v. Mississippi*[115] in a somewhat different, though analogous, setting as a danger of constitutional magnitude). The judge might defer to the jury and the jury defer to the judge, with the result that the capital defendant falls between the stools.[116]

A second factor, just as important as the divided sentencing structure, was that Bundy's jury was *misled* as to the vital importance of its penalty decision. To cite one example from among many, during jury selection the following exchange took place between the prosecutor and a prospective juror:

PROSECUTOR:

Do you understand that the judge, Judge Jopling, in this case, as the trial judge, would have the ultimate responsibility for determining which punishment to impose?

PROSPECTIVE JUROR:

Yes, I do.

PROSECUTOR:

In other words, the jury would render an advisory opinion only, just that, an opinion.

PROSPECTIVE JUROR:

Yes, sir.[117]

Such admonitions by the prosecutor could well have led reasonable jurors to conclude (incorrectly, under Florida law) that their sentencing recommendation would not carry much weight with the trial judge. Further, the prosecutor's statements were reinforced by the judge, who told the prospective jurors that the jury's decision "is a recommendation only. The law places the awesome burden upon the judge to decide what final disposition is made or penalty is imposed in a capital case." The judge's sentencing instructions to the jury cemented the legal misconception that "as you have been told, the final decision as to what punishment shall be imposed is the responsibility of the judge."

At no time was Bundy's sentencing jury given the *accurate* information that a jury recommendation of life imprisonment must by law be given great weight by the court and indeed must be followed, save in the rarest of cases. Thus, (1) Bundy's sentencing jury was misled as to its role in Florida's three-step capital sentencing scheme, and (2) the misleading information was of a kind that tended to diminish the jury's sense of its own sentencing responsibility.

You may wonder: So what? Should we really care if Bundy's jury had a diminished sense of the importance of its role or if sentencing responsibility was divided? No reasonable sentencer could possibly have sentenced the infamous Bundy to anything less than death. But recall that the Chi Omega jury, culled of all strong death penalty opponents and marinated with relentless pretrial publicity, did reportedly for a time split six–six on whether to recommend death for Bundy. Recall that the prosecutors offered life pleas in both the Chi Omega and Kimberly Leach cases. Recall why: the evidence of Bundy's guilt was gossamer.

In any event, on Friday, January 20, 1989, four days before the scheduled Tuesday morning execution and only hours after the Florida Supreme Court had denied a stay sought on other grounds, Coleman decided to investigate seriously the issue of diminished sentencing responsibility (why, apart from reasons of fatigue and pressure, it was not identified and explored earlier remains a mystery; Wilmer, Cutler & Pickering had litigated an identical claim in another Florida capital habeas case, that of Roy Harich, before the *en banc* Eleventh Circuit Court of Appeals in 1987 and 1988).[118] I was to dictate a bare-bones statement of the abstract legal claim (devoid of record support, since at that point no one knew the depth of the issue's basis in the trial record), to be included in a federal habeas corpus petition that Coleman planned to file the next morning (Saturday) in the Orlando federal district court[119] before Judge G. Kendall Sharp. (This was after Judge Sharp's congressional testimony focusing on Bundy, mentioned above. I do not know if Coleman moved for Judge Sharp's recusal, founded on the bias revealed in his earlier congressional appearance; I do know that Coleman was aware of Judge Sharp's previous congressional testimony regarding Bundy.) Meanwhile, Coleman would comb the 15,000-page trial transcript[120] to bolster the argument of diminished sentencing responsibility. It was a weird plan, ripe with madness and a sort of low-tech desperation that none of us were proud of.

Also on Friday, Bundy began meeting with police detectives from several states, reportedly to confess to crimes,[121] against Coleman's advice and apparently in the bizarre belief that confessions would delay the execution. These confessions received substantial national media attention.

On Saturday morning, I received an unexpected telephone call from Dr. Michael Radelet, a Gainesville criminologist and *pro bono* paralegal[122] working with Coleman. Bundy had asked, through Radelet, for my thoughts or advice about his case and its likely course over the next few days. My messages to Bundy centered on his reported meetings with detectives and on the atmosphere those meetings were creating in the media. My advice was blunt and threefold: "Shut up; shut the fuck up; and shut the fuck up right now." Bundy's reported confessions were devastating his legal case. Michaud and Aynesworth reported that Coleman had counseled Bundy not to speak with law enforcement representatives.[123] This may not be quite accurate. Coleman did tell Bundy not to confess in the glare of national publicity, regardless of the general wisdom of cooperating with the police. Rule was probably closer to the truth when she wrote, "Coleman said he was aware that there was the possibility of a deal to delay—confessions for time—but that he was not involved in it, and would not comment."[124]

Bundy's question and my answers were unsettling. It seemed as though we were probing the outer limits of the adversarial system. On the one hand, who was a lawyer to tell Bundy not to confess if confession salved his soul and made things right with his deity? And as a citizen I was pleased that his statements might be solving cases and, perhaps, giving the victims' families the sense of closure necessary for people to get on with their lives.

On the other hand, such confessions, even if factually untrue, sabotaged Bundy's case in the courts. The statements, or more precisely the manner in which they were being reported in the limelight of publicity, were offensive. Bundy appeared to be trading on the bodies of his victims to prolong his own life; Von Drehle called it "Bundy's bones-for-time" scheme.[125] Judges are human, I told Bundy through the paralegal, and they will be revolted by the circumstances under which the confessions were being made. Such revulsion must have influenced the judicial decisions affecting Bundy's life. Significantly, at that moment he *had* a legal case to devastate, a strong constitutional claim that should, in a rational and calm world, result in a stay in his case as it had in others. For a time Bundy ceased the meetings with police, but by the following evening he had resumed them.

His lawyers filed the stay application and habeas petition in federal district court on Saturday morning. Judge Sharp held an evidentiary hearing on one of Bundy's claims, beginning at 9:00 A.M. This issue alleged that the state sentencing judge had received improper, *ex parte* information.[126] The claim was unrelated to the issue of diminished sentencing responsibility. After a hearing lasting 40 minutes, the court rendered its decision denying all requested relief, initially from the bench and subsequently in a 17-page opinion released at two minutes past noon. The denial was no surprise, given Judge Sharp's congressional testimony about Bundy's cases. Coleman immediately filed a notice of appeal to the Eleventh Circuit.[127]

The Eleventh Circuit reportedly gave Bundy's attorneys two hours to file a brief.[128] By the magic of fax machines, they filed it on time. The three judges (who had their chambers in three different cities)[129] conferenced by telephone.[130] Bundy seemed safe for the night. He had raised a powerful constitutional challenge to his death sentence, and the record was massive. Surely the court would want some time to sort it out correctly.

In fact, the Eleventh Circuit unanimously denied a stay late Saturday afternoon.[131] The Supreme Court was now the last remaining hope, and Bundy's advocates spent Sunday crafting the diminution of sentencing responsibility claim and buttressing it with quotations from the trial transcript as they found them. Full review of the record revealed that the issue was far stronger than suspected—considerably stronger than in the cases that had previously received stays on the basis of the claim. Bundy raised the issue in stay papers filed in the Florida Supreme Court and the U.S. Supreme Court. Procedurally, the issue was raised as an original habeas corpus petition in the Florida Supreme Court. The application presented to the U.S. Supreme Court sought a stay of execution pending the filing and disposition of a certiorari petition requesting review of the Eleventh Circuit's decision.

Monday we waited. While Coleman was en route to the prison to visit Bundy, I became the contact person for the Florida Supreme Court and the U.S. Supreme Court. Bundy lost in the state supreme court at approximately 6:00 P.M., but on balance the news was hopeful. Atypically, the Florida Supreme Court published no opinion explaining its decision to deny the stay. Although that court rejected the claim of diminished sentencing responsibility, it did so based on the merits of the issue; the court had not applied a procedural bar. Since the state court had decided the issue on its merits, the federal courts would be expected to do so as well.[132] Bundy seemed fairly safe; had he not *been* Bundy, he likely would have been.

At Coleman's direction I activated (and so filed) a previously lodged stay application in the U.S. Supreme Court. The only issue before the Justices was diminished sentencers' responsibility. The mood among Bundy's lawyers was guardedly nonpessimistic, but as the night dragged on apprehension increased. The Court was taking too long. A stay would have come early, if Bundy had garnered the requisite five votes.

The air was nervous the night before Bundy was destroyed. Around 10:30 P.M. I called the clerk's office to check in. Chris Vasil, the deputy clerk and a friend, suggested that we remain on the line, since a decision by the Court appeared imminent. Chris and I made small talk for the next five minutes or so, as we had done many times in the past, waiting for the Justices to issue their decisions. I remember that we talked about the weather in D.C. and Vermont. After momentarily putting me on hold, the deputy clerk told me that Bundy had been denied a stay by a vote of five–four.[133] It took a moment to sink in: Bundy had lost by *one vote* in the *Rehnquist*

Court, on the claim that had been identified by his lawyers a mere three days earlier and meaningfully investigated only one day before: the issue of diminished sentencing responsibility. The deputy clerk read me Justice Brennan's dissent.[134]

It was over. There would have been no point in filing a petition for plenary Supreme Court review, which, under the "rule of four," requires four votes to grant (a stay, by contrast, requires five votes; a "hold" pending disposition of another case involving similar issues requires three votes).[135] The Justices would not have considered a certiorari petition until the Court's next regularly scheduled conference.[136] By then Bundy would already have been dead, and the Court would have dismissed the certiorari petition as moot.[137]

I telephoned the prison with the news but was not permitted to speak with Bundy. Regulations. He was in a meeting. The message presumably was relayed to him, one way or the other. I took a long drink of Wild Turkey, smoked a Dominican cigar, and took a walk in the iron January Vermont night.

Bundy was executed shortly after 7:00 A.M. the next day, on schedule. James Coleman witnessed the killing of his client.[138] Outside the death chamber, much of Florida rejoiced. A reporter described the tailgate party atmosphere:

> Ted Bundy went out with a cheer.
> Across Florida, radio stations bade "Bye, Bye, Bundy," while next door to the Chi Omega sorority, where Bundy killed two young women, a campus bar was offering "Bundy fries" and "Bundy fingers"—actually, french fries and strips of alligator meat.
> At the Florida State Prison [in the town of Starke, where Bundy was executed], Ted Bundy haters arrived by the hundred as a traffic jam snaked across State Road 16 from Starke. The field across from the prison, where people were hawking pins of the electric chair and offering coffee and doughnuts, had all the trappings of a late-night county carnival.
> Except it was a chill dawn morning, and the reason for gathering was darker than any fair. Take the signs.
> "Chi-O, Chi-O, it's off to Hell I go," read one, referring to the sorority murders.
> "Bundy BBQ," read another.
> As the crowd gathered, [radio station] Q-Zoo deejay Cleveland Wheeler was back in Tampa Bay pouring Jolt Cola and playing uncharacteristically uncommercial songs for the occasion—including Peter Gabriel's Shock the Monkey. Then, when word from the prison arrived, Wheeler put on Eddy Grant's churning Electric Avenue. Simultaneously in Starke, revelers set off fireworks and sang a chorus of "Na Na Na Na, Na Na Na Na, Hey, Hey, [Hey,] Goodbye."[139]

When Bundy was killed, it was a powerful thing to see. There was a fast and terrible speed to it. Margaret Vandiver, a criminologist who worked as a *pro bono* paralegal on Bundy's behalf and who witnessed the scene outside the prison following his execution, characterized the scene as

> terrible and entirely banal at the same time. It was like being at the county fair, if you didn't know what was going on. There were so many cables crossing the ground that it was hard to walk. Generators made a lot of noise and there were large vans and trucks parked at different angles. There were several satellite dishes, and people were milling around in large groups.
>
> Before the execution and during it I tried to ignore everything, protesters, celebrators, media. I left the crowds and went over to the fence at the east of the field. It was a perfect winter dawn. I noticed one man walking, alone, along the fence. He seemed very sad, and I wondered if he might be a relative of a victim. I saw him again when Dennis [Adams] was killed a few months later, walking slowly and alone by the fence, with the sun coming up behind him.
>
> When a reporter left the prison and waved a white handkerchief [indicating that Bundy was dead], the crowd began singing and cheering. I tried then to turn myself into a videorecorder. I left the area of the protestors and went to the section where the pro execution crowd gathered, and walked back and forth through the area, trying to remember everything. But it's hard now to remember, and even harder to write. It breaks language. The jeering faces were familiar: Breughel's painting of the mocking of Christ, some of Bosch's work. People were selling doughnuts and coffee. There were beer cans on the ground. At least one person had constructed a model electric chair, and a full sized effigy of Ted, and was carrying them around in the back of a pick up truck. There were little pins or models of the electric chair being sold. People had signs, sparklers, firecrackers.[140]

Florida anthropologists Anthony Paredes and Elizabeth Purdum, astute observers of the subtexts of executions,[141] viewed the Bundy carnival as a "false catharsis of a classic sort—'purging ourselves.' "[142] The European witch craze comes to mind, the torture and murder of up to nine million women in the cause of "purifying the body of Christ."[143] Vandiver went on to describe what she saw as "something very ancient, and the modern setting only made it more bizarre. The ritual which was being repeated had elements of human sacrifice, of placing the sins of all on one victim and killing him, of celebratory lynching mobs, and of public executions. And all of those probably have their roots in the attempt to control the fear of death through ritually imposing it on one selected victim."[144]

Theodore Bundy's story did not quite end with his death. Three days after he was electrocuted, the Eleventh Circuit stayed by unpublished order a scheduled execution of another Florida death row prisoner. The sole basis of the stay was the issue of diminished sentencing responsibility that had come within one vote in the Supreme Court of securing a stay for Bundy.[145]

Soon after Bundy was executed, his habeas petition in the Chi Omega case was dismissed as moot.[146]

The Mirror, the (Scrambled) Metaphor: Bundy as Cultural Construction, Bundy as the "Crystallization of Culture"

> This is the story of how we begin to remember . . .
> —Paul Simon, "Under African Skies"

> A Man with Vision. A Man with Direction. A Prophet of Our Times . . . Bundy: The Man, The Myth, The Legend.
> —Campus poster

The foregoing discussion suggests that a tremendous gap exists between the super-due-process public perception and the minimal-due-process legal reality of Bundy's attempts to stay alive. The gap can partially be explained by public ignorance about the workings of the capital punishment system.[147] Lack of information is not a sufficient account, however; the question is how the public processed the information it *did* have.

I suggest here that the disparity between perception and reality can be explained, at least in part, by the fact that Bundy became a symbol of death row and of the type of person the United States most wants to execute. He has become the symbol of death row for the cultural consciousness of the United States. For this generation, Bundy rivals Hitler and Eichmann as the personification of evil and, therefore, as the embodiment of who should be on death row. He touched a nerve.

Specifically, this section shows the complexity of two related and superficially straightforward questions: Why did Bundy come to symbolize death row? Precisely what does he symbolize? I make no pretense of answering these questions completely. The modest thesis of this section is that the explanations are not as simple as one might expect.

The mythic Bundy energizes death penalty supporters, and he makes more than a few death penalty opponents squeamish and defensive. Capital punishment advocates gleefully cite Bundy as the ultimate justification for the ultimate sanction. Conversely, Bundy is a recurring nightmare for people advocating abolition of the death penalty. I have heard colleagues, male and female, who profoundly believe in the abolition of capital punishment murmur that in their hearts they might make an exception for Bundy.[148] Such death penalty opponents distance abolitionist sentiments from Bundy, pointing out, accurately, that most capital cases are not nearly so heinous.[149]

On one level, Bundy appears an unlikely candidate for death row symbol. Bundy and his cases are strikingly atypical of capital inmates and their cases generally. Unlike most death row prisoners, he was perceived by the culture to be a relatively bright,[150] articulate, middle-class, well-educated (college degree and one year of law school),[151] physically attractive[152] and charming[153] white man[154] who was apparently not the victim of childhood sexual abuse.[155]

Bundy seemed so relentlessly middle class. He appeared to have a promising future. He had done well in college and poorly in a year of law school.[156] By his late twenties, Bundy was a rising figure within the Seattle Republican party;[157] Richard Larsen quoted a letter from the former governor of Washington State to the admissions committee of the University of Utah Law School, summarizing Bundy's "outstanding" performance as a member of the governor's campaign staff;[158] Larsen himself thought Bundy might someday run for public office.[159] Bundy did volunteer work, writing a rape prevention pamphlet for women,[160] and working on a crisis hotline while in college.[161] These majoritarian attributes distinguish Bundy from almost everybody else living on death row. Vickie Karp, in her poem "One Hundred Well-Cut Leaves," got it right: "The brother you loved who fought in the Boxer Rebellion / And kept the gray photographs, a modest vault of evil / Beneath the bed where he slept."

Part of the explanation for Bundy's symbolic role lies in his savvy ability to attract and manipulate media attention. His jaunty air before the television cameras, and his intuitive grasp of the sound bite, made Bundy ripe for stardom as a *bête noire*. His trial was the first ever to be televised in Florida.[162]

Ultimately, however, two facts caused Bundy to stand out as a renowned symbol: his very atypicality on death row and his recognizability by the dominant culture in this country. Bundy's recognizability as "one of us,"[163] "everyone's son," the "boy next door," made him singularly threatening and feared. This phenomenon is reflected in the titles of books written about him: *The Stranger Beside Me*, *The Killer Next Door*, *The Phantom Prince*.[164] Bundy mirrored the United States' worst nightmares because he was so close to images valued by this society.

Race

> Evil is a mirror.
> —Editorial: "Accomplices to Genocide,"
> *New Republic*, August 7, 1995

Race factored into his recognizability by the dominant culture. It is paradoxical, though unsurprising, that death row's symbol should be white.

113

The pervasiveness of racism in this country requires no citation, and its persistence in the legal machinery of capital punishment should be expected and has been documented,[165] though it has been trivialized by the courts as constitutionally insignificant.[166] The Census Bureau reports that African Americans represent 12 to 15 percent of the present U.S. population; since the abolition of the slave trade, they have never represented less than 9 percent. Yet of the 3,589 people put to death for all crimes between 1930 and 1967, 54.6 percent were African American or members of other racial minority groups.[167] Statistics on execution for rape are even more dramatic. Of the 455 people put to death for the crime between 1930 and 1972, 89.5 percent were nonwhite.[168]

These execution figures remained relatively constant over time, but their message changed as the culture of the United States redefined their significance. Throughout the history of capital punishment, peaking in the 1930s, few people gave the racial dimension of the death penalty system much thought. The 1960s civil rights movement transformed the culture's awareness of race. The national sense of unease that blacks were bearing the brunt of executions increased apace.

Such unease manifested itself early in Florida. John Spenkelink, a run-of-the-mill killer if ever there was one, became the first person executed under the state's present-day capital statute. Victor Streib contextualized the case:

> Spenkelink, raised on an Iowa farm, had a traumatic childhood. At the age of twelve, he personally found the body of his alcoholic father who had committed suicide. At age fourteen, his criminal record began with an arrest for driving a stolen car. His record grew to include armed robbery and escape from prison.
>
> In early 1972, Spenkelink began traveling around the country with Joseph J. Szymankiewicz, a hitchhiker Spenkelink had picked up. Having been forcibly sodomized and otherwise mistreated by Szymankiewicz, Spenkelink devised a plan to recover the personal property which Szymankiewicz had stolen from him and to terminate his relationship with his abusive companion. Following his plan, Spenkelink shot Szymankiewicz in the back while he was asleep in their motel room in Tallahassee, Florida, on February 4, 1973.
>
> One week later, Spenkelink was arrested in Buena Park, California, for armed robbery. A police search of the apartment in which he was arrested uncovered the handgun used in the Florida killing. Soon thereafter, Spenkelink was returned to Florida and tried for first degree murder. Convicted under a felony-murder statute for the robbery-killing of Szymankiewicz, he was sentenced to death on December 20, 1973.[169]

Spenkelink's prosecutor at the postconviction stages of the case, Raymond Marky, was quoted as explaining: "contrary to a lot of belief, I had no animus toward Mr. Spenkelink at all. . . . In fact, I really felt that he was probably the least obnoxious on death row in terms of the crime he committed. . . . I didn't have some hideous monster . . . who strangled three generations of women. We had a guy who killed a faggot."[170]

Though Florida's New South governor reportedly explained that Spenkelink went first because his case had been in the courts the longest,[171] speculation persists that race was an important consideration in his decision to sign Spenkelink's death warrant. Karen Gottlieb, a Miami attorney involved in the case, wrote of the "widely-held belief among Mr. Spenkelink's attorneys and others who assisted in the litigation in his case that the extraordinary efforts by the state of Florida to have Mr. Spenkelink executed were prompted by two factors: the relatively non-heinous nature of his crime and the fact that Mr. Spenkelink was white, the theory of the state being that if Mr. Spenkelink could be executed, then everyone on death row would be destined for execution."[172] An anonymous central Florida lawyer (later identified as Larry Helm Spalding, the first director of Florida's CCR) was quoted by a journalist as saying: "I'll tell you why they wanted to kill him. He was white. No one in the South wants to kill a black man first. They don't want to be labeled racist. I think the next person who gets it will also be white. And then it's watch out blacks."[173]

In the same way that executing whites insulates a criminal justice system susceptible to charges of being racist, so too does designating Bundy as death row's symbol. His race reinforced his identification as a member of the dominant culture.

Sex

> Mirrors are crafty.
> —Margaret Atwood, "Tricks with Mirrors"

Beyond his physical attributes and background, Bundy was a creation of the culture in more subtle and troubling respects. The Bundy symbol is inseparable from matters of sex and gender—that complex amalgam of meanings which society creates and imposes upon biological sex by acculturation and socialization. Researchers and theorists usually speak of gender as socially constructed, not biologically determined.[174] Certainly maleness is the one obvious trait shared by all known serial sexual killers. "There has never been a female [Yorkshire Ripper]. Women have committed very brutal murders; they have killed repeatedly; they have killed at random. But in all the annals of recorded crime, no woman has done what [the Yorkshire Ripper] did."[175] "Only men, it seems, are compulsive lone hunters, driven by the lust to kill—a sexual desire which finds its outlet in murder."[176]

115

No such serial sexual murderers appear in Ann Jones's history of female killers in the United States.[177] Jones documented that "unlike men, who are apt to stab a total stranger in a drunken brawl or run amok with a high-powered rifle, we women usually kill our intimates: we kill our children, our husbands, our lovers."[178] Interestingly, a series of Florida murders of men has been linked to a woman, Aileen Wuornos.[179] In January 1992 Wuornos was sentenced to death for the murder of Richard Mallory, her first alleged victim, and in September 1994 the Florida Supreme Court unanimously affirmed the conviction and death sentence on direct appeal.[180] No evidence has yet emerged suggesting a *lust* murder dimension to these killings, however.

Feminism?

> Over and over, the chauvinist draws a portrait of the other which reminds us of that part of his own mind he would deny and which he has made dark to himself. . . . The chauvinist cannot face the truth that the other he despises is himself. This is why one so often finds in chauvinist thinking a kind of hysterical denial that the other could possibly be like the self.
> —Susan Griffin, *Pornography and Silence*, 161–62

The remainder of this section draws upon feminist[181] scholarship, notwithstanding its controversial reputation and notwithstanding some hesitation. The hesitation arises because of my male gender and because feminist learning is grounded so strongly in the experiences of women. When writers who are men appropriate the writings of women, readers should be on their guard.[182] Feminism is everywhere, but it is not monolithic. Leslie Bender is correct that labels and categorization should be resisted as divisive.[183] "As soon as labels are imposed, stereotypes and preconceived ideas become fixed instead of remaining fluid and growing."[184] This section of the chapter thus does not subdivide feminism into radical feminism, African American feminism, Latina feminism, liberal feminism, Marxist feminism, socialist feminism, lesbian feminism, and so on. Bender wryly observed that "feminism is a dirty word. I never fail to be amazed at the strength of the hostility the word generates. . . . Professor Lucinda Finley likens it to the 'F' word."[185] New dissenting voices have been raised; Katie Roiphe, Rene Denfeld, Camille Paglia, and Christine Hoff Sommers have joined the debate with longtime critics like Midge Decter.[186]

It seems to me that despite cogent criticisms of "feminism" and feminist scholarship, any intelligible discussion of sexual murder or serial murder[187] must bring questions of gender to the fore. Traditional literature on the topic all but ignores it. And to disregard gender buries the fundamental issue of who is doing the killing and who is doing the dying. Only such scholarship recognizes the centrality of gender to any meaningful inquiry into serial sexual murder.

Second, feminism employs the mirror as a metaphorical device in ways similar to those in which I am using it. For example, in *A Room of One's Own*,[188] Virginia Woolf powerfully described how women serve as mirrors reflecting a magnified view of masculinity back to men rather than acting for themselves, existing in their own right, and defining themselves on their own terms. This is one manifestation of the culture's definition of woman as other, inessential, deviant, abnormal in comparison to the male. The idea of woman as other (at least in its contemporary form) seems to have originated with Simone de Beauvoir, who argued in *The Second Sex* that in patriarchal culture the masculine is the norm and the feminine is defined negatively, in terms definitionally nonmasculine—in terms of otherness. The concept of other is prominent in feminist discourse,[189] though not only in feminist discourse.[190] Polarity is the seed of gender definition and of the self/other dichotomy. Each gender is constructed as the opposite of the other. Contrast is the point. Opposition and negative definition are the sources of the definition of the other. The concept of otherness underlies categories of contrasting characteristics labeled masculine and feminine.

Third, feminist scholarship at its best is useful because it tends to be interdisciplinary and inclusive rather than insular. Deborah Cameron and Elizabeth Frazer, for example, write: "One further sign of our commitment to feminism is the consciously interdisciplinary focus of *The Lust to Kill* and the fact that we have felt able to venture into academic territory where we have no special claims to expertise. Feminists are notorious for not respecting the 'proper' boundaries of academic disciplines, and in our opinion that is all to the good."[191]

Feminist learning typically employs gender as a fundamental organizing category of human experience. It stresses that men and women have different perceptions or experiences in the same contexts (the male perspective having been dominant, if not exclusive, in fields of knowledge) and that gender is not a natural biological fact but a social construct, a learned quality, an assigned status—and therefore subject to identification by humanistic disciplines. Some poststructuralists, reacting to liberal feminism's focus on the experiences of white, middle-class, heterosexual women, question the preeminence of gender. They posit that there is no essential womanness, "no woman but many women."[192] These writers appear not to reject gender as a frame of reference. Rather they claim that gender cannot be understood in isolation; experiences based on gender cannot be separated from experiences based on race, class, sexual preference, cultural identity, and the like.[193] These poststructuralists have as their goal the crafting of "a synthesis of class, race and gender perspectives into a holistic and inclusive feminist theory and practice."[194] Their challenge goes to the heart of the matter of gender. Esmeralda Thornhill, for one, demands that white feminists revise their work so that the "experiences of Black women are not 'merely tacked on as window dressing, diminished in parentheses, or hidden in footnotes.' "[195] Feminist theory often "begins by describing, defining, and exposing patriarchy. 'Patriarchy' is the feminist term for the ubiquitous phenomenon of male domination and hierarchy."[196] The word is a wide conceptual umbrella that covers systems of male dominance that oppress women through social, political, and economic institutions.

Feminism resonates here because most of the people who represented Bundy and judged him were male. His alleged victims were female.

In the area of criminal law, feminists have attempted to demonstrate that "what is perhaps the most paradigmatic expression of patriarchical force—rape—is not, as common sense might insist, a crime of desire, passion, frustrated attraction, victim provocation or uncontrollable biological urges."[197] Rape isn't about sex. Rape is about power and violence and domination.

Less convincingly, feminists such as Susan Brownmiller, author of *Against Our Will,* assert that sexual violence against women is culturally condoned and widespread. Because of the possibility of rape as well as its pervasive actuality, Brownmiller describes the crime as "nothing more or less than a conscious process of intimidation by which *all men* keep *all women* in a state of fear."[198] She included all men because any man could be a rapist, and because even men who do not rape are the beneficiaries of the climate of coercion created by those who do. Andrea Dworkin[199] argues that the driving engine of male history is male violence. In *Intercourse,*[200] she also contends (unpersuasively, I believe) that pornography underpins male supremacy.

Feminist theory is right, then, it seems to me, to define rape not only as a violent act but also as a social institution that can have the effect of perpetuating patriarchal domination. The perpetrators are thus not "an aberrant fringe. Rather, rape is a social expression of sexual politics, an institutionalized and ritualized enactment of male domination, a form of terror which functions to maintain the status quo." Jane Caputi further (and more problematically) reasons that, like rape, "sexual murder is not some inexplicable explosion/epidemic of an extrinsic evil or the domain only of the mysterious psychopath. On the contrary, such murder is an eminently logical step in the procession of patriarchal roles, values, needs, and rule of force."[201]

Many feminist writers, including Caputi and Catharine MacKinnon, think they see a connection between pornography and violence against women, including rape. They argue that the pervasive pornographic dimension of U.S. culture creates enduring images that glorify (or at least condone) sexual violence against women—up to a point.[202] The pornography debate is complicated,[203] divisive, and easily oversimplified. MacKinnon, Susan Griffin, and Dworkin do not argue that there are direct, empirically demonstrable causal relationships between pornography and rape. Feminists, particularly critics in science, contend at the outset that concepts such as "objectivity," "empiricism," and "neutrality" are themselves suspect.[204] According to Maria Mies, for example, identification with the research subject is essential to feminist investigation. Such conscious partiality contrasts with "objective" spectator knowledge, which purports to take a "neutral," independent attitude toward the research subject. As to pornography itself, MacKinnon, Griffin, and Dworkin contend that the images it creates shape desires by making available certain objects and meanings, given that desire itself is to some degree a cultural construct.[205] Even terms like "censorship" are not clear-cut. MacKinnon, Griffin, and Dworkin see pornography itself as a form of censorship, arguing that it silences the authentic voices of women. Other feminists find these antipornography efforts distracting and diffusing. Mary Dunlap, for example, claims that the important issue is the reality of rape, not the image of rape contained in pornography. "If we take on pornography as the image of rape, and we destroy it, we will have destroyed, I suspect, nothing more than the image of rape. . . . Let us end rape."[206] Amen.

One need not subscribe to Caputi's entire worldview (I prefer to remain agnostic at the moment) to appreciate her insight that sexual murderers, like rapists, are not so different from the rest of us as we might like to believe. A 1990 *Newsweek* cover story on rape suggested that sexual violence "may now be an emblem of the American way." "After two decades of the newly 'sensitive,' nurturing male, the macho stud seems to have come back in magnum force."[207]

Bundy's typicality as an all-American guy was hammered home to me early in his postconviction litigation. A male psychiatrist who had observed him closely saw parallels between Bundy and the masculine characters created by Norman Mailer[208] (who transparently identifies with his literary creations). The comparison between Bundy's persona and Mailer's characters shocked me at first, but I gradually began to appreciate its haunting logic. I had forgotten the comparison until I read Cameron's and Frazer's excellent feminist study of sexual murderers.[209] They analyzed Mailer's 1957 essay "The White Negro"[210] as a highly articulated expression of the psychopathic killer as ultimate individualist,[211] existential rebel, and cultural hero—a social outlaw who celebrates murder as a liberating event and who sees the murderer as catalyst of social change.[212] He begins to resemble a latter-day incarnation of Nietzsche's *Übermensch*[213] or Dostoyevsky's Raskolnikov:[214] a Faustian figure who transcends conventional morality in the cause of his own liberation.[215]

There is more than a grain of truth in the notion that misogyny, grounded in the dominant culture, together with the Mailer paradigm of masculinity, also rooted in the prevailing culture, combine to make possible the serial sexual murderer in the United States. Cameron and Frazer observed that such a murderer is a peculiarly North American invention. Other societies have had their serial killers and have developed a discourse within which to define them. But "the real reason why the concept of serial murder has arisen in North America and not elsewhere is its dependence on a certain representation of North America itself, its culture, its symbols, its heroes. The serial killer . . . is the American counterpart of [Jean] Genet's[216] or [Colin] Wilson's existential rebel."[217]

Cameron and Frazer discuss in fascinating detail existentialism and the theme of murder as the ultimate act of transcendence (and will and freedom and defiance) of the constraints that normally determine human destiny.[218] They trace the theme of sexual murderer as rebel/hero from the writings of the Marquis de Sade, whom they denote as the father of the sexual murderer. "The aspect of Sade's life and work which has converted the Western imagination is the idea that the individual who transgresses [man-made laws] is a rebel, in search of a freedom and pleasure—a 'transcendence'—which society, in its ignorance and repressiveness, denies him. Thus the way is paved for the sexual murderer to become the quintessential modern hero."[219] Cameron's and Frazer's treatment of Sade's modern interpreters among the existentialists—Sartre, Beauvoir, Genet, Gide, Wilson—as well as their thoughtful critique of the existentialists' account of (and celebration of) the murderer, are particularly interesting.[220] Indeed, "the sort of figure who is celebrated in Mailer's essay—hip, cool, psychopathic—has in fact become a touchstone" of American masculinity. "He is an up-to-date exemplar of the 'outlaw' tradition which appears in a variety of representations in North America."[221] A male novelist opined a few years ago that "America's greatest contribution to pop literature is the tough-guy hero, that hard-punching, hard-drinking, hard-loving macho mensch who can't help annoying the bad guys, even while he makes every woman swoon."[222] The serial killer therefore becomes a "transformation of the traditional loner on his unending journey, a perverse incarnation of the 'Man with No Name.' Traditional North American individualism sorts well with the existentialist theme of the free man's right to transcend ordinary constraints on behavior."[223] Cameron and Frazer conclude that this quest for transcendence through lust murder, combined with misogyny reinforced and validated by societal norms, best accounts for serial sexual murders.[224]

Cameron and Frazer are describing the murderer-as-rebel/hero generally; Caputi and others make the point as to Bundy particularly. While awaiting trial in Aspen, Colorado, for kidnapping and murdering Caryn Campbell, he twice escaped[225] and eventually made his way to Florida. Before the escapes, Bundy had been convicted of kidnapping and publicly connected with many sexual murders in the Pacific Northwest.[226] Yet when he escaped the second time much of Aspen rooted for him. "All observers concur;" Caputi accurately notes: " 'In Aspen, Bundy had become a folk hero.' 'Ted achieved the status of Billy the Kid at least'; or 'Aspen reacted as if Bundy were some sort of Robin Hood instead of a suspected mass murderer.' "[227] T-shirts proclaimed "Bundy is a one night stand"; a radio station adopted a Bundy request hour, playing songs such as "Ain't No Way to Treat a Lady"; a restaurant advertised a Bundyburger, a plain roll because, the sign explained, "the meat has fled."[228] He was even memorialized in doggerel:

> So let's salute the mighty Bundy,
> Here on Friday, gone on Monday.
> All his roads lead out of town,
> It's hard to keep a good man down.[229]

It is especially interesting that this outburst of enthusiasm followed Bundy's *escape* from custody.[230]

Looking through the lens of gender provided by such writers as Caputi, Cameron, and Frazer, one can hypothesize that Bundy remained part of the culture precisely because of—not in spite of—his crimes. The very acts we want to think set him apart in fact reinforced his definition as one of us. He thus remains a symbol of evil, although not of evil alone. He represents something far more insidious and therefore far more frightening. He can best be understood as a multifaceted symbol: a demon, but a demon all too recognizable as a societal construct of masculinity, albeit a construct perhaps containing aspects bordering on caricature. Perhaps.

Yet precisely because Bundy was recognized as part of the dominant culture, one might have expected him to be exempt from capital punishment. Psychological distancing, the dehumanizing essential to the determination that a fellow human deserved to die, was less apparent here than in most capital cases. Still, he became the symbol of death row. Why?

The easy and comfortable explanation is that Bundy committed horrible crimes against helpless white women. That answer rings false. Conviction of awful crimes is perhaps a necessary, but certainly not a sufficient, condition for being designated as the symbol of those whom we want to execute—for the creation of a symbol as enduring as Theodore Bundy.

Consider as a cautionary tale the case of Gerald Stano,[231] another accused serial killer on Florida's death row. Like Bundy, he is alleged to have murdered many women during the 1970s. Have you ever heard of Gerald Stano? Most people, even most Floridians, have not. Stano's cases have resulted in no movies, comparatively little media attention, and only one trashy book, written by the mother of his prosecutor.[232] Even scholarly studies of serial murder tend to dwell on Bundy and to ignore Stano.[233] This is curious, given the similarities between their alleged crimes. Stano would respond that he differs from Bundy because he is innocent. But, as was suggested above, the evidence of Bundy's guilt presented at trial was also far from overwhelming.

The difference may be that Stano lacks the qualities of stardom. He is overweight, whereas Bundy was viewed as trim and attractive. Stano is balding, whereas Bundy was viewed as rakish and photogenic. Stano is undereducated, inarticulate, and quite possibly crazy, whereas Bundy the former law student[234] was viewed as eloquent and artful in his use of the "mask of sanity."[235] Herbert Cleckley, a psychiatrist, reportedly examined Bundy and testified at his pretrial hearing that Bundy was competent to stand trial but that he exhibited antisocial behaviors.[236] Caputi devilishly switched Cleckley's terms and referred to the psychopath's mask of *insanity,* deftly making her point that Cleckley's designation obscures the real similarities between sexual killers and at least some "normal" men in the United States.[237] One of my male academic colleagues insists that Bundy can only be explained by mental illness: Bundy *must* have been crazy to have done those things. To the extent that this view is widespread, it seems to me to say more about our fears (or our hopes) than it says about Bundy's actual mental condition. Stano is one of "them." Bundy was one of "us."

The Stano comparison underscores that Bundy's notoriety did not result from public revulsion over what he did to women, that he did not become death row's symbol because of his peculiar contempt for women. It is true that Bundy's victims were comparatively valued by the dominant society (college students rather than prostitutes, white women rather than women of color), while Stano's alleged victims were women marginalized by society (prostitutes, runaways). Cameron and Frazer surveyed the criminology literature and concluded that the "callous treatment of prostitute murder victims, which excuses—or rather, erases—male sadism, recurred in practically every source we looked at."[238] Still, the identities of Bundy's victims provide little meaningful insight into the culture's reaction to him.[239] The contrast between the media coverage of the impending Bundy and Stano executions was revealing. Every event and nonevent in Bundy's litigation received the coverage of Armageddon. The Stano litigation, when mentioned at all, was usually discussed as an appendage to the Bundy case.

Again feminist learning illuminates, and again the image emerges of

Bundy as a Norman Mailer character carried a bit too far, a difference of magnitude rather than kind. Few men would do what Bundy did, but more men than we want to admit share his lusts. Or as one writer who contributes often to horror magazines phrased it (satirically?): "Most men just hate women. Ted Bundy killed them."[240]

The reasons Bundy came to symbolize death row, as well as the identification of precisely what he does symbolize, thus are matters both complex and paradoxical. This chapter does not attempt to resolve such questions in any satisfactory way; it need not do so for my purposes here. The fact remains that, regardless of the explanations, Bundy does personify death row. That personification helps explain both the legal system's actual treatment of his cases and the popular misconceptions about that treatment. I am not excusing Bundy's alleged crimes by putting them in cultural context. My reasoning condemns the culture for being more like its image of Bundy than polite society wants to realize.

To the person who resembles you closely, yet is not really your double, you might easily end up saying: "You are almost like me. The similarity between us is so plain that in the eyes of the world you are my brother. But, to speak honestly, you are not my brother. My identity, in relation to you, consists precisely in the ways in which I am different from you. Yet the more you resemble me, the harder it is for anyone else to see those crucial differences. Our resemblance threatens to obliterate anything that is special about me, so you are my false brother. I have no alternative but to hate you, because by working up rage against you, I am defending everything that is unique about me." Martin Luther King, Jr., wrote along similar lines in "Letter from Birmingham City Jail" when he described segregation as wrong in part because it "ended up relegating persons to the status of things. . . . To use the words of Martin Buber, segregation substitutes an 'I-it' relationship for the 'I-thou' relationship."[241]

Conclusion: Bundy as Other, Bundy as Almost the Same, Bundy as Us

> The power of a metaphor is that it colors and controls our subsequent thinking about its subject.
> —Stephen L. Winter, "The Metaphor of Standing and the Problem of Self-Governance"

> Socrates, I must confess, is so close to me that I am almost constantly fighting him.
> —Friedrich Nietzsche, *The Origin of Philosophy*

Despite the grotesquely misleading media hyperbole about "10 years of repetitive judicial review," the legal system failed in Bundy's case. At the time of his electrocution, it had cost Florida taxpayers millions of dollars to

123

execute him.[242] Von Drehle wrote that as of 1988 there were 55 prisoners on the state's death row, more than one-sixth of Florida's condemned population, who had been there longer than Bundy.[243]

Bundy the man was destroyed on schedule—well *ahead* of schedule, if you accept the chronology set out earlier in this chapter. The capital assembly line bureaucrats in *Bundy* acted coarsely and thoughtlessly, and then they refused to consider critically what they had done. Few mourned Mr. Bundy's electrocution, but I did; I still do. We had failed as attorneys by not identifying the dispositive constitutional issue in his case sooner. The courts had failed as well. Judging a metaphor is as complicated as being his lawyer. Bundy's growth into a myth made it difficult for judges to judge.[244]

"Now I believe they will leave me alone" declares Lyman Ward in the opening line of Wallace Stegner's *Angle of Repose*. Since Bundy was so atypical of the death row population (in being seen as attractive, comparatively smart, white, recognizably middle class), how is it that he came to be the emblem of death row, the poster child for capital punishment? The paradoxical explanation is that he attained this status precisely because he was so atypical of the condemned, and so typical of, and therefore recognizable by, the dominant culture in the United States. He was "one of us."[245]

It may well be that Bundy was executed because his crimes set him apart, although his offenses may simply be located on the continuum of masculine violence at a point that society cannot explicitly tolerate. In any case, he became death row's symbol not because he was different from the usual violent male offender but rather because he was similar.[246] The manic festival celebrating Bundy's execution reflected what Susan Griffin terms "the hysterical denial that the other could possibly be like the self."[247] Likewise (and ironically, given Bundy's apparent preoccupation with pornography)[248] a functionally similar process of cultural deletion permitted him to become defined as other, negated, killed. Writing of women, but making a point also true of Bundy and other condemned people, Cameron and Frazer observe, "What turning persons into objects is all about, in our culture, is, in the final analysis, killing them."[249]

By "inventing a figure different from self"—here, our image of death row—we construct "an allegory of self" that contains the values the culture defines as positive.[250] This construction, however, depends on difference and distance. The other can never be permitted to resemble the self. The line between the two must remain distinct. Bundy hit an exposed cultural nerve, and the culture needed not merely to kill him but to dance merrily on his grave: Bundy blurred the line between self and other, between us and them.

Because he was so recognizably "one of us," Bundy was a mirror for each of us—but only because we were looking. He unflinchingly and remorselessly reflected our deepest fears. We have seen the enemy, to paraphrase Walt Kelly's *Pogo*, and he is us. We hated seeing the things he made us see in ourselves. So we shattered the mirror in our attempt to destroy the image it contained. *We* still look the same. *Our* ignorance and fear and hatred remain unchanged. But with Theodore Bundy dead, we are no longer forced to see ourselves.

Or are we?

5

Why I Did Deathwork
Pressing the Law to Keep Its Promises

And the executioner's face is always well hidden.
—Bob Dylan, "Hard Rain Gonna Fall"

Lawyers must continue to bear witness to the shameful injustices which are all too
routine in capital cases.
—Stephen Bright, "Counsel for the Poor: The Death Sentence Not for the Worst
Crime but for the Worst Lawyer"

But this phase in our history won't last forever. We will regain our faith in our ability
to address our problems as a society, and our sense of shared responsibility and of a
shared destiny as a people. And as we do, the inexorable progress of abolition will
resume.

I can't say that this is the most important legal work one could be engaged in. But I
do think it needs to be done. If there are some law students here tonight who think
you'd like to put your shoulder to this wheel, welcome. Don't be discouraged. Push.
It'll move.
—David Bruck, "Does the Death Penalty Matter?"

"When it comes to death," wrote Ralph Waldo Emerson, "all of us are
children." I lack the language to capture in words how personally reward-
ing and satisfying, as well as how terrifying and stressful and beautiful,
capital postconviction work can be. I'm at best a mediocre writer with a
hell of a story to tell. It is difficult to talk about representing people who are
litigating for their lives without sounding cartoonish. But the reason it is
hard to talk about it, is the reason I keep doing it. I wonder if questions of
motive would be so difficult were I a construction worker, a secretary, or a
nuclear physicist.

"Why do you represent the condemned? Isn't it depressing? What
about the victims?" Particularly when I was a public defender I was asked
such questions so often, by so many people with different degrees of seri-

126

ousness, that I have tried to find some pat answers, or at least one pat answer suitable for wineglass repartee.

These attempts have been unsuccessful. This is not because I am ashamed of what I do, or because I am unwilling to debate the merits of the death penalty, or because I fail to appreciate the impact of the violent crimes committed by most of my clients; casual chatter about deathwork is awkward because I have been unable to find a way to express succinctly, in a sound bite, the intensity, the breathtaking emotional highs and sometimes heartbreaking, savage lows, of working for people who are litigating for life itself; the existential angst that comes with burying our dead: people we represent, of course, but also comrades as different as Craig Barnard[1] and Mark Evans, who also count among our casualties.

Doing deathwork means that every now and again, not often but often enough, you get to be a part of justice being done. I do not mean to sound Pollyannishly altruistic, though I hope that public spirit is part of it. The satisfaction derived from doing deathwork is, in a big way, quite selfish. Much of the public hates lawyers, and the lawyers themselves are none too happy these days: polls and personal experience convince me that many, if not most, attorneys are unhappy with their jobs. I loved my job as a Florida public defender representing people on death row. My cases involved real people with horrifyingly real problems; I was able to help them in very tangible ways, and they and their loved ones were grateful for my help.

My postconviction practice permitted—*required*—me to deconstruct such foundational social and political matters as race, gender, and class. The first job of a good postconviction litigator is to find out and understand who this prisoner is, what his story is, what more there is to him beyond the fact (usually, but not always) of a brutal crime. There is more to all of us than what we did on the worst day of our lives. Our job is to find the missing pieces of the puzzle, to contextualize the offense by filling out the rest of the offender's picture.

And, not to sound too sappy, my practice allowed me to pursue justice in an unjust world; more, to work for perfect justice in a perfectly unjust world. I learned from Judge Vance, a veteran of the civil rights wars, that it just feels pretty damned good to be *proud* of the work you do, to be able to look at yourself in the bathroom mirror at the end of the day, to feel no guilt when you deposit your paycheck at the end of each month—and if there isn't much money to deposit, if you are still driving a VW bug while your law school classmates are driving BMWs, then, oh, well.

Capital postconviction representation today and for the foreseeable future involves not so much debates about the wisdom of the death penalty in theory—its abstract morality or immorality or wisdom as a matter of public policy—but rather case-by-case constitutional attacks upon the legal system that selects which citizens die.

America's capital punishment system is beyond unjust and beyond unfair. The thing is dysfunctionally baroque. A clear sense of the system's basic unfairness is an important motivating factor. Few other paying jobs permit one to spend one's working time and energy fighting the theory and practice of government-sponsored homicide in this country. I believe this system is an unambiguous disgrace to civilized humanity; besides being classist and indecent, it is racist.

Another motivation is the knowledge that effective postconviction advocacy can, without a doubt, ameliorate the harshness of the capital punishment system in individual cases by pressuring the law to keep its promises. That helps death-eligible and death-sentenced people in concrete ways; it saves lives that *ought* to be saved in the eyes of the law. Attorneys for people litigating for their lives can pressure the law to keep its promises of justice and fairness and equality, even while knowing in our bone marrow that the law *won't* keep its promises, that the law lies, or, perhaps, that the law simply *can't* keep the promises it has made, that its reach here exceeds its grasp. It is work that yields tangible results, one way or the other.

Effective participation in the capital collateral system can, and often does, reveal latent injustices and therefore force the court system to work as it should, even in the most apparently hopeless and seemingly clearcut cases. There is even some room for legal jujitsu—for using the legal system's weight and resources against the system itself. And, for a long, long time, I thought that if the best of the bar shun these cases, or conscientiously abstain from taking them, then less competent and less committed lawyers might well end up representing the condemned.

Another reason for doing deathwork is the web of people you become connected with and the complex geometry of relationships among them (although it's better to read Russian novels than to live in one): from the grand chessmaster visionaries who seem touched with fire; to the poets and the historians; to the investigative and organizational geniuses; to the gifted trench warriors and appellate wizards; to the pit-bull investigators; to the real-world-grounded eggheads; and the people who held it all (and us all) together.

I also *like* most of my condemned clients. I identify with many of them: there, but for the grace of God and impulse control, go I. I've never killed anyone—so far as I know—but I *could* have, and, had a few details been different, I might have. We all tell stories of the crazy things we did in our 20s, at least all of us do who were lucky enough to have done crazy things in our 20s and, luckier yet, survived them.

In a nation and in an epoch as riven by classism, racism, sexism, and homophobia as ours, it's a stupid thing to have spent your time fighting, I often think. One great tragedy is that the incandescent energy of people like Henry Schwartzschild[2] and Anthony Amsterdam had to be spent here, on this issue, in this way. But, to me, state killings are the rawest example of the exercise of governmental power against the culture's most marginalized citizens. The whole Frankenstein monster of federal government machinery involved with the business of crime and punishment doesn't work any better when the stakes are life and death than it does when the stakes are freedom versus many years' confinement to a cage. And once you know that and once you've lived within the reality of capital punishment as a legal system for any appreciable time, it's virtually impossible, for me, at least, to turn your back on it and move on to other work. The death penalty system is so hideous and so unfair, and so few people give a tinker's damn about it, that it's difficult just to walk away. I know that I can't change the system; I can't even get Joe Spaziano, who is innocent, off death row. And yet I have to keep trying, keep writing, and keep thinking about Joe and about the others.

To work with people like Schwartzschild, Mark Olive, Scharlette Holdman, Richard Jorandby, and Craig Barnard on a cause so vital is a privilege, and this was so in part because it was never a "cause" or an abstract issue; it was concrete work to keep the state from killing some of its citizens, particular people we came to know *as* people. They were clients, and those clients had cases, but first and last they were human beings with dignity as people.

The cadence of the attorney-client relationship will be influenced greatly by how far along in the legal process the inmate's case has progressed when we first meet. Most have committed heinous crimes against innocent victims. All have already been convicted of capital murder and sentenced to death, and all have had their convictions and death sentences affirmed on direct appeal by a state appellate court. At the early stages of the postconviction process, when we can expect that the execution will not happen for several years—if it happens at all—our relationship evolves at its own speed and with its own rhythm. It is, of course, impossible to generalize about a population as diverse as the fraternity of the condemned, as every prisoner is unique, and that uniqueness defines the contours of our relationship. Sometimes we become close; in other cases we do not. It all depends. This is an aspect of deathwork I didn't expect. Some inmates are intensely interested in every legal development; others want to know, but they want the attorney to broach the subject and to pursue it; still others want to talk only about their families, their lives on death row, or the state of the world in general. Death row, in its randomness, includes poets and artists. Joseph Spaziano is a talented painter; Stephen Booker published a book of poetry; Joseph Giarratano is a shrewder legal tactician than many people licensed to practice law. Florida's death row included a whippet-thin man who spoke with the power of Ezekiel and whose Old Testament demons were as real as breakfast and as terrifying as the electric chair. He pictured his boot on the tail of Satan in Goyaesque word-etchings polluted with freaks: depraved, slobbering bats and goblins and ghouls (think of the *Disasters of War* in Madrid's Prado Museum, engraved with an almost sadistic attention to detail).

A few condemned prisoners are just not very interesting, not many, but some. Many more are mentally ill in one form or another, ranging from gentle neurosis to flamboyant talking-to-space-ships delusional psychoses, crippling mental retardation or depression, and in one case brain damage so severe that the man's lawyer exhorted the Florida Supreme Court justices to "just look at the MRI. Part of his brain is literally damaged or missing. You can *see* the holes in his brain." (The court denied the stay of execution anyway.) And so on. Again, it is impossible to generalize; death row is more reflective of the diverse culture of the United States than one might expect. Early in the legal process, the death penalty does not eclipse all other subjects, although it provides the subtext for much of our conversation. We can be expansive and talk about a wide spectrum of subjects, including my reasons for being there.

The client and I have not always had the luxury of getting to know each other through a slowly evolving relationship, however. The scarcity of death row attorneys in Florida in the mid-1980s, and the frequency with which execution dates were scheduled by its governors, meant that at that time I often met the inmate for the first time when the execution date had been set for the forthcoming month. Regardless of the circumstances, my job required that I get to know the prisoner fast and gain his trust, so that he would rely on my judgment and, more important, share information with my colleagues and me. The first step in any postconviction investigation is to piece together a complete history of the condemned person, from embryo to death row. Often the information needed is of the most intimate sort and may require the inmate to confront and share painful feelings and long-buried memories. The urgency of an impending execution date means that the legal team must develop, and sometimes force, trust and closeness at an accelerated pace. This requires time, but time is compressed when the metaphorical clock is ticking.

Unearthing new evidence in postconviction factual reinvestigation does not translate into judicial *consideration* of the evidence. Courts are loath to revisit cases in light of such newly discovered evidence, even if such evidence goes to factual innocence. However discouraging it may be when courts reject such legal claims, the litigation is still making a record for the future. Taken as a whole, these cases form a historical record of whom the state is killing and under what circumstances. The cases document that the "modern" death penalty is just as unfair as ever, just as random as ever. Jordan Steiker wrote in a perceptive essay that Thurgood Marshall always regarded the Court's 1976 cases upholding the constitutionality of capital punishment as provisional—as authorizing the death penalty only to the extent that the new statutes and procedures actually redressed the inequalities and arbitrariness of the *ancien* capital punishment regime. Marshall as Justice was a trial lawyer building a record: Marshall attempted to ground his opposition in the apparent failure of states to fulfill the particular promises upon which the modern death penalty statutes had been approved. He sought to demonstrate that, notwithstanding the seemingly scientific language of the redrafted statutes, states' administration of the death penalty remained arbitrary and discriminatory.

Primarily, though, we are litigating for the courts, or at least *in* the courts. Here, timing is everything. The most wrenching cases are those in which the inmate is running out of legal possibilities for relief. Such cases have been through the entire postconviction legal process in both state and federal courts at least once, and are called "successors." When an execution date is set in a case requiring successive litigation, both the inmate and the lawyer know that the chances of obtaining a stay of the execution are slim. Some Georgia deathworkers decided a few years ago not to bring successors as a matter of routine. We must strike our own balance between ephemeral hope and hard reality.

The improbability of securing stays of execution, which is linked to the increasing hostility of the courts to successors, presents lawyers with intractable dilemmas, given their finite resources. Should scarce defense resources (material as well as credibility capital) be expended on cases in which we will probably not succeed in preventing the execution? The question is not without consequences, because undertaking such a litigation effort requires enormous investments of time, work, and emotional energy—scarce resources that otherwise might be spent in aid of other clients with a greater likelihood of ultimate success in the courts. For me, one important component of this decision is the impact on the person waiting to be killed, and on his loved ones, of a last-ditch effort: does the litigation effort, which inevitably raises the man's hopes that he will escape his imminent execution date, impede his ability to work through the (uncertain) fact of impending death? Does such litigation—such literally last-minute litigation—foster denial of the reality of his impending death?

These issues are not abstract. Deathworkers confront them every day, and whether one wants to deal with these sorts of conundra should be given hard thought by anyone considering doing deathwork in the first place.

Some years ago David Bruck was researching the death penalty for juveniles:

> In the National Archives I came across the certiorari petition filed in the United States Supreme Court on behalf of two black teenage murderers in a Mississippi case in 1947. The petition had weak legal claims—the papers seemed desperate, and succeeded only in postponing that double execution for a few months. I think I can imagine the sense of humiliation and defeat that their lawyer must have felt the night of that execution, when he watched the clock and knew he had failed so completely to stop the inexorable grinding of that racist system.
>
> The signature at the bottom of that cert petition was Thurgood Marshall's. His work for the NAACP Legal Defense Fund may seem to have been glamorous and exciting now, when so many of the battles he fought have been at least partly won. But that night, his hopeless campaign to stop Mississippi from executing those two black teenagers must have seemed pointless, marginal, a humiliating enactment of political weakness.
>
> Justice Marshall was the lone dissenter last week [in 1990] when Virginia electrocuted a man named Wilbert Evans.[3] This stubborn stand again seems forlorn, and so, I suppose, it is.
>
> But this phase in our history won't last forever.[4]

Death row needs lawyers desperately. As death row continues to grow and as more condemned inmates enter the postconviction process,[5] states with the death penalty must decide whether condemned inmates wishing to pursue postconviction remedies should be provided lawyers at the states' expense. This aspect of capital punishment was masked during the de facto moratorium on executions between 1967 and 1977, and by the slow resumption of executions in the late 1970s and 1980s. But as capital punishment becomes a genuinely national phenomenological reality, and as executions resume in earnest, the counsel question takes on increasing urgency. It is an urgency with two quite different aspects. The state must decide whether to give condemned people lawyers. And lawyers must decide whether they can, and should, do this work.

The principal aims of the remainder of this chapter are to begin a definition of the counsel crisis and to explore one state's legislative "solution." The chapter proceeds in three sections. First, access to the courts in the postconviction process must remain open to the condemned: the postconviction system reveals injustices not detected earlier in the criminal justice process. Second, the chapter explores Florida's counsel crisis and the reality of inmates facing imminent execution without the assistance of counsel. Third, it traces how the counsel crisis in Florida culminated in the legislative creation of a state agency, the Office of the Capital Collateral

Representative (CCR), to provide direct representation to Florida's condemned. The chapter concludes with a critique of CCR today.

Texas in 1996 was Florida circa 1985: Texas is experiencing a postconviction counsel crisis of escalating magnitude caused by the shrinking pool of volunteer lawyers and the accelerated scheduling of execution dates for unrepresented death row inmates. Roughly 125 of Texas' death row prisoners remained lawyerless as of May 1996.[6] In a situation eerily reminicent of Florida in the mid-1980s, almost all the lawyers in Texas capital postconviction proceedings are volunteers.[7] In Texas, the extraordinary numbers of postappeal execution orders, accelerated postconviction litigation schedules, and decreasing numbers of volunteer attorneys effectively nullify the state postconviction process for many death-sentenced prisoners. These problems are magnified when execution dates have been set. To stay the execution, counsel must master a substantial record and a complex area of law while simultaneously litigating both the merits and the stay request in federal and state forums, often before more than one court in each. This sometimes involves a literal race from court to court to meet deadlines.

The Texas capital representation crisis has been building for several years. In 1987, a Texas committee chaired by a judge of the Texas Court of Criminal Appeals concluded that "the absence of a system to insure that death-sentenced inmates have counsel throughout the appeals process has had a detrimental effect upon all the parties and upon the quality of justice in both our state and federal courts." The absence of a counsel system affected the state ("cases have not progressed smoothly or at a reasonable pace through the court system"), the defendant ("he or she has not had the means to test the fairness of his or her conviction and sentence of death"), the courts ("it has meant high-pressure decision making because an execution is imminent and sometimes briefs and arguments have been inadequate"), and "society at large" ("the larger issues present in many of the death cases receive inferior adversarial testing").[8]

The representation problem became significantly worse in 1991 when "the Court of Criminal Appeals suddenly stopped granting stays to allow additional time for the [Texas Resource] Center to recruit volunteer counsel," and, at the same time, "state trial courts began setting execution dates in unprecedented numbers": 64 in 1991; 111 in 1992; and 89 in 1993 (as of October 26, 1993).[9] Now, "more than 75 death row prisoners do not have attorneys." As a result, "no attorney has examined these individuals' cases for potential postconviction appeals."[10]

A 1993 study confirmed these conclusions, stating, "in the strongest terms possible, that Texas has already reached the crisis stage in capital representation and that the problem is substantially worse than that faced by any other state with the death penalty." The Texas problem is "desperate" because the number of cases is "overwhelming," "no funds are allocated for payment of counsel or litigation expenses," and "the number of available attorneys and firms remains limited." The problem will get worse. "We estimate that the number of persons on death row will continue to grow at an even higher rate in the next few years."[11]

And get worse it has. Although there had been a resource center in Texas, for many reasons it was incapable of representing all, or even most, Texas death-sentenced prisoners; in any event, in 1995 the center was defunded by Congress. No state provides less financial support for state postconviction counsel in capital cases than does Texas.[12] No state, through its death warrant policy, provides more work for defense attorneys. By generating approximately 75 percent of the nation's first-time postconviction death warrants (outside of California),[13] Texas forces attorneys to dedicate enormous amounts of time to "satellite litigation" that "occurs at every court level."[14] "Few good attorneys are willing to litigate in such harried and compressed circumstances." In sum, "despite enormous effort in a wide variety of areas, the Resource Center is simply not equipped to handle the kind of work required of it by current practices regarding the appointment of counsel in capital cases."[15]

Prosecutors responded that the "crisis" was manufactured by the Texas Resource Center, and that the center opposed legislation that would have created a CCR-type entity to provide direct representation for Texas' condemned population. In the 1993 session of the Texas legislature, Representative Pete Gallego introduced legislation that would have amended state habeas procedure in capital cases. The legislation, which was passed by the House of Representatives, provided for counsel, who were to be compensated, to be appointed immediately after the entry of judgment to assist death-sentenced inmates in state habeas review. The final version of the bill provided for a "semi-unitary" procedure in which the state habeas application would be filed 150 days after the state's brief was filed on direct appeal. The final bill also foreclosed the setting of an execution date until after the Court of Criminal Appeals had entered judgment on an initial petition for writ of habeas corpus and required execution dates to be set at least 60 days in advance. The bill was opposed by the organized defense bar, including the Texas Criminal Defense Lawyers Association and the Texas Resource Center.[16] According to its sponsor, the bill died in the Texas Senate as a consequence of this opposition.[17] Representative Gallego reintroduced the bill in the 1995 session of the Texas legislature. It passed.

As of January 1996, Pennsylvania had 187 inmates on its death row, of whom 100 to 125 have no postconviction lawyers.[18] Nine months earlier a state supreme court justice, speaking before the Philadelphia Bar Association Criminal Justice Section, estimated that 57 of the 187 are "probably" underrepresented, and 130 of them may or may not have completed their full appeals.[19] A Pittsburgh School of Law professor said, "There are about 190 people on death row right now, and almost none are represented after the direct appeal stage."[20]

Of the 401 inmates on California's death row as of May 1995, 108 (27 percent) were without counsel.[21] According to the *Harvard Law Review*, in "September 1993 about 105 of California's 370 death row inmates had no counsel."[22] The ABA reported that as of the fall of 1994, hundreds of death row prisoners across the United States were without lawyers. With a handful of exceptions, few states with large death row populations, including Texas, Georgia, Alabama, and Virginia, formally provide for counsel in capital postconviction litigation. A claimed Texas counsel crisis reached the U.S. Supreme Court in 1994, but the Court decided the case on different grounds that permitted it to avoid addressing the counsel crisis. Until mid-1985, Florida also did not provide for counsel in capital post-conviction proceedings.

Nationally, hundreds more are already in the postconviction process, and many more will be there soon. Virtually all of these inmates are indigent and cannot afford to hire lawyers. The overwhelming majority of capital defendants are paupers.[23] The ABA has estimated that 99 percent of death row prisoners are poor; because many of them can neither read nor write, it is virtually impossible for them effectively to investigate and to file meaningful petitions and otherwise pursue remedies in the postconviction process.[24] As Steve Bright testified before Amnesty International's Commission of Inquiry into the Death Penalty, poverty is a "crucial factor that determines who receives the death penalty. The major consequence of poverty for those facing the death penalty is having a court-appointed lawyer. Just having a judge who may have made his way from district attorney to judge by discriminating, by seeking and using the death penalty as a political tool, and who is now the person who appoints the lawyer for the poor person accused of a death-eligible crime. Poor people accused of crimes do not pick their lawyers. They are stuck with their lawyers. But any mistake the lawyer makes is held against the person accused, not against the lawyer."[25]

The shortage of qualified counsel willing to represent death row prisoners was crucial to the 1997 resolution passed by the ABA. The resolution "calls upon each [state] that imposes capital punishment not to carry out the death penalty," unless and until that state "implements policies and procedures that (1) ensure that death penalty cases are administered fairly, and (2) minimize the risk that innocent persons may be executed." Among the "policies and procedures" highlighted by the ABA was the need for guidelines to encourage competency of lawyers to handle capital cases.

The Death Penalty Assembly Line, and the Importance of Meaningful Access to the Capital Postconviction System

> SIR THOMAS MORE:
>> The law, Roper, the law. I know what's legal not what's right. And I'll stick to what's legal. . . .
>
> WILLIAM ROPER:
>> So now you'd give the Devil benefit of law!
>
> MORE:
>> Yes. What would you do? Cut a great road through the law to get after the Devil?
>
> ROPER:
>> I'd cut down every law in England to do that!
>
> MORE:
>> Oh? And when the last law was down, and the Devil turned round on you—where would you hide, Roper, the laws all being flat? This country's planted thick with laws from coast to coast—Man's law, not God's—and if you cut them down—and you're just the man to do it—d'you really think you could stand upright in the winds that would blow then?
>
> —Robert Bolt, *A Man for All Seasons*

> Capital punishment is to the rest of all law as Surrealism is to Realism. It destroys the logic of the profession.
>
> —Norman Mailer

In virtually all jurisdictions, capital trials occur in two stages. First there is a traditional trial to determine guilt or innocence. This is followed by a penalty phase, which constitutes in essence a separate trial on the issue of sentencing. Following conviction of a capital offense and imposition of the death penalty, the condemned has a right to a direct (plenary) appeal to the state court of appeals.[26] Counsel must be provided at trial[27] and on this direct appeal.[28] Beyond this point, however, the right to counsel is unclear.

After the direct appeal, the death row inmate is entitled to seek certiorari in the U.S. Supreme Court and then to seek postconviction relief in state court. State postconviction provides a procedural mechanism for raising claims that were not or could not have been raised on the direct appeal.[29] For this reason, at least as to these issues, it is fair to characterize the state postconviction process as an extension of and a supplement to the direct appeal. Depending on the type of claims raised and the requirements of local procedure, a state postconviction proceeding may be initiated in the state trial court and, if denied, appealed to the state appellate court, or state postconviction litigation may be initiated in the state appellate court.

Following completion of state postconviction litigation, the inmate is entitled to file a petition for writ of habeas corpus in federal district court and, if denied, to appeal the denial to the appropriate Circuit Court of Appeals. At least since *Brown v. Allen*,[30] the controversial[31] Great Writ of habeas corpus permits the relitigation of federal constitutional claims, even if their substance was presented previously to the state courts.[32]

The postconviction process in Florida is functionally typical of the collateral systems in most states. In Florida, the litigation stages, from imposition of death sentence to execution, can be diagrammed as in Figure 1.

At any point beyond the plenary direct appeal (between steps 3 and 4), an execution date may be set by the governor. In most states, Louisiana and Texas, for example, execution dates are set by the state courts. In other states, such as Florida and New Hampshire, dates are set by the governor. Once a date is set, the condemned inmate must obtain a stay of execution in order to remain alive to pursue postconviction remedies in state and federal courts.

The postconviction process is of paramount importance to the condemned. The figures on success rates in the state postconviction system are incomplete, but the success rate of noncapital habeas petitions is low, with estimates ranging from 0.25 percent[33] to 3.2 percent to 7 percent.[34] The success rate in capital habeas is much higher, however: 70 percent as of 1983,[35] 60 percent as of 1986,[36] and 40 percent as of today.[37] Between 1976 and 1983 federal appellate courts ruled in favor of the condemned inmate in 73.2 percent of the capital habeas appeals heard, compared with

Trial and Sentence in State Trial Court STEP 1	State Postconviction Motion in State Trial Court STEP 4	Federal Habeas Corpus Petition in Federal District Court STEP 7
Affirmance of Conviction and Sentence on Plenary Appeal to State Court STEP 2	Appeal to State Appellate Court of State Postconviction Motion; Filing of Original Proceedings in State Appellate Court STEP 5	Appeal to Federal Circuit Court STEP 8
Request for Plenary Review in U.S. Supreme Court STEP 3	Request for Plenary Review in U.S. Supreme Court STEP 6	Request for Plenary Review in U.S. Supreme Court STEP 9

Executive Clemency

Figure 1. Litigation Stages in Florida

137

only 6.5 percent of the decisions in noncapital habeas cases. Of the 56 capital habeas appeals decided by the U.S. Court of Appeals for the Eleventh Circuit between 1981 and 1987, half of the inmates were granted relief.[38] The significance of these figures cannot be overemphasized:

> In every one of these cases, the inmate's claims had been rejected by a state trial court and by the state's highest court, at least once and often a second time in state postconviction proceedings; the Supreme Court had usually denied *certiorari* at least once and sometimes twice; and a federal district court had then rejected the inmate's claims of federal constitutional error infecting his conviction and/or death sentence. Yet [as of 1983] in over 70 percent of the cases, a federal court of appeals found merit in one or more of the inmates' claims.[39]

The success rates of capital postconviction litigation tell only part of the story, however: Of great significance are the *reasons* for these successes. Postconviction courts remove inmates from death row for a wide variety of reasons, including ineffective assistance of counsel at the guilt/ innocence phase of trial, for conceding the defendant's guilt; ineffective assistance of counsel at the penalty phase, for failure to investigate or present *any* evidence in mitigation; and violation of due process, by putting a mentally incompetent defendant on trial. Posttrial investigation resulted in the conviction, in Texas in 1992, of a pathologist who faked autopsies. He performed hundreds of autopsies a year, and at least 20 death penalty convictions were obtained with the aid of his testimony. For more than a decade, he worked closely with prosecutors and the police and apparently tailored his findings to conform with their theories of the cases. "If the prosecution theory was that death was caused by a Martian death ray, then that was what he reported," said the special prosecutor who handled the investigation.[40]

A forensic dentist in Mississippi who has testified in numerous capital cases was censured in April 1994 by the American Academy of Forensic Sciences for misrepresenting evidence and failing to meet professional standards. Yet in August 1994 he was still scheduled to be an expert witness in three upcoming capital murder trials.[41]

And so on. As the following case studies suggest, these reasons for granting postconviction relief are intuitively troubling; they are not "legal technicalities."

Charles Young

Charles Young was convicted in 1976 by a Georgia jury of malice murder. Six years later, the U.S. Court of Appeals for the Eleventh Circuit ordered that habeas relief be granted, finding that Young had been deprived of effective assistance of counsel at his state court trial. Young's counsel conceded his client's guilt to all charges during the guilt/innocence phase of the trial, adopted unsupportable defenses, ignored obvious defenses, and was unaware of Georgia's bifurcated proceedings in death penalty cases. The lawyer apparently believed that such a strategy was necessary to make a strong plea for mercy. In addition, the Eleventh Circuit affirmed the federal district court's holding that there was legally insufficient evidence to support the jury's finding of aggravating factors necessary to support a death sentence under Georgia's death penalty statute. The Eleventh Circuit held that the state could not attempt to impose the death penalty on Young in his retrial.

Young's trial counsel had decided that he would defend his client by establishing an affirmative defense of insanity. Trial counsel could not support this defense, however, because Young's confession to FBI agents following his arrest gave no indication that he was insane at the time he assaulted his victim. Moreover, counsel did not uncover or present any evidence that pointed to insanity, and counsel never had a psychiatrist examine Young to determine his mental capacity at the time of the alleged offenses. Counsel "thus proceeded to trial on an insanity defense he could not possibly establish," as the Eleventh Circuit put it.

Of the 12 witnesses initially called by the state prosecutor, Young's trial counsel failed to cross-examine four. The Eleventh Circuit wrote that defense counsel's questioning of all but one was "cursory and superficial." Counsel failed to appear for a night session of court and, while informing the trial judge that he would not be present, neither asked for a continuance nor informed his client that he would be absent. A trial counsel assistant who had only a cursory role in the proceedings filled in for counsel at the night session even though he was not prepared to cross-examine the state's witnesses.

During the course of the trial, counsel never attempted to persuade the jury to find Young guilty of manslaughter rather than malice murder on the theory that the homicide was committed during a heated argument. The Eleventh Circuit concluded that, given the state's evidence, trial counsel neglected a very strong argument that Young killed in the heat of passion. Similarly, counsel neglected to refute an armed robbery charge despite a lack of evidence; Young did not rob by use of an offensive weapon and thus could not be guilty under the Georgia statute. Counsel also abandoned, for lack of proof, the defense that Young was insane at the time of the offense.

Because trial counsel was unaware of Georgia's bifurcated proceedings in death penalty cases, he chose a strategy of conceding Young's guilt to malice murder and other charges during the guilt/innocence phase of the trial and begged the jury for mercy then. The trial judge admonished counsel to save his argument on punishment for the sentencing phase of the trial, but counsel ignored this warning and continued to plead for mercy. As the Eleventh Circuit noted, "With both the prosecution and the defense advising it that Charlie Young had committed malice murder, the jury promptly found Young guilty of that offense and armed robbery and robbery by intimidation as well."

Immediately following Young's conviction, the court declared a recess so that the parties could prepare for the presentencing hearing on the death penalty. Seeing that defense counsel did not comprehend the purpose of the proceeding, the trial judge instructed counsel's assistant to explain it to him. Despite substantial favorable mitigating evidence that might have led the jury to recommend against the death penalty, counsel failed to present any of this evidence and refused to let Young take the stand on his own behalf.

Jack Carlton House

Jack Carlton House's case is another example of the life-or-death importance of the capital postconviction process. House was a 27-year-old father of three who lived in Atlanta with his wife and daughters. Although he had a history of alcoholism, he was regularly employed and had no criminal record other than traffic violations.

After four hours of police interrogation without an attorney present, House signed a confession stating that he had raped and killed two young boys who had followed him into a wooded area when he was drunk. House later maintained that he had signed the confession only to stop the beating conducted by his interrogators and that the police fabricated the statement concerning the crime. During postconviction proceedings, both of his lawyers testified that following the interrogation House's body was badly bruised, including the area around his groin. One lawyer testified that House begged her, when she first visited him in jail, not to let the police beat him anymore. Neither attorney, however, took any pictures or asked any medical personnel to witness House's condition.

Despite substantial doubt about House's guilt, his trial lawyers, who were real estate attorneys, failed to interview any witnesses, including the police officers and medical witnesses listed in the indictment. The lawyers did not attempt to obtain documents from the prosecutor during discovery. They did not visit the neighborhood or scene of the crime, and they spoke only to House's mother and his wife. Although there was physical evidence that substantiated House's innocence, including hair samples and nail scrapings, his attorneys failed to introduce it.

House's counsel did not file pretrial motions. Neither attorney had ever read the new Georgia death penalty statute; both were unaware that there was to be a separate sentencing phase until it arrived. The lead attorney cross-examined a police officer who was a key witness on the confession issue, even though the lawyer was not present during the officer's direct examination. The lawyer also was not present for half of the prosecution's closing argument. The closing argument for the defense consisted of a short Bible verse asking for forgiveness.

After the jury found House guilty and rendered a binding recommendation of the death sentence, the defense attorneys filed a boilerplate motion for a new trial. The attorneys, however, failed to mention that they had received new testimony volunteered by two residents of the victims' neighborhood who stated that they had seen the victims playing in the yard of one of the witnesses two hours *after* they were seen going into the woods after a drunk man (identified as House only by his dark hat) and well after House was home in bed.

The Eleventh Circuit ordered a new trial. When the case was returned to the state trial court, the prosecutors offered House a negotiated plea of life imprisonment with parole eligibility. The prosecutors emphasized that they would seek the death penalty at retrial. Confronted with this Sophie's choice, House accepted the plea while continuing to maintain his innocence. On the day he accepted the plea arrangement, rather than take another chance at being given the death penalty, House told the Georgia court:

> I am pleading guilty today although, as God is my witness, I am innocent. I swear before Heaven itself that I did not kill or molest those boys. I am pleading guilty today, after fighting for over 12 years, because I want to live. I want to see my family again. I want to serve God, and I hope and pray that some day I will be released and free to do His work. I am pleading guilty because although I did not commit this crime, and have witnesses who will testify to that, my lawyers tell me that there is a chance, maybe even a good chance, that I may be convicted again and sentenced to death. The D.A. has witnesses who say I confessed. I swear I have never confessed to this crime. I could never have because I am innocent. The police forced me to sign the statement they now say is my "confession." The Lord will judge these men who bear false witness against me, but I will not die to satisfy their aims. I do not feel right pleading guilty to a crime I did not commit, but my attorneys have explained that the state has enough evidence to convict me, and it is worse to risk death where there is hope for life. [The following sentence was added to the typed text; it is in Jack House's handwriting.] You all will never know the real peace of mind I got by knowing I have no such sin against my soul.
>
> When I was arrested in 1973 I had never been convicted of any crime. I was married and had three little daughters. Now I have been in jail for over

12 years. I have spent 10 and one-half years on death row, never knowing when or if I would be executed for another man's crime. I have stood on death row and heard Van Solomon beg on his knees for life without parole before he was executed. I have heard my little daughter beg me to choose life for her sake. If the penalty I faced were life imprisonment, even without any chance of parole, I would not be pleading guilty today. But the penalty is death. [The next sentence was added in House's hand.] I will not put my Momma and Daddy and babies through that type of hell again. After all these years, after all I know, I cannot fight. [The rest of the paragraph was added in House's handwriting.] My baby told me she was going to have another baby. Well, she won't have to worry. Her child will never have to say Grandpa died in the electric chair. That is worth living for.

From the bottom of my heart I thank my attorneys who brought me back from death row and who would have defended me if I had chosen to fight. God bless the people who came forward to offer their evidence that I am innocent. Someday, if God wills, I will be released and can show you I am indeed the man you believe I am.

Joseph Green Brown

Joseph Green Brown spent 13 years on death row and came within 15 hours of being executed before his attorney obtained a stay from the Eleventh Circuit; Brown had eaten his "last meal" and had been measured for the suit of clothes he would have worn for his funeral. Ultimately the Eleventh Circuit overturned Brown's conviction based on prosecutorial misconduct.[42] In ordering that Brown's habeas petition be granted, the Eleventh Circuit found that the prosecutor knowingly allowed and exploited perjured testimony from the state's star witness.

Brown was 24 years old in 1974 when he was convicted of the rape, robbery, and murder of Earlene Barksdale, a Tampa, Florida, shop-owner. He was sentenced to death for the murder. The state's case against Brown hinged on the testimony of Ronald Floyd, the only witness who placed Brown at the crime scene and the only witness to testify to Brown's alleged admission that he committed the rape and murder.

According to Floyd's testimony, he, Brown, and a man identified as "Poochie" (who was never located) drove to the Barksdale shop; Brown and Poochie entered the shop while Floyd waited in the car outside. Floyd testified that he did not know what Brown and Poochie intended to do once they were inside the shop. Floyd testified that he did not see a gun, but he did notice a bulge under Brown's shirt that looked like a gun. Floyd testified that after waiting in the car for 15 minutes, he went to the shop door to look in, heard a shot, entered the store, and saw the foot of a body lying inside. Floyd testified that Brown and Poochie emerged from the shop and that all three men got into the car and drove away. In the car, Floyd testified, Poochie told Brown, "Man, you didn't have to do that." Floyd also testified that the next day, he, Brown, and another man were together and heard a radio broadcast about the Barksdale murder. According to Floyd, Brown subsequently admitted to him that he killed the woman.

On the evening after the murder, Brown and Floyd robbed a couple at a Holiday Inn motel. Brown also tried to sexually assault the woman, but stopped and fled. After the robbery, Brown, not yet a suspect in the Barksdale murder, turned himself in to the police and implicated Floyd as his accomplice in the motel robbery. Noting similarities between the Barksdale and Holiday Inn crimes—timing, location, robbery, and sexual assaults—the police offered Brown immunity if he testified against Floyd. Brown refused, saying he knew nothing about the Barksdale crime. When Floyd was arrested and heard that Brown had implicated him in the Holiday Inn robbery, he implicated Brown in the Barksdale murder.

Floyd's testimony was the key to the state's case. Absent his testimony, there was little evidence linking Brown to the rape and murder, "possibly not even sufficient evidence to submit the case to the jury."[43] During the trial, Brown's attorney attempted to impeach Floyd's testimony by casting doubt on his credibility. The attorney questioned Floyd on whether he entered into a plea agreement with the state that was beneficial to him. Floyd testified that he had not entered into any plea agreement, nor was he promised immunity or leniency with regard to either the Barksdale or the Holiday Inn cases. In his closing argument to the jury, the Eleventh Circuit noted, the prosecutor used Floyd's denial of any promises to bolster Floyd's testimony: "I submit that there have been no promises made to Ronald Floyd for his testifying in this case. . . . He has absolutely nothing to gain by testifying against this particular individual."

The only other link between Brown and the murder was that a .38 Smith & Wesson revolver traced to Brown allegedly was the murder weapon.[44] In fact, however, Brown's weapon had not fired the shot, and the prosecutor knew it. The prosecutor deliberately led the jury to believe that the .38 Smith & Wesson Brown used during the Holiday Inn robbery was the murder weapon, when the prosecutor knew that Brown's gun could not chamber or fire the .38 "Special" bullet that killed Earlene Barksdale. The FBI ballistics reports conclusively ruled out any possibility that Brown's .38 Smith & Wesson could have fired the .38 "Special" bullet, because it could not fit into Brown's gun. Nevertheless, the prosecutor deliberately misled the jury in his opening and closing statements, arguing that Brown's .38 Smith & Wesson *was* the murder weapon.[45]

The prosecutor had included the FBI agent who prepared the ballistics report on his pretrial list of witnesses. Because the agent was already listed as a witness, Brown's attorney did not himself subpoena the agent.[46] However, the prosecutor never called the agent to the stand. On the last day of the trial, and without notifying Brown's attorney, the prosecutor released the agent back to the vacation from which he had been summoned and where he could not be reached on short notice. Brown's attorney requested a continuance so he could locate and subpoena the agent, but his request was refused.[47]

The prosecutor's statement that Floyd had cut no deals with the state was also untrue. Agreements *had* been reached between Floyd and prosecutors on both the Holiday Inn and Barksdale crimes prior to Floyd's testifying at Brown's trial. Floyd was never indicted for the Barksdale murder, and he received probation for the Holiday Inn robbery. The Eleventh Circuit directed that the habeas writ be granted "because the prosecution knowingly allowed material false testimony to be introduced at trial, failed to step forward and make the falsity known, and knowingly exploited the false testimony in its closing argument to the jury."

The state decided not to retry the case, primarily because by that time Floyd had recanted his trial testimony, without which the state had virtually no real evidence to make a case against Brown.[48] Floyd first tried to retract his trial testimony two weeks after the trial ended, when he signed an affidavit saying he had lied in that testimony. At a subsequent hearing, the judge and prosecutor warned Floyd about perjury, incorrectly informing him that the sentence for perjury was life in prison. Floyd backed down from his recantation. During the course of Brown's postconviction litigation, Floyd came forward again and, in a videotaped sworn statement, testified that police had put him under pressure to testify against Brown at trial; that detectives showed him pictures of the murder scene before he agreed to testify; and that he had been promised probation in the Holiday Inn case if he agreed to testify against Brown in the murder case. He further testified that he agreed to testify against Brown in part because he was angry at Brown for implicating him in the motel robbery, that he had invented "Poochie" because police told him a third assailant was involved in the crime, and that he had retracted his 1975 recantation because the judge and prosecutor threatened him with perjury charges.

Brown was released from prison in March 1987, after spending 13 years on death row and coming within 15 hours of being executed for a murder he most likely did not commit. Today Brown is married and living and working outside Florida.[49]

These cases presenting questions of innocence are not isolated. A study by Hugo Bedau and Michael Radelet produced evidence of 450 cases since 1900 where actually innocent people were wrongly convicted of offenses punishable by death. In most of the cases, the convictions were upheld on appeal, but new evidence later emerged. The study included 50 cases occurring after 1970, including several in which death sentences were imposed under post-*Furman* statutes and one—the case of James Adams in Florida in 1984—that resulted in execution.[50]

Effective postconviction advocacy can reveal latent injustices by exposing errors, thereby forcing the criminal justice system to work as it should, even in seemingly clearcut cases. The cases of Joseph Green Brown, Jack House, and Charles Young provide human texture to the capital postconviction litigation success rate statistics discussed at the outset of this section. The statistics, and the humanity that lies behind the statistics, show why death row inmates must have meaningful access to postconviction procedures and remedies.[51]

Why Meaningful Access to the Capital Postconviction Process Requires Lawyers for the Condemned

> Granting prisoners the use of a law library without the interpretive expertise of a lawyer may be analogized to giving prisoners surgical equipment without a physician.
> —Position of the Florida Bar By and Through Its Legal Aid and Indigent Defendant Committee, 1973

> [Capital habeas litigation] is the most complex area of the law I deal with.
> —Judge John C. Godbold, " 'You Don't Have to Be a Bleeding Heart' "

> There was only one catch and that was Catch-22.
> —Joseph Heller, *Catch-22*

I suggested above that, as a practical matter, condemned inmates must have meaningful access to postconviction remedies. Otherwise, grave injustices will remain uncorrected by the criminal justice system. Only a meaningful capital postconviction system can vindicate fundamental rights and maintain the integrity and appearance of fairness in our legal system.

Meaningful access to the capital postconviction system requires lawyers.[52] Although the factors I identify parallel the factors identified by courts in determining whether counsel is constitutionally required in specific settings, I am not conducting a doctrinal analysis of the possible sources of a right to counsel—I am trying to show that in this context meaningful access to courts means the provision of counsel. To require condemned inmates to litigate without lawyers is to foreordain failure.

Counsel should be provided to death row inmates because these inmates cannot meaningfully pursue postconviction litigation on their own. Even lawyers find capital postconviction work to be among the most complex, nuanced, and rapidly changing cases of litigation. Experienced practitioners find these cases difficult enough, a fact evidenced by the time lawyers require to do postconviction litigation. But imagine if you were isolated on death row, physically unable to conduct the factual investigation or legal research essential to minimally effective capital post-conviction advocacy. Add to that illiteracy, mental impairment, lack of any formal legal training, or all of these. Further, imagine that you, the condemned, are to be the "lawyer" for yourself, with a "fool for a client" as the saying goes. Finally, imagine that you must do all of this under the pressure of an imminent execution date and that you must get it right the first time, because the courts look with grave disfavor on "successive" postconviction challenges.

The quality of the defense can play a large role in prosecutors' decisions to seek death and juries' decisions to impose it. In 1992, Indiana instituted a law that radically improved its neglected indigent defense. Now, each capital defendant gets two attorneys, each paid $70 an hour, and money for reasonable expenses. Since its passage, juries, which used to return five or six death penalties a year, have returned one in three years. "That law has swayed prosecutors not to ask for death," says Larry Landis, executive director of the Indiana Public Defender Council. "Requests for death have been cut in half."

When Philadelphia judges realized that the pool of lawyers willing to take homicide appointments had shrunk to about 50, public defenders were brought in to take one case in five. A defendant who draws them is lucky indeed: two attorneys, a mitigation specialist, and an investigator work on each case, and there is a psychiatrist on staff and a fund for expert witnesses. Since the public defenders began taking murder cases in April 1993, their clients have not been given a single death sentence, while 33 of those privately represented—most, if not all, court appointed—have been given one.

The outcome of all of this is fairly obvious and has been empirically tested in the noncapital postconviction setting: Lawyers make a difference. Studies show that the difference is substantial. In the capital setting, the difference can mean the difference between life or death.

Singly, death penalty jurisprudence and postconviction law bedevil the practitioner and the theoretician. In combination, the two areas are a minefield for the unwary.

Please don't be alarmed if you find the next several paragraphs incomprehensibly complex. It isn't you, and you aren't alone. Many judges and most lawyers won't be able to follow them either.

In fact, your confusion can be a useful mind experiment. Imagine you are on death row trying to figure out the labyrinth discussed below. Imagine you are doing so alone, without a lawyer. Imagine that the cost of any mistake you make in understanding and following these arcane rules will, quite literally, be your life. Now imagine, finally, that you have 28 days to live. Go . . .

The Supreme Court's ambivalence over the death penalty has resulted

146

in murky standards and an inability to predict with any precision where the Court will go next. In 1971 the Court held that the due process clause of the Fourteenth Amendment did not mandate standards to guide a capital sentencer's discretion. One year later, the Court held that the Eighth Amendment's cruel and unusual punishments clause did require such standards.[53] Then, in 1976 the Court approved the standards adopted in Georgia, Florida, and Texas, even though these standards were more cosmetic than real. The "standards" of Georgia[54] and Florida[55] contained exceptions that threatened to engulf the guidelines in unlimited discretion. In 1978, despite Justice Rehnquist's charge that the Court was going from "pillar to post," and despite Chief Justice Burger's recognition that the Court's death penalty decisions were far from consistent, the Court held that the sentencer must be permitted to consider any relevant evidence proffered in mitigation, a notion reaffirmed in subsequent cases. The Court has since fine-tuned the capital system it approved in 1976, sometimes vacating death sentences and sometimes, more frequently since the 1982 term, upholding them. Litigators and commentators seldom can predict what the Court will do with any given array of facts.

If the Court's capital jurisprudence is opaque, its habeas corpus jurisprudence is Byzantine. The habeas litigator must understand the intricacies of the exhaustion doctrine, as codified by Congress and construed by the Court.[56] The doctrine can "operate[ ] as a trap for the uneducated and indigent *pro se* prisoner-applicant." It is "one of the most difficult procedural obstacles for state prisoners to overcome when seeking federal habeas corpus relief."[57] Exhaustion requires the inmate to travel a maze of state postconviction procedures before seeking federal habeas corpus relief. In Florida,[58] for example, claims that were raised or could have been raised earlier on direct appeal are estopped from being presented in collateral state review.[59] The Florida Supreme Court has stated repeatedly that a state postconviction proceeding is "neither a second appeal nor a substitute for appeal," and that absent fundamental error the postconviction court will not readdress claims raised on direct appeal and decided against the defendant. Further, "any matters which could have been presented on appeal are similarly held to be foreclosed from consideration" in postconviction. And, as of January 1985, all state postconviction proceedings must be initiated within two years of termination of direct appeal litigation. Also beginning in 1985, all state postconviction claims must be brought in a single collateral proceeding.

Prior to these 1985 changes, a successive postconviction challenge in Florida could "not be summarily dismissed solely on the basis" that the prisoner had previously filed a postconviction motion, and was allowed if it "stat[ed] substantially different legal grounds." The Florida Supreme Court's recent amendment to the state postconviction rule provides, essentially, that issues that could have been raised in an earlier postconviction motion cannot be litigated in a successive motion. Claims not known or reasonably knowable to the prisoner at the time an initial postconviction motion was filed, however, may be raised in a successive motion. In addition, errors based on "fundamental grounds" may be raised at any time, on the original appeal or collaterally in postconviction proceedings.

The Florida Supreme Court has applied the fundamental error principle to numerous and varied issues, including the failure of an indictment or information to allege one or more essential elements of a crime, failure to allege venue, jury instructions on and conviction of a nonexistent crime, or conviction of a crime that is "totally unsupported by evidence." The court has also found fundamental error in failure to give jury instructions on the elements of underlying felonies in a first degree felony murder conviction; failure to define premeditation; sentencing court departures from noncapital sentencing guidelines; failure to make the specific factfindings required by the noncapital sentencing guidelines statute; and improper retention of jurisdiction over noncapital sentencing. Florida's intermediate courts of appeal have found fundamental error where: improper jury deadlock instructions coerced the jury to reach a verdict and to contemplate such extraneous factors as the state's fiscal well-being; the jury was erroneously instructed that the defendant had a duty to retreat prior to acting in self-defense; the prosecutor improperly argued to the jury that the defendant "manipulated the judicial system" and made "chumps out of the jury and judicial officers"; prosecutorial misstatements and improper jury instructions told the jury that they could convict the defendant even if the crime took place at a time outside the statement of particulars; the error violated a "defendant's substantive constitutional double jeopardy rights"; and a capital defendant claimed that the waiver of a twelve person jury was invalid.

Following proper exhaustion, the inmate then faces the intricacies of federal habeas corpus law, including the rule of *Stone v. Powell,* with its extensions, lack of extensions,[60] and exceptions.[61] The inmate also faces the legislative and judicial rules of federal court deference to certain types—but only to certain types—of state court fact finding.[62] The standards governing a petitioner's right to an evidentiary hearing have their own complexity, as do the rules on burdens of proof at such hearings. Obtaining a certificate of probable cause to appeal is no simple matter. If the postconviction petition is not the inmate's first, then state and federal principles precluding successive petitions must be responded to, along with subsidiary rules governing whether the current petition presents a "new" claim, whether prior claims were resolved on the merits, whether the failure to raise the claim earlier was attributable to inexcusable neglect or deliberate bypass, and whether the ends of justice require relitigation.

But perhaps most important—as well as most confusing—are the procedural default doctrine of *Wainwright v. Sykes* and the retroactivity doctrine of *Teague v. Lane,* which is fatal even to many death row inmates represented by counsel.[63] Justice Stevens has described the *Sykes* doctrine as a "procedural maze of enormous complexity," which has caused the Court to lose its way.

The Court in *Sykes* held that if a state court relies upon an adequate and independent state procedural ground to bar a federal claim, then a federal court in habeas generally may not consider the merits of the claim, unless the habeas petitioner can show "cause" for and "actual prejudice" resulting from the default. While the Court in *Sykes* declined to define the parameters of this cause-and-prejudice standard, it has done so in subsequent cases. The Court has explained that "the existence of cause for a procedural default must ordinarily turn on whether the prisoner can show that some objective factor external to the defense impeded counsel's efforts to comply with the State's procedural rule." The failure of an attorney to raise a federal claim in state court in a timely manner will not constitute cause unless the attorney error rises to the level of violation of the Sixth Amendment right to the effective assistance of counsel; these claims are best treated under an ineffective assistance of counsel analysis rather than under a cause-and-prejudice *Sykes* analysis.

Novelty of a federal constitutional claim constitutes cause for a failure to raise a claim in state court in a timely fashion, but only if the constitutional tools for framing the claim were unavailable at the time. In proving prejudice, at least as to jury instructional error, a habeas petitioner must "shoulder the burden of showing, not merely that the errors at his trial created a possibility of prejudice, but that they worked to his actual and substantial disadvantage, infecting his entire trial with error of constitutional dimensions."

To further complicate matters, the standards established in *Sykes* are not the exclusive analysis that a federal court confronted with a state procedural default must undertake. The Supreme Court, in *Smith v. Murray,* made it fairly clear that determining that a petitioner cannot satisfy the cause test "does not end our inquiry." In "appropriate cases, the principles of comity and finality that inform the concepts of cause and prejudice must yield to the imperative of correcting a fundamentally unjust incarceration." This fundamental fairness exception to *Sykes* is satisfied if a petitioner makes a colorable claim of innocence: "Where a constitutional violation has probably resulted in the conviction of one who is actually innocent, a federal habeas court may grant the writ even in the absence of a showing of cause for the procedural default." Although a petitioner in this circumstance presumably satisfies the prejudice test of *Sykes,* the fundamental fairness inquiry is best treated as an analysis separate from *Sykes,* one that is triggered only upon a conclusion that *Sykes* has not been satisfied. The Court took this approach in *Sykes* and in at least one case since then.

Although the fundamental fairness inquiry is subsequent to the *Sykes* cause-and-prejudice analysis, other inquiries could obviate the need to undertake the cause-and-prejudice inquiry. If the state court explicitly forgave any procedural default, then the federal courts must do so as well. If the state court possessed the discretion and the power to forgive the default, that alone should permit federal review, even though the state court declined to exercise such discretion in the capital case at hand. Even if the state court explicitly relied upon a procedural ground to deny relief, the *Sykes* cause-and-prejudice analysis still may not apply. Before making a cause-and-prejudice examination, the federal court must make a threshold determination that the state procedural rule being invoked is both an adequate and an independent state ground that would bar direct U.S. Supreme Court review of the federal constitutional claim. The adequate and independent state ground doctrine, as developed in the context of direct review by the U.S. Supreme Court of state court judgments, provides that where a state court decision rests on two grounds—one purely federal law and one purely state law—and where either ground, standing alone, is sufficiently strong to support the result reached by the state court, then the Supreme Court will not decide the federal issue.

The Court's recent retroactivity decisions form another obstacle to habeas petitioners. These decisions, taken together, appear to stand for the proposition that the right of habeas will be unavailable to inmates basing their constitutional claims on "new rules" articulated in decisions rendered after the date their convictions become final on direct appeal.

In *Teague v. Lane*[64] in 1989, a plurality of the Supreme Court adopted a new approach to retroactivity that profoundly changed the law of habeas corpus and narrowed the range of relief that is available in habeas corpus proceedings.[65] The *Teague* doctrine (which a majority of the Court has ratified on several occasions since *Teague*)[66] can be briefly stated as follows: With two exceptions, a prisoner[67] may not seek to enforce a "new rule" of law in federal habeas corpus proceedings if the new rule was announced after the petitioner's conviction became "final" (or if the petitioner is seeking to establish a wholly new rule or to apply a settled precedent in a novel way that would result in the creation of a new rule).[68] The first exception permits retroactive application of new rules that "place[ ] 'certain kinds of primary, private individual conduct beyond the power of the criminal law-making authority to proscribe,' "[69] including "rules forbidding criminal punishment of certain primary conduct [and] . . . rules prohibiting a certain category of punishment for a class of defendants because of their status or offense."[70] The second exception permits retroactive application of new rules that "require[ ] the observance of 'those procedures that . . . are "implicit in the concept of ordered liberty." ' "[71]

This good faith exception to the habeas statute is sophistry, but it could have a devastating impact on death row inmates who are confined in violation of the Constitution. The retroactivity decisions craft an elegant box. If the inmate must rely on a "new rule," then she loses under the retroactivity holdings. But if she is not relying on a new rule, then how can an inmate explain why her claims failed in state court?

Much of the law and procedure summarized in the preceding discussion would be incomprehensible to the *pro se* petitioner in the best of circumstances. It is confusing and inaccessible to many lawyers. But to the death row inmate, it is inaccessible in a more direct way: Many condemned inmates are prohibited from gaining physical access to the prison law library, which itself often is inadequate. In Florida, for example, death row inmates must request specific legal materials from their cells and are generally limited to one request per week and three citations per request. Such limited access makes it practically impossible for a condemned inmate even to keep current with the highly nuanced and rapidly changing law of death and habeas corpus, much less to research issues such as jurisdiction, exhaustion of remedies, and types of relief available.[72]

As one court noted in the noncapital context:

> Simply providing a prisoner with books in his cell, if he requests them, gives the prisoner no meaningful chance to explore the legal remedies he might have. Legal research often requires browsing through various materials in search of inspiration; tentative theories may have to be abandoned in the course of research in the face of unfamiliar adverse precedent. New theories may occur as a result of a chance discovery of an obscure or forgotten case. Certainly a prisoner, unversed in the law and the methods of legal research, will need more time or more assistance than the trained lawyer in exploring his case. It is unrealistic to expect a prisoner to know in advance exactly what materials he needs to consult.[73]

Another court underscored the inadequacy of existing prison law library programs:

> In this court's view, access to the fullest law library anywhere is a useless and meaningless gesture in terms of the great mass of prisoners. The bulk and complexity [of the law] have grown to such an extent that even experienced lawyers cannot function efficiently today without the support of special tools, such as . . . computer research systems. . . . To expect untrained laymen to work with entirely unfamiliar books [to which they have only limited access and] whose content they cannot understand, may be

worthy of Lewis Carroll, but hardly satisfies the substance of the constitutional duty.

Access to full law libraries makes about as much sense as furnishing medical services through books like: "Brain Surgery Self-Taught," or "How to Remove Your Own Appendix," along with scalpels, drills, hemostats, sponges, and sutures.[74]

If legal research for indigent death row inmates is virtually impossible, factual investigation is out of the question.[75] A former justice of the Florida Supreme Court was fond of asking at oral argument why, if he could read a trial transcript in a few hours, it took so much time to put together a postconviction petition in a capital case. The answer is that reading the transcript is only the first step in the process of constructing a proper postconviction litigation.

Posttrial investigation almost always discloses important factual information not discovered by trial attorneys, who often work with extremely limited resources. Sometimes new evidence of innocence is found. Sometimes factors beyond the inmate's control, such as mental illness or a childhood of extreme abuse or neglect, may explain the crime. Sometimes evidence of a defendant's positive qualities is found, making it less simple to reduce the defendant to someone who has no right to live.

Effective postconviction litigation requires a complete reinvestigation of the case, with a focus on material not in the trial transcript. What evidence was not presented and why? What evidence was not investigated and why? The trial transcript provides clues, but those clues mark only the beginning of the postconviction litigator's task. Even with access to a prison law library, inmates have little or no access to outside sources, such as expert witnesses (ballistic, forensic, medical, psychiatric), character witnesses, and prior counsel, that may be vital to their cases. Inmates pursuing postconviction relief also have difficulty pursuing claims of ineffective assistance of trial counsel. To establish this claim an inmate must produce evidence of the "background, character and reputation, of appointed trial counsel and of what [counsel] did and failed to do," evidence that confined death row inmates have no way of obtaining. In fact, inmates may have difficulty even obtaining a copy of their own trial transcripts.

The person litigating the postconviction case must review the trial court docket sheets, files, and records that are maintained in the trial court, including physical evidence, exhibits, and notes of the court clerk about proceedings not designated as part of the formal record on direct appeal. Witnesses must be located and interviewed, including co-defendants and prior counsel. Records of proceedings relevant to co-defendants must be obtained and reviewed. Media coverage must be gathered and reviewed.

Often collateral litigation must be initiated to obtain discovery of these matters. In most cases a postconviction psychiatric examination must be arranged and efforts must be made to ensure that such examination is conducted properly. Any prior conviction that played a role at trial or penalty phase must also be reinvestigated for validity.

Because capital postconviction litigation often turns on trial counsel's failure to investigate mitigating evidence, the postconviction investigation requires not only an informed evaluation of trial counsel's performance, but also a complete background investigation of the inmate's life, literally from embryo to death row. This investigation often requires counseling with the inmate's family members, loved ones, and friends in order to reveal intimate information critical to the litigation. Such an investigation must cover the inmate's upbringing, education, relationships, important experiences, and overall psychological makeup. Many crucial witnesses, such as childhood friends, teachers, ministers, and neighbors may be "scattered like a diaspora of leaves along the tracks of the defendant's travels," yet they must be located and interviewed within a short period of time if they are to offer favorable postconviction evidence. Throughout this process, the inmate's lawyer at trial must be treated with care and sensitivity. It is virtually impossible for a condemned inmate to handle this crucial potential witness properly.

This essential investigation simply cannot be done from death row, even if the inmate possessed the competence to conduct it. As discussed below, most inmates do not possess such competence.

The sheer complexity of habeas corpus proceedings is enough to defeat an inexperienced or overworked death penalty attorney, not to mention a death row inmate without counsel. But in recent years several federal courts, including the Supreme Court, have made the task of capital postconviction litigation all the more difficult by greatly compressing the time allowed for briefing and arguing habeas corpus petitions and appeals. In the 1983 case of *Barefoot v. Estelle,* the Supreme Court held that a federal circuit court may, by summarily deciding the merits of the appeal along with the stay application, provide death-sentenced petitioners/appellants with significantly less time for briefing and argument than is provided to all other federal appellants.[76]

Thomas Barefoot, a death-sentenced Texas inmate, filed a federal habeas corpus petition challenging his conviction and sentence on several constitutional grounds. The district court rejected his claim, but on December 3, 1982, issued a certificate of probable cause to appeal. Unwilling to await the outcome of the appeal, the state trial court on December 20 set Barefoot's execution date for January 25, 1983. On January 14, three days after the Texas Court of Criminal Appeals refused to grant a stay of execution,[77] Barefoot's counsel filed a hastily prepared application with the U.S. Court of Appeals for the Fifth Circuit for a stay of execution pending disposition of his habeas corpus appeal to that court. Three days later, the court scheduled oral argument on the stay application for January 19.

Only two out of the three judges hearing the appeal had seen the papers in the case, and none of them had seen the 1,400-page state trial transcript. In addition, neither the judges nor Barefoot's counsel had seen the transcript of the habeas corpus hearing, even though the Texas attorney general had received a copy. Nevertheless, on the following day the court handed down an opinion both rejecting Barefoot's claims on the merits and refusing to stay his execution.[78]

The Supreme Court upheld the lower court's action by a 5–4 vote.[79] The Court stated that although it was not the "norm" or the "preferred procedure," "a practice of deciding the merits of an appeal . . . together with the application for a stay, is not inconsistent with our cases."[80] Thomas Barefoot was executed several months after the Supreme Court issued its opinion in his case. In the wake of *Barefoot,* some federal courts have devised new rules under which the time between the district court's ruling and the appeals court's disposition of a capital case can be less than one day. Under the Fifth Circuit's rules, at least one death row inmate, Johnny Taylor of Louisiana, had his habeas appeal heard (and rejected) by the federal circuit court on the same day he lost in the district court, and only three days after he lost in state postconviction proceedings.[81]

In contrast to the frenetic procedure approved in *Barefoot,* in noncapital felony cases defense counsel have 10 days after the district court's judgment to file a notice of appeal and 40 days thereafter to prepare a brief. Counsel has two weeks to reply to the state's responsive brief and usually has a month or more before oral argument.

The isolation of death row means that even a condemned inmate with the skills of Clarence Darrow could not mount a proper postconviction effort. But many inmates, and particularly many death row inmates, are illiterate, uneducated, mentally impaired, or any combination of the three.

Statistics on death row education, intellectual capacity, and mental capacity are incomplete, but existing data indicate that condemned inmates lack the ability to serve as their own lawyers. A 1962 study found that none of the 19 inmates on death row in Sing Sing had an education beyond the tenth grade and that some were illiterate.[82] A 1979 study of Florida's condemned estimated that the mean education level was approximately the ninth grade and that 15 percent of the inmates had an IQ of less than 90.[83]

Intelligence and educational levels among prisoners as a group are very low.[84] A 1968 study of federal and state prisons found that in most states the average prisoner had only eight years of education.[85] In states with large death row populations, the figures were even more troubling: 49 percent of Florida inmates completed less than nine years of education; Louisiana inmates averaged six years of schooling; and Texas inmates had an average educational level of 5.1 years. The average inmate IQ in Alabama and Louisiana was 80, while in Texas it was 86. Thirty percent of South Carolina inmates had IQs less than 80, while 49 percent of North Carolina inmates had IQs less than 90. The study found that prisoners are three times more likely to be mentally disabled than members of the general population.

In 1982 a federal district court, following extensive evidentiary hearings, found that more than half of Florida's inmates were functionally illiterate. The court also found that 22 percent of the total prison population had an IQ of less than 80, which is considered to be borderline retarded. One witness at the hearing testified that "for more than 50 percent of the inmates, attempting to read a law book would be akin to attempting to read a book written in a foreign language."[86]

Between capital punishment's restoration in 1976 and February 1997, at least 30 of the 108 prisoners executed had serious mental deficiencies.[87] Thirteen of the inmates fit into the current definition of mentally retarded with IQs lower than 70, and the remaining 17 were "borderline," with IQs ranging from 70 to the low 80s.[88] Accurate figures do not exist on how many mentally retarded inmates are currently on death row. The Georgia Clearinghouse on Prisons and Jails suggested that there may be at least 250 such inmates nationwide out of the 1,900 prisoners on death row at the time of the estimate.[89] One expert on corrections and retardation estimated that 3.5 to 5.0 percent of the national prison population, amounting to between 17,000 and 24,000 inmates, is mentally retarded.[90]

The mentally retarded prisoner is usually not capable of assisting his attorney in conducting postconviction litigation, much less litigating on his own.[91] Often the inmate is unable to recall crucial details about events. His ability to communicate a complex chain of events prevents him from explaining to his attorney his role, if any, in crimes.[92] Moreover, wishing to camouflage the fact that he is mentally retarded, or acting defensively about it, "the mentally retarded defendant may boast about how tough he is or how he outsmarted a victim, when in fact he accomplished neither feat."[93] Finally, the ability of the mentally retarded defendant to present arguments is questionable; when "verbally or physically challenged, most retarded persons will go to great lengths to please their challengers, thereby hoping to avoid the antagonistic situation."[94]

A mentally retarded death row inmate may not comprehend the gravity of his situation or truly understand evidentiary criminal justice proceedings, let alone the complexities of the postconviction process. The attorney for Morris Odell Mason, an inmate with an IQ of 65 who was executed in

1985, said that Mason did not understand what it meant to be executed.[95] Denied a new trial or sentence reduction to life in prison, death row inmate Limmie Arther, who had an IQ of 65, responded to attorney David Bruck's question about how he felt: "I ain't too sure . . . I feel good anyway . . . I got a new trial."[96] In an interview, Arther was asked what it would mean if he were executed. He answered: "What happens? That's a tough one. For one thing, that learning what I just learned, what I learned in [the penitentiary] that would amount to nothing . . . and my GED [high school equivalency degree], I wouldn't see no GED. I wouldn't get my GED."[97]

Further, many death row inmates suffer from mental illness.[98] While many of these inmates were mentally ill prior to being condemned, others became that way while on death row,[99] perhaps in part due to the intense physical and psychological pressures caused by death row confinement.[100] Scharlette Holdman, a layperson experienced with death row inmates, estimated that half of Florida's death row population may become intermittently insane.[101] These mental disorders can directly affect an inmate's ability to proceed *pro se*. Two commentators, for example, have found that death row inmates minimize the gravity of their legal situation as a psychological defense mechanism.[102] Another researcher, Robert Johnson, has found in condemned prisoners a pattern of shock, denial, and depression, coupled with "a fatalistic belief that the person is a pawn in the process that will coldly and impersonally result in his death."[103]

These findings confirm the 1969 statement of the Supreme Court that "jails and penitentiaries include among their inmates a high percentage of persons who are totally or functionally illiterate, whose educational attainments are slight, and whose intelligence is limited." It should come as no surprise that death row does as well.

The federal courts are applying the "abuse of the writ" doctrine, governing successive habeas petitions, with increasing stringency even in capital cases. The deliberate bypass standard established in *Sanders v. United States*[104] was fairly forgiving, and the lower courts often applied it that way in death cases.[105] More recently, however, courts have, in effect, replaced the deliberate bypass test with a harsher standard—drawn from the virtually insurmountable cause-and-prejudice test of the *Wainwright v. Sykes* procedural default cases—that imputes habeas counsel's knowledge and decisions to his client.[106] Furthermore, after *McCleskey v. Zant*,[107] relitigation of issues rejected in a prior habeas petition will be all but impossible absent factual innocence.

The consequence of the increasingly stringent rules against successive postconviction challenges is that a habeas petitioner cannot proceed in his first petition in the hopes that issues or facts discovered later can be litigated in a subsequent round of postconviction litigation. Thus, the postconviction petitioner must get it right the first time.

Few people can simultaneously prepare to die and direct litigation intended to permit them to live. The two efforts require entirely different mindsets.

As former Justice Powell observed, "Most men and women value the opportunity to prepare, mentally and spiritually, for their death."[108] People pass through identified psychological stages when they face impending death, including denial, anger, depression, and acceptance.[109] Frequently, however, the dying may "work through" these stages by taking care of "unfinished business," mourning the impending loss of all that is known to be meaningful and making peace with their God. As Dr. Elisabeth Kübler-Ross recounts, the end of this process is a "time when the patient has switched off all external input, when he begins to wean off, when he becomes very introspective, when he tries to remember incidents and people important to him, and when he ruminates once more about his past life in an attempt to, perhaps, summarize the value of his life and to search for meaning."[110] Through this process, people achieve peace and a state of acceptance; in short, they are allowed to die with dignity.

Acceptance is, however, antithetical to the mindset essential to victory in crisis capital litigation. To be a forceful advocate, one can never view the impending execution as inevitable. While a realistic appraisal of the legal landscape is essential to effective capital advocacy, the zealous presentation of the case before the courts requires a belief in victory. The litigation at this state is uniquely rough-and-tumble, with many of the trappings of judicial decorum suspended. Often virtually all of the other actors in the system, from prosecutors to judges to courtroom personnel to prison officials, expect the execution to go forward and resent the interference by the inmate and his lawyer. Stopping that momentum requires a belief that the scheduled execution will not occur.

John Charles Boger, then an attorney with the capital punishment project of the NAACP Legal Defense and Educational Fund, put it well:

> [The] prospect of facing death or having to come to terms with an execution date or a date certain for one's demise is [such a] serious . . . emotional and personal crisis that even an inmate who was a law graduate[,] and who otherwise had the capability to do legal and factual research, probably does not have the detachment and dispassion to litigate under those circumstances. I have had lots of clients in those last 60 day time periods, and what they are forced to do is to prepare themselves mentally and spiritually and emotionally to deal with their family and their children, all of whom see them as about to die. And that is a full time job.
>
> And very few of them, I think, even have the emotional resources to talk with you meaningfully at that point about their case. Much less to take it over.[111]

When a person must prepare to die and, at the same time, litigate to live, that person is denied the process that leads to dying with peace in a state of acceptance. He is denied the opportunity to die with dignity.

The demands of capital postconviction litigation perhaps are measured best by examining the time and energy that lawyers, particularly those working as volunteers, expend on the postconviction process. If lawyers find these cases difficult, time-consuming, and complex, then laypersons working under difficult circumstances will surely find them far more so.

In 1986, the ABA conducted a national survey of private attorneys providing representation in postconviction death penalty cases to calculate realistically the time spent and expenses incurred in the postconviction process.[112] The results of this study (the first of its kind) provide information about 114 death-penalty postconviction cases. Of the 114 cases surveyed, 73 occurred in Florida.

To conduct this survey, lawyers with substantial postconviction experience designed a written questionnaire that collected data about time and expenses for private attorneys and their support staff, together with figures concerning court reimbursement of expenses. Public defenders, trial level counsel, and attorneys who only had experience with clemency proceedings were excluded from this survey. (Appellate public defender systems involved in capital postconviction representation were examined in a separate study discussed below in this chapter.)

The ABA study concluded that the most reliable index of time and expense for postconviction litigation is the median number of hours required to litigate at each level of the process. Because postconviction is a lengthy process involving many distinct procedural segments frequently handled by different lawyers over time, the study concluded that this technique produces more reliable figures than attempts to track each case to its conclusion.

Out of the entire sample of 114 lawyers, 96 had conducted capital postconviction litigation in state trial courts. In this group, the estimated number of hours expended on a single case at that level ranged from 4,116 to 65 hours. The average number of hours consumed by state trial court proceedings was 582, while the median was 400 hours. Similarly, of the 75 attorneys who worked at the state appellate court level, the hours expended ranged from 1,214 to 10, with an average of 288 and a median of 200 hours.

The variance in these figures may be due to the greater complexity of some cases, particularly those requiring evidentiary hearings. Furthermore, cases that go into postconviction litigation under the pressure of outstanding execution dates will demand greater time commitments because of the unavoidable duplication of effort involved in filing simultaneously in different courts.

The ABA study also produced separate figures for the state of Florida. In Florida, of 37 lawyers working at the circuit (trial) court level, the maximum number of attorney hours reported was 4,116, while the minimum was 65. The median number of hours was 500 and the average 763. For the Florida Supreme Court, the maximum hours reported was 1,214, and the minimum was 30; the median reported figure was 240 hours, and the average was 406. Florida cases that sought review by the U.S. Supreme Court directly from state court postconviction litigation were represented by seven lawyers, who reported a maximum of 178 hours, a minimum of 25, a median of 77 hours, and an average of 88 hours at this level.

Florida cases that then reached federal district court on habeas corpus brought 20 responses, with an estimated maximum of 2,557 hours, a minimum of 45, a median of 388, and an average of 516 hours worked at this level. Eighteen Florida cases went to the federal court of appeals. Study respondents reported a maximum of 1,278 hours, a minimum of 80, a median of 318, and an average of 471. Seven cases that sought review in the Supreme Court required a maximum of 350 hours, a minimum of 110, an average of 206, and a median of 160 hours.[113] Table 1 compares the median hours for documented cases with those for the entire sample, as well as with the Florida cases.

The study showed that Florida's median attorney time was roughly 25 percent higher than the sample figures taken as a whole. Although the study provided no explanation for this occurrence, several attorneys volunteered the suggestion that postconviction time in Florida was increased by the short time period between the setting of execution dates and the carrying out of the executions, which, until recently,[114] was approximately 28 days.

The figures used in the ABA study were based on estimates by attorneys. The study indicated that these figures probably were conservative; attorney hours documented in hard data substantially exceeded those in the entire sample, except at the U.S. Supreme Court level. The documented

Table 1. Median hours: entire sample, Florida cases, and documented cases

Court level	Entire sample	Florida cases	Documented cases
State Trial Court	400	500	494
State Supreme Court	200	240	369
U.S. Supreme Court (1)	65	77	100
Federal District Court	305	388	500
Federal Circuit Court	320	318	437
U.S. Supreme Court (2)	180	160	100

Source: Spangenburg Group, "Time and Expense Analysis in Post-Conviction Death Penalty Cases" (1987).

median hours exceeded even the heavy Florida estimates at all but two court levels.

In state trial court, the 33 documented respondents reported a maximum of 4,116 hours, a minimum of 196, a median of 494, and an average of 887 hours. In state appellate court, the documented maximum of 24 attorney respondents was 1,214 hours, with a minimum of 21, a median of 369, and an average of 506 hours. For the U.S. Supreme Court, nine attorneys produced a documented maximum of 304 hours and a minimum of 20; there was a median of 100 hours and an average of 123 hours.

At the federal district court level, 17 documented attorneys reported maximum hours of 1,920, minimum hours of 94, median hours of 500, and average hours of 606. For the federal courts of appeals, the 13 documented responses had a maximum of 1,263 hours, a minimum of 25, a median of 437, and an average of 573 hours. Of five Supreme Court petitions in the documented sample, the maximum number of hours worked was 1,575, the minimum 20, the median 100, and the average 428 hours.[115]

Twenty-two of the 38 states with the death penalty have state appellate defender programs. These programs provide representation to indigent defendants appealing their convictions after trial. The ABA surveyed these programs as part of its effort to determine how much time is expended on representation of capital cases in postconviction litigation.[116]

The study identified two types of state programs. One type of program consisted of an office that was part of an integrated state public defender program, and the other type of program was a distinct state appellate defense office. The latter sort of program was found in states having no statewide public defender system.[117]

Not all state programs have had experience with capital postconviction cases. Of those states having statewide systems, the programs in Colorado, Connecticut, Delaware, Missouri, New Hampshire, New Jersey, and Vermont had not yet handled capital postconviction cases at the time of the ABA study. Of those states with separate appellate programs, no capital postconviction work was done in Illinois, North Carolina, Oregon, or Washington. Statewide systems with capital postconviction experience included Kentucky, Maryland, Nevada, New Mexico, and Wyoming. Separate programs with capital postconviction experience included California, Florida, Indiana, Ohio, Oklahoma, and South Carolina.[118]

The importance of support staff hours should not be underestimated. Staff costs affect the willingness of private attorneys and law firms to take on capital cases at the postconviction stage. The ABA study unfortunately provided relatively crude data on support staff time because few respondents were able to document staff hours or to divide them reliably by staff categories; the study's authors regard its results as conservative estimates.[119]

Across the entire sample, support hours for state trial court proceedings were based on 89 responses, with a maximum of 2,592 hours, a minimum of 20, a median of 150, and an average of 257 hours. For state appellate courts, 68 respondents produced a maximum estimate of 986 hours, a minimum of 5, a median of 80, and an average of 160 hours. In certiorari petitions to the U.S. Supreme Court, 30 respondents reported a maximum estimate of 250 hours, a minimum of 5, a median of 40, and an average of 67 hours.

In federal habeas proceedings, 59 respondents at the district court level reported a maximum of 2,200 hours, a minimum of 10, a median of 150, and an average of 275 hours. Thirty-eight respondents at the federal court of appeals level produced a maximum of 796 hours, a minimum of 24, a median of 166, and an average of 237 hours. Seventeen cases that sought certiorari in the Supreme Court yielded a maximum of 803 staff hours, a minimum of 10, a median of 75, and an average of 133 hours.

In Florida state trial court, 34 proceedings required staff hours estimated at a maximum of 2,592 hours, a minimum of 37, a median of 168, and an average of 343 hours. At the Florida Supreme Court level, 28 responses yielded a maximum of 986 staff hours, a minimum of 5, a median of 78, and an average of 235 hours. Certiorari from Florida state courts to the U.S. Supreme Court yielded six responses, with a maximum of 175 hours, a minimum of 20, a median of 45, and an average of 79 support hours.

On federal habeas, Florida support hours were based on 18 responses for the district court level, with a maximum of 1,647, a minimum of 10, a median of 145, and an average of 312 hours. In the federal Court of Appeals, 17 Florida respondents reported support hours with a maximum of 700, a minimum of 24, a median of 182, and an average of 193 hours. At the Supreme Court certiorari level, seven replies estimated support hours at a maximum of 75 hours, a minimum of 10, a median of 45, and an average of 44 hours.

The ABA study also produced data on expenses, such as travel, obtaining transcripts, expert witnesses, depositions, outside investigators, duplicating, secretarial overtime, meals, transportation, and computerized legal research. In some states lawyers are reimbursed for these expenses, while other states require court-appointed attorneys to use their own office funds and resources. Data collected for the ABA study covered both situations. The expense data presented in the study were not complete because many of the cases were and are ongoing.

Across the entire sample, 101 replies revealed a maximum cost estimate of $96,667, a minimum of $100, a median of $4,000, and an average of $11,887 in expenses. In Florida, 37 replies revealed a maximum cost estimate of $83,874, a minimum of $1,623, a median of $10,000, and an average of $18,467. In the 39 documented cases, the maximum cost estimate was $96,667, the minimum $354, the median $13,556, and the average $20,068.[120]

The ABA study provides some concrete data validating what every capital postconviction practitioner worth her salt knows: This sort of litigation is among the most difficult and time-consuming around.

The various alternatives to attorney assistance suggested by the courts, including assistance by prison inmate writ-writers, paralegals, and law clerks,[121] cannot take the place of attorneys in providing effective representation for the condemned in postconviction proceedings.

The initial problem facing a petitioner seeking the assistance of an inmate writ-writer is one of access. Lacking a legal education, a writ-writer must spend much of his time plunging aimlessly through a jungle of constitutional law, criminal law and procedure, extraordinary remedies, and countless other details before he is able intelligently to prepare and present his case to the courts. The average writ-writer is left with little free time and is therefore unable to assist others.[122] Moreover, courts and commentators have noted the tendency of many writ-writers to condition their services on receiving favors from fellow inmates.[123]

Even if every condemned inmate were guaranteed access to an inmate writ-writer, there is no assurance that inmates who claim to be able to prepare pleadings have adequate legal ability, or that they will have their clients' interests rather than their own as their primary objective.[124] While some inmate writ-writers may genuinely believe themselves competent, many merely pretend to have extensive knowledge and "play upon the false hopes of naive inmates."[125] Some writ-writers may deliberately misstate facts so that it appears the petitioning inmate might get relief, while others may employ tricks or fabricate citations.[126] Whether well-intentioned or unscrupulous, inmate writ-writer pleadings are "heavily larded with irrelevant legalisms—possessing the veneer but lacking the substance of professional competence."[127] In short, writ-writers often are incompetent,[128] and several cases indicate that their advice may be useless or damaging to a prisoner's suit.[129]

Further, writ-writers labor under the same logistical problems that disable the *pro se* litigant. They cannot conduct factual investigations, interview witnesses, appear in court, or even make long-distance telephone calls.[130] They may have limited access to the prison law library and have to rely on antiquated law books.[131]

The above discussion should also make it clear why assistance by paralegals or law students is an inadequate substitute for attorney representation. Paralegals receive only limited legal training and are not intended to replace lawyers, but merely to assist them in practicing law.[132] Because of time constraints and rapid turnover, law student programs often are not

162

equipped to handle the subtle complexities of large-scale capital post-conviction litigation.[133] Not that paralegals, law clerks, investigators, or law students ought to be excluded from the process of capital postconviction litigation—on the contrary, these individuals can provide critical and indispensable support for the lawyer directing that effort. The ideal capital litigation team should include nonlawyers as well as lawyers. Still, attorneys trained in capital postconviction practice must direct the litigation.

Common sense should teach that lawyers matter here. Empirical data support this intuition. I know of no study of the importance of counsel in capital habeas particularly, but one study of noncapital habeas, commissioned by the Federal Justice Research Program, concluded that "the most surprising and dramatic finding of the study was the effect at every stage of the habeas process of the presence of counsel."[134] Another study found that counsel was "quite valuable" to the habeas petitioner.[135]

The Federal Justice Research Program study reviewed all of the federal habeas corpus petitions filed by state prisoners in four districts during a two-year period. The 1,899 cases studied—nearly one in eight state prisoner petitions filed during the relevant period—were analyzed for 39 variables.[136] Although counsel was no less likely than *pro se* petitioners to satisfy the exhaustion of state remedies requirement, counsel showed an ability to avoid dismissals on this ground and to exhaust state remedies without successive filings.[137] Also, counsel was more likely to use the proper form in filing habeas corpus claims. The presence of counsel "dramatically influenced almost every aspect of the court's consideration of the petition," including securing hearings, avoiding procedural denials, inducing the courts to issue written opinions, and, most importantly, winning relief to which the petitioner was entitled.

The study revealed a "dramatic correlation between counsel involvement and a petitioner's chances for winning relief": Counsel's success rate was more than 15 times greater than that of *pro se* petitioners (12.6 percent as compared with 0.8). The disparity in success rates continued into the appellate stage of the habeas process. In fact, "counsel involvement influenced the circuit court's dispositions even more dramatically than it affected the district court's dispositions." In sum, the "finding that counsel involvement improved a petitioner's chances of success at almost every stage of the habeas process was perhaps the most astonishing and disturbing finding in the study." These conclusions confirmed the findings of an earlier study that the presence of counsel raised the success rate from 3 to 12 percent.[138]

The U.S. Supreme Court's own capital decisions bear out the numbers. In *Amadeo v. Zant*,[139] a unanimous Supreme Court reversed an Eleventh Circuit decision that had denied Amadeo habeas corpus relief. A local prosecutor had instructed the jury commissioner "to underrepresent black people and women on the master jury lists" from which Amadeo's grand jury and petit jury had been drawn. At a federal habeas evidentiary hearing, Amadeo's postconviction lawyers, one of whom had represented him continuously in the postconviction process,[140] established the fact-based "cause" and "prejudice" that excused Amadeo's failure to raise the jury issues before indictment and voir dire,[141] and introduced extra-record evidence of the underlying underrepresentation scheme. The Supreme Court reversed the circuit court for failing to give appropriate weight to the district court's evidentiary findings.

In 1982–83 Alvin Ford "was reporting that 135 of his friends and family were being held hostage in the prison" and that prison guards, acting in conspiracy with the Ku Klux Klan, "had been killing people and putting the bodies in the concrete enclosures used for beds."[142] Without representation of counsel prior to filing his federal habeas corpus petition and time to investigate and present his constitutional claims, Ford could not have developed the extra-record evidence of his insanity,[143] challenged the testimony of three state psychiatrists who summarily and collectively "examined" him, or researched and marshaled the centuries-old common law tradition that persuaded the Supreme Court to hold that the "Eighth Amendment prohibits a state from carrying out a sentence of death upon a prisoner who is insane."[144] In addition, without counsel, Ford surely would have been executed before the Supreme Court could have considered and resolved the important issues that he presented.[145]

With legal representation provided well prior to filing his federal habeas corpus petition,[146] Samuel Johnson successfully challenged his death penalty because it was based in part on an unrelated, illegally imposed New York felony conviction.[147] Postconviction lawyers conducted the extra-record investigation that revealed that Johnson's New York sentence was illegal, and then initiated the New York proceeding that invalidated it.[148] Without legal representation and adequate time, Johnny Penry could not have vindicated, through federal habeas corpus, his constitutional right to have his capital sentencer consider important nonstatutory mitigating evidence: that Penry's IQ was "between 50 and 63"; that he had "the mental age of a 6½-year-old"; that his "ability to function in the world was that of a 9- or 10-year-old"; and that he had been physically abused as a child.[149]

In three cases, counsel for Dale Yates analyzed and applied a variety of complex constitutional and criminal law principles first to identify an erroneous burden-shifting jury charge; then to establish that the decision invalidating such instructions applied retroactively; and finally to persuade the Supreme Court that the error was not harmless.[150] With representation, and through federal habeas corpus, William Cartwright successfully challenged the finding that his homicide was "especially heinous, atrocious, or cruel."[151] Counsel argued that the Oklahoma Court of Criminal Appeals had not construed this enhanced aggravating circumstance in a way that sufficiently channeled the discretion of the capital sentencer. Similarly, it was only with prefiling representation, and through federal habeas corpus, that Robert Parker enforced the constitutionally based obligation of supreme courts in "balancing" states to reweigh aggravating circumstances against nonstatutory mitigating evidence after they strike an aggravating circumstance.[152] The Court granted James Hitchcock's habeas corpus petition because Hitchcock's lawyer, who had represented him for over five years, established that the sentencing judge had erroneously believed that he could not consider evidence that might establish nonstatutory mitigating circumstances and because he so instructed the sentencing jury.[153]

Habeas cases in which petitioners failed to prevail are as instructive as cases in which they succeeded. For example, in *McCleskey v. Zant,* the Supreme Court held that McCleskey had abused the writ by failing to allege a claim in his first habeas petition that he asserted in his second, based on newly discovered evidence. The district court had granted the writ, holding that McCleskey had not abused the writ because, when he filed his first petition, he had not known about a series of facts that helped establish the claim: Therefore, he had not deliberately withheld the claim. The Eleventh Circuit reversed, and the Supreme Court affirmed the Eleventh Circuit decision. The Supreme Court's analysis of its abuse-of-the-writ doctrine provides compelling support for providing first-time habeas petitioners with counsel to draft that petition and for giving counsel reasonable time to investigate and present habeas corpus claims. To establish "cause" for a first petition omission, "petitioner must [have] conduct[ed] a reasonable and diligent investigation aimed at including all relevant claims and grounds for relief in the first federal habeas petition." If what petitioner later learns "supports a claim for relief in a federal habeas petition," but "*could [have been] discover[ed] upon reasonable investigation,*" petitioner may not assert the claim in a second habeas petition.

If habeas corpus petitioners are to be bound by what they "could discover upon reasonable investigation," they should be given the assistance of counsel guaranteed by federal statutes and reasonable time to conduct that "reasonable investigation." When they get them, they often prevail in the Supreme Court. When they do not, some will be executed even though their convictions or sentences were imposed unconstitutionally.

Thus, death row needs lawyers for effective postconviction litigation. Practically, lawyers are necessary to make the postconviction process work for the condemned; inmates with lawyers are far more likely to get the relief to which they are entitled under law. As discussed earlier, equally important are the reasons for the relief: The postconviction system uncovers fundamentally unjust convictions and death sentences, sometimes involving innocent citizens condemned to die, sometimes involving "trial" in form only. In a larger jurisprudential sense, this means that a meaningful capital postconviction process—which in the real world means a process with lawyers for the condemned—is a necessary check on the functioning of the legal system at trial. The capital postconviction process is necessary to the integrity of the legal system, and lawyers are a sine qua non of the capital post-conviction process.

A System in Crisis: Unrepresented Inmates Facing Imminent Execution, and What the Florida Legislature Did about It

> Finding the lawyers to represent the flood of condemned [Florida men in the mid-1980s] was like bailing the Titanic with a teaspoon. The teaspoon had a name: Scharlette Holdman. Scharlette Holdman had a title: Director of the Florida Clearinghouse on Criminal Justice.
>
> —David Von Drehle, *Among the Lowest of the Dead:*
> *The Culture of Death Row*

Given the complexity of capital postconviction litigation and the need for the kind of factual investigation that cannot be done from a death row cell, there would be a counsel crisis even if execution dates were not set for inmates without lawyers. What elevates the problem from abstract crisis to dire emergency is that execution dates *are* set for such inmates. No inmate has yet been executed without a lawyer, but many condemned prisoners have come perilously close. Far more have been represented by inexperienced or hopelessly overburdened lawyers working desperately against the clock.[154]

I now explore the counsel crisis in a state where the crisis was, and may well still be, a reality: Florida. The demographics of Florida's death row population made Florida the first state where the counsel problem became acute. Florida pioneered a legislative solution to the problem of postconviction representation for death row inmates by creating a publicly funded state agency to provide direct representation for the condemned. Further, during the evolutionary process that culminated in the creation of the agency, Florida experimented with another possible solution to the counsel crisis: a resource center to provide support for members of the private bar who represent individual death row inmates *pro bono*.

From the mid-1970s until the mid-1980s, the only institutionalized mechanism[155] for locating *pro bono* lawyers for Florida death row inmates was a small, nonprofit community organization called the Florida Clearinghouse on Criminal Justice.[156] The Clearinghouse, which received no government funds and relied for financial support on contributions from private citizens, religious groups, and foundations, consisted of a director, Scharlette Holdman, and a one- or two-person staff. Neither Holdman nor any of her staff were attorneys. The primary responsibility of the Clearinghouse was to attempt to recruit and assist volunteer counsel for condemned inmates whose convictions and sentences had been affirmed by the Florida Supreme Court.[157] Holdman described the nature of the recruitment work as "pretty informal."[158] David Von Drehle described it in this way:

> All day, every day, Holdman sat at her telephone in her shabby office at the FOG Building, chain-smoking Benson and Hedges cigarettes with one hand and dialing with the other. Quite a sight she was: Hair frizzed, feet bare, body rocking in a cheap swivel chair, face lost in a cloud of smoke. She called the heads of local bar associations and asked for recommendations. She called managing partners at big law firms and inquired about their pro bono programs. She got rosters of various liberal organizations and cross-indexed them with the state legal directory, targeting potentially friendly lawyers for calls. She haunted law conferences, scouting for likely prospects. Holdman spent so much time on the telephone in search of lawyers that one Christmas her secretary gave her a cushion for the receiver to prevent cauliflower ear.
>
> Luckily for Holdman—and, more to the point, for her clients—she had a glorious gift of the gab. From the moment a lawyer answered the phone, Holdman kept up a steady line of pleading, cajoling, flattering and noodging, all spiced with a dark but hilarious wit. Scharlette Holdman talking was a natural force, like a hurricane or a rockslide; she was unstoppable. If she was in the mood to tell the truth, she would ask the lawyer for "three years of your life and ten grand out of your pocket," which was her estimate of what a decent capital appeal might take. But Holdman was rarely so candid. Instead, she'd say that so-and-so on death row was in danger of dying unless a simple appeal was filed, and couldn't the lawyer just give her a week . . . just three days, maybe . . . a weekend . . . to draw up the brief? The lawyer on the other end of the line might start stammering for an excuse, but it had not taken Holdman long before she had heard every imaginable excuse, and had learned how to cut in quickly and quash each one. She'd promise to gather all the files. She'd arrange all the typing. If the lawyer protested that he knew next to nothing about criminal appeals, Holdman would answer, in her sweetest former cheerleader's drawl: Don't worry, we'll get somebody to help you.
>
> At the end of each call, she made a notation on an index card and added it to the pile she kept beside her ledger. "A street fighter," she wrote on the card of one eager prospect. "Will help us but only in a crunch," she noted on the card of a less enthusiastic possibility. "Only into $$$$$," she scribbled under the name of one unpromising target. Most of the time, she had nothing to note but an outright rejection. But Holdman kept going, fueling herself with Kentucky Fried Chicken and coffee in the daytime, cheap whis-

key or jug wine at night. Sometimes, during a frantic day of phone calls, she'd look up and it was 8 p.m. and she'd realize she had nothing in the refrigerator for the kids to eat. On such days, Holdman would make a mad dash to McDonald's and then hurry back to work. More than once, her electricity was cut off because she had been too busy to pay the bill.[159]

Execution dates are set in Florida by the governor's signing of a death warrant. During the 1980s, the number of death warrants increased dramatically at the same time that the pool of available volunteer counsel decreased. Between 1979 (when Florida inmate John Spenkelink[160] became the first nonconsensual execution in the post-*Furman* era) and December 1983, the Florida governor signed 65 warrants. Fifty-one (78 percent) of those cases required volunteer counsel. Six warrants were issued in 1979; 20 were issued in 1983. Of the six inmates scheduled for execution in 1979, five (83 percent) were continuously represented by volunteer counsel; all six had counsel at the time the warrants were signed. By 1982, when 23 warrants were signed, fifteen (65 percent) were without counsel at the time of the warrants. Table 2 illustrates the increase in both the number of cases in need of counsel and the unavailability of counsel to take the cases.

Von Drehle describes what these numbers meant to the Clearinghouse:

> For Holdman, Graham's accelerated schedule of death warrants was crushing. It ruined her life and played havoc on her mind. . . .
> And daily her flock worked their desperate paths through the ten steps toward death in her handwritten ledger. Every one of them needed a lawyer. It was true that stays were coming easily—but that might end any day. Anyway, to get a stay someone had to file an appeal, and if the lawyers didn't get every available issue, large and small, into the first appeal, they

Table 2. Availability of counsel in Florida capital cases, 1979–1983

Year	Number of warrants signed	Without counsel at time of warrant	With volunteer counsel at time of warrant	With public defender or retained counsel at time of warrant
1979	6	0	5	1
1980	6	0	3	3
1981	10	1	7	2
1982	23	15	7	1
1983	20	3	10	7
	65 (100%)	19 (29%)	32 (49%)	14 (22%)
1982	23	15	7	1
1983	20	3	10	7
	43 (100%)	18 (42%)	17 (40%)	8 (19%)

might not get a second chance. Each death warrant required a full-scale legal response. So many cases, so few lawyers.[161]

A few examples will illustrate the accelerating counsel problem in Florida during the 1980s, which is being replicated today in Texas, Pennsylvania, and other death penalty jurisdictions.

Freddie Lee Hall

When Freddie Lee Hall's direct appeal to the Florida Supreme Court was decided in 1981,[162] and the Clearinghouse added Hall to the list of condemned inmates in need of counsel, Holdman contacted at least 100 lawyers without success.[163] When Hall's death warrant was signed in September 1982, he was still without an attorney. Execution was scheduled for October 6.

On September 20—16 days before the scheduled execution—the state judge who sentenced Hall to death ordered the local public defender's office to consult with Hall to determine whether he wished to pursue available postconviction remedies.[164] No lawyer in the office had ever litigated a postconviction case.

The public defender's office assigned the task of representing Hall to Jerry Lockett, who at that time had been an assistant public defender for one year and was chief trial supervisor for the office.[165] Although Lockett had considerable legal experience as a civil litigator and as a law school professor, he had never been involved in any criminal case on direct appeal or in collateral proceedings.[166] In handling Hall's case, Lockett was assisted by T. Michael Johnson, an assistant public defender who had one year of criminal trial experience in the public defender's office. Like Lockett, Johnson had never handled any criminal appeal or postconviction matter.[167]

Following the meeting with Hall, the attorneys returned to their office and prepared a report to the trial judge advising him of their compliance with his order. The court then appointed the public defender's office to represent Hall and set a deadline of September 27, which was later extended to September 28, for the filing of all state postconviction motions.[168] Counsel promptly moved for a stay of execution, but the stay request was denied on September 22.[169]

Lockett and Johnson had seven days to confer with their client, advise him of his rights, prepare pleadings, outline a strategy for the hearing, interview witnesses, and develop a case to present at the hearing.[170] Between their initial meeting with Hall on September 21 and the evidentiary hearing on the postconviction motion, which was ultimately held on September 30, Lockett and Johnson reviewed the 1,100-page transcript of Hall's trial, familiarized themselves with the complex law and procedure governing postconviction relief proceedings, prepared a 60-page state postconviction motion, drafted and filed numerous other state and federal court pleadings, attended several hearings, and attempted to begin an investigation of the facts and circumstances surrounding Hall's trial.[171]

Lockett and Johnson did all they could in the time before the hearing, but much remained to be done. After the initial consultation with Hall on September 21, counsel was unable to conduct any other substantive discussions with Hall concerning his case prior to the September 30 hearing.[172] The trial transcript reflected the fact that Hall's trial attorneys presented no evidence on his behalf at the sentencing phase of his trial.[173] Lockett and Johnson were able to conduct only the most preliminary investigation of whether mitigating evidence could have been presented, and they did not have time to review the results of the small amount of investigation that was done prior to the September 30 hearing.[174] Moreover, although the trial transcript alerted Lockett to the possibility that Hall had been prejudiced by the apparent incompetence of defense counsel with respect to the state's use of certain scientific evidence that was discussed in the presence of the jury but never introduced into evidence, Lockett did not have enough time to investigate any of the scientific evidence involved.[175] Between Lockett's appointment and the September 30 hearing, neither he nor Johnson interviewed any potential witness, other than trial counsel, whose testimony might have been relevant to Hall's claim of ineffective assistance. They did not have time.[176]

The state trial court denied postconviction relief. Within the next week, Lockett and Johnson frantically prepared and filed pleadings in the Florida Supreme Court[177] and the federal district court. The district court stayed Hall's execution and subsequently denied relief. The Court of Appeals for the Eleventh Circuit remanded Hall's case for an evidentiary hearing to determine whether Lockett's and Johnson's refusal to present evidence at the state evidentiary hearing was a "deliberate bypass"—a finding that would preclude a federal hearing on the merits of Hall's claim of ineffective assistance.[178] Incredibly, the district court found that it was, and the Eleventh Circuit affirmed.[179] The Florida Supreme Court subsequently granted Hall's successive motion for state postconviction relief.[180]

Aubrey Dennis Adams

Aubrey Dennis Adams, a former client of mine, was convicted of murdering a child, and condemned. On August 21, 1984, Adams' execution was scheduled for September 19.[181] He had no lawyer.[182] Although the civil law firm of Ausley, McMullen, McGhee, Carothers and Proctor had no experience in capital criminal proceedings, the firm agreed to undertake Adams' representation on August 27 after determining that no other counsel was available.[183] The Ausley Firm would serve as Dennis Adams' Last Aid kit.

Kenneth Hart, a partner at Ausley McMullen, assumed primary responsibility for Adams' case.[184] At that time, no assistance was available from groups with extensive postconviction experience.[185] Hart personally had none.[186] He reviewed the extensive record of the trial and direct appeal. No investigation of facts outside the record was done, complete psychological or psychiatric evaluations were never conducted, and the files of Adams' trial attorneys were never sought or obtained.[187]

Twenty-three days remained before the execution was scheduled to occur. The time was spent as follows.[188]

On Wednesday, September 5 (Day 9), Adams' volunteer lawyers filed an extensive state motion for postconviction relief to vacate judgment and sentence in the Florida trial court. Various other postconviction motions were also filed in the state trial court, including: (1) an application for stay of execution; (2) a memorandum in support of the application for stay of execution; (3) a motion for an evidentiary hearing and for the production of Adams at that hearing; (4) a motion for order of insolvency; (5) a motion for appointment and payment of experts and investigators; and (6) a conditional motion for continuance to allow time for discovery.

On Friday, September 7 (Day 11), the state postconviction judge entered the courtroom and immediately began reading an order denying relief.

On Monday, September 10 (Day 14), the denial of the postconviction motions was immediately appealed to the Florida Supreme Court. The following materials were filed with that court: (1) an application for stay of execution; (2) a brief on appeal; (3) a petition for state writ of habeas corpus; and (4) a reply brief to the State's extensive answer brief.

On Tuesday, September 11 (Day 15), oral argument was held before the Florida Supreme Court. The same day, the Florida Supreme Court rendered its opinion denying all relief sought.[189] One justice dissented. The dissenter believed the death penalty was improper and disproportionate in view of the mitigating circumstances and the highly questionable aggravating factors. He also believed the trial court should have held an evidentiary hearing regarding claims relating to ineffectiveness of trial counsel and mental incompetency of Adams to stand trial.[190]

On Friday, September 14 (Day 18), Adams' counsel filed a petition for writ of habeas corpus in the U.S. District Court. In the petition, Adams again requested an evidentiary hearing.[191]

On Sunday, September 16 (Day 20), the State filed a detailed motion for summary denial and memorandum of law in support of the motion. Ad-

ams' counsel was notified by telephone that there would be a nonevidentiary hearing held before the federal district judge. The State filed a
response to Adams' application for stay of execution.

On Monday, September 17 (Day 21), Adams' lawyers filed a motion to
amend the habeas petition that the court granted the same day. The amendment alleged further facts—Adams' incompetence to stand trial or participate in the sentencing phase of trial—and that these matters required an
evidentiary hearing.[192] Less than 48 hours before Adams' scheduled execution, a nonevidentiary oral argument on the petition was held before the
federal district judge.

On Tuesday, September 18 (Day 22), the federal district judge issued a
27-page opinion denying the habeas petition and also denying the application for stay. Counsel was notified by telephone of the opinion at approximately 3:00 A.M.[193] Later in the day, Adams' counsel filed with the district
court the following: (1) a motion to stay execution pending appeal; (2) an
application for certificate of probable cause to appeal; and (3) an application for certificate to appeal *in forma pauperis*. The State filed an opposition to Adams' application for a certificate of probable cause to appeal.
The same day, the district court granted Adams' certificate of probable
cause and leave to appeal *in forma pauperis* and denied the motion for stay
pending appeal. Adams immediately filed (1) a notice of appeal to the Eleventh Circuit and (2) an emergency motion for stay of execution. The motion for stay of execution pending appeal was granted by the Eleventh
Circuit.

Wednesday, September 19 (Day 23), was Adams' scheduled execution
date. The State moved in the Eleventh Circuit to reconsider the stay, and
the Eleventh Circuit denied its request that same day. The U.S. Supreme
Court also denied attempts by the State to have the stay lifted.[194] Voluminous motions and responses were filed in the Supreme Court by both sides.

In an affidavit filed at a subsequent stage of the Adams litigation, Kenneth Hart described the circumstances under which he originally agreed to
represent Adams and his efforts—under the most intense time pressure—
to become familiar with a new body of substantive and procedural law:

> Had Mr. Adams been given adequate time, rather than compelled to
> present life and death issues within a three-week time frame, the course of
> litigation would have been altered significantly. An independent investiga-
> tion of facts outside the record would have been conducted. A thorough
> psychiatric history and evaluation would have been developed. These ef-
> forts have now been seen. . . . Meritorious issues would have been more
> accurately identified, researched, developed and presented to reviewing
> courts. Assistance from those experienced and knowledgeable in capital
> and criminal defense litigation would have been sought and provided.[195]

172

The Eleventh Circuit eventually ruled against Adams on the appeal,[196] and the Supreme Court denied certiorari.[197] A second execution date was scheduled. By this time, Florida had created CCR to provide direct representation of Florida's condemned. CCR and Hart initiated litigation on several fronts,[198] and the U.S. Supreme Court eventually stayed the execution less than 15 hours before it was to have been carried out.[199] The Eleventh Circuit, in 1986, mandated resentencing in Adams' case.[200] The Supreme Court granted certiorari to review the Eleventh Circuit's decision in Adams' case,[201] and ultimately reversed on the basis of a procedural technicality.[202]

The procedural technicality: Adams' previous lawyers had not raised his constitutional claims soon enough. It was a fatal technicality. Adams was executed in 1989.[203]

James David Raulerson

James David Raulerson was convicted and sentenced to die for the murder of a Jacksonville, Florida, police officer. Raulerson had no lawyer when his execution date was set early in August 1983.[204] The Clearinghouse's Holdman called 50 lawyers before she prevailed upon Stephen Bright, director of the Southern Prisoners' Defense Committee (now the Southern Center for Human Rights) in Atlanta, Georgia, to represent Raulerson.[205] That was on August 8.

It took Bright a week to obtain the trial records from a recalcitrant public defender in Tallahassee, Florida.[206] By August 25 Bright had filed a postconviction motion in the state trial court. It was denied on August 30. The next morning, at 8:30 A.M., Bright argued the case in the Florida Supreme Court. Later that same day, the Florida Supreme Court denied all relief.[207]

The next morning, Bright filed a petition for writ of habeas corpus in federal district court in Jacksonville. Following oral argument (and the Labor Day weekend), the district court granted a 48-hour stay but dismissed the habeas petition. The Eleventh Circuit granted an indefinite stay.[208]

The Eleventh Circuit eventually affirmed the denial of habeas relief,[209] but the stay gave Bright time to investigate Raulerson's case in a way that was impossible when the execution date loomed. He learned that Raulerson's trial had been conducted amidst tremendous publicity[210] and that the trial lawyer had conducted no investigation into mitigating evidence despite the ready availability of such evidence. Bright also learned that the prosecutor's penalty phase argument that Raulerson was part of a multistate crime spree was based on the belief of one person who said he could identify Raulerson as the perpetrator of an Alabama robbery. Ten other witnesses to the Alabama robbery could not identify Raulerson as the robber.[211] The trial lawyer meekly summed up the case by emphasizing how hard it was for him to ask the jury not to execute his client:

> It is awfully hard to argue for a man's life. I have done it too many times, it never gets easy. . . . I feel as though I fell down on my job yesterday and I do not feel as though I can persuade you now. . . . It's terribly difficult when a man is facing 12 citizens of your community who found him guilty of unlawful homicide, guilty of murder in the first degree and, in this case, the killing of a police officer. . . . I feel as though my effectiveness is at a very low end. It is very hard. You heard all of the testimony. I'll say nothing further on behalf of my client other than just weigh and consider your decision. Thank you.[212]

Raulerson's trial lawyer also emphasized that the jury's sentence was only advisory and that "whatever you do will not—may not be followed by the court."[213]

Bright attempted to raise these issues in a second round of post-conviction litigation, but the courts dismissed Raulerson's claims as an abuse of the habeas writ.[214] Raulerson was executed in January 1985 as 75 police officers stood outside the prison wearing t-shirts saying, "Raulerson Make My Day," clapping and cheering as the hearse bearing Raulerson's body passed by.[215]

Alvin Bernard Ford

Alvin Bernard Ford, formerly a client of mine, was convicted of the capital murder of a police officer who was attempting to prevent Ford from robbing a Red Lobster restaurant in Fort Lauderdale. Ford's certiorari petition after direct appeal[216] was denied in April 1980.[217] Thereafter, no attorney represented Alvin Ford for approximately one year. Then Larry Wollin, a volunteer lawyer, agreed to prepare Ford's executive clemency proceeding and to represent him in collateral proceedings. Wollin had not actively practiced law for a number of years, having become a criminologist and faculty member at Florida State University in Tallahassee.

When Ford's death warrant was signed in November 1981, no postconviction proceeding litigation had been developed. A handful of issues had been identified, but that was all. Through consulting with other lawyers, a postconviction pleading was developed and filed. Less than one week before Ford's scheduled execution, when state remedies had been exhausted[218] and the district court proceedings had begun, only Wollin, the inexperienced postconviction lawyer, represented Ford. Wollin was still struggling to develop a working knowledge of death penalty law and postconviction litigation techniques. At that point, a more experienced lawyer became co-counsel, but only in the midst of a federal habeas corpus proceeding on the merits, with the execution date only four days away. Nevertheless, despite never having read Ford's trial record, the second lawyer was better equipped to litigate the district court proceeding. When the district court denied relief, the new lawyer took Ford's appeal to the U.S. Court of Appeals for the Eleventh Circuit. It was not until this second lawyer was in the midst of preparing Ford's brief on an expedited briefing schedule that he read for the first time the trial record.

The Eleventh Circuit denied Ford's claims, the Supreme Court denied certiorari, and a second execution date was set.[219] Ford's new attorneys with the West Palm Beach public defender's office initiated postconviction litigation, arguing that during Ford's time on death row he had become insane and that for this reason he could not be put to death. In a matter of a few hectic weeks, Ford's claim was rejected by the state trial court, the Florida Supreme Court,[220] and the federal district court. The Eleventh Circuit stayed the execution[221] but eventually denied relief.[222] The U.S. Supreme Court, however, granted certiorari and reversed the Eleventh Circuit, agreeing with Ford's claim that the insane may not be executed and remanding the case for further consideration to determine if Ford was in fact sane enough to be executed.[223] The district court found that he was.[224] While Ford's case was pending on appeal, he died in prison.[225]

Anthony Antone

Anthony Antone was sentenced to death on August 27, 1976, for carrying out a gangland-style execution, allegedly on orders of the organized crime family with which he was employed.[226] On direct appeal, the Florida Supreme Court, after remanding Antone's case to the trial court for determination of whether the state had violated the rules of pretrial discovery,[227] affirmed Antone's conviction and sentence in 1980. The U.S. Supreme Court denied certiorari on October 14, 1980.[228]

On January 6, 1982, Governor Bob Graham signed a death warrant requiring that Antone be put to death between the dates of January 29, 1982, and February 5, 1982.[229] The prison scheduled the execution for February 2, 1982. Thomas McCoun was the attorney (in a two-person law firm) who would ultimately represent Antone through two rounds of state and federal postconviction litigation. Before the governor signed Antone's death warrant, McCoun had no knowledge of Antone's case.

On January 11, 1982, a lawyer contacted by Holdman asked McCoun to render voluntary, *pro bono* assistance to Antone in the preparation of state and federal postconviction litigation. McCoun had been a member of the Florida bar and an attorney since 1977, having served for three years as a state prosecutor. When he began representing Antone, McCoun was in practice with one other attorney in a predominantly criminal trial practice. Although he had handled state court appeals both as a prosecutor and as a defense attorney, and had prosecuted and defended murder cases, he had never previously litigated a collateral attack under the state postconviction rule or the federal habeas corpus statute. Despite his lack of experience at the appellate level, McCoun recognized that "the urgency of the situation and the finality of the punishment required that an attorney begin working on Antone's case," and therefore he agreed to represent Antone.[230]

McCoun's first contact with the record in Antone's case was on January 12, 1982. On that day, McCoun met one of Antone's trial attorneys for the first time. McCoun learned at that meeting that this lawyer and a second attorney had jointly defended Antone at trial. One of the trial attorneys had represented Antone throughout the direct appeal pursuant to a court appointment and had also filed a certiorari petition for Antone in the U.S. Supreme Court.

Trial counsel informed McCoun that a witness with knowledge of and involvement in the case had contacted them. Based on this potential witness's testimony, trial counsel and his law partner were preparing a state postconviction motion and a petition for writ of *error coram nobis,* raising the single issue of newly discovered testimony. It was obvious to McCoun, however, that other legal issues, including ineffective assistance of trial counsel, had to be raised. It was equally apparent to McCoun that trial counsel could not argue that he himself was ineffective. At that point, McCoun informed trial counsel that McCoun would prepare a separate state postconviction motion raising any other legal claims that could be found in the record.

Between January 12 and January 19, 1982, McCoun reviewed the 2,000-page record of Antone's case. McCoun also reviewed the court file and researched numerous legal issues. He spent from 12 to 15 hours each day on Antone's case. His law practice was put on hold.

McCoun completed the state postconviction motion at 1:30 A.M. on January 20. The motion was filed later that day. Trial counsel had filed his state postconviction motion on January 15, and had begun conducting discovery.

A hearing on both postconviction motions was set for January 21, at 3:00 P.M. McCoun spent the 37 and one-half hours remaining between his completion of the postconviction motion and the hearing attempting to locate witnesses to testify on the various legal issues raised, preparing additional motions, memoranda of law, and proposed orders, and continuing to research the issues raised.

During the time he had to prepare for the hearing, McCoun persuaded

176

one attorney to testify on limited aspects of the issue of ineffective assistance of trial counsel and secured documents in support of these issues. He was, however, unable to find any attorneys who could, in the time remaining, review the record adequately to testify on other important dimensions of the issue. There was insufficient time to meet with trial counsel or to plan a strategy for the presentation of evidence at the hearing. During the period immediately prior to the hearing, Antone was in transport and thus unavailable to McCoun.

At the outset of the hearing, McCoun requested a continuance because he had had insufficient time to conduct discovery, contact witnesses, and prepare for the hearing. The motion was denied, and the hearing proceeded. McCoun called Antone and one other witness. He did not call either trial attorney, because he had lacked sufficient time to discuss with them the case or their participation in it. He had no knowledge of what their testimony would be and was simply unprepared to present their testimony. In addition, one trial attorney informed the court that he would refuse to testify at the hearing because he was still acting as Mr. Antone's attorney.[231]

Both state postconviction motions, as well as an application for stay of execution, were denied on January 21.[232] McCoun immediately filed a notice of appeal to the Florida Supreme Court. He filed his appellate brief on January 26, 1982, the same day oral argument was heard in the Florida Supreme Court.

When he was preparing the state court pleading, McCoun was also preparing a petition for writ of habeas corpus for filing in the U.S. District Court, along with an application for stay of execution. On January 22, while the state postconviction appeal was still pending in the Florida Supreme Court, McCoun filed the petition for writ of habeas corpus in federal district court. On January 28, the federal district court held oral argument on the habeas petition.[233] During the course of the argument, the Florida Supreme Court entered an order denying Antone's appeal.[234] The federal district court denied Antone's request for an evidentiary hearing, but allowed oral argument to continue on the legal issues presented.

On January 29, the federal district court denied the habeas petition and the stay request. Because of the nearness of the execution date, the district judge read his order orally into the record and ordered the transcript to be forwarded to the U.S. Court of Appeals for the Eleventh Circuit. McCoun immediately filed a notice of appeal as well as an application for stay of execution. These documents were completed at 1:00 A.M. on January 30. McCoun flew the pleadings and attachments to Atlanta for filing on Saturday, January 30, in the Eleventh Circuit.

On February 1, at 5:00 P.M., the Eleventh Circuit stayed Antone's execution and remanded the case to the district court for more complete and reviewable findings of fact and conclusions of law.[235] Several weeks later, the district court filed a memorandum of decision in the Eleventh Circuit. The Eleventh Circuit heard Antone's case on an expedited appeal schedule. McCoun filed his principal brief on April 9, 1982.

Following oral argument, a panel of the Eleventh Circuit affirmed the judgment of the district court on June 13, 1983.[236] A petition for rehearing was filed on July 1, and denied on September 6. McCoun filed a petition for writ of certiorari in the U.S. Supreme Court, which was denied on November 28, 1983.

The cycle then repeated itself. On January 4, 1984, the governor signed a second death warrant, requiring Antone's execution between January 20 and January 27, 1984.[237] Once again Antone had no lawyer other than McCoun, and so once again McCoun litigated the case *pro bono*. The state postconviction motion was filed on January 19 and denied that same day.[238] The following day, the Florida Supreme Court heard oral arguments on the appeal of the trial court's denial of the state postconviction motion and denied all relief.[239] The federal courts thereafter also denied all relief, finding that Antone and McCoun had "abused the writ" during the first postconviction litigation for not raising all available claims at that time.

The U.S. Supreme Court denied a stay and denied certiorari. In a footnote, the Court said that the time pressures were no excuse for failing to raise claims in the first habeas corpus proceeding because Antone really had had a lawyer all along.[240] Antone was executed the morning after the Supreme Court denied the stay. At the time of his electrocution, Antone was the oldest man on Florida's death row.

Stephen Todd Booker

Stephen Todd Booker, a former client of mine, was sentenced to die for the rape and stabbing-murder of Dolores Harmon, an elderly woman living in Gainesville, Florida. On March 22, 1982, the governor of Florida signed Booker's death warrant.[241] The execution was scheduled for 7:00 A.M. on April 21.[242]

When the warrant was signed, Booker was not represented by a lawyer.[243] The lawyer who had represented him at trial, on direct appeal, and in filing a petition for a writ of certiorari in the U.S. Supreme Court had filed a motion in the Florida Supreme Court asking to be relieved of responsibility for the case. Booker's trial counsel eventually agreed to represent Booker in collateral proceedings after Holdman and the Clearinghouse, despite extensive efforts, failed to locate other counsel.[244]

Trial/postconviction counsel filed a state postconviction motion on the afternoon of April 13, 1982.[245] On that same date, counsel also filed a petition for writ of habeas corpus in federal district court. On April 14 the state trial court denied Booker's postconviction motion. This decision was made without affording Booker the opportunity for an evidentiary hearing or even an opportunity to submit a memorandum in support of the claims. Counsel filed a notice of appeal from the trial court's decision to the Florida Supreme Court on April 14.

On April 15, Booker's counsel filed with the Florida Supreme Court an application to stay his scheduled execution so that he could adequately brief the issues raised by the denial of the postconviction motion and so that the court could review those issues.[246] On April 19 the Florida Supreme Court issued an opinion denying Booker's application for a stay of execution pending full appellate consideration and affirming the denial of the postconviction motion.[247] The Florida Supreme Court made this decision without affording Booker an opportunity to file a brief on the merits.

Simultaneously with the state court litigation, Booker was pursuing his federal habeas corpus litigation. The federal district court denied Booker's request for a stay of execution and dismissed his habeas corpus petition on April 19.[248] On April 20 the Eleventh Circuit stayed Booker's execution pending its consideration of the district court's denial of federal habeas corpus relief.[249] The Eleventh Circuit eventually affirmed the district court's decision, and the U.S. Supreme Court denied Booker's petition for a writ of certiorari on October 17, 1983.[250]

On October 27, Governor Bob Graham signed a second death warrant against Booker,[251] only 10 days after the U.S. Supreme Court declined to review the federal courts' denial of habeas corpus relief. Booker's execution was scheduled for 7:00 A.M. on November 17.[252]

When this warrant was signed, Booker again was not represented by counsel. Booker did not obtain counsel until November 1, nearly one week after the new warrant was signed and little more than two weeks before he was scheduled to be executed.[253] Before obtaining counsel, the Clearinghouse and others unsuccessfully asked approximately 150 attorneys to represent him.

Represented by new counsel (James Coleman, Marion Lindberg, and Jeffrey Robinson of the District of Columbia firm Wilmer, Cutler & Pickering), Booker filed a state postconviction motion in the trial court on November 8.[254] Counsel also filed an application for a stay of execution, a supporting memorandum, and a motion for an evidentiary hearing on claims made in the postconviction motion. On the evening of November 8, the state trial judge scheduled a hearing for November 10 at 9:00 A.M. On the morning of the hearing, the State filed a written response to Booker's motion.

At the hearing the trial judge ruled, and the State conceded, that Booker was entitled to an evidentiary hearing on his claim of ineffective assistance

179

of trial counsel. Booker's prior postconviction counsel, who had also been his trial counsel, could not have brought this claim earlier because the attorney would have been claiming his own ineffectiveness at trial, which is impermissible under Florida law.[255] The state trial court ruled that Booker was barred from raising any claims other than ineffective assistance in the motion without giving Booker an opportunity to respond in writing to the State's written submission upon which the court's ruling was based.

The judge initially ordered Booker's new postconviction counsel to conduct an evidentiary hearing on the ineffective assistance of counsel claim at the November 10 hearing.[256] The court had not notified counsel that it would hear evidence at that time. The judge eventually reversed himself and scheduled an evidentiary hearing for November 14, the next Monday following a holiday weekend.[257] In doing so, the court denied Booker's request for a continuance to allow his counsel adequate time to locate and interview witnesses for the hearing. Because of the holiday, a subpoena issued to obtain documents located in New York could not be served until the day of the rescheduled hearing.

The evidentiary hearing was held on November 14, 1983.[258] Booker presented the testimony of his trial counsel and that of three other attorneys who had been qualified as expert witnesses. Additional witnesses whose testimony was relevant to Booker's claim, and who were present in court, were not allowed to testify because the judge apparently had set an unannounced deadline for ruling on Booker's motion—the close of business on the day of the hearing. For the same reason, the court denied Booker's renewed request for a continuance to allow counsel adequately to develop and prepare other evidence.

Shortly before 5:00 P.M. on the day of the hearing, the judge denied Booker's postconviction motion from the bench, without giving Booker's counsel an opportunity to submit a brief and without taking a recess at the close of testimony. The court relieved the State of the burden of having to present any evidence at the hearing. Three days remained until the scheduled execution.

Immediately after the trial court opened for business on November 15, Booker filed a notice of appeal from the trial judge's rulings. On the same day, Booker also filed with the Florida Supreme Court an application for a stay of execution, a petition for a writ of habeas corpus, and a petition for a writ of mandamus.

The Florida Supreme Court stayed Booker's execution until noon on November 16. The prison subsequently rescheduled Booker's execution for 7:00 A.M. on November 18.

Shortly after noon on November 15, the Florida Supreme Court ordered Booker's counsel to file an appellate brief on the merits of Booker's appeal by the morning of November 16, even though no written order

180

from the trial court was then available and even though the record on appeal had not been filed. Counsel complied with this order and filed an appellate brief without seeing the trial court's order or the record on appeal.

The Florida Supreme Court held oral argument at 8:00 A.M. on November 17, the day before the rescheduled execution.[259] At approximately 2:00 P.M. on the day of the argument, the court issued a unanimous decision affirming the trial court and denying Booker's application for a stay and his petitions for mandamus and habeas corpus.[260]

The Florida Supreme Court's decision was made without reviewing the full record from the trial court. At the oral argument before the Florida Supreme Court, the attorney representing the State candidly informed the court that it did not have the full record of the trial court proceeding, primarily because the court reporter preparing the record was exhausted. The attorney went on to say that "if the court finds [the complete record] relevant, we could take some type of drastic action to get her going again."[261] The court stated in its opinion, however, that its review had been based on the "record."[262]

Booker's counsel had previously prepared and lodged a petition for a writ of habeas corpus and an application for a stay of execution in the U.S. District Court on November 16; those pleadings were activated and filed immediately following the Florida Supreme Court's decision. That same day, arguments on the application for a stay of execution were held before a federal district court judge. The judge stayed Booker's execution at 5:00 P.M. on November 17, 14 hours before the execution was to have occurred.[263]

The district court subsequently denied Booker's habeas petition, and a panel of the Eleventh Circuit affirmed.[264] While Booker's petition in the Eleventh Circuit for rehearing *en banc* was pending, a third death warrant was signed and a new execution date was set. The Eleventh Circuit denied rehearing[265] but granted a stay to permit Booker to petition the Supreme Court for certiorari. The Supreme Court dissolved the stay.[266]

Booker then moved in the state trial court to reopen the 1983 state postconviction litigation, arguing that his trial attorney had lied during the 1983 evidentiary hearing and therefore had committed a fraud on the court. He also filed a motion in federal district court to set aside judgment pursuant to Federal Rule of Criminal Procedure 60(b). The trial judge granted an indefinite stay, which the State unsuccessfully sought to dissolve.[267] Following an evidentiary hearing, the state trial court denied the motion to reopen. The Florida Supreme Court affirmed.[268] The federal district court also denied the Rule 60(b) motion, and the Eleventh Circuit affirmed.[269] In August 1987 Booker filed an original proceeding in the Florida Supreme Court, raising an issue he raised in his first round of postconviction litigation.[270] The Florida Supreme Court agreed that

Booker's sentencing proceeding was tainted with error of constitutional magnitude but held the error harmless.[271] Booker filed a fourth habeas petition in federal district court. The governor signed a death warrant. The district judge granted a stay and ordered resentencing; the Eleventh Circuit affirmed;[272] the Supreme Court denied review.[273] Before the resentencing could occur, the state filed a motion in federal district court to reopen the habeas case in light of a recent U.S. Supreme Court decision. On March 18, 1994, the district court denied the state's motion and reiterated Booker's entitlement to resentencing.[274] The state appealed to the Eleventh Circuit, which ruled against the state in the fall of 1996.

Prosecutors and other politicians often trash defense attorneys for causing "delay" in capital cases—an average of eight years. Booker won his new sentencing order in 1988. Yet *state* appeals prevented him from getting his resentencing trial. As of this writing, those state appeals have taken nine years. And counting.

The Solution: CCR

Three systematic efforts, two in the form of litigation and one in the form of legislation, have been mounted to deal with the counsel problem in Florida. In 1985 these efforts culminated in the creation of a state agency, the Office of the Capital Collateral Representative, to provide direct representation to Florida's condemned.

The first litigation effort seeking a systemwide solution to Florida's emerging counsel crisis was initiated in 1979, at the beginning of the crisis, when only three Florida death warrants had been signed in the post-*Furman* era: two against John Spenkelink and one against Willie Jasper Darden. The lawsuit, styled *Graham v. State,*[275] was brought as an original proceeding in the Florida Supreme Court, on behalf of nine condemned inmates with volunteer or public defender lawyers, seeking appointment of counsel for state postconviction and federal habeas corpus proceedings. The actual petitioners were volunteer attorneys who either represented one of the nine condemned men or who had represented John Spenkelink.[276] Five of the nine condemned inmates had previously filed state post-conviction motions,[277] and one had filed a federal habeas petition.[278] The petitioners/attorneys had examined the records of the nine condemned men and argued to the court that each record contained issues that had sufficient merit to warrant collateral review.[279]

The petition catalogued the legal steps taken by the NAACP Legal Defense and Educational Fund, Inc. (LDF) and other volunteers to attempt to prevent the execution of John Spenkelink.[280] The petition specified that LDF was unable to continue the support it had provided during the

Spenkelink litigation and discussed other possible sources of lawyers. As to volunteer counsel, the petition said:

> The Petitioners herein represent the bulk of Florida attorneys willing to volunteer time and expertise to secure collateral review in death cases. The volunteer attorneys have learned, as a result of the Spenkelink/Darden experience, that a single lawyer is wholly insufficient in a death case. Additionally, because of Spenkelink and Darden, the volunteers are exhausted and their funds depleted. In short, volunteers are incapable of seeking the collateral review required to be sought on behalf of the condemned. It is unfair and unreliable that condemned persons must rely upon representation by unpaid volunteer attorneys.[281]

The petition gave two reasons why public defenders could not assume responsibility for such representation. First, the public defenders' authority to represent inmates in federal courts was questionable.[282] Second, "the public defenders are simply not equipped to expend the effort and resources that the Spenkelink execution proved mandatory. Neither the budget nor the staff of the public defenders' offices are adequate to handle such cases."[283]

The petition was based solely upon the due process clause of the Fourteenth Amendment.[284] No claim based on the Eighth Amendment or on the state constitution was advanced. The Florida Supreme Court denied the petition, holding that "no court has determined that there is a constitutional right to the assistance of counsel to aid in the preparation of a petition for postconviction relief."[285] The court appeared to deny the existence of a counsel problem in Florida, noting that the petitioners in *Graham* were all persons who, in the court's view, had had considerable judicial attention given to their cases.[286]

The court did seem to recognize that counsel ought to be appointed generally: "The adversary nature of the proceeding, its complexity, the need of an evidentiary hearing, or the need for substantial legal research are all important elements which may require the appointment of counsel."[287] Nevertheless, the court reiterated that the State of Florida has no obligation to provide counsel or pay the costs of federal proceedings.[288]

The court analyzed in more detail the need to provide counsel for state postconviction proceedings. The court explained that Florida had been progressive on the right to counsel issue ever since *Gideon v. Wainwright*,[289] noting that the state had established a public defender system within weeks of that decision, as well as comprehensive postconviction relief proceedings.[290] Given that the state also supplied counsel in postconviction proceedings once a defendant was able to make a prima facie case for relief, the court concluded that "there is no constitutional requirement for the appointment of individual counsel for an application for postconviction relief until a colorable or justiciable issue or meritorious grievance . . . appears in the appellant's petition."[291]

The second attempt to secure a systemwide solution to the then-growing counsel crisis in Florida occurred in 1982. Timothy Palmes, a condemned inmate facing impending execution, sought a stay of execution and appointment of counsel based on the decision in *Hooks v. Wainwright*.[292] The federal district court in *Hooks* had entered an order finding that the Florida Department of Corrections was denying inmates the constitutionally guaranteed right of meaningful access to the courts. The court found that to satisfy the inmates' right to access, Florida must provide a plan that would give indigent inmates access to attorneys for the purpose of representing and advising them in state and federal judicial proceedings attacking their convictions and sentences.[293] At the time Palmes filed his action, all proceedings in *Hooks* had been stayed pending appeal. Palmes was a member of the *Hooks* class, and his motions for stay of execution and appointment of counsel were brought as part of the *Hooks* litigation.[294]

Palmes' case was an appropriate vehicle to raise the constitutional implications of Florida's counsel crisis: He was facing an imminent execution date and he had no lawyer. On May 18, 1982, the clemency attorneys representing Palmes and Ronald Straight, Palmes' co-defendant, telephoned the Clearinghouse and left messages for Holdman. Before Holdman could return their phone calls, Mrs. Anna Palmes, Timothy Palmes' mother, telephoned the Clearinghouse to tell Holdman that she had learned that the governor had signed death warrants against her son and Ronald Straight, and that they were to be executed on June 15. Holdman told her not to worry, because Palmes' clemency attorney had assured Holdman that he would represent Palmes in postconviction proceedings and in obtaining a stay of execution so that those proceedings could go forward.

By the next day, Holdman had talked with the clemency attorneys. Both told her that they would not represent Palmes or Straight, and that Holdman should try to find other volunteer counsel. She asked them to help find counsel for these men.

Holdman immediately began telephoning members of the private bar, asking them to consider representing either Palmes or Straight, and asking for names of other attorneys whom she might contact to ask for assistance. During the next week, she spoke with 40 attorneys and explained the dire need for *pro bono* help for these two men who faced imminent execution with no counsel. She explained that neither prisoner had been represented in any state postconviction or federal collateral proceeding and that, given their own educational backgrounds and abilities and the conditions of confinement at Florida State Prison, it was virtually impossible for them to represent themselves. She also explained that no state-funded agency provided counsel to death-sentenced prisoners after the Florida Supreme Court affirmed their convictions and sentences on direct appeal. These two prisoners, she told them, like others on death row, were entirely dependent on the private bar to provide representation as part of their *pro bono* obligation, and there were no guaranteed financial resources, either state or private, to offset the substantial out-of-pocket expenses related to the cases.

Several of the attorneys agreed to consider representing one of the two prisoners if their law firms agreed. Only one attorney, Raymond Makowski, agreed to represent either prisoner. Makowski agreed to represent Ronald Straight.

Attorneys frequently gave Holdman the same reasons for not representing either Palmes or Straight:

1. Inexperience with the prevailing law. Some criminal defense attorneys felt they did not have sufficient experience in capital law and habeas litigation to allow them to research and review relevant state and federal law; review the transcripts; interview the client, his prior counsel, co-defendants, and other relevant people; and investigate and prepare the pleadings necessary to obtain the stay of execution in the time available before the execution.
2. Financial costs. Some attorneys did not have the financial resources to cover out-of-pocket expenses such as printing, travel, telephone, and express mail, all necessary for investigation and consultation with the inmate, his prior counsel, potential witnesses, and potential experts.
3. Scheduling. Several attorneys expressed deep concern and said they wished they could offer their services. But their immediate calendar and commitments to fee-paying clients precluded their representing these two men on such short notice when it was apparent that a tremendous amount of time would have to be spent reviewing the record, interviewing the client, researching the law, investigating the merits of possible claims, and preparing the multiple pleadings that would have to be filed in several courts.
4. Conflicts. Some attorneys had been employed by the state prosecutor's office at the time the cases were prosecuted and thus had a conflict of interest. Others had represented one of the co-defendants who received immunity in exchange for testifying for the state. Others had personal relationships with the victim's family.[295]

Two lawyers eventually agreed to represent Palmes in his efforts to secure counsel. These lawyers refused, however, to represent Palmes in his underlying challenges to his conviction and sentence. The lawsuit seeking counsel (and stay of Palmes' execution) was brought as part of the ongoing *Hooks* litigation.

The district court eventually granted a stay but denied Palmes' claim under *Hooks*. The court treated Palmes as moving through his attorneys[296] and noted that "it was certainly somewhat incongruous that a person claiming he is unable to obtain the assistance of counsel is currently represented by at least two able attorneys."[297] This view clearly influenced the court's reasoning in rejecting Palmes' claims:

> Accompanying his motion is a well-orchestrated array of affidavits intended to show that all efforts to secure counsel to represent him have been unsuccessful. The affidavits include veiled pleas for judicial assistance on behalf of various organizations devoted to representing defendants convicted of capital crimes. The content of these affidavits reflects a broader purpose than merely securing the assistance of counsel for Timothy Palmes. They are replete with general information as to the burgeoning number of capital cases and the inability of the organizations to obtain adequate funds to cover even the expenses of volunteer attorneys.
>
> The motion and attached affidavits are well-intentioned but, unfortunately, misdirected.[298]

The court held that it lacked jurisdiction to issue a stay of execution absent a pending habeas petition.[299] It reasoned that particularly during "these times of growing friction and disagreement concerning the proper working relationship between the state and federal courts,"[300] federal courts ought to operate only through "prescribed mechanisms," such as habeas corpus proceedings.[301]

The court was careful to stress that it was in no way adjudicating the merits of Palmes' claim that he was entitled to counsel.[302] The court recognized that its opinion in *Hooks* was "clearly relevant" to Palmes' claim and found the idea that a person might be executed without the benefit of some form of attorney-assistance to aid him in pursuing remedies prescribed by law "repugnant to the spirit, if not the letter, of the federal Constitution."[303] In addition, the court found it difficult to discern how a person confined to death row could be afforded meaningful access to the courts without the benefit of some professional legal assistance.[304]

The court put the burden right back where it always had been: on the backs of the volunteer lawyers. "Fortunately," the court wrote with a wink to reality, "at least in the past, there have been adequate numbers of qualified volunteer attorneys to represent capital defendants in postconviction proceedings."[305] The court "trusted" that Palmes' present counsel would continue to represent him until a habeas petition had been filed, which most likely also meant until exhaustion could be completed, at which time a determination of appointment of counsel would be appropriate.[306]

Eventually, Thomas McCoun, who had represented Anthony Antone, volunteered to represent Palmes. He did so throughout two rounds of state

186

and federal postconviction proceedings. Palmes was executed in 1984,[307] two years before his co-defendant, Ronald Straight.[308]

Despite the outcome of the *Palmes/Hooks* litigation, change was in the air. In 1982 the ABA approved a resolution calling for the appointment of counsel for capital postconviction litigation in state and federal court.[309] In January 1984 the Florida State-Federal Judicial Council, led by Eleventh Circuit Chief Judge John Godbold, squarely addressed the counsel problem. Concluding that the basic problem with the capital postconviction process was the inadequate number of volunteer lawyers, the Council passed a unanimous resolution to ask the Florida bar to create a mechanism within the bar to recruit private counsel in this area. In May 1984, in response to this request, the Florida bar appointed a Special Committee on Representation of Death Sentenced Inmates in Collateral Proceedings.[310] The Committee consisted of 15 lawyers representing 15 of the largest civil law firms in the state.[311]

The Committee first met in June 1984 and developed a plan of action centering on the recruitment of volunteer attorneys, particularly from large civil law firms in Florida.[312] The idea behind tapping the resources of civil law firms was twofold. First, the small pool of criminal defense attorneys able and willing to handle collateral proceedings in capital cases had been exhausted. Second, large civil law firms were in a better position, relative to small firms or sole practitioners, to absorb the huge expenditures of time and money required by such litigation.[313]

At the June meeting, the Committee discussed how many *pro bono* counsel would be needed, at which level of the proceedings recruited counsel should enter the case, and what guidelines should be developed to ensure effective representation without unethical or improper activity designed solely to burden the courts or oppose the death penalty philosophically. The Committee also discussed the idea that they would be better able to recruit civil attorneys if they could (1) develop an information base or research institute to assist volunteers; (2) pair civil lawyers with experienced capital postconviction attorneys in the role of co-counsel or "mentor"; and (3) establish some sort of funding base for partial reimbursement of legal fees and expenses in connection with representation. Finally, the Committee discussed working toward the development of a permanent, state-supported agency to handle postconviction proceedings.[314]

The day of the June organizational meeting, Committee Chairman James C. Rinaman, Jr., appeared before the Florida State-Federal Judicial Council to address the problems he perceived would confront the Committee. These problems included difficulty in getting civil trial lawyers into complex criminal law, the appearance to death penalty opponents that a "train to execution" was being created, and the attitude of death penalty advocates that collateral proceedings are largely frivolous. Rinaman also wondered whether it was really in the best interest of inmates to file timely collateral petitions and have them considered in a deliberative manner, or to wait until the last minute to file, which makes the death penalty difficult to enforce. Finally, Rinaman posited that if the Committee performed its job well, Florida would be less likely to provide a long-term solution in the form of a state-funded agency.[315]

The Committee immediately began its effort to recruit volunteer attorneys, develop a list of attorneys with expertise in death penalty collateral litigation, and establish and fund a resource center. On June 29 the Committee had its first success in recruiting a civil law firm—that of a Committee member—to represent a death row inmate scheduled for execution in 13 days. The Committee paired the firm with an attorney who had some criminal defense experience and who had volunteered to represent the inmate, but whose small firm did not have the resources to allow her to undertake the representation alone. An assistant public defender with experience in collateral proceedings was found to serve as a consultant to the team.[316]

Meanwhile, Rinaman had begun discussions with Talbot D'Alemberte, dean of Florida State University Law School, to see whether FSU would consider serving as a resource center for lawyers recruited by the Committee. FSU was interested in the project but concerned about the controversial nature of the Committee's work and the appropriateness of the law school's involvement. D'Alemberte suggested that the Committee obtain assurances from Florida's political leadership that the resource center would not be "offensive" to anyone.[317] Later, when FSU agreed to take on the resource center, the dean asked Chairman Rinaman to help generate letters from bar leaders, political leaders, and judges thanking FSU for undertaking the project. "This will help me a great deal with the administration here at FSU and those who remain skeptical on the faculty and student body," he explained.[318]

Although the Committee presented itself as neither for nor against the death penalty,[319] the controversial nature of death penalty representation, especially at the collateral proceedings stage, would, as Rinaman foresaw, constantly confront the Committee as it sought to find volunteer attorneys and establish funding for the resource center. In an apparent attempt to appease the concerns of the pro-death-penalty majority in the Florida state government, legislature, and citizenry, then-Florida Bar President William Henry made a number of public comments offensive to death penalty opponents and attorneys representing death-sentenced inmates. Henry referred to the latter group as including too many ideologues "more interested in thwarting the death penalty than in representing their clients,"[320] and suggested that they engaged in frivolous litigation to secure stays of execution. On the other hand, in a memorandum to the newly appointed Committee,

Henry told members that "the results of your work may not be popular (although I hope it [*sic*] is) but it is essential that the constitutional rights of every person be carefully reviewed before the state imposes its ultimate penalty for a crime."[321]

The Committee met again in September 1984 and established general policies assuming the need for 15 to 20 *pro bono* counsel for death row inmates annually:

1. Civil trial firms would be utilized only when experienced criminal defense attorneys could not be found.
2. Civil trial lawyers would be appointed as co-counsel with experienced criminal defense lawyers wherever possible to provide assistance and expenses. Where a co-counsel arrangement could not be established, an experienced criminal defense lawyer would be assigned as a consultant or "mentor" to the civil trial lawyers.
3. Lawyers would establish individual lawyer–client relationships upon accepting a case.
4. Civil lawyers would not be asked to accept sole responsibility for any case where an execution warrant had been signed. Lawyers would attempt to become involved in cases prior to clemency proceedings, which, in Florida, occur prior to the initiation of postconviction litigation.
5. Manuals and other training and research materials on the law of state postconviction and federal habeas corpus would be developed by a resource center at FSU Law School to provide research support for recruited firms.
6. A fund would be created for minimal expense reimbursements ($2,000 to $3,000 per case) as incentive for firms to undertake representation.
7. The long-term objective was to establish legislative funding for public defenders offices, or some other publicly funded representation, in the postconviction stage.[322]

By early fall 1984, the law school at FSU had committed itself to establishing a resource center. In September, the Florida Bar Foundation approved an application for $90,600 to fund the resource center and $25,000 as a fund for minimal cost reimbursements. By mid-September, the Committee had matched civil trial firms as co-counsel with criminal defense lawyers in four cases in response to emergency requests for assistance.[323]

Although the Committee successfully recruited civil law firms to ensure that every inmate subjected to a death warrant between June 1984 and November 1985 was provided with counsel,[324] the Committee met with skepticism and refusals to participate along the way. Some Committee members themselves were skeptical. At an August 1984 meeting of large civil law firms and several prominent criminal law attorneys, two Committee members who had organized the recruitment meeting told Chairman Rinaman that they were disappointed and pessimistic about the prospects of succeeding in such a task.[325]

The positions that the civil litigators took at the August meeting had three consistent themes.[326] First, the civil attorneys were concerned about the financial commitment involved in taking on representation of a death row inmate, especially given the emergency nature of these proceedings and the short notice involved. When it was suggested that these emergencies could be avoided by the timely handling of collateral proceedings before a death warrant was signed, the criminal attorneys voiced objections that any such effort hastened the imposition of the death penalty and would be contrary to the interests of the death row inmate.[327]

Second, the civil litigators voiced a lack of desire to work with anti-death-penalty groups. The criminal law attorneys, however, were adamant: Someone who supports the death penalty probably could not give the type of commitment required to provide proper representation of a death row inmate.[328]

Would the civil litigators asked to help have any idea what representing a death row inmate entailed? The criminal attorneys felt that representing death row inmates in collateral proceedings was such a highly specialized area of the law (none of the criminal law attorneys present considered themselves fully capable of handling such cases) that civil litigators could not be expected to do a competent job. Their conclusion was that no civil litigator could provide effective and competent representation to a death row inmate.[329]

It was clear to the Committee that in order to accomplish the recruitment they hoped for, the resource center and a pool of "mentors" had to be made immediately available to the civil law firm volunteers. This was accomplished in February 1985 when the Volunteer Lawyers' Resource Center received final approval from the Florida Bar and was put into place at FSU Law School. By that time the Committee had sent recruitment letters to 30 criminal defense attorneys nominated by the Florida Institute for Criminal Justice as lawyers capable of serving as mentors/consultants or co-counsel with civil trial firms in the representation of death row inmates in collateral proceedings.[330] While many of the attorneys who responded to the letter indicated that they could not serve as co-counsel, either because they were already lead counsel in death penalty cases or because there was a conflict of interest, almost all of the attorneys solicited agreed to serve in a consultant capacity.[331]

By early March 1985, with the Resource Center open and a pool of available mentors on hand, Chairman Rinaman reported to the Committee that they were ready to begin full-scale recruiting to obtain representation for death row inmates in pre- and postclemency status.[332] At that time 30 death row inmates were in need of representation. Out of those 30, the Committee identified six whose death warrants were expected to be signed within the next several months and who needed counsel right away. Nine inmates were identified whose clemency hearings were scheduled for June 1985 and whose death warrants, therefore, would not be expected to be signed until late 1985 to 1986.[333]

By the end of May 1985, the Committee had recruited 17 civil trial firms to represent death row inmates.[334] In an interim report to the Florida Bar Board of Governors, Rinaman estimated that the Committee would need to recruit at least another 12 to 15 civil firms in order to keep the program operating until a state-funded office could be established.[335] The Committee had just barely kept up with providing representation to inmates with warrants pending. Now, it was trying to plan ahead to assign firms before or immediately after clemency hearings so that the civil firms would have sufficient time to review the cases and prepare petitions and briefs before the urgency of a death warrant intervened.[336] It was clear, however, that the Committee could now do no more than keep pace with the death warrants being signed.

Furthermore, the pool of civil law firms willing to undertake representation was rapidly diminishing, and the Resource Center found itself severely overworked, understaffed, and underfunded.[337] A more comprehensive solution to the counsel problem would be required.

Faced with the continuing counsel crisis, the Florida legislature created the Office of the Capital Collateral Representative (CCR) in June 1985.[338] This action was widely supported, including among its proponents the Florida attorney general, the governor, the Florida Bar Association, and the Florida Public Defenders Association.[339]

Two events in early 1985 transformed the debate over the counsel crisis into concrete legislative proposals for a solution.[340] First, Florida amended its state postconviction rule to require that collateral proceedings be brought within a specified time following final judgment on direct appeal. As a result, the 34 unrepresented persons then on death row would have been required to initiate their collateral actions before January 1, 1986.[341]

The second event was a counsel crisis involving two death row inmates, James Agan and Robert Waterhouse. State trial judges had stayed the executions of Agan and Waterhouse because of the unavailability of postconviction counsel, despite the efforts of the Committee to find volunteer counsel to represent them.[342] The state appealed the stays, but the Florida Supreme Court refused to dissolve them.[343] In the Florida Supreme Court, Waterhouse was represented by counsel who had entered the case only days before. Agan, however, remained without counsel to oppose the state's attempt to lift the stay: The chairs at the defense table were empty.[344]

The Florida Attorney General's Office interpreted the action of the Florida Supreme Court in *Agan* and *Waterhouse* to mean that the court would not vacate a stay of execution issued between affirmance of the sentence on direct appeal and the scheduled execution when the inmate had no counsel, even though a volunteer attorney was found shortly before the scheduled execution.[345] Attorney General Jim Smith, therefore, became the principal proponent of the bill providing for the creation of an office for capital collateral representation.[346] Smith's Kafkaesque state senate testimony in support of the bill bears quotation at some length:

> I'd like to take just a minute or two to talk with you about a Catch-22 that . . . relates to capital punishment in Florida. I'm sure all of you are aware the state is required to provide counsel for death row inmates through the appeals to the Florida Supreme Court and for their opportunity to petition the United States Supreme Court to hear their case. After that process is completed, there is no legal requirement at the federal level or state level that death row inmates be provided representation.
>
> We had our first execution in modern times in Florida in 1979. Since that time, death row inmates have been represented by essentially volunteer lawyers. We've got a lot of lawyers from out of state come into Florida and represent these people. The Florida Bar now for about a year has been working diligently to provide attorneys to represent death row inmates for what we call "collateral appeals." We're at a point in time now, though, where that category of volunteer lawyers is really running out.
>
> In two recent cases before the Florida Supreme Court, . . . one of the inmates obtained an attorney just hours before a hearing before the court and he was granted a stay on the promise that "if you give me some time to look at the file, I might represent this individual." Another stay was granted. Unfortunately, the Court did not write an opinion in either case so I can't stand here and tell you exactly what they meant by their action, but my interpretation of their action is these people did not have attorneys.[347] There will be stays and I can see capital punishment in Florida coming to a grinding halt. Obviously, there is no incentive now for a death row inmate to try to obtain a lawyer.
>
> We're still pretty much in an evolutionary process of capital punishment in the development of that law. In the old days, the federal courts really didn't second guess the final judgments of state courts. Obviously, in the capital punishment area there will be an exhaustive review by the federal courts after . . . action. Frankly, I anticipated this problem about four years ago and I recommended to the legislature then that we begin to require public defenders to provide this representation, but the public defenders strenuously opposed that suggestion and legislation did not get anywhere. What you have before you is essentially a new recommendation that we create under the state courts administrator an office for capital collateral appeals where the state essentially would provide attorneys to represent death row inmates in collateral proceedings.
>
> If we are going to continue to have executions in Florida, I think there is obviously still broad support for that state policy, I think this is a step we should take.[348]

A senator asked Smith if he could guarantee that CCR would speed up executions. Smith replied:

> I can't guarantee anything. . . . I think clearly with this representation provided that claims will be advanced much sooner, there will be no excuse that we can't find lawyers, and frankly, it's been rather embarrassing to me at clemency hearings for the last six and a half years to have legal work lawyers coming down here and have them defend people on death row in Florida. You know, we're a big state. The people in this state want capital punishment and I think we ought to provide the resources to make it happen. As a lawyer and as Attorney General it has been embarrassing that we've had these volunteers coming down here always making snide remarks about the legal processes in our state like we're trying to rush these people to judgment, that kind of thing which is clearly not true. But, I . . . am standing here to say we need to spend this money to make it happen.[349]

One senator appeared satisfied:

> Senator: It certainly removes that element of lawyers coming in on the 11th hour because of the glitch that we've got now. At least now you'll have a continuous flow of these people coming in that are retained literally in the 11th hour and suddenly you've got a brand new lawyer on the case that's never even looked at the file and they get another stay granted because the attorney obviously has not had a real chance to review the case.
>
> Now, you should have a continuous, smooth flow all the way through and the whole process should stay on schedule rather than having these delays in the 11th hour.

Smith also thought that eventually the courts would hold that condemned inmates have a right to counsel in capital postconviction:

> I don't think before *Wainwright v. Gideon* [sic] there was no requirement that states provide lawyers for poor people. I think ultimately we're going to see the Supreme Court of the United States say what value is the right of collateral relief for death row inmates if they have to advance it themselves and I think we're just, you know, 3, 4, 5, 6, 7 years away from the Supreme Court of the United States saying the states are going to have to provide this kind of representation. I don't think we want to see this kind of process stagnate and us get to the point where we got five- or six-hundred people on death row writing to the courts on this issue. I think Florida, as we have been on this issue, should stay ahead of the curve and let's appropriate the money and get on with it.
>
> The Senator: Yes. If we provide this, are these people still going to be allowed to go lawyer shopping? For volunteers . . . themselves? Are they going to be restricted to go ahead and utilize it?
>
> Mr. Smith: I think we will see—and again I'm just guessing at what I

think will happen—but I think we will see the state courts and the federal courts, if representation is made available, not allow that. Now is right for that kind of sensationalism. If the states provide lawyers, I think we'll see the courts not allow that.[350]

Smith's reasons for supporting the creation of CCR put death row's advocates in a delicate position.[351] Nevertheless, the prevailing system clearly was on the brink of collapse, and CCR seemed the best solution. Even if CCR made the process faster, it would also make it fairer. Ultimately, the CCR bill received the support of opponents as well as advocates of the death penalty.[352]

Florida's CCR office opened on October 1, 1985, with a budget of $860,000. The CCR legislation contemplated a CCR staff of 21 individuals, including the Capital Collateral Representative and nine attorneys. It was initially assumed that it would take approximately three months for the office to become fully established and staffed; however, the office's attorney staff did not reach its full complement until approximately March 1, 1986, five months after its inception.[353] During this time period, the Volunteer Lawyer's Resource Center effectively merged with CCR.

Within the first eight days of CCR's operation, Governor Bob Graham signed four death warrants. On November 4, 1986, he signed two more.[354] During 1986 and 1987, the governor increased his average number of death warrants from 24 to 35.[355] At any given time during this period, four CCR clients would be scheduled for execution.

When the CCR legislation was passed and the office began operation, it was contemplated that the volunteers recruited by its predecessor Bar Committee would continue to represent inmates whose collateral proceedings they had undertaken.[356] According to CCR director Larry Spalding, however, nearly one-third of the private law firms recruited by the Bar's Special Committee tried to turn their cases over to CCR within the first year of its existence,[357] at a rate of about one case per month.[358] CCR managed to persuade some firms, but not all, to continue as counsel in their cases. One prominent Florida law firm that was supposed to file pleadings by a certain date called CCR one month before the papers were due to say that the firm would not represent the client any longer.[359] Now that there was a state agency, many private firms and potential volunteers decided, their services were no longer needed.

A Dangerous Law Firm: "There's No Substitute For Life Insurance"

At CCR I worked for Mark Olive. We all worked for Mark Olive, and for Scharlette Holdman. Holdman's and Olive's criticism of the legal system focused on what it left out: the family history that contextualizes the crime and the criminal. At a time when litigation in the minds of much of the public is synonymous with preening, highly paid legal guns (O. J. Simpson's "dream team" comes to mind), it is useful to recall that Holdman's and Olive's contributions came in the form of factual investigation—gumshoe work—on a low budget. Olive was the Norman Mailer of deathwork: brilliant, brave, original, and quirky. He liked to shock. Olive is an old-timey litigator, a throwback to the times of Clarence Darrow, before the days of television. He projects in a court room that rarest of qualities in lawyers: an awesome sense of integrity and commitment and utter conviction. That is pure magic in capital postconviction litigation. When it comes to cutting through the muttering haze of an oral argument in certain courts at certain times, Olive has no peer.

There were some days (and nights) when CCR was the best public defender office in the world. Most days at CCR were slow. Wild things happened to all of us some of the time, and to some of us almost all of the time, but not always. They were not the norm. The daily diet is lean for the infantry.

On paper, neither Olive nor Holdman ran CCR; that title belonged to Larry Helm Spalding. With the warrants and the infighting on all fronts, it has suddenly become chic to ridicule Spalding. Spalding got his head handed to him by a gang of upstarts: He knows what it feels like to be the rich boy at the wedding in *The Graduate*. I believe Spalding did some good at CCR. But none of that good can ever come close to compensating for Spalding's fatal decision in the late 1980s, to fire Scharlette Holdman, knowing that Mark Olive would be forced to resign in protest.

CCR under Holdman and Olive was a precarious place at best; CCR without Holdman and Olive was like a ship taking on water and threatening to sink in 90 feet of water. CCR had as its statutory mandate the representation of all Florida death row inmates in state and federal postconviction proceedings.[360]

The Florida legislature set the size of the CCR staff and its budget with the expectation that the office would handle about 30 cases in its first year of operation. Instead, it handled about 150 cases.[361] Even though CCR attorneys were routinely working 60- to 90-hour weeks, and some private attorneys remained available as volunteers, CCR was having trouble keeping up with the increase in Florida's death row population.[362] CCR's crushing caseload raised serious ethical dilemmas—dilemmas that have led courts[363] and commentators[364] to find that staggering caseloads can result in ineffective representation.

Despite this caseload, CCR did not fulfill Attorney General Smith's expectations and speed up the execution process, at least in its early years. In its first year and a half of existence, only three executions occurred in Florida.[365] CCR or CCR-assisted volunteer counsel won retrials or resentencings in several cases.[366] Further, stays of execution were usually obtained in state court far earlier in the postconviction process than had been true previously. Ironically, once CCR had become operational and had succeeded in preventing a string of executions, some legislators complained that CCR had violated the legislative intent behind its creation.[367]

Mary Chapin Carpenter has a song called "Heroes and Heroines" that nails the sense of the CCR. Not that *I* was a hero, by *any* stretch of the imagination—affidavits demonstrating exactly how unheroic I was would be very easy to come by—though I *worked* with genuine heroes and heroines. It's hard to describe our sense of fragility, and flickering vulnerability, in the face of a prosecutorial state colossus willing to tax and spend itself into the ground to kill our clients, and our sense of loneliness and isolation and otherness, a siege mentality akin to self-imposed exile, combined with an omnipresent and always unspoken fear, working the high wire without a net, never really knowing what the rules of the game would be, and never completely sure what the hell we were doing, because the game could change daily and without advance notice from the judges who *did* set the rules; only knowing for certain that when we made mistakes—and we *all* make mistakes—our clients would die.

Florida was the "capital of capital punishment," as a recent campaign ad put it—proudly number one in the nation in terms of the numbers of people on death row, actual executions, and raw public zeal for more and faster executions. The office had as its statutory mandate to represent all Florida death row cases in the "endless" postconviction habeas corpus stages of litigation; all of our clients' cases had been affirmed once in the state supreme court.

The Office of the Capital Collateral Representative sounds more like an insurance underwriting outfit than a death row defense agency, a perception not discouraged by our location in the Independent Life Insurance Building on South Pensacola Street (motto on the window: "There's No Substitute For Life Insurance"). Such camouflage was not entirely accidental. The protective coloration was useful because our Tallahassee office was a political lightning rod. It was an easy walk to the Florida Supreme Court, the legislature, the law library at FSU, the Hilton bar, and the Chi Omega Sorority.

When I was at CCR, it seemed as though just about everyone (except our clients) hated us: the public, the media, the prosecutors, the governors and their staff, the judges, the legislators who decided every year how much (or whether) to fund us. I always thought of such universal animosity as a good thing, or at least as a hopeful thing.

"A hungry army's enough to spook the dead."[368] Everyone at CCR in those days worked extraordinarily long hours and shared a deep commitment to the office's mission. But what made the office work in the early years was the presence of two certifiable geniuses: Scharlette Holdman and Mark Olive. Olive and Holdman made the CCR of the mid-1980s a dangerous law firm: dangerous to the powerful, the dishonest, and the deceitful.

It's hard to describe what made CCR dangerous, but I do know that it had little to do with levels of funding or resources. Perhaps it was a matter of attitude: What Olive and Holdman brought to CCR, in addition to skills and experience, was a fearless will. I asked Olive once what it was that stopped executions from occurring. He told me that it wasn't good facts (although those helped); it wasn't good law (although that helped); it wasn't even having an innocent client (which didn't help at all, it just made the state actors more determined not to admit they had made a mistake). What stopped executions was will: an iron determination that *this killing will not happen.*

Florida's counsel crisis may or may not be resolved. CCR's early record justified guarded nonpessimism. Although each annual CCR appropriations debate has the potential to bring back the scramble for counsel that predated the creation of the agency, that potential will be balanced against the bureaucratic inertia of an extant agency that fulfills a genuine need. In 1987 CCR's budget was increased to $1.4 million.[369] At the same time, the governor announced new policies that would greatly increase the number and frequency of death warrants signed.[370] The same political give-and-take occurred in fiscal years 1993–94, 1995–96, and 1996–97.[371]

The United States has reached a crossroads on capital punishment. Broad-based challenges to the death penalty are not likely to succeed in the foreseeable future. Because capital punishment is here to stay, the judiciary has the task of seeing to it—case by case—that the punishment is administered in as fair and reliable a manner as is possible.

The postconviction process has become an integral part of the system of capital punishment. The postconviction component of the system is necessary because it exposes injustices. This stage is an essential check on the functioning of the judicial system at trial. It is necessary to the integrity of a legal system that strives to tame the death penalty within the rule of law.

In turn, lawyers are essential to the integrity of the capital postconviction process. Each jurisdiction enforcing the death penalty must recognize this and must craft its own mechanism of providing counsel to its condemned population. There is much room for creativity. In some states, the best solution will be a Florida-type agency or unit within a public defender office to provide direct representation to death row inmates. In other states, the best solution will be a resource center to support private appointed or *pro bono* counsel. Elsewhere, the best solution will be a hybrid of more than one model. But some solution must be found for every jurisdiction with the death penalty. That solution should be devised and put in place before a crisis similar to Florida's converts the need into an emergency. Florida's experience should serve as a firebell in the night to all states recognizing the death penalty but not having a mechanism for providing capital postconviction counsel. The counsel crisis Florida experienced can be ameliorated or avoided in other states by crafting counsel solutions before the crisis reaches the fever pitch Florida experienced in mid-1985.

Pseudoreality Prevails

I first drafted this chapter in early 1987. CCR was only two years old, and Olive and Holdman were still working miracles there. At that time, I felt strongly that the right place for abolitionist defense lawyers was in CCR or in places like it. I now believe I was wrong about that. After more than two decades of extraordinarily expensive work, Florida's high-powered capital punishment system is a smoking ruin, a disaster. It's humiliating to be a part of that mess. The whole structure should be plowed under, for landfill.

I now believe that attorneys and others of conscience should opt out of the postconviction machinery of death. We should—we *must*—continue to fight capital punishment in the venues of electoral politics and public sentiment. We must continue in our roles as storytellers and historians. And trial lawyers. But not as postconviction litigators. The time of the lawyer is past.

I've come to the position of conscientious abstention slowly and painfully. As discussed in Chapter 6, I've been raising it as a possible course of action since 1991. But I *acted* on it in late 1995 when I realized, finally, how totally and carelessly the system of "legal" homicide had treated one of my clients—my *last* client, in fact—Joseph Spaziano, whose case I explore in some depth in Chapter 6.

Mr. Spaziano's 1995 brush with Florida's electric chair made me realize that by entrusting the "legal" system with his life I had been less than useless to my longtime friend and client. By my participation I granted my implicit blessing and validation to a legalistic system that was, in fact, immoral and lawless. The legal system is determined to kill the residents of death row; the participation of defense lawyers imbues an essentially lawless "system" with the veneer of justice and fairness. I will no longer play that role.

A 1961 movie was the beginning of the end of my life as a capital postconviction litigator. During Mr. Spaziano's last death warrant, I rented *Judgment at Nuremburg*. I lack the vocabulary or the grammar or the syntax to describe what it felt like for me to hear my own self-justificatory rationales for my own participation in an immoral "legal" system come out of the mouths of Ernst Janning and Herr Rolff. So, in the words of Grant Gilmore, I revoke.

I can hear the voices of CCR's current bureaucrats now: "You're killing your clients," they will doubtless say. Maybe that's true. But their illusion, their pretense, is that by being good and dutiful lawyer/bureaucrats—by thinking they can use the master's tools to destroy the master's house, to paraphrase Audre Lorde—they *aren't* "killing" *their* clients. The truth is, of course, that neither I nor CCR is killing anybody. The *state* is doing the killing, and the right question is what our individual consciences compel us to do in the face of the state's attempts to kill people we care about. The hard question is whether we can *prevent* the state from getting on with the killing. On a micro level, in individual cases, the answer clearly is yes. But that "yes," and the participation it inexorably commands, comes at a price. By participating, and perhaps saving a few individual lives, we make it easier for the "legal" machinery of death to kill the rest. Whether that price is worth paying is a question each man or woman can answer for themselves, by peering into their own souls and consciences. Many, many, people can—and, I am confident, *will*—disagree with the choice I have made for myself. Reasonable people can disagree on the answer to the question of conscientious abstention. Reasonable people of conscience cannot, in my view, disagree that the question must be posed, and that it must be taken seriously. Conscious ignorance is not a defense to complicity in homicide.

6

"On Strike, Shut It Down"
An *Apologia* for Conscientious Abstention from the Machinery of Death

The Duties of a Law-Abiding Capital Postconviction Defense Lawyer

How ought capital postconviction defense lawyers to respond to the system I have been describing? This being America, capital punishment the social issue has become capital punishment the legal and constitutional issue. For a time (roughly 1972 to early 1983), the Supreme Court seemed determined to scrutinize states' capital punishment systems with some degree of care. No longer. The Court today has all but given up its earlier project of bringing rationality, order, and coherence to capital punishment as a legal system. In this era of deregulated death, states are more or less free to run the death penalty as they see fit.

The lower courts, state and federal, have gotten the message. Defense lawyers who are too aggressive have learned to expect the sting of the judge's wrath: threats of sanctions; abuse at oral arguments; even, as I learned in 1995, firing.

It is a terrible thing to strive for a professional lifetime, and come to the final realization that you have failed. For 14 years, my lifetime as a lawyer, I have participated in a legal system I knew was wrong if not evil. Banal evil, but evil nonetheless. I represented death row prisoners; encouraged other lawyers to do the same; wrote in favor of the creation of public defender offices to provide lawyers for the condemned; advocated the creation of such an office in Florida;[1] and, when the Florida legislature finally *did* create such an office, I started working at the place the day it opened its doors.

There was a larger question of my own complicity in Florida's legal system of state-sponsored killing, and there is a more painful paradox to this deal with the devil. I raised this question publicly at a 1991 symposium organized by Professor James Acker, the *Albany Law Review,* and the Albany School of Criminal Justice: Do I *want* to increase the comfort level of the Florida Supreme Court justices by my presence, participation, and tacit acquiescence? Do I *want* to alleviate the judges' squeamishness and help them sleep at night? Do I *want* to be part of the reason those justices can look in the bathroom mirror at the end of the day and say, "I'm OK; the system works, because look at how well these people were represented?" Once, during one of my oral arguments in the Florida Supreme Court, one of the justices went off on a rambling frolic about the wisdom of capital punishment as social policy. The others tried to pretend that it wasn't happening. I was, after all, in the South—and in some tangled way I knew that I was the justices' *guest.* Or maybe they were *mine.* Who knows? We southern people can be strange about manners. But there was no doubt that *somebody* was drifting over the line into unacceptable behavior, and I didn't think it was *me.*

I'm not sure I want to help the system to work by joining a game so rigged against my clients. With the dice so loaded against our clients, ought we play at all? "On Strike, Shut It Down?" Except that it *wouldn't* shut down, it would just keep chugging along. (When doctors in Los Angeles went on strike in 1976, the death rate declined, Lewis Lapham observed in *Harper's.*) Still, maybe we are only responsible for our own souls; better to open a frozen yogurt stand at the Hoboken train station or a used bookstore in Burlington. To paraphrase Westbrook Pegler, I used to be a member of the rabble in good standing. Uptown lawyers and judges would reply that I never left the rabble, even though the card I carry might have expired; and if truth be known, I hope they'd be right about that; they wouldn't mean it as a compliment, but that's how I'd take it. Fuck 'em if they can't take a joke. What the hell, as McWatt used to say in *Catch-22,* as he turned back to make another bomb run.

But then, on the other hand, how would I begin to explain to Joseph Spaziano that I had decided to abstain conscientiously from doing deathwork? Postconviction defense lawyers *do* make a difference.

In a paper I presented (but didn't publish) at the 1991 Albany symposium[2] on reinstating capital punishment in New York, I hoped to use the need for effective defense counsel in capital cases—at trial, on appeal, and in the postconviction process—as a frame of reference through which to explore the respective roles that scholars and defense lawyers can play in the capital punishment system envisioned by New York's then-proposed death penalty statute.[3] Using the lens of lawyers, I hoped to illuminate two essential points. First, high-sounding aspirational rhetoric aside, restoration of capital punishment in New York State would result in lousy representation for many people on trial for their lives. This is so because New York's indigent defense system is *today* incapable of providing decent lawyering services to people on trial for their liberty. This system would be taxed, perhaps to the point of disintegration, if capital punishment were added to its already crushing burden. Scholars, particularly empiricist social scientists, can and must document this reality. Is it credible to expect that New York, which *already* appears unwilling or unable to deliver quality defense services in *noncapital* cases, will keep its promises to provide quality legal aid in the exponentially more complex (and expensive) death penalty cases? Second, if New York's capital punishment system will be as underfunded as I predict, should defense lawyers conscientiously abstain from participating in such a sham of a system; do attorneys risk giving the system a (false) aura of fairness and legality by their very participation in the charade?

In my 1991 talk in Albany, I addressed some of the dilemmas confronting defense lawyers who must choose whether to participate in this system, and thereby lend it legitimacy. The issue, bluntly, was whether we do more harm than good by lending our efforts to holding this mess of a legal system together; or whether the better part of valor might be conscientious abstention from participation in a system that will be a nightmare of the capital punishment bureaucracy no matter *what* we do.

But would things really be so bad were New York to restore capital punishment? There is pretty solid legislative history that New York *intended* its death-eligible and death-sentenced citizens to receive the best legal services that money could buy. The statutory language itself was impressive, and provided as to counsel significantly more protection than that accorded under the federal Constitution as presently construed. The federal Constitution only guarantees a right to counsel at trial and on the first nondiscretionary direct appeal. Yet the New York statute—otherwise offensive to the federal Constitution—goes much further than the federal constitutional minimum in this area. It guarantees a right to counsel in postconviction as well: state postconviction and federal habeas corpus. The legislative history promised even more. New York citizens at risk of execution would be entitled to the *best:* F. Lee Bailey and Percy Foreman, if those legal lights would agree to take the cases. Those two kahunas were mentioned *by name* in the legislative history of past versions of the bill.

It sounded great. But what was wrong with this picture? What was wrong is that it was a bait and switch scam. And scholars, particularly social scientists and historians, must expose and document the scam. Scholars can identify the reality. The reality is that New York does not *today* provide the resources necessary to provide decent legal services in *noncapital* cases. By this I mean not the slightest disrespect to the hundreds of dedicated New York defense lawyers who work daily to do the impossible. That their job *is* impossible is the *system's* fault, not theirs; my point in Albany was that New York today is experiencing a *systemic* failure in its process of delivering legal services to the poor. As the New York State Defender's Association Back-Up Center wrote wryly in 1982, "Those who are familiar with New York's defense system may find it anomalous that while New York continues to rank 45th in its assigned counsel structure for non-capital cases, its legislature has declared that it will pay whatever is necessary in death penalty cases."[4]

I suggested that scholars were in a unique position to build upon the data compiled by the Center and presented in the its brilliant *amicus* brief to the New York Court of Appeals in 1984 in the Lemuel Smith case.[5] Anyone seriously interested in this problem must read this Brandeis brief. It documented five areas where New York public defense practice fell below national standards: availability and provision of counsel to eligible defendants; availability of skilled practitioners, investigators, and experts; political and professional independence; compensation; scope and duration of representation. So, realistically, one must begin with the premise that the indigent defense system—again, with emphasis on *system,* as opposed to individual actors within that system—is inadequate *now.* Then one must appreciate the enormous cost, quantifiable and hidden, of introducing capital punishment into the calculus. These costs have been documented to some extent; again, the pioneering work was done by the New York State Defender's Association Back-Up Center. Social scientists ought to build upon that and other studies.

If capital punishment is added to New York's already straining criminal defense delivery system, two outcomes are likely. First, an overloaded system will become totally swamped, with the result that *non-capital* cases will receive less resources than they do today. Much of the limited resources available today for noncapital cases will be diverted to capital cases. At the same time, *capital* cases will not receive the resources necessary to litigate them in a minimally effective way. This is what has happened in many other states, as documented by the ABA.

My point in Albany, at least the point I wanted to direct to social scientists, is that these are *factual* questions amenable to empirical study.[6] The New York death penalty bills denied the phenomenological reality. Scholars can document that reality. And they can do it in good conscience and in good faith, using the tools of their trade. All they need to do is report: Honest reportage condemns the process as it is and as it would be. "Just the facts, ma'am."

But what about defense lawyers? How ought defense lawyers to respond to the restoration of capital punishment in New York in the way I've described? In my Albany presentation, I conceded at the outset that I didn't know. Here, doing right becomes much more murky, at least in my view and my experience. I was emphatic that nothing I said ought to be construed as a plea for lawyers not to take capital cases. All I was saying was that lawyers must think about some of the implications of becoming a component of the death penalty system. Because, like it or not, that is what we become. I can't even answer these questions for myself. We all have to work out our own answers. My modest goal was to try to convey the complexity of the questions. Scholars absolutely have a role to play here. Do lawyers? Maybe. I wasn't sure. I didn't know. I still don't know, although, for myself, the case for conscientious abstention is far, far stronger today than it was in 1991.

Michael Radelet and George Barnard in 1988 and Richard Bonnie in 1990 published articles that spoke strongly, if obliquely, to the issue of conscientious abstention by defense lawyers.[7] They evaluate the ethical case for abstention by mental health professionals from the practice of restoring insane death row inmates to mental health, so that the state can execute them.[8] But, as Bonnie argues, the professional parallels between law and medicine are disturbingly close here. William Geimer addresses the issue directly in a recent article.[9]

I will revisit New York's capital punishment story near the end of this chapter. But now I want to return us to Florida.

The Defense Lawyer as a Punching Bag: Judge Edith Jones Gets Her Daily Aerobic Exercise

It is beyond serious dispute that innocent people are condemned to die. So are retarded people and crazy people. Lawyers for death row have shown again and again that race, poverty, wildly incompetent counsel, and popular passions send people to the electric chair, the gas chamber, the hangman's scaffold, the firing squad, and the lethal injection gurney.

No capital postconviction litigator worth his/her salt will be popular among their peers or the judges who decide whether their clients should be killed. For example, one candidate for a Texas judgeship campaigned for the court on promises of "sanctions for attorneys who file frivolous appeals especially in death penalty cases."[10]

Most often judges keep their frustrations to themselves, but occasionally they go public. A few years ago in *Franklin v. Lynaugh*,[11] the U.S. Court of Appeals for the Fifth Circuit (the court with jurisdiction over Texas, Mississippi, and Louisiana, three states with large death row populations) lectured lawyers for the condemned:

> It is plain our repeated admonitions to counsel against deliberately withholding [successive] filings until the last minute have fallen on deaf ears. . . .

Such tactics constitute not only an abuse of the writ but of the Court. We need not and will not tolerate them further. . . .

Grateful for the selfless efforts of counsel on behalf of the condemned, and conscious of the deeply-held convictions that often motivate those efforts, we have hesitated to act thus far. Deliberate withholding of claims until the eleventh hour has now become all but a standard tactic in these cases, however; and we can tolerate it no longer. Counsel are therefore admonished against such abuses and warned that in the future we will not hesitate to impose sanctions.[12]

It's a tired trope, but it plays well in the provinces. A few months earlier, in *Bell v. Lynaugh,*[13] Fifth Circuit Judge Edith Jones—whom President Bush interviewed for a seat on the Supreme Court before selecting David Souter[14]—delivered a lecture with rather a different tone. Judge Jones sputtered: "The veil of civility that must protect us in society has been twice torn here. It was rent wantonly when Walter Bell robbed, raped and murdered Fred and Irene Chisum. It has again been torn by Bell's counsel's conduct, inexcusable according to ordinary standards of law practice. . . . His motive in late-filing must have been to play 'chicken' with the state and federal courts on the eve of execution. . . . At a minimum, I would suggest that counsel who have engaged in delaying tactics should be struck from the rolls of the Fifth Circuit and not be allowed to practice in our court for a period of years. I would not rule out imposition of other sanctions as well."[15] Writing on *Bell v. Lynaugh,* a *New York Times* reporter observed that volunteer lawyers "say last-minute filings are necessities rather than cynical strategems [*sic*]. Lawyers handling death appeals are scarce and overworked."[16] A law professor at the University of Texas Law School asked about *Bell:* "If Judge Jones' remarks come to reflect the Fifth Circuit's view, how can we ask lawyers to devote themselves to these gut-wrenching cases? How can we ask them to devote thousands of hours of uncompensated time if their efforts are met with hyperbolic condemnation and threats to their livelihood?" The attorney for Mr. Bell was quoted as saying: "What I object to is the personal attack on my integrity." He said that he had spent "hundreds of hours" on the case, along with nearly $10,000 of his own money. "You have the judiciary begging us to take these cases, and when we do, they slam-dunk us all over the place for simply doing our jobs." In January 1994 the Fifth Circuit again threatened that sanctions, albeit in milder forms than the shunning suggested by Judge Jones, might be appropriate deterrence against late filings.[17]

The district court will be required to hold a hearing at some future date to determine whether and in what amount fees are to be awarded [the condemned inmate's] appointed counsel. As the district court is already aware, counsel waited more than ten weeks from the time the Court of Criminal

Appeals denied [the prisoner] relief on his second state habeas petition to file a second federal habeas petition and a motion to be appointed with the district court—only a few days before [the] scheduled execution. At the hearing, the district court should determine whether counsel, as an officer of the court, had good cause for delay in filing [the] second habeas petition and if not, whether the amount of fees to which counsel would otherwise be entitled should be reduced as a sanction.

Who's Sandbagging Whom: Killing Frog

The hydraulic nature of high-velocity crisis litigation renders and defines the psychic topography of litigators like me, people serving in the capacity of advocate. Viewing the impending execution as inevitable could become a rather nasty self-fulfilling prophecy.[18]

Yet confidence in victory against the odds has retarded my own process of dealing with the killing of my clients. This was brought home to me forcefully in the case of Ronald ("Frog") Straight, who was executed in May 1986 following a round of successive postconviction litigation. Ronnie Straight was a violent man, and his reputation stood out even against the background of Florida's condemned population. His violence could be casual and random, and he romanticized danger, "as if danger were a joke with a distant / and corny punchline, a huge shaggy dog / he'd risk his life to rise / to scratch behind the ears of."[19] When friends die, it feels as though a chunk of yourself has been ripped away in the darkness.

Before discussing how the Supreme Court disposed of Mr. Straight's case—and thus of Mr. Straight himself—I want to provide a few background facts, lest you think I sentimentalize the crimes of my clients. This is what Ronald Straight did. On July 30, 1976, Straight received a mandatory conditional parole from the Florida Parole and Probation Commission. By early September, he had drifted to Jacksonville, where he moved into an apartment occupied by Timothy Palmes, Jane Albert, and Albert's seven-year-old daughter. Jane Albert worked as a secretary for James Stone, who owned a furniture store. After discussing Mr. Stone's business with Albert, Straight and Palmes proposed that they would collect old debts of Stone's customers in exchange for 40 percent of the monies collected. Stone rejected their offer because they contemplated using violence against the uncooperative debtors. But Stone did offer Straight one hundred dollars for new clothes, and he told Palmes there might soon be a full-time job opening in the store.

By late September, Stone had decided not to employ Palmes, who then told Straight and another, "You know, I'm going to kill him." Straight replied that he should have that opportunity because Mr. Stone's offer of money was insulting. They agreed to wait until after the first of October, when customers' monthly payments would be in the store. On Sunday, October 3, 1976, Straight, Palmes, and Albert purchased lumber, cement, metal supports, and screws to construct a heavily weighted coffin. The next morning, Albert lured Mr. Stone from the store to her apartment, where her daughter told him to go to the back bedroom. Straight and Palmes were waiting for him and there struck him with a hammer, bound his hands and feet with wire and placed him in the box. For approximately 30 minutes, they beat him, amputated several of his fingers, and otherwise tortured him. During this time the victim repeatedly begged for his life. Finally, with a machete and butcher knife, Straight and Palmes stabbed Mr. Stone 18 times, eventually killing him. They took his watch, money and car. Meanwhile, Albert took $2,800 from the store. The weighted coffin with Mr. Stone's corpse was dumped into the St. Johns River. Albert, her daughter, Palmes, and Straight then left for California. When police there apprehended them, Straight resisted arrest by firing a weapon at the officers. Albert was granted immunity from prosecution by the state in exchange for her testimony as a witness. Palmes confessed, and the coffin was recovered from the river. Tried separately, Palmes and Straight were convicted of first degree murder and sentenced to death. Palmes was executed in 1984, Straight two years later.

Please forgive me, but for a moment I must get legalistic. Some of the law's technicalities are in this instance indispensable to appreciating what the U.S. Supreme Court did to Ronnie Straight—and why I so fear and loathe Mr. Justice Lewis Powell. At the time that Governor Graham signed Ronald Straight's death warrant and the prison scheduled Straight's execution, the U.S. Supreme Court had under consideration another Florida capital case, *Darden v. Wainwright;*[20] the Court also was deciding whether to grant plenary review in a third Florida case, *Hitchcock v. Dugger.* I filed, on Mr. Straight's behalf, a petition for writ of habeas corpus claiming that, at the time of his trial, Florida's capital sentencing procedure was constitutionally defective. We asserted that this claim was also presented in *Darden* and asked the Court to stay his execution pending the decision in that case (stays require five votes). We also petitioned for plenary review of his case, or certiorari (certiorari requires four votes). Finally, we asked for a "hold," until the Court could decide *Darden,* or at least until the Court could decide whether to decide *Hitchcock* (at that time, "holds" required three votes).

By a 5–4 vote, the Court denied Straight's application for a stay.[21] Justice Powell filed an opinion concurring in the denial of the stay, which was joined by Chief Justice Burger and Justices Rehnquist and O'Connor.[22] Justice Brennan dissented in an opinion joined by Justices Marshall and Blackmun.[23] Both the concurrence and the dissent addressed the question of the Court's obligation to stay an execution where the petition for certiorari presents an issue on which certiorari has already been granted and on which decision is pending.[24] Justice Brennan's dissent revealed that "four Justices have voted to 'hold' Straight's petition because they believe that it presents an issue sufficiently similar to *Darden* to warrant delaying disposition of Straight's case until a decision is reached in that case."[25] If the Court had actually granted certiorari in *Straight,* the posture of the case would have been identical to that of *Darden,* and the central question on the stay application would have been, as it was in *Darden,* whether the fact that four Justices had voted for certiorari triggers a duty for the remaining Justices to vote for a stay in order to preserve the Court's jurisdiction. Here, however, the vote of the four Justices was not for certiorari, but rather to postpone consideration of the petition until after the decision on the merits of Darden's claims. The question before the Court, then, was whether this difference was relevant for the purpose of determining whether the execution should be stayed.

In Joseph Heller's novel, *Catch-22,* Yossarian, a World War II flier, can't bear to go on any more missions, so he asks Doc Daneeka to declare him insane. The doctor tells Yossarian that a sane person would beg out of the missions, so Yossarian can't be insane. Only insane people wouldn't ask. That's Catch-22.

Justice Brennan viewed *Darden* and *Straight* as similar cases in all relevant respects. He argued that, for purposes of staying an execution, a vote to hold should be treated no differently than a vote to grant plenary review (certiorari):

> A "hold" is analogous to a decision to grant a petition for certiorari. The Court's "hold" policy represents the conviction that like cases must be treated alike. Like the Rule of Four, it grants to a minority of the Court the power to prevent the majority from denying a petition for certiorari when the minority is persuaded that the issues or questions presented in the case to be held are similar to a case that the Court is to decide. The principle is apparent: whether an individual obtains relief should not turn on the fortuity of whether his papers were the first, the second or the tenth to reach the Court. What counts is the merits. A vote to "hold" is a statement by a number of Justices that the disposition of the granted case may have an effect on the merits of the case which is to be held. The fact that a majority of the Justices disagree with the decision to "hold" does not warrant subversion of the "hold" rule any more than does disagreement by five with the decision to grant a petition for certiorari justify departure from the Rule of Four.[26]

Apparently referring to the Court's disposition of the stay application in *Darden* earlier that term, he added: "It is unthinkable to me that the practice that four votes to grant certiorari trigger an 'automatic' fifth vote

208

to stay an execution should not apply to a 'hold' when a man's life is in the balance."[27] For the dissenters, then, the requirement that held cases be treated identically to granted cases arises from the ancient common law principle that "like cases be treated alike."[28] Generalizing from the particular context of *Straight,* if the Court has granted certiorari in one case to resolve a particular issue, and, before it has reached a decision on the merits of that case, the same issue is presented in a second certiorari petition, the latter petition must be held pending the adjudication of the first case to enable both petitioners to be treated alike. Otherwise, the treatment of the two petitioners will depend on the "fortuity" of who filed first: the petitioner in one case will benefit from the rule, but the petitioner in the other will not.[29]

Justice Powell, joined by Chief Justice Burger and Justices Rehnquist and O'Connor, strongly disagreed with the claim that because the Court issues stays when four Justices have voted to grant certiorari, it must also do so when three (or four) have voted to hold. This conclusion rested on two arguments. First, Justice Powell stated that a vote to grant certiorari reflects a decision that the case raises an issue worthy of plenary consideration and creates the possibility that the petitioner will obtain a favorable outcome. Thus, the petitioner in a granted case has been found, in a sense, to "merit" the Court's consideration. In contrast, according to Justice Powell, a decision to hold may not reflect any such opinion regarding the "merit" of the petitioners' claims: "the Court often 'holds' cases for reasons that have nothing to do with the merits of the cases being held, as when we wish not to 'tip our hand' in advance of an opinion's announcement."[30] Justice Powell's second reason for treating held cases differently from granted cases is no more persuasive. Turning to the merits of Straight's particular claims, Justice Powell stated: "In this case, my vote to deny Straight's petition for certiorari—and therefore not to hold the petition for *Darden*[—] reflects my view that *no matter how Darden* is resolved, the judgment [in *Straight*] will be unaffected."[31] This rationale fully and properly explains why Justice Powell voted against holding the petition in *Straight.* That, however, was not the issue to which his opinion was supposed to be addressed. Instead, the question before the Court was whether the five Justices who voted against holding nevertheless had an independent duty to protect the Court's jurisdiction once their colleagues invoked the hold rule.

Fast-forward to the fall of 1994. That summer I spent some time working through the recently released papers of Justice Thurgood Marshall; in a way, I was relieved to find nothing in the papers concerning the *Straight* case. However, Marty McClain, CCR's Chief Assistant, found something I missed: four internal memoranda from Justice Lewis Powell to "The Conference": that is, to the other Justices. These memoranda, dated May 16,

May 19, and May 20, 1986,[32] and reproduced in the notes to this chapter, were never intended to be made public so soon after the event; the Marshall papers do not present a happy picture of the Justices behind the scenes, and one can see why Chief Justice Rehnquist was so angered by their release to the public.

Mr. Justice Powell's memos accused me of "sandbagging" (Powell's word choice). His *Straight* memos reveal a mind that was either stupid or malicious, I'm not sure which, and I don't much care. What I *am* sure about is that Powell was wrong; I didn't delay filing; I didn't sandbag or drag my feet in that or any other case, simply because sandbagging is an ineffectual tactic. Recently I ran across a transcript of an oral argument that Mark Olive, my former boss, and I did in the case of Joseph Spaziano, from that same period. The judge was concerned that we were sandbagging.

> MR. OLIVE: Judge, we knew, and Mr. Mello, when he first came to [the newly created public defender office] was screaming and shouting at me, "if we don't file this, we are going to be hit with, 'why hasn't it been filed?'" If we can get it filed without there being a [death] warrant in the case, which we should do and which I want to do," Mr. Mello said, "then we won't face this appearance of dilatoriness." Unfortunately, the day he walked in the door, or within a week, we had six warrants, and there were some more emergencies that we had to handle.[33]

There's more. Three weeks after Straight was killed the Supreme Court granted plenary review in *Hitchcock v. Dugger.* James Hitchcock, a former client of mine, was challenging the Florida standard jury instruction on mitigating circumstances. To oversimplify Hitchcock's constitutional claim, the trial judge's instruction, in essence, told the jury to consider *only* those portions of Hitchcock's mitigating evidence that bore relevance to the seven mitigating circumstances listed in Florida's capital statute, and so to ignore all "nonstatutory" mitigating circumstances in the case; since virtually all of the mitigating evidence presented by Hitchcock at trial was relevant only to *nonstatutory* mitigating circumstances, in effect the jury had been instructed to disregard most of his favorable evidence. Straight's jury had received an all but identical jury instruction, but I had been unable to persuade the Supreme Court to consider the issue in *Straight.* And when the Court *did* finally consider the claim, in *Hitchcock,* Justice Scalia, the Court's conservative Rottweiler, wrote for a *unanimous* Supreme Court that Mr. Hitchcock was right: "We think it could not be clearer" that Hitchcock's judge and jury believed they could consider only a few favorable facts, that the Florida standard jury instructions given in *Hitchcock* (and *Straight*) violated the same constitutional issue in both cases: the jury instruction on consideration of favorable evidence. (I intend no canine slur on Rottweilers, those large black and tan dogs named after a town in southwest Germany and known for their fearsome aspect, though lacking any vicious trait; these dogs have become the second most popular breed in America, and are panting hard after the most popular, the kinder, gentler Labrador retriever.) Mr. Hitchcock and Mr. Straight raised that selfsame issue in the same procedural posture: the issue was properly before the federal courts, on a first habeas petition (in *Straight,* the Florida Supreme Court had decided the issue on its merits, thus requiring the federal courts to do so as well—a fact we all but screamed at the Justices).

The Court issued its 9–0 opinion in *Hitchcock* in the spring of 1987. I learned about the *Hitchcock* decision exactly one year to the day after Ronald Straight was executed. I had raised the *Hitchcock* jury instruction in *Straight;* I knew the issue cold, because earlier in my legal career I had been co-counsel for none other than James Hitchcock himself; a year or so prior to my raising the jury instruction in *Straight,* I had helped write the jury instruction portion of Mr. Hitchcock's brief in the Eleventh Circuit. It didn't matter. None of it mattered. None of us mattered. Powell intoned in *Straight:*

> To the extent that Straight is repeating arguments made in his first habeas petition, there have been no changed circumstances that would justify rehearing and deciding those arguments again. (I note that we denied cert on Straight's *Lockett* claim only six weeks ago. No. 85–6264, cert. denied 3/31/86.) And to the extent he is adding new arguments, this is plainly an abuse of the writ. Straight has been relying on various versions of his *Lockett* argument since 1981. He and his lawyers have been fully aware of that argument's significance. The Court has repeatedly stated that it will not tolerate this kind of sandbagging of the judiciary in capital cases.
>
> For the reasons stated above, this is not a hold for *Darden* or *Hitchcock,* or for any other pending case. My vote therefore is to deny the application for a stay. If the case is held, I will write [an opinion in dissent].

The memos' dismissive and disgusted and exasperated tone, the bloodless, legalistic content, and the sense of vanity and moral cowardice evince Justice Powell's belief that Ronald Straight (meaning Mr. Straight's *lawyer,* meaning me) had strategically withheld potentially winning issues until the eleventh hour. Stay denied. Ronald Straight dies. Thus did Justice Powell elide responsibility and absolve *himself* of responsibility for the execution of Ronald Straight. It wasn't Justice Powell's outcome-determinative vote that killed Straight. It was me.

Lewis, Lewis, Lewis, as Felix Unger might say, with the resigned weariness of a spouse. Powell and I had been through this drill so often that I sometimes felt as though we were an old married couple, that we'd had the

211

same conversation so many times, it was so rotely familiar, that we could speak in shorthand, completing each other's sentences. I had lived for months in his mind; at times it was a very civilized place to be. But the Thurgood Marshall papers provide a unique window into Mr. Justice Powell and into the private thinking of the reticent racist from Richmond; Powell's *Straight* memos strike a tone of imperious and patronizing arrogance reminiscent of W. C. Field's routine: "Go away, kid, you bother me." Redacted of its camouflage of legalese, Powell was saying: "You lost because you got here a few weeks late, so go away and die quietly, get over it, stop bothering us with your constitutional kvetching."

Of course, in our pleadings we had to be polite to the likes of Lewis Powell. We *should* have beat him like a gong. Or maybe put a brick through the plateglass window in his house. It makes a wonderful noise, and the people inside run around like rats in a firestorm. It's *fun*. Smashing windows is *art*. The trick is getting *paid* for it. Of course, if I'd followed my own instincts, I'd be *shooting* at Mr. Justice Powell, instead of just smashing his windows.

Mr. Powell, as much a killer but with a different choice of weapons— Waterman fountain pen, rather than butcher knife—is alive and prospering in retirement. Had I to choose between Ronald Straight and the Phillip Morris tobacco company, Powell's longtime client, give me the remorseful killers anytime. At least Ronald Straight had the grace to admit that *he* killed his victim, rather than trying to fob off his responsibility on someone else. Mr. Straight, he dead.

But even assuming that Powell was correct, and that I was as clever as he suggested I was, his *Straight* memos evince a coldness of heart and barrenness of soul that is extraordinary. Fine: If the court thinks I am playing unethical games with the Justices, then punish *me;* sanction *me;* disbar *me;* but don't take your frustrations out on my indigent, condemned client. I am, and was in 1986, a member of the bar of the U.S. Supreme Court, and thus subject to sanctions for unethical behavior. It beggars the imagination—or at least *my* imagination—to think that even Mr. Justice Lewis Powell would send a man to his death because of a mistake, in Powell's own denuded view, made by the man's lawyer.

Powell's complaint was that we raised the winning constitutional issue a few weeks too late for his delicate sense of propriety. I thought of Powell when Ann Richards likened her opponent's criticism of her record to a husband's criticism of his wife's ironing: He says, "Why did you fold 'em and put 'em in a drawer? I like 'em on the hanger." Or, as Strother Martin, the boss in *Cool Hand Luke,* said to his chain-gang constituent, Paul Newman, "What we've got here is a failure to communicate."

It was more than that, of course. The legalistically arid affect and tone of the Supreme Court's internal memoranda in *Straight* didn't obscure the essential narrative theme; Justice Lewis Powell's subtext all but says, "This guy's lawyer (i.e., me) is sandbagging us. We're the highest court in the most powerful nation on earth; we're the *Supreme* Court, doggone it, and we will not be trifled with. We'll show that uppity attorney we mean business. We'll kill his client." Well, I guess Powell showed *us*.

Thus did Lewis Powell—legal technician, laconic hack of low cunning—turn the prose of law poisonous. Not only was there no poetry, but there was no visible trace of humanity in Powell's imperious pronouncements. In a different, less mortal context, the fatuous bleatings of this enraged domehead might appear comic, or at least ironic. Reading the Marshall papers is a bit like reading somebody else's mail: The closeness between writer, text, and reader is so claustrophobic, so intimate that it turns into violence—the violence of the word, as Robert Cover put it, and a violence so rabid that it almost becomes farce. Almost. But not quite, because those words killed a man, and words like them killed other men.

Soon after James Hitchcock won in the Supreme Court, he sent me a letter I will always cherish:

To: Michael Mello   6–4–87
Dear Sir:
    I just wanted to drop you a line or 2 to say thanks for all your help in my appeal. I know your work rarely shows appreciation. But know your efforts are appreciated deeply by me.
    Thanks to you and a lot of other people who worked on my case together you gave me a new lease on life.
    Even if I get resentenced to Death—It will have bought me valuable time. Which I was nearly out of. And I hold life precious And where theres life and time—theres possibility of change and hopes for things to get better.
    So thanks—And take care and keep punching.
                    Sincerely
                    James Hitchcock No. 058293 R-3-5-9
                    P.O. Box 747
                    Florida State Prison
                    Starke, Fla. 32091

But it wasn't enough to save Ronald Straight. Or the other Florida prisoners executed prior to 1987. Once again, David Von Drehle got it exactly right:

    The courts can change their minds very quickly. That was the message of the second death penalty ruling published on that April day in 1986, Hitchcock v. Dugger. Technically, the U.S. Supreme Court had never ruled on whether Florida's death penalty law limited a defendant's right to present evidence in favor of a life sentence. But the Court had been asked repeatedly to take the question under consideration, and repeatedly the Court had refused. And sixteen people went to Old Sparky. That suggests the majority had made up their minds. Now they changed them: The justices ruled unanimously—all of them, the conservatives, the moderate, the liberals—that the law had been "authoritatively interpreted by the Florida Supreme Court" to mean that mitigating evidence was limited.

Craig Barnard was right. The Florida Supreme Court had denied this for some eight years—sixteen executions—but Barnard had kept at it, kept hammering, despite scolding and even ridicule from judges and prosecutors. The public complained bitterly about lawyers like him, with their delaying tactics and technicalities. Politicians had proposed all sorts of bills to limit his access, and the access of his colleagues, to the appellate courts.

Now the U.S. Supreme Court said unanimously that Barnard had been right all along. Justice Scalia, the new conservative tiger, wrote the opinion. "We think it could not be clearer . . . " he intoned, in his confident, definitive way, that the judge and the jury believed they could consider only a few favorable factors. It could not be clearer.

The Court's opinion in Hitchcock was brief, scarcely hinting at the years of litigation that had gone into Barnard's victory. In the end, the subtle shift Barnard had made in his argument was the fig leaf the justices grasped to cover their sudden change of heart. . . .

The opinion was written to make it seem that a very small point had been decided, but Craig Barnard could see that a new generation of appeals had been opened for the men who had been on Florida's death row the longest. What was true for James Hitchcock was at least arguably true for all of them . . . dozens of them, and they were the men closest to Old Sparky. And Hitchcock had an even larger meaning for Barnard. After the ruling, he proudly told his troops: "When people ask why we keep appealing, why we raise these issues over and over, why we never give up fighting . . . tell them to look at Hitchcock."[34]

So James Hitchcock lives, and wins a unanimous decision in the U.S. Supreme Court; Ronald Straight, who had the identical issue, is electrocuted. I raised the same issue in both cases in virtually identical language; were the mortally different outcomes caused by my failings as a defense lawyer? Or was it just pure, dumb luck? The legal issues were everywhere; the constitutional tools necessary to craft those legal issues into winning constitutional claims was there all along in both cases. "Water, water, everywhere / and all the boards did shrink; / water, water, everywhere, / nor any drop to drink," Samuel Coleridge wrote in *The Rime of the Ancient Mariner.*

Mr. Straight's execution was particularly painful for me because in the final few weeks I'd become unusually close to my client and to his family. He was so frightened of dying, but more frightened to show it. I know that my friend wanted to cry, but wouldn't in front of another man. I knew this because, as his lawyer, I had to educate myself about his history, including his father, the breakfast-table sadist who would make men out of boys. This meant not bringing your friends into the fire zone you called home. It meant going to school with fingerprints on your face and arms.

The final gasps of Ronald Straight's litigation felt like a savage street fight. I, at least, have never recovered from it. When he did finally come to appreciate that they *were* going to kill him, and soon, he asked me to witness his execution. (His words seared: "Man, I don't want to look out from that chair and see only cops, prison guards and reporters.")

Mr. Straight and I spent hours on the phone and finally agreed that I wouldn't witness it: "That would fuck you up, man, just *fuck* you *up,* and the other guys need help. You can't get fucked up for David. He thinks he's going down." This from a lifer who had committed a murder-for-money of unusual brutality, whose *nom de row* was "Frog" because he was always jumping on people. Not to sentimentalize the man or his crime, but *Jesus.* His was an act of pure selfless altruism; he didn't have to do that, and until now only one or two other people knew about it at all. The man's poise and quiet dignity in the face of almost certain impending electrocution took my breath away. He and I had this conversation around dusk on the evening before he was scheduled to be, and in fact was, killed. So we agreed that I wouldn't witness the execution itself; Larry Spalding, our office's chief administrator, would serve as our designated execution eyewitness, as he had in all other executions of the office's clients. But I would be a pall-bearer at Straight's funeral, and I'd comfort his momma as best I could, and I'd try to tell his story. Those are promises I'll spend the rest of my life trying to keep. This book constitutes partial performance, as we say in the contracts biz. I still think about him every day.

The legal endgame went down to the wire, and Straight's lawyers had to stay glued to our office phones in Tallahassee to juggle the fast-breaking decisions by courts in Jacksonville, then courts in Atlanta, and finally the U.S. Supreme Court in the District of Columbia; the case circled the drain for a long time, as the Supreme Court Justices entered a series of baby stays of ever shorter duration. The last stay application was denied by the U.S. Supreme Court, 5–4, less than half an hour before the killing occurred; by that time he was already strapped into the electric chair, and there wasn't even time for us to say goodby. I followed my usual post-execution ritual of taking myself out to a restaurant for a meal of steak and good red wine, although that was just going through the motions of grieving. Eight years after the execution, I learned that Ronald Straight had died at peace; to reverse the genders in Virginia Woolf's *Orlando,* "he lay content. The scent of the bog myrtle and the meadowsweet was in his nostrils."

Mr. Straight's repose was in large measure made possible because he

215

was able to confess to his priest shortly before the killing took place. This confession was dicey because in the final stages of Phase II of Deathwatch, the prisoner's visits are monitored by prison guards; to allow Mr. Straight a modicum of privacy during his last confession, two of his final visitors broke into spontaneous song, thus providing enough white noise that the guards were unable to hear the confession; by the time they figured out what was happening, it was over. Mr. Straight's visitors also brought him a bouquet of gardenias; unable to find a place to buy flowers on Route 121, the visitors picked a handful of gardenias from a local garden ("Now, remember, if someone calls the law, you're a *nun*"—which was true; and they *did* knock on the front door before liberating the flowers). "His rest shall be glorious." Isaiah 11.10.

At the time of Mr. Straight's electrocution, I had been out of law school for four years, a judicial clerk for 12 months, and a practicing attorney for a little more than two years. That was 11 winters ago. I was 28 years old; he was 43 years old; I remember thinking: I'm too young for this shit.

The grief took me by the throat like an LAPD chokehold and wouldn't let go. I was the little boy in Lincoln's graceful story, who stubbed his toe and said he was too old to cry and it hurt too much to laugh.

I don't have the words; only poets might. Poetry attempts to cheat reality; it pretends that it takes reality's worries seriously. It shakes its head knowingly. Oh, it says, another earthquake. Injustice again. Floods, revolutions. Once again someone has reached old age. Poetry fears that its secret will be discovered. One day reality may notice that the heart of poetry is cold. That poetry has no heart at all, just big eyes and an excellent ear. Reality will suddenly understand that it was only a bottomless source of metaphors for poetry, and it will vanish. Poetry will remain alone in the world, mute, empty, sad, and incommunicable.

At the time Ronald Straight was killed in 1986, there really wasn't *time* for me to grieve; our public defender office was mandated by statute to represent *everyone* on Florida's death row who needed our services (then about 200; oh, that seems so long ago!). The weird and twisted mathematics of death row's demographics in the 1980s meant that our office had other clients with other execution dates, and with other briefs to write and other facts to investigate.

As in battlefield triage, the most critically wounded got the highest priority, until they died. Then their priority became zero, and you moved on to the next case. Quickly. Preferably without looking back.

But that's exactly what Powell's deadly memos in *Straight* forced me to do: look back, long and hard, and *remember*. Amnesia was better, or at least it felt healthier. Reading Mr. Justice Powell's words in 1994, eight years after he wrote them, in what he undoubtedly believed was the secrecy of the Court's Conference, I identified with the protagonist in the terrible aircraft scene in *Catch-22,* where Yossarian tries to save the fatally wounded radio gunner, bandaging the wrong wound as Snowden dies ("I'm cold," Snowden whimpers, "I'm cold." "There, there," Yossarian says. "There, there."). Time was, I feared and loathed Mr. Justice Powell for what he did to my clients under pretense of law. Now I just loathe him. No, actually, it's deeper than that. I hate him.

As grotesque as it was to read Lewis Powell's lies about me, there was a thrill to it, also. Perhaps the final insult would have been for him simply to have ignored me: Hunter Thompson wrote in the summer of 1973 of the "Gross sense of injury I felt when I saw that my name was not included on the infamous 'enemies of the White House list.' "

Powell's bankrupt and worthless and useless defense must, it seems to me, have been driven by his craving for a "place in history," a place that is even now being etched out in acid by eager historians and former law clerks at the University of Virginia Law School. The left and right forks of Powell's tongue were each fed by the same venomous vein.

On balance, I'm glad I found Mr. Justice Powell's *Straight* memos, and I'm glad I read them: Tim O'Brien is right that "you got to *listen* to your enemy." Powell's memos suggest that Camus was also right: "This is a world without God—this is a world of hypocrites affecting the language of justice and moral outrage." And surely one can feel pity for an arid, constipated figure who writes (and thinks) about death cases like a lugubrious bureaucrat and then inflicts a moralistic cliche upon someone whose job it is to try to persuade the Justices that *his* client's case is just like that *other* prisoner's case—an argument that turned out to have been right all along. Yet those memos made me hate Lewis Powell, visceral hate, bone marrow hate, the kind of hate that stays with you in your dreams. To be precise (a vice of my trade) and honest (a personal vice, which runs counter to the ethos of my trade), I *possess* hatred. I don't think that this makes me a hater, in the sense I referred to earlier, because *I* possess the hatred, rather than vice versa. But maybe that's just wishful thinking. I've tried to live an archetype of forgiveness, but I can't forgive Powell. Not for this. Not this time.

Enabling: The Ghost in the Machinery of Death

Reading Powell's memos concerning the destruction of Ronnie Straight brought home the reality that although I am a participant who advocates for the condemned, I am a participant nonetheless—a genuinely Faustian bargain.[35] Powell's memos made me wonder about the extent to which I was serving to legitimize the system by helping to provide sanitized executions, executions with the aura of legalism and therefore the appearance of fairness.

To paraphrase Millard Farmer, had I become the mask of the executioner? I sure felt like it, as I stood beside Mr. Straight's mother at his graveside. Her sobs were like nothing I've ever heard before. I surrendered, I took it in, let it fill me up: this chorus of regret and despair, her grand artillery of grief. And again when I sat in the Reading Room of the Manuscripts Division of the Library of Congress, reading and rereading Powell's deadly memos. As the poet Samuel Hazo has written, obscurity, like fame, equally has a story to tell.[36] If Ronald Straight is forgettable, we're all forgettable.

Make no mistake: The participation of good defense lawyers in the capital punishment process *does* make the system, legal and beyond, feel more comfortable about executions. This is especially so when the resources provided for defense services are grossly inadequate and when the law, substantive and procedural, is increasingly hostile to the claims of death row inmates. We are complicit. We do the best job we can do, but by participating in this process we risk, to borrow a term from the recovery industry, becoming "enablers."

Enabling is our expected role, our *demanded* role. Departures from this role are not received warmly by courts, legislatures, or the public.[37] Given the sheer numbers and complexity, as well as the emotional power, of these cases, perhaps it is inevitable that death row attorneys will be attacked as unethical and unprofessional by opposing attorneys representing the state, and that some of this almost prosecutorial rhetoric will find its way into the utterances of judicial officers. The most common charges (brought against me by Lewis Powell in *Straight,* for example), include the intentional thwarting of justice by strategically withholding winning issues until the last moment, by raising frivolous claims, and by using all available procedures to obtain a stay. In particular, it is becoming increasingly common to hear accusations that legal papers are intentionally filed so close to the scheduled execution date that courts must grant stays simply to consider the claims raised—which usually turn out to lack merit anyway.

Capital postconviction work is hard enough without being trashed by the judges whose job it is to decide whether our clients deserve to die. Deathwork is debilitating, emotionally draining, complex work; low pay at best, often no pay plus covering all your expenses out of your own pocket; long hours; criticism at best and vilification at worst from your friends, family, business associates, prosecutorial opponents, media; zero prestige.

Ignorant and misleading criticism from judges won't be the only reason defense lawyers will shun death row clients, but it might well be the last straw. It sure can be one reason among many. For instance, Charles Sevilla represented Robert Alton Harris in federal court before Harris was killed in the California gas chamber in 1992. Four years later, Sevilla still refused to discuss the case and says he probably will never represent another death row inmate. "You're not going to get any accolades—except possibly from some of your peers—nor any understanding from the public," Sevilla was quoted as telling a *Los Angeles Times* reporter. "If the case becomes a high-profile one, you will be vilified in every way imaginable. It's a painful and frustrating experience."[38]

Two events proved the catalysts for my decision to become a conscientious objector in the capital postconviction wars: the near-killing of "Crazy Joe" Spaziano and the death of CCR. The unifying narrative theme connecting these two events was my complicity in the capital punishment system, a system I have come to believe is evil. Thus, the resonance of Hannah Arendt's *Eichmann in Jerusalem*.

Killing "Crazy Joe" and Jerry White

Were it up to the legal machinery of death, Joseph ("Crazy Joe") Spaziano would have been electrocuted by the state of Florida at 7:00 A.M. on June 27, 1995, for a crime he did not commit. This portion of the chapter tells the story of why he is, for the moment, still alive.

I tell "Crazy Joe" Spaziano's story for four reasons. First, his case is emblematic of much that is wrong with capital punishment as a legal system: rogue cops, tunnel-visioned prosecutors, inept defense lawyers, and formulaic judges all contribute to the ultimate danger that the state will execute an innocent person. Second, I have represented Joe, on and off, for 14 years. I believe he is innocent.

Third, until Mr. Spaziano's case deteriorated into a parody of justice, I believed that the Office of the Capital Collateral Representative, the agency created by the Florida legislature to serve as counsel for the condemned, was beneficial for death row inmates. I am now convinced that having CCR as your lawyer is worse than having no lawyer at all.

Fourth, this case and, more precisely, the ways in which the courts and CCR treated that case, led to my decision to stop participating in the postconviction system of capital punishment. Mr. Spaziano's is my last capital case.

Lies I Told My Client

No. 83–5596
Spaziano v. Florida

Dear John,

Thurgood, you and I are in dissent in the above. Would you mind "oinking" for us dissenters?

Sincerely,
["Bill"]

Dear Bill:
Oink!

Respectfully,
["John"]

—Memoranda exchanged by Justices William Brennan and John Paul Stevens near the end of the Court's 1983 term.

Capable counsel has in effect subsidized injustice; they have given skillful and vigorous defense at great personal and financial costs to themselves; faced with provision of inadequate resources with which to mount a defense, they have done the best they could with what they had. This is an honorable choice by competent attorneys, but it is not the only choice. . . . Perhaps it is legitimate for competent counsel to consider whether their laudable efforts are helping to mask injustice, and therefore delay the day when "close enough for government work" will be rejected by the courts and by the profession.

—William Geimer, "A Decade of Strickland's Tin Horn: Doctrinal and Practical Undermining of the Right to Counsel"

The toughest test in writing about Joseph Spaziano's case is to convey the scale of the event. Some things are easily quantified. One can write of a plane crash that took 68 lives or a hurricane that wiped out a trailer park in Homestead. But how to quantify 20 years on death row for crimes you didn't commit? Five death warrants? Being strapped into an electric chair to pay for somebody else's crime?

Consider:

- There was absolutely no physical evidence linking Mr. Spaziano to the brutal murder of a young woman named Laura Lynn Harberts. Mr. Spaziano's conviction was based solely on the testimony of a teenager who did not "remember" anything relevant about Spaziano or the alleged crime until police removed him from a juvenile detention facility, dropped pending investigations on breaking and entering charges, and then "refreshed" his memory with grossly suggestive hypnosis sessions, conducted by a self-styled police "ethical hypnotist." This teenager, Anthony DiLisio, is now 37 years old. In 1995, DiLisio and his lawyer

220

formally joined Mr. Spaziano in asking the governor for clemency and in asking the courts for a new trial on *both* the Harberts homicide conviction and on a previous, unrelated rape and mutilation of Vanessa Dale Croft, of which Mr. Spaziano was convicted in 1975— again, based in large part on the purchased testimony of Anthony DiLisio. Today, DiLisio has, under oath, disavowed his testimony in *both* cases, saying he had been "brainwashed" by the police at the time.

• At his trial, the prosecution withheld evidence that police had better suspects in the murder case and in the rape case.

• The prosecution offered only one piece of circumstantial evidence at trial; the prosecutor knew the evidence was false but withheld the truth from the defense, judge, and jury.

• A postconviction investigation showed that the jury had serious doubts that Mr. Spaziano was guilty, but because he was a member of the Outlaws motorcycle brotherhood, a frightening presence in south Florida in the early 1970s, the jurors voted him guilty to keep him off the streets. As a hedge against the real possibility that Joe Spaziano was innocent, and in an effort to show mercy, they recommended a life prison sentence, but the judge overrode their recommendation and sentenced Joseph Spaziano to death in Florida's electric chair.[39]

• Less than a decade after Mr. Spaziano's conviction, and shortly after his conviction became final on direct appeal, the Florida Supreme Court ruled that testimony gathered through the use of hypnosis cannot be used as evidence because it is unreliable and potentially harmful. The court relied on experts who said that subjects who undergo hypnosis become extremely vulnerable to suggestion and form hardened beliefs that what they "remembered" while in the trance, no matter how true or false, is absolutely accurate. The ruling, which came during Theodore Bundy's appeals, was not retroactive. So even though the Florida Supreme Court indirectly discredited the *only* evidence used to convict Joseph Spaziano, he has been sitting on death row for 20 years, a victim of lies, incompetent counsel, police collusion, and a court system's cowardly reluctance to admit error and reverse itself; a victim of a "clemency" board that dispenses mercy based on polling data and that hears only from those who want executions carried out more swiftly than ever, who regard all claims of innocence as equally dubious, who see electrocution of human beings as the last proof that Florida's government can do something right, after all.

Joseph Spaziano is not on death row because he's a murderer or because he's a rapist. He's on death row because he's an Outlaw—president, *in absentia,* of the Outlaws motorcycle brotherhood, Orlando Chapter. Joe Spaziano will not be killed by one individual, but by the silence of many.

Enter the Miami Herald

You may fairly ask, if it is so certain that Mr. Spaziano is innocent or deserving of a new trial, why have the courts, after 19 years of considering well-crafted appeals, not said so? The answer is not that the courts were not convinced one way or the other, but that they are bound by the procedural rules they created. It is a court rule that if the defense attorney did not make proper objections during the trial, then the error cannot be raised on appeal.[40] Also, federal courts must defer to state procedural rules.[41] Because of this, no court has ever ruled on the merits of the evidence demonstrating Mr. Spaziano's innocence.

I wrote my first legal paper on Joseph Spaziano's behalf in 1983, 14 years ago. That document was a petition for plenary review (certiorari) in the U.S. Supreme Court, and it did not have my name on it because it was written and filed before I had passed the bar exam. In the decade-plus since, I have filed on Mr. Spaziano's behalf postconviction petitions, stay applications, and appellate briefs in state and federal courts. None of them made the slightest difference. The only thing I have ever written for Mr. Spaziano that mattered was an opinion-editorial piece for the *Miami Herald.* My editorial was followed up by a series of brilliant investigative articles by Lori Rozsa, with Gene Miller and Warren Holmes, and by equally superb editorials and columns by James J. Kilpatrick, Tony Proscio, Tom Fiedler, Martin Dyckman, Tom Blackburn, the *Gainesville Sun, Tampa Tribune, St. Petersburg Times,* and *Palm Beach Post.*[42] This investigation and reporting, and not anything done by lawyers or judges, caused Governor Chiles to stay Mr. Spaziano's death warrant. A follow-up piece by a team of ABC's *World News Tonight* journalists, along with pieces in *The Nation, New Republic,* the *Washington Post,* and *The Economist,* caused the governor to continue the stay.[43] When the U.S. Supreme Court denied plenary review in Joseph Spaziano's case, in January 1995, I did something I have never done before, and will never do again, in a capital case: I attempted to take the case to the media.

Specifically, I took the case to Gene Miller. Twenty-one years ago, in 1975, Miller published a magnificent book, *Invitation to a Lynching,* that resulted in the pardon and release of two black men, Freddie Pitts and Wilbert Lee, who had been railroaded onto death row for a crime they did not commit.[44] I had never met Miller before, but I was thoroughly intimidated by his reputation in Florida as a skeptic when it came to death row claims of innocence. After his book was published in 1975, Miller was contacted by countless prisoners, all of whom attempted to enlist his aid in their causes. Miller stated at the time, and in the two intervening decades, that he would never again become involved in a capital case.

A friend of mine from our Florida deathwork days knew Mr. Miller's daughter. My friend persuaded the daughter to persuade Mr. Miller to accept a short telephone call from me. During that 10-minute telephone conversation, Mr. Miller was gracious but firm. He appreciated Mr. Spaziano's dilemma, but, although my desperation appeared genuine, it was extremely unlikely that he or the *Miami Herald* would insert themselves into Mr. Spaziano's case. Mainly as a courtesy to his daughter, I think, Miller agreed to read a book chapter I had written on Joseph Spaziano's case. I Federal Expressed the chapter, and I fully expected never to hear from him again.

To my surprise and delight, Miller called me the following day. My memory is that the telephone conversation went something like this. Miller asked, "What aren't you telling me in your book chapter? You can't be telling me the whole story here, because no case, not even a Florida capital case tried 20 years ago, could possibly be as bad as you describe in your chapter."

I replied that the book chapter I had written was as close as I was capable of coming to objective reporting. Because anyone reading my book would know my biases and predispositions, in that chapter I had bent over backward to construe every piece of evidence and every single logical inference that could reasonably be drawn from that evidence in favor of the prosecution and against Mr. Spaziano's claim of innocence. After letting me speak my piece, Miller politely reiterated his belief that there must be something I was leaving out of the chapter, such as the credible evidence that my client was guilty of murder. I repeated that there was nothing else. Miller repeated that there must be something else. We paused. I then suggested that there really was only one way that he could determine whether I had left anything out. I offered to send him the trial transcripts.

Mr. Miller was adamant about what he was willing to read, and, specifically, what he was not willing to read. "I want the trial transcripts, the police reports, the transcripts of the hypnosis sessions of the State's star witness, the audio tapes of those hypnosis sessions, and nothing more. I don't want briefs. I don't want legal memoranda. I don't want anything else written by any of Mr. Spaziano's defense lawyers—especially not anything written by you." Fair enough. More than fair. I promised to arrange to have the materials he wanted Federal Expressed that very day.

A few days later, Governor Lawton Chiles signed Spaziano's death warrant. The warrant was signed on May 24, 1995. The prison scheduled the execution for approximately four weeks hence, at 7:00 A.M., June 27, 1995. I fully expected, and Mr. Spaziano fully expected, that he would be killed on schedule.

But he was not, and it was not because of anything that I or any other lawyer did, or anything that any court did. Rather, it was solely because of the efforts of Gene Miller and his colleagues at the *Miami Herald*. I later learned that Miller had given the raw documents in the case to Warren Holmes, his investigator on the Pitts and Lee case. Mr. Holmes's skepticism about claims of innocence is, if such is possible, greater than that of Gene Miller. On the Friday of Memorial Day weekend, Miller dropped the trial transcripts, police reports, and other material on Holmes's desk and asked him, as a personal favor, to glance through them. As Warren Holmes told me later, he was not pleased. He hoped, and fully expected, to spend about half an hour reading through the trial transcript of the murder case and concluding, as he has concluded in virtually every other capital case he has investigated, that Mr. Spaziano is, in fact, as guilty as the prosecution argued he was at trial. But a half-hour became an hour, became two hours, became four hours, became eight hours, became 10 hours. There just was not any evidence there. Warren Holmes knew that Spaziano had also been convicted of the rape and mutilation of Vanessa Dale Croft, and so he dug into the trial transcript of the rape case. And, *mirabile dictu*, Holmes concluded that Spaziano did not commit the rape, either.

I wish I had a tape recording of the first conversation I had with Warren Holmes in connection with the case. It went something like this. Mr. Holmes asked me whether I was a defense lawyer. I answered in the affirmative. There was a long pause. Mr. Holmes then asked me whether I happened to have any problems with the rape case. I told him that I did. He asked me whether I had mentioned those problems to Mr. Miller. I told him that I had not. Incredulous, he asked me why. And I confessed. I was afraid that if I had told Miller that I thought that the police had framed Joseph Spaziano for the rape, in addition to framing him for the homicide, Miller would dismiss me as a flake. What else, I visualized Miller asking me at the time, did the state frame your client for? JFK? Jimmy Hoffa? Elvis?

I then had a telephone conversation with Warren Holmes of the sort that a defense lawyer has maybe once in her life, if she lives right and is very, very lucky. In essence, Holmes laid out for me in his own words why he thought that Spaziano was innocent of both the homicide and the rape. He told me that he had reviewed between 1,200 and 1,400 trial transcripts in his time as a law enforcement officer and as a private investigator. Out of all of those transcripts, he had thought three men were innocent. Pitts. Lee. And Joseph Robert Spaziano.

I thought we were home free. Surely, now that the legendarily skeptical Gene Miller and the even more legendarily skeptical Warren Holmes were convinced there was significant doubt about Spaziano's guilt on the homicide, the *Miami Herald* would jump into the case. Eventually, the *Herald* did jump in, with both feet and with guns blazing. But even with the vociferous advocacy of Gene Miller and Warren Holmes, for a time—which to me seemed interminable—the powers-that-be at the *Herald* remained unconvinced. It wasn't Miller's call; it was John Pancake's call, the *Herald's* state editor. Miller and Holmes fought like wildcats to persuade Pancake to assign a team of reporters to conduct a top-down reinvestigation of the factual circumstances of Joseph Spaziano's conviction and condemnation, but there did not seem to be enough time. The killing was scheduled for only a month away. I had come to them too late. My errors in judgment and timing had contributed to the imminent execution of a man who I believed was innocent.

Gene Miller called me with a proposition. He and Holmes had persuaded the *Herald* to publish, in its "Viewpoint" section, an opinion piece that I would write and that would appear under my byline. Miller then followed up on a point that I had made in my first telephone conversation with him. Had I really meant it when I told him that, of the 70 or so condemned prisoners I have been involved with over the past 12 years, Mr. Spaziano was my only innocent client? I told him yes. He told me that I needed to say that, explicitly and forcefully, in the first paragraph of the opinion piece that the *Herald* was willing to publish.

I told Mr. Miller that there were 70 reasons why I could not write such an opinion piece in the pages of Florida's flagship newspaper. The first 69 reasons were my other 69 clients. How would they feel, how would their families feel, to read in the pages of the *Miami Herald* that their former lawyer believed, at least implicitly, that they were in fact guilty all along? It was unethical, according to the rules and regulations governing the ethical behavior of lawyers admitted to practice before the courts of Florida. More importantly, it was wrong.

My seventieth reason for not wanting to write the opinion piece was personal and selfish. I was already in hot water with the Florida bar in connection with my short-lived representation of Paul Hill on his direct appeal challenging his murder conviction and death sentence for the assassination of an abortion doctor and his armed escort. One of Mr. Hill's "pro-life" movement lawyers had filed a complaint against me with the Florida bar. The complaint was, in my opinion, patently frivolous. But it did not seem an opportune time for me to engage in an act of civil disobedience against the rules and regulations governing the behavior of Florida bar members.

Miller said he understood and appreciated my reticence. He would fully understand if I chose not to write the opinion piece. All he was doing was informing me of the factual reality. The *Miami Herald* would not insert itself into Mr. Spaziano's case and the paper would not assign a group of reporters to investigate the crimes unless I wrote, and they published, the opinion piece. I tried to bargain. Let me write it, but let it appear under someone else's byline—his, any name other than my own. No. It had to be written by me. It had to be written in the first person. It had to appear under my own name.

So, of course, I agreed to write it, and to write it in time for it to appear in the Sunday, June 4, 1995, edition of the *Miami Herald*. Over the next few days, I tried to write it as best I could and, with the critical assistance of Laura Gillen, Deanna Peterson and Bob Trebilcock, we got it in on time.

Mr. Miller not only reworked, edited, and polished the piece, but he decided that he could not, in good conscience, treat Mr. Spaziano's story as competitive. Consequently, and undoubtedly causing some controversy within the newspaper itself, Mr. Miller arranged for my Viewpoint piece to appear simultaneously, on June 4, in the *Miami Herald*, the *St. Petersburg Times*, and the *Orlando Sentinel*.[45] This is what I submitted to the *Herald*:

> This is a story about failure, the systemic failure of Florida's assembly line of death in general, and my own personal failure in particular.
>
> Allow me cut to the chase: I want to tell you about a former client of mine, Joseph Robert Spaziano. For the past 19 years Mr. Spaziano has lived on Florida's death row. Joseph ("Crazy Joe," to quote from his murder indictment) Spaziano is scheduled to be executed in Florida's electric chair at 7:00 a.m. on June 27. That is in 19 days—less than three weeks hence.
>
> Mr. Spaziano is, I believe in the very marrow of my bones, innocent. By "innocent" I mean exactly that: the state got the wrong man. I'm not referring to "legal technicalities"; I'm not saying he did it, but he was crazy; I'm not saying he did it, but he had a bad upbringing.
>
> I'm saying he's innocent the old fashioned way, as my mother would put it. Joe Spaziano didn't do the crime, period. This fact makes him unique among my death row clients. When I was a Florida appellate public defender in the mid 1980s, my caseload was 35 capital cases, more or less; in all, over the past 11 years, I have been closely involved in approximately 70 death row cases.
>
> Now, let me introduce myself. This is the first time I have written on behalf of a former client in an attempt to focus public attention on a very real person with an impending execution date. I don't try my cases in the media, and I am writing this with full knowledge of the potential consequences to my license to practice law in Florida. I write as a private citizen and not as Joseph Spaziano's attorney, which I no longer am.
>
> There're a lovely couple of lines in Harper Lee's *To Kill a Mockingbird*. Atticus Finch tells his daughter: "Scout, simply by the nature of the work, every lawyer gets at least one case in his lifetime that affects him personally. This one's mine, I guess." This one's mine, I guess.
>
> I am telling you about Joseph Spaziano's case for two reasons. First, Mr. Spaziano is most likely going to be killed in Starke, on schedule, notwithstanding the powerful likelihood that he's an innocent man. He's going to be killed, not because his trial was fair or because his execution is

lawful. That doesn't matter. What matters is that his case has already been "reviewed" by the courts. Because the courts have "reviewed" his case once, they are loath to do so again—notwithstanding inflated political rhetoric about "10 years of repetitive review." For this reason, and this reason alone, his death warrant will probably be carried out. His head and right ankle will be shaved; he will be measured for his funeral suit; he will say goodbye to his mother and niece and daughter and friends; he will be strapped into Florida's electric chair in full view of two dozen witnesses selected by the prison, most of whom will be strangers to him. He will be electrocuted by an executioner whose anonymity will be protected by the prison, and who will be paid $150 for his services rendered. Joe Spaziano will be electrocuted in our name. In your name. And in my name.

The second reason I am telling you about Joseph Spaziano is because his story is emblematic of much that is wrong with the jury override, in part because his jury recommended against death due to their nagging doubts that he was guilty at all. The judge disregarded the jury's recommendation and imposed death, yet now we know that the jury's doubts were well founded. Post-trial discovery of the facts surrounding the hypnotism of the state's key witness destroys any confidence in the conviction of Mr. Spaziano.

For the past 11 years, I've been a dutiful and polite little lawyer who played by the rules and trusted the legal system to correct the monstrous injustice in this case. I told my client that the state courts would not permit an innocent man to be destroyed, but I was wrong. They will, and they are: they've used legal technicalities to ignore the critical aspects of this case. The hypnotically-manufactured evidence against Mr. Spaziano would be per se inadmissible today—but the decision saying so came too late to benefit Joe Spaziano; what ought to be an unceasing search for truth has devolved into a morbid game of "Gotcha."

Then I told my client that the federal courts wouldn't permit an innocent man to be killed, but, again, I was wrong. Judge Carnes' opinion in Joe Spaziano's case spent more pages whining about the length of the brief I was not permitted to file than it spent addressing the points about innocence I wanted to make in the brief.[46] In 1992, the United States Supreme Court held that innocence is not an issue cognizable in a habeas corpus proceeding; four Justices, in a subsequent case, did not even want to give Lloyd Schlup, who had a videotape showing him somewhere else at the time of the murder for which he was condemned to die, a hearing to consider the new videotaped evidence. The Court, in effect, was saying: "Go to the governor and seek clemency if the criminal justice system has miscarried." So I did.

Finally, I told my client that executive clemency was a fail safe designed to prevent execution of an innocent man, but I shouldn't have bothered, because, for all practical purposes, "clemency" in Florida does not exist. As Martin Dyckman has written, while Florida governors in the past weren't afraid to grant life sentences in cases involving credible claims of innocence, there have been no clemencies for Florida's death row since the third year of Bob Graham's first term—14 years ago. One final time I was wrong: Governor Lawton Chiles said that it's the court's job—not his job—to see to it that the right person is being executed. So the courts deny responsibility and say it's up to the governor; the governor denies responsibility and says it's up to the courts.[47] The outcome of this deadly game of blind man's bluff is that Joe Spaziano will be executed for a crime he did not commit, and nobody is willing to take responsibility for this abominable perversion of justice.

Mr. Spaziano is no Boy Scout. He's an unreconstructed biker (President, in absentia, of the Outlaws Motorcycle Brotherhood, Orlando Chapter), and a convicted rapist (that conviction is also highly questionable, but it's another story). He is also a self-taught artist, and he is my friend. His family is my family.

I am convinced that Mr. Spaziano is innocent, but I can't prove it with certainty. I have no compelling physical or testimonial evidence proving that Mr. Spaziano did not commit the crime for which he is condemned to die. What my investigators and I have done is more a matter of vaporizing the State's case of guilt than proving his innocence, which, I know, isn't the same thing.

Mr. Spaziano was accused of murdering Laura Lynn Harberts, a vibrant young woman whose body was discovered in a garbage dump in Seminole County, Florida, on August 21, 1973. She was identified by dental records, and was last seen alive on August 5, 1973.

Beverly Fink was Laura Harberts' roommate in Orlando. According to Ms. Fink, the last time she saw Ms. Harberts was on a Sunday afternoon, about August 5, 1973. The previous night, Ms. Fink and her boyfriend, Jack Mallen, were preparing to leave their apartment. At that time, Ms. Harberts was on the phone and, as Fink and Mallen were leaving, Ms. Harberts said, "Hold on a minute, Joe," and then waved goodbye. Ms. Fink stated she and Mallen returned to the apartment about 2:30 or 3:00 a.m. and Ms. Harberts was asleep on the couch.

Later that same night, someone knocked at the door. Ms. Harberts asked Jack Mallen to go to the door but not open it, and tell whoever it was to go away; it was too late at night, and she did not want to talk to him. Mr. Mallen complied with the request and the person went away. Ms. Fink further testified that she had spoken briefly with Mr. Spaziano once sometime in July 1973, when he came by the apartment on a weekend afternoon and asked to talk to Ms. Harberts. According to Ms. Fink's recollection, the man said he had met Ms. Harberts in Eola Park. After talking for a few minutes, the man left.

On cross-examination, Ms. Fink testified that Ms. Harberts was not dating Mr. Spaziano, and there was another "Joe" who worked at the hospital with Ms. Fink and Ms. Harberts. Ms. Fink could not say which "Joe" Ms. Harberts was referring to on the phone the night before she was last seen.

228

William Coppick and Michael Ellis testified that approximately two years prior to Ms. Harberts' disappearance, Mr. Spaziano lived in a trailer in the same general area where Ms. Harberts' body was found. Mr. Coppick also testified that Mr. Spaziano told him about finding some bones, but Mr. Coppick did not say where or exactly when the alleged conversation took place. Mr. Ellis further stated that Mr. Spaziano took him to the general area where the body had been found. He concluded that Mr. Spaziano went to get some marijuana "stashed" there. Again, Mr. Ellis was unsure of the date when this took place.

The State's chief witness was an acquaintance of Mr. Spaziano named Anthony DiLisio, who was sixteen years old at the time of the events in question. He testified that he accompanied Mr. Spaziano to a dump, for the ostensible reason, according to DiLisio, that Mr. Spaziano could show him some women that he had raped and tortured. DiLisio testified that he saw two female bodies in the dump. He did not at the time report what he had seen to the police.

DiLisio testified he never believed Mr. Spaziano and that he thought Mr. Spaziano was bragging to impress him. DiLisio further indicated that he idolized Mr. Spaziano and that he wanted to ride motorcycles with him. DiLisio said he did not report what he had seen because he wanted to become a member of the Outlaws Motorcycle Club.

Tony DiLisio was the State's case. The prosecutor told the trial court during a motion to preclude DiLisio's testimony that "if we can't get in the testimony of Tony DiLisio, we'd absolutely have no case here whatsoever—So either we're going to have to have it through Tony, or we're not going to have it at all." And as the State argued to the jury in closing argument, if they did not believe Mr. DiLisio, they had to acquit Mr. Spaziano. This closing argument proved prophetic. After lengthy deliberation, the jury stated that it was having trouble reaching a verdict. The jury was told to continue deliberations and was told by the court that it was their duty to try to agree upon a verdict (a so-called "dynamite charge"). They tried again and reported they still did not believe they could reach a verdict. The court gave a more emphatic "dynamite charge," late in the evening, and a verdict of guilty was returned within minutes. The only evidence that could have possibly convicted Mr. Spaziano was Mr. DiLisio's testimony, and the reason for the juror uncertainty was accurately portrayed by the State: They "struggled so diligently with Mr. DiLisio's testimony."

In contrast to the difficulty the jury had in reaching its guilty verdict, it reached an almost immediate sentencing verdict of life imprisonment. This verdict suggests strongly that the jury was attempting to use the life verdict as its only available safeguard against the overall weakness of the evidence. If it had believed the State's evidence, the jury would have believed that Mr. Spaziano had committed a brutal crime. Yet the jury voted for life.

What was not revealed to the jury that convicted Mr. Spaziano, or to the judge that sentenced him to death, was that there was a strong likelihood that the singularly devastating DiLisio testimony was manufactured.

229

Mr. DiLisio did not "remember" his story until he was under police hypnosis, and the hypnosis sessions were conducted in such a suggestive and unprofessional manner that the resulting "recall" and testimony deserve no respect. Indeed, the Florida Supreme Court eventually held (several years after Mr. Spaziano's direct appeal) that hypnotically refreshed evidence is so unreliable as to be inadmissible by law in Florida. But the state courts said this decision came too late for Mr. Spaziano.

At trial, counsel for Mr. Spaziano attacked DiLisio's testimony by using the traditional tools of cross-examination. He stressed that DiLisio was an admitted drug user before, during, and after the alleged dump incident. DiLisio admitted that while on LSD he sometimes hallucinated, especially when he combined marijuana and LSD. In closing argument, counsel urged the jury to feel sorry for DiLisio but not to believe him. He suggested that DiLisio might have honestly been confused, either by drugs or by the police. This strategy of discrediting Mr. DiLisio was central to any hopes of a defense victory in this case, but in pursuing it counsel failed to employ his most potent weapon. Counsel did not reveal the fact that DiLisio never "recalled" the alleged incident at the dump until after he went to a police hypnotist.

Courts now recognize that testimony extracted by hypnosis is untrustworthy and should be treated with skepticism. The testimony of any witness is subject to the inaccuracies of observation, and hypnosis exacerbates this unreliability. There is a public misconception that hypnosis acts as a form of truth serum, preventing a witness who has been hypnotized from lying. To the contrary, "the commentators and experts are united in the view that hypnotized subjects can and occasionally do prevaricate." Hypnotized subjects engage in "confabulation," the invention of details to supply unremembered events in order to make the account complete, logical, and acceptable to the hypnotist. This tendency to fill in the gaps of memory is extremely difficult to detect, because "[a] witness who is uncertain of his recollections before being hypnotized and who has confabulated during hypnosis will become convinced that the post-hypnotic recollections are absolutely accurate. Such a belief can be unshakable, last a lifetime, and be immune to all cross-examination."

In 1985, Florida joined the growing roster of jurisdictions which hold that hypnotically-produced testimony is per se inadmissible. But that court decision came too late for Mr. Spaziano; the Florida Supreme Court refused to apply its 1985 hypnotism decision to Mr. Spaziano's case. Thus, Mr. Spaziano will be electrocuted on June 27 due to a legal technicality.

Had Spaziano's trial lawyer investigated available sources, he would have found an abundance of medical scientific evidence proving the inherent unreliability of hypnotically-generated testimony. By reading Gene Miller's magnificent 1975 book *Invitation to a Lynching*, counsel would have learned that Joe McCawley, the hypnotist who hypnotized DiLisio, was a laughable mountebank, and that McCawley's hypnotic skills had previously sent two innocent men to Florida's death row, in the infamous

230

case of Freddie Pitts and Wilbert Lee. By 1976, when Mr. Spaziano went to trial, scientists had advanced several arguments for excluding hypnotically-warped testimony, including (1) hypnosis was not widely accepted as a reliable method of "refreshing" memory; (2) subjects respond according to what they perceive as the response likely to please the hypnotist; (3) subjects "confabulate," or fill gaps in their memories; (4) the recall induced by hypnosis may be totally incorrect; (5) the subject can willfully lie; (6) cross-examination of a hypnotized witness is virtually ineffective; and (7) no set of procedural safeguards is effective in eliminating these problems. Mr. Spaziano's trial counsel could and should have made the same arguments at trial.

I have a juror affidavit that says that the jury recommended life imprisonment rather than death because they weren't so certain that he was guilty at all, but their only choices at the guilt/innocence stage were acquittal or conviction of first degree murder. They knew he was an Outlaw (his club colleagues attended the trial, in full biker regalia), and they were squeamish about letting him loose. The trial took place in the mid-1970s when bikers were considered by many "normal" people to be domestic terrorists, and they didn't want him running loose on the streets of Orlando. So the jury found him guilty of first degree murder, but voted (9–3 or 10–2, according to the juror's affidavit) against the imposition of death. There was a catch, however: the trial judge didn't know the reason for the jury's life recommendation, and Florida law does not permit a judge to factor such lingering doubt into a capital sentencing decision. A defendant "cannot be a little bit guilty," in the memorable words of former Florida Supreme Court Chief Justice Joseph Boyd.

Former Spaziano juror Lena Lorenzana was in her eighties when I met with her on the porch of her home in Orlando. Ms. Lorenzana signed an affidavit for me, discussing the jury's recommendation of life imprisonment instead of the death penalty. It said:

> One of the major reasons for [nine or ten] of us favoring a life sentence was our doubts about whether Mr. Spaziano was guilty of the crime as charged. I distinctly remember this being expressed as a factor in many of the jurors' minds.
>
> One of our major concerns was the testimony of the 16-year-old boy, Tony Dilisio, which we didn't entirely believe at the time of the trial. Had we known his testimony was prompted by hypnosis, I believe it would have made a difference.

The post-trial investigation did more than reveal the hideous unreliability of DiLisio's hypnotically-warped testimony. As mentioned previously, the victim—Laura Harberts—had a roommate, Beverly Fink. At trial, Ms. Fink testified that Ms. Harberts had received a telephone call from "Joe" just before the time of her disappearance. The State implied and argued that the telephone call was from Joe Spaziano. Although Mr. Spaziano was able to argue that the call may have been from any other "Joe," including Joe Suarez, the exhibitionist whom Laura Harberts dated from time to time, the jury was clearly led to believe that the fact that the caller may have been Mr. Spaziano was an incriminating piece of circumstantial evidence. Yet, we now know from recently disclosed police files that the police had determined that the caller was indeed Joe Suarez and that the state failed to disclose this fact. In addition, Joe Suarez denied to the police that he had been with the decedent on August 5, 1973. Yet, in an undisclosed documented interview, the police were able to conclude that Suarez was with the decedent on the night of her disappearance.

During the investigation, the State believed that Laura Harberts' killer was Lynwood Tate, although none of the documents suggesting Mr. Tate's guilt were disclosed to the defense at trial. Mr. Tate was given several polygraph tests about his role in the killing, which he failed. He was a known rapist and all of the investigators involved concluded that Tate had committed the murder. Tate told the investigators "on several occasions" that "he didn't know whether he committed the murder" and "that if he did, he would like to know it." At one time, "an indication was made [by Tate] that there was a possibility that he may have done this and did not know it." Most important, the police located an eyewitness, Mr. William Enquist, who positively identified Tate as the individual he observed at the scene of the crime with several women near the time of the killing. None of the documents containing this information were disclosed to the defense at trial.

The State also failed to disclose the contents of an interview with Mr. DiLisio conducted in October 1974 (about six months before the first disclosed interview). Although only police notes confirm this interview (as opposed to a transcript or tape), it appears that this was the first police interview with DiLisio where the subject of the murders in the dump arose. The police notes indicate that all Mr. Spaziano had ever (allegedly) said to DiLisio was "man, that's my style." The report does not indicate that Spaziano admitted to the murder or that he gave any other information to Mr. DiLisio, but he only supposedly claimed that it was his "style." Of course six months later, in the first recorded statement of DiLisio, the story had radically changed. By the time of the trial DiLisio claimed even more extensive statements were made by Mr. Spaziano. Yet, defense counsel did not have available the contents of the first interview which would have constituted strong impeachment of DiLisio's trial testimony.

By now you are probably wondering: So what's Spaziano's alibi? Where was he, if he wasn't killing Laura Lynn Harberts? It's a fair question, and Mr. Spaziano wishes, more than you'll ever know, that he knew the answer—and so do I. But the truth is that he doesn't know where he was on the day Laura Harberts was murdered. Recall that police suspicion did not focus on Mr. Spaziano until two years after Ms. Harberts was killed. Now, quick: Can you say where you were, and with whom, two years ago today—on June 4, 1993? I don't know either, but I keep a journal, so I could find out. Joe Spaziano didn't keep a journal in 1972, so he didn't remember where he was or what he was doing when he was questioned by the police two years later.

Mr. Spaziano is not a good personal historian. Part of the reason for this is that at the time of Ms. Harberts' disappearance in 1972, Mr. Spaziano was living the nomadic and chaotic life of an Outlaw. But there is another reason Mr. Spaziano is not a good historian, and it's a subject about which Mr. Spaziano is, to this day, embarrassed. He would rather be executed for a crime he didn't commit than let me tell the world why his nickname was "Crazy Joe" long before he joined the Outlaws. You see, Mr. Spaziano is crazy. That's the truth. It's a truth that shames and humiliates him in his own eyes.

Mr. Spaziano's medical history shows that on May 29, 1966, he suffered a severe head injury as a result of being run over by an automobile. He was admitted to Rochester, New York, General Hospital on May 29, 1966, with a "fracture of the skull in the right parietal area, contusion of the brain with accompanying coma, contusion of the urinary bladder, a fracture of the right ulna, a right peripheral facial paralysis, a 4 inch laceration of the scalp, and a 1 inch laceration of the right wrist." Mr. Spaziano was in a coma for several weeks and was discharged on June 20, 1966. Upon discharge, however, Mr. Spaziano "was still somewhat confused and only semioriented. In general he appeared rather indifferent to his mental difficulties." The significance of this injury in relation to the recent evaluations of Mr. Spaziano by medical experts cannot be overstated. "Closed head injuries," such as Mr. Spaziano suffered, "are the most common cause of organic personality syndromes in peacetime." Temporal lobe seizures, classically manifested as dream-like states which Mr. Spaziano experienced after his head injury, augment the development of an organic personality syndrome.

Most importantly, recent medical literature demonstrates that the symptomatology of the kind of head trauma suffered by Mr. Spaziano includes deficits in short and long term memory. That's why, when he was arrested in 1975, he had no alibi for his whereabouts two years previously, when Laura Harberts disappeared.

This case haunts me like no other. If you're like most folks I know, I am the kind of capital criminal defense lawyer you probably love to hate. Between 1983 and 1986, I was a capital appellate public defender, initially in West Palm Beach and later in Tallahassee, at the Office of the Capital Collateral Representative (CCR). Over the past couple of years, I've free-lanced with CCR, representing a handful of condemned clients. I first represented Mr. Spaziano in 1983–87. When I left Florida in January 1987, I turned Mr. Spaziano's case over to a Tallahassee attorney, but promised to re-enter the case if it reached the federal court of appeals.

I tried to persuade the state trial judge, the justices of the Florida Supreme Court, a federal district judge, three judges on the Eleventh Circuit Court of Appeals, and the Justices of the Supreme Court of the United

States. I have failed utterly to convince a court to look at any of this. They let me file briefs and listen politely to my oral arguments. But I can't get them to hear me. No one has listened.

I like to think that I represent all my clients, guilty or not, as zealously as humanly possible within the bounds of the law. I didn't think it would make a difference to me that one particular client is innocent. But it does; losing feels worse, and it's harder to convince myself that I ought to participate in a system so crassly and hideously and grotesquely unfair that it can't even ensure that the person being executed is actually guilty of the crime. That matters. It matters to me.

I have had fairly extensive contact with Mr. Spaziano throughout the course of working on his case. I corresponded with him and visited him on death row. In numerous conversations with me, Mr. Spaziano has always forcefully maintained his innocence of the murder of Laura Harberts. He has never suggested that he was involved in any way in that crime, not even to the point of asking or answering "hypothetical" questions that might assume his guilt. On the contrary, Mr. Spaziano has insisted that he was in no way involved in the crime. In fact, Mr. Spaziano's firm assertions of his innocence have, on occasion, been a source of some tension in our relationship. From the time that I first became involved with his case (in the fall of 1983), up until now, the case has not been in a posture that permitted us to introduce evidence of Mr. Spaziano's innocence. By the time the case reached our hands, the legal issues had "narrowed" to the constitutional challenges to his conviction and sentence. Accordingly, I had to tell Mr. Spaziano—more than once—that, at least for the time being, our hands were tied; we were limited to those constitutional issues in our appeals.

While expressing frustration at the slow pace of his appeals, and anger that the courts have failed so utterly to uncover the truth about the crime, Mr. Spaziano has continued steadfastly to maintain his innocence, and has never wavered in his belief that if the truth about the crime were brought to light, he would be exonerated and released.

As discussed above, even a jury that was not told about DiLisio's hypnotism had serious doubts about Joe Spaziano's guilt. That jury recommended life imprisonment as a hedge against the very real possibility that an innocent man had been convicted; the judge disregarded the jury's recommendation and imposed death. Yet now we know that the jury's doubts were well founded. Our post-trial discovery of the facts surrounding the hypnotism of the State's key witness destroys any reasonable confidence in the conviction of Joe Spaziano.

Joe Spaziano has steadfastly maintained his innocence. From his personal history, particularly the car accident and its aftermath, it is easy to understand why no alibi has ever been established. Joe Spaziano's memory and incoherence explain why he is a terrible personal historian. The most recent psychological and neuropsychological evaluations completed note that his "blanking out" during conversations is probably the result of petit mal seizures, one of the lingering results of the severe head injuries suffered in the car accident.

I have won some cases, but those aren't the ones that haunt my dreams. The cases I revisit nightly are the near misses, the cases I lost by a one vote margin. I can't shake the feeling that if only I had been smarter, or a better lawyer, or if I could make language sing the way David Von Drehle does, then maybe that would have meant life rather than death for a human being I had come to know better than a spouse knows her husband. Our roles— lawyer and damned—could, and often did, require us to become that intimate. As I mentioned above, I often became close with my clients. But Joe Spaziano's case is different, because he's innocent and because I've failed so completely to convince any Florida governor or any court anywhere of that fact.

I've done the best I'm capable of doing, but it hasn't been enough. Mr. Spaziano will be destroyed at 7:00 a.m. on June 27, and there's not a thing I can do to stop it.[48]

Miller also contacted people he knew at the *New York Times,* the *Washington Post,* and *Newsweek,* and James Jackson Kilpatrick, the conservative columnist from my own native commonwealth of Virginia.[49]

Most importantly, Miller and Holmes persuaded the *Herald* to assign a crack team of investigators, led by Lori Rozsa, to reinvestigate the case. Ms. Rozsa pulled off a number of miracles over the ensuing couple of weeks, but I must mention one. The State's case against Joseph Spaziano rested, as noted above, on the testimony of Anthony DiLisio. In 1985, my investigator had tracked DiLisio down to a small town in California. DiLisio refused to talk to my investigator about the case. In March 1995, CCR's investigator tracked DiLisio down to Pensacola, Florida. Not only did he strike out with DiLisio; his heavy-handed approach made it extremely unlikely that DiLisio would talk to anyone about Spaziano's case. So, when I gave Lori Rozsa Mr. DiLisio's address in Pensacola, I fully expected that she would strike out as well. The first time she approached DiLisio, he slammed the door in her face. The second time she approached him, he slammed the door on her foot. The third time she approached him, he let her into his kitchen, and spoke with her for several hours about Joseph Spaziano and himself.

The ensuing news stories written by Rozsa and her colleagues at the *Miami Herald,* combined with columns and editorials in other newspapers in and outside of Florida, caused Governor Chiles to stay the execution of Mr. Spaziano—an execution Chiles had ordered by signing the death warrant in the first place.[50]

I want to be very, very clear on this point. As surely as I live and breathe, but for the intervention of Gene Miller, Warren Holmes, and Lori Rozsa,

Joseph Robert Spaziano would have been executed, as scheduled, at 7:00 A.M. on June 27, 1995.

After the stay came down, other media picked up the story. Jeffrey Rosen wrote an editorial in the *New Republic*. Bruce Shapiro wrote a beautiful piece in *The Nation*. In the *National Law Journal,* Linda Gibson traced the *Herald*'s role in the case. The *Washington Post,* the *Christian Science Monitor,* and *The Economist* all wrote substantial news stories about it. And ABC's *World News Tonight* conducted its own, extremely thorough, factual reinvestigation.[51] Producers Nina Alvarez and Beth Grossbard, along with reporters Mark Potter and Michelle Genessy, generated a meaty and accurate account of the case.

The *Miami Herald* was responsible for obtaining the stay of execution. And ABC News was responsible for holding the stay of execution for as long as it held. During my 12 years as a capital postconviction litigator, I swore that I would never try any of my cases in the media. Now, I swear that I will never again try one in court.

When I first decided to take Mr. Spaziano's case to the *Miami Herald,* one of my friends and colleagues in deathwork asked me whether I had lost my mind. I had not lost my mind; I had found my courage. And I had found my voice.

Giving Up on the Federal Courts

By 1995, 12 years of deathwork had left me extremely distrustful of reporters, and, in a few instances, that intuitive distrust was confirmed by my experiences in Joseph Spaziano's case. A few, but only a few, reporters who called me were only interested in a quickie story. But those were not the reporters with whom I chose to deal.

The reporters with whom I chose to deal all met two simple criteria. First, they did their own homework, their own prosaic, gumshoe reporting. Second, if their own independent reporting confirmed my contentions that Mr. Spaziano was, in fact, innocent and that he had been framed by the State, then those reporters would not be intimidated by the governor, or the Florida Department of Law Enforcement, or the courts, or the prosecutor. They would report what they found in their own investigation of the case. These reporters knew they were getting into a marathon, not a sprint. They were in it for the long haul. They were looking for the long view, the wide-angle lens shot.

The State, under the auspices of the Florida Department of Law Enforcement (FDLE), also did an investigation that was limited to one narrow focus: the credibility of Anthony DiLisio, the State's only witness of substance against Mr. Spaziano at the murder trial and the rape trial. The

FDLE spent two months investigating, at an undisclosed expense to Florida taxpayers, to generate a report.

However, there was a catch. The FDLE report was ordered sealed,[52] an order upheld by the Florida Supreme Court.[53] Once again, Lori Rosza's investigative reporting exposed the FDLE report as a fraud.[54] But the secret police report was enough for Chiles. He signed a new death warrant on August 24, 1995.[55]

In investigating Joe Spaziano's case after the legal system's abdication of responsibility for killing this innocent man, the newspaper saved that legal system from its own spinelessness in cases where death is the punishment. If the Florida judiciary ends up sparing Joe Spaziano's life, it will be said: The system worked. In fact, it was reporters who worked. The legal system did its powerful best to kill. It still will likely succeed in that effort.

So I gave up on the postconviction courts. I tried to explain why in a memo written shortly before Joe was scheduled to be killed on his fifth death warrant.

CONFIDENTIAL MEMORANDUM

DATE: August 27, 1995
TO: Pat, MO, Jenny, Matthew, Steve, and George
FROM: Mello
RE: Why I will *not* take Joe Spaziano's case back into federal court on a successive habeas, or into the state trial court on a fifth Rule 3.850 motion

All of you are understandably skeptical about my decision not to take Joe's case into Federal court. I'll try here to sort out my thought processes.

There is an undeniable legal benefit in going into every possible court to seek a stay: The system of capital punishment is random, and we might get lucky and get a stay from the federal courts—if we don't ask, we don't get. There is also a psychological benefit: we feel better, because we've done all we can do as lawyers; our client feels better, knowing that we've knocked on every legal door; the judges feel better, because they can tell themselves "the defense system worked because the defense lawyers scurried like rats from court to court raising every conceivable issue (we chide them for doing that, but we don't mean it)"; ditto, the public feels better.

So the benefits of the eleventh hour dash are clear and familiar to us; we've all been through the drill before. But every litigation decision we make—be it to go into court or not to—entails risks as well as benefits. The risks are as unquantifiable as the benefits. The best I can do here is try to *identify* the risk as well as the benefits in choosing whether to take Joe's case into federal court under a fifth (count 'em) warrant.

First, the costs of foregoing the federal courts are minimal: to paraphrase Lincoln in 1862, for Joe Spaziano, there is no North—not on a successive habeas petition, at any rate. The "federal courts" here mean Kendall Sharp, Ed Carnes, and the Big Bill Rehnquist Court. Sharp has never granted CPC [Certificate of Probable Cause to Appeal], much less a stay or evidentiary hearing. In 13 years on the bench, Brother Sharp has not once found a single claim by a condemned prisoner to be non-frivolous—to say nothing of sufficiently potentially meritorious to justify a stay. Ed Carnes—the Alabama capital prosecutor cross-dressing as a federal appellate judge—requires no comment. Mr. Ed wrote the Eleventh Circuit's opinion on Joe's case, and he spent more energy bitching about the page limit for my brief than he devoted to my evidence of innocence I *raised* in the goddamn brief. So we clear the Eleventh Circuit on a successive habeas petition in a 20-year-old case on which the Court granted plenary review in 1984, with no stay and no CPC. The innocence-based cert. petition I filed in November did not get a single vote for cert. And that was on a first habeas—a habeas based on pretty compelling evidence of innocence, some of which wasn't procedurally defaulted.

Our evidence on innocence is pretty powerful, but we don't have a videotape showing that Joe was elsewhere at the precise time of the murder. The videotaped alibi isn't a hypo, of course; that's what Lloyd Schlup had in his successive habeas petition. And all Schlup got out of the Rehnquist/Scalia/Thomas Court was an evidentiary hearing—and that only by a razor margin of 5–4, the same number of votes we'd need (5, not 4; remember *Streetman* and *Herrera?*) for a stay in Joe's case.

So the real legal test, as opposed to the black letter law, is: If you have a videotaped alibi, and you're in successor habeas status, then you might be able to scrape together five votes for a *chance* to prove your claim at an evidentiary hearing—a hearing which, in Joe's case, would occur before Judge Kendall Sharp. And a hearing before Sharp is the *most* we can expect to get out of the federal judiciary. We have little chance of getting even that, it seems to me. We don't have a videotaped alibi, or anything close. Like *Schlup*, we're a successor; unlike *Schlup*, Joe ran innocence as the centerpiece of his first habeas—and of the 13 federal judges who could have considered that evidence, none did—not a single one. In federal court, innocence is irrelevant. The Supreme Court says so, and the lower listen—as they're required to do.

So I think we give up little by foregoing the federal courts. Let's take their procedural default/retroactivity/abuse-of-the-writ rhetoric seriously. Fuck 'em.

On the other hand, the risks of going into federal courts are great. We waste our scarce time and energy on essentially hopeless litigation before judges who don't think we belong there—and, if the Supreme Court's pronouncements in *Teague* and *Sykes* and *McCleskey* and *Coleman* and *Parks are* the law, then those judges are right. We *don't* belong in federal court. The Supreme Court has said so again and again. Maybe it's time to start *listening* to those robed assholes.

More significantly, it seems to me, by doing the 50-yard dashes from court to court, we shift attention from Chiles and from the FSC [Florida Supreme Court]. Most critically, we diffuse responsibility among Chiles, the FSC, and the federal courts. It's an interstitial, systemic manifestation of the Private Slovik syndrome and the *Caldwell* problem: If everyone shares some responsibility for the killing of this innocent man, then no one does.

I have long thought that diffusion of responsibility was the fundamental systemic and institutional problem with this case. The jury wasn't sure Joe was guilty, but they knew he was an Outlaw, and it was Orange County in the mid-1970s. So they split the difference, and they found Joe guilty but recommended life. The trial judge didn't know about the jury's lingering doubt about guilt, so he overrode the imposed death. So the jury shifted responsibility to the judge, and vice versa. And the same thing happened at each other sequential step along the capital assembly line. The FSC deferred to the jury and trial court, as principles of appellate practice dictate. And the federal courts deferred to the state judiciary, as principles of federalism command.

Finally, the judiciary (state and federal) deferred to the clemency authority of the governor—which, under *Herrera* and *Graham* they were supposed to do, no matter how idiotically unrealistic *Herrera* and *Graham* might seem to us. Finally, in 1995, the responsibility for executing this innocent man rested on the shoulders of one person: Lawton Chiles. The buck stopped there, and he knew it. That's why the *Herald*'s coverage persuaded him to stay the warrant in June, I'm convinced.

And, I'm afraid, I erred in giving Chiles an out when I filed in the FSC. FDLE and the *Orlando Sentinel* gave him all the political cover he needed. We were back in the FSC, so it was the courts' problem—not his. If we lost in the FSC, Chiles would expect us to dash into FDC [Federal District Court], then the 11th Circuit and the Supreme Court. With thudding predictability, the stay would be denied the night before the scheduled execution, and all of the attention—and any blame would stick to the judges and not to Governor Chiles. As we all know, that's the expected drill: the motherfuckers run us ragged from court to court, then they kill our clients and blame it on us for filing at the eleventh hour.

In my opinion, Joe has *some* (very little) chance of getting a stay from either of two places: the FSC and Chiles. If the FSC has any interest in doing right in this case, they have the opportunity to do so with the out-of-time rehearing motions pending before them. If the FSC has any inclination now—and they have never shown the slightest inclination in the eight other times Joe's case has come before them—in cutting through the procedural screens the court itself has erected to avoid even considering the evidence of innocence here, now they have the chance. I have no reason to think they will suddenly seize that opportunity. If they don't, I see no reason to give either the FSC or the trial court yet another chance to default and abuse us.

That leaves Chiles as our best shot at a stay. It is a very depressing thought, and I want to be clear that I do not for a moment think that Chiles will grant a stay out of any impulses of justice or fairness or decency. I keep hearing what a decent fellow Chiles is, but the May warrant, the stay (in the wake of public pressure), and the present warrant (now that the media attention has died down; remember Larry Joe Johnson?) leave me convinced that Chiles uses the killing machinery of the state according to the crass political calculus perfected by Bob Graham, the original wimp who transformed himself into a national political force, and who did so on the charred bodies of our clients.

That political calculus is, I believe, our only real chance for a stay. It's not much of a chance, but neither are the courts. It worked in June, to the amazement of us all (especially me). It may well not work again, as it wasn't supposed to work last time, either. What we must do is to maximize the pressure on Chiles.

The key to maximizing the pressure on Chiles is to eliminate any opportunity for him to pass the buck to the courts, to close off all possible escape routes. Thus, it seems to me, our chance with Chiles hinges on our ability to keep the responsibility for killing this innocent man squarely on Chiles and on Chiles alone. That's why I won't go to federal court. That's why, should we lose in the FSC, I won't file a new 3.850 in the trial court.

The magnitude of the pressure Chiles will face will depend, more than anything else, on our (and the media's) ability to discredit FDLE's secret, Star Chamber "process." That means getting access to FDLE's report and its underlying materials and exposing them as the product of a whitewash with a foreordained conclusion. Perhaps the combination of the report and the *Orlando Sentinel* will provide Chiles with enough political cover regardless of what we are able to ferret out. But I still think that Joe's best shot at a stay—and his only shot at any real, substantive relief—lies in my joint investigative venture with the *Herald*. The paper isn't beholden to me or to Joe of course; if they discover evidence Joe is guilty, they'd print it; they'd *have* to print it. Still, I plan to continue to treat the *Herald* as my investigative partner, giving them full and open access to my files and my thinking. By now, I trust Miller's, Holmes' and Rozsa's ability to distinguish the real, reliable evidence from FDLE's smoke screens and McCarthyesque guilt by association.

It's terrifying to think that Joe's life is in the hands of a politician—a politician who has signed two warrants on him within three months, notwithstanding the evidence of innocence. But I believe our best shot is in keeping the responsibility on Chiles and on Chiles alone.

If Joe is killed, I want there to be no doubt that the final responsibility rests with one man, a man who must be thinking about his place in history. I want him to know that, no matter how much good he did in the Senate and in the governor's mansion, it will all be eclipsed by this; it will all be outweighed by his killing this man. Tony Proscio was right that this really *is* a defining moment for America; it will, I can only hope, be the moment for Lawton Chiles to define how he is to be remembered. This will be the ultimate measure of the grain of his character and the content of his soul.

This will be his obituary, no matter how few column inches he rates when he dies.

Wayne Gretzky (cameo star of *Mighty Ducks II*), asked the secret of his success in hockey, said "I always skate to where the puck is going, not to where it's been." The continuity of our litigation strategy under warrant contrasts sharply with the discontinuity of events—the "federal courts," especially *our* lower federal courts, have been packed with hacks by Reagan and Bush—suggests that perhaps we, by continuing to do the death warrant *Shinkansen* through the federal courts, are skating to where the judicial puck has been. Or maybe it's the *political* puck. Or maybe I'm just plain wrong about all of this, and maybe my wrongheadedness will cause the death of my one innocent client and close friend. Gene Miller accused me yesterday of "playing games" with Joe's life, and maybe he's right. On some level this *is* all a high-stakes game—so is Russian Roulette, and so are Pentagon war exercises in the Persian Gulf—but if it *is* all a game, then I think we need to consider changing the rules. My recent experiences with CCR convince me now—and better late than never, I guess—that Millard was right when he said at Airlie in 1986 that we risk becoming "the mask of the executioner." Better that Joe have no lawyer at all—and that the world clearly sees that he has no lawyer—than that Joe have the *illusion* of a lawyer, a hack PD office like CCR that plays by the rules laid down by the people whose job it is to kill their clients.

One final word about taking responsibility. This call is mine (and Joe's). I've been privileged to have the input and advice of many, many people far smarter than I, and for that I am deeply grateful. But the final responsibility is mine alone. I hope I'm making the right decision on this; I hope even more that we won't need to find out, because the FSC will grant a stay to consider the rehearing motions now pending before it. Gulp.

God help Joe. God help us.

The Hard Part of Playing "Chicken" Is Knowing When to Flinch

"If this court intends to kill this innocent man by depriving him of the effective assistance of counsel," I wrote the Florida Supreme Court on September 8, 1995, "then it will do so without my complicity. I will not participate in a sham evidentiary 'hearing.' " To stop the machinery of death from claiming my client, I had to throw myself on the gears. By refusing to show up for a hearing for which I had been given less than a week to prepare—and highlighting that, in my opinion, my client was being denied effective assistance of counsel—I tried to shame the court into granting a stay of execution and time to prepare properly.

Joe Spaziano was to die September 21. On September 5, the Florida Supreme Court told me to be in Tallahassee for oral argument on September 7. So I went to the Florida Supreme Court seeking a stay of execution and an evidentiary hearing concerning DiLisio's recantation. The next day, on September 8, the court granted the hearing, but refused to order a stay of execution. Instead, by a 4–3 vote, the court ordered me, an appellate lawyer with very little trial experience, no associates, and no investigators, to handle an evidentiary hearing one week later, on September 15. The court also ordered CCR, a public defender's office devoted to capital postconviction appeals, to assist me. I refused to comply. In a memo written two days later I wrote, "We could have thrown a hearing together, put on enough evidence so that the justices could say, 'Yeah, you had your hearing,' we would have lost, the [trial-level] judge would have made killer fact-findings against us, and . . . Joe would have been dead on time and as scheduled."[56]

In a handwritten fax sent from my motel to the supreme court on the night of September 8, I just said no. I wrote, among other things, that CCR and I could not provide competent assistance with just six days' preparation. I also pledged that I would not surrender my 25 boxes of case files to CCR or to any other attorney in time for the hearing. "If you are going to kill an innocent man without a lawyer," I wrote, "you will do so in such a way that the whole world will see what you are doing . . . I will not be your mask."

The hard part about playing chicken is knowing when to flinch. The high court blinked. On September 12 it threw me off the case, but granted Joe Spaziano an indefinite stay. Then, in January, after new *pro bono* attorneys from the 470-lawyer firm of Holland & Knight took over the case—and the supreme court allowed them four months to prepare—Circuit Judge O. H. Eaton, Jr., of Sanford, Florida, heard a week's worth of evidence.

The Canary in the Mine: CCR Today

Let me begin my critique of the modern-day CCR with a vignette. On January 19, 1996, the State of Florida filed a motion in Joseph Spaziano's case. The state was asking the court to compel the law firm then representing Mr. Spaziano to send its files to CCR, and not to send them to me. Forget for a moment the legalities of the state's motion to choose which lawyer, CCR or me, would represent Spaziano; I will return to these legalities in a moment. My point is that the state, a state salivating to get Spaziano into the electric chair, was *demanding* a court order dictating that CCR be the state's opponent. Think about this for a moment. When the state *really* wants to kill a death row inmate in Florida, *the state wants its opposition counsel to be CCR.* What does this say about CCR?

The alternative to aggressive defense lawyering is an unbearable coziness with power. CCR has suffered the same homogenizing doom suffered years ago by the Legal Service Corporation. With one eye on the governor and legislature to whom they owe their jobs and with the other shut tightly, CCR lawyers have gone the way of deadening mediocrity. Everything that cannot be made palatable to the institutional powers is killed outright. Spoiled and corrupted by the illusion that it had the "ear" of Governor Chiles, CCR seemed to have no patience to hear my declaration that 96 hours is an absurdly paltry amount of time to prepare for a complex evidentiary hearing. CCR's cowardice and mediocracy kill CCR's clients, no less than their sociopathic friend who actually signs the death warrants.

The blame for CCR's devolution into a hack public defender office rests with its leadership, not with its front-line litigators. This leadership constrained the aggressive litigators, making CCR a pariah among the best capital defenders. CCR's director has a good heart, but this is life and death.

Now CCR, although vastly overfunded and underworked, feeds the deadly illusion that Florida does not have a counsel crisis, because Florida has CCR. The fact is that Florida has a counsel crisis worse than Texas precisely *because* of CCR. In Texas, everyone can see that death row has no lawyers. In Florida, it is worse than having no lawyers: CCR provides the comfortable illusion that death row *has* aggressive lawyers.

How is it possible for CCR to mistake for an ally the governor who signs the death warrants on CCR's clients? Perhaps the answer is simply stupidity. Perhaps the answer is bureaucratic inertia. Or perhaps Archimedes was right: From inside the hull of a ship, it's impossible to know if the vessel is moving.

CCR's belief that at all costs it must remain on "good terms" with the governor and the Florida Supreme Court resembles the Leninist doctrine that peace is always better than war. But peace is not always better than war. Hitler and Eichmann taught us that—taught *me* that, at any rate. When the peace is morally and practically crippled; when CCR's lawyers are put in the impossible position of litigating aggressively and then being told to subvert that representation by following rules that kill their clients; and when CCR's Faustian bargain with the powers that be will almost certainly lead in the long run to the annihilation of more and more of CCR's clients, it is far worse than CCR's present refusal to cooperate—its civil disobedience, if you will. However, CCR will continue to play the role of collaborator.

CCR's special blend of cowardice and ineptitude came very close to killing Joe Spaziano. It *did* kill a man named Jerry White in December 1995. The parallels between *White* and *Spaziano* are frightening, and Mr. White's fate shows what would have happened to Mr. Spaziano had I followed the Florida Supreme Court's *dictats* and handed the case to CCR for an evidentiary hearing under death warrant. Like Spaziano, White had, prior to the warrant, been represented by volunteer, *pro bono* counsel. As in *Spaziano,* CCR told the Florida Supreme Court that it could not competently represent White due to CCR's caseload.[57] The Florida Supreme Court disbelieved CCR's overload representations and ordered CCR to represent Mr. White anyway, under warrant. As in *Spaziano,* CCR then folded its counsel arguments and undertook the representation, under circumstances that CCR itself had just told the Florida Supreme Court rendered effective assistance of counsel impossible. And, like Spaziano's, Jerry White's case raised compelling constitutional issues—compelling enough for White to lose in the Florida Supreme Court by only one vote (4–3), the same vote by which the court denied a stay and ordered me to put on an evidentiary hearing on 96 hours notice.

There the comparison between *White* and *Spaziano* ends. In *Spaziano,* I refused to permit CCR to take over as counsel. No one was there to prevent CCR from taking over *White.* So it did. CCR dashed from court to court, pretending that it could represent White effectively, and was doing so.[58] White was executed on December 4. (The electric chair malfunctioned during Mr. White's electrocution; he screamed, and his scream was heard by the execution witnesses.[59] Another CCR client, Phillip Atkins, was executed less than 24 hours later.)[60] Whether effective counsel could have prevented White's execution we will never know. Jerry White's killing makes it a moot point anyway.

What happened in *White* is precisely what I feared would happen in *Spaziano,* had I acquiesced in an evidentiary hearing "assisted" by CCR under warrant. Jerry White was the canary in the mine.

CCR's ineptitude in *White* carried through to the very end. CCR's director, Michael Minerva, had asked Richard Jorandby, the Public Defender in West Palm Beach, to witness Mr. White's execution. Jorandby drove from West Palm to Starke for that sad reason. He arrived in Starke the night before the execution occurred. But, on the morning of the killing, when Jorandby arrived at the prison to witness the electrocution of Jerry White, the prison personnel told Jorandby that he was not on the witness list. Bureaucratic foul-up, but not the prison's. CCR had forgotten to put Jorandby on the witness list. He was escorted off prison grounds by five prison guards.

In *White,* CCR had told the Florida Supreme Court it could not render the effective assistance of counsel. Yet CCR represented Mr. White anyway, after the Florida Supreme Court ordered it to do so. This means that CCR either (1) lied to the Florida Supreme Court about its inability to represent Mr. White effectively, or (2) failed to represent Mr. White effectively. It's either/or; it's one or the other. There are no other possibilities.

Perhaps I overstate in saying that CCR "killed" Jerry White, but I don't think so. CCR did not pull the switch, yet neither did Governor Chiles or the Florida Supreme Court. CCR is one with Spaziano's other, more obviously identifiable executioners among the executive and judiciary. CCR's collaboration and cowardice were conditions precedent to the electrocution of its client. CCR's actions were necessary (if not sufficient) conditions, causes-in-fact, and proximate causes of White's execution.

Then it happened again. On March 25, 1997—after this book was set in galleys—a man named Pedro Medina was executed in Florida's electric chair. Like "Crazy Joe" Spaziano, Pedro Medina sought a stay based on his claim of newly discovered evidence proving his total factual innocence of the capital murder for which he was about to be put to death. Like Spaziano, Medina was denied a stay by the narrowest of margins in the Florida Supreme Court—four votes to three—the three dissenters would have stayed Medina's execution until an evidentiary hearing could be held to explore Medina's claim of innocence. And like Jerry White's execution, the electric chair at Florida State Prison malfunctioned. A few hours after the botched execution, I spoke by phone with Professor Michael Radelet, a good friend and chair of the sociology department at the University of Florida. Sounding shellshocked, Radelet said of the Pedro Medina execution, "They burned him alive . . . after losing by only one vote in the Florida Supreme Court."

An Associated Press wire story entitled "Flames Erupt from Inmate's Head," dated March 26, 1997, provided a few more details: "A mask concealing" the face of Medina "burst into flames. . . . There was no indication Medina felt the flames, Gov. Lawton Chiles said. 'We've had an occasion of smoke before,' Chiles said. 'But the question is really, Is this something that is torturous or painful?' " the AP wrote. However, Florida Attorney General Bob Butterworth said Medina's "gruesome death would be a deterrent. 'People who wish to commit murder, they better not do it in Florida, because we may have a problem with our electric chair.' "

"Medina's last words were: 'I am still innocent.' Medina was convicted of the 1982 killing of Dorothy James. . . . James' daughter, Lindi James, opposed the execution, saying she never believed Medina killed her mother," the AP reported.

CCR's modern mandarins like to boast about the agency's "success rate," and, on their face, the numbers appear impressive. Look beneath the surface of CCR's "success rates," however, and you'll find an artifice typical of hack public defender offices: CCR has in the past farmed out the hardest cases to outside lawyers (by finding that it has a "conflict of interest"), while keeping the easier cases in-house, as CCR clients. This tactic worked so long as the Volunteer Lawyers' Resource Center existed to provide expertise and support for the outside attorneys. Now that VLRC is dead, many of these cases will revert back to CCR. This happened to Jerry

White. As CCR takes over more of the former Center's cases, one can expect CCR's "success" statistics to change accordingly.

Many on Florida's death row fear and loathe CCR, but what choice do they have about who shall represent them?[61] As the Florida Supreme Court made clear in *Spaziano v. State* in 1995, Florida's condemned can be represented (1) by CCR; or (2) by volunteer, *pro bono* counsel (fat chance since the death of the Volunteer Lawyers' Resource Center); or (3) by themselves, *pro se*. In other words, death row had best shut up and be satisfied with whatever hack law firm the state, in its generosity, decides to bestow upon them. Most on Florida's death row get the message and don't dare criticize CCR in public. But don't confuse their silence with ignorance or with acceptance.

When I first argued for CCR's abolition in 1995, I never thought it could happen any time soon. The Agency and its patron Governor Chiles seemed entrenched as ever. But things can change in Florida with dizzying speed.

The politics of death in Florida can make the strangest of bedfellows. In early 1997, my critique of CCR's ethics received support from a surprising source. As discussed in Chapter 5, in 1985 I was allied with Governor Bob Graham and Attorney General Jim Smith—two politicians who built their public careers upon the dead bodies of my clients—in arguing for the creation of CCR. In 1997 I found myself allied with a thing called the McDonald commission in its call to abolish CCR and replace the agency with an alternative model of providing death row with legal aid. The commission was charged with reviewing Florida's system of providing postconviction counsel for death-sentenced prisoners; the commission's goal was to trim a significant amount of time from the average time it takes for death sentences to be carried out. The McDonald commission was chaired by former Florida Supreme Court Justice Parker Lee McDonald (who loathed CCR from soon after it was created in 1985), and included several members of the legislature. The commission's formal name was the Commission for Review of Postconviction Representation, and it was created by Governor Lawton Chiles, the president of the state senate, and the speaker of the state house of representatives.

The McDonald commission issued its report on February 13, 1997—after this book had been set in galleys. The commission and I agreed on two propositions, although we approached them from entirely different frames of reference. First, the commission and I agreed that CCR had engaged in a longstanding pattern of violations of Florida's rules of professional responsibility. Second, we agreed that CCR ought to be replaced.

The McDonald commission found that CCR's "reputation has been tarnished" by "many unethical tactics and abuses." But where I fault CCR for tepid and inept representation of its clients, the commission concluded that "CCR has engaged in abusive public records requests and dilatory litigation tactics, including the failure to reveal adverse legal representation to the court."

The McDonald commission and I agreed that CCR's ethical abuses suggested that the agency ought to be abolished. "The commission finds that based on CCR's lack of institutional integrity, [the Florida legislature] should consider other models of postconviction representation," the commission wrote in its report. In addition, the commission's report included a section captioned "Additional Recommendations to Improve the Administration of Justice in Florida." The first such recommendation was: "The Commission Strongly Encourages the Florida Bar and the Florida Supreme Court to Strictly Enforce the Canons of Ethics and Professionalism in Death and Penalty Cases." The commission explained:

> The Commission is disturbed by the credible information demonstrating litigation abuses committed by the office of the Capital Collateral Representative. The Commission urges the Florida Supreme Court and all other state courts to require all attorneys to comply with the Canons of Ethics, regardless of the nature of the case. No justification exists to allow any attorneys to violate the rules binding on the legal profession.

Whether CCR will indeed be abolished is an open question as this book goes to press. If the agency is abolished, whether it will be replaced by something worse for death row is another open question. Regardless, the ethically challenged agency I encountered in 1995 in Joe Spaziano's case has been identified as such by the McDonald commission. If CCR is abolished, I'll file that news under "Be careful what you ask for, because you might get it."

In any event, the McDonald commission's findings that CCR is ethically challenged beyond repair reinforced my September 1995 refusal to obey the Florida Supreme Court's demand that CCR replace me as Joe Spaziano's attorney. The ethically obtuse CCR described by the McDonald commission is the same CCR I refused to allow to take over Joe's case.

Privatizing Legal Services for Death Row Prisoners: A Case for Replacing Florida's CCR with a Volunteer Lawyers' Resource Center

Trying to "reform" CCR today is like attempting to repair a ship at sea. Some, but not all, of CCR's systemic defects might be corrected by adopting an alternative model: a resource center. *Anything* is better for death row than CCR. My model of choice is nothing: a general strike by capital postconviction lawyers. A resource center might be a way of crafting a less radical compromise.

247

For one remarkable moment, more than a decade ago, supporters and opponents of capital punishment in Florida were in rare agreement: The twin goals of speeding up executions and ensuring that those executions were lawful and fair required the legislative creation of a public defender office with statewide jurisdiction to provide direct representation for condemned prisoners in postconviction proceedings in state and federal court. Although Governor Bob Graham, Attorney General Jim Smith, Scharlette Holdman, Craig Barnard, and I could agree on no other issue concerning capital punishment in 1985, we all agreed that the legislature should create the Office of the Capital Collateral Representative.

I now suggest that in 1997, 12 years after CCR's creation, this same diverse constellation of supporters and opponents of capital punishment ought to agree again: this time on the abolition of CCR and its replacement with a reborn Volunteer Lawyers' Resource Center (VLRC) to provide logistical support and intellectual resources to private law firms wishing to discharge their *pro bono* obligations by representing death row inmates or to seek court appointment.

Supplanting CCR with a VLRC makes sense for two sorts of reasons. First, it would be cheaper for Florida's taxpayers—*much* cheaper. Second, it would result in better legal representation for death row, thus maximizing the likelihood that the people being executed are the *right people* who are at least guilty of the crimes for which they are being executed. My basic thesis is that Florida's experiment with CCR has failed, notwithstanding the legislature's willingness to give the agency ever-greater levels of annual funding. And while CCR has been failing, resource centers—in Florida and 20 other states—were succeeding, at least until Congress decided to end their funding in October 1995.[62]

The governor and the Florida Supreme Court want to move in the opposite direction. In an extraordinary report requested by the Florida Supreme Court, former Attorney General Robert Shevin proposed the complete deprivatization of legal services for death row.[63] Shevin reported that CCR's annual budget for 1996 is in the neighborhood of $2.9 million and that that level of funding contemplates 22 full-time lawyer positions.[64] At the time VLRC was defunded, VLRC's budget was $1.5 million in federal funds[65] and provided for eight lawyer positions. Shevin reported that CCR's assuming VLRC's caseload would require the legislature to increase CCR's annual budget by $730,000 to $1 million;[66] CCR, by contrast, insists that its existing budget must be *doubled* (to approximately $6 million) to allow it to absorb VLRC's caseload.[67] The governor's proposed 1996–97 budget increases CCR's annual funding by $730,000.

Under the plan proposed by Shevin and the budget submitted by Governor Chiles, CCR would represent *everyone* on Florida's death row. The private bar would be relieved of any responsibility for representing condemned prisoners in Florida. That responsibility—and its cost of at least $3.5 million each year—will be borne totally by Florida's taxpayers. In an era when all sorts of public services—from prisons to schools—are being privatized, Florida would move in the opposite direction: Legal services for death row inmates would be entirely deprivatized. Such deprivatization would be bad public policy and a waste of taxpayers' money.

Whether there is a constitutional right to counsel in capital post-conviction proceedings was unclear when CCR was created in 1985. It remains unclear today. The Florida Supreme Court's statements on the matter have gone both ways,[68] as have the opinions of the U.S. Supreme Court.[69]

Although some legislative history supports the notion that CCR was created in an attempt to anticipate an expected U.S. Supreme Court determination that states must provide lawyers for condemned prisoners,[70] my own involvement with the political culture that created CCR suggests that the agency was created primarily as a response to an increasingly volatile counsel crisis.[71]

As described in Chapter 5, the counsel crisis came about because Governor Graham signed death warrants on prisoners who were without counsel. In the past, Scharlette Holdman's Florida Clearinghouse on Criminal Justice had been able to find volunteer, *pro bono* lawyers to jump into the fray to represent prisoners with warrants and without attorneys.[72] By 1984, however, the pool of volunteer attorneys was running dry.[73] The Florida bar, as well as the state and federal judiciaries, began searching for a more permanent solution to the counsel problem.[74]

The Florida bar came up with a then-novel solution: create VLRC to recruit volunteer attorneys and guide them through the labyrinth of state and federal postconviction practice and procedure.[75] When the first-generation Florida VLRC was created in 1984, it was the first such operation in the nation.

The first Florida VLRC was blessed with a brilliant director, Mark Olive, but it soon became clear to the bench and bar that VLRC couldn't do the job alone. There were simply too many cases and too many death warrants.[76] That VLRC was swamped came home in two cases, *Agan* and *Waterhouse*, described in Chapter 5 and (in more detail) in my own history of the creation of CCR.[77]

So the legislature created CCR. Olive and Holdman (and I) went to work there. Under Florida law, CCR is automatically appointed to represent all indigents in capital cases after the direct appeal becomes final, and the condemned person's petition for certiorari is denied. The CCR director is appointed to a four-year term by the governor from a list of three or more nominees submitted by the elected circuit public defenders. Recently the governor of Florida rejected the incumbent, who was first on the list, and appointed another person from the list. If there is a conflict of interest, or if the CCR cannot accept a new case because its attorneys are overloaded, the CCR must notify "the sentencing court." The sentencing court must appoint "one or more members of the Florida Bar to represent one or more [indigent] persons."

While CCR's enabling statute provides that "appointed counsel shall be paid from dollars appropriated to the Office of the Capital Collateral Representative," the Florida legislature has not appropriated funds to pay the expenses of "volunteer" counsel appointed by the sentencing court. "Volunteers" to represent indigents in state and federal post-conviction proceedings were recruited by the VLRC, the agency that had been funded by Congress at the request of the Committee on Defender Services.

In 1988, three years after CCR was created, the second-generation VLRC was created to supplement CCR's efforts. Thanks to the leadership of the Florida state bar and Attorney General Jim Smith, the governor and the Florida legislature responded to the needs of Florida's death row population by creating and funding the original VLRC. Again, those same allies responded to the needs of the CCR. The CCR was originally funded to handle 12 to 15 cases per year. It was funded for 12 lawyers. When the Florida Supreme Court increased its affirmances to 25 cases per year, the CCR staff was increased to 22 lawyers. The staff can absorb one new case every two weeks, or approximately 26 cases a year. The Supreme Court affirmed 43 cases in the first 11 months of 1994. The CCR has requested 10 more attorneys to handle an approximately 50 present increase in its caseload. At 32 attorneys, the CCR will be able to handle all indigent postconviction petitions in both state and federal courts where there is no conflict, if the affirmance rate remains at approximately 43 cases per year. Without an increase, 18 volunteer attorneys will be required to handle the overload on the CCR office. To demonstrate the support given to the CCR office by the governor and the Florida legislature, the attorney general's office handles all direct appeals, petitions for certiorari, and postconviction matters in state and federal court with only 14 lawyers—as compared with CCR's 22, whose jurisdiction is limited to postconviction matters.

The 1988 version of VLRC performed several functions. It provided direct representation for some indigents who filed for postconviction collateral review in cases where CCR had a conflict, or where the CCR attorney staff was overloaded. VLRC did not receive federal funding for direct representation in state court. VLRC lawyers who appeared in state court did so on personal leave time! The VLRC also recruited "volunteers" to represent inmates on death row in postconviction matters. As an inducement, the VLRC provided support including research, consultation, and investigation services.

The support services performed by the VLRC were consistently cited as the most important factor in Florida's remarkable success in providing counsel for indigents on death row. As of January 1, 1994, Florida had 332 persons on death row. Seven were without counsel.[78] California had 381, of whom 118 were without counsel.[79] The budget request for fiscal year 1995 for Florida's death penalty resource center was $1,527,000.[80] California's requested $5,485,000.[81] Florida's resource center recruited "volunteers" for state and federal postconviction proceedings, and it provided some direct representation in the federal courts. The California resource center does not recruit lawyers for state postconviction proceedings in death penalty cases.

Private volunteer counsel recruited by VLRC for work in federal court were entitled to reimbursement for their direct representation of death row inmates. Most members of the Florida Bar who were recruited from the civil bar do *not* request compensation for their representation.[82] They consider it to be a professional responsibility, and a *pro bono* contribution to the good reputation of the legal profession. A report on voucher payments for fiscal year 1993 reflects that seven Florida lawyers received a total of $185,907.95, for an average payment of $26,558.28 per client.[83] The same report shows that 54 California attorneys received $4,735,099.30, for an average payment of $87,687.02 per client.[84] Either it costs three times as much to practice L.A. Law or California federal judges are three times as generous as their Florida counterparts.

Most folks with experience in the capital postconviction system agree that a VLRC costs less, much less, than CCR. The reason is commonsensical: It will always be cheaper to help a law firm with their capital case than to investigate and litigate the entire case yourself.

Congress got this point exactly wrong when in 1995 it voted to defund all 21 VLRCs. In its rush to overhaul our system of death penalty appeals, the left hand of Congress undid what its right hand had appropriately done. Even in this era of budget cutting, no one would argue that the decision to cut funding for the resource centers is fiscally sound. With a total budget of less than $20 million, the resource centers were a drop in the bucket. In fact, the federal courts estimated that eliminating them and using more expensive private lawyers appointed by the courts would not result in cost saving. Judge Richard Arnold, my hero in *Stanley*, noted, "If these [resource] centers are eliminated, the cost to the taxpayer will go up."[85]

Why? The reason, according to the House, was to cut down on delay. Yet the House's action will have precisely the opposite effect. Finding enough qualified lawyers to handle these unpopular and time-consuming cases is almost impossible. Federal judges and bar associations know that sad truth. In the late 1980s, when the federal death penalty caseload started climbing, the shortage of lawyers slowed the appeals process to a crawl and then to a standstill. To keep appeals moving, the courts created the resource centers.

CCR's annual budget is in the neighborhood of $3 million; as noted, it employs at least 22 attorneys. Still, CCR routinely complains that it lacks the resources to represent its clients effectively. The Florida Supreme Court has ignored CCR's representations about case overload. Perhaps the legislature should hold hearings on the question of CCR's purported "overload" before appropriating more money for the agency. At a minimum, the legislature could insist that CCR provide it with sworn affidavits setting out their personnel time records.

Although I was an early supporter and longtime (and often solitary) ally of CCR, my recent experience with the agency has led me to the personally sad conclusion that under its current leadership CCR has become incompetent. Here, I hope to offer some general thoughts on why—structurally and institutionally—a VLRC model makes more sense than a CCR model.

First, as I suggested above, a VLRC would do the job more cost-effectively than does CCR, because the firms, rather than the taxpayers, shoulder the bulk of the substantial expenses associated with death row representation. Second, replacing CCR with VLRC would encourage private lawyers and law firms to experience capital punishment as a legal system. This benefits both the lawyers and their condemned clients.

It benefits the VLRC lawyers as well by bringing the insights and experiences of the private practitioners into the collective corpus of capital punishment knowledge. It also mitigates the bunker mentality that explains, in part, what CCR has become: an isolated and insular Masada, fearful of the outside world and, in the end, of its own clients. The interaction between VLRC lawyers and the volunteers they assist keeps both groups of lawyers on their toes.

Third, the creation of a VLRC today would draw on a fairly extensive body of experience that simply did not exist in 1984 when the first Florida VLRC was created. Between 1988 and 1995, a total of 21 VLRCs existed—not the least of which was Florida's.

CCR's Conflicts

CCR labors under conflicts of interest, some of which are inherent in the structure of the agency and some of which are inherent in any office that specializes in direct representation of a state's death row population. An example of the former type is the fact that the CCR director is appointed by the governor (who also signs the death warrants on CCR's clients) and that the agency gets its funding from the Florida legislature (the same legislature that created CCR as a device to speed up executions).

The first species of conflicts could be fixed by making CCR a more independent entity. The second sort of conflict is not so easily remedied.

The latter type of conflict of interest can best be illustrated by a hypothetical. Assume a lame duck Florida governor who wants to end his political career on a moral high note of mercy and forgiveness. Our governor decides to commute the death sentences in 10—but no more than 10—capital cases. The governor also wants to commute the 10 most deserving people. Knowing that the CCR is the expert on who those lucky 10 are, our governor sets up a meeting with his old friend the CCR director, whom our governor appointed to his job as head of the CCR law firm.

It's just the two them in the conference room in the governor's mansion, these two old veterans of Florida's political battles. The governor says to the director: "I've decided to commute 10 of your 100 clients. You know best which of your clients are the most deserving, because you have access to all kinds of confidential information I don't. All I want from you is the 10 names; I don't want reasons or explanations or justifications. I know you're an honorable man, and you'll give me the 10 best cases. Don't say anything now. Go back to your office and think about it. I need the 10 names two weeks from today. Don't worry that the Executive Cabinet must concur if clemency is to be granted; I've got them on board because I'll take all the political heat, which will be considerable. I can live with the heat, if I'm convinced I've commuted the 10 most deserving cases, and only *you* have the information to identify those cases. And I'll keep this strictly confidential between you and me; no one outside this room needs to know about this. But you need to understand: If you refuse to give me the 10 names, then the deal's off. I won't commute *any* death sentences."

What would you do if you were the CCR director? Reject the governor's proposition and entrust your clients' lives to the vagaries of the courts, knowing that you *may* win 10 of your 100 cases in the courts, if you're lucky? Or would you provide the list? If so, how would you go about selecting the fortunate 10? Would you choose the 10 most deserving, according to your own moral calculus: the 10 most likely to be innocent, or perhaps the 10 with the most unfair trials? Or would you choose the 10 *worst* cases, factually and legally, based on the idea that the more sympathetic cases are also the most likely to win at least some kind of relief in the courts? Would your pool be limited to CCR's clients, or would it include death row prisoners represented *pro bono* by law firms that CCR assists? And what about disclosure, to the 10 you choose or the 90 you don't?

This hypothetical is not as outlandish as it might appear at first blush; something similar happened in another state (not Florida) a few years ago. More to the point, the species of conflict illustrated by the hypothetical arises whenever a single law firm (like CCR) represents many death row prisoners in one state (like Florida) and must appear before the same court (like the Florida Supreme Court) in case after case after case raising the same legal issue.

I experienced this phenomenon first-hand when I was a CCR attorney in the mid-1980s.[86] Bob Graham was governor, and he typically signed two 28-day death warrants every two weeks; this meant that at any given time, four of CCR's clients were scheduled to die in the near future. Also at that time, for about five months, the U.S. Supreme Court had under consideration *Lockhart v. McCree*. Because *McCree* was a challenge to the way in which capital juries were selected, virtually every capital case raised a *McCree* issue, in one form or another. The strongest *McCree* cases had several potential jurors removed during the "death qualification" process. The weakest *McCree* cases had no venirepeople removed; there the argument was that the *process* of death qualification itself (asking the voir dire questions and eliciting the answers) resulted in a jury unnaturally, and therefore unconstitutionally, prone to convict.

Because *McCree* claims were based on social science research, the CCR lawyers decided that only one of us really needed to work through the studies. I ended up being that one. During the pendency of *McCree* in the Supreme Court, I did the oral arguments in the Florida Supreme Court asking for stays of execution based on the pendency. In every one of these cases I was arguing before the same seven Florida Supreme Court justices.

The problem was that I *knew* which of my cases presented the stronger *McCree* claims, and I also knew which cases did not. Before every oral argument in every death warrant case, I asked myself: What ought I do when the justices ask me—as they invariably did—whether the case at hand was a strong *McCree* claim or a weak one, compared with the case I was arguing last week and the case I'd be arguing next week? I ultimately decided to answer that question, in part because I knew I'd be appearing before the justices in many future cases; I didn't want to imperil my reputation as a straight shooter. But in so doing I was less aggressive in some stay cases than I would have been otherwise. Some of those clients did not get a stay. I was laboring under a conflict of interest at the time.

The most difficult problem in crafting the VLRC I envision is to keep the center autonomous and independent from the politics of the death penalty in Florida. The way in which CCR's director is selected is simply absurd: The public defenders (whose offices are often alleged by CCR to have been ineffective at the trial level) sends three names to the governor, who makes the first selection. The governor (who of course is the same person who signs death warrants on CCR's clients) thus chooses who will run the agency. I have suggested that this conflict of interest—in which the governor gets to decide who his opponent in court will be—explains, in part, why CCR under its current director has become a lapdog law firm.

The Florida Supreme Court correctly noted that Joseph Spaziano did not (and does not now) want CCR as his lawyer,[87] but the court ignored the good reasons why Mr. Spaziano reasonably believes that having CCR as your lawyer is worse than having no lawyer at all. CCR's performance in Mr. Spaziano's case does not just suggest that that the agency is over-worked; it suggests the agency is inept. Two weeks in advance of Mr. Spaziano's scheduled execution—on a fourth death warrant—CCR had conducted no fact investigation of any use (notwithstanding a wealth of leads, provided mainly by the *Miami Herald*'s independent investigation, which was initiated over the strong misgivings of CCR and with no help whatsoever from that office), CCR had drafted no pleadings, CCR had developed no strategy, and CCR's director was telling reporters (and the governor) that all he wanted for his factually innocent client ("innocent" in that he did not commit the crime) was a reduction in sentence from death to life in prison.

As I told the Florida Supreme Court, I would rather go to jail for contempt than allow CCR to handle Mr. Spaziano's case. This is because CCR has become a pawn of the institutional powers in Florida attempting to kill Mr. Spaziano.

When the Florida Supreme Court stayed Joseph Spaziano's September 1995 execution date and remanded the case for an evidentiary hearing on Mr. Spaziano's factual innocence claim, his representation was undertaken by Greg Thomas and Kim Stott of Holland & Knight (Florida's largest and richest law firm), James Russ, an Orlando criminal defense lawyer, and, perhaps most important of all, Lori Lakeman, Russ's paralegal.

Steve Hanlon was quoted after the hearing as saying that without VLRC, "we're reaching the point now where there's a very serious question about whether private law firms should volunteer to do this work."[88] Without VLRC, he said, "There's a great and justified concern in my view that unless you have that kind of legal expertise and that kind of investigative ability to back you, *then you are merely greasing the skids.*" Hanlon told the reporter that he would advise his firm to stay out of death penalty cases in the future because of the burden, and that he had even resisted taking on the "relatively easy" Spaziano case.[89]

When Florida's VLRC shut down in 1995, it was providing support in about 41 death cases. Without VLRC's help, "many of their volunteer lawyers are trying to bail out of their cases."[90] Joe Spaziano was one such client. Many of the remainder will end up as CCR clients—with their lawyers' efforts paid for *entirely* by Florida's taxpayers, as opposed to being represented by Florida pro bono lawyers receiving essential *support* from a Center funded by tax dollars and, perhaps, by Florida bar money as well. Keep in mind my basic fiscal point: It is always cheaper to provide support for private law firms representing death row prisoners than to represent the condemned clients yourself.

As I have explained elsewhere, my recent experience with the "Crazy Joe" Spaziano case led me to conclude that CCR is worse for death row than no lawyers at all. The *illusion* of having a lawyer is worse than having no lawyer.

One way or another, Florida will have to find a way to provide logistical support and expertise for *pro bono* lawyers willing to take these cases when the bar and the Supreme Court come asking for help. And they *will* come asking. We've been through this drill before.

But they best not come to me, not that I expect they will. After I worked for 2,000 *pro bono* hours, and went into personal debt that maxed out all my credit cards, the Florida Supreme Court's response was to "fire" me from the case. At the end of the day, however, the court's relentless determination to make it physically impossible for me to continue as Mr. Spaziano's lawyer did me a great personal service. The court's shameful treatment of Spaziano's attempts to prove his innocence was a *mitzva* for me, because it cemented a decision I have been moving toward for years: to conscientiously abstain from participation in a legal "system" so grotesquely skewed and unfair and morally corrupt that it won't even *consider*—really consider, as opposed to pretending to consider—evidence of innocence.

I can no longer, in good conscience, participate in a legal "system" so rigged that it can't even be trusted to ensure that it is killing the right person. The reasons for my decision are beyond the scope of this book, but they relate directly to my conclusion that CCR has become the mask of the executioner.

The coming counsel crisis in Florida provides an opportunity to explore how defense lawyers ought to respond to the system of capital punishment as it is. The capital defense bar is entering a crucial time, one that offers a chance to define our agenda for the coming crisis. For myself, the *Spaziano* case suggests that the ideas, answers, theories, and institutions of the past are no longer adequate to the challenges and questions before us.

Thomas Kuhn, in *The Structure of Scientific Revolution,* described such a time as a "crisis" that precedes a paradigm shift. For Kuhn, a crisis occurs when an old theory fails to answer the questions posed by new observations and realities.

And so it is with us. For decades, Florida defense lawyers responded by jumping in and representing condemned prisoners. The *Spaziano* case suggests, to me at least, that the time has come for us to stop pretending that capital punishment is a legal system at all. If the system is as worthless as we say it is, perhaps the best response is to refuse to play the game anymore. Perhaps the time has come to say, On strike. Shut it down.

"All is flux; nothing stays still," Heraclitus wrote. Nowhere in capital punishment is this dictum truer than it is for CCR. The CCR of today bears little resemblance to the CCR of the Olive/Holdman days. The name is the same. Everything else—all that matters—is so different as to be unrecognizable.

Yet, yes, all is flux. CCR may still find its roots. But if I were on Florida's death row, I wouldn't bet my life on it. The place that cradled me is burning, and Florida's death row is alone.

Florida Then, New York Now

Florida's experience with capital punishment matters, because many other states are headed today into territory Florida clearcut decades ago. New York is one such state. New York's 1995 death penalty statute purported to fix the most serious problems identified in my 1991 Albany paper, discussed at the beginning of this chapter. Like its predecessors, the bill that became New York law in 1995 promised a well-financed and independent capital defense delivery system. The statute provides for the formation of a Capital Defender Office (CDO).[91] The Committee Bill Memorandum[92] spoke of the "Creation of a New Public Defense System in Capital Cases." The statute requires that "full state funding is provided in recognition of the very high costs associated with capital defense."[93] The bill establishes a Capital Defender Office governed by a three-member board of directors. The board members are appointed by the Chief Judge of the Court of Appeals, the Temporary President of the Senate, and the Speaker of the Assembly. The Capital Defender Office is authorized, within the amounts appropriated by law, to represent indigent defendants in capital cases, provide training for attorneys who will represent indigent defendants, to determine minimum standards for the qualification of assigned counsel, and to participate in establishing a pool of attorneys qualified to represent defendants. By detailing the specific functions of the Capital Defender Office, the bill precludes the Office from performing other unauthorized activities, such as lobbying. Payment of expenses for investigative, expert, and other services is also provided for. Moreover, the bill, on its face, guarantees that indigent defendants will receive state-financed representation and other such services beyond the trial, including other services on appeal from a death sentence, in connection with an initial motion for postconviction relief, and in connection with an appeal relating to such a motion.

The bill also amends the County Law and the Executive Law to provide for reimbursement to district attorneys for expert witness fees in the prosecution of capital cases and for investigative services in connection with sentencing proceedings and mental retardation hearings. In addition, the Division of Criminal Justice Services is authorized to contract with an organization to develop and provide continuing legal education, training, advice, and assistance to prosecutors. There is also created a

"Capital Prosecution Extraordinary Assistance Program," from which funds may be distributed to a district attorney upon a determination that the nature or number of cases being prosecuted has placed a significant financial burden on a particular district attorney's office.

In an April 1996 *New Yorker* profile of the new office and its first head, Kevin Doyle, the writer asked, perhaps rhetorically, whether Governor Pataki "knew what he was doing when he agreed to the well-financed office."[94] My guess is he did. First, the statute provided for $750,000 in start-up costs.[95] This seems to be a popular amount for legislatures creating a death row defense organization: That's how much the Florida legislature initially provided for CCR—a decade earlier and in a state that already *had* a statewide public defender system and had had one since 1963, shortly after *Gideon v. Wainwright* (a Florida case) was decided.

Second, the appointment of counsel will be made by the trial judge, not the Capital Defender Office; the Office will be limited to nominating four teams consisting of only two lawyers each, with one such team having to be from the local judicial department. Only two trial lawyers, at most two appellate lawyers, and only one postconviction lawyer can be appointed pursuant to the new Section 35-b of the Judicial Law.

Governor Pataki, in signing the statute, stressed that the interests of justice "can be satisfied only if the standards [governing the competency of defense lawyers] are not set at unrealistically high levels."[96] The statute guarantees that "the fee schedules are not set at unduly high levels,"[97] Pataki explained. To this end, "the bill mandates that the compensation paid to all such [capital] attorneys—not just privately retained attorneys but also attorneys provided at public expense—be considered. Moreover, considerable care must be taken so that the fee schedules do not affect adversely the supply of attorneys representing defendants in non-capital cases."[98] The governor also pointedly noted that "the New York State District Attorney's Association played a particularly significant role in developing the bill."[99] So did the attorney general.[100] And long before the death penalty bill was even introduced, headlines attacked the supposedly liberal judges on the Court of Appeals as a threat to any capital punishment statute. Public outrage at judicial invalidation of death sentences has thrown judges in California and Mississippi out of their jobs.[101]

According to a Public Defender Backup Center report, the counsel provisions of the new statute were "worked-over repeatedly during the negotiation process, and the final version is more a product of political compromise than a coherent system designed to provide first-rate lawyers to persons the state seeks to execute."[102] The statute creates a maze of requirements for assignment and compensation of counsel and experts. "Threats to a capital defendant's right to effective and zealous representation lurk at every turn of this maze."[103]

There was no talk about Percy Foreman or F. Lee Bailey in the legislative history this time around. The first few capital trials will be high-profile and will attract high-caliber legal talent at the CDO.[104] The first New York State Capital Defender, Kevin Doyle, is a veteran of the Alabama death penalty resource center who in five and a half years in Alabama never had a client whom he had defended at trial sentenced to death. In the April 1996 *New Yorker* profile, Doyle and others are quoted as saying that New York death sentences will be a rarity.[105] The reason is that the office is "well-financed," as the report put it.[106]

But after a while the novelty will wear off, as it did in Florida and Georgia and Texas and most everywhere else.[107] When Florida's CCR was created in 1985, it attracted the best in the business: Scharlette Holdman and Mark Olive. The second CCR generation was not quite as good. The third was worse still.

Geology is the study of pressure and time. What's the difference between New York's CDO today and Florida's CCR today? Ten years.[108]

It Takes a Nun: Sunset on the Day of the Lawyers

> Monsieur Camus, you gave
> the stone of our absurdity a name.
> Daily we roll it to our graves.
> There's no reprieve.
> Later, you wrote that we are best
> when we rebel—against the casual
> unfairness of this world, against
> acceptance and the cowardice
> it hides, against rebellion
> itself.
> Rebelling with your pen,
> you called the evil of our age
> our willingness to kill within
> the law.
> —Samuel Hazo, "Stop and Be Stopped in Lourmarin"

Because I am a healer, all that I do heals.

—Martin Amis, *Time's Arrow*

"Legal interpretation takes place in a field of pain and death," Robert Cover wrote.[109] Part of this violence is metaphorical and linguistic, but only part. "Law is built on more than metaphors, and the capital trial is a vivid reminder of that fact."[110] Modern law is a creature of a "literal, bone-crushing violence," as well as of "imaginings and thoughts of force, disorder and pain."[111] Capital trials are thus both the field of pain and death upon which law plays and the field of its discursive representation. Such trials provide a "representational medium that serves as a grammar of social symbols. The criminal trial is a 'miracle play' of government in which we can carry out our inarticulate beliefs about crime and criminals within the reassuring formal structure of disinterested due process."[112]

It is perhaps fitting, and not so unsurprising, that the most eloquent and *listened-to* abolitionist voice in the national conversation about capital punishment is not that of a lawyer or a judge or a politician; it's the voice of a nun, Sister Helen Prejean. The film *Dead Man Walking* grossed more than $30 million in two months. Sister Helen's book sold 30,000 copies before the film was released, and 10 times that number since. Susan Sarandon's portrayal of Sister Helen won an Oscar for Best Actress. Sister Helen averages 25 media interviews per week.[113]

Dead Man Walking has gotten more people thinking and talking about capital punishment than four decades of academic articles written by legal eggheads like me. And working as a capital postconviction litigator today seems to me even more marginalized; postconviction defense lawyers, as lawyers, are becoming less and less relevant to the struggle against capital punishment in the United States.[114] The substantive law is bad and getting worse. The habeas corpus procedural law is worse and becoming abysmal. By conscientiously abstaining from postconviction deathwork, I'm not giving up the fight.

What this struggle needs now are storytellers and poets, as I said in Chapter 1. Lawyers can, of course, *be* storytellers and poets; some of our best capital postconviction litigators are both: Mark Olive, David Bruck, Millard Farmer, Joseph Nursey, George Kendall, Bryan Stevenson, Clive Stafford-Smith, Tim Ford.

In the past decade, I have volunteered my time to the struggle against America's legal system of capital punishment; of necessity, this devotion has, in part, been a public act. But not *too* public and no more public than I felt was necessary to zealously represent my clients within the bounds of the law. I rarely went to the demonstrations held on the cow pasture across from Florida State Prison during executions. My excuse was logistics: As often as not, I ended up being the contact person on the telephone, coordinating and keeping in touch with the desk clerk in the U.S. Supreme Court and his counterparts in the Eleventh Circuit in Atlanta and District Courts throughout Florida. The real reason I didn't go was because of the counterdemonstrators who also invariably turned out to egg the state on in its killing business. The scenes in the cow pasture were especially dramatic, during the festival celebrating the execution of Theodore Bundy, but the punks were always there. Our people, with their candles and hymns, were dignified and respectful. The others were pigs, a useless mob of ignorant chickenshit ego junkies whose only accomplishment was to embarrass the whole tradition of public protest. They were hopelessly disorganized, they had no real purpose in being there other than to be assholes, and about half of them were so wasted on beer and cheap wine that they couldn't say for sure whether they were raising hell in Starke or Miami or Jacksonville.

Attending rallies and demonstrations—even the earnest rallies and dignified demonstrations—to amplify a private belief or witness or confession makes some people feel uncomfortable. I'm one. This might be a reaction to the relentless herding and sound-bite process of today's television and advertising, to the age of orchestration and simplification of opinion and events, the creating of instant cohorts of peers. I mean no disrespect to the people who bear witness in Florida State Prison's cow pasture to Florida's killing of some of its citizens, and I don't mean to minimize the central importance that their community—*our* community—plays in my own emotional universe. But it's not as important to me as a community of three or four veterans of Florida's deathwars sitting around a table in Tallahassee or Arlie or Atlanta trying to understand what went wrong or right in their lives yesterday. Deathworkers have "words they only said to themselves by the fire."[115] The one funeral I did attend could have been any strained family gathering: awkward small talk, the crazy attempt to normalize an unbearable moment, the pointless cheerfulness.

I have also given a lot of my soul to the struggle, which has been an intensely private act. This book discusses some of the interior life, in the hope that people might better understand what the death penalty does to the people it touches.[116] That has always been at the core of my opposition to state killing: What it does to *people,* and not just to the person who is killed. We're *all* part of the collateral damage caused by capital punishment, if I may borrow an image from military nomenclature. Thomas Fowell Buxton is right that "one of the ill effects of cruelty is that it makes the bystanders cruel."

Except that in our Republic, *none* of us are merely bystanders. State-sanctioned killing is done in our name. To paraphrase Terry Tempest Williams, "We are all *hibakusha*": We are all "down winders" in Hiroshima, and in capital punishment as well. Bad karma tends to generate its own kind of poison, which—like typhoid chickens and rotten bread cast out on the waters—will usually come home to roost, fester, or mutate very close to its own point of origin. Good Morning, Mr. Bundy.

But doing deathwork by serving as a postconviction attorney . . . I just can't. Not in the age of the Rehnquist/Thomas/Scalia Court. Not in a death machine so eager to kill Joe Spaziano and to fob off that responsibility on Joe's lawyers—on *me.*

I have long thought that in understanding and appreciating the reality of capital punishment as an American legal system today—a system of premeditated, state-sponsored killing—details matter; particularly, it seems to me, bureaucratic institutional details matter. The devil is in those details. Support for capital punishment is often based on rhetorical generalities. Camus wrote, in his savage essay "Reflections on the Guillotine": "The survival of such a primitive rite has been made possible among us only by the thoughtlessness or ignorance of the public, which reacts only with the ceremonial phrases that have been drilled into it. When the imagination sleeps, words are emptied of their meaning. But if people are shown the machine, made to touch the wood and steel and to hear the sound of a head falling off, then public imagination will repudiate both the vocabulary and the penalty." In the postmodern world, of course, heads don't "fall off"; technology and medicine have provided more "humane," albeit less picturesque, mechanisms for putting down adult human beings: lethal injections, gas chambers, electric chairs, and the like. My hope is that, presented with some of the true war stories from America's death rows, you will feel, not the shock of spectacle, but rather, perhaps, the shock of recognition.

The politicians who capitalize on capital punishment—and for me that includes many judges, state and federal—will tell you that legal homicide is legitimate because it is *legal,* because executions occur under color of law, and, in a sense, they're right. Lawyers and judges run capital punishment as a legal system. In my experience, however, most of those judges, governors, and lawyers, including many defense lawyers, are cowardly sociopaths who seek refuge in the positive law to rationalize and justify (first and foremost to themselves) their evil actions.

"Evil" may strike you as too strong a word, but I think it's exactly the right word. Executing an innocent man is evil. If there's more justice in Heaven than there is on earth, these homicidal clowns will join some of my clients in hell (I dream so). I don't mean that these politicians and judges are stupid people; many sociopaths are quite intelligent. Ask Ted Bundy. I am not among those who believe the Florida executive branch has the collective intelligence of the beef jerky manufactured by my sister-in-law, Norma.

The governor who signed Joseph Spaziano's death warrant is not a stupid man; the Florida Supreme Court justices who would send Mr. Spaziano to his death are not stupid men. They are accomplices to murder, and they are cowards. But they are not stupid.

I think Arendt's "banality of evil" frame of reference possesses useful explanatory content when applied to capital punishment today. As I hope the following pages make clear, I have harsh words for the governmental bureaucrats—particularly when those bureaucrats are public defenders and call themselves "defense lawyers"—who make capital punishment a day-to-day operational reality in this country. If Camus is right that we are all either "victims" or "executioners," then the people being executed are clearly the victims. The judges and lawyers who make the capital bullet trains run on time are not victims; *they* are the ones I criticize in these pages.

I hope this book also makes clear that the word "they" in the preceding sentence includes myself. I am not a victim of the death penalty. Under Camus's dichotomy, I am an executioner. The CCR office I helped establish has become our *Judenrat*. I suggest in this book a better metaphor for my collaboration in a legal system I know is evil: I have become the executioner's mask. I have become the evil thing itself.

Capital punishment as a legal system is evil. Banal evil, to be sure, but evil nonetheless. The term "banality of evil" comes, of course, from Arendt's *Eichmann in Jerusalem*. Let me begin by saying the obvious: I am not, in any manner, comparing capital punishment today with the Shoah. I find *any* comparison with the Shoah deeply offensive, for personal family history reasons as well as for intellectual and historigraphical reasons. For my purposes, it is unfortunate that Arendt chose Eichmann as the subject for her treatment of evil's banality. Her choice of subject made it awkward to apply her insights to other contexts.

Arendt's *Eichmann* book is justly controversial because she appears to blame the Shoah's victims—particularly the Jewish Councils, the *Judenrat*[117]—for the decimation of European Jewry. That she passed such harsh judgments from her safe sinecure in the United States added to the insult. Arendt's long devotion to Martin Heidegger, father of postwar existentialism, great-uncle to the opacities of deconstruction, enthusiastic supporter of Nazism, also has not helped.[118] Arendt's book generated a sad, bitter, and pointless debate about who were "good Jews" and who were "bad Jews" under National Socialism. Even to undertake such a conversation is painful for the living and disrespectful of the dead; it seems to minimize the totalizing atmosphere of terror created by the Nazis and their real collaborators.

Still, there was truth in her observation that Eichmann was not the devil incarnate but an even more terrifying figure, an ordinary, conventional bureaucrat of the killing machine. More recent scholarship[119] reinforces the idea in *Eichmann* that the perpetrators of the Final Solution were, by and large, ordinary men and women, workers, merchants, and so on, who, millions strong, ravaged the ghettos, brutally supervised the death camps, and enthusiastically carried out Hitler's plan to obliterate world Jewry in all its manifestations—its people, of course, but also its culture, its history, and its memory. The inescapable, fundamental truth is that for the Shoah to have occurred, an enormous number of ordinary, law-abiding Germans had to become Hitler's willing executioners.[120]

Arendt was wrong in characterizing Eichmann's evil as "banal"; she came closer the first time, I think, in *Totalitarianism* when she characterized Nazism as "radical evil." Radical evil is never banal, but the men and women who do evil things are often chillingly ordinary. Killing hundreds of thousands of innocent people with the stroke of a pen, or killing one innocent person with the stroke of a pen, for that matter, is not a banal activity, but Eichmann was not a freak. He was not even very interesting. And yet we *want* him to be interesting, we need him to be different from us. To discover that there was no identifiable flaw in his character that made him different is unsettling, because that means he could be one of us.

Eichmann in Jerusalem was a reporter's account of the first major Nazi trial in Israel and also, for much of its length, a product of evident pain and anger. Anna Pierpont observed that it was Arendt's contemptuous treatment of the Jewish Councils' cooperation with Nazi authorities, a well-documented and complex and anguishing matter, that proved to be the truly incendiary element in her book. Mixing techniques of emphasis and omission, Arendt stressed the culpability of these wretched councils, while removing them from their equally wretched context of torturing decisions and hopes. By these means, Arendt mounted the accusation—head-on and inescapable this time—that the Jews were in part accountable for their own destruction. She argued that without direct Jewish cooperation, the number of Jews murdered during the war would have been drastically reduced. For Arendt, one must assume, even the awful burden of responsibility was preferable to the humiliation of the helpless victim. To deliver blame to one's own people was to deliver control and to suggest that a future was possible. And yet her pitiless righteousness, and the great height from which she peered down on those whose choices she had never faced, makes reading her judgments, even today, an unnerving experience.

In a chapter entitled "Duties of a Law Abiding Citizen," Arendt wrote that Eichmann's opportunities for feeling like Pontius Pilate were many, and as the months and the years went by, he lost the need to feel anything at all. This was the way things were, this was the new law of the land, based on the Führer's order; whatever he did he did, as far as he could see, as a law-abiding citizen. He did his *duty,* as he told the police and the court over and over again; he not only obeyed *orders,* he obeyed the *law.* There was not the slightest doubt that in one respect Eichmann did indeed follow Immanuel Kant's categorical imperative: A law was a law, and there could be no exceptions.

Arendt wrote that the trouble with Eichmann was precisely that so many were like him, and that the many were neither perverted nor sadistic: that they were, and still are, terribly and terrifyingly normal. From the viewpoint of our legal institutions and of our moral standards of judgment, this normality was much more terrifying than all the atrocities put together, for it implied (it had been said in Nuremberg over and over again by the defendants and their counsel) that this new type of criminal, who was in actual fact *hostis generis humani,* commits his crimes under circumstances that make it well nigh impossible for him to know or to feel that he is doing wrong. In describing the subtitle of her book, *A Report on the Banality of Evil,* Arendt wrote that she was reporting on the strictly factual level, pointing to a phenomenon that stared one in the face at the trial. Eichmann was not Iago and not Macbeth, and nothing would have been further from his mind than to strive with Richard III "to prove a villain." Except for an extraordinary diligence in looking out for his personal advancement, he had no motives at all. And this diligence was in no way criminal; he certainly would never have murdered his superior in order to inherit his post. He *merely,* to put the matter colloquially, *never realized what he was doing.* It was precisely this lack of imagination which enabled him to sit for months on end facing a German Jew who was conducting the police interrogation, pouring out his heart to the man and explaining again and again how it was that he reached only the rank of lieutenant colonel in the SS, and that it had not been his fault that he was not promoted. In principle, he knew quite well what it was all about, and in his final statement to the court he spoke of the "reevaluation of values prescribed by the Nazi government." He was not stupid. It was sheer thoughtlessness—something by no means identical with stupidity—that predisposed him to become one of the greatest criminals of the period. And if this is "banal" and even funny, if with the best will in the world one cannot extract any diabolical or demonic profundity from Eichmann, that is still far from calling it commonplace. That such remoteness from reality and such thoughtlessness can wreak more havoc than all the evil instincts taken together which, perhaps, are inherent in man— that was, in fact, the lesson one could learn in Jerusalem. But it was a lesson, neither an explanation of the phenomenon nor a theory about it. What came to light in the Eichmann trial was neither nihilism nor cynicism, as one might have expected, but a quite extraordinary confusion over elementary questions of morality, as if an instinct in such matters were truly the last thing to be taken for granted in our time.

Arendt's characterization of Eichmann as a government bureaucrat operating within the framework of existing law resonates throughout Ingo Müller's study *Hitler's Justice: The Courts and the Third Reich.* Written by a German lawyer and former law professor, first published in Germany, Müller's troubling book documents how and why the judges, lawyers, and law professors of a civilized state succumbed to a lawless regime. By presenting one horrific perversion of justice after the other, Müller effectively destroys one pious myth found in postwar legal literature: that judges never wavered from the positivistic tradition of German law and did no more than apply existing codes.

While Müller's book describes what happened to liberalism and the rule of law under the Third Reich in Germany, Richard Weisberg's research into the case of Vichy France offers an even more disturbing portrait of what Weisberg calls *"Cartesian lawyers and the unspeakable."*[121] His research into Vichy law indicates how free and creative Vichy was in both finding and persecuting Jews. In most key respects, Vichy racial policy was self-created; and it so often surpassed the German models that it was extended to the occupied zone and to conquered foreign territories such as the British Channel Islands. Through a legalistic triad of statutory definition, judicial interpretation, and administrative fiat, many individuals and some entire groups left alone by the Nazis were victimized by the French. On occasions the Germans slapped the wrists of French courts and agencies that they felt had been unnecessarily harsher than their own courts on the subject of racial definition. Weisberg writes that to Vichy, which created and then scrupulously implemented its own version of the racial laws, "resistance" to German pressure had nothing to do with savings Jews. It had everything to do with saving the French government, French traditions, French law. Central to this enterprise was Pierre Laval, himself a lawyer.

Weisberg makes a powerful case that the German lust for Jewish bodies continued to be mediated in France by a reliance on what he calls "legalistic Vichy." Law, not passion, informed Vichy's approach to the Jews. Anti-Semitism alone does not explain Vichy's racial policies, except as they satisfied the average Frenchman's need to find a scapegoat for the humiliating military defeat. The enormity of Vichy's extensive and complex persecution of the Jews was more a function of a kind of desiccated rationalism, embodied in the web of laws, decrees, judicial opinions, and learned articles that fill the pages of French law books for the years 1940–44. These legalisms, wrought with the delicate and often superficially eloquent subtlety of French culture, eventually extended to both French zones a unique opportunity for the Nazis to minimize their own manpower requirements and watch the French "do it themselves." At the same time, it gave the French the illusion of preserving a part of their precious heritage, the logic of Descartes and the aesthetically pleasing rhetoric of the Codes.

Weisberg argues that the "Cartesian lawyers," not the virulent Jew-haters, accounted for the high "kill rate" in France. Once their own racial laws were inscribed, hundreds of relatively normal people in the legal and administrative domains collectively worked through the grotesque structure to its logical conclusion. If, in many areas, these conclusions exceeded anything the Nazis themselves had wrought, so be it. The system of laws, minutely elaborated and scrupulously followed, had taken on a life of its own, cerebral and utterly lacking in any sense of common justice—but a life, nonetheless. Weisberg quotes an internal German memorandum of January 21, 1941: "The French believe in the letter of the law . . . they do not understand the idea of a clean sweep." Every arrest and subsequent deportation from then on was linked in the German mind to the development of French law, allowed to work autonomously according to a Gallic model that the Germans cleverly realized would give them what they wanted, almost effortlessly.

Fifty years ago René Bousquet was head of the police at the height of the mass deportation of French Jews. When he was killed in 1993, the initial guess was that the killing must have been the work of a descendant of one of his victims, unable to bear the idea that such a scoundrel should be living comfortably, untormented by conscience. As it turned out, however, the "avenger" was a frustrated scrivener who craved celebrity rather than justice. The media gave him the limelight he was seeking, but in killing Bousquet he deprived France of a trial that would have thrown light on the complicity of high-level officials in Nazi crimes.

Bousquet was one of three elderly Frenchmen facing trial for crimes against humanity committed during the Nazi occupation. He was, however, the crucial one. Paul Touvier, for so long protected by the Catholic clergy, was a sort of junior Klaus Barbie, a bloody torturer who operated on a local scale in the Lyons area. Maurice Papon, who became an influential politician after the war, was also a local figure, whose atrocities were confined to Bordeaux. Bousquet was much more than a provincial, anti-Semitic thug. He was a brilliant member of the establishment and, as head of the French police in 1942–43, was responsible for repression and deportations throughout France. His example shows how far *raison d'etat* combined with ruthless ambition can lead. Singer concluded that his case is worth examining because it tells us a great deal about the ambiguous relationship between postwar French politics and wartime collaboration. The trial of Klaus Barbie simply confirmed the criminality of the Germans. To bring a Bousquet to court was quite a different matter. A trial would adduce evidence of French complicity in those crimes at the highest level. It was likely to lead to a real debate about the state, its institutions, its function, and its morality.

Weisberg concludes that Vichy's lesson for us is particularly acute because the values of French constitutional law, most of which remained on the books during Vichy, are similar to many that we hold dear. Yet first principles are often redefined during moral crises. What happens, particularly among professionals like lawyers and scholars, is that the rational bases of their training become a moral end in themselves, while previously precious principles become devalued. People like you and me put on our professional masks. Paradoxically, this is simpler when the system (as in France and the United States) appears to have been idealistic to begin with. Thus people who were hitherto morally sensitive might actually use their allegiance to law to propound a system that would have seemed grotesque just months or years before. Their idealism was focused on a narrow band of issues: "Is an individual with two Jewish and two non-Jewish grandparents to be considered a Jew?" replaced "Does our legal system permit such an inquiry?" An equally legalistic question, but one asked only by a tiny minority of French lawyers during the Vichy period.

And Weisberg asks: "Could the same thing happen here? Well, a look at American antebellum law books indicates that it already has." As Eugene Genovese has argued, slaveholders were not uniquely evil; rather they were "good and decent people who tried to live decently with their slaves." In this they were doomed to fail, "for at the bottom their relations with their slaves rested on injustice and violence."[122] It should be recalled of the Declaration of Independence that a slaveholder wrote it, and that slaveholders signed it.

Perhaps the first lesson of Vichy is that we must rip away the mask of professional narrowness in times of crisis and force ourselves to see and address the larger issues that are in fact a part of that practice. "Moral neutrality" does not exist in professional practice. Think of all the doctors[123] and lawyers who served Hitler. Think not of thugs like Julius Strieker. Think of Martin Heidegger[124] and Paul de Man.

We, like Laval, are always powerful enough to define our own professional perspective. Like the French who served Vichy, we are solely responsible for the focus we bring to our words and deeds.

Capital punishment is here to stay, in one form or another. But the forms themselves fall along a surprisingly broad spectrum of possibilities. All capital punishment schemes are not created awful, and, while they are all, in my opinion, bad to a greater or lesser degree, some are much worse than others, and the degree of hideousness does make a life or death difference. Some states, like California, do attempt to provide high-quality legal representation at trial, on appeal, and throughout the capital post-conviction process. Many states, like Texas, seem quirkily proud of how lazily and stupidly they impose, review, and carry out death sentences.

To be sure, important constitutional legal issues remain to be resolved in individual cases. Such claims, however, are different from the basic, systemic challenges that once typified death penalty litigation. Prior challenges revolved around such questions as whether retribution is a legitimate goal of a decent, civilized penal system, whether the death penalty is arbitrary, whether the imposition of capital punishment is so racist that it offends the federal Constitution, whether capital punishment deters crime more effectively than lengthy imprisonment, and so on. This narrowing of claims from the systemic to the individual is exemplified by the present state of litigation surrounding deterrence. It is no longer viable to litigate that the evolving social scientific evidence demonstrates that the death penalty does not deter. Instead, advocacy concerns the right of an individual person on trial for his life to present social scientific evidence at that trial.

268

The goal is to save the individual rather than to attack the core jurisprudential assumptions or federal constitutionality of the death penalty itself. In fact, to the extent that specific cases present issues of broader-gauge application, it may be wise to deemphasize the larger questions and market one's case as presenting the smallest target possible. The question I most dread from judges at oral argument is: "Counsel, if we rule your way, won't we also have to grant relief in a lot of other cases that present the same claim?" The correct answer to this venomous question is always some form of the word "no." To sanitize a line from Richard Pryor, "I want to be in *that* line," that short line of people moving off death row and on to (into) life.

The demarcations are not as clear as I'm making them sound. No clear lines exist between "systemic" defects in capital punishment as a system and "individual" defects in specific cases. The unfairness of a particular death sentence is often symptomatic of more general flaws in the death penalty system itself. There has, however, been a paradigm shift in the ways that courts and litigants conceptualize and confront these problems. No longer are courts interested in broad-based attacks on the death penalty. The fight is for one life at a time, playing for time in the hope of keeping our people alive until we can come up with the magic admixture of new facts and new law and good luck that we can file in *exactly* the right court at *exactly* the right time and in *exactly* the right manner that will get them off death row altogether. The irony is the need to convince the courts that granting relief in a particular case will not "open the floodgates" to granting relief in many other cases.

"Let's get small," quipped Steve Martin. He was not referring to constitutional issues in capital cases, of course, but his admonition fits this context like a fingerprint. The paradigm shift from the macro to the micro, from the mega-constitutional claim to the microscopic constitutional claim, along with the shifting battleground from the broad issue to the individual case and the increasing impatience with capital cases generally, must be understood in terms of a burgeoning death row. Never before in American history have so many people awaited death as a punishment. There are presently more than 3,000 men and women under sentence of death in the United States, spread over 38 states and federal custody. There are nearly 400 in Florida alone. State and federal courts in the southeastern United States, where the concentration of condemned inmates is the greatest, have in the past decade and a half been swamped by the sheer number and complexity of the appeals and collateral proceedings. Judges, being human, may begin to tire of these cases and become numbed by the volume. Our society's desire to make executions easier may make us forget that we are dealing with people's lives. Taking life becomes routine, if not boringly banal, bureaucratically, tediously monotonous.

The precedents defining the landscape of present capital litigation form the closed universe within which the zealous advocate must operate "within the bounds of the law." It is a world within which state-sponsored killing is accepted as legally permissible. Legalistic resistance to executions therefore becomes paradoxical. The system is attacked, but this attack becomes institutionalized and thus, to some extent, domesticated. We're not lapdogs (or potted plants), but we're not arsonists or bomb throwers, either. We're lawyers. We're only lawyers. We make mistakes. Those mistakes ought not to kill people. But they do.

My fear is that the above discussion about "conscientious abstention" from deathwork might appear to be—might in fact *be*—a self-justifying rationalization, an illusion that allows me to explain (to myself, mostly) why I am a tenured law professor, teaching at a sometimes indulgent institution, while people are being killed at an ever-increasing rate in the South of my birth. If the need for lawyers is as acute as I argue that it is; if the capital punishment system is as god-awful as I believe it is, what the hell am I doing in Vermont?

I'm here because I can no longer, in good conscience, participate in this deformed legal system. I'm not "burned out," although I won't deny the pain.[125] Bringing a very finite me to bear on an infinite punishment, where mistakes—*my* mistakes, because I take these things personally—could be and were the proximate cause of death of a person I'd grown close to, was simply too much to bear. Maybe it's too much to expect *anyone* to bear; often at CCR I thought of Robert E. Lee's statement after the third day of Gettysburg: "All this has been my fault. I asked more of men than should have been asked of them." Whatever. I also thought a lot about *M*A*S*H* during the time I did in Tallahassee.

At CCR in the mid-1980s, triage was the way of life: death warrant cases that had already been through the federal courts took top priority; followed by warrant cases that hadn't; followed by the nonwarrant briefs, petitions, investigations, hearings, and all the rest. And overlaid on the case triage was our own emotional triage. No matter how hard we worked, no matter how good we were, no matter how clever we were, the state was going to kill some of the people we represented. As I said at the beginning of this book, battles remain (that military imagery again!), but the war is over, and we lost. I miss the work.

Be clear: Nothing I write here should be construed as insisting that others not take on capital cases; to the contrary, in every year before 1995, I encouraged my best students to do deathwork. I don't know how I'll advise them now. Each person must listen to and follow her own conscience. The actions we take dictate the life we lead.

At a minimum, we all need to be conscious of the implications of becoming a component of the death penalty system. Because, inevitably, to some degree that *is* what we become. Eventually, individual consciousness—abstention or an organized strike—might become preferable to enablement. For myself that time is now. For others, not now, but maybe by and by. Maybe not. Maybe yes.

Of course, my becoming a conscientious objector means that people I might have represented may be electrocuted, injected, hanged, or shot. Correctly or not, I am convinced that had I made this decision two years ago, Joe Spaziano would have been killed on schedule.

But maybe that's OK in the long run. The idea is that only an increase in the number and frequency of "mistaken" executions will exceed the public's tolerance for capital punishment itself. David Cole made the point that what truly could bring about serious movement toward abolition is "the accelerated pace of executions, together with the elimination of the death penalty resource centers and restrictions on federal court review, [insuring] that the years to come will see more and more errors in the administration of death."[126]

Cole is also right that the prospect of adopting such a "strategy" is "almost too terrible to contemplate." By the time Joe Spaziano's fifth death warrant was signed in August 1995, it was clear to me that the political cause of abolition would have been served best by his execution. The media and much of the public would not have forgotten soon the electrocution of this innocent man whose trial was a joke. After all, England abolished the death penalty in the 1950s following public revulsion over the execution of an innocent man. When Joe's execution was stayed, capital punishment supporters, including the *Miami Herald,* felt reinforced in their sense of security that *really* innocent men aren't put to death in this day and age. Similarly, my next law review article will argue that states probably can, consistent with the court's recent proportionality cases, execute rapists.[127]

We are killing people who are innocent, people who were children when they committed their crimes, people who are crazy, people who just don't deserve to die. We also killed Ted Bundy, and maybe that makes all the rest of it worthwhile. But not for me, and not in my name. I must agree with Theodore Dreiser, who asked, in *An American Tragedy,* "Are we, the public, the ones who really committed this crime?" *We* are responsible, you and I and Lawton Chiles and CCR and the judges and lawyers who delude themselves by thinking that participating in an evil system makes them anything other than evil, even if the evil thing is the law. My *experience* over the past decade convinces me that, as presently practiced, the death penalty is anathema to civilization. I believe that basic decency negates any justification for our system of institutionalized homicide.

This book is one I have dreaded writing; it is one I've resisted writing for at least half a decade. I hope I am wrong, and that others will show how wrong I am, in deciding to conscientiously abstain from representing death row prisoners in postconviction proceedings.

Over the next few years, capital punishment will become ever more entrenched in our national politics and in our national psyche. More states will adopt death penalty statutes, and the existing capital punishment states will join the federal judiciary in deregulating death, streamlining the system, and expediting executions. We will execute a few monsters like Bundy, and a few innocents like "Crazy Joe" Spaziano, but mostly we will execute run-of-the-mill killers.

Eventually, however, this pointless killing by our government will end in this country—as it has ended in most of the rest of the "civilized" world. I have enough faith in the soul of the American people to hope, even now, in the midst of the capital punishment juggernaut, that such a time will come for us. Someday we will make our national peace with legal homicide. But some kinds of peace can only be found on the other side of war.

Postscript

In January 1996, Seminole County, Florida, Circuit Judge O. H. Eaton, Jr., conducted an eight-day evidentiary hearing in *Spaziano v. State*. After the hearing, Judge Eaton ordered a new trial for Mr. Spaziano. Judge Eaton's unpublished opinion reads as follows:

IN THE CIRCUIT COURT OF THE
EIGHTEENTH JUDICIAL CIRCUIT
IN AND FOR SEMINOLE COUNTY,
FLORIDA
CASE NO. 75 – 430-CFA

STATE OF FLORIDA,
    Plaintiff,

vs.

JOSEPH R. SPAZIANO,
    Defendant.

ORDER VACATING JUDGMENT AND SENTENCE
AND
SETTING TRIAL DATE

On September 12, 1995, the Supreme Court of Florida entered an order treating two out-of-time motions for rehearing as a successive Rules of Criminal Procedure 3.850–3.851 motion based upon newly discovered evidence of the recantation of the testimony of a significant witness and remanded this case to this court for consideration of that issue. *Spaziano v. State,* 660 So. 2d 1363 (Fla. 1995). By separate order dated October 12, 1995, the Supreme Court directed this court to commence an evidentiary hearing no later than January 15, 1996. The hearing commenced on January 8, 1996, and was completed on January 15, 1996. At that time the matter was taken under advisement.

273

Postscript

THE ISSUE

The issue to be decided is whether, due to the newly discovered evidence of the recanted testimony of Anthony Delisio, the defendant is entitled to a new trial.

THE LAW OF NEWLY DISCOVERED EVIDENCE
AND RECANTED TESTIMONY

In order to prevail on newly discovered evidence the defendant must prove:

1. the evidence has been discovered since the former trial;
2. the evidence could not have been discovered earlier through the exercise of due diligence;
3. the evidence is material to the issue;
4. the evidence goes to the merits of the case and not merely impeachment of the character of a witness;
5. the evidence must not be merely cumulative; and
6. the evidence must be such that it would probably produce a different result in retrial.

Jones v. State, 591 So. 2d 911 (Fla. 1992); *Henderson v. State,* 195 So. 625 (Fla. 1938); *Smith v. State,* 158 So. 91 (Fla. 1934); *Beasley v. State,* 315 So. 2d 540 (Fla. 2d DCA 1975); *Weeks v. State,* 253 So. 2d 459 (Fla. 3d DCA 1971).

In determining whether a new trial is warranted due to recantation of a witness's testimony, a trial judge is to examine all the circumstances of the case, including the testimony of the witnesses submitted on the issue. *Armstrong v. State,* 642 So. 2d 730 (Fla. 1994); *Bell v. State,* 90 So. 2d 704 (Fla. 1956). Moreover, recanting testimony is exceedingly unreliable, and it is the duty of the court to deny a new trial where it is not satisfied that such testimony is true. Especially is this true where the recantation involves a confession of perjury. *Id.* at 705; *Henderson v. State, supra.*

FINDINGS OF FACT

Trial judges are taught to determine the credibility of a witness and the weight to be given to testimony by considering the demeanor of the witness; the frankness or lack of frankness of the witness; the intelligence of the witness; the interest, if any, that the witness has in the outcome of the case; the means and opportunity the witness had to know the facts about which the witness testifies; the ability of the witness to remember the events; and the reasonableness of the testimony considered in light of all of the evidence in the case. Additionally, trial judges attempt to reconcile any conflicts in the evidence without imputing untruthfulness to any witness. However, if conflicts cannot be reconciled, evidence unworthy of belief must be rejected in favor of evidence which is worthy of belief. These principles have been applied here, although it has not always been easy.

The crucial testimony at the trial of this case in 1976 came from the mouth of Anthony Delisio. It was he who provided the only evidence of the cause of death of the decedent and it was he who supplied the jury with the evidence connecting this tragic event to the defendant. Without his testimony, there simply is no corroborating evidence in the trial record that is sufficient to sustain the verdict—not even any evidence from the medical examiner who performed the autopsy.

Delisio now testifies that he did not tell the truth during the trial and provides a complicated explanation of the events which led up to his trial testimony. This testimony is credible and is corroborated by other evidence to a significant extent.

Delisio testified that he and his five siblings lived in a dysfunctional family ruled by his father, Ralph Delisio, who physically abused them. Delisio tried to please his father but he never succeeded. His father owned a boat dealership known as Maitland Marine and Delisio frequented the business as a young teenager.

Ralph Delisio started an affair with a younger woman employee named Keppy who seduced Delisio when he was fifteen and with whom he had frequent sexual intercourse for about two and one half years. His father and Keppy ultimately married. Delisio had sex with her for the last time on their wedding day. It was during this time that Delisio started using drugs including marijuana, hash and alcohol.

The defendant worked at the marina and Delisio knew who he was. There is a conflict as to just how close their relationship was but none of the witnesses who testified were able to establish a fast friendship.

Not surprisingly, Keppy began to have a sexual relationship with the defendant. Ralph Delisio found out and became angry. At some point Keppy accused the defendant of raping her. It was about that time that Ralph Delisio asked his son if the defendant had told him that he mutilated women. Delisio testified that the defendant never said anything like that to him. But the idea was planted in his mind.

Delisio's mid-teenage years included several brushes with the law. He ran away from a drug treatment center in a stolen car with two other juveniles and ended up in Volusia's House. It was there that Detectives Abbgy and Martindale, who were investigating the homicide in this case, approached Delisio for information. After being encouraged by his father to cooperate with the police, he agreed to be hypnotized in order to refresh his memory.

The detective induced Delisio to cooperate by inferring that his cooperation would get him out of Volusia House and would result in several serious criminal charges being dropped. They also supplied him with bits of information prior to the hypnosis session. He was scared. He went along with the police in an effort to please them and his father.

After the first hypnosis session was over, Delisio did not think the police believed he cooperated. In fact, he "recalled" very little during the first session. It was then that the police took him to the scene of the homicide. A second hypnosis session was scheduled the next day.

275

Tapes of the sessions are in evidence, as are the transcripts. The hypnotist does not give the listener confidence in his abilities. The defense experts who testified about the sessions and procedures agreed. One of them gave the hypnotist a "double F" and the other rated his skill level at "zero." It is plain from the testimony of these two distinguished experts that the reliability of the procedure used should be seriously doubted and that the information which was produced as a result was unreliable. Both experts agreed that hypnosis cannot improve recall beyond that which can be recalled through conscious efforts and that is exactly what the hypnotist thought he could do. It is most likely that the crime scene depicted by Delisio is a scene that he created for the purpose of pleasing the police and his father. One of the experts even pointed out that the actual crime scene did not match Delisio's depiction in several material respects.

The State called several witnesses in order to attack Delisio's testimony and destroy his credibility. Many of these witnesses had major credibility problems themselves. One of the witnesses, a murderer in the Federal witness protection program, testified that he and the defendant were in prison together after the defendant was sentenced to life for rape but before the trial in this case. The witness heard the defendant express concern over a young boy whom he had taken to see some dead bodies. The reliability of that statement is questionable. If the statement was made, it is likely that the defendant was discussing the testimony he had learned Delisio was going to give at trial. That is the only way to reconcile the testimony with Delisio's version of the events without rejecting it as being untruthful.

Another witness, Bill O'Connell, was a counselor at the Volusia House and knew Delisio while he was there. He stated that Delisio was having trouble sleeping and told him that he had taken the police to a grave site. However, that statement, if made, does not agree with other credible evidence in the case unless it was made after Delisio had developed his testimony for the trial. The same is true of the statement Annette Jones says Delisio made to her and the statement Delisio says he made to Sandy Vehman.

CONCLUSION OF LAW

In the United States of America every person, no matter how unsavory, is entitled to due process of law and a fair trial. The defendant received neither. The validity of the verdict in this case rests upon the testimony of an admitted perjurer who had every reason to fabricate a story which he hoped would be believed. The courts of this country should not tolerate the deprivation of life or liberty under such circumstances. A fair trial requires a determination of the truth by an informed jury. The verdict of an uninformed jury results in an unfair trial. An unfair trial is an unlawful trial because it produces an illegal result.

The evidence of recantation in this case is newly discovered evidence which could not have been discovered earlier through the exercise of due diligence. It is material evidence which goes to the merits of the case. It is not cumulative evidence and it would probably produce a different result on retrial. As Justice Kogan stated in his concurring opinion remanding this case to this court:

"Today we are presented with a grossly disturbing scenario; a man facing imminent execution (*a*) even though his jury's vote for life imprisonment would be legally binding today, (*b*) with his conviction resting almost entirely on testimony tainted by a hypnotic procedure this Court has condemned; (*c*) with the source of that tainted testimony now swearing on penalty of perjury that his testimony was false, and (*d*) without careful consideration of this newly discovered evidence under the only legal method available, Rule of Criminal Procedure 3.850 or 3.851." *Spaziano v. State, supra* at 1367. That careful consideration has now been given and the validity of the Judgment and sentence has been found to be so questionable that it cannot stand.

IT IS ADJUDGED:

1. The Judgment rendered on January 23, 1976, and the sentence entered on June 4, 1981, are vacated.

2. This case is set for trial during the trial period commencing March 25, 1996, with docket sounding on March 12, 1996.

ORDERED at Sanford, Seminole County, Florida, this 22nd day of January, 1996.

O. H. Eaton, Jr.
Circuit Judge

The state appealed Judge Eaton's new trial order to the Florida Supreme Court. Briefs were filed in the spring and summer of 1996. The court heard oral argument in December 1996, and ruled against the state in April 1997. The new trial is scheduled to begin in October.

Notes
Index

Notes

Chapter 1. Deathwatch: A Sort of Introduction

Welcome to the underbook, where the author cites his sources, points out controversies, justifies his own judgments, and makes clear where reporting ends and imagination begins. The primary purpose here is to separate fact from opinion. This is where you see that, to borrow a line from Dave Barry, "I am not making this up."

1. Michael Mello, "Facing Death Alone," 37 *American University Law Review* 513 (1988); Michael Mello, "Is There a Federal Constitutional Right to Counsel in Capital Postconviction Proceedings?" 79 *Journal of Criminal Law and Criminology* 1065 (1989).

2. Albert Camus, *Notebooks, 1942–1951,* at 146 (1991).

3. I dearly hope Camus was right when he wrote in his notebooks for November 1942: "Let's suppose a philosopher who after having published several works declares in a new book: 'Up until now I was going in the wrong direction. I am going to begin all over. I think now that I was wrong.' No one would take him seriously any more. And yet he would then be giving proof that he is worthy of thought." *Supra* n. 2.

4. Michael Mello, *Against the Death Penalty: The Relentless Dissents of Justices Brennan and Marshall* (1996).

5. E.g., Saundra Torry, "Juggling the Issue of Representing Death Row Inmates," *Washington Post,* March 4, 1996.

6. E.g., Vivian Berger, "The Chiropractor as Brain Surgeon: Defense Lawyering in Capital Cases," 18 *New York University Review of Law and Social Change* 245, 249 (1991); see also Jack Greenberg & Jack Himmelstein, "Varieties of Attack on the Death Penalty," 15 *Crime and Delinquency* 112, 114 (1969) (noting that nearly 100 percent of those executed from 1930 until 1967 were indigent); Michael G. Millemann, "Financing the Right to Counsel in Capital Cases," 19 *Loyola of Los Angeles Law Review* 383, 384 (1985) (reporting that in California fewer than 2 percent of death row inmates were represented by retained counsel); William P. Redick, "The Crisis in Representation of Tennessee Capital Cases," *Tennessee Bar Journal,* March/April 1993, at 22, 23 (estimating that more than 75 percent of all capital defendants in Tennessee are indigent at the trial stage); Ronald

J. Tabak & J. Mark Lane, "The Execution of Injustice: A Cost and Lack-of-Benefit Analysis of the Death Penalty," 23 *Loyola of Los Angeles Law Review* 59, 70 (1989) (reporting that approximately 90 percent of those on death row in 1985 had appointed counsel when convicted) (citing John Conyers, Jr., "The Death Penalty Lottery," *New York Times,* July 1, 1985).

7. Mack Reed, "Dearth of Attorneys Creates Backlog on California's Death Row," *Los Angeles Times,* April 6, 1996.

8. Death Penalty Information Center, *With Justice for Few: The Growing Crisis in Death Penalty Representation* 21 (1995); see also Steven Keeva, "Justice on Death Row," *American Bar Association Journal,* April 1996, at 105 (quoting Professor Michael Millemann, "More than 100 death row inmates in Pennsylvania alone will not have representation."); Kathleen Berexa, "The Coming Crisis in Death Penalty Cases," *Pittsburgh Legal Journal,* May 18, 1995, at 32; Hank Grezlak, "Castille: Death-Row Inmates Need Lawyers Now," 18 *Pennsylvania Law Weekly* 484 (April 24, 1995). On the counsel crisis generally see, e.g., Editorial, "A Good Defense," *Pittsburgh Post-Gazette,* Aug. 20, 1995; Stephen Maskaleris, "Cavalier Defense Leads to Death for Many," *National Law Journal,* Feb. 12, 1996, at A21; Anthony Lewis, "Cruel and Reckless," *New York Times,* Aug. 11, 1995; Torry, *supra* n. 5.

9. President Clinton signed the bill on the first anniversary of the Oklahoma City bombing; victims of the bombing and other terror attacks flanked the president as he signed the bill. On the habeas provisions of the crime bill generally, see "Habeas Proposal Stresses Only Appeals Counsel," *National Law Journal,* April 1, 1996, at A14; Editorial, "Terrorist Victory," *Rutland Herald,* April 23, 1996; Editorial, "Grave Trouble for the Great Writ," *New York Times,* April 8, 1996; Anthony Lewis, "Stand Up for Liberty," *New York Times,* April 15, 1996; Anthony Lewis, "How Terrorism Wins," *New York Times,* March 11, 1996; Anthony Lewis, "Mr. Clinton's Betrayal," *New York Times,* July 7, 1995; Anthony Lewis, "Is It a Zeal to Kill?" *New York Times,* Dec. 8, 1995; Stephen Labarton, "Effort to Derail Anti-Terrorism Bill Fails," *New York Times,* April 17, 1996; Peter Rubin, "Terror Struck," *New Republic,* Sept. 4, 1995, at 17. For an argument that aspects of the statute are unconstitutional, see Michael Mello and Donna Duffy, "Suspending Justice," 18 *New York University Review of Law and Social Change* 451 (1990–91).

The Supreme Court expedited review of the new statute's constitutionality. Linda Greenhouse, "Justices, with Rare Speed, Agree to Review New Law on Appeals," *New York Times,* May 4, 1996.

10. Report of the Subcommittee on Death Penalty Representation, Judicial Conference of the United States (June 1995); Carol Castaneda, "Death Penalty Centers Losing Support, Funds," *USA Today,* Oct. 24, 1995; Marcia Coyle, "Death Resource Centers Reborn as Private Groups," *National Law Journal,* Jan. 15, 1996; Lis Wiehl, "Program for Death-Row Appeals Facing Its Own Demise," *New York Times,* Aug. 11, 1995; *National Law Journal,* Aug. 7, 1995; *National Law Journal,* July 31, 1995; Editorial, *Washington Post,* July 22, 1995.

11. Michael Radelet, Hugo Bedau, and Constance Putnam, *In Spite of Innocence* (1992).

12. Bryan Marquard, "Lawyer Pushes Ethics Envelope," *Valley News* [Lebanon, N.H.], Oct. 8, 1995.

13. Diane Rado, "Spaziano's Lawyer Says State Lied," *St. Petersburg Times,* Sept. 1, 1995.

14. Letter from Michael Mello to Gov. Lawton Chiles (Aug. 3, 1995). Camus, of course, suggested that there is no difference between capital punishment and murder. Albert Camus, *Reflections on the Guillotine* 123, 126 (1957).

15. William Stringfellow, *Free in Obedience* (1964); Martin Luther King, Jr., "Letter from Birmingham Jail," in *A Testament of Hope* 289 (1986); Henry David Thoreau, "Civil Disobedience," in *Walden* 85 (1962).

16. Andrew McThenia, "Civic Resistance or Holy Obedience?" 48 *Washington and Lee Law Review* 15, 15–16 (1991); Robert Cover, "Foreword," 97 *Harvard Law Review* 4, 46–47 (1983).

17. Thomas Shaffer, *American Legal Ethics* 541 (1981); see also David Luban, *Lawyers and Justice* (the later chapters).

18. For some lovely thoughts on lawyers, see Sister Helen Prejean, Symposium, 23 *Hofstra Law Review* 627, 652–53 (1995).

19. Margaret Radin, "Cruel Punishment and Respect for Persons: Super Due Process for Death," 53 *Southern California Law Review* 1143 (1980).

20. E.g., Daniel Goldhagen, *Hitler's Willing Executioners* (1996).

21. Michael Mello, "On Mirrors, Metaphors and Murders: Theodore Bundy and the Rule of Law" in Colloquium: Challenging the Death Penalty, 18 *New York University Review Law and Social Change* 889 (1990–1991).

22. Callins v. Collins, 114 S. Ct. 1127 (1994).

23. E.g., Hugo Bedau, *Death Is Different* (1987); Leon Shaskolsky Sheleff, *Ultimate Penalties: Capital Punishment, Life Imprisonment, Physical Torture* (1989); Walter Berns, *For Capital Punishment* (1979); Glen King, "On Behalf of the Death Penalty," in *The Death Penalty in America* (H. Bedau ed. 1982); Anthony Amsterdam, "Capital Punishment," in *The Death Penalty in America* (H. Bedau ed. 1982); Ernest van den Haag & Joseph Conrad, *The Death Penalty: A Debate* (1983); William Bowers, *Legal Homicide* (1984); Franklin Zimring & Gordon Hawkins, *Capital Punishment and the American Agenda* (1986); Kimberly J. Cook, "Punitiveness and Public Opinion on Abortion and Capital Punishment" (1994) (unpublished Ph.D. dissertation, University of New Hampshire).

24. Charles Black, *Capital Punishment* (1974).

25. Susan Smith in South Carolina was the highest-profile female defendant in a potentially capital case in recent years. E.g., Abbe Smith, "The Law vs. Women," *Boston Globe,* Feb. 27, 1995; AP, "Smith Testimony Poses Risk for Defense," *Myrtle Beach Sun News,* June 26, 1995; Stephanie Saul, "In Union, Passing Time Tempers Demand for Death in Smith Case," *Newsday,* June 26, 1995; Steven Roberts, "The Murderer Who Was Too Pathetic to Kill," *U.S. News & World Reports,* Aug. 7, 1995, at 9; Rick Bragg, "Sheriff Says Prayer and a Lie Led Susan Smith to Confess," *New York Times,* July 18, 1995; Rick Bragg, "Touching and Grim Testimony in Smith Trial," *New York Times,* July 20, 1995; Rick Bragg, "Mother Was Remorseful, Witness Says," *New York Times,* July 21, 1995; AP, "Susan Smith Is Spared," *St. Petersburg Times,* July 29, 1995; Rick Bragg, "Susan Smith Verdict

Brings Relief to Town," *New York Times,* July 30, 1995; Christopher Allen, "Union, S.C., Looks to Heal," *Valley News,* July 30, 1995; Brian McGory, "After Smith Trial, S.C. Town Begins to Heal," *Boston Globe,* July 30, 1995; "Who Deserves to Die?" *Newsweek* (cover story), Aug. 7, 1995; Anne Hull, "At the Water's Edge," *St. Petersburg Times,* July 9, 1995; Rick Bragg, "Carolina Jury Rejects Execution for Woman Who Drowned Sons," *New York Times,* July 29, 1995; Brian McGory, "Smith Given Life Term for Sons' Death," *Boston Globe,* July 29, 1995.

For an excellent analysis of why relatively few women are sentenced to death, see Joan Howarth, "Feminism, Lawyering, and Death Row," 2 *Southern California Review of Law & Women's Studies* 401 (1991). According to the indispensable archival and tracking work done by Watt Espy of Headland, Alabama, and Victor Streib of Cleveland State University Law School, and updated regularly by Streib, both the female death-sentencing rate and the female death row population remain very small in comparison to the figures for males. Streib observed that actual execution of female offenders is quite rare, with only about 520 documented instances, beginning with the first in 1632. These 520 female executions constitute less than 3 percent of the total of approximately 18,600 confirmed executions since 1608. The most recent female offender executed was Velma Barfield in North Carolina on November 2, 1984 (see generally Velma Barfield, *Woman on Death Row* [1985]), the only female among the 248 offenders executed in the post-*Furman* era (1973–94). Prior to this current era, the last female offender executed was Elizabeth Ann Duncan, executed by California on August 8, 1962. Streib reported that the annual rate of death sentences for female offenders has remained around five (or under 2 percent of the annual total) for many years. A total of 101 female death sentences have been imposed, under 2 percent of the total of about 5,198 death sentences for all offenders. Despite some fluctuations, particularly in the early years of this period, the death sentencing rate for female offenders was typically about five per year beginning in the 1980s.

Streib noted that in 1989 this annual death sentencing rate doubled for reasons unknown. In 1990 and 1991, the sentencing rate seemed to have returned to just above the pre-1989 levels. The rate then surged to 10 in 1992, portending an annual rate again nearly double that of the 1980s. This is about 4 percent of the death sentences imposed in 1992, suggesting a significant increase in the rate of the death sentencing of female offenders. However, four of these 10 death sentences were imposed on the same person (Aileen Wuornos in Florida, a prostitute who was herself a victim of child abuse, found guilty of luring male travelers off Florida highways, Interstate 4 or Interstate 75, and killing them; see generally Wuornos v. State, No. 79, 484 (Fla. Sept. 22, 1994) (opinion on direct appeal affirming one of Wuornos' murder convictions and death sentences for the killing of Richard Mallory; the court's opinion noted that the sentencing jury's recommendation for death was unanimous, 12–0, and that "at trial, the state was allowed [by trial judge Uriel "Bunky" Blount] to introduce similar-crimes evidence about Wuornos' alleged involvement in several other murders": Charles Richard Humphreys, Peter Siems, Walter Jeno Antonio, Troy Burress, David Spears, Charles Clarkaddon); Wuornos v. State (Fla. Oct. 6, 1994) (unanimous opinion on direct appeal, rejecting challenges to Wuornos' three other first degree murder convictions and death sentences for the killings of Troy Burress, Charles Humphreys, and David Spears; Wuornos had pleaded no contest in these murders); Michael Reynolds, *Dead Ends* (1993); Dolores Kennedy, *On a Killing Day* (1992)), leaving only six other female death sentences during 1992. Total female death sentences then returned to the normal level: five in 1993. Streib reported that in any event, the number of female offenders sentenced to prison death rows each year remains under 0.2 percent of the approximately 3,700 women sentenced to prison each year.

Of these 101 death sentences for female offenders, Streib reported that only 36 sentences (imposed upon 33 females) remain currently in effect (*Ms.* reported, without verifiable documentation, that "of the 35 women on death row in 1993, almost half were there for the murder of an abusive partner"; "Where Do We Go from Here? An Interview with Ann Jones," *Ms.*, Sept.–Oct. 1994, at 62; on domestic violence generally, see Angela Browne, *When Battered Women Kill* (1987); Ann Jones, *Next Time, She'll Be Dead* (1994)). One such sentence resulted in an execution (Velma Barfield), and another 64 death sentences were reversed or commuted to life imprisonment, according to Streib. Thus, for the 65 death sentences finally resolved (excluding the 36 still in effect and still being litigated), the reversal rate for female death sentences in the current era is over 98 percent (64/65). These 101 death sentences for female offenders have been imposed in 23 states, making up well over half of the death penalty jurisdictions.

Two states (Florida and North Carolina) account for over one-quarter of all such sentences. The first 10 states have imposed three-quarters of female death sentences. These dominant sentencing states range from North Carolina to California and from Texas and Florida to Ohio. The 36 female offenders on death row constitute only 1.2 percent of the total death row population of about 2,870 and less than 0.1 percent of the approximately 50,000 women in prison in the United States.

26. Abbe Smith, "The Jailing of America," *Boston Globe,* Dec. 10, 1995.

27. John Gonzalez, "Texas' 100th Execution Could Be in October or November," *Fort Worth Star-Telegram,* Sept. 26, 1995; NAACP Legal Defense and Education Fund, Inc., "Death Row, USA" (unpublished compilation).

28. David Barstow, "Executions Rise Sharply as Appeals Dry Up," *St. Petersburg Times,* Dec. 5, 1995.

29. See generally Michael Meltsner, *Cruel and Unusual* (1974); Burton Wolfe, *Pileup on Death Row* (1973); Herbert Haines, *Against Capital Punishment* (1996).

30. Barstow, *supra* n. 28.

31. James Brooke, "Utah Debates Firing Squads in Clash of Past and Present," *New York Times,* Jan. 14, 1996.

32. AP, "56 Executions This Year Are Most Since 1957," *New York Times,* Dec. 30, 1995.

33. *Id. See also* Brooke, *supra* n. 31.

34. AP, "After Debate, Virginia Executes Murderer with IQ of Only 68," *New York Times,* Jan. 6, 1996; Denis Keyes, William Edwards, and Robert Perske, "People with Mental Retardation are Dying, Legally," *Mental Retardation,* Feb. 1997.

35. *Id.* On the *Garcia* case, see Don Terry, "After a Life of Desperation, a Female Inmate Asks to Die," *New York Times,* Jan. 8, 1996. A few hours before Ms. Garcia was to have been executed, the governor of Illinois commuted the sentence to life imprisonment. Don Terry, "Clemency Given to Woman Who Wanted Death Sentence Carried Out," *New York Times,* Jan. 17, 1996; AP, "Condemned Woman Spared in Illinois," *Boston Globe,* Jan. 17, 1996.

36. "Word for Word/The Condemned, As Executions Mount, So Do Infamous Last Words," *New York Times,* July 31, 1994: "Three men who killed a man in front of his family were executed one by one yesterday as the Supreme Court rejected arguments that they were treated 'like hogs at a slaughter.' It was the nation's first triple execution in 32 years." "Arkansas Conducts Triple Execution," *Washington Post,* Aug. 4, 1994; see also AP, "2 Die By Lethal Injections as Third Awaits in Arkansas," *Los Angeles Times,* Aug. 4, 1994. Earlier in 1994 Arkansas put to death two men in a single day. "Arkansas Carries Out Nation's First Triple Execution in 32 Years," *New York Times,* Aug. 5, 1994.

Writing of the 1994 triple execution, Jim Hightower noted: "The last state to manage a 'triple play' execution of criminals was California, 1962. But three was not even close to the record. Virginia electrocuted eight men during one long night in 1951—and federal agents sponsored a hangfest in Mankato, Minnesota, back in 1862, stringing up 39 Dakota Indians in a single day." Jim Hightower, "Making Executions Fun," *Texas Observer,* Sept. 16, 1994.

By 1997 the novelty of triple executions had worn off. The January 8, 1997, triple header made headlines in the newspaper of the National Coalition to Abolish the Death Penalty, see Steven Hawkins and Don Cabana, "Ringing in the New Year in Arkansas: Triple Execution neither Cheap nor Soothing," *Lifelines* (undated) at p. 1.

37. "The Continuing Crisis," *American Spectator,* Jan. 1996, at 12.

38. AP, "Inmate Executed after Sedative Overdose," *Dallas Morning News,* Aug. 12, 1995; AP, "Oklahoma Killer Up for Execution Overdoses," *Dallas Morning News,* Aug. 11, 1995; AP, "Murderer Is Revived, Then Executed," *St. Petersburg Times,* Aug. 12, 1995.

39. Al Brumly, "Broadcast Blunder," *Dallas Morning News,* July 7, 1995.

40. "The Executioner's Docudrama," *Harper's,* May 1995, at 22.

41. Brooke, *supra* n. 31.

42. Richard Bierck, "Eyewitness, You," *Pittsburgh City Paper,* Aug. 9–15, 1995.

43. Christopher Hitchens, "The Clemency of Clinton," *The Nation,* March 1992. Even to those of us used to "New South" politicians (like Florida's Bob Graham; see Robert Sherrill, "The Sunshine Executioner," *The Guardian,* 1979) playing the politics of capital punishment, the obviousness of Clinton's tactical and strategic thinking in the Rector case was arrestingly base and hungrily cunning. For an excellent description of the events culminating in Rector's execution, see Marshall Frady, "Death in Arkansas," *New Yorker,* Feb. 22, 1993.

44. Mark Ballard, "Death's Right-Hand Man," *Texas Lawyer,* May 29, 1995.

45. Jennifer Lightsy, "Executions to Change from Witching Hour to Noon," *Huntsville Newcomers Guide* [Tex.], Sept. 1995, at 83.

46. See Sam Verhovek, "Judge's Optimistic Signature on a Grim-Faced Death Row," *New York Times,* July 28, 1993.

47. Rebecca Fowler, "Eating His Way Off of Death Row? 409 Pound Man Appeals Sentence, Says Hanging May Decapitate Him," *Washington Post,* August 4, 1994. See also "Obesity Brings Stay of Execution," *Boston Globe,* Sept. 21, 1994; Rebecca Fowler, "Inmate Ruled Too Heavy to Be Hanged: 410 Pound Man May Get Death Sentence Reduced," *Washington Post,* Sept. 21, 1994; Christopher Hitchens, "Minority Report," *The Nation,* Feb. 1, 1993, at 114. On recent hangings, see also Robert Sullivan, "Lynchburg: Walla Walla Postcard," *New Republic,* Feb. 1, 1993, at 12; Editorial, "End of the Rope?" *The Nation,* June 6, 1994, at 772.

48. Letter to the Editor, "Chain Gangs Are the Law," *St. Petersburg Times,* July 15, 1995; see also William Booth, "Chain Gang Show and Tell," *Washington Post* (National Weekly Edition), Dec. 25–31, 1995, at 31; Mireya Navarro, "Chain Gangs, with Limits, Return to Florida Today," *New York Times,* Nov. 21, 1995; Martin Dyckman, "Chained to Flawed Logic," *St. Petersburg Times,* June 29, 1995; Anne Hull, "Chained to a New Kind of Justice," *St. Petersburg Times,* June 25, 1995.

49. "Alabama to Make Prisoners Break Rocks," *New York Times,* July 29, 1995.

50. AP, "Arizona Death Sentence: 40-hour Work Week," *Boston Globe,* Dec. 7, 1995.

51. E.g., Robert Connolly, "Governor to Ask Legislature to Restore Death Penalty," *Boston Herald,* March 9, 1995; Doris Sue Wong, "Governor Refiles Bill for Death Penalty; Says 'Moral Consensus' Favors Its Reinstatement," *Boston Globe,* March 11, 1995; AP, "Wisconsin Tries Again on Death Penalty with a Narrow Bill," *New York Times,* March 19, 1995; Mike Blecha, "Is It Time for Death Penalty?: Push Is On in Wisconsin for Capital Punishment," *Green Bay Press-Gazette,* March 19, 1995; James Baraniak, "It's Morally Wrong to Use Violence to Fight Violence," *Green Bay Press-Gazette,* March 19, 1995; Editorial, "Tougher Laws Should Be First Option," *Green Bay Press-Gazette,* March 19, 1995; "About Wisconsin's Death Penalty Legislation," *Green Bay Press-Gazette,* March 19, 1995; Allen Lasee, "Sponsor: Killers Deserve Same Fate; It's Only Justice in Heinous Crimes," *Green Bay Press-Gazette,* March 19, 1995; Dave Hutchison, "Killing Doesn't Teach a Lesson: It's Also Not a Deterrent to Crime," *Green Bay Press-Gazette,* March 19, 1995; Harold Compton, "Bring Balance Back into Justice System," *Green Bay Press-Gazette,* March 19, 1995; "People's Forum—On the Death Penalty," *Green Bay Press-Gazette,* March 19, 1995; Ian Fisher, "Clamor over Death Penalty Dominates Debate on Crime," *New York Times,* Oct. 9, 1994; Ian Fisher, "Cuomo's Crime Plan: Longer Terms, Treatment Efforts," *New York Times,* Oct. 13, 1994; Patricia Nealon, "Life Terms for Murderers Favored in New State Poll," *Boston Globe,* Oct. 13, 1994; Editorial, "Cross-Fire over Public Safety," *Boston Globe,* Oct. 11, 1994; David Nyhan, "Election '94 Comes Down to a Battle of the Bucks," *Boston Globe,* Oct. 7, 1994; Frank Phillips, "Trooper's Dad Blasts Kennedy in Romney Ad," *Boston Globe,* Oct. 5, 1994; B. Drummond Ayers, "In Race for California Chief, No Candidate Is Favorite,"

New York Times, Sept. 19, 1994; Don Aucoin, "Democrats Questioned on Capital Punishment," *Boston Globe,* Sept. 11, 1994, at 33; Doris Wong, "At State House Rally, Weld Renews Call for Death Penalty," *Boston Globe,* Sept. 9, 1994; Don Aucoin, "Roosevelt Says He Misspoke on Death Penalty," *Boston Globe,* Aug. 25, 1994; Peter Howe, "Bachrach: Weld Playing Politics with Cooper's Death," *Boston Globe,* Sept. 8, 1994; Editorial, "How to Honor a Fallen Trooper," *Boston Globe,* Sept. 8, 1994; Michael Matza, "Ted Kennedy Faces Biggest Fight of His Life," *Sunday Rutland Herald,* Oct. 9, 1994; Todd Gillman, "Nightbeat, Students' Chant Make Executions Surreal," *Dallas Morning News,* Sept. 22, 1994; Todd Gillman, "Lott Executed for Two Killings," *Dallas Morning News,* Sept. 20, 1994; Selwyn Crawford, "Lott Set to Die Tuesday for Court House Deaths," *Dallas Morning News,* Sept. 16, 1994; Wayne Slater, "New Bush Ad Assails Richards on Crime: Governor's Campaign Calls TV Spot a 'Lie,' " *Dallas Morning News,* Aug. 23, 1994; AP, "One in Three State Legislators Favors Death Penalty," *Green Bay Press-Gazette,* Oct. 2, 1994; California for Huffington, Paid Political Ad, "Feinstein v. Huffington: Here Are the Facts in a *Real* Murder Case: See if You Agree with the Judge's Decision," *Los Angeles Times,* Sept. 22, 1994; Amy Chance, "Kathleen Brown's No-No on Death Penalty: Criticizes Five Demos for Shift in Position; Retracts Comment about Feinstein," *San Francisco Examiner,* Sept. 27, 1994; Sean Schultz and Kathleen McGillis, "Death Penalty Is an 'Answer': The Families of Kora, Jones and Amy Breyer Pushed for Capital Punishment," *Green Bay Press-Gazette,* Sept. 22, 1994; Ronald Poppenhagen and Brian Kerhin, "Candidates Debate Death Penalty at a Distance," *Green Bay News Chronicle,* Sept. 29, 1994; Leslie Boellstorff, "Crime Fuels Iowa Death Penalty Debate," *Omaha World Herald,* Sept. 11, 1994; Richard Tapscott, "Sauerbrey Attacks Bentley on Death Penalty: Targeting Certain Minor Drug Dealers Is 'Unrealistic,' Says Candidate for Maryland Governor," *Washington Post,* Sept. 7, 1994; Michelle McPhee, "Slaying Renews Debate on Executions," *Boston Globe,* Sept. 5, 1994; Maura Leveritt, "Rites to Kill: A Behind-the-Scenes Account of the First Triple Execution in Recent U.S. History," *Arkansas Times,* Aug. 11, 1994, at 15; Bob Egelko, "Lawyers, Scholars Agree: Wealthy Are Able to Escape Death Row," *Fresno Bee,* Aug. 14, 1994; Ken Chavez, "Political Fur Flies at Wilson Anti-Crime Rally," *Sacramento Bee* Aug. 9, 1994; Gary Siegel, "Defending Killer Who Seeks to Die," *Los Angeles Times,* July 31, 1994; Gary Siegel, "Lawyers Take Offense at Peer's Unorthodox Defense: Utah Public Defender Elliott Levine Faces Possible Disbarment for Respecting His Client's Wish to Be Executed," *Los Angeles Times,* Aug. 1, 1994; Letter to the editor from Alan Walker, "Past Time to Restore Iowa Death Penalty," *Cedar Rapids Gazette,* Sept. 4, 1994; Ronald Brownstein, "Death Penalty Debate Roils Campaign: Seldom-Used Punishment a Potent Symbol," *San Francisco Chronicle,* Aug. 31, 1994; Jane Harper, "One for the Books—Six Death Cases in a Week," *Houston Post,* Sept. 11, 1994; Editorial, "A Death Penalty, Now," *Boston Herald,* Sept. 12, 1994; Tom Held, "Kunicki to Push Death Bill: Says Killing of Girl, Officer Changed Views," *Milwaukee Sentinel,* Sept. 16, 1994; Phil Nero, "Racial Bias Is among Reservations of Three Law Makers to Death Penalty Bill," *Milwaukee Journal,* Oct. 5, 1994; Tom Still, "Death Penalty Being Used as Major Political Issue," *Sheboygan Press,* Sept. 10, 1994;

Kent Biffle, "Women Don't Often Meet the Executioner," *Dallas Morning News,* Nov. 13, 1994; Robert Scheer, "Death Penalty: Fashionable Idea for the '90s," *Los Angeles Times,* Nov. 6, 1994; Editorial, "Of Punks and Old Sparky," *Hartford Courant,* Nov. 6, 1994; Denis Horgan, "Capital Punishment: A Capital Idea for Today's Candidates," *Hartford Courant,* Nov. 2, 1994; Editorial, "The Phony Use of Genuine Grief," *New York Times,* Oct. 28, 1994; Ellen Goodman, "Political Hobgoblins," *Boston Globe,* Oct. 27, 1994; AP, "TV Ads in Governor's Race Focus on Crime: Is Jeb Bush Borrowing from His Father's Willie Horton Tactic?" *New York Times,* Oct. 27, 1994; Antony Flint, "Voters' Fear of Violence May Decide Senate Race," *Boston Globe,* Oct. 24, 1994; Russell Baker, "Howl from the Jungle," *Rutland Daily Herald,* Nov. 9, 1994; Kevin Sack, "Pataki, Backing Executions, Assails Cuomo at Murder Site," *New York Times,* Nov. 5, 1994; Sean Loughlin, "Candidates Duel over Anti-Crime Credentials, the Death Penalty: A Hot-Button Issue," *Sarasota Herald Tribune,* Oct. 29, 1994; Derrick Z. Jackson, "Susan Smith's Other Crime . . . The South Carolina Tragedy: Victims of Stereotypes," *Boston Globe,* Nov. 9, 1994; Tim Cornwell, ". . . And One of Her Victims," *Boston Globe,* Nov. 9, 1994; Gary Trudeau, *Doonesbury,* Nov. 8, 1994; Lantz McClain, "Criminal Appeals Judge Should Not Be Retained," *Oklahoma Gazette,* Oct. 27, 1994; Steve Daley, "Bush Sons Whip Up Execution Fever: Texas, Florida Voters Rally around Capital Punishment," *San Francisco Examiner,* Oct. 30, 1994; Bob Minzesheimer, "Executioner's Song Heard in Governor Races," *USA Today,* Oct. 27, 1994; Editorial, "Mr. Pataki's Odd Attack," *New York Times,* Nov. 7, 1994; Dan Wasserman, Editorial Cartoon, *New York Times,* Nov. 6, 1994; Robert Yoakum, "Everyspeech," *New York Times,* Nov. 2, 1994; Diego Ribadeneria, "Like Father, Like Son—Jeb Bush Ad Evokes Willie Horton," *Boston Globe,* Oct. 30, 1994. The politicization of capital punishment continued after the election, of course. See Doris Wong, "AG Rejects Death Penalty Ballot Item," *Boston Globe,* Sept. 9, 1995; Editorial, "Debating Death to Death," *Boston Herald,* Sept. 7, 1995; Editorial, "Harshbarger's Patriotic Decision," *Boston Globe,* Sept. 7, 1995; Stuart Taylor, "The Politics of Death: Governing by Tantrum," *Texas Lawyer,* Sept. 11, 1995; Frank Phillips, "Massachusetts House Votes Down Death Penalty," *Boston Globe,* June 29, 1995.

52. E.g., Diane Derby, "Costle, Backus Exchange Barbs with a Week to Go," *Rutland Daily Herald,* Sept. 7, 1994; Ross Sneyd, "Sharp Exchanges between Backus, Costle," *Valley News* Sept. 7, 1994; Editorial, "Mr. Moneybags," *Rutland Daily Herald,* Sept. 1, 1994.

In the Massachusetts race for lieutenant governor, "Robert K. Massie said he remains opposed to the death penalty and his running mate, gubernatorial candidate Mark Roosevelt, said that he has no plans to pressure Massie to change his mind. . . . Massie said, 'Mark has known since we first met' that he opposes capital punishment, 'and I remain opposed to it.' " Peter Howe, "Massie Won't Quit Death Penalty Opposition," *Boston Globe,* Sept. 28, 1994.

53. Diane Derby, "Backus Beats Costle, Kelley Leads GOP," *Rutland Daily Herald,* Sept. 14, 1994; see also Editorial, "*Backus vs. Jeffords,*" *Rutland Daily Herald,* Sept. 15, 1994; Betsy Liley, "Backus Takes Costle in Primary: Democrat Will Challenge Jeffords," *Burlington Free Press,* Sept. 14, 1994; Ross Sneyd, "Ver-

mont Democrats Backing Backus," *Boston Globe,* Sept. 14, 1994. Doug Costle reportedly expended $300,000, Backus only $30,000. Janice Prindle, "Costle Says 'Money Thing' Hid Identity from Voters," *Valley News,* Sept. 16, 1994; Jack Hoffman, "Why Did Costle Lose the Primary?" *Rutland Sunday Herald,* Sept. 18, 1994; Jack Hoffman, "Jeffords Lead Slims to 45–38," *Rutland Herald,* Oct. 26, 1994; AP, "Women Call on Jeffords to Pull Ad," *Valley News,* Oct. 25, 1994; Diane Derby, "Jeffords Is Sorry for Flyer on Crime," *Rutland Herald,* Nov. 1, 1994.

54. Rich Barlow, "Backus Defeats Costle," *Valley News,* Sept. 14, 1994. Maybe it's just Vermont, which since 1992 has had as its only member of the House of Representatives Bernard Sanders, an independent socialist.

55. Ben Sheffner, "Loopy Tuesday," *New Republic,* Oct. 10, 1994, at 11.

56. Mac Gordon, "Execution Goes Back on Agenda," *Jackson Clarion-Ledger,* Aug. 13, 1994; Gina Holland, "Special Session Looks at Crime," *Biloxi Sun Herald,* Aug. 14, 1994; Sister Therese Jacobs, BVM, "Readers' Views, Pro/Con: Is Capital Punishment Needed?" *Jackson Clarion-Ledger,* Aug. 24, 1994; see also Adam Nossiter, "Making Hard Time Harder," *New York Times,* Sept. 17, 1994.

57. Curtis Wilkie, "Mississippi Debates Death Penalty Shortcuts," *Boston Globe,* Aug. 21, 1994.

58. Terry Cassreino, "House Strips Inmates of Perks," *Biloxi Sun Herald,* Aug. 20, 1994.

59. *Id.; accord* Emily Wagster, "Bill Bans TV, Radio in Prisons," *Jackson Clarion Ledger,* Aug. 20, 1994; Nossiter, *supra* n. 56; see also Senate Bill No. 2005 (as sent to the governor by Senators Smith, Huggins, Thames, Minor, Gunn, and Dickerson), Mississippi Legislature, First Extraordinary Session, 1994; House Bill No. 21, by Representative Blackmon, Mississippi Legislature, First Extraordinary Session, 1994.

60. The phrase "the devil is in the details" was popular among members of Congress and their staffers during the legislative negotiations that resulted in the 1994 federal crime bill. The term is an inversion of the phrase "God is in the details," an aphorism popular with the architect Ludwig Mies van der Rohe and the art historian Aby Warburg; William Safire reported that it has been attributed, without verification, to Gustave Flaubert ["Le Bon Dieu est dans le detail"]. William Safire, "On Language: Who's in Those Details?" *New York Times Sunday Magazine,* July 30, 1989, at 8.

61. See generally Wendy Lesser, *Pictures at an Execution: An Inquiry into the Subject of Murder* (1993).

62. Letters to the Editor, "Let Victims' Kin See Executions?" *Houston Chronicle,* Apr. 1, 1995; Christy Hoppe, "Rules Would Let Victims' Kin Watch Executions," *Dallas Morning News,* Nov. 11, 1995; Jo Ann Zuniga, "Execution-Witness Bill Dies in House," *Houston Chronicle,* May 25, 1995; Christy Hoppe, "Senate Panel Might Lift Ban on Victims' Families Viewing Executions," *Dallas Morning News,* Sept. 14, 1995; Christy Hoppe, "Morales to Allow Victims' Families to Witness Murderers' Executions," *Dallas Morning News,* Sept. 27, 1995.

63. Jeremy Epstein, "Require Judge and Jury to Witness Executions," *National Law Journal,* Dec. 11, 1995.

64. See generally Martin Gardner, "Execution and Indignities," 39 *Ohio State Law Journal* 96 (1978) (discussing methods of execution); George Ryley Scott, *The History of Capital Punishment* (same); *Royal Commission on Capital Punishment, 1949–53, Minutes of Evidence,* at 8405–10 (finding that hanging is the most humane method of execution); Glass v. Louisiana, 471 U.S. 1080 (1985) (Marshall, J., dissenting from denial of certiorari) (discussing electrocution); Campbell v. Wood, 18 F.3d 662 (9th Cir. 1994) (hanging); Gray v. Lucas, 710 F.2d 1048 (5th Cir. 1983) (gassing); Gomez v. United States District Court, 112 S. Ct. 1652 (1992) (gassing).

65. Disturbingly, the best research on the effects of poison gas on human subjects was done by the Nazis; see, e.g., *Nazi Mass Murder: A Documentary History of the Use of Poison Gas* (Eugen Kogon, Herman Langbein, and Adalbert Rucker, eds. 1994); *Anatomy of the Auschwitz Death Camp* (Yisrael Gutman and Michael Berenbaum, eds. 1994).

66. James Coates writes that "the most striking feature of the reformation [of the Mormon Church] was the revival of the concept of blood atonement, the principle that there are certain sins, the most noteworthy being the spilling of innocent blood and heresy against the prophet, that can only be forgiven once the sinner's own blood is shed and flows into the ground," so that "the smoke thereof might ascend to the heavens as an offering." *In Mormon Circles: Gentiles, Jack Mormons, and Latter Day Saints* 64, 66 (1991). Mikal Gilmore (Gary Gilmore's brother) explored the fascinating connections among Mormondom and Utah's capital punishment culture in *Shot in the Heart* 10–23 (1994); see also Stephen Nafeth and Gregory Smith, *The Mormon Murders* 44–45, 48, 276, 478 (1989); "Note, Impartial Jury as Determined by Religious Affiliation," 1972 *Utah Law Review* 250.

In an 1856 sermon Brigham Young thundered from the pulpit: "There are sins that men commit for which they cannot receive forgiveness in this world, or in that which is to come, and if they had their eyes open to see their true condition, they would be perfectly willing to have their blood spilt upon the ground, that the smoke thereof might ascend to heaven as an offering for their sins; and the smoking incense would atone for their sins, whereas, if such is not the case, they will stick to them and remain upon them in the spirit world." Coates, *supra* at 64–65.

Blood atonement has arisen as an issue in capital cases. In 1994 James Wood, a capital defendant in Pocatello, Idaho, moved to recuse the trial judge based on the latter's Mormon beliefs. Coates reported an earlier case where, in an effort to avoid death sentences, lawyers for Ron and Dan Lafferty brought in expert witnesses to show that the basic idea of blood atonement that drove the brothers to murder might also drive the Mormons on the jury to vote for the death penalty so that a firing squad could mix the Laffertys' blood with the earth to atone for the brutal murders of a young woman and her infant. These witnesses explained most emphatically to the Mormon jurors that their church's current teaching bans blood atonement even though it was once Mormon frontier tradition. Dr. Jess Groesbeck, a Provo psychiatrist who has studied Mormon beliefs, testified on behalf of Ron Lafferty that he has found in dozens of interviews with church members a prevailing belief that the doctrine of blood atonement stands today just as it did when Brigham Young tamed an unforgiving salt valley. He noted that the common misperception was that the church proper teaches that those who commit murder must atone for the act by having their blood spilled on the ground, preferably from a head wound or a slit throat. Groesbeck testified that in his experience, "most rank and file Mormons believe this." Dan Lafferty was found guilty of murder and sentenced to life in prison. Ron, however, was sentenced to death by his jury, and Judge Boyd Park of the Utah District Court in Provo subsequently ordered execution by firing squad. Coates, *supra* at 157–58. See Amended Petition for Post-Conviction Relief, James Edward Wood v. The State of Idaho, Case Number 42257-D, in the District Court of the Sixth Judicial District of the State of Idaho, in and for the County of Bannock (filed June 17, 1994). Coates, *supra* at 157–58. I am grateful to Lissa Gardner and Indian of the Vietnam Vets Motorcycle Club (VNVMC) of Las Vegas, for bringing the Coates book and other materials on Mormondom to my attention.

67. See generally Victor Streib, *Death Penalty for Juveniles* (1987); Stanford v. Kentucky, 491 U.S. 617 (1989); Suzanne Strater, "The Juvenile Death Penalty," *Human Rights*, Spring 1995, at 10. Victor Streib notes that the leading source for these and other data on lawful executions throughout American history is Watt Espy, director of the Capital Punishment Research Project in Headland, Alabama. According to Streib, four juvenile offenders were executed in the last six months of 1993, as many as had been executed in the entire preceding seven years. During this same six-month period, Florida made national and international headlines with high-profile homicide arrests of juveniles, some as young as 13. In the past decade, homicide arrests of adults have risen about 25 percent. In that same period, homicide arrests of juveniles have risen about 170 percent.

Streib notes that more than a few observers of this recent wave of juvenile homicide have announced that the death penalty for juvenile offenders is or should be the American people's solution of choice for this criminal justice nightmare. The spate of recent executions of juvenile offenders seems to suggest that they are right. However, the data compiled by Streib suggest that these prognosticators are wrong. In fact, a juvenile arrested for homicide today is less likely to be sentenced to death than in the past.

Streib documents over 21 years of juvenile death sentencing under modern death penalty statutes in the United States. Consistent with the general pattern over this 21-year period, both the annual juvenile death sentencing rate and the juvenile death row population remain very small in comparison to the figures for adults, each being between 1 and 2 percent of the totals. For purposes of consistency, a juvenile crime is defined as one committed while the offender was under age 18, the most common age-jurisdictional dividing line between juvenile and criminal courts. A juvenile death penalty is one imposed for a juvenile crime. The spiraling number of arrests of juveniles for potentially capital crimes has resulted neither in a comparable rise in juvenile death sentencing nor a rise in the number of juvenile offenders on death row. Streib observes that nine of these executions for juvenile crimes have been imposed during the current era (1973–94). These nine recent executions of juvenile offenders are only 4 percent of the total of about 250 executions through August 1, 1994, a somewhat higher rate than had been experienced prior to 1973.

68. Emily F. Reed, *The Penry Penalty* (1993); Penry v. Lynaugh, 492 U.S. 302 (1989).

69. Kent Miller and Michael Radelet, *Executing the Mentally Ill* (1993); Ford v. Wainwright, 477 U.S. 399 (1986); Rick Bragg, "Killer Rocked by Delusions Is Put to Death in Alabama," *New York Times,* May 13, 1995.

70. Beverly Petigrew Kraft, "Schizophrenic's Execution Argued," *Jackson Clarion-Ledger,* Oct. 5, 1994.

71. See generally Louisiana v. Perry, 610 So. 2d 746 (La. 1992).

72. Stephen Adler, "The Cure That Kills," *American Lawyer,* Sept. 1986, at 1, 29–33; American Public Health Association, Policy Statement 85201: Participation of Health Professionals in Capital Punishment, 76 *American Journal of Public Health* 339 (1986); George Annas, "Nurses and the Death Penalty," 1 *Nursing Law and Ethics* 3 (May 1980); Paul Appelbaum, "Competence to Be Executed: Another Conundrum for Mental Health Professionals," 37 *Hospital and Community Psychiatry* 682 (1986); Charles Ewing, "Diagnosing and Treating 'Insanity' on Death Row: Legal and Ethical Perspectives," 5 *Behavioral Science and Law* 175 (1987); Douglas Mossman, "Assessing and Restoring Competency to Be Executed: Should Psychiatrist Participate?" 7 *Behavioral Science & Law* 397 (1987); Michael Radelet and George Barnard, "Ethics and the Psychiatric Determination of Competency to Be Executed," 14 *American Academy of Psychiatry and Law* 37 (1986); Michael Radelet and George Barnard, "Treating Those Found Incompetent to Be Executed," 16 *Bulletin of the American Academy of Psychiatry and Law* 197 (1988); Note, "Medical Ethics and Competency to Be Executed," 96 *Yale Law Journal* 167 (1986); Barbara Ward, "Competency for Execution; Problems in Law and Psychiatry," 14 *Florida State University Law Review* 35 (1986); Donald Wallace, "Incompetency for Execution," 8 *Journal of Legal Medicine* 265 (1987).

73. Ronald Bayer, "Lethal Injections and Capital Punishment: Medicine in Service of the State," 4 *Journal of Prison and Health Reform* 7 (1984); Barbara Bolsen, "Strange Bedfellows: Death Penalty and Medicine," 248 *JAMA* 518 (Aug. 6, 1982); William Curran and Ward Casscells, "The Ethics of Medical Participation in Capital Punishment by Intravenous Drug Injection," 302 *New England Journal of Medicine* 226 (Jan. 24, 1980); Jack Kevorkian, "Medicine, Ethics, and Execution by Lethal Injection," 4 *Medicine and Law* 407 (1985).

74. The oath: "I will follow that system of regimen which, according to my ability and judgment, I consider for the benefit of my patients, and abstain from whatever is deleterious and mischievous. I will give no deadly medicine to anyone if asked, nor suggest any such counsel; . . . Into whatever houses I enter, I will go into them for the benefit of the sick, and will abstain from every voluntary act of mischief and corruption." Hippocrates, *The Physician's Oath* (trans. W. H. Jones) (Loeb Classical Library).

75. Telephone conversation with Dr. Morris Bol, Wilder, Vermont (Sept. 23, 1994).

76. John Burnett, All Things Considered (National Public Radio broadcast Official Transcript at 19–20), "Carrying Out Capital Punishment" (Sept. 27, 1994).

77. Gilmore v. Utah, 429 U.S. 1012 (1976); Grasso v. Oklahoma, 857 P.2d

802 (Okla. Crim. App. 1993); Norman Mailer, *The Executioner's Song* (1977); Richard Bonnie, "Dignity of the Condemned," 74 *Virginia Law Review* 1383 (1988); Richard Strafer, "Volunteering for Execution: Competency, Voluntariness and the Propriety of Third Party Intervention," 74 *Journal of Criminal Law and Criminology* 860 (1983); Note, "The Death Row Right to Die," 54 *Southern California Law Review* 575 (1981).

78. This happened in the District of Columbia in March 1995. At the urging of U.S. Attorney General Janet Reno, D.C. U.S. Attorney Eric Holder announced that he would seek the death penalty for an alleged killer of a Washington police officer a few days after Christmas 1993. See Editorial, "Choosing the Death Penalty," *Washington Post,* March 25, 1995. Even though the District of Columbia does not have a death penalty, a federal statute was available allowing capital punishment in cases where a law enforcement officer working on a narcotics case has been killed.

The *Washington Post* editorialized, however, that the decision by Mr. Holder at the urging of Attorney General Reno was "unfortunate." *Id.* Both professed to be "personally opposed to capital punishment. Both are familiar with the views of the citizens of the District of Columbia on the subject: the death penalty was resoundingly defeated by the voters in a referendum in 1992. This is not simply a question of enforcing a personally repugnant law, as Mr. Holder and Ms. Reno would have us believe. It's not like collecting a tax you think is unfair or submitting to the draft when you oppose the war. The only way to comply with the law in these cases is to set aside personal objections and do what the law has made mandatory. But a prosecutor's decision to ask for the death penalty is a choice, not a requirement. In this case, Mr. Holder had options. He could have chosen to seek a life sentence, but he made a personal decision to go beyond that and to ask for a penalty that has not been imposed in this city for almost 40 years." The public "should be spared the complaints of the prosecutor and the attorney general that this was for them a difficult responsibility carried out against their personal inclinations in order to uphold the law. They did not have to make this choice, but they did. It was the wrong one." *Id.* See also Toni Locy, "U.S. to Seek Death in D.C. Case; Prosecutor Accedes to Reno's Decision in Officer's Slaying," *Washington Post,* March 21, 1995.

Although Holder endorsed the death penalty in the case, he settled for six consecutive life sentences, without possibility of parole, at the federal prison in Marion, Illinois. Bill Gifford, "Good Cop," *New Republic,* May 1, 1995, at 15.

79. See generally Hartman, " 'Unusual' Punishment: The Domestic Effects of International Norms Restricting the Application of the Death Penalty," 52 *University of Cincinnati Law Review* 655 (1983).

80. Christy Hoppe, "Death Row Appeal Bill Endorsed," *Dallas Morning News,* May 19, 1995.

81. The controversy of such review is difficult to exaggerate. For example, in the Alday family cases, the U.S. Court of Appeals for the Eleventh Circuit unleashed a firestorm of criticism, much of it directed specifically at the court, when a three-judge panel ordered new trials for three Georgia death row inmates. The three inmates, Wayne Carl Coleman, George Elder Dungee, and Carl J. Isaacs, were condemned to death for murdering several members of the Alday family. The Elev-

enth Circuit's opinions are reported as Coleman v. Kemp, 778 F. 2d 1487 (11th Cir. 1985), *cert. denied,* 476 U.S. 1164 (1986); Isaacs v. Kemp, 778 F. 2d 876 (11th Cir. 1985); Dungee v. Kemp, 778 F. 2d 914 (11th Cir. 1985).

Three days after the rulings, one newspaper reported that with one notable exception, editorial pages across Georgia "blasted the 11th U.S. Circuit Court of Appeals decision." "Most State Editorial Pages Decry Alday Ruling," *Macon Telegraph and News,* Dec. 12, 1985. E.g., Resch, "Midstate Judge Has Tried His Share of 'Glamour Cases,' " *Macon Telegraph and News,* July 21, 1986 (quoting state judge assigned to retry Alday case as saying "I'm completely put out by the federal government on the death system. . . . The general public equates the inability of federal courts to establish finality on death verdicts with the entire court system"); Grimm, "We'll Never Be the Same: Court's Decision Granting New Trial to Defendants in Alday Rulings Case Has Opened Old Wounds," *Macon Telegraph and News,* June 10, 1986 ("those rulings are regarded as the inexplicable acts of madmen. They solidified all the local mistrust of everything urban and Washington, of slick lawyers and their technical maneuvering, of ivory tower judges and their niggling fascination with the seemingly irrelevant. 'Ought to hang them judges' "); "Measure Hits Court Ruling in Alday Case," *Atlanta Const.,* Jan. 18, 1986 (40 members of the Georgia House of Representatives signed, as co-sponsors, resolution condemning Alday rulings); "Justice Left on Legal Scrap Heap," *Macon Telegraph and News,* Dec. 20, 1985 (letter to the editor) ("it is just such stupid decisions by men such as [the Eleventh Circuit panel of judges] that one day will force the very best of men to begin to take revenge, for most good men in America have about come to feel that there is no justice at all left in America"). But cf. "Decision Shocking but Also Necessary," *Macon Telegraph and News,* Dec. 12, 1985 (state courts "dropped the ball. Finally, after all these years, the federal appeals court had to pick it up and do what the state courts apparently lacked the courage to do— something unpopular, yet important to our freedoms"); Teepen, "Buck Stopped at 11th Circuit," *Atlanta Constitution,* Dec. 12, 1985; "Tough, but Correct, Alday Ruling," *Atlanta Constitution,* Nov. 11, 1985.

A Georgia grand jury accused the Eleventh Circuit judges of "callous disregard for the rights of crime victims and their families." "Lowndes Grand Jury Faults Judges' Lifetime Appointment," *Atlanta Constitution,* Feb. 15, 1986. In a voluminous petition, 100,000 citizens asked Congress to impeach the three Eleventh Circuit judges who took part in the Alday decisions. See "A Stand on Judicial Principle," *Atlanta Constitution,* Oct. 29, 1986; see also numerous articles on the case that appeared in the *Atlanta Constitution,* the *Macon Telegraph and News,* and the *Atlanta Journal* in 1986.

At the retrials, two of the three Alday defendants, Wayne Coleman and George Dungee, were resentenced to life imprisonment. Carl Isaacs was resentenced to death. See also "Blocked Executions Roll Tennessee," *Boston Globe,* June 14, 1995.

82. Megan Rosenfeld, "Condemned to Silence?" *Washington Post,* May 18, 1995. The book at issue was Mumia Abu-Jamal, *Live from Death Row* (1995). Abu-Jamal's case attracted enormous publicity, including media analysis of the media coverage of the case. I must confess to the sin of jealousy. At the time Mr.

Abu-Jamal was dominating the media with an innocence claim (bogus, I thought), Joseph Spaziano, my client in Florida—a man who *really* is innocent, I am convinced—was heading for execution. I made the connection between the two cases in Michael Mello, "Death and His Lawyers," 20 *Vermont Law Review* 19 (1995). For a sampling of the articles on the Abu-Jamal case, see Marc Kaufman, "Abu-Jamal's Long Climb to a World Stage," *Philadelphia Inquirer,* Aug. 13, 1995; Jeff Cohen, "Silencing Rights of Prisoners," *Arizona Republic,* Aug. 7, 1995; Patricia Smith, "Abu-Jamal's Case Haunts Event," *Boston Globe,* Aug. 21, 1995; Zachary Dowdy, "Convict's Cause Gains Local, Global Support," *Boston Globe,* Aug. 2, 1995; Marc Kaufman, "From Condemned to Cult Hero," *Rutland Herald,* Aug. 20, 1995; Mike Royko, "A Way with Words Can Win Sympathy If You're on Death Row," *St. Petersburg Times,* Aug. 5, 1995; Paul Mulshine, "Abu-Jamal's 'Innocence' Is Just a Legal Tactic," *Valley News,* Aug. 25, 1995; Editorial, "The Case of Abu-Jamal," *New York Times,* Aug. 17, 1995; E. L. Doctorow, "From Here to Death Row," *New York Times,* July 14, 1995; Lena Williams, "Pending Execution of Ex-Reporter Divided Black Journalists," *New York Times,* July 17, 1995; Derrick Jackson, "Compounding the Crime," *Boston Globe,* July 26, 1995; Derrick Jackson, "Death Row's Ugly Truths," *Boston Globe,* July 28, 1995; Diane Derby, "Wild Protest at Sheraton Ends in Arrest of 15," *Rutland Herald,* July 31, 1995; Brian McGory, "A Condemned Pennsylvania Man Becomes Cause to Many," *Boston Globe,* Aug. 4, 1995; Don Terry, "With Execution Pending, Clashes in a Courtroom," *New York Times,* July 30, 1995; Cornel West, "Free Mumia?" *Boston Globe,* Aug. 6, 1995; Don Terry, "Black Journalist Granted a Stay by the Judge Who Sentenced Him," *New York Times,* Aug. 8, 1995; Francis Clines, "The Case That Brought Back Radical Chic," *New York Times,* Aug. 13, 1995; Lynne Abraham, "Mumia Abu-Jamal, Celebrity Cop Killer," *New York Times,* Aug. 12, 1995; "Mumia Abu-Jamal Must Have a New Trial" (full-page ad), *New York Times,* Aug. 9, 1995; at A13; Erika Duckworth, "Why Is NABJ Silent on Abu-Jamal?" *St. Petersburg Times,* Aug. 8, 1995; Nat Hentoff, "Due Process Gets Short Shrift in Pennsylvania," *Valley News,* Aug. 7, 1995.

83. Michael Graczyk, "U.S. Supreme Court Grants Stay of Texas Execution Set for Today," *Dallas Morning News,* April 28, 1995; "Morales Right to Support Deadline on Appeals," *Dallas Morning News,* March 30, 1995; Worl Pinkston, "Morales Urges Speeding Up Appeals of Death Penalty," *Dallas Morning News,* March 29, 1995; David Jackson, "U.S. Supreme Court Rejects Plea on 17-year Death Row Stay; But Two Justices' Objections Could Continue to Delay Execution," *Dallas Morning News,* March 28, 1995; Joan Biskupic, "Justice Stevens Urges New Examination of Capital Punishment," *Valley News,* March 28, 1995; Linda Greenhouse, "Court to Review Forfeiture in Drug Case," *New York Times,* March 28, 1995. Willie Lloyd Turner unsuccessfully raised this claim. Charles Hall, "15-Year Wait to Die Cruel and Usual, Virginia Prisoner Says," *Washington Post,* May 21, 1995. On the fascinating Turner case, see Peter Boyer, "The Genius on Death Row," *New Yorker,* Dec. 4, 1995, at 64.

In March 1995 Supreme Court Justice John Paul Stevens questioned whether a prisoner who had spent 17 years on Texas' death row had already been punished enough. Stevens, joined in part by Justice Steven Breyer, called upon lower federal courts to begin examining whether executing a prisoner who had spent many years on death row violates the Constitution's prohibition on cruel and unusual punishment. The question is significant because on average a prisoner endures 10 years between sentencing and execution.

"Though novel, petitioner's claim is not without foundation," Justice Stevens wrote. In a somewhat rare public commentary on the court's refusal to hear the case, Justice Breyer wrote that he agreed with Justice Stevens that the issue is "an important undecided one." The memorandum urged lower courts to take a hard look at the legality of lengthy death penalty delays. Stevens noted that the Court has allowed capital punishment, in part, because it serves social purposes of retribution and deterrence. "It is arguable that neither ground retains any force for prisoners who have spent some 17 years under a sentence of death," he wrote. "After such an extended time, the acceptable state interest in retribution has arguably been satisfied by the severe punishment already inflicted." Stevens noted that English jurists have ruled that execution after an inordinate delay is unlawfully cruel. Justices Stevens and Breyer, however, did not dissent from the full Court's rejection of the petition for plenary review by murderer Clarence Lackey, who abducted a 25-year-old secretary from her Lubbock apartment, beat her, raped her, and cut her throat. Stevens suggested that lower courts "served as laboratories" to determine whether the death penalty has become pointless and unnecessary. Stevens' statement follows a recent pattern of public soul searching about the death penalty and recalls comments from retired Justices Harry Blackmun and Lewis F. Powell, Jr., criticizing capital punishment.

84. In a seven-month span in 1984–85, Georgia executed five black men—Ivon Ray Stanley, Alpha Otis Stephens, Roosevelt Green, Van Solomon, and John Young. John Vodicka, "The Death Penalty: A Georgia Update," *Hospitality,* Aug. 1995; McCleskey v. Kemp, 481 U.S. 279 (1987). See generally Michael Mello, "Defunding Death," 32 *American Criminal Law Review* 933 (1995); Dwight Sullivan, "Military Death Row: Separate, not Equal," *National Law Journal,* Nov. 6, 1995, at A19; Ava Plakins, "A Dark Cloud over the Courts," *Connecticut Law Tribune,* Aug. 14, 1995, at 1; Barbara Ransby, "The Black and White of the Death Penalty," *Las Vegas Review-Journal,* Aug. 6, 1995.

Racial bias isn't limited to the capital punishment subsystem of the criminal justice system. One out of three black men is either under some form of court supervision or in jail or prison. Smith, *supra* n. 26. If one-third of all *white* males were either in prison or jail or under court supervision, the dominant culture would find it intolerable.

85. See the poems by Adrienne Rich, "Pierrot Le Fou," in *The Fact of a Doorframe* 126 (1984), and "From the Prison House," *id.* at 158.

86. Richard Posner, *Overcoming Law* (1995).

87. Joan Howarth, "Deciding to Kill: Revealing the Gender in the Task Handed to Capital Jurors," 1994 *Wisconsin Law Review* 1345, 1383 n.193.

88. *Id.* at 1386.

89. *Id.* at 1386–87.

90. Robert Cover, "Violence and the Word," 95 *Yale Law Journal* 1601, 1601 (1986).

91. Max Lerner, *Nine Scorpions in a Bottle: Great Judges and Cases of the Supreme Court* (1994).

92. Coleman v. Thompson, 111 S. Ct. 2546, 2548 (1991). *Time* magazine didn't quite see it that way. "Roger Coleman Claimed He Was Innocent," *Time*, May 2, 1991 (cover story). He was executed on January 23, 1992.

93. Callins v. Collins, 114 S. Ct. 1127 (1994).

94. E.g., Feguer v. United States, 302 F.2d 214 (8th Cir. 1962); Pope v. United States, 372 F.2d 710 (8th Cir. 1967).

95. Subsequent to the U.S. Supreme Court's denial of a stay, a lower court stayed Callins' execution.

96. As described by his biographer and former judicial clerk, Powell in retirement came to believe capital punishment unconstitutional. John Calvin Jeffries, *Justice Lewis F. Powell, Jr.* 451–52 (1994). I prefer the view of Powell held by Scharlette Holdman and Gail Rowland of the Florida Clearinghouse on Criminal Justice, an operation (described in Chapter 5) existing to find and help lawyers willing to represent Florida death row inmates *pro bono:*

> By Spring of 1984, Holdman was spending an hour a day just keeping her ledger [of condemned Florida inmates] up to date. And the work kept expanding. Every few weeks another family would arrive in North Florida to face the possible extinction of a son, a brother, a father. Scharlette Holdman raised their bus fares, found them someplace to stay. Some of those sons and brothers and fathers did die; Holdman arranged the funerals. Gail Rowland became an overnight expert in the laws governing interstate transportation of corpses. Holdman, as always, worked the phone: "I need $300 for a funeral; can your church group handle it?" Or "You've got six acres out there; can we bury somebody on your land?" Holdman's son Tad came home one day to find a station wagon in the carport with a big box in the back. "Is that what I think it is?" he asked. It was—the dead followed her home.
>
> She worked constantly—her first day off that year came in November—but she confided that she cried as much as she worked. She cried though she hated to be seen crying. (When a photographer got a picture of her sobbing at a vigil for Anthony Antone, Holdman announced that she would no longer attend such protests.) Death became her life, and it subsumed the lives of those around her. "I got to the point where all I did was buy black clothes," said Gail Rowland. "I learned so many damn funeral songs. I hope I never sing 'Amazing Grace' or 'Will the Circle Be Unbroken' again."
>
> There were moments when the tension broke, moments of bitter laughter. Gail Rowland's puppet, for example. At the U.S. Supreme Court, one justice was assigned to each region of the country to handle emergency appeals. Florida's justice was Lewis Powell; naturally he became a particular target of Holdman's scorn. So Rowland made a hand-puppet that she called "Mr. Justice Powell," and the puppet offered running commentary on events in the office. Say Holdman and Craig Barnard were talking about filing an appeal based on an inmate's deprived background. Mr. Justice Powell would pop up and shout, "Oh, shut up! Not another bed-wetting darkie!" Or Jimmy Lohman would strum a folk tune on his guitar, and Mr. Justice Powell would chime in with some grossly racist, sexist lyrics. Holdman either laughed or cried; it was a time of emotional extremes; her nerves glowed like incandescent filaments.

David Von Drehle, *Among the Lowest of the Dead: The Culture of Death Row*

(1995). I reviewed Von Drehle's book in Michael Mello, "The Sunshine Executioner," 23 *Journal of Contemporary Law* 1 (1997).

As Henry Schwartzschild put it, "There is a special place in hell reserved for people who are shits when they're in power and then are lovely human beings when they're out." Telephone conversation with Henry Schwartzschild, Aug. 17, 1994.

97. David Von Drehle, "When Harry Met Scalia: Why the Death Penalty Is Dying," *Washington Post*, March 6, 1994.

98. See generally Mello, *supra* n. 4.

99. Gregg v. Georgia, 428 U.S. 153 (1976); Proffitt v. Florida, 428 U.S. 242 (1976); Jurek v. Texas, 428 U.S. 262 (1976).

100. Herrera v. Collins, 113 S. Ct. 853 (1993).

101. Roger Parloff, "When Worlds Collide," *American Lawyer*, June 1, 1995. The Florida Supreme Court upheld Hill's death sentence. See Associated Press, "Death Sentence Upheld for Abortion Clinic Killer," March 6, 1997.

Paul Hill, a former minister, opened fire with a shotgun July 29, 1994, outside the Ladies Center in Pensacola, where he had been protesting against abortion for six months, killing a doctor, Dr. John Britton, and his escort, retired Air Force Lt. Col. James Barrett. At trial Hill represented himself and attempted to argue that the killing of Britton and Barrett constituted "justifiable homicide." Following Hill's conviction of first degree murder, his sentencing jury rendered a unanimous recommendation of death as the appropriate penalty. He was sentenced December 6, 1994, to die in the electric chair. Initially Hill and his family wished me to represent him on his appeal to the Florida Supreme Court. I drafted an appellate brief focussing on two issues: (1) the bearing of Hill's motives for killing Dr. Britton and Col. Barrett—Hill's belief that in killing his victims he was preventing them from committing the greater evil of destroying more than two "unborn human beings"; (2) whether Hill's reasons for killing meant that he was acting under a "*pretense* of moral or legal justification" such that he did not deserve to die. Although personally prochoice, I drafted a brief making these arguments on Hill's behalf. Unfiled Draft Initial Brief of Paul Jennings Hill, in Hill v. State, no. 84, 838 (Florida Supreme Court Jan. 1995).

Hill fired me as his appellate attorney, see Parloff, *supra*, and his case was handled by others. In Oct. 1996, the court rejected Hill's arguments and unanimously upheld Hill's murder convictions and death sentences, reasoning, "As a practical matter, permitting a defendant to vindicate his or her criminal activity in this manner would be an invitation for lawlessness."

102. Roger Rosenblatt, *The Man in the Water: Essays and Stories* (1995).

103. Gary Gilmore and Jesse Bishop volunteered for execution by waiving legal challenges to their death sentences. Gilmore was executed in 1977, Bishop in 1978. See NAACP, Legal Defense and Educational Fund, Inc., "Death Row, U.S.A." (unpublished compilation); Victor Streib, "Executions under the Post-*Furman* Capital Punishment Statutes," 15 *Rutgers Law Journal* 431 (1984); see also Mailer, *supra* n. 77.

104. John Arthur Spenkelink was executed at Florida State Prison on May 25,

1979. Bowers, *supra* n. 23 at 427; Welsh S. White, *The Death Penalty in the Eighties* 55 (1987). For views on the Spenkelink execution, see Robert A. Burt, "Disorder in the Court," 85 *Michigan Law Review* 1741, 1805–13 (1987); Streib, *supra* n. 103 at 449–51 (1984); Ramsey Clark, "Spenkelink's Last Appeal," *The Nation,* Oct. 27, 1979, at 385.

105. Roy Stewart was executed on April 22, 1994. "Death Row, U.S.A," *supra* n. 103. The state trial court had stayed Mr. Stewart's execution. The Florida Supreme Court dissolved the stay on April 18. Texas executed more people than Florida in 1986, a trend that extended into 1987 and beyond. "Death Row, U.S.A.," at 7. Louisiana executed eight people in 10 weeks in mid-1987, during which time there was only one execution in Florida. *Id.*

106. Subsequent to the creation of the agency, a resource center was created to take some pressure off CCR and to help private, mostly *pro bono*, attorneys represent death row prisoners.

107. Curtis Wilkie, "Mississippi Debates Death Penalty Shortcuts," *Boston Globe,* Aug. 21, 1994.

108. E.g., William Geimer and Jonathan Amsterdam, "Why Jurors Vote for Life or Death," 15 *American Criminal Law Review* 1 (1988).

109. Jack Bass, *Taming the Storm: The Life and Times of Judge Frank M. Johnson, Jr., and the South's Fight over Civil Rights* 454 (1993).

110. These papers may be found at the Manuscripts Division of the Library of Congress.

111. For discussions of the quality of the Florida Supreme Court's review of death cases, see generally George E. Dix, "Appellate Review of the Decision to Impose Death," 68 *Georgetown Law Journal* 97, 123–41 (1979); Michael L. Radelet and Margaret Vandiver, "The Florida Supreme Court and Death Penalty Appeals," 74 *Journal of Criminal Law and Criminology* 913 (1983). For the most comprehensive and critical comment, see Neil Skene, "Review of Capital Cases: Does the Florida Supreme Court Know What It's Doing?" 15 *Stetson Law Review* 263 (1986).

112. E.g., Espinosa v. Florida, 112 S. Ct. 2926 (1992) (challenge to aggravating circumstance); Sochor v. Florida, 112 S. Ct. 2114 (1992) (same); Parker v. Dugger, 111 S. Ct. 731 (1991) (jury override); Hitchcock v. Dugger, 481 U.S. 393 (1987) (holding that sentencing jury and judge's refusal to consider evidence of nonstatutory mitigating circumstances rendered death sentence invalid); Darden v. Wainwright, 106 S. Ct. 2464 (1986) (upholding prosecutor's inflammatory closing argument and approving exclusion of prospective juror because of prospective juror's moral opposition to the death penalty); Wainwright v. Witt, 469 U.S. 412, 423–26 (1985) (setting standard for exclusion of prospective juror based on venireperson's death penalty views); Spaziano v. Florida, 468 U.S. 447 (1984) (upholding constitutionality of judge overriding jury's recommendation of life imprisonment); Strickland v. Washington, 466 U.S. 668, 687 (1984) (articulating standard for claim of ineffective assistance of trial counsel); Barclay v. Florida, 468 U.S. 939 (1983) (holding that capital sentencer's consideration of nonstatutory aggravating circumstances does not violate Constitution); Enmund v. Florida, 458 U.S.

782 (1982) (reversing death sentence of accomplice who did not kill, attempt to kill, or intend to kill victim); Gardner v. Florida, 430 U.S. 349 (1977) (precluding death sentences based on secret evidence).

113. Mac Gordon, "Governor Fordice Signs on Prison Construction Bill," *Jackson Clarion-Ledger*, Aug. 25, 1994.

114. The journalist Ann Rule recorded that in 1977 Millard Farmer "called the State of Florida 'the Buckle of the Death Belt.' " Ann Rule, *The Stranger Beside Me* 336 (1986). This evocative metaphor has been appropriated by others to refer to other parts of the South. E.g., Death Penalty Information Center, *Chattahoochie Judicial District: Buckle of the Death Belt* (1991). Kimberly J. Cook, Letter to the Editor, "Facts on Death Penalty Show It Ineffective, Costly," *Jackson Clarion-Ledger*, Sept. 7, 1994.

115. Memorandum from Margaret Vandiver to Michael Mello, April 1, 1990, at 1.

116. Richard Kluger, *Simple Justice* 710 (1975). Thurgood Marshall, architect of the 1954 Brown v. Board of Education school desegregation case, was appointed by President Johnson to the Supreme Court in 1967. As a justice, Marshall, along with William Brennan, consistently voted against imposition of the death penalty. See generally Mello, *supra* n. 4.

The *Groveland* case is described more fully in Steven Lawson, David Colburn, and Darryl Paulson, "Groveland: Florida's Little Scottsboro Case," 16 *Florida Historical Quarterly* 1 (1986). The *Scottsboro* case in Alabama, in turn, is described in James Goodman, *Stories of Scottsboro* (1994); Dan Carter, *Scottsboro: A Tragedy of the American South* (rev. ed. 1979); Langston Hughes, *Scottsboro Limited: Four Poems and a Play in Verse* (1932); Clarence Norris and Sybil Washington, *The Last of the Scottsboro Boys: An Autobiography* (1979); Hayward Patterson and Earl Conrad, *Scottsboro Boy* (1950); Morris Shapiro, "Behind the Scenes at Scottsboro," 145 *The Nation*, Aug. 14, 1937, at 170.

117. David Von Drehle, *supra* n. 96 at 318.

118. Hatcher, "Florida Builds State-of-the-Art Death Row," *San Francisco Journal*, Dec. 16, 1992, at 11. I have written elsewhere about various dimensions of Florida's death penalty. E.g., Michael Mello and Nell Joslin Medlin, "Espinosa v. Florida: Constitutional Hurricane, Lambent Breeze, or Idiot Wind?" 22 *Stetson Law Review* 907–1029 (1993); Ruthann Robson and Michael Mello, "Ariadne's Provisions: A 'Clue of Thread' to the Intricacies of Procedural Default, Adequate and Independent State Grounds, and Florida's Death Penalty," 76 *California Law Review* 87 (1988).

119. Paul Monette, *West of Yesterday, East of Summer* 27 (1994).

120. Owen wrote:

This book is not about heroes. English poetry is not yet fit to speak of them.
Nor is it about deeds, or lands, nor anything about glory, honour, might, majesty, dominion, or power, except War.
Above all I am not concerned with Poetry.
My subject is War, and the pity of War.
The Poetry is in the pity.

Yet these elegies are to this generation in no sense consolatory. They may be to the next. All a poet can do today is warn. That is why the true Poets must be truthful.

(If I thought the letter of this book would last, I might have used proper names; but if the spirit of it survives—survives Prussia—my ambition and those names will have achieved themselves fresher fields than Flanders . . . .)

Wilfred Owen, Preface to *The Collected Poems of Wilfred Owen* 31 (1963).

121. Kate Millett, *The Politics of Cruelty* 15 (1994).

122. The culture of lawyering—and of writing scholarship on lawyering and its work products—purports to banish emotion from the temple of the law. Immersion in the world of "thinking like a lawyer" tends to lead legal professionals to think in terms of rules and proofs only. Yet operating in a vacuum tube of pure logic has its costs.

Fred Rodell fingered the problem in his 1937 *Virginia Law Review* piece, "Goodbye to Law Reviews":

There are two things wrong with almost all legal writing. One is its style. The other is its content. That, I think, about covers the ground . . . The average law review writer is peculiarly able to say nothing with an air of great importance.

The explanatory footnote is an excuse to let the law review writer be obscure and befuddled in the body of his article and then say the same thing at the bottom of the page the way he should have said it in the first place . . . .

It is the probative footnote that is so often made up of nothing but a long list of names of cases that the writer has had some stooge look up and throw together for him. These huge chunks of small type, so welcome to the student who turns the page and finds only two or three lines of text above them, are what make a legal article very, very learned. They also show the suspicious twist of the legal mind. The idea seems to be that a man cannot be trusted to make a straight statement unless he takes his readers by the paw and leads them to chapter and verse. Every legal writer is presumed to be a liar until he proves himself otherwise with a flock of footnotes.

In any case, the footnote foible breeds nothing but sloppy thinking, clumsy writing, and bad eyes. Any article that has to be explained or proved by being cluttered up with little numbers until it looks like the Acrosses and Downs of a cross-word puzzle has no business being written.

Fred Rodell, "Goodbye to Law Reviews," in *Rodell Revisited: Selected Writings of Fred Rodell* (1994).

123. David Mason, "Eighty Acres," *Hudson Review,* Summer 1995, at 228.

124. Mason, again, expresses this in "Eighty Acres." *Id.* at 228.

125. Stephen Dobyns, "Dead Curtain," 108 *Salmagundi* 91, 93 (Fall 1995).

126. See Symposium, "Lawyers as Storytellers and Storytellers as Lawyers: An Interdisciplinary Symposium Exploring the Use of Storytelling in the Practice of Law," 18 *Vermont Law Review* 565 (1994); Symposium, "Legal Storytelling," 87 *Michigan Law Review* 2073 (1989); "Symposium Speeches from the Emperor's Old Prose: Reexamining the Language of Law," 77 *Cornell Law Review* 1233 (1992).

127. See, e.g., Clark D. Cunningham, "A Tale of Two Clients: Thinking about Law as Language," 87 *Michigan Law Review* 2459, 2463 (1989); Steven Lubet,

"The Trial as a Persuasive Story," 14 *American Journal of Trial Advocacy* 77, 77 (1990); Sharon Creeden, "Telling Your Client's Story to the Jury," *Tennessee Bar Journal*, May–June 1991, at 10.

128. See, e.g., Charles R. Lawrence III, "The Word and the River: Pedagogy as Scholarship as Struggle," 65 *Southern California Law Review* 2231, 2278 (1992); Kim Lane Scheppele, "Foreword: Telling Stories," 87 *Michigan Law Review* 2073, 2073 (1989). The relationship between law, storytelling, and progressive lawyering is brilliantly portrayed by Gerald López, *Rebellious Lawyering: One Chicano's Vision of Progressive Law Practice* (1992). For a thoughtful analysis of López's ideas, see Anthony V. Alfieri, "Practicing Community," 107 *Harvard Law Review* 1747 (1994) (book review). The idea of voice and narrative is also the focus of much academic literature from other disciplines, including literature, anthropology, political science, and history. See, e.g., James McPherson, *Battle Cry of Freedom: The Civil War Era* at ix–x (1988). For a critique of the legal narrative movement, see Daniel A. Farber and Suzanna Sherry, "Telling Stories Out of School: An Essay on Legal Narratives," 45 *Stanford Law Review* 807, 840–54 (1993) (arguing that objective standards should be used to evaluate narratives and that much narrative scholarship falls short of these standards).

129. Michael Mello, "Death and His Lawyers," 20 *Vermont Law Review* 19 (1995). See also Michael Mello, *"Crazy Joe" Spaziano* (forthcoming, The University of Wisconsin Press).

130. The judicial opinions in *Spaziano* are not worth citing, because they are not worth reading. The media's coverage of the case—with the exception of the *Orlando Sentinel*—comes far closer to the truth than anything yet by a judge or a law clerk. E.g., Bruce Shapiro, "Not for Burning Probability of Habeas Corpus Reform," *The Nation*, July 17/24, 1995, at 79; James Kilpatrick, "Florida May Execute Innocent Man," *Miami Herald*, June 8, 1995; ABC's *World News Tonight*, "Hypnotized Witness Recants Story," Transcript no. 5130–5 (June 30, 1995), at 21; William Booth, "Gov. Chiles Halts Execution after Witness Recants," *Washington Post*, June 17, 1995; Larry Rother, "A Witness Says He Lied, but the Execution Is On," *New York Times*, Oct. 1, 1995; Linda Gibson, "Court Gives 'Crazy Joe' 11th Hour Reprieve," *National Law Journal*, Sept. 25, 1995, at A10; Bryan Marquard, "Lawyer Stretches the Ethics Envelope," *Valley News*, Oct. 8, 1995; Editorial, "Time Is Running Out," *St. Petersburg Times*, June 15, 1995; Editorial, "Too Much Doubt in Spaziano Case," *Tampa Tribune*, June 17, 1995; Editorial, "Chiles Spared Florida from a Capital Crime," *Palm Beach Post*, June 16, 1995; Editorial, "Less 'Panic' for Spaziano," *Miami Herald*, Sept. 13, 1995; John McKinnon, "Spaziano Lawyer: Hearing a 'Sham,'" *Miami Herald*, Sept. 10, 1995; Lori Rozsa, "'Crazy Joe' Is Granted a Reprieve," *Miami Herald*, Sept. 13, 1995; Larry Kaplow, "Legal Gamble Wins Spaziano Stay," *Palm Beach Post*, Sept. 13, 1995; Jackie Halifax, AP, "Court Hears Spaziano's Death Appeal," *Tallahassee Democrat*, Sept. 12, 1995; Diane Rado, "Justices Grant Stay to Spaziano," *St. Petersburg Times*, Sept. 13, 1995; Lori Rozsa, "For Death Row Inmate, Another Day in Court," *Miami Herald*, Sept. 9, 1995; Diane Rado, "Spaziano's Lawyer Says State Lied," *St. Petersburg Times*, Sept. 1, 1995; Mark Silva, "Court Faces

Quandry on Spaziano," *Miami Herald,* Sept. 8, 1995; Kevin Metz, "Spaziano Gets Stay of Execution," *Tampa Tribune,* Sept. 13, 1995; David Greenberg, "Attorney Problems Complicate Spaziano Case," *Gainesville Sun,* Sept. 13, 1995; Mark Silva, " 'Crazy Joe' Lawyers to Square Off Today," *Miami Herald,* Sept. 7, 1995; Lori Rozsa, " 'Crazy Joe' Is Guilty, Must Die, Chiles Says," *Miami Herald,* Aug. 25, 1995; Kevin Metz, "Chiles Orders Execution of Killer," *Tampa Tribune,* Aug. 25, 1995 Kevin Metz, "Clemency Sought in Death Case," *Tampa Tribune,* June 29, 1995: Beth Taylor, "Essay-writing Lawyer Rejoins Killer's Case," *Orlando Sentinel,* June 18, 1995; Jim Leusner, "Lawyer Takes Spaziano Case to Top U.S. Court," *Orlando Sentinel,* Sept. 10, 1995; Colin Wentworth, "Justice in a Trance," *Moon Magazine,* June 14, 1995; Editorial Cartoon, *Miami Herald,* Aug. 31, 1995; Lori Rozsa, "A Witness Recants, but Electric Chair Looms," *Miami Herald,* Sept. 6, 1995; Tony Proscio, "Anatomy of a Lie," *Miami Herald,* Sept. 8, 1995; Tony Proscio, " 'Memory' of Murder, Mockery of Justice," *Miami Herald,* June 14, 1995; Lori Rozsa, "Case # 75–430," *Miami Herald,* Nov. 19, 1995; Lori Rozsa, "Over Time, Spaziano Witnesses' Tales Shifted," *Miami Herald,* Nov. 21, 1995; Lori Rozsa, "Chiles Got a Flawed Report on 'Crazy Joe,' " *Miami Herald,* Sept. 17, 1995; Editorial Cartoon, *Miami Herald,* Aug. 31, 1995; Tom Fiedler, "Taking the Politics Out of Capital Punishment," *Miami Herald,* June 18, 1995; Editorial, "Death Unwarranted," *Miami Herald,* June 16, 1995; Editorial, "Recover a Little Justice: Give Spaziano a New Trial," *Palm Beach Post,* Sept. 12, 1995; Lori Rozsa, " 'Crazy Joe' Psychic Offers More Information," *Miami Herald,* Oct. 15, 1995; Lori Rozsa, " 'Crazy Joe' Trial Witness Told Pastor That He Lied," *Miami Herald,* Sept. 12, 1995; David Von Drehle, "A Hypnotized Witness," *Washington Post,* Sept. 15, 1995; "Change of Heart," *The Economist,* June 24, 1995, at 28; Editorial, "The Secret Trial," *Gainesville Sun,* Aug. 29, 1995; Editorial, "Death by Secret Evidence," *Miami Herald,* Aug. 25, 1995; Martin Dyckman, "A Man May Die under Cover of Secrecy," *St. Petersburg Times,* Aug. 27, 1995; Bill Moab, "Joe Spaziano Gets Fifth Death Warrant," *St. Petersburg Times,* Aug. 25, 1995; Jim Leusner, "Chiles Keeps FDLE Records of Spaziano Review," *Orlando Sentinel,* Aug. 26, 1995; Lucy Morgan, "Spaziano Report to Remain Secret," *St. Petersburg Times,* Aug. 26, 1995; Editorial, "Justice for Spaziano," *Orlando Sentinel,* Aug. 25, 1995; Editorial, *New Republic,* July 17, 1995, at 9; Lori Rozsa, "Witness: Don't Kill Convict," *Miami Herald,* June 11, 1995; Lori Rozsa, "Chiles Considers Staying Execution of Joe Spaziano," *Miami Herald,* June 15, 1995; Lori Rozsa, "A Case Built on Hypnosis Crumbles," *Miami Herald,* June 16, 1995; Lori Rozsa, "Governor Chiles Steps in: Execution Called Off," *Miami Herald,* June 16, 1995; Lori Rozsa, "Governor Asked to Free 'Crazy Joe,' " *Miami Herald,* June 30, 1995; Brad Barnes, "Execution Case Hangs on Witness' Credibility," *Pensacola News Journal,* July 19, 1995; Michael Griffin, "Spaziano Asks Chiles, Cabinet for Clemency Hearing," *Orlando Sentinel,* June 29, 1995; Coleman McCarthy, "The Case of the Hypnotized Witness," *Washington Post,* Aug. 5, 1995; Carl Hiaasen, "Even Crazy Joes Deserve to Live," *Gainesville Sun,* July 27, 1995; Martin Dyckman, "Call Again for Clemency," *St. Petersburg Times,* June 13, 1995; Editorial, "Tick-Tick for 'Crazy Joe,' " *Miami Herald,* Aug. 30,

1995; Liz Balmaseda, "Chiles' Logic, Like This Case, Is Full of Holes," *Miami Herald*, Aug. 31, 1995; Tom Blackburn, "The Hypnotic Case of Crazy Joe," *Palm Beach Post*, Aug. 28, 1995; Editorial, "A Death Penalty Mistake," *St. Petersburg Times*, June 4, 1995; Michael Griffin, "Chiles to O.K. Spaziano's Death," *Orlando Sentinel*, Aug. 24, 1995; Editorial, "The Clemency Factor," *Gainesville Sun*, June 14, 1995; Lori Rozsa, " 'Crazy Joe' Trial Witness Told Pastor That He Lied," *Miami Herald*, Sept. 21, 1995.

The Florida Supreme Court ordered an evidentiary hearing on one aspect of Mr. Spaziano's innocence claim. Spaziano v. State, 660 So. 2d 1363 (Fla. 1995). The best accounts of the hearing are unfortunately unavailable on NEXIS: John McKinnon, "Tables Turned, State Grills Ex-star Witness," *Miami Herald*, Jan. 11, 1996; Lori Rozsa, "Ex-Girlfriend: 'Crazy Joe' Forced Me to Lie," *Miami Herald*, Jan. 12, 1996; John McKinnon, "Witness: Truth Was Told In '76," *Miami Herald*, Jan. 14, 1996; John McKinnon, "One Judge Holds Key to Crazy Joe's Fate," *Miami Herald*, Jan. 16, 1996; Editorial, "Retry 'Crazy Joe,' " *Miami Herald*, Jan. 17, 1996; Carl Hiaasen, "Fairly Convict Crazy Joe—or Let Him Live," *Miami Herald*, Jan. 11, 1996.

By far the worst accounts of the hearing are unfortunately available on NEXIS: the "coverage" provided by the *Orlando Sentinel*." Michael Griffin, "Spaziano's Life Hinges on Whether Judge Believes Witness's Latest [*sic*] Story," *Orlando Sentinel*, Jan. 7, 1996; Jim Leusner and Michael Griffin, "Former Outlaw: Spaziano Enjoyed Killing [*sic*]," *Orlando Sentinel*, Jan. 8, 1996; Michael Griffin, "Spaziano Brothers: Joe Said He Killed a Nurse [*sic*]," *Orlando Sentinel*, Jan. 9, 1996; Beth Taylor and Michael Griffin, "DiLisio: I Wronged Spaziano," *Orlando Sentinel*, Jan. 10, 1996; Michael Griffin and Beth Taylor, "DiLisio's Facts Wobbly [*sic*]," *Orlando Sentinel*, Jan. 11, 1996; Michael Griffin, "Spaziano's Former Girlfriend Contradicts [*sic*] DiLisio's Story," *Orlando Sentinel*, Jan. 12, 1996; Jim Leusner and Michael Griffin, "Stepmother Disputes DiLisio's New [*sic*] Version," *Orlando Sentinel*, Jan. 13, 1996; Michael Griffin and Beth Taylor, "Brother against Brother," *Orlando Sentinel*, Jan. 14, 1996; Jim Leusner and Michael Griffin, "Spaziano's Future Is Now in Hands of Circuit Judge," *Orlando Sentinel*, Jan. 16, 1996.

For my own earlier writings on Joe Spaziano's case, see Michael Mello, "Outlaw Executive," 1 *Journal of Contemporary Law* 1 (1997); Michael Mello, "Outlaw Judiciary," 23 *City University of New York Law Review* 104 (1996); Michael Mello, "A Letter on a Lawyer's Life of Death," 38 *South Texas Law Journal* 121 (1997); Mello, *supra* n. 129.

131. "Terms for Assessment: An ABA Journal Roundtable," *American Bar Association Journal*, July 1994, at 53 (quoting Pamela Karlan, professor of law at the University of Virginia Law School).

132. *Id.* at 56 (quoting Harold Koh, professor of international law, Yale Law School).

133. Tim O'Brien, *The Things They Carried* (1990).

134. Laurie Lee, *A Moment of War* (1986).

135. Robert Burt, "Disorder in the Court," 85 *Michigan Law Review* 1741, 1764 (1987).

Chapter 2. Judge Robert S. Vance: The Hanging Judge Who Hated Capital Punishment

1. By this I don't mean The Shoah. Although it touched my family, I have no right to write about that event. I don't mean "event"; referring to it in that way forgets that the Shoah is outside history. As Steven Katz has demonstrated in volume 1 of his planned multi-volume treatise, the Holocaust is outside history in its singularity.

2. John Leonard, *Private Lives in the Imperial City* (1979).

3. Abner J. Mikva and John C. Godbold, " 'You Don't Have to Be a Bleeding Heart,' Representing Death Row: A Dialogue," 14 *Human Rights* 22, 23 (Winter 1987) (quoting Judge John Godbold, former Chief Judge, United States Court of Appeals for the Eleventh Circuit).

4. 408 U.S. 238 (1972); 428 U.S. 153 (1976); 481 U.S. 279 (1987).

5. Jack Bass, *Taming the Storm: The Life and Times of Judge Frank M. Johnson, Jr., and the South's Fight over Civil Rights* 454 (1993).

6. *Id.* at 453.

7. Remarks of Robert S. Vance, Jr., "In Praise of Life's Enjoyment: A Tribute to the Spirit of My Father," 42 *Alabama Law Review* 951, 953 (1991).

8. Telephone conversation with Ray Jenkins, August 21, 1994. Mr. Jenkins generously shared with me the manuscript of his splendid book about Robert Vance: *Blind Vengeance* (1997). The Vance family cooperated in this undertaking, as did the family of Robbie Robinson in Savannah and, surprisingly, even the family of Walter Moody. Letter from Ray Jenkins to Michael Mello (Sept. 16, 1993). On June 28, 1991, Walter Leroy Moody, Jr., was convicted in a federal courtroom in St. Paul, Minnesota, on all 71 counts of an indictment charging him with the murder of Robert S. Vance and Robert Robinson.

9. My tribute to Judge Vance appears as Michael Mello, "Rough Justice: Reflections on the Capital Habeas Corpus (Anti) Jurisprudence of Judge Robert S. Vance," 42 *Alabama Law Review* 1197 (1991).

10. Evans v. Britton, 639 F.2d 221 (5th Cir. 1981), *rev'd sub nom.* Hopper v. Evans, 456 U.S. 605 (1982).

11. *Id.* The Alabama statute precluding consideration of lesser included offense instructions in death penalty cases was invalidated in Beck v. Alabama, 447 U.S. 625 (1980). In reversing the former Fifth Circuit in *Evans,* the Supreme Court held that under *Beck* "due process requires that a lesser included offense instruction be given only when the evidence warrants such an instruction." Hopper v. Evans, 456 U.S. 605, 611 (1982). The court reasoned that because John Evans had not been prejudiced by the preclusion clause, he was not entitled to a new trial. *Id.* at 613–14. Thus Evans' conviction and sentence, as well as all other convictions and death sentences imposed under Alabama's 1975 capital statute, were not invalidated by implication.

12. Ford v. Strickland, 696 F.2d 804 (11th Cir. (en banc)), *cert. denied,* 464 U.S. 865 (1983); McClesky v. Kemp, 753 F.2d 877 (11th Cir. 1985) (en banc), *aff'd,* 481 U.S. 279 (1987).

13. Washington v. Strickland, 693 F.2d 1243 (5th Cir. Unit B 1982) (en banc), *rev'd,* 466 U.S. 668 (1984).

14. Strickland v. Washington, 466 U.S. 668, 686–91 (1984).

15. Two Eleventh Circuit panels, both of which included Judge Vance, re-manded the Theodore Bundy cases for evidentiary hearings. Bundy v. Wainwright, 808 F.2d 1410 (11th Cir. 1987); Bundy v. Dugger, 816 F.2d 564 (11th Cir.), *cert. denied*, 484 U.S. 870 (1987).

16. Richard Posner, *Overcoming Law* 465 (1995).

17. Levit, "Expediting Death," 59 *UMKC Law Review* 55 (1990).

18. *Id.* at 495–96.

19. *Id.* at 496.

20. Posner, *supra* n. 16 at 456.

21. *Id.* at 460.

22. A. T. Denning, *The Family Story* 183 (1981).

23. Posner, *supra* n. 16 at 465.

24. 693 F.2d 1243 (5th Cir. Unit B 1982) (en banc), *rev'd,* 466 U.S. 668 (1984).

25. Stanley v. Zant, 697 F.2d 955 (11th Cir. 1983). I realized, while writing this note, that I have memorized the full citation to this opinion.

26. *Id.* My only victory in Ivon Stanley's case was persuading Judge Vance to include this letter in a footnote to the published opinion in *Stanley v. Zant.*

Chapter 4. On Metaphors, Mirrors, and Murders: Theodore Bundy and the Rule of Law

1. I do not for a moment suggest that mine is the only or the most important account of Bundy's cases. Bundy's chief postconviction counsel, for example, has written of his experiences as Bundy's lawyer, James Coleman, "Litigating at the Speed of Light," 16 *Litigation* 14 (Summer 1990); one of Coleman's assistants also wrote a memoir: Polly Nelson, *Defending the Devil: My Story as Ted Bundy's Last Lawyer* (1994). Telling the story from my perspective and in my voice is all I can do here.

2. "Serial murderer" refers to one who kills a number of people over a long period, as opposed to a "mass murderer," who kills a number of people in a single crime. See Donald T. Lunde, *Murder and Madness* 47 (1976).

3. Richard Larsen, *Bundy: The Deliberate Stranger* 2 (1986).

4. Elizabeth Kendall, *The Phantom Prince: My Life with Ted Bundy* (1981); Ann Rule, *The Stranger Beside Me* (rev. ed. 1989); Stephen Michaud and Hugh Aynesworth, *The Only Living Witness: A True Account of Homicidal Insanity* (rev. ed. 1989) [hereinafter *Witness*]; Stephen Michaud and Hugh Aynesworth, *Ted Bundy: Conversations with a Killer* (1989); Steven Winn and David Merrill, *Ted Bundy: The Killer Next Door* (1980); Polly Nelson, *Defending the Devil* (1994). Rumor has it that one of the many police detectives assigned to Bundy is also writing a book about the case.

5. Michael Perry, *The Stranger Returns* (1992); C. Terry Cline, *Missing Persons* (1981).

6. E.g., Daly, "Murder! Did Ted Bundy Kill 36 Young Women and Will He Go Free?" *Rolling Stone,* Dec. 14, 1978, at 58; Horwitz, "Ted Bundy—Portrait of a Compulsive Killer," *Cosmopolitan,* Nov. 1980, at 328; MacPherson, "The Roots

of Evil," *Vanity Fair,* May 1989, at 140; Jon Nordheimer, "All-American Boy on Trial," *New York Times,* Dec. 10, 1978, sec. 6.

7. *The Deliberate Stranger* (two-part NBC television broadcast, May 5 and 7, 1986). The U.S. Supreme Court denied plenary review in Bundy's case on May 6, 1986—the day between the airing of parts one and two of the NBC mini-series.

8. Klass, "Ted Bundy Serial Murders Inspire New Dance Drama," *Valley News* (Lebaon, N.H.), March 13, 1991.

9. Larsen, *supra* n. 3 at 300–301 (describing the "media army" that covered Bundy's first Florida trial); *Witness, supra* n. 4 at 4, 260–61 (describing television coverage of same trial); Rule, *supra* n. 4 at 352 (same).

10. E.g., Daniel Franklin, "The Right Three Strikes," *Washington Monthly,* Sept. 1994, at 29. Examples from 1991 alone include Gow, "Stopping Murderers," *Chicago Tribune,* Aug. 15, 1991, at 24 (editorializing that state has "moral right to authorize the executions of sadistic murders like Richard Speck, Ted Bundy, John Gacy and Jeffrey Dahmer"); T. Squitieri, "Drifter: I Killed 60 People," *USA Today,* Aug. 15, 1991 (author Ann Rule quoted as fearing glamorization of Theodore Bundy and fictional character Hannibal Lecter in the film *Silence of the Lambs* may spark imitators); Warren, "Race to Publish Case of Milwaukee Serial Killer Inspires Several Quickie Books," *Chicago Tribune,* Aug. 11, 1991, Tempo Section (Lindy Dekoven of Lorimar Pictures quoted as explaining lack of Hollywood interest in Dahmer case: "Someone like Ted Bundy was a more complex, appealing character"); Montgomery, "FBI Expert Says 'Signature' Links 3 Eastside Murders," *Seattle Times,* Aug. 8, 1991 (prosecutors in Seattle serial murder cases reportedly sought testimony of John Douglas, chief of FBI National Center for the Analysis of Violent Crime, who worked for government on Bundy case); Williamson, "The Smell of Death and Indifference," *Seattle Times,* Aug. 6, 1991 (in opinion column, writer cited experts who point to common traits among such alleged serial murders as Theodore Bundy, John Gacy, and Jeffrey Dahmer); Curt Suplee, "Serial Killers: Frighteningly Close to Normal," *Washington Post,* Aug. 5, 1991 (forensic psychiatrist Emanuel Tanay, who examined many alleged serial killers including Bundy, quoted as saying they were not copycats but are "very attentive to their predecessors"); Warren, "Walking Papers," *Chicago Tribune,* Aug. 4, 1991, Tempo section (editor of gay publication argued that lifestyles of reported heterosexual killers like Bundy tend not to be implicitly questioned as they are when killers or victims are gay); Barron and Tabor, "17 Killed and a Life Is Searched for Clues," *New York Times,* Aug. 4, 1991, sec. 1 (some criminal psychologists reported as seeing traits in Jeffrey Dahmer that they studied in Bundy); Germani, "Serial Killers Are Rare, but Increasing Sharply," *Christian Science Monitor,* Aug. 2, 1991, at 9 (Dr. James Fox of Northwestern University College of Criminal Justice quoted as saying, "We make our serial killers into celebrities," noting movie made about Bundy); Johnson, "Microscope on Monsters at Serial Killer Seminar," *Chicago Tribune,* Aug. 1, 1991 (describing all-day panel on serial crime sponsored by FBI, including a tape in which Bundy reportedly claimed that "basically, I'm a normal person"); Worthington and McMahon, "Anger Building over Role of Police in Dahmer Case," *Chicago Tribune,* July 29, 1991 (Bundy included in list of well-known serial murder cases); Howlett, "Milwaukee Mass Murder: Jeffrey

Dahmer," *USA Today,* July 24, 1991, sec. A (contrasting the confused, loner-type serial killer such as Edward Gein with "the cold, calculating Bundy-esque killer"); Susan Okie, "Profiles in Murder: The Art of Psychological Crime-Solving Is Evolving into a Science," *Washington Post,* June 16, 1991, sec. B, at 3 (describing FBI unit specializing in compiling psychological portraits; quoting sources as saying the man who taught them most was Bundy, who talked with members of the unit repeatedly over several years); Kilian, "The Murdering Mind: FBI Experts Make It Their Business to Know Mass Killers," *Chicago Tribune,* April 19, 1990, Tempo section ("Buffalo Bill" character in film *Silence of the Lambs* used cast on arm to fool victims, the same ruse was reportedly used by Bundy, the "smooth-talking, clean-cut ladies' man"); Achenbach, "Serial Killers: Shattering the Myth," *Washington Post,* April 14, 1991, Style section (top-grossing movie *Silence of the Lambs* made mass murder a growth industry; noting that in earlier TV, Bundy was played by Mark Harmon, the actor once labeled "the sexiest man alive"); Gelmis, "On the Twisted Trail of the Serial Killer," *New York Newsday,* April 1, 1991, at 43 ("Buffalo Bill" character's arm cast in *Silence of the Lambs* reportedly was based on Bundy's method of operation); Roberts, "The Most Baffling Serial Killer Hunt," *Chicago Tribune,* March 26, 1991, Tempo section (reporting that Bundy wrote from prison offering to help Seattle police in serial murder investigation); Berson, "A Culture of Violence—Murder and Mayhem Are Everywhere, and People Can't Seem to Get Enough," *Seattle Times,* March 12, 1991, sec. B (creator of dance performance, *Killer,* reportedly drew on publicized murders of women by Charles Campbell and Theodore Bundy); James, "Now Starring: Killers for the Chiller 90's," *New York Times,* March 10, 1991, sec. 2 (reviewer of *Silence of the Lambs* and Bret Easton Ellis' *American Psycho* argued that these works show "an obsession with the criminal mind" and pander to audiences used to reading letters of Son of Sam and seeing Theodore Bundy played on television by actor Mark Harmon); Trebble, "The Manhunter behind 'Lambs,' " *USA Today,* March 1, 1991, Life section (FBI investigator John Douglas quoted as saying *Silence of the Lambs* is "reality," pointing out that "Buffalo Bill" character in movie used Theodore Bundy's reported cast-on-arm ruse); Emerson, " 'Silence' Is Golden: Hopkins Lands a Role He Can Sink His Teeth Into," *Chicago Tribune,* Feb. 17, 1991, Arts section (actor Anthony Hopkins quoted as telling interviewer that he started reading a book about Theodore Bundy in preparing for role, but could not finish it: "I'm not interested in these guys"); "Cozying Up to the Psychopath That Lurks Deep Within," *New York Times,* Feb. 10, 1991, sec. 2 (actress Kathy Bates, who plays deranged nurse in movie *Misery,* quoted as telling interviewer that she read books in preparing for the role and learned that psychopaths "are often extremely charming like Ted Bundy").

11. Wendy Lesser, *Pictures at an Execution:An Inquiry into the Subject of Murder* 19, 21, 77, 192, 222–23, 245 (1993).

12. E.g., John Grisham, *The Chamber* (1994); Patricia Cornwell, *Post Mortem* 76, 79 (1990); Jaqueline Girdner, *The Last Resort* 8 (1991); Sharyn McCrumb, *If I Return, Pretty Peggy-O* 211 (1991); M. Perry, *supra* n. 5.

13. Jonathan Groner, *Hillary's Trial* 148 (1991).

14. Lion, "Coming to Grips with Our Fascination with Serial Murderers," *Valley News,* Sept. 18, 1990.

15. Guskind, "Hitting the Hot Button," *National Law Journal,* Aug. 4, 1990; see also "Ad Features Bundy," *Advertising Age,* March 12, 1990, at 23 (describing ad); Spears, "Bob Graham Criticizes Ads for Martinez," *Tallahassee Democrat,* Mar. 8, 1990 (Martinez, in his reelection advertising, "declare[d] his support of the death penalty in a 30-second TV spot that also shows a smirking Ted Bundy, who was electrocuted at Martinez's order"); Minzesheimer, "Campaign '90 Notebook," *Gannett News Service,* March 5, 1990 (describing ad); Balz, "New Campaign Ads: Grim Focus on Fear of Crime," *Washington Post,* March 4, 1990 (describing ad).

The 1990 election was not the first time Bundy was used in state electoral politics. Bundy's "name—*and* continuing survival—[also had been] subjects raised often in both the [1986] gubernatorial and attorney general races in Florida." Rule, *supra* n. 4 at 461 (emphasis in original). According to press accounts, Bundy at one point sought a stay of execution in part based on his assertion that Governor (now U.S. Senator) Robert Graham scheduled Bundy's execution to enhance Graham's campaign for the Senate. See Hardy, "Bundy Blames Graham for Pending Execution," *United Press International,* June 24, 1986 (Bundy's motion for postconviction relief claimed that "the governor's action in signing this [death] warrant can only be viewed as an attempt to profit politically from taking action against Mr. Bundy").

16. Remarks of Chief Justice William H. Rehnquist at the American Bar Association Mid-Year Meeting (Feb. 6, 1989), at 13–14, 16.

17. Statement of G. Kendall Sharp, Federal District Court Judge, Middle District of Florida, Orlando Division, "Who Is on Trial? Conflicts between the Federal and State Judicial Systems in Criminal Cases," Hearing before a Subcommittee of the Committee on Government Operations, 100th Cong., 2d Sess. 62 (1988).

18. *Id.* at 78; see also Cotterell, "Death-appeals Process Examined," *Tallahassee Democrat,* Feb. 27, 1988.

19. Moline, "Graham and Cabinet Consider Clemency for Bundy," *United Press International,* Dec. 19, 1985.

20. Hamilton, "Mass Killers Back in Death Row Cells," *United Press International,* July 3, 1986.

21. *Id.*

22. "Graham Urges Time Limit on Death Appeals," *United Press International,* Jan. 26, 1989. See also, e.g., Donald D. Hooks and Lothar Kahn, *Death in the Balance: The Debate over Capital Punishment* 119 (1989) ("Theodore Robert Bundy was *finally* electrocuted after a decade on Florida's death row.") (emphasis added); Leguire, "Grant Blasts Bundy Delays," *Lake City Reporter* (Fla.), Feb. 22, 1988 ("Saying that convicted murderer Ted Bundy has made a mockery of the law, Congressman Bill Grant, D- [Madison County, Florida], is calling for an overhaul of the judicial system which would hasten executions").

23. As Von Drehle's book says, he and I spent a good bit of time discussing my understanding of Florida's capital punishment system. I am not, however, in my opinion, a "legal egghead." See David Von Drehle, *Among the Lowest of the Dead: The Culture of Death Row* 216 (1995).

24. Rule, *supra* n. 4 at 461.

25. *Id.* at 470. *See infra* (discussing cost of Bundy litigation).

26. *Id.* (discussing Supreme Court's denial of Bundy's certiorari petition).

27. Carolyn Forché, "The Recording Angel," in *The Angel of History* 55 (1994).

28. Albert Camus, *Notebooks, 1942–1951,* at 10 (1991).

29. Letter from Michael Radelet to Michael Mello, July 19, 1994. Nelson's book treats my minor role in Bundy's case fairly accurately. The firm (where I later worked as an associate) took on the case at my prodding, because firm attorneys James Coleman, Jeffrey Robinson, and Marian Lindberg *did* do a magnificent job representing Stephen Booker (whose case is described in Chapter 5). I *did* indeed think Nelson's Eleventh Circuit brief was misguided, and I *was* visibly aghast at the (never realistic) possibility that she might do the appellate oral argument.

30. *Id.* at 259 (capitalization in the original).

31. *Id.* at 257.

32. E.g., *id.* at 127–28, 73.

33. Id. at 69.

34. Polly Nelson, Bookmark, "Ted Bundy and Earthworms: Compassion [*sic*] for the Lower Orders of Life," *Los Angeles Times,* Aug. 21, 1994. Nelson's excerpt inspired the following response from a reader in Irvine, California: "Ted Bundy is a person that deserved and received his just reward. The excerpt from Polly Nelson's book "Defending The Devil" (Bookmark, August 21) wanted us to show compassion to earthworms and Bundy. Well, Ms. Nelson, I think we did both. One, by executing Bundy we showed compassion for the victims and their families. Two, putting him in the ground keeps your lowly earthworms company." Letter to the editor from Shannon Burns, "Death Penalty," *Los Angeles Times,* Sept. 29, 1994.

35. Nelson, *supra* n. 1 at 319.

36. Less than a month after Bundy's execution, a letter was sent above Nelson's signature to Roy D. Matthews; Dorothy Otnow Lewis, M.D.; Arthur Norman, Ph.D.; and Michael Radelet, Ph.D. reminding them that their "services on behalf of the attorneys for Theodore Robert Bundy are subject to the ethical requirements of attorney-client confidentiality," so that any communications "by Mr. Bundy personally or through his lawyers that were not made public by Mr. Bundy or by his counsel in the course of legal proceedings. . . . must be kept confidential." The confidentiality requirement she reminded them, "survives Mr. Bundy's death and cannot be waived by the client's personal representative or heirs."

The day before, attorney Diane A. Weiner sent a letter to Michael Radelet, informing him that as personal representative of Bundy's estate, she had "the responsibility under Florida law to assert and protect all privileges, including the attorney-client privilege, which exist in favor of Mr. Bundy." Weiner stressed that confidential communications with Bundy "remain inviolate and undisclosable to any individual or entity" no exceptions.

37. Margaret Radin, "Cruel Punishment and Respect for Persons: Super Due Process for Death," 53 *Southern California Law Review* 1143 (1980).

38. This chapter does not attempt a scholarly treatment either of the nature of metaphor or the role of metaphor in law. For brilliant expositions of both, see Stephen L. Winter, "Transcendental Nonsense: Metaphoric Reasoning and the

Cognitive Stakes for Law," 137 *University of Pennsylvania Law Review* 1105 (1989); Stephen L. Winter, "The Metaphor of Standing and the Proplem of Self-Governance," 40 *Standford Law Review* 1371 (1987).

39. See NAACP, Legal Defense and Educational Fund, "Death Row, USA," (unpublished compilation).

40. The office's crushing caseload raised serious ethical dilemmas, which have led courts and commentators to conclude that such workloads render effective representation impossible. E.g., Cooper v. Fitzharris, 551 F.2d 1162 (9th Cir. 1977), *modified,* 586 F.2d 1325 (9th Cir. 1978); State v. Smith, 140 Ariz. 355, 362, 681 P.2d 1374, 1381 (1984) (en banc); Schwarz v. Cianca, 495 So. 2d 1208, 1209 (Fla. Dist. Ct. App. 1986); State ex rel. Escambia County v. Behr, 354 So. 2d 974, 975 (Fla. Dist. Ct. App. 1978), *aff'd,* 384 So. 2d 147 (Fla. 1980); Note, "The Right to Counsel and the Indigent Defense System," 14 *New York University Review of Law and Social Change* 221, 221–23, 240–41 (1986).

41. The executive schedules execution dates only in New Hampshire and Florida. In the remaining 36 capital punishment states, (see "Death Row, U.S.A," *supra* n.39) execution dates are set by the state courts.

42. Larsen, *supra* n. 3 at 351.

43. See Larsen, *supra* n. 3 at 245–54; *Witness, supra* n. 4 at 213–19; Rule, *supra* n. 4 at 264–80.

44. Bundy v. State, 455 So. 2d 330 (Fla. 1984), *stay granted,* 475 U.S. 1041 (1986), *cert. denied,* 476 U.S. 1109 (1986).

45. Bundy v. State, 471 So. 2d 9 (Fla. 1985), *cert. denied,* 479 U.S. 894 (1986).

46. For descriptions of the DeRonch case trial, see Larsen, *supra* n. 3 at 134–49; *Witness, supra* n. 4 at 153–71; Rule, *supra* n. 4 at 187–90. Bundy was sentenced to 1 to 15 years in prison. Rule, *supra* n. 4 at 206. The Utah Supreme Court affirmed the conviction. State v. Bundy, 589 P.2d 760 (Utah 1978), *cert. denied,* 441 U.S. 926 (1979).

47. Von Drehle, *supra* n. 23 at 285.

48. See A. Rule, *supra* n. 4 at 375, 383; see also *id.* at 365 ("the word was that Bundy might win").

49. *Id.* at 317.

50. *Id.*

51. Bearak and Thompson, "Jurors Have Varied Reasons for Deciding Bundy's Guilt," *Miami Herald,* July 31, 1979.

52. E.g., Darden v. Wainwright, 477 U.S. 168 (1986) (exclusion from the jury in a capital trial of a member of the venire for expressing beliefs in opposition to capital punishment not error; proper test is whether a prospective juror's views on capital punishment would impair performance of her duties as a juror); Wainwright v. Witt, 469 U.S. 412 (1985) (same); see also Lockhart v. McCree, 476 U.S. 162 (1986) (process of death-qualification of capital juries held not to violate Constitution). For an analysis of death qualification in Florida, see Winick and Witherspoon, "In Florida: Reflections on the Challenge for Cause of Jurors in Capital Cases in a State in Which the Judge Makes the Sentencing Decision," 37 *University of Miami Law Review* 825 (1983).

53. Bearak and Thompson, *supra* n. 51.

54. Rule, *supra* n. 4 at 392.

55. See Fla. Stat. § 921.141(3) (Harrison Supp. 1989).

56. See Patten v. State, 467 So. 2d 975, 979 (Fla. 1985), *cert. denied,* 474 U.S. 876 (1985); Rose v. State, 425 So. 2d 521, 525 (Fla. 1983), *cert. denied,* 461 U.S. 909 (1983).

57. Rule, *supra* n. 4 at 340.

58. *Witness, supra* n. 4 at 265; *cf.* Larsen, *supra* n. 3 at 327 (by the time the Leach trial began in January 1980, "Florida and other states had been saturated with publicity about Ted Bundy, the 'multiple murder suspect,' convicted killer of the Chi Omega" women).

59. Larsen, *supra* n. 3 at 296.

I draw no conclusions about Bundy's factual guilt or innocence, much less about his legal culpability (even assuming that such concepts can be reasonably defined, which here they may well not; see generally Charles Black, *Capital Punishment* [2nd ed. 1981]). Popular writers studying Bundy's case, including some ostensibly predisposed to find him innocent, have universally concluded that he was factually guilty of at least several sexual homicides. Much of the material relied upon by these writers was not presented at Bundy's trials, and thus it has never undergone adversarial testing. However, the cumulative weight of the cases made against Bundy by Michaud, Aynesworth, Rule, and Larsen cannot be dismissed for that reason alone. Cf. Carrie Menkel-Meadow, "Portia in a Different Voice: Speculations on a Women's Lawyering Proces," 1 *Berkeley Women's Law Journal* 39 (1985) (questioning the efficacy of the adversarial model as a way of solving problems and ascertaining truth); Carrie Menkel-Meadow, "Toward Another View of Legal Negotiation: The Structure of Problem Solving," 31 *UCLA Law Review* 754 (1984) (same).

60. *Witness, supra* n. 4 at 273; *accord* Bearak and Thompson, *supra* n. 51.

61. *Witness, supra* n. 4 at 9. "In fact, in the dozens of cases from Seattle to Florida in which the police have sought to implicate Bundy there has not been a single bit of physical evidence that incontrovertibly demonstrates his involvement in anything more sinister than car theft." *Id.*

62. Bundy v. State, 471 So. 2d 9, 18 (Fla. 1985), *cert. denied,* 479 U.S. 894 (1986); Bundy v. State, 455 So. 2d 330 (Fla. 1984), *cert. denied,* 476 U.S. 1109 (1986).

63. Coleman, *supra* n. 1 at 17 (describing hypnotized testimony in Leach case and the court's application of harmless error standard to admission of witness's hypnotically "refreshed" testimony in that case).

64. See Larsen, *supra* n. 3 at 296–300; *Witness, supra* n. 4 at 255–58; Rule, *supra* n. 4 at 343–44.

65. Larsen, *supra* n. 3 at 298–300; *Witness, supra* n. 4 at 255–59; Rule, *supra* n. 4 at 344.

66. Larsen, *supra* n. 3 at 343–46; *Witness, supra* n. 4 at 250–52, 258–59, 266; Rule, *supra* n. 4 at 345; see also Coleman, *supra* n. 1 at 16.

67. Immediately prior to closing arguments in the Chi Omega trial, Bundy's lawyers moved to revisit the competency issue. The court refused. Larsen, *supra* n. 3 at 314.

68. Rule, *supra* n. 4 at 373; see generally Bundy v. Rudd, 581 F.2d 1126 (5th Cir. 1978) (finding no federal constitutional error in Florida's refusal to permit Farmer to represent Bundy), *cert. denied,* 441 U.S. 905 (1979); cf. Larsen, *supra* n. 3 at 294–95 (discussing Farmer's attempts to represent Bundy).

69. *Witness, supra* n. 4 at 252, 254; Farmer v. Holton, 245 S.E.2d 457, 146 Ga. App. 102 (1978) (upholding contempt citation and describing facts), *cert. denied,* 440 U.S. 958 (1979).

70. Rule, who was present for the Chi Omega trial, characterized Bundy's lawyers as "all young, all determined to do their best, and all woefully inexperienced." Rule, *supra* n. 4 at 346; see also *id.* at 360, 375; *accord Witness, supra* n. 4 at 262–63, 269, 270–71. For example, the attorney who, at Bundy's insistence, did the closing argument in the Chi Omega case was an appellate lawyer with no previous felony trial experience. Larsen, *supra* n. 3 at 316; *Witness, supra* n. 4 at 262.

71. E.g., Larsen, *supra* n. 3 at 296, 298–300, 310, 313–14; *Witness, supra* n. 4 at 256–58; Rule, *supra* n. 4 at 335, 344–46, 372–73, 375.

72. Rule, *supra* n. 4 at 335–38, 373. Bundy continued throughout the trial to request Farmer. *Id.* at 342, 373, 389.

73. Soon after denying certiorari in Bundy's case, the Supreme Court granted review in another case to examine the constitutional consequences of hypnotically affected testimony. See Rock v. Arkansas, 483 U.S. 44 (1987) (criminal defendant's testimony on her own behalf cannot be excluded because it was hypnotically affected).

74. Rule, *supra* n. 4 at 438.

75. Bundy v. Florida, 475 U.S. 1041 (1986). The events leading up to the stay are described in Rule, *supra* n. 4 at 438.

76. Bundy v. Florida, 476 U.S. 1109 (1986).

77. Rule, *supra* n. 4 at 448.

78. Bundy's lawyers unsuccessfully attempted to persuade the governor to wait before signing a warrant. Coleman, *supra* n. 1 at 18.

79. *Id.;* see also *id.* at 18–19 (describing efforts).

80. Rule, *supra* n. 4 at 458.

81. Coleman, *supra* n. 1 at 18.

82. Bundy v. State, 490 So. 2d 1257 (Fla. 1986) (decided June 26, 1986); Bundy v. State, 490 So. 2d 1258 (Fla. 1986) (decided June 30, 1986).

83. Bundy v. Wainwright, 651 F. Supp. 38 (S.D. Fla. 1986) (decided July 2, 1986), *rev'd,* 808 F.2d 1410 (11th Cir. 1987).

84. Bundy v. Wainwright, 808 F.2d 1410, 1414 (11th Cir.1987); Coleman, *supra* n. 1 at 18.

85. Bundy v. Wainwright, 794 F.2d 1485 (11th Cir. 1986) (decided July 2, 1986); Rule, *supra* n. 4 at 451.

86. Coleman, *supra* n. 1 at 52.

87. Bundy v. Florida, 479 U.S. 894 (1986).

88. Coleman, *supra* n. 1 at 19; see Emergency Application for Stay of Execution to Preserve Jurisdiction Pending Filing and Disposition of Petition for Writ of Certiorari, at 2, Bundy v. Florida, 488 U.S. 1036 (1989).

89. Letter from Margaret Vandiver to Michael Mello, Aug. 14, 1990, at 3. See also Bundy v. State, 497 So. 2d 1209 (Fla. 1986) (decided Nov. 17, 1986); Bundy v. Wainwright, 805 F.2d 948 (11th Cir. 1986) (decided Nov. 18, 1986). The federal district court's opinion of November 17, 1986, denying the stay, is unpublished. See Order, Bundy v. Wainwright, No. 86–968- CIV-ORL-18 (date-stamped at 10:48 P.M., Nov. 17, 1986); see also Coleman, *supra* n. 1 at 19.

90. Bundy v. Wainwright, 805 F.2d 948 (11th Cir. 1986).

91. Wainwright v. Bundy, 479 U.S. 978 (1986) (summary order).

92. Witness, *supra* n. 4 at 316.

93. Rule, *supra* n. 4 at 458.

94. Michael Mello, "Rough Justice: Reflections on the Capital Habeas Corpus (Anti) Jurisprudence of Judge Robert S. Vance," 42 *Alabama Law Review* 1197 (1991).

95. Rule, *supra* n. 4 at 457–58; Rule's quotations confirm conversations I had with Judge Vance, for whom I clerked in 1982–83, shortly after the *Bundy* argument. Based upon Judge Vance's descriptions to me of what he said and what he meant by lambasting the prosecutor, it appears that Rule's account captured the flavor of the exchanges between judge and counsel. See also United Press International, "Smith Blasts Federal Court in Bundy Case," Oct. 24, 1986 (same); United Press International, Oct. 23, 1986 (quoting Judge Vance as saying that "this case is going to be reversed on a stupid error").

Eleventh Circuit oral arguments are not available to the public in either recorded or transcript form.

96. Rule, *supra* n. 4 at 458.

97. Bundy v. Dugger, 816 F.2d 564 (11th Cir.), *cert. denied,* 484 U.S. 870 (1987) (Kimberly Leach case); Bundy v. Wainwright, 808 F.2d 1410 (11th Cir. 1987) (Chi Omega case).

98. According to Rule, Bundy's was his first capital habeas case since becoming a federal judge. Rule, *supra* n. 4 at 458. It showed.

99. Coleman, *supra* n. 1 at 53 (summarizing Bundy's claim of mental incompetency); see also *Witness, supra* n. 4 at 317–23 (same); Rule, *supra* n. 4 at 462–70 (summarizing Bundy's incompetency claim and the prosecution's counterarguments).

100. Bundy v. Dugger, 675 F. Supp. 622 (M.D. Fla. 1987), *aff'd,* 850 F.2d 1402 (11th Cir. 1988), *cert. denied,* 488 U.S. 1034 (1989).

101. Rule, *supra* n. 4 at 470.

102. Coleman, *supra* n. 1 at 53.

103. Bundy v. Dugger, 675 F. Supp. 622 (M.D. Fla. 1987).

104. Bundy v. Dugger, 850 F.2d 1402 (11th Cir. 1988), *cert. denied,* 488 U.S. 1034 (1989).

105. Bundy v. Dugger, 488 U.S. 1034 (1989).

106. Emergency Application for Stay of Execution to Preserve Jurisdiction Pending Filing and Disposition of Petition for Writ of Certiorari [to the United States Court of Appeals for the Eleventh Circuit], at 3; see also Coleman, *supra* n. 1 at 14 (warrant signed less than 15 minutes after certiorari denial); cf. *Witness, supra* n. 4 at 331 (governor signed warrant "within the hour" of the Court's

certiorari denial); Rule, *supra* n. 4 at 473 ("the Supreme Court denied [review], and [Governor] Martinez immediately signed that death warrant").

107. *Witness, supra* n. 4 at 331–34; *id.* at 333–34 (summarizing issues raised by the stay application).

108. The court's opinion denying the stay is reported as Bundy v. State, 538 So. 2d 445 (Fla. 1989).

109. By this time I had left Florida, worked at the Wilmer, Cutler & Pickering law firm for a time (1987–88), and was living and writing in Vermont.

Von Drehle characterizes this as my "brainstorm," and I wish it were true. In fact, applying *Caldwell* to Florida's trifurcated capital sentencing scheme *was* a brainstorm, but it wasn't mine. It was Steve Malone's, and it occurred in 1985— four years before Bundy's lawyers raised the issue for the first time, three days before the execution.

By the time of Bundy's last death warrant, the "*Caldwell* claim" in Florida was a matter of common knowledge, and was being raised routinely by defense attorneys inside and outside Florida.

110. Ordinarily, the late discovery of the issue (following trial, direct appeal, state postconviction and federal habeas corpus review) would have foreclosed federal judicial consideration of its merits. E.g., Coleman v. Thompson, 111 S. Ct. 2546 (1991); McCleskey v. Zant, 111 S. Ct. 1454 (1991); Lewis v. Jeffers, 110 S. Ct. 3092 (1990); Dugger v. Adams, 489 U.S. 401 (1989); Murray v. Carrier, 477 U.S. 478 (1986); Wainwright v. Sykes, 433 U.S. 72 (1977); Ira P. Robbins, "Whither (or Wither) Habeas Corpus? Observations of the Supreme Court's 1985 Term" 111 *Federal Rules Digest* 265 (1986). The state courts in Bundy forgave the procedural default, however, and decided the claim on its merits. See Bundy v. Dugger, 488 U.S. 1036 (1989) (Brennan, J., dissenting from denial of stay) (explaining why no procedural bar foreclosed federal judicial review of Bundy's constitutional claim). Still, the untimely discovery of the issue undoubtedly reduced the likelihood of persuading a court to grant a stay or more substantive relief based on the claim.

111. Constitutional developments after Bundy's execution would have foreclosed his entitlement to relief under this claim. E.g., Preston v. Florida, 487 U.S. 1265 (1988) (order granting stay of execution pending the filing and disposition of a timely petition for writ of certiorari) (cited in Bundy v. Dugger, 488 U.S. 1036 [1989]) (Brennan, J., dissenting from denial of stay). The Supreme Court's order granting the stay in Robert Preston's case did not explain the basis of the Court's action. Preston's stay application raised only one issue, however, and that was the claim that subsequently failed to secure a stay in Bundy. The "Question to Be Presented" in Preston's eventual petition for plenary review was:

> Whether the decision of the Florida Supreme Court refusing to apply this Court's holding in Caldwell v. Mississippi, 472 U.S. 320, [105] S. Ct. 2633 (1985), to the facts of Mr. Preston's case fundamentally and irreconcilably conflicts with the decisions of the United States Court of Appeals in Adams v. Dugger, 816 F.2d 1493 (11th Cir. 1987), modifying on rehearing Adams v. Wainwright, 804 F.2d 1526 (11th Cir. 1986), cert. granted Dugger v. Adams, 108 S. Ct. 1106, 56 U.S.L.W. 3601 (1988); Mann v. Dugger, 844 F.2d 1446 (11th Cir. 1988) (en banc); and Harich v. Dugger, 844 F.2d 1464 (11th Cir. 1988) (en banc).

Application for a Stay of Execution Pending Review of Petition for a Writ of Certiorari to the Supreme Court of Florida, at 2–3, Preston v. Florida, 487 U.S. 1265 (1988) (No. A-216) (copy on file with author).

The Court granted the stay in *Preston* on September 23, 1988. Sawyer v. Smith, 110 S. Ct. 2822 (1990) (holding case relied upon by Bundy nonretroactive); on retroactivity generally, see Butler v. McKellor, 494 U.S. 407 (1990); Saffle v. Parks, 494 U.S. 484 (1990); Penry v. Lynaugh, 492 U.S. 302 (1989); Blume and Pratt, "Understanding *Teague v. Lane,*" 18 *New York University Review of Law and Social Change* 325 (1990–91); Goldstein, "Chipping Away at the Great Writ: Will Death Sentenced Federal Habeas Corpus Petitioners Be Able to Seek and Utilize Changes in the Law?" 18 *New York University Review of Law and Social Change* 357 (1990–91); James S. Liebman, "More Than 'Slightly Retro': The Rehnquist Court's Rout of Habeas Corpus Jurisdiction in *Teague v. Lane,*" 18 *New York University Review of Law and Social Change* 537 (1990–91); Robert Weisberg, "A Great Writ While It Lasted," 81 *Journal Criminal Law and Criminology* 9 (1990). It was an issue then under active consideration by the U.S. Supreme Court in another Florida capital case.

That other case had been orally argued months before Bundy raised the virtually identical constitutional claim. The case, decided subsequent to Bundy's execution, was Dennis Adams' case, Dugger v. Adams, 489 U.S. 401 (1989).

Soon after Bundy's execution, the Supreme Court decided *Adams*. The Court ruled against the inmate, Dennis Adams, on grounds of procedural default and thus avoided the merits of the constitutional question presented by Adams as well as by Bundy. Ironically, Bundy's case was not burdened by the procedural defect that proved literally fatal in *Adams*. See *Bundy,* 488 U.S. at 1036 (Brennan, J., dissenting from denial of stay) (explaining why Bundy's case presented no procedural bars foreclosing federal judicial review of the asserted constitutional defects in his sentence). However, retroactivity decisions rendered by the Court subsequent to Bundy's execution would have had the same effect as the application of a procedural bar. Sawyer v. Smith, 110 S. Ct. 2822 (1990).

Dennis Adams was executed several weeks after the Supreme Court's procedural default ruling in his case. "Death Row, U.S.A.," *supra* n. 39 at 8; see also Adams v. Dugger, 490 U.S. 1061 (1989) (order denying stay of execution).

112. Tedder v. State, 322 So. 2d 908, 910 (Fla. 1975); see also Cochran v. State, 547 So. 2d 928, 933 (Fla. 1989). "That the [Florida Supreme Court] meant what it said in *Tedder* is amply demonstrated by the dozens of cases in which it has applied the *Tedder* standard to reverse a trial judge's attempt to override a jury recommendation of life." Florida has executed three people notwithstanding their jury "recommendations" of life imprisonment: Ernest Dobbert in 1984, Buford White in 1987, and Robert Francis in 1991.

113. This is similar to the Private Eddie Slovik syndrome: the belief that in a multi-layered system of sequential decision-makers, someone, somewhere, sometime down the line of the process will make a "saving" decision. In Slovik's case, however, that never happened, and Slovik was executed. On Slovik's case generally, see William Bradford Huie, *The Execution of Private Slovik* (1954). On the Slovik syndrome generally, see Paduano and Smith, "Deadly Errors: Juror

Misperceptions Concerning Parole in the Imposition of the Death Penalty," 18 *Columbia Human Rights Law Review* 211, 213 n. 3 (1987) ("perhaps a majority of jurors" refuse to believe that the death sentence they impose will be carried out); "Special Project: Parole Release Decisionmaking and the Sentencing Process," 84 *Yale Law Journal* 810, 812 (1975) (describing the "Slovik Syndrome" as a juror's expectation that the sentence will not be fully carried out).

114. The early results of the Capital Jury Project were presented at a national conference on juries held at the Indiana University School of Law, Bloomington, on February 24, 1995, and sponsored by the Indiana University School of Law and the Law and Society program. Papers presented at the conference included: William Bowers, "The Capital Jury Project: Rationale, Design and Prospects"; James Luginbuhl and Julie Howe, "The Inadequacy of Capital Sentencing Instructions"; Austin Sarat, "Violence, Representation and Responsibility in Capital Trials: The View from the Jury"; Joseph Hoffmann, "Where's the Buck?—Juror Misperception of Sentencing Responsibility in Death Penalty Cases"; Marla Sandys, "Cross-Overs: Capital Jurors Who First Believe the Defendant Deserved to Die (Live) and Then Vote for Life (Death)."

Robert Weisberg has analogized capital jurors to the subjects of the famous Milgram experiment. Like the Milgram subjects, the typical death penalty juror is placed "in a novel and disorienting situation that pose[s] for him a distressing moral dilemma." And, like the Milgram subjects, the juror in a death penalty case may seek "a professional, symbolic interpretation of the situation to reorient himself"—in short, the "mystifying language of legal formality" may lead the juror to conclude that the sentencing decision falls outside the scope of the juror's personal moral responsibility, and may therefore distort the juror's "moral sense." The experiments involved volunteers who are asked to serve as "teachers" in a study of learning. The "teachers" were told to ask questions of a "subject" and to administer a painful electric shock to a "subject" who gave the wrong answer. The stated purpose of the study was to see how negative reinforcement affected learning. In reality, however, Milgram wanted to study the willingness of the "teachers" to administer pain: the shocks were not real, and the "subjects" were trained actors who only pretended to suffer from the shocks. Milgram found that the "teachers" showed a troubling ability to administer various levels of pain that in their perception ranged from relatively mild to very severe, even potentially fatal. According to Milgram, this ability to engage in conduct that, under normal circumstances, would seem sadistic and cruel was triggered by an abdication of personal moral responsibility: whenever they balked, the "teachers" were told that "the experiment must go on," and the responsibilities for the outcome lay with the scientists and not with the "teachers." Robert Weisberg, "Deregulating Death," 1983 *Supreme Court Review* 305. The experiments themselves are described in Stanley Milgram, *Obedience to Authority* (1974); Stanley Milgram, "Some Conditions of Obedience and Disobedience to Authority," 18 *Human Relations* 57 (1965); Stanley Milgram, "Behavioral Study of Obedience," 67 *Journal of Abnormal Psychology* 371 (1963). I am grateful to Joseph Hoffman's symposium paper, cited above, for bringing this aspect of Weisberg's work to my attention.

115. Caldwell v. Mississippi, 472 U.S. 320 (1985) (prosecutor's and judge's

comments to jury regarding appellate review held to constitute violation of Eighth Amendment). The Court has held that *Caldwell* is not retroactive. Sawyer v. Smith, 110 S. Ct. 2822, 2827 (1990).

It does not matter for my purposes that ultimate relief under *Caldwell* could have been denied to Bundy based on *Sawyer*. The point is that Bundy was treated differently. Other inmates raising *Caldwell* claims, such as Robert Preston (see *supra* n. 111), received stays. Bundy did not.

116. Joan Cheever, an editor for the *National Law Journal*, and, for five years, counsel to a condemned killer, described how this worked. Cheever tracked down 10 of the 12 jurors to discuss the mitigating evidence she had unearthed in the postconviction investigative stage of the case. In discussing the evidence that never was presented to them, all the jurors were sympathetic, and three invited Cheever into their homes for hour-long chats. "One was visibly shaken by the abundance of mitigating evidence that had never been presented. He agreed to sign an affidavit saying that had he known Walter had no prior record of violence and that had he heard testimony from the character witnesses, he would have voted for a life sentence (he was troubled by the lack of guidance provided by the defense attorney. He was sure, he said, that other jurors would be, too). But the next day he retracted his offer to testify. He didn't want to have anything to do with overturning the verdict. But he was *sure*, he said, that [Cheever and her colleagues] could find a way to get the case reversed—based on the *law*."

117. Emergency Application for Stay of Execution to Preserve Jurisdiction Pending Filing and Disposition of Petition for Writ of Certiorari to the Supreme Court of Florida, at 6, Bundy v. Florida, 488 U.S. 1036 (1989); *see also id.* at 6–10 (cataloguing many other examples of the sorts of comments quoted in the text).

118. Harich v. Dugger, 844 F.2d 1464, 1473 (11th Cir. 1988) (en banc).

119. It is unclear how this issue could have been raised in the habeas petition, since as of that time the claim had never been presented to the state courts and thus was an unexhausted claim. E.g., Vasquez v. Hillary, 474 U.S. 254 (1986); Rose v. Lundy, 455 U.S. 509 (1979) (exploring exhaustion rules requiring that claims must be presented to state courts before being presented to federal courts). Perhaps the state waived exhaustion. In any event, the federal courts in *Bundy* seemed untroubled by this comity difficulty.

120. Emergency Application, *supra* n. 106 at 7, Bundy v. Dugger, 488 U.S. 1036 (1989).

121. *Witness, supra* n. 4 at 329, 333–44, 346–52; Rule, *supra* n. 4 at 474–88.

122. Dr. Radelet, a professor of sociology and criminology at the University of Florida, and a leading scholar on capital punishment, had volunteered his services on Bundy's behalf.

123. See *Witness, supra* n. 4 at 332.

124. Rule, *supra* n. 4 at 474.

125. Von Drehle, *supra* n. 23.

126. *Witness, supra* n. 4 at 333–34 (discussing arguments raised in stay application); *id.* at 336, 342–43 (discussing evidentiary hearing).

127. The facts outlined in this paragraph come from Emergency Application, *supra* n. 106 at 5; see also *Witness, supra* n. 4 at 342–43.

128. *Witness, supra* n. 4 at 343.

129. Judge Thomas Clark has his chambers in Atlanta, Georgia; Judge Frank Johnson has his in Montgomery, Alabama; the late Judge Robert Vance had his in Birmingham, Alabama.

130. *Witness, supra* n. 4 at 343.

131. Emergency Application, *supra* n. 106 at 6. The Eleventh Circuit, contrary to its customary practice, never published an opinion explaining its decision to deny the stay.

132. E.g., Wainwright v. Greenfield, 474 U.S. 284, 289 n. 3 (1986).

133. Bundy v. Dugger, 488 U.S. 1036 (1989) (order denying stay of execution).

134. *Id.* (Brennan, J., dissenting from denial of stay). Justices Marshall, Blackmun, and Stevens also voted to grant the stay. *Id.*

135. That was the "hold" rule in existence at the time Bundy was executed, at any rate. On May 21, 1991, Chief Justice Rehnquist issued a "Memorandum to the Conference" entitled Re: Procedural Changes Agreed Upon at Today's Conference. The memo began "1. Henceforth, it will require four votes, rather than three, to 'hold' cases pending disposition of another case." *Source:* Papers of Thurgood Marshall, Manuscripts Division, Library of Congress, Container 518, Folder 4.

136. See generally Revesz and Karlan, "Nonmajority Rules and the Supreme Court," 136 *University of Pennsylvania Law Review* 1067 (1988). According to a media report, in at least one case (decided subsequent to Bundy's execution) even four votes for certiorari did not guarantee the fifth vote necessary to grant a stay of execution and thus to prevent the mooting of the certiorari grant. James Smith was executed on June 26, 1990. "Death Row, U.S.A.," *supra* n. 39 at 8. The Washington, D.C., *Legal Times* reported that hours before Smith's execution "William Brennan indicated that he and three other justices—Thurgood Marshall, Harry Blackmun, and John Paul Stevens—had voted to grant cert." in Smith's case. Robert Mauro, "Death in Texas: Why Cert. Didn't Work," *Legal Times* (D.C.), Nov. 19, 1990, at 10. On the first Monday of October 1990, four months after Smith's execution, the Court dismissed Smith's certiorari petition as moot: "Buried in a grave in Indianapolis, Smith can no longer benefit from the Court's review." *Id.*

137. Cf. Mauro, *supra* n. 136.

138. Rule, who was not present, wrote that immediately before Bundy's execution "Ted's flat eyes locked onto Jim Coleman and Reverend [Fred] Lawrence and he nodded. . . . 'Jim . . . Fred,' he said. 'I'd like you to give my love to my family and friends.' " Rule, *supra* n. 4 at 493; see also *Witness, supra* n. 4 at 356–57.

139. Koff, "Revolted by Bundy's Life, People Celebrate His Death," *St. Petersburg Times,* Jan. 25, 1989; see also Jane Caputi, *The Age of Sex Crime* 446 (1987) Anthony Paredes and Elizabeth Purdum, " 'Bye-Bye Ted . . . :' Community Response in Florida to the Execution of Theodore Bundy," 6 *Anthropology Today* 9 (April 1990); David von Drehle, "Execution Ends Bundy Horror; Macabre Carnival outside Prison Celebrates Murderer's Death: Slaying Toll May Be as High as 50," *Miami Herald,* Jan. 25, 1989; *Washington Post,* Jan. 29, 1989; *New York Newsday,* Jan. 27, 1989.

140. Memorandum from Margaret Vandiver to Michael Mello (Apr. 1, 1990) at 1 [hereinafter Vandiver Memorandum]. Most of the celebrants were men.

141. E.g., Anthony Paredes and Elizabeth Purdum, "Rituals of Death: Capital Punishment and Human Sacrifice," in *Facing the Death Penalty* (M. Radelet, ed. 1989).

142. Paredes and Purdum, *supra* n. 139 at 10.

143. Mary Daly, *Gyn/Ecology: The Metaethics of Radical Feminism* 178 (1978); see also Anne L. Barstow, *Witchcraze* (1994); Caputi, *supra* n. 139 at 96–102; Carlo Ginzburg, *Ecstasies: Deciphering the Witches' Sabbath* (1991); H. C. E. Midelfort, *Witch Hunting in Southwestern Germany, 1562–1684* (1972); H. R. Trevor-Roper, *The Crisis of the Seventeenth Century*, ch. 3 (1967).

144. Vandiver Memorandum, *supra*. n. 140. Others have commented on the collective madness surrounding public executions and the insight it provides into fears of death and the possible vileness of one's self. E.g., Arthur Koestler, *Reflections on Hanging* 9 (1957); Wendy Lesser, *Pictures at an Execution* (1993); James A. McCafferty, *Capital Punishment* 9 (1973); Negley Teeters, "*. . . Hang by the Neck . . .*" 30–46 (1967).

145. Clark v. Dugger, No. 89–3065 (11th Cir. Jan. 27, 1989) (unpublished order granting stay of execution and certificate of probable cause to appeal, limited to the sentencer's responsibility issue) (copy on file with author). The court's unpublished order reads in its entirety:

> BY THE COURT:
> Certificate of [probable] cause [to appeal] is GRANTED but limited to petitioner's claim based on Caldwell v. Mississippi, 472 U.S. 320 (1985).
> Briefing is stayed pending the decision of the Supreme Court in Adams v. Dugger, 816 F.2d 1493 (11th Cir. 1987), cert. granted sub nom. Dugger v. Adams, 108 S. Ct. 1106 (1988).
> The execution of petitioner is ORDERED stayed pending further order of this court.

The court ultimately rejected Raymond Clark's *Caldwell* claim. Clark v. Dugger, 901 F.2d 908 (11th Cir.), *cert. denied,* 111 S. Ct. 372 (1990). Clark was executed on November 19, 1990. "Death Row, U.S.A.," *supra* n. 39; see also Clark v. Dugger, 111 S. Ct. 422 (1990) (order denying stay of execution).

Like Bundy, Clark raised the *Caldwell* issue in a successive habeas petition. Two Eleventh Circuit judges, Vance and Kravitch, sat on both the *Bundy* and *Clark* panels.

146. *Cf.* Mauro, *supra* n. 136 (following stay denial and execution of Texas prisoner, Court dismissed inmate's certiorari petition as moot).

147. See generally Levit, "Expediting Death," 59 *UMKC Law Review* 481, 498–502 (1990).

148. Three years before Bundy was executed, I attended a conference of death row advocates. After several speakers used Bundy as a foil ("in dealing with the media, be sure to show that while the crime in your case was bad, your client was no Bundy," for example), Polly Nelson evoked an uncomfortable silence by reminding the audience that even Bundy had people who cared about him and that it was inappropriate to suggest that Bundy ought to be put to death.

149. See Testimony of Dr. Michael Radelet, "Death Penalty: Hearings before the Committee of the Judiciary of the United States Senate," 101st Cong., 1st Sess.

201 (Sept. 19, 1989) ("I know many people in Florida who oppose the death penalty but, then, would say except for Ted Bundy"); Coleman, *supra* n. 1 at 15 ("If ever the death penalty were warranted, even some lifelong opponents of capital punishment agreed, Ted Bundy would have been an appropriate candidate for execution.").

150. Bundy reportedly graduated from the University of Washington with a 3.51 grade point average. Rule, *supra* n. 4 at 36. At least some of his teachers thought very well of him. *Id.* at 19 (quoting a letter from a psychology professor placing Bundy in "the top 1% of undergraduate students with whom I have interacted both here at the University of Washington and at Purdue University. He is exceedingly bright, personable, highly motivated, and conscientious."). Bundy won a scholarship to Stanford University to study Chinese for a summer. *Id.* at 15.

Rule consistently referred to him as "brilliant." *Id.* at i, 28, 72, 155, 396. Larsen called him "bright," *supra* n. 3 at 12, 293, and observed that his academic record in college was erratic. *Id.* at 108–9. Michaud and Aynesworth concluded that Bundy was "only middling bright (IQ 124)," also pointing to Bundy's mixed academic career. *Witness, supra* n. 4 at 7, 56–60, 65–67, 71. "The image of brilliance owes much to the newspeople who fostered it. Ted made very good copy." *Id.* at 252.

"Brilliant," "bright," or simply cognitively unimpaired, Bundy was different from most death row inmates.

151. Most death row inmates grew up in poverty. In 1987 the American Bar Association calculated that 99 percent of condemned inmates were indigent. Blodgett, "Death Row Inmates Can't Find Lawyers," 73 *American Bar Association Journal* 58 (Jan. 1, 1987); see also Hugo Bedau, *The Death Penalty in America* 187–88 (1982).

Many death row inmates are illiterate, retarded, and/or mentally ill. E.g., Stanford v. Kentucky, 492 U.S. 361, 398 (1989) (noting that a 1988 diagnostic evaluation—the 1988 Lewis, Pincas, et al study, cited *infra*—of the 14 juveniles on death row in four states revealed that seven were "psychotic when evaluated or had been so diagnosed in earlier childhood; four others had histories consistent with diagnoses of severe mood disorders; and the remaining three experienced periodic paranoid episodes during which they would assault perceived enemies"); Hooks v. Wainwright, 536 F. Supp. 1330, 1337–38 (M.D. Fla. 1982) (more than half of Florida's prison inmates were functionally illiterate, and 22 percent of the total inmate population had IQ of less than 80, which is considered to be borderline retarded), *rev'd on other grounds*, 775 F.2d 1433 (11th Cir. 1985), *cert. denied,* 479 U.S. 913 (1986); Statement of James Ellis, President, American Association on Mental Retardation, "Death Penalty: Hearings before the Committee of the Judiciary of the United States Senate," 101st Cong., 1st Sess. 396 (Sept. 27, 1989) ("of the 118 people executed since 1976, at least seven had mental retardation"); Bluestone and McGahee, "Reactions to Extreme Stress: Impending Death by Execution," 119 *American Journal of Psychiatry* 393 (1962) (study finding that none of 19 condemned inmates on Sing Sing's death row had an education beyond the tenth grade and that some were illiterate); John Blume, "Representing the Mentally Retarded Defendant," *The Champion,* Nov. 1987, at 32; John Blume and David

Bruck, "Sentencing the Mentally Retarded to Death," 41 *Arkansas Law Review* 725, 725 n. 4 (1988); Jacob and Sharma, "Justice after Trial," 18 *University of Kansas Law Review* 493, 508–9 (1970) (intelligence and educational levels among prisoners as a group are lower than those of the population at large); Lewis, "Killing the Killers: A Post-*Furman* Profile of Florida's Condemned," 25 *Crime and Delinquency* 200, 211 (1979) (estimating that the mean education of Florida's condemned population was approximately ninth-grade level, and that 15 percent of the inmates had an IQ of less than 90); Lewis, Pincus, Bard, Richardson, Prichep, Feldman, and Yeager, "Neuropsychiatric, Psychoeducational and Family Characteristics of 14 Juveniles Condemned to Death in the United States," 145 *American Journal of Psychiatry* 584 (1988); Lewis, Pincus, Feldman, Jackson, and Bard, "Psychiatric, Neurological and Psychoeducational Characteristics of 15 Death Row Inmates in the United States," 143 *American Journal of Psychiatry* 838, 840–44 (1986) (discussing mental illness among certain death row inmates); Ream, "Capital Punishment for Mentally Retarded Offenders: Is It Morally and Constitutionally Impermissible?" 19 *Southwestern University Law Review* 89, 112–13 (1990) ("Current research [as of 1989] indicates that possibly as many as 250 of the [then] 2,000 people on death row in the United States are mentally retarded. Other research shows that since the death penalty was reinstated by Gregg in 1976, at least 5 of the 70 people executed [between 1977 and 1986] were arguably retarded"); Reid, "Unknowing Punishment," 15 *Student Lawyer* 18, 23 (May 1987) (discussing retarded inmates who have been executed); Ronald J. Tabak and J. Mark Lane, "The Execution of Injustice: A Cost and Lack-of-Benefit Analysis of the Death Penalty," 23 *Loyola of Los Angeles Law Review* 59, 94 (1989) ("more than twelve percent of the inmates currently on death row have been diagnosed as either retarded or of borderline intelligence"); Weiner, "Interfaces between the Mental Health and Criminal Justice Systems," in *Mental Health and Criminal Justice* 36 (Linda Teplin, ed. 1984) ("estimates of the mentally ill within prisons range from 14 percent who are considered psychotic to as high as 50 percent when behavior disorders are included. Between 10 and 29 percent of the prison population is also estimated to be mentally retarded"); Note, "Prison 'No Assistance' Regulations and the Jailhouse Lawyer," 1968 *Duke Law Journal* 343, 347–48, app. (intelligence and educational levels among prisoners as a group are lower than those of the population at large; one source of data analyzed by Jacob and Sharma, *supra*); "Items of Interest," 6 *Mental Disability Law Reporter* 52, 53 (Jan.–Feb. 1982) ("studies have shown that from 20 to 60 percent of the 142,000 persons in jail on a given day have mental health problems").

152. Larsen wrote that Bundy "had the good looks to be an actor." *Supra* n. 3 at 131; see *id.* at 133. Rule repeatedly called Bundy "handsome." *Supra* n. 4 at 28, 396.

By portraying the antagonistic characters as physically deformed, the 1990 movie *Dick Tracy* reinforced Western culture's association of badness with unattractiveness. Michaud and Aynesworth referred to the "hunchback" lurking beneath Bundy's facade of normality. *Witness, supra* n. 4 at 6. Similarly, Carl Sutcliffe, on being told that his brother was the "Yorkshire Ripper" (who killed and mutilated 13 women in England between 1975 and 1980), remarked: "I imagined [the killer] to be an ugly hunchback with boils all over his face, somebody who couldn't get women and resented them for that. Somebody with totally nothing going for him." Deborah Cameron and Elizabeth Frazer, *The Lust to Kill: A Feminist Investigation of Sexual Murder* 35 (1987).

Cameron and Frazer observe that the powerful popular stereotype of the sexual murderer as physical beast is "an important means by which the extraordinary acts of sexual killers can be slotted into our culture's scheme of things. . . . It has profoundly affected our responses to cases of sexual murder." *Id.* The authors' use of "our culture" is explained in their introduction. They "decided to concentrate on our own time and culture . . . twentieth-century England." *Id.* at 2–3.

The lens through which we view attractiveness is distorted by our own race, gender, class, and appearance.

153. Many encountering Bundy remarked on his urbanity and apparent intelligence. Immediately before pronouncing a sentence of death upon Bundy, Florida judge Edward Cowart advised Bundy to "take care of yourself. . . . You're a bright young man. You'd have made a good lawyer. I'd have loved to have you practice in front of me." Larsen, *supra* n. 3 at 321; *accord* Rule, *supra* n. 4 at 394. Judge Cowart then added: "But you went the wrong way, pardnuh." Larsen, *supra* n. 3 at 321; *accord* Rule, *supra* n. 4 at 394.

154. The relevance of Bundy's race and gender are discussed *infra*.

155. My experience was that in addition to poverty, the single most pervasive characteristic of death row inmates was that they were victims of childhood sexual abuse. Some data support this anecdotal observation. E.g., Lewis, Pincus, Bard, Richardson, Prichep, Feldman, and Yeager, *supra* n. 151 at 586–87.

156. Larsen, *supra* n. 3 at 43; Rule, *supra* n. 4 at 122, 138.

157. E.g., Larsen, *supra* n. 3 at 4–12, 109–10; *Witness, supra* n. 4 at 61, 67–69; Rule, *supra* n. 4 at 34, 39; see also *id.* at 101–2.

158. Larsen, *supra* n. 4 at 44 (same).

159. *Id.* at 11–12, 127–28.

160. Caputi, *supra* n. 139 at 51.

161. Larsen, *supra* n. 3 at 109; Rule, *supra* n. 4 at 23–32.

162. Coleman, *supra* n. 1 at 16.

163. The terms "one of us," "our," or "we" refer to the dominant culture, i.e., male gender, white race, heterosexual sexual orientation, comparatively affluent class. Below I discuss the relevance of gender and race in thinking about Bundy the symbol.

164. Caputi wrote in a similar vein of London's Jack the Ripper. See *supra* n. 139 at 17.

165. Georgia has been the most closely studied U.S. jurisdiction in this regard. One of the most accessible yet sophisticated treatments of the Georgia data is Samuel Gross, "Race and Death," 18 *University of California at Davis Law Journal* 1275 (1985). For studies of Georgia and other jurisdictions, see David C. Baldus, George Woodworth, and Charles Pulaski, *Equal Justice and the Death Penalty* (1990); William Bowers, *Legal Homicide* (1984); Samuel Gross and Robert Mauro, *Death and Discrimination: Racial Disparities in Capital Sentencing* (1989); David C. Baldus, George Woodworth, and Charles Pulaski, "Arbitrariness

and Discrimination in the Administration of the Death Penalty," 15 *Stetson Law Review* 133 (1986); David C. Baldus, George Woodworth, and Charles Pulaski, "Monitoring and Evaluating Contemporary Death Sentencing Systems: Lessons from Georgia," 18 *University of California at Davis Law Journal* 1375 (1985); David C. Baldus, George Woodworth, and Charles Pulaski, "Comparative Review of Death Sentences: An Empirical Study of the Georgia Experience," 74 *Journal of Criminal Law and Criminology* 661 (1983); William Bowers, "The Pervasiveness of Arbitrariness and Discrimination under Post-*Furman* Capital Statutes," 74 *Journal of Criminal Law and Criminology* 1067 (1983); Samuel Gross and Robert Mauro, "Patterns of Death: An Analysis of Racial Disparities in Capital Sentencing," 37 *Stanford Law Review* 27 (1984); Jacoby and Paternoster, "Sentence Disparity and Jury Packing: Further Challenges to the Death Penalty," 73 *Journal of Criminal Law and Criminology* 379 (1982); Keoniger, "Capital Punishment in Texas, 1924–1968," 15 *Crime & Delinquency* 132 (1969); Raymond Paternoster, "Prosecutorial Discretion in Requesting the Death Penalty: A Case of Victim-Based Racial Discrimination," 18 *Law and Society Review* 437 (1984); Raymond Paternoster, "Race of Victim and Location of Crime: The Decision to Seek the Death Penalty in South Carolina," 74 *Journal of Criminal Law and Criminology* 754 (1983); Paternoster and Kazyaka, "Racial Considerations in Capital Punishment: The Failure of Evenhanded Justice," in *Challenging Capital Punishment* (Kenneth C. Haas and James A. Inciardi, eds. 1988); Michael Radelet, "Racial Characteristics and the Imposition of the Death Penalty," 46 *American Sociological Review* 918 (1981); Michael Radelet and Glenn Pierce, "Choosing Those Who Will Die: Race and the Death Penalty in Florida," 43 *Florida Law Review* 1 (1991); Michael Radelet and Glenn Pierce, "Race and Prosecutorial Discretion in Homicide Cases," 19 *Law and Society Review* 587 (1985); Hans Zeisel, "Race Bias in the Administration of the Death Penalty: The Florida Experience," 95 *Harvard Law Review* 456 (1981).

These studies quantify the different ways in which the criminal justice system responds to the racial identity of the murder *victim*. The Baldus study of capital sentencing patterns in Georgia, for example, showed that a person of any race who has been convicted of murder is far more likely to be condemned if the victim was white than if the victim was of any other race. Killers of whites received the death penalty in 11 percent of the cases studied by Baldus and his colleagues, but only 1 percent of those who murdered blacks were sentenced to die. If the murderer was black and the victim white, the killer received the death penalty 22 percent of the time. If a black killed another black, that figure dropped to 1 percent. Even controlling for 230 other variables, the death sentence was four times more likely to be imposed when the victim was white. Gross put these numbers into common sense perspective: "Smoking cigarettes increases the risk of death by heart disease greatly, but by a considerably smaller amount than the race-of-victim effects" revealed by the Baldus study. Gross, "Race and Death," *supra* at 1308. A *New York Times* article also brought the studies' impact home dramatically. "Nearly half a century and at least 1,000 executions since it last happened in the United States, a white person was executed [on Sept. 6, 1991] for killing a black." David Margolick, "White Dies for Killing Black for the First Time in Decades," Sept. 7,

1991. When South Carolina executed Donald Gaskins on September 6, 1991, the *Times* wrote that not since 1944 "has a white person in the United States received the death penalty for killing a black. No white has been executed in South Carolina for such a killing since 1880. The total number of executions in the state is unclear, but 245 people have been sent to the state's electric chair since 1912." *Id.*

166. McCleskey v. Kemp, 481 U.S. 279 (1987) (purporting to accept as valid studies demonstrating discrimination in Georgia capital sentencing patterns, but finding no constitutional significance in the statistical disparities shown by the studies). *McCleskey* was "immediately beset by sharp criticism and, in some instances, outright denunciation." Kennedy, "*McCleskey v. Kemp:* Race, Capital Punishment, and the Supreme Court," 101 *Harvard Law Review* 1388, 1389 (1987) (collecting examples). For criticisms of *McCleskey* by the authors of the study at issue in *McCleskey* as well as by others, see, e.g., Baldus, Woodworth, and Pulaski, *supra* n. 165; Gross and Mauro, *supra* n. 165; Carter, "When Victims Happen to Be Black," 97 *Yale Law Journal* 420 (1988); Holland, "*McCleskey v. Kemp:* Racism and the Death Penalty," 20 *Connecticut Law Review* 1029 (1989); Johnson, "Unconscious Racism in the Criminal Law," 73 *Cornell Law Review* 1016 (1988); Mikel, "*McCleskey v. Kemp:* Whether Georgia's Capital Punishment Statute Is a Vehicle for Discrimination," 1988 *Detroit College of Law Review* 1029 (1988); "The Supreme Court, 1986 Term—Leading Cases," 101 *Harvard Law Review* 119, 153–59 (1987).

167. Wolfgang and Riedel, "Racial Discrimination, Rape, and the Death Penalty," in *The Death Penalty in America* 194 (Hugo Bedau, ed. 1982).

168. *Id.;* see also Partington, "The Incidence of the Death Penalty for Rape in Virginia," 22 *Washington and Lee Law Review* 43 (1965) (finding that between 1908 and 1964, 41 men, all African American, were executed for rape in Virginia); Wolfgang and Riedel, "Rape, Race, and the Death Penalty in Georgia," 45 *American Journal of Orthopsychiatry* 658 (1975).

The Supreme Court in 1977 held the death penalty unconstitutional disproportionate for the crime of rape of an adult woman. Coker v. Georgia, 433 U.S. 584 (1977). An amici curiae brief filed by the American Civil Liberties Union and several women's rights organizations (and written by then-Professor Ruth Bader Ginsberg) focused on the racial and gender aspects of the issue. None of the *Coker* opinions referred to these dimensions of the case, stressing instead matters of proportionality.

169. Victor Streib, "Executions under the Post-*Furman* Capital Punishment Statutes," 15 *Rutgers Law Journal* 443, 450 (1984) (footnotes omitted). Larsen characterized Spenkelink's crime as a "cruel, rather undistinguished murder." *Supra* n. 3 at 295. For views on the Spenkelink execution, see Robert Burt, "Disorder in the Court," 85 *Michigan Law Review* 1741, 1805–16 (1987); Ramsey Clark, "Spenkelink's Last Appeal," *The Nation*, Oct. 27, 1979, at 385.

170. Stephen Adler, "Death Specialists: Florida's Zealous Prosecutors," *American Lawyer*, Sept. 1981, at 36. Marky's prosecutorial colleague in *Spenkelink*, George Georgieff, volunteered this memorable explanation of how he became convinced that the death penalty works: "I know it's a deterrent because many years ago I was having a spat, a physical fight, with one of my ex-wives, and I found

myself choking her, and I saw her eyes start to pop out, and suddenly off to the left or right I saw the electric chair. It deterred *me.*" *Id.* Reading Georgieff's comment sure made *me* feel safer living in Tallahassee.

171. Sherrill, "Death Row on Trial," *New York Times Magazine,* Nov. 13, 1983, at 108–9.

172. Letter from Karen Gottlieb to Michael Mello (July 31, 1990). In 1979 Gotlieb, today a highly respected freelance appellate attorney in Florida, was employed as an assistant state public defender in Miami. She "had an opportunity many times to consult with the lawyers who represented Mr. Spenkelink in post conviction proceedings, including his attorneys in the litigation which immediately preceded his execution in May of 1979." *Id.*

173. Sherrill, *supra* n. 171 at 109; *cf.* Zeisel, *supra* n. 165 at 465–66 (documenting that Florida prosecutors altered charging decisions in apparent attempts to influence results of statistical studies of racism in the capital punishment process).

174. E.g., Judith Butler, *Gender Trouble: Feminism and the Subversion of Identity* (1990); Gayle Rubin, "Thinking Sex: Notes for a Radical Theory of the Politics of Sexuality," in *Pleasure and Danger: Exploring Female Sexuality* (Carole Vance, ed. 1984); see also Ruth Bleier, *Science and Gender* (1984); L. Davidson and L. Gordon, *The Sociology of Gender* 1–33 (1979); Simone de Beauvoir, *The Second Sex* 1–47 (1953); Anne Fausto-Sterling, *Myths of Gender* (1985); Evelyn Fox Keller, *Reflections on Gender and Science* (1985); Suzanne Kessler and Wendy McKenna, *Gender: An Ethnomethodological Approach* (1978).

175. Cameron and Frazer, *supra* n. 152 at 1.

176. *Id.;* see also *id.* at 23–26, 144–48.

177. See Ann Jones, *Women Who Kill* (1980).

178. *Id.* at xv; see also Jack Levin and James Alan Fox, *Mass Murder: America's Growing Menace* 53 (1985) ("It is obvious that certain types of mass killings—for example, serial raping and murdering—are the sole province of men"); R. Morneau and R. Rockwell, *Sex, Motivation, and the Criminal Offender* 223 (1980) (advising police that "the sadistic murderer is almost always male. Generally, do not waste time looking for a female").

179. "Femme Fatale," *New York Times,* Feb. 2, 1991 (editorial); Holmes, "8 Men Slain, and Now a Suspicion That the Killer Is a Woman," *New York Times,* Dec. 17, 1990.

180. See generally Wuornos v. State, No. 79, 484 (Fla. Sept. 22, 1994); Michael Reynolds, *Dead Ends* (1993); Dolores Kennedy, *On a Killing Day* (1992). Wuornos was convicted of and condemned for the murder of Richard Mallory; the Florida Supreme Court opinion noted that the sentencing jury's recommendation for death was unanimous, 12–0, and that "at trial, the State was allowed [by trial judge Uriel "Bunky" Blount] to introduce similar crimes evidence about Wuornos' alleged involvement in several other murders": those of Charles Richard Humphreys, Peter Siems, Walter Jeno Antonio, Troy Burress, David Spears, Charles Clarkaddon.

181. To paraphrase Walter Kaufmann's characterization of existentialism, feminism is less a unified philosophy than a label for several different revolts

against traditional modes of thought—including a revolt against labeling. *Existentialism from Dostoyevsky to Sartre* 11 (1975).

182. For a particularly offensive example of appropriation wearing the mask of sensitivity, see Fraser, "What's Love Got to Do with It? Critical Legal Studies, Feminist Discourse and the Ethic of Solidarity," 11 *Harvard Women's Law Journal* 53 (1988).

183. Bender, "A Lawyer's Primer on Feminist Theory and Tort," 38 *Journal of Legal Education* 3, 5 n. 5 (1988).

184. *Id.*

185. *Id.*

186. E.g., Wendy Kaminer, "Feminism's Identity Crisis," *The Atlantic*, Oct. 1993, at 51; see also Katie Roiphe, *The Morning After* (1933); Christina Hoff Summers, *Who Stole Feminism?* (1994); Rene Denfeld, *The New Victorians* (1995); Camille Paglia, *Sex, Art and American Culture* (1992); Midge Decter, *The New Chastity and Other Arguments against Women's Liberation* (1972).

187. E.g., R. Ressler, A. Burgess, and J. Douglas, *Sexual Homicide: Patterns and Motives* (1987); Levin and Fox, *supra* n. 178.

188. Virginia Woolf, *A Room of One's Own* 35 (1929) ("Women have served all these centuries as looking-glasses possessing the magic and delicious power of reflecting the figure of man at twice its natural size"). Woolf's metaphor has roots in Mary Wollstonecraft, *Thoughts on the Education of Daughters* (1787), and Mary Wollstonecraft, *A Vindication of the Rights of Women* (1789).

Feminists, of course, are not alone in their use of the mirror as metaphor. E.g., Rodolphe Gasché, *The Tain of the Mirror: Derrida and the Philosophy of Reflection* (1986); Richard Rorty, *Philosophy and the Mirror of Nature* (1979); "Vision, Veritable Reflections," in *Reading Rorty: Critical Responses to Philosophy and the Mirror of Nature* 47 (Alan R. Malachowski, ed. 1990); Yoltom, "Mirrors and Veils, Thoughts and Things: The Epistemological Problematic," in *Reading Rorty* 58 (Alan R. Malachowski, ed. 1990).

189. E.g., Nancy Chodorow, *The Reproduction of Mothering* (1978); Andrea Dworkin, *Pornography: Men Possessing Women* (1981); Susan Griffin, *Pornography and Silence: Culture's Revenge against Nature* 156–99 (1981).

190. See Edward Said, "Michel Foucault, 1926–1984," in *After Foucault* 5 (Jonathan Arac, ed. 1988); see also R. Boyne, *Foucault and Derrida: The Other Side of Reason* (1990). On feminism and Foucault, see *Feminism and Foucault* (I. Diamond and L. Quinby, eds. 1988).

191. Cameron and Frazer, *supra* n. 152 at xv.

192. For treatments of the debate, see Diana Fuss, *Essentially Speaking* (1989); E. Spellman, *Inessential Women: Problems of Exclusion in Feminist Thought* (1988); Harris, "Race and Essentialism in Feminist Thought," 42 *Stanford Law Review* 581 (1990). For an accessible discussion of how poststructuralist thought might influence feminist jurisprudence, see Ashe, "Mind's Opportunity: Birthing a Poststructuralist Feminist Jurisprudence," 38 *Syracuse Law Review* 1129 (1987).

193. E.g., Combahee River Collective, "A Black Feminist Statement," in *All the Women Are White, All the Blacks Are Men, but Some of Us Are Brave* 13 (Gloria Hull, ed. 1982).

194. Maxine B. Zinn, Lynn Weber Cannon, Elizabeth Higginbotham, and Bonnie Thornton Dill, "The Costs of Exclusionary Practices in Women's Studies," in *Making Face, Making Soul: Haciendo Caras: Creative and Critical Perspectives by Women of Color* 35 (Gloria Anzaldúa, ed. 1990).

195. Kline, "Race, Racism, and Feminist Legal Theory," 12 *Harvard Women's Law Journal* 115, 117 (1989) (quoting Esmeralda Thornhill, "Focus on Black Women," 1 *Canadian Journal of Women and the Law* 153, 160 [1985]). For other critiques of white feminist theory and practice, see, e.g., *Common Differences* (Gloria Joseph and Jill Lewis eds., 1981); *Home Girls: A Black Feminist Anthology* (Barbara Smith ed. 1983); bell hooks, *Ain't I a Woman: Black Women and Feminism* (1981); bell hooks, *Feminist Theory: From Margin to Center* (1984).

196. Bender, *supra* n. 183 at 5–6.

197. Caputi, *supra* n. 139 at 3. E.g., Susan Brownmiller, *Against Our Will: Men, Women and Rape* (1976); Susan Estrich, *Real Rape* (1987); Nancy Gager and Cathleen Schurr, *Sexual Assault: Confronting Rape in America* (1976), Susan Griffin, *Rape: The Politics of Consciousness* (1986); Catharine MacKinnon, *Toward a Feminist Theory of the State* 171–83 (1989); Andra Medea and Kathleen Thompson, *Against Rape* (1974); Kate Millett, *Sexual Politics* 44, 184, 335 (1970); Diana Russell, *Rape in Marriage* (1982); Diana Russell, *The Politics of Rape: The Victim's Perspective* (1975); C. Smart, *Feminism and the Power of Law* 26–49 (1989); Susan Estrich, "Rape," 95 *Yale Law Journal* 1087 (1986).

198. Brownmiller, *supra* n. 197 at 5 (emphasis in original).

199. Andrea Dworkin, *Woman Hating* (1974), and Dworkin, *supra* n. 189.

200. Andrea Dworkin, *Intercourse* (1987).

201. Caputi, *supra* n. 139 at 3.

202. E.g., Kathleen Barry, *Female Sexual Slavery* 174–214 (1984); Dworkin, *supra* n. 189; Zillah Eisenstein, *The Female Body and the Law* 162–74 (1988); Griffin, *supra* n. 189; Catharine MacKinnon, *Only Words* (1994); MacKinnon, *supra* n. 197 at 195–214; Catharine MacKinnon, *Feminism Unmodified: Discourses on Life and Law* (1987); Smart, *supra* n. 197 at 114–137 (1989); *Take Back the Night: Women on Pornography* (L. Lederer ed. 1980); cf. Linda Lovelace and Mike McGrady, *Ordeal* (1980) (describing Linda Lovelace's experiences as a pornography star).

203. See Richard Posner, "Obsession," *New Republic,* Oct. 18, 1993, at 31; Leanne Katz, "Censor's Helpers," *New York Times,* Dec. 4, 1993; Floyd Abrams and Catharine MacKinnon, "The First Amendment, Under Fire from the Left," *New York Times Magazine,* March 13, 1994; David Horowitz, "Cuss Me Kate: The Lunacy of Catharine MacKinnon," *Heterodoxy,* Nov. 1993; Jeffrey Toobin, "XRated," *New Yorker,* Oct. 13, 1994, at 70.

204. E.g., Chodorow, *supra* n. 189; Dorothy Dinnerstein, *The Mermaid and the Minotaur: Sexual Arrangements and Human Malaise* (1976); M. Eichler, *The Double Standard: A Feminist Critique of Feminist Social Sciences* (1980); Eisenstein, *supra* n. 202 at 42–51 (1988); *Feminist Praxis: Research, Theory, and Epistemology in Feminist Sociology* (L. Stanley ed. 1990); Sandra Harding, *Whose Science? Whose Knowledge?* (1991); Sandra Harding, *The Science Question in Feminism* (1986); Keller, *supra* n. 174 at 67–115; *The Prism of Sex: Essays in the*

Sociology of Knowledge (J. Sherman and E. Beck eds., 1979); see also *Doing Feminist Research* (H. Roberts ed. 1981); MacKinnon, *Only Words supra* n. 197 at 120–24, 162–63, 183; MacKinnon, *Only Words supra* n. 197 at 54–55; Maria Mies, "Towards a Methodology for Feminist Research," in *Theories of Women's Studies* (G. Bowles, ed. 1983); Minow, "Supreme Court Forward: Justice Engendered," 101 *Harvard Law Review* 10 (1987); Reinharz, "Experimental Analysis: A Contribution to Feminist Research," in *Theories of Women's Studies* (G. Bowles ed. 1983); Scales, "The Emergence of a Feminist Jurisprudence: An Essay," 95 *Yale Law Journal* 1373 (1986); Stanley and Wise, "Back Into the Personal, or Our Attempt to Construct 'Feminist Research,' " in *Theories of Women's Studies* (G. Bowles ed. 1983).

205. E.g., Coward, "Introduction," in *Desire: The Politics of Sexuality* (Ann Snitow ed. 1984).

206. Ellen Carol DuBois, Mary Dunlap, Carol Gilligan, Catharine MacKinnon, and Carrie Menkel-Meadow, "Feminist Discourse, Moral Values, and the Law—A Conversation," 34 *Buffalo Law Review* 11, 81 (1985). See also Nadine Strassen, *Defending Pornography* (1995); Nat Hentoff, *Free Speech for Me—but Not for Thee* (1992); Paglia, *supra* n. 186; Camille Paglia, *Vamps and Tramps* (1994).

207. Gelman, "The Mind of the Rapist," *Newsweek,* July 23, 1990, at 52.

208. For an illuminating treatment of Mailer's position in the literary culture of the United States, see Millett, *supra* n. 197 at 9–16, 314–35. Millett's book also has interesting discussions of D. H. Lawrence, Henry Miller, and Jean Genet. *Id.* at 237–313, 336–61.

209. Cameron and Frazer, *supra* n. 152.

210. Norman Mailer, "The White Negro," in Mailer, *Advertisements for Myself* 337 (1959).

211. In literature, "the male metaphor, and the male travail, is individualist." Sherry, Civic Virtue and the Feminine Voice in Constitutional Adjudication, 72 *Virginia Law Review* 543, 586 (1986).

212. Cameron and Frazer, *supra* n. 152 at 36, 160; Caputi, *supra* n. 139 at 110; Griffin, *supra* n. 189 at 90–91, 94 (discussing Norman Mailer, *The American Dream* [1965]); Millett, *supra* n. 197 at 9–16 (same). For a trashing of Mailer generally, see Millett, *supra* at 314–35; Germaine Greer, "My Mailer Problem," in *The Madwoman's Underclothes* 78 (1986).

213. Friedrich Nietzsche, *Beyond Good and Evil* (R. Hollingdale trans. 1981); Friedrich Nietzsche, *Ecce Homo* (R. Hollingdale trans. 1979). See generally Laurence Lampert, *Nietzsche and Modern Times: A Study of Bacon, Descartes and Nietzsche* (1993); Steven Aschniem, *The Nietzsche Legacy in Germany, 1890–1990* (1992); *Nietzsche, Feminism and Political Theory* (P. Patton ed. 1993); Irvin D. Yalom, *When Nietzsche Wept* (1993); L. Thiele, *Friederich Nietzsche and the Politics of the Soul: A Study of Heroic Individualism* (1990); Walter Kaufman, *Nietzsche: Philosopher, Psychologist, Antichrist* (4th ed. 1974).

Sophomoric attempts to emulate Nietzsche's superman apparently played a role in the notorious Leopold and Loeb "thrill killing," for which the two stood trial in 1924. Clarence Darrow represented Leopold and Loeb. In one of the first modern capital sentencing proceedings (Darrow pled his clients guilty and made penalty the main event of the trial), Darrow argued that Leopold had been strongly influenced by reading Nietzsche's philosophy at the University of Chicago. See Clarence Darrow, *The Story of My Life* (1932); Clarence Darrow, *Attorney for the Damned* 70 (A. Weinberg ed. 1957); H. Higdon, *The Crime of the Century* 341 (1975); I. F. Stone, *Clarence Darrow for the Defense* 387–88 (1941); Kevin Tierney, *Darrow: A Biography* 341 (1979).

214. Fyodor Dostoyevsky, *Crime and Punishment* (1866) (D. Magar-Shack trans. 1951).

215. Cameron and Frazer, *supra* n. 152 at 160–61.

216. For a thoughtful discussion of Genet in this regard, see Millett, *supra* n. 197 at 336–61.

217. Cameron and Frazer, *supra* n. 152 at 158.

218. *Id.* at 58–66.

219. *Id.* at 58.

220. *Id.* at 58–66.

221. *Id.* at 161.

222. Kent, "The Governor Did It," *New York Times,* Aug. 19, 1990 (reviewing Stephen Pett, *Sirens* [1990]).

223. Cameron and Frazer, *supra* n. 152 at 161.

224. *Id.* at 166–70.

225. Larsen, *supra* n. 3 at 206–21, 242–43; *Witness, supra* n. 4 at 178–200; Rule, *supra* n. 4 at 434.

226. Larsen, *supra* n. 3 at 94 (describing media coverage); *Witness, supra* n. 4 at 153 (same).

227. Caputi, *supra* n. 139 at 51 (footnotes omitted).

228. *Id.;* see also Larsen, *supra* n. 3 at 210–11, 221; *Witness, supra* n. 4 at 187; Rule, *supra* n. 4 at 238, 255–56.

229. Caputi, *supra* n. 139 at 46, 47, 50; Rule, *supra* n. 4 at 255–56. Cameron and Frazer noted a similar reaction in England to the Yorkshire Ripper. "Many women reported casual comments from men that implied they shared the Ripper's pleasure in female fear. In Leeds, football crowds adopted 'Jack' as a folk hero and chanted at one stage 'Ripper eleven, police nil'." Cameron and Frazer, *supra* n. 152 at 33. While this information refers to events involving the Yorkshire Ripper, the term "Jack" indicates the legacy left by "Jack the Ripper." "Several later killers have been called after him [Jack the Ripper]." *Id.* at 181.

230. "After his first escape, the male identification was with Bundy as outlaw rebel-hero. But subsequently, Bundy did the supremely unmanly thing of getting caught." Caputi, *supra* n. 139 at 447. Similarly, a partial explanation for Jack the Ripper's unparalleled ability to generate mythology, see Caputi, *supra* n. 139 at 50–55, can be attributed to the fact that he was never caught.

231. See generally Stano v. State, 520 So. 2d 278 (Fla. 1988); Stano v. State, 497 So. 2d 1185 (Fla. 1986); Stano v. State, 473 So. 2d 1282 (Fla. 1985); Stano v. State, 460 So. 2d 890 (Fla. 1984); see also Stano v. Dugger, 901 F.2d 898 (11th Cir. 1990) (en banc) (remanding for evidentiary hearing).

I emphasize that Stano maintains his innocence, a fact underscored by a panel of the Eleventh Circuit's decision (albeit short-lived) mandating a new trial in one series of Stano's cases. See Stano v. Dugger, 889 F.2d 962 (11th Cir. 1989) (remanding for issuance of habeas corpus writ commanding retrial), *vacated pending reh'g en banc,* 897 F.2d 1067 (11th Cir. 1990) (en banc), *rev'd in part and remanded to panel for further consideration,* 921 F.2d 1125 (11th Cir. 1991) (en banc).

232. Anna Flowers, *Blind Fury* (1993).

233. For example, the index to Jane Caputi's book listed a single reference to Stano and 24 to Bundy, and one of the book's introductory epigraphs contained a reference to Bundy. See *supra* n. 139, at 239, 245. The Cameron and Frazer work had no references to Stano but one to Bundy. *Supra* n. 152 at 204, 207. This may reflect the latter authors' interest in cases arising in the United Kingdom.

234. Rule wrote that Bundy's "I.Q. alone nearly equalled Stano's and [another condemned inmate's] combined." *Supra* n. 4 at 434. This is hyperbole, but it illustrates the public perception that Bundy was brilliant while Stano is not.

235. This evocative term apparently originated in Herbert Cleckley, *The Mask of Sanity: An Attempt to Clarify Some Issues About the So-Called Psychopathic Personality* (5th ed. 1976).

236. Larsen, *supra* n. 3 at 345–46; Rule, *supra* n. 4 at 345.

237. Caputi, *supra* n. 139 at 109.

238. Cameron and Frazer, *supra* n. 152 at 31–33 (emphasis in original); see also Caputi, *supra* n. 139 at 46–47.

239. Bundy and Stano were at one time scheduled to be executed on the same day in 1986. Former Florida Governor, and now U.S. Senator, Robert Graham often signed death warrants in pairs, sometimes adopting warrant "themes." The Bundy/Stano theme apparently was serial killers. On another occasion, Graham signed simultaneous warrants on two inmates with the last name Thomas: Daniel Thomas and Edward Thomas. Daniel Thomas was executed; Edward Thomas received a stay. Graham's apparent cuteness was lost on the family of Edward Thomas, whose life had been spared. Media reports that "Thomas" had been executed in Florida prompted frantic calls to CCR from Edward Thomas's sister to determine if the executed man was *their* family's Thomas. Rule, *supra* n. 4 at 450.

240. McDonough, "I Can Teach You How to Read the Book of Life," 3 *Bill Landis' Sleazoid Express,* no. 7, at 3–5 (1984) (quoted in Caputi, *supra* n. 139 at 1). For Caputi's description of McDonough, see *id.* at 61–62.

241. Martin Luther King, "Letter from Birmingham Jail," in *A Testament of Hope* 293 (1986). For an interesting discussion of Buber's I-Thou idea as it might apply to law, see Ciampi, "The I and Thou: A New Dialogue for the Law," 58 *University of Cincinnati Law Review* 881 (1990).

242. The media quoted an unidentified prosecutor's estimation that executing Bundy cost the State of Florida approximately $6 million. Stott, "No Way to Tell If Bundy's a True $6 Million Man," *Florida Times Union* (Jacksonville), Jan. 13, 1988; Crawford, "Trying to Kill Bundy Costs Millions More Than Life in Prison," *Orlando Sentinel,* Dec. 18, 1987. The state attorney general's office declined an academic's request to estimate officially the cost of killing Bundy. See Letter from Walter Meginniss, Director, Criminal Appeals, Office of the [Florida] Attorney General, to Dr. Michael Radelet, Associate Professor, University of Florida (Dec.

30, 1987) ("You are advised that a study of the costs in the Bundy case has not been conducted in this office and consequently, your request for a copy must be declined.")

243. See David Von Drehle, "End Nearing for Death Row's No. 1 Killer: Ted Bundy Makes His Last Stand," *Miami Herald,* Dec. 11, 1988; see also "Death Row U.S.A., *supra.* n. 39.

244. The public outrage over judicial invalidation of capital sentences can be intense, as is evidenced by the events surrounding the successful recall of California Supreme Court Chief Justice Rose Bird and her two colleagues. See Ronald J. Tabak, "The Death of Fairness: The Arbitrary and Capricious Imposition of the Death Penalty in the 1980's," 14 *New York University Review of Law and Social Change* 797, 847 (1986).

245. Remember that "one of us," "we," or, "our" refers to the dominant culture, i.e., male, heterosexual, white, comparatively affluent.

246. *Cf.* Griffin, *supra* n. 189 at 174.

247. *Id.* at 162.

248. See Rule, *supra* n. 4 at 494–95; *Witness, supra* n. 4 at 65, 105, 107, 117; Bullough and Kuntz, "On Ted Bundy, Pornography, and Capital Punishment," 9 *Free Inquiry,* no. 9, at 54 (Spring 1989).

249. Cameron and Frazer, *supra* n. 152 at 176.

250. Griffin, *supra* n. at 162.

Chapter 5. Why I Did Deathwork: Pressing the Law to Keep Its Promises

1. Craig Barnard's story is told throughout David Von Drehle, *Among the Lowest of the Dead: The Culture of Death Row* (1995).

2. Unfortunately, we lost Henry just as this manuscript was being submitted for publication.

3. In 1995, I learned from one of Mr. Evans' lawyers that Mr. Evans asked to be buried with a copy of the dissenting opinion written by Thurgood Marshall. See Michael Mello, *Against the Death Penalty: The Relentless Dissents of Justices Brennan and Marshall* (1996).

4. David Bruck, "Does the Death Penalty Matter?" (Address given at Austin Hall, Harvard Law School, Oct. 22, 1990) (published at 1 *Reconstruction* 35 [1991]).

5. According to the most up-to-date compilation to which I have access, as of the summer of 1987 at least 487 capital cases were in the state postconviction system or federal habeas corpus process; these figures do not include Texas, Arizona, or Virginia, three states with substantial death row populations. See 1987 Airlie Status Report (unpublished compilation prepared by the NAACP Legal Defense and Educational Fund, Inc.).

In 1983, the Supreme Court noted that "it is a matter of public record that an increasing number of death-sentenced petitioners are entering the appellate stages of the federal habeas process." Barefoot v. Estelle, 463 U.S. 880, 892 (1983); see also Brief of Amicus Curiae, NAACP Legal Defense and Educational Fund, Inc., at

35, Barefoot v. Estelle, 463 U.S. 880 (1983) (No. 82–6080) ("approximately 60 [capital] cases have already reached the federal courts of appeal, and roughly 100 more are pending in the federal district courts").

6. Haftali Remauid, "A Punishing New Regime," *Legal Times,* May 6, 1996; McFarland v. Scott, 114 S. Ct. 2785 (1994) (Blackmun, J., dissenting from denial of cert.); see also Brief Amicus Curiae, ABA, McFarland v. Scott, No. 93–6497.

7. Spangenberg Group, "A Study of Representation of Capital Cases in Texas," i, viii, 161–63 (March 1993) [hereinafter 1993 Texas Capital Representation Study]. This study was requested by the State Bar of Texas and funded by the Texas Bar Foundation. *Id.* A summary of the study's findings is contained in Mark Ballard, "Texas' Capital Representation," *Texas Lawyer,* April 26, 1993, at 3.

8. Texas State Bar Ad Hoc Committee Regarding Legal Representation of Those on Death Row, Texas Plan 1 (1987).

9. Texas Resource Center Board of Directors, "Crisis in Representation of Texas Death Row Inmates" 5 (Oct. 26, 1993) (paper provided to the Clerk, U.S. Supreme Court) (footnote omitted). In 1992, there also was a marked increase in the "rate of affirmances of death sentences by the Court of Criminal Appeals." *Id.*

10. *Id.* at 6.

11. 1993 Texas Capital Representation Study, *supra* n. 7.

12. *Id.* at 127 (Table 9–4). Even in those states in which there is no "clear responsibility to provide counsel and compensation," funds still are provided "in the vast majority of cases." *Id.* The State of Texas provides no financial support to the resource center. *Id.* at 6–9.

13. 1993 ABA Counsel Study, at Executive Summary.

14. ABA Criminal Justice Section, "Report to the House of Delegates" (1989), reprinted in 40 *American University Law Review* 1, 9, 138 (1990) ("ABA Habeas Report") (footnotes omitted).

15. *Id.*

16. See Policy Statement of Texas Criminal Defense Lawyers Association and endorsements and minutes of the April 14, 1993, meeting of the House Committee on Criminal Jurisprudence.

17. See Press Release, "Gallego Will Try Again to Eliminate Unwarranted Delays in Capital Murder Cases" (in the author's files).

18. Michael Riccardi, "Death Row Inmates to Race the Clock," *Legal Intelligencer,* Jan. 8, 1996. See also Steven Keeva, "Justice on Death Row," *American Bar Association Journal,* April 1996.

19. Hank Grezlak, "Castille: Death Row Inmates Need Lawyers Now," 18 *Pennsylvania Law Weekly* 484 (April 24, 1995)

20. Kathleen Berexa, "The Coming Crisis in Death Penalty Cases," *Pittsburgh Legal Journal,* May 18, 1995.

21. Steve Albert, "Condemned, Without Counsel," *The Recorder,* May 26, 1995. For additional treatments of the counsel crisis, see Marcia Coyle, "Death Counsel Shortage Grows," *National Law Journal,* Sept. 27, 1993; David Elliot, "Death Row Work Offers Attorneys Few Incentives," *Austin [Texas] American-Statesman,* Sept. 26, 1993; Ronald Smothers, "A Shortage of Lawyers to Help the

Condemned," *New York Times,* June 4, 1993; Faye Silas, "Death Row: A Cry for Help," *Bar Leader,* May/June 1988; Scott Howe, "More Texas Law Firms to Represent Death Row Inmates," *Texas Bar Journal,* Sept. 1988; James Sales, "Indigent Death Row Inmates," *Texas Bar Journal,* Sept. 1988; William Choyke, "Legal Crisis on Death Row," *Dallas Morning News,* June 25, 1989; Victoria Lee, "*Coloradans Taking Texas Cases*", July 28, 1992; Sue Lindsay, "Local Lawyers to Help Inmates Awaiting Execution in Texas," *Rocky Mountain [Colorado] News,* July 26, 1992; Jan Hoffman, "Wanted: A Few Good Lawyers for Tough Cases in 'the Death Belt,' " *New York Times,* May 10, 1992; Harriet Chang, "Lawyers Shun Death Row Cases," *San Francisco Chronicle,* April 16, 1992; David Elliot, "Death Row in Texas 'in Crisis,' " *Austin American-Statesman,* May 9, 1992.

22. Note, "The Eighth Amendment and Ineffective Assistance of Counsel in Capital Trials," 107 *Harvard Law Review* 1923, 1294 (citing Marcia Coyle, "Death Counsel Shortage Grows as Executions Speed Up," *National Law Journal,* Sept. 27, 1993, at 3).

23. *Id.* at 1923 n.2 (1994); Gary Hengstler, "Attorneys for the Damned," *American Bar Association Journal,* Jan. 1, 1987, at 56, 57.

24. "Death Row Inmates Can't Find Lawyers," 73 *American Bar Association Journal* 58, 58 (Jan. 1, 1987) (quoting Steven Raiken, Staff Director, ABA Section of Individual Rights and Responsibilities); see also Hooks v. Wainwright, 536 F. Supp. 1330, 1337–38 (M.D. Fla. 1982) (one-half of Florida's inmates as of 1981 were functionally illiterate and 95 percent were indigent), *rev'd on other grounds,* 775 F.2d 1433 (11th Cir. 1985), *cert. denied,* 107 S. Ct. 313 (1986).

25. Stephen Bright, "Waste, Poverty and Disadvantage in the Infliction of the Death Penalty in the Death Belt," in *The Machinery of Death,* 124–125 (Amnesty International, 1995). See also Stephen Bright, "Counsel for the Poor: The Death Sentence Not For the Worst Crimes But for The Worst Lawyer," 103 *Yale Law Journal* 1835 (1994).

26. See Larry Yackle, *Postconviction Remedies* 1–2 (1981) (explaining that all states provide for direct review of state criminal judgments).

27. Gideon v. Wainwright, 372 U.S. 335 (1963).

28. Douglas v. California, 372 U.S. 353 (1963).

29. See, e.g., McCrae v. State, 437 So. 2d 1388, 1390 (Fla. 1983) (finding that issues which were raised or could have been raised on direct appeal cannot be relitigated in state postconviction proceeding); Atkinson v. United States, 366 A.2d 450, 452–53 (D.C. 1976) (same).

30. 344 U.S. 443 (1953).

31. For a sampling of the academic debate surrounding the federal courts' redetermination of federal questions decided in state criminal proceedings, see generally James Liebman and Randy Hertz, *Federal Habeas Corpus Practice and Procedure* (2nd ed. 1994 and 1997 supp.); Paul Bator, "Finality in Criminal Law and Federal Habeas Corpus for State Prisoners," 76 *Harvard Law Review* 441 (1961); Brennan, "Federal Habeas Corpus and State Prisoners: An Exercise in Federalism," 7 *Utah Law Review* 423 (1963); Friendly, "Is Innocence Irrelevant? Collateral Attack on Criminal Judgments," 38 *University of Chicago Law Review* 142

(1970); James Liebman, "Apocalypse Next Time?" 92 *Columbia Law Review* 1997 (1992); Daniel Meltzner, "Habeas Corpus Jurisdiction," 66 *Southern California Law Review* 2507 (1993); Bert Neuborne, "The Myth of Parity," 90 *Harvard Law Review* 1105 (1977); Gary Peller, "In Defense of Habeas Corpus Relitigation," 16 *Harvard Civil Rights–Civil Liberties Law Review* 579 (1982); Ira Robbins, "The Habeas Corpus Certificate of Probable Cause," 44 *Ohio State Law Journal* 307 (1983); Jordan Steiker, "Innocence and Federal Habeas," 41 *UCLA Law Review* 303 (1993); Larry Yackle, "Explaining Habeas Corpus," 60 *New York University Law Review* 991 (1985); "Developments in the Law," 83 *Harvard Law Review* 1038 (1970).

32. At some point between direct appeal and execution, the condemned inmate may seek executive clemency. On clemency generally, see Edmund Brown, *Public Justice, Private Mercy* (1989); Hugo Bedau, "The Decline of Executive Clemency in Capital Cases," 18 *New York University Review of Law and Social Change* (1990–91); "Clemency and Pardons Symposium, 27 *University of Richmond Law Review* 177–371 (1993); DiSalle, "Comments on Capital Punishment and Clemency," 25 *Ohio State Law Journal* 71 (1964); Note, "Executive Clemency in Capital Cases," 39 *New York University Law Review* 136 (1964).

33. Guttenberg, "Federal Habeas Corpus, Constitutional Rights, and Procedural Forfeitures: The Delicate Balance," 12 *Hofstra Law Review* 617, 678 (1981).

34. Paul Robinson, *An Empirical Study of Federal Habeas Corpus Review of State Court Judgments* 23 (1979); Allen, Schachtman, and Wilson, "Federal Habeas Corpus and its Reform: An Empirical Analysis," 13 *Rutgers Law Journal* 675, 683 (1982).

35. Barefoot v. Estelle, 463 U.S. 880, 915 (1983) (Marshall, J., dissenting).

36. Interview, "Death Penalty Lawyer Jack Boger," 7 *Defender* 15, 17 (July–Aug. 1986) (publication of the New York State Defenders' Association, Inc.).

37. James Liebman and Randy Hertz, *Federal Habeas Corpus Practice and Procedure* (2nd ed. 1994 and 1997 Supp.).

38. Abner J. Mikva and John C. Godbold, " 'You Don't Have To Be a Bleeding Heart,' Representing Death Row: A Dialogue," 14 *Human Rights* 22, 23 (Winter 1987) [hereinafter " 'You Don't Have To Be a Bleeding Heart' "].

39. Anthony Amsterdam, "In Favorem Mortis: The Supreme Court and Capital Punishment," 14 *Human Rights* 13, 51 (Winter 1987).

40. Paul Giannelli, "When the Evidence is a Matter of Life and Death," *New York Times,* Aug. 21, 1994.

41. *Id.*

42. Brown v. Wainwright, 785 F.2d 1457 (11th Cir. 1986). For accounts of Brown's case, see Blumenthal, "If An Innocent Person Can Be Executed, the Death Penalty is Unworkable," *Hartford Courant,* May 17, 1987; Styron, "Death Row," *New York Times,* May 10, 1987; Blumenthal, "If the Death-Penalty System Works, Why Did It Almost Make a Fatal Error?" *Advocate,* April 26, 1987, at A23; Fink, "Given New Life After Death Row, Man Fights Capital Punishment," *Hartford Courant,* March 19, 1987; Meehan, "When an Error Can Mean Execution," *Advo-*

cate, March 15, 1987; Deitz, "He's Unsure About New Life," *Tampa Tribune,* March 14, 1987; Krasnow, "Ex-Inmate Wants Story To Be Told," *Florida Times-Union/Jacksonville Journal,* March 14, 1987; Port, "Freed Prisoner Talks of Brush With Death," *St. Petersburg Times,* March 14, 1987.

43. Brown v. Wainwright, 785 F.2d at 1466 (11th Cir. 1986).

44. *Id.* at 1464–67.

45. *Id.*

46. *Id.*

47. *Id.* at A19; Brief for Appellant at 6–7, Brown v. Wainwright, 785 F.2d 1457 (11th Cir. 1985) (No. 85–3217).

48. Krasnow, *supra* n. 42.

49. Conversation with Shabaka Waglini (Joseph Green Brown) in Washington, D.C. (July 1987).

50. Michael Radelet, Hugo Bedau, and Constance Putnam, *In Spite of Innocence* (1992); Hugo Bedau and Michael Radelet, "Miscarriages of Justice in Potentially Capital Cases," 40 *Stanford Law Review* 21 (1987). The *Brown* case would have been included in the study had relief been granted during the study's time frame. Telephone conversation with Michael Radelet, University of Florida, Gainesville, Florida (July 1987). The Bedau and Radelet study as published in the *Stanford Law Review,* described *Adams* in this way:

> Witnesses located Adams' car at the time of the crime at the home of the victim, a white rancher. Some of the victim's jewelry was found in the car trunk. Adams maintained his innocence, claiming that he had loaned the car to his girlfriend. A witness identified Adams as driving the car away from the victim's home shortly after the crime. This witness, however, was driving a large truck in the direction opposite to that of Adams' car, and probably could not have had a good look at the driver. It was later discovered that this witness was angry with Adams for allegedly dating his wife. A second witness heard a voice inside the victim's home at the time of the crime and saw someone fleeing. He stated this voice was a woman's; the day after the crime he stated that the fleeing person was positively not Adams. More importantly, a hair sample found clutched in the victim's hand, which in all likelihood had come from the assailant, did not match Adams' hair. Much of this exculpatory information was not discovered until the case was examined by a skilled investigator a month before Adams' execution.

Bedau and Radelet, *supra* app. A at 92. These facts came to light in connection with the postconviction litigation in Adams' case.

51. These materials refute the statements of some Supreme Court Justices that expedited capital postconviction procedures are a necessary response to a flood of frivolous litigation. See Stephens v. Kemp, 464 U.S. 1027, 1032 (1983) (Powell, J., dissenting from grant of stay of execution) ("Once again . . . a typically 'last minute' flurry of activity is resulting in additional delay of the imposition of a sentence imposed almost a decade ago"); Gray v. Lucas, 463 U.S. 1237, 1240 (1983) (Burger, C.J., concurring in denial of certiorari and denial of application for stay of execution) ("This case illustrates a recent pattern of calculated efforts to frustrate valid judgments after painstaking judicial review over a number of years.").

52. For a brilliant treatment of this issue, see Ira Robbins, "Toward a More Just and Effective System of Review in State Death Penalty Cases," 40 *American University Law Review* 1 (1990) [hereinafter "ABA Task Force Report and Background Paper"].

53. Furman v. Georgia, 408 U.S. 238 (1972). The effect of *Furman* was to hold the death penalty unconstitutional as then administered in the United States. In response, the states enacted two kinds of capital punishment statutes: mandatory statutes requiring the death penalty for certain classes of crimes and guided-discretion statutes calling for comparison of specified aggravating and mitigating factors. In 1976, the Court held mandatory capital punishment statutes unconstitutional, except in the most extraordinary situations.

54. The Georgia statute authorized the death penalty if the crime was "outrageously or wantonly vile, horrible or inhuman in that it involved torture, depravity of mind, or an aggravated battery to the victim." *Georgia Code Ann.* § 27–2534.1(b)(7) (Supp. 1975); *see* Godfrey v. Georgia, 446 U.S. 420, 428–29, 432–33 (1980) (reversing death sentence when defendant's crimes "cannot be said to have reflected a consciousness materially more 'depraved' than that of any person guilty of murder," because victims were killed instantaneously, their deaths caused defendant extreme emotional trauma, and defendant admitted responsibility shortly after crimes).

55. Florida's statute authorized the death penalty if the crime was "especially heinous, atrocious, or cruel." *Fla. Stat.* § 921.141(5)(h) (Supp. 1976–1977); see Michael Mello, "Florida's 'Heinous Atrocious or Cruel' Aggravating Circumstance," 13 *Stetson Law Review* at 528–50 (1984) (arguing that on its face and as applied, § 5(h) is arbitrary).

56. See Rose v. Lundy, 455 U.S. 509 (1982) (adopting a total exhaustion rule requiring dismissal of mixed habeas petitions containing both exhausted and unexhausted claims). The exhaustion doctrine requires that the prisoner present the substance of his federal claim to the state courts; it is not, however, necessary to exhaust "book and verse" of the claim. Picard v. Connor, 404 U.S. 270, 278–79 (1971). It is unnecessary to exhaust when recourse to state remedies would be futile. *Ex parte Hawk,* 321 U.S. 114, 118 (1944); Piercy v. Black, 801 F.2d 1075, 1077–78 (8th Cir. 1986). The presentation of new facts in federal court does not abridge the exhaustion requirement. Vasquez v. Hillery, 106 S. Ct. 617, 620–22 (1986). The exhaustion rule, though strictly enforced, is not jurisdictional. Strickland v. Washington, 466 U.S. 668, 684 (1984). It is a doctrine of comity. Thompson v. Wainwright, 714 F.2d 1495, 1503–08 (11th Cir. 1983), *cert. denied,* 466 U.S. 962 (1984).

The exhaustion doctrine probably does not *require* states to fashion reliable procedures to vindicate federal rights. See Note, "Effect of the Federal Constitution in Requiring State Post-Conviction Remedies," 53 *Columbia Law Review* 1143, 1147–50 (1953) (arguing that although the Supreme Court has jurisdiction to do so, it has not required states to create postconviction procedures). The exhaustion doctrine *does* mandate plenary federal review in the absence of reliable state procedures; given, however, that because sufficient state procedures may generate fact-findings that are generally presumed correct in federal court (see *infra*), states have a strong incentive to create reliable procedures for the vindication of federal rights. See, e.g., Jones v. State, 446 So. 2d 1059, 1062–63 (Fla. 1984) (encouraging state trial courts to hold evidentiary hearings in state postconviction matters because factfindings generated by such proceedings would be entitled to presumption of correctness in subsequent federal habeas corpus litigation).

57. Allen, Schachtman and Wilson, *supra* n. 34 at 690 (1982).

58. See generally Roy v. Wainwright, 151 So. 2d 825, 827–29 (Fla. 1963) (outlining Florida procedures for postconviction relief); Brown, "Collateral Post-Conviction Remedies in Florida," 20 *University of Florida Law Review* 306, 324, 329 (1968) (discussing Florida's postconviction procedures and their complexity); Note, "Trial Court and Prison Perspectives on the Collateral Post-Conviction Relief Process in Florida," 21 *University of Florida Law Review* 503 (1969) (same); Comment, "The Right to Appointed Counsel at Collateral Attack Proceedings," 19 *University of Miami Law Review* 432 (1965) (same).

59. Ineffective assistance of trial counsel and prosecutorial failure to disclose exculpatory information are typical claims cognizable in state postconviction proceedings. See, e.g., Squires v. State, 513 So. 2d 138, 139 (Fla. 1987) (claim that police report was improperly withheld by prosecutor); Smith v. State, 400 So. 2d 956, 962–64 (Fla. 1981) (police report withheld); Washington v. State, 397 So. 2d 285, 286–87 (Fla. 1981) (claim of ineffective assistance). Both types of claims usually involve facts outside the trial record and therefore cannot be litigated on direct appeal.

60. To date, the Court has not extended the principles of *Stone* beyond the Fourth Amendment setting. See, e.g., Withrow v. Williams, 507 U.S. 680 (1992); Rose v. Mitchell, 443 U.S. 545, 559–64 (1979); Jackson v. Virginia, 443 U.S. 307, 321–24 (1979); Brewer v. Williams, 430 U.S. 387, 395–97, 406 (1977). *Stone*, however, "may only be a sleeping giant, and not a dead one." Ira P. Robbins, "Whither (or Wither) Habeas Corpus? Observations on the Supreme Court's 1985 Term," 111 *Federal Rules Digest* 265, 292 (1986). Four Justices would extend *Stone* to certain confession claims and to claims of racial discrimination in grand jury selection. Vasquez v. Hillery, 106 S. Ct. 617, 631–34 (1986) (Burger, C. J., Powell, and Rehnquist, JJ., dissenting); *id.* at 625 (O'Connor, J., concurring); Maine v. Moulton, 106 S. Ct. 477, 495–96 (1985) (Burger, C.J., White, Rehnquist, and O'Connor, JJ., dissenting).

61. The decision in *Stone* does not bar a claim if the petitioner did not have "an opportunity for full and fair litigation of [the] . . . claim" in the state courts. Stone v. Powell, 428 U.S. 465, 494 (1976); see, e.g., Riley v. Gray, 674 F.2d 522, 526–27 (6th Cir. 1982) (finding no full and fair opportunity when state appeals court failed to remand to establish defendants' standing to bring claim), *cert. denied,* Shoemaker v. Riley, 459 U.S. 948 (1982); Doescher v. Estelle, 616 F.2d 205, 207 (5th Cir. 1980) (holding no full and fair opportunity when state procedure subsequently was declared unconstitutional); Gates v. Henderson, 568 F.2d 830, 840 (2d Cir. 1977) (en banc) (noting there is no full and fair opportunity if no state procedures or if state procedures break down), *cert. denied,* 434 U.S. 1038 (1978).

62. 28 U.S.C. § 2254(d) (1982) provides that a state court's findings of historical fact are entitled to a presumption of correctness unless the state fact-finding

procedure was deficient in one of eight specified respects. For examples of the application of 28 U.S.C. § 2255(d), see Ford v. Wainwright, 106 S. Ct. 2595, 2602–3 (1986); Miller v. Fenton, 106 S. Ct. 445, 450–51 (1985); Wainwright v. Witt, 469 U.S. 412, 426–30 (1985); Patton v. Yount, 467 U.S. 1025, 1036–40 (1984); Sumner v. Mata, 449 U.S. 539, 545–47 (1981). Subsection (d) was added to the habeas statute in 1966. See S. Rep. No. 1797, 89th Cong., 2d Sess. (1966), reprinted in 1966 *U.S. Code Cong. & Admin. News* 3663. The amendment is best understood as supplementing the standards enunciated in Townsend v. Sain, 372 U.S. 293 (1963), which govern when a federal evidentiary hearing is mandatory in habeas proceedings. *Townsend* controls when an evidentiary hearing is required, while subsection (d) controls the burden of proof at such a hearing. Thomas v. Zant, 697 F.2d 977, 980, 983–86 (11th Cir. 1983). On federal evidentiary hearings generally, see Wright & Sofaer, "Federal Habeas Corpus and State Prisoners: The Allocation of Fact-finding Responsibility," 75 *Yale Law Journal* 895 (1966).

63. For examples of capital cases in which procedural defaults in the state system barred federal habeas relief, see Straight v. Wainwright, 772 F.2d 674, 678 (11th Cir. 1985) (no cause), *cert. denied*, 475 U.S. 1099 (1986); Francois v. Wainwright, 741 F.2d 1275, 1280–83 (11th Cir. 1984) (no prejudice); Palmes v. Wainwright, 725 F.2d 1511, 1524–26 (11th Cir.) (no cause), *cert. denied*, 469 U.S. 975 (1984); Dobbert v. Strickland, 718 F.2d 1518, 1524–25 (11th Cir. 1983) (no cause), *cert. denied*, 468 U.S. 1220 (1984); Shriner v. Wainwright, 715 F.2d 1452, 1457 (11th Cir. 1983) (no prejudice), *cert. denied*, 465 U.S. 1051 (1984); Antone v. Strickland, 706 F.2d 1534, 1536–38 (11th Cir.) (no cause or prejudice), *cert. denied*, 464 U.S. 1003 (1983); Sullivan v. Wainwright, 695 F.2d 1306, 1311 (11th Cir.) (no cause on one claim, no prejudice on another), *cert. denied*, 464 U.S. 922 (1983).

Bob Sullivan was executed in 1983; Anthony Antone, Ernest Dobbert, Timothy Palmes, and Carl Shriner were executed in 1984; Francois was executed in 1985; and Straight was executed in 1986. The procedural default dimensions of *Antone, Shriner,* and *Sullivan* are discussed in Catz, "Federal Habeas Corpus and the Death Penalty: Need for a Preclusion Doctrine Exception," 18 *University of California at Davis Law Review* 1177, 1198–1205 (1985).

64. 489 U.S. 288 (1989). See generally Arkin, "The Prisoner's Dilemma: Life in the Lower Federal Courts After Teague v. Lane," 69 *North Carolina Law Review* 371 (1991); Bender, The Retroactive Effect of an Overruling Constitutional Decision: Mapp v. Ohio," 110 *University of Pennsylvania Law Review* 650 (1962); Berger, "Supreme Court Review: Little Sympathy for Defendants in Capital Cases," *National Law Journal,* Aug. 13, 1990, at S12; Beytagh, "Ten Years of Non-Retroactivity: A Critique and a Proposal," 61 *Virginia Law Review* 1557, 1558 and n. 3 (1975) (citing authority); Blume and Pratt, "Understanding *Teague v. Lane,*" 18 *New York University Review of Law and Social Change* 325 (1990–91); Corr, "Retroactivity: A Study in Supreme Court Doctrine 'As Applied,' " 61 *North Carolina Law Review* 745 (1983); Dubber, "Prudence and Substance: How the Supreme Court's New Habeas Retroactivity Doctrine Mirrors and Affects Substantive Constitutional Law," 30 *American Criminal Law Review* 1 (1992); Fallon and Meltzer, "New Law, Non-Retroactivity, and Constitutional Remedies," 104 *Har-*

vard Law Review 1731 (1991); Faust, Rubenstein, and Yackle, "The Great Writ in Action: Empirical Light on the Federal Habeas Corpus Debate," 18 *New York University Review of Law and Social Change* 637 (1990–91); Freeman, "The Protection Afforded Against the Retroactive Operation of an Overruling Decision," 18 *Columbia Law Review* 230 (1918); Goldstein, "Chipping Away at the Great Writ: Will Death Sentenced Federal Habeas Corpus Petitioners Be Able to Seek and Utilize Changes in the Law?" 18 *New York University Review of Law and Social Change* 357 (1990–91); Hartman, "To Be Or Not To Be A 'New Rule': The Non-retroactivity of Newly Recognized Constitutional Rights After Conviction," 29 *California Western Law Review* 53 (1992); Hoffman, "Retroactivity and the Great Writ: How Congress Should Respond to Teague v. Lane," 1990 *Brigham Young University Law Review* 183; Hoffman, "The Supreme Court's New Vision of Federal Habeas Corpus for State Prisoners," 1989 *Supreme Court Review* 165; James S. Liebman, "More than 'Slightly Retro': The Rehnquist Court's Rout of Habeas Corpus Jurisdiction in Teague v. Lane," 18 *New York University Review of Law and Social Change* 537 (1990–91) (presenting a version of this chapter); Mishkin, "Foreword: The High Court, the Great Writ, and the Due Process of Time and Law," 79 *Harvard Law Review* 56 (1965); Patchel, "The New Habeas," 42 *Hastings Law Journal* 941 (1991); Powers, "State Prisoners' Access to Federal Habeas Corpus: Restrictions Increase," 25 *Criminal Law Bulletin* 444 (1989); Richardson and Mandell, "Fairness Over Fortuity: Retroactivity Revisited and Revised," 1989 *Utah Law Review* 11; Schwartz, "Retroactivity, Reliability, and Due Process: A Reply to Professor Mishkin," 33 *University of Chicago Law Review* 719 (1966); Ronald J. Tabak and J. Mark Lane, "Judicial Activism and Legislative 'Reform' of Federal Habeas Corpus: A Critical Analysis of Recent Developments and Current Proposals," 55 *Albany Law Review* 1 (1991); Traynor, "Quo Vadis Prospective Overruling: A Question of Judicial Responsibility," 28 *Hastings Law Journal* 533 (1977); Weisberg, "A Great Writ While It Lasted," 81 *Journal of Criminal Law and Criminology* 9 (1990); Note, On With the Apocalypse: The Supreme Court's New Approach to Old Problems of Equity, Novelty and Death," 29 *American Criminal Law Review* 1045 (1992); Note, "*United States v. Johnson:* Reformulating the Retroactivity Doctrine," 69 *Cornell Law Review* 166 (1983); Note, "Retroactivity, Habeas Corpus, and the Death Penalty: An Unholy Alliance," 41 *Duke Law Journal* 160 (1991); Note, "Limitation of Judicial Decisions to Prospective Operation," 46 *Iowa Law Review* 600 (1961); Note, "The Evolution of the Supreme Court's Retroactivity Doctrine: A Futile Search for Theoretical Clarity," 80 *Journal of Criminal Law and Criminology* 1128 (1990); Note, "Retroactive Application of Statutes: Protection of Reliance Interests," 40 *Maine Law Review* 183 (1988); Note, "Prospective Overruling and Retroactive Application in the Federal Courts," 71 *Yale Law Journal* 907 (1962); Recent Developments, "The Court Declines in Fairness—Teague v. Lane," 29 *Harvard Civil Rights–Civil Liberties Law Review* 164 (1990).

65. On one view, the rule of *Teague* and its progeny is not properly understood as merely an innovation in retroactivity doctrine. Rather, the rule may be seen as a full-fledged, if self-imposed, limitation on the federal courts' jurisdiction to grant habeas corpus relief. In recent *Teague* decisions, in fact, the Court hardly mentions

the word "retroactivity," preferring to describe the doctrine in quasi-jurisdictional terms. See, e.g., Gilmore v. Taylor, 113 S. Ct. 2112, 2119 (1993) (eschewing word "retroactivity" in favor of formulation that new rules "cannot provide the basis for federal habeas relief").

66. Gilmore v. Taylor, 113 S. Ct. 2112 (1993); Graham v. Collins, 113 S. Ct. 893 (1993); Stringer v. Black, 112 S. Ct. 1130 (1992); Sawyer v. Smith, 497 U.S. 227 (1990); Saffle v. Parks, 494 U.S. 484 (1990); Butler v. McKellar, 494 U.S. 407 (1990); Penry v. Lynaugh, 492 U.S. 303 (1989).

67. After some equivocation (see *Teague,* 489 U.S. at 314 n. 2), the Court in Penry v. Lynaugh applied the doctrine to capital as well as noncapital prisoners. See Penry v. Lynaugh, 492 U.S. at 313–14. See also Graham v. Collins, 113 S. Ct. at 897.

68. See, e.g., Gilmore v. Taylor, 113 S. Ct. at 2116; Grahma v. Collins, 113 S. Ct. at 897 (" 'Under *Teague,* new rules will not be applied or announced in cases on collateral review unless they fall into one of two exceptions' " (quoting Penry v. Lynaugh, 492 U.S. at 313)); Stringer v. Black, 112 S. Ct. at 1135. The "rules" to which the *Teague* doctrine refers may be rules announced by or sought in either the Supreme Court (see, e.g., Sawyer v. Smith, 497 U.S. 227 [1990] (analyzing retroactivity of Court's prior ruling in Caldwell v. Mississippi, 472 U.S. 320 (1985)), or a lower federal court, see, e.g., Gilmore v. Taylor, 113 S. Ct. at 2116–18 (analyzing retroactivity of 7th Circuit's prior ruling in Falconer v. Lane, 905 F.2d 1129 (9th Cir. 1990)); Parke v. Raley, 113 S. Ct. 517, 521 (1992) (noting, but avoiding as forfeited by state's failure to raise, question of retroactivity of 6th Circuit's prior ruling in Dunn v. Simmons, 877 F.2d 1275 (6th Cir. 1989), *cert. denied,* 494 U.S. 1061 (1990), based on which circuit had granted petitioner relief). By "seek to enforce a 'new rule' " is meant either (1) an attempt in a later case to rely on a principle announced in an earlier case (see, e.g., Sawyer v. Smith, discussed above), or (2) an attempt to secure the announcement of a new rule in the case at hand (see, e.g., Graham v. Collins, 113 S. Ct. at 895, 897). See generally, Lockhart v. Fretwell, 113 S. Ct. 838, 844 (1993) (*Teague* doctrine applies to new rules "announced or applied on collateral review").

69. *Teague,* 489 U.S. at 307 (plurality opinion), quoting Mackey v. United States, 401 U.S. 667, 692 (1971) (Harlan, J., concurring in part and dissenting in part)). *Accord* Penry v. Lynaugh, 492 U.S. at 329.

70. Penry v. Lynaugh, 492 U.S. at 330. *Accord* Sawyer v. Smith, 497 U.S. at 241; Saffle v. Parks, 494 U.S. at 494.

71. *Teague,* 489 U.S. at 307 (plurality opinion) (quoting Mackey v. United States, 401 U.S. at 693) (Harlan, J., concurring in part and dissenting in part).

72. See Note, "Trial Court and Prison Perspectives on the Collateral Post-Conviction Relief Process in Florida," *supra* n. 58 at 507–9 (discussing prisoners' lack of knowledge in preparation of habeas corpus proceedings).

73. Williams v. Leeke, 584 F.2d 1336, 1339 (4th Cir. 1978); see also United States *ex rel.* Wolfish v. Levi, 439 F. Supp. 114, 130 (S.D.N.Y. 1977) (describing inadequacies of prison library facilities), *aff'd,* 573 F.2d 118 (2d Cir. 1978).

74. Falzerano v. Collier, 535 F. Supp. 800, 803 (D.N.J. 1982).

75. See Note, "The Jailed Pro Se Defendant and the Right to Prepare a

Defense," 86 *Yale Law Journal* 292, 295, 306 (1976) (describing inability of jailed defendant to perform pretrial legal and factual research in preparation of defense).

76. Barefoot v. Estelle, 463 U.S. 880 (1983).

77. Amsterdam, *supra* n. 39. The Texas Court of Criminal Appeals first denied a stay in *Barefoot* on December 21, but the court failed to notify Barefoot's counsel of its decision until January 7, 16 days later. On January 10, counsel renewed the stay motion, based in part on the delay in notification. This motion was denied on January 11. Id.

78. Anthony Amsterdam observed that the court's opinion relied in part upon "incorrect statements of what witnesses had testified in the court below." This was no surprise, given that the Fifth Circuit judges took less than a day to study the voluminous record. *Id.*

79. Barefoot v. Estelle, 463 U.S. 880 (1983).

80. *Id.* at 889–90. Amsterdam points out that the irony of the Court's decision in *Barefoot* is that a "death-sentenced appellant who has obtained a certificate of probable cause can have his appeal decided on the merits under guise of denying a stay of execution *without* the full time for briefing, argument and judicial deliberation that would be permitted in a five-dollar tax case or a two-dollar social security case." Amsterdam, *supra* n. 39 at 53–54 (emphasis in original).

81. Taylor v. Maggio, 727 F.2d 341, 344 (5th Cir.), *stay and certif. of prob. cause denied,* 465 U.S. 1075 (1984). At his trial, Taylor's counsel failed to exercise any of his available challenges against the impaneling of an all-white jury for Taylor, who was black. Taylor's counsel also failed to present *any* mitigating evidence, such as the fact that Taylor had never before committed a violent crime. In addition, Taylor's counsel failed to call any character witnesses even though Taylor's family was present at the trial. Counsel failed to argue at any time that Taylor did not deserve the death penalty. *Id.*

Taylor's new volunteer postconviction counsel, who was in his first year of practice, had less than two weeks to review the record and file an ineffective assistance of trial counsel claim in four different courts. Ronald J. Tabak, "The Death of Fairness: The Arbitrary and Capricious Imposition of the Death Penalty in the 1980's," 14 *New York University Review of Law and Social Change* 797, 836–37 (1986). Despite the substance of the claim, the postconviction case was rushed through the courts pursuant to a post-*Barefoot* rule. *Id.* Only two days after his hearing in the federal Court of Appeals and 14 days after securing his new volunteer counsel, Taylor was executed.

In inviting the federal appeals courts to adopt expedited procedures in capital habeas appeals, the Supreme Court in *Barefoot* assumed that a death row inmate's attorney does not need much time to prepare the federal appeals brief because he could basically resubmit the brief used in the direct appeal to the state supreme court—even though such briefs are often of poor quality. *Id.* at 835. Furthermore, the habeas brief must consider any significant decisions rendered since the direct appeals brief was prepared.

82. Bluestone and McGahee, "Reactions to Extreme Stress: Impending Death by Execution," 119 *American Journal of Psychiatry* 393, 393 (1962).

83. Lewis, "Killing the Killers: A Post-*Furman* Profile of Florida's Condemned," 25 *Crime and Delinquency* 200, 211 (1979).

84. Jacob and Sharma, "Justice After Trial," 18 *University of Kansas Law Review* 493, 508–10 (1970). According to statistics compiled in 1974 by the Justice Department, 32 percent of all state prisoners had no more than a high school education and only 26 percent had a high school diploma when they entered prison. About 10 percent earn a high school diploma while in prison. National Criminal Justice Information And Statistics Service, U.S. Department of Justice, "Profile of State Prison Inmates: Sociodemographic Findings from the 1974 Survey of Inmates of State Correctional Facilities" 9–12 (1979).

85. Note, "Prison 'No-Assistance' Regulations and the Jailhouse Lawyer," 1968 *Duke Law Journal* 343, 347–48.

86. Hooks v. Wainwright, 536 F. Supp. 1330, 1336–37 (M.D. Fla.), *rev'd on other grounds,* 775 F.2d 1433 (11th Cir. 1985), *cert. denied,* 107 S. Ct. 313 (1986).

87. Denis Keys, William Edwards, and Robert Perske, "People with Mental Retardation are Dying Legally," *Mental Retardation,* Feb. 1997, at 60–61; Clearinghouse On Georgia Prisons And Jails, "Fact Sheet on Execution of the Mentally Retarded" (Nov. 1986).

88. Denis Keys, et al., *supra* n. 87, at 60–61; Reid, "Unknowing Punishment," 15 *Student Lawyer* 18, 23 (May 1987). Morris Mason, executed in Virginia in 1985, had an IQ of 66 and a mental age of eight. Jerome Bowden, executed in Georgia in 1986, had an IQ between 59 and 65. James Terry Roach, executed in South Carolina in 1986, had an IQ between 69 and the low 70s. James Dupree Henry, executed in Florida in 1984, had an IQ in the low 70s. Ivon Ray Stanley, executed in Georgia in 1984, had an IQ that ranged from 61 when he was younger to 81 at the time of his trial. *Id.*

89. Clearinghouse on Georgia Prisons and Jails, "Preliminary Survey" (1986).

90. Reid, *supra* n. 88 at 18 (quoting Miles Santamour, a Los Angeles-based consultant on corrections and mental retardation).

91. See generally Ellis and Luckasson, "Mentally Retarded Criminal Defendants," 53 *George Washington Law Review* 414, 479–84 (1985) (describing difficulties facing mentally retarded defendants at trial); Mickenberg, "Competency to Stand Trial and the Mentally Retarded Defendant: The Need for a Multi-Disciplinary Solution to a Multi-Disciplinary Problem," 17 *California Western Law Review* 365, 387–401 (1981) (enumerating essential mental abilities for any defendant to stand trial and noting mentally retarded defendant's inability to reach these capacities).

92. Ellis and Rice, "Retarded Inmates Imprisoned in Legal Limbo," *Dallas Times Herald,* March 31, 1985.

93. Ellis and Luckasson, *supra* n. 91 at 430. Mentally retarded inmates sometimes confess to crimes they did not commit in order to gain the approval of police interrogators or other perceived authority figures, or because they do not understand, and may be incapable of understanding, the ramifications of a confession and the right not to confess. *Id.*

94. Mickenberg, *supra* n. 91 at 397 (citing Robert B. Edgerton, *The Cloak of Competence* 2–4, 204 (1967)).

95. Reid, *supra* n. 88 at 23.

96. Marcus, "Retarded Killer's Sentence Fuels Death-Penalty Debate," *Washington Post,* June 22, 1987. For further discussion of Limmie Arther's reaction to his death sentence, see O'Shea, "Mental Age At Issue In Death Row Case," *State* (Columbia, S.C.), June 15, 1987; Lang, "Arther Again Sentenced to Death," *News & Courier* (Charleston, S.C.), May 14, 1987; "Retarded Man Gets Death Penalty Again," *State* (Columbia, S.C.), May 14, 1987.

97. Marcus, *supra* n. 96.

98. Lewis, Pincus, Feldman, Jackson, and Bard, "Psychiatric, Neurological and Psychoeducational Characteristics of 15 Death Row Inmates in the United States," 143 *American Journal of Psychiatry* 838, 840–44 (1986); Lewis, Pincus, Bard, Richardson, Feldman, Prichep, and Yeager, "Neuropsychiatric, Psychoeducational and Family Characteristics of 14 Juveniles Condemned to Death in the United States" (paper presented to American Academy of Child and Adult Psychiatry, Oct. 1987).

99. For a graphic illustration, see the gradual mental deterioration of the condemned inmate in Ford v. Wainwright, 106 S. Ct. 2595, 2598–99 (1986).

100. For discussions of the mental and physical effects of death row confinement, see Furman v. Georgia, 408 U.S. 238, 288 (1972) (Brennan, J., concurring); Solesbee v. Balkcom, 339 U.S. 9, 14 (1950) (Frankfurter, J., dissenting); Groseclose v. Dutton, 594 F. Supp. 949, 961 (M.D. Tenn. 1984); Hussain & Tozman, "Psychiatry on Death Row," 39 *Journal of Clinical Psychiatry* 183 (1979); Johnson, "Under Sentence of Death: The Psychology of Death Row Confinement," 5 *Law and Psychology Review* 141, 157–60 (1979); Michael Radelet, Margaret Vandiver, and Berardo, "Families, Prisons and Men With Death Sentences," 4 *Journal of Family Issues* 593, 595–600 (1983); Richard Strafer, "Volunteering for Execution: Competency, Voluntariness and the Propriety of Third Party Intervention," 74 *Journal of Criminal Law and Criminology* 860, 867–69 (1983); West, "Psychiatric Reflections on the Death Penalty," 45 *American Journal of Orthopsychiatry* 689, 694–95 (1975); Note, "Mental Suffering Under Sentence of Death: A Cruel and Unusual Punishment," 57 *Iowa Law Review* 814, 826–31 (1972).

101. Barbara Ward, "Competency for Execution: Problems in Law and Psychiatry," 14 *Florida State University Law Review* 35, 42 (1986) (quoting Robert Sherrill, "In Florida, Insanity Is No Defense," *The Nation,* 551, 555–56 (Nov. 24, 1987) (quoting Scharlette Holdman, director, Florida Clearinghouse on Criminal Justice) ("[Death row inmates] go in and out. Like most people with mental illnesses, they have crisis periods and other periods when they can function. A lot depends on bad diet, lack of medication, lack of exercise . . . . Unless you can manipulate the environment, they can only deteriorate").

102. Bluestone and McGahee, *supra* n. 82 at 395.

103. Robert Johnson, *Condemned to Die* 94 (1981).

104. 373 U.S. 1 (1963).

105. See Potts v. Zant, 638 F.2d 727, 736–38 (5th Cir. 1981).

106. McCleskey v. Zant, 111 S. Ct. 1454 (1991); Jones v. Estelle, 722 F.2d 159, 167 (5th Cir. 1983).

107. 499 U.S. 467 (1991).

108. Ford v. Wainwright, 477 U.S. 399, 421 (1986) (quoting Lord Coke).

109. See generally Orville G. Brim, et al., *The Dying Patient* (1970); Elisabeth Kübler-Ross, *On Death and Dying* (1969); Robert H. Williams, *To Live and to Die—When, Why And How* (1973).

110. Elisabeth Kübler-Ross, *Questions on Death and Dying* 92 (1974).

111. Testimony of John Charles Boger, Trial Transcript at 33–34, Giarratano v. Murray, 668 F. Supp. 511 (E.D. Va. 1986) (No. 85–0655R), *rev'd by panel,* 836 F.2d 1421 (4th Cir.).

112. Spangenburg Group, "Time and Expense Analysis in Post-Conviction Death Penalty Cases" (1987) [hereinafter "Spangenburg Group Analysis"].

113. *Id.* A typical lawyer in private practice devotes approximately 1,600 hours per year to active law practice. Thus, a median figure of 400 hours spent on one case in state trial court equals roughly one-fourth of a lawyer's time for a year in providing representation of one inmate for this one level of postconviction alone.

114. In 1987 the warrant periods were extended to 60 days or more.

115. "Spangenburg Group Analysis" at 15.

116. Spangenburg Group, "Caseload and Cost Projections for Federal Habeas Corpus Death Penalty Cases in FY 1988 AND FY 1989," at 44 (1987) (citing Spangenburg Group, "A Caseload/Workload Formula for Florida's Office of the Capital Collateral Representative" 53 (1987)) [hereinafter "Caseload/Workload Formula"].

117. "Caseload/Workload Formula," *supra* n. 116 at 51.

118. Until 1986, the Oklahoma appellate defender program could not, by statute, represent postconviction death-sentenced individuals, although the office has had considerable experience in arranging for such representation by the private bar. In some Oklahoma localities, the office was restricted to providing postconviction representation in state court and was not permitted to provide representation in federal court.

119. See "Spangenburg Group Analysis," *supra* n. 112 at 16 (explaining that few respondents to the study provided documented totals of support hours).

120. *Id.* The study reported that given the incomplete status of many of the cases, the Florida figures were "noteworthy," because, in Florida as in many other states, attorneys at the time of the study were not reimbursed for their expenses. *Id.*

121. Federal courts have stressed that without the aid of trained paralegals and law librarians, prison libraries cannot be used adequately. Cruz v. Hauck, 627 F.2d 710, 720–21 (5th Cir. 1980); Battle v. Anderson, 457 F. Supp. 719, 736–37 (E.D. Okla. 1978) (enumerating alternative methods for assuring inmate access to courts, including training inmates as paralegals).

122. Larsen, "A Prisoner Looks at Writ-Writing," 56 *California Law Review* 343, 356 (1968).

123. Johnson v. Avery, 393 U.S. 483, 499 (1969) (White, J., dissenting); G. Alpert, *Legal Rights of Prisoners* 7–8 (1978); Larsen, *supra* n. 122 at 351–56; Spector, "A Prison Librarian Looks at Writ-Writing," 56 *California Law Review* 365, 365–66 (1968); Note, "A Prisoner's Constitutional Right to Attorney Assis-

tance," 83 *Columbia Law Review* 1279, 1282 (1983) [hereinafter "Attorney Assistance"].

124. See Hooks v. Wainwright, 536 F. Supp. 1330, 1348 (M.D. Fla. 1982) (discussing obstacles to inmate law clerks such an inability to prepare logical arguments and draw legal conclusions), *rev'd on other grounds*, 775 F.2d 1433 (11th Cir. 1985), *cert. denied*, 107 S. Ct. 313 (1986); Johnson v. Avery, 393 U.S. 483, 499 (1969) (White, J., dissenting) (stating that inadequate inmate assistance in writ-writing is as useless as receiving no help at all).

125. Zeigler and Hermann, "The Invisible Litigant: An Inside View of Pro Se Actions in the Federal Courts," 47 *New York University Law Review* 157, 174 (1972).

126. Larsen, *supra* n. 122 at 355.

127. Bounds v. Smith, 430 U.S. 817, 836 (1977) (Stewart, J., dissenting).

128. Hooks v. Wainwright, 536 F. Supp. 1330, 1348 (M.D. Fla. 1982), *rev'd on other grounds*, 775 F.2d 1433 (11th Cir. 1985), *cert. denied*, 107 S. Ct. 3133 (1986); Alpert, *supra* n. 123 at 7–8; Jacob and Sharma, *supra* n. 84 at 591; Larsen, *supra* n. 122, at 351–56.

129. Storseth v. Spellman, 654 F.2d 1349 (9th Cir. 1981); *In re* Green, 586 F.2d 1247, 1249–50 (8th Cir. 1978), *cert. denied*, 440 U.S. 922 (1979); "Attorney Assistance," *supra* n. 123 at 1312.

130. *Hooks*, 536 F. Supp. at 1348.

131. Larsen, *supra* n. 122 at 354.

132. Voorhees, "Paralegals: Should the Bar Employ Them?" 24 *Vanderbilt Law Review* 1151, 1158–59 (1971).

133. Bounds v. Smith, 430 U.S. 812, 831 (1979); Jacob and Sharma, *supra* n. 84 at 493; ABA Resource Center on Correctional Law and Legal Services, "Providing Legal Services to Prisoners," 8 *Georgia Law Review* 363, 400–404 (1974); "Attorney Assistance," *supra* n. 123 at 1312.

134. Allen, Schachtman, and Wilson, *supra* n. 34 at 731.

135. Shapiro, "Federal Habeas Corpus: A Study in Massachusetts," 87 *Harvard Law Review* 321, 368 (1973).

136. Allen, Schachtman, and Wilson, *supra* n. 34 at 678–79.

137. *Id.* at 740. The study also indicated that *pro se* petitioners were more likely to exhaust state remedies only after filing successfully in state or federal court. *Id.* at 740–41.

138. Robinson, *supra* n. 34 at 58.

139. 486 U.S. 214 (1988).

140. Amadeo v. State, 384 S.E.2d 181, 181 (Ga. 1989). In this 1989 decision, rendered after the Supreme Court's *Amadeo* decision, the Georgia Supreme Court noted that one of Amadeo's lawyers had represented him for 10 years. *Id.*

141. State law imposed these time limits. Amadeo v. Zant, 486 U.S. at 218 n. 2.

142. Ford v. Wainwright, 477 U.S. 399, 402 (1986).

143. His insanity developed after conviction and imposition of sentence. Ford v. Wainwright, 477 U.S. at 401–2.

144. *Id.* at 409–10. The Supreme Court also found unconstitutional Florida's procedures for determining whether death-sentenced prisoners are competent to be

executed. *Id.* at 410–18. See also *id.* at 424 (Powell, J., concurring); *id.* at 427 (O'Connor, J., concurring).

145. Prior to the Supreme Court's *Ford* decision, Ford's postconviction attorneys obtained orders staying two scheduled executions. See Ford v. Strickland, 676 F.2d 434, 437 (11th Cir. 1982); Ford v. Wainwright, 477 U.S. at 404; Response to Petition for Writ of Habeas Corpus, Ford v. Wainwright, No. 84–6493-Civ.-NCR (S.D. Fla. May 29, 1984), *cited in* Joint Appendix, at 26–27, Ford v. Wainwright, 477 U.S. 309 (1986) (No. 85–5542). When the Supreme Court granted Ford relief, one of his attorneys had been representing him for over five years. See Ford v. State, 407 So. 2d 907, 907 (Fla. 1981); Ford v. Wainwright, 451 So. 2d 471, 473 (Fla. 1984); Ford v. Wainwright, 752 F.2d 526, 526 (11th Cir. 1985); Ford v. Wainwright, 477 U.S. at 401.

146. The lawyer who represented Johnson on the direct appeal of his conviction (see Johnson v. State, 511 So. 2d 1333, 1335–36 n.1 (Miss. 1987)), continued to represent Johnson throughout the next two years, including during the state habeas proceedings (*id.*) and the final successful appeal to the Supreme Court, although he did not argue the case in the Supreme Court. Johnson v. Mississippi, 486 U.S. 578, 580 (1988).

147. Johnson v. Mississippi, 486 U.S. 578 (1988).

148. See People v. Johnson, 506 N.E.2d 1177, 1178 (N.Y. 1987); Johnson v. State, 511 So. 2d 1333, 1337 (Miss. 1987). Postconviction counsel also obtained orders staying two scheduled executions so that they could investigate and present Johnson's ultimately successful federal habeas corpus claims. See Joint Appendix, Chronological List of Relevant Docket Entries at 1–2, Johnson v. Mississippi, 486 U.S. 578 (1988) (No. 87–5468).

149. Penry v. Lynaugh, 492 U.S. 302, 307–9, 319 (1989).

150. See Yates v. Aiken, 474 U.S. 896 (1985); Yates v. Aiken, 484 U.S. 211, 216–18 (1988); Yates v. Evatt, 111 S. Ct. 1884, 1891–97 (1991).

151. Maynard v. Cartwright, 486 U.S. 356, 359–60 (1988).

152. Parker v. Dugger, 498 U.S. 308 (1991). Robert Link was Parker's counsel on direct appeal of his conviction in 1984, and he represented Parker for seven years, throughout the state and federal postconviction process. See Parker v. State, 458 So. 2d 750, 751 (Fla. 1984); Parker v. State, 491 So. 2d 532, 532 (Fla. 1986); Parker v. Dugger, 876 F.2d 1470, 1471 (11th Cir. 1989); Parker v. Dugger, 498 U.S. 308, 309 (1991). Parker's postconviction attorney also obtained orders staying two executions prior to the Court's 1991 decision.

153. Hitchcock v. Dugger, 481 U.S. 393 (1987). Hitchcock's postconviction lawyers obtained an affidavit from his trial attorney that supported their contention that the trial attorney believed he was legally precluded from producing nonstatutory mitigating evidence at Hitchcock's sentencing hearing. Hitchcock's postconviction attorneys also proffered to the District Court "significant evidence of nonstatutory mitigating factors [that] could have been presented at his sentencing hearing." Hitchcock v. Wainwright, 745 F.2d 1332, 1344 (11th Cir. 1984) (Johnson, J., dissenting), *aff'd en banc,* 770 F.2d 1514 (1985) (en banc) *reversed,* 481 U.S. 393 (1987).

154. Marshall, "Remarks on the Death Penalty Made at the Judicial Conference of the Second Circuit," 86 *Columbia Law Review* 1, 1–2 (1986).

155. Other individuals in, for example, the office of the NAACP Legal Defense and Educational Fund, Inc., and the West Palm Beach Public Defender's Office attempted on an ad hoc basis to locate volunteer attorneys for condemned inmates without counsel.

156. For one of the best contemporary descriptions of the Florida Clearinghouse on Criminal Justice, see Robert Sherrill, "Death Row on Trial," *New York Times Magazine,* Nov. 13, 1983, at 80. The Clearinghouse operated "out of a rundown, $100-a-month room in a one-story, cement-block building full of . . . non-profit 'cause' organizations near the state Capitol in Tallahassee. The clearinghouse is, for all practical purposes, one person: Scharlette Holdman, who, behind an affected neo-redneck pose, is a sophisticated genius at marshaling volunteer lawyers." *Id.* at 98.

157. Letter from Scharlette Holdman to Honorable John C. Godbold, Jr. (Dec. 14, 1983) at 1 [hereinafter Holdman Letter]. The letter was written in response to the Eleventh Circuit's invitation to submit comments on its proposed rules to expedite capital habeas cases.

158. Testimony of Scharlette Holdman, Transcript of Evidentiary Hearing, at 56, Hall v. Wainwright, No. 82–195-CIV-OC-14 (M.D. Fla. Sept. 19, 1985). Holdman explained:

> What we do is on Thursday, when the State Supreme Court issues opinions in capital cases, we go over and pick them up, and for cases that are affirmed we try to contact the last known attorney to see if that attorney can assist us in finding replacement counsel or continue in the representation.
>
> And about probably 80 or 90 percent of the cases, the appellate attorney declines further representation because there is no money available from the courts or the state or any state agency, and it's going to become a pro bono case, then we move that case on to a list that we try and maintain of other people on death row whose cases have been affirmed who need counsel in order to initiate state and federal post conviction.

Id.

159. Von Drehele, *supra* n. 1 at 126–27.

160. Spenkelink was executed at Florida State Prison on May 21, 1979.

161. Von Drehle, *supra* n. 1 at 227–29.

162. Hall v. State, 403 So. 2d 1321, 1325 (Fla. 1981); Hall v. State, 403 So. 2d 1319, 1321 (Fla. 1981).

163. Testimony of Scharlette Holdman, *supra* n. 158 at 59.

164. Testimony of Jerry Lockett, Transcript of Evidentiary Hearing, at 87, Hall v. Wainwright, No. 82–195-CIV-OC-14 (M.D. Fla. Sept. 19, 1985).

165. *Id.* at 81, 86.

166. *Id.* at 88.

167. *Id.* at 155–56.

168. *Id.* at 103

169. *Id.* at 98–99.

170. Hall v. Wainwright, 733 F.2d 766, 776 (11th Cir. 1984).

171. Testimony of Jerry Lockett, *supra* n. 164 at 95–121.

172. *Id.* at 107, 164.

173. *Id.* at 114.

174. *Id.*

175. *Id.* at 117.

176. *Id.* at 115, 118.

177. Hall v. State, 420 So. 2d 872 (Fla. 1982).

178. Hall v. Wainwright, 733 F.2d 766, 778 (11th Cir. 1983), *cert. denied,* 471 U.S. 1107 (1984).

179. Hall v. Wainwright, 805 F.2d 945, 948 (11th Cir. 1986).

180. Hall v. State, 541 So. 2d 1125 (Fla. 1989).

181. Brief of Appellant at 34, Adams v. Wainwright, 804 F.2d 1526 (11th Cir. 1986) (No. 86–3207) [hereinafter Adams Brief].

182. *Id.*

183. *Id.*

184. *Id.* at 12.

185. *Id.*

186. *Id.*

187. *Id.*

188. This chronology is drawn from Affidavit of Kenneth Hart, Appendix to Brief of Appellant, Adams v. Wainwright, 804 F.2d 1526 (11th Cir. 1986) (No. 86–3207).

189. Adams v. State, 456 So. 2d 888, 891 (Fla. 1984).

190. *Id.* at 892.

191. Adams v. Wainwright, No. 84–170-CIV-OC-16 (M.D. Fla. Sept. 18, 1984).

192. *Id.* at 13.

193. *Id.*

194. Wainwright v. Adams, 468 U.S. 1261 (1984).

195. Adams Brief, *supra* n. 181 at 38.

196. Adams v. Wainwright, 764 F.2d 1356 (11th Cir.), *cert. denied,* 474 U.S. 1073 (1985).

197. 474 U.S. 1073 (1986).

198. Adams v. State, 484 So. 2d 1216 (1986); Adams v. State, 484 So. 2d 1211 (1986); Adams v. State, 484 So. 2d 580 (1986).

199. Adams v. Wainwright 475 U.S. 1062 (1986).

200. Adams v. Dugger, 804 F.2d 1526 (11th Cir. 1986), *cert. granted,* 56 U.S.L.W. 3601 (U.S. Mar. 8, 1988) (No. 87–121), *reversed,* 490 U.S. 1059 (1989).

201. *Id.*

202. Dugger v. Adams, 490 U.S. 1059 (1989).

203. NAACP Legal Defense and Educational Fund, "Death Row, U.S.A.," (unpublished compilation).

204. A federal district court previously had ordered Raulerson resentenced. Raulerson v. Wainwright, 508 F. Supp. 381 (M.D. Fla. 1981). Raulerson subsequently was resentenced to death. He was executed in 1984.

205. Holdman Letter, *supra* n. 157 at 43–45.

206. *Id.* at 150.

207. Raulerson v. State, 437 So, 2d 1105 (Fla. 1983).

208. Testimony of Scharlette Holdman, *supra* n. 158 at 154.

209. Raulerson v. Wainwright, 732 F.2d 803 (11th Cir.), *cert. denied,* 469 U.S. 966 (1984).

210. Testimony of Scharlette Holdman, *supra* n. 158 at 168, 169.

211. *Id.* at 19, 22.

212. Quoted in James Ridgeway, *Village Voice,* April 6, 1985, at 20.

213. *Id.* This argument seems to violate the constitutional prohibition against diminishing the capital sentencer's sense of responsibility for sentencing. See Caldwell v. Mississippi, 472 U.S. 320, 329 (1985); Adams v. Wainwright, 804 F.2d 1526, 1529 (11th Cir. 1986), *modified,* Adams v. Dugger, 816 F.2d 1493 (11th Cir. 1987), *cert. granted,* 56 U.S.L.W. 3601 (U.S. March 8, 1988) (No. 87–121), *reversed on other grounds,* 490 U.S. 1059 (1989).

214. Raulerson v. State, 462 So. 2d 1085, 1087 (Fla. 1985); Raulerson v. Wainwright, 753 F.2d 869, 871 (11th Cir. 1985).

215. "A Day's Work on Death Row," *Manchester Guardian Weekly* (N.H.), Feb. 10, 1985, at 9; "Florida Executes Killer of Officer," *New York Times,* Jan. 31, 1985; Mary Anne Rhyne, "Cop Killer Dies in Florida Electric Chair," Associated Press, Domestic News, Jan. 30, 1985 (LEXIS: NEXIS).

216. Ford v. State, 374 So. 2d 496, 503 (Fla. 1979), *cert. denied,* 445 U.S. 972 (1980).

217. Ford v. Florida, 445 U.S. 972 (1980).

218. Ford v. State, 407 So. 2d 907, 909 (Fla. 1981).

219. Ford v. Strickland, 696 F.2d 804 (11th Cir.) (en banc), *cert. denied,* 464 U.S. 865 (1983).

220. Ford v. Wainwright, 451 So. 2d 471 (Fla. 1984).

221. Ford v. Strickland, 734 F.2d 538 (11th Cir. 1984).

222. Ford v. Wainwright, 752 F.2d 526 (11th Cir. 1985), *rev'd,* 477 U.S. 399 (1986).

223. Ford v. Wainwright, 477 U.S. 399 (1986).

224. AP, "Killer Dies During Death-Row Wait," *St. Petersburg Times,* March 9, 1991.

225. Kent Miller and Michael Radelet, *Executing the Mentally Ill* (1993).

226. These facts come from Affidavit of Thomas McCoun, Appended to Petition for Writ of Habeas Corpus, Antone v. Dugger, No. 82–61-CIV-T-CC (M.D. Fla. filed Jan. 22, 1984) [hereinafter McCoun Affidavit].

227. Antone v. State, 355 So. 2d 777 (Fla. 1978).

228. Antone v. State, 382 So. 2d 1205 (Fla.), *cert. denied,* 449 U.S. 913 (1980).

229. Memorandum at 4, Antone v. Dugger, No. 84–3058 (M.D. Fla. 1984).

230. McCoun Affidavit, *supra* n. 226 at 1.

231. *Id.* at 5.

232. Memorandum, *supra* n. 229 at 4.

233. *Id.*

234. Antone v. State, 410 So. 2d 157 (Fla. 1982), *cert. denied,* 464 U.S. 1003 (1983).

235. Memorandum, *supra* n. 229 at 5.

236. Antone v. Strickland, 706 F.2d 1534 (11th Cir. 1983), *cert. denied,* 464 U.S. 1003 (1983).

237. Memorandum, *supra* n. at 5.

238. *Id.* at 6.

239. Antone v. Wainwright, 444 So. 2d 959 (Fla. 1984).

240. Antone v. Dugger, 465 U.S. 200, 206 n. 21 (1983).

241. Brief of Appellant at 2, Booker v. Wainwright, 764 F.2d 1371 (11th Cir. 1985) (No. 84–3306).

242. *Id.* at 3.

243. *Id.*

244. *Id.*

245. *Id.*

246. *Id.* By rule, appellants in Florida state postconviction cases normally are allowed 30 days after the filing of the record in which to file a supporting brief. *Fla. R. App. P.* 9.700. The record is not required to be filed until 50 days after the trial court's decision. *Id.*

247. Booker v. State, 413 So. 2d 756 (Fla. 1982).

248. Brief of Appellant, *supra* n. 241 at 3.

249. Booker v. Wainwright, 675 F.2d 1150 (11th Cir. 1982), *cert. denied,* 464 U.S. 922 (1983).

250. Booker v. Wainwright 703 F.2d 1251 (11th Cir. 1982), *cert. denied,* 464 U.S. 922 (1983).

251. Brief of Appellant, *supra* n. 241 at 3.

252. *Id.* at 4.

253. *Id.*

254. *Id.*

255. Adams v. State, 380 So. 2d 421 (Fla. 1980).

256. Brief of Appellant, *supra* n. 241 at 5.

257. *Id.*

258. *Id.*

259. *Id.*

260. Booker v. State, 441 So. 2d 148 (Fla. 1983).

261. Audio Tape of Oral Argument, Booker v. State, 441 So. 2d 148 (Fla. 1983).

262. *Booker,* 441 So. 2d at 151.

263. Brief of Appellant, *supra* n. 241 at 5.

264. Booker v. Wainwright, 764 F.2d 1371 (11th Cir.), *cert. denied,* 474 U.S. 975 (1985).

265. Booker v. Wainwright, 770 F.2d 1084 (11th Cir.), *cert. denied,* 474 U.S. 975 (1985).

266. Wainwright v. Booker, 474 U.S. 975 (1985).

267. State v. Crews, 477 So. 2d 984 (Fla. 1985).

268. Booker v. State, 503 So. 2d 888 (Fla. 1987).

269. Booker v. Dugger, 825 F.2d 281 (11th Cir. 1987), *cert. denied,* 108 S. Ct. 2834 (1988).

270. Booker v. State, 503 So. 2d 888 (1987).

271. *Id.*

272. Booker v. Dugger, 922 F.2d 633 (11th Cir. 1991).

273. Singletary v. Booker, 112 S. Ct. 277 (1991).

274. Booker v. Singletary, No. TCA 88–40228-MP (N.D. Fla. March 18, 1994).

275. 372 So. 2d 1363 (Fla. 1979).

276. Petition for Writ of Habeas Corpus at 1 n.*, Graham v. State, 372 So. 2d 1363 (Fla. 1979).

277. *Id.* at 2–3.

278. *Id.* at 3.

279. *Id.*

280. *Id.* at 5–6.

281. *Id.* at 4.

282. *Id.* at 4–5. This question was resolved in favor of representation in Brummer v. State, 467 So. 2d 1091 (Fla. 1985).

283. *Id.* at 5.

284. Memorandum of Law in Support of the Petition, at 1–2, Graham v. State, 372 So. 2d 1363 (Fla. 1979) (No. 56,947).

285. Graham v. State, 372 So. 2d 1363, 1364 (Fla. 1979).

286. "Each of these named death row defendants has been through the entire trial and appellate process in the state court system, and each has had his application for review denied at least once by the United States Supreme Court." *Id.*

287. *Id.* at 1366.

288. *Id.* at 1365.

289. 372 U.S. 335 (1963).

290. Graham v. State, 372 So. 2d 1363, 1365 (Fla. 1979).

291. *Id.* at 1366.

292. 536 F. Supp. 1330 (M.D. Fla. 1982), *rev'd,* 775 F.2d 1433 (11th Cir. 1985), *cert. denied,* 107 S. Ct. 313 (1986).

293. *Hooks* was based on the right of access to courts articulated in Bounds v. Smith, 430 U.S. 817 (1977). See generally Note, "A Prisoner's Constitutional Right to Attorney Assistance," 83 *Columbia Law Review* 1279 (1983).

294. This discussion of the genesis of Palmes' counsel motion comes from Affidavit of Scharlette Holdman, Attached to Motion for Emergency Relief, Palmes v. Wainwright, Nos. 71–144-CIV-J-S and 71–1011-CIV-J-S (M.D. Fla. filed June 2, 1982) [hereinafter Affidavit of Holdman].

295. *Id.*

296. Palmes v. Wainwright, 540 F. Supp. 652, 654 (M.D. Fla. 1982). Two attorneys, Steven Goldstein and Bruce Rogow, signed Palmes' motion.

297. *Id.* at 1.

298. *Id.* at 654.

299. *Id.* The federal courts were split on this jurisdictional issue. *Compare* McFarland v. Collins, 7 F.3d 47 (5th Cir. 1993) with Brown v. Vasquez, 952 F.2d 1164 (9th Cir. 1992). The Supreme Court resolved the matter in McFarland v. Scott (1994).

300. *Id.* at 655.

301. *Id.*

302. *Id.* at 656.

303. *Id.*
304. *Id.*
305. *Id.*
306. *Id.*
307. "Death Row, U.S.A.," *supra* n. 203; see also Palmes v. Wainwright, 747 F.2d 599 (11th Cir. 1984). For additional background on the *Palmes* habeas litigation, see Palmes v. Wainwright, 725 F.2d 1511 (11th Cir. 1984); Palmes v. Wainwright, 460 So. 2d 362 (Fla.), *cert. denied,* 469 U.S. 873 (1984); Palmes v. State, 425 So. 2d 4 (1983).
308. "Death Row, U.S.A.," *supra* n. 203; see also Straight v. Wainwright, 791 F.2d 830 (11th Cir. 1986).
309. The ABA first recognized the impending crisis in 1979. At its 1979 midyear meeting, the ABA House of Delegates adopted the following resolution:

> Be It Resolved, That the American Bar Association recommends that the United States Supreme Court adopt a rule providing for appointment of counsel to prepare petitions for discretionary review of state court convictions, including appropriate postconviction or clemency petitions if necessary, in death penalty cases where the defendant cannot afford to hire counsel; and
>
> Be It Resolved, That the American Bar Association offer to assist the United States Supreme Court in identifying qualified attorneys who are willing to accept appointment to prepare and file a petition for discretionary review in state death penalty cases, and to urge the Court to begin making appointments in state death penalty cases immediately; and
>
> Be It Further Resolved, That the American Bar Association recommend to Congress that the Criminal Justice Act (18 U.S.C. Section 3600A) be amended to provide for the payment of adequate compensation to counsel appointed by the United States Supreme Court to prepare and file petitions for discretionary review in state death penalty cases.

In 1982 the ABA approved a second resolution which reads as follows:

> Be It Further Resolved, That the American Bar Association should support the prompt availability of competent counsel for both state and federal court proceedings, essential in many instances to enable the federal courts fairly and expeditiously to evaluate the merits of a claim presented in a habeas corpus petition.
>
> (a) There should be prompt appointment of competent counsel to pursue state appellate process, state postconviction remedies, or unified review process;
>
> (b) There should be appointment of counsel other than trial counsel should any question of trial counsel's competence be an issue;
>
> (c) Counsel in the state appellate process, postconviction review process, or unified review procedure should be trained to present in the state courts the facts and legal precedents which form the basic federal constitutional issues raised by the case;
>
> (d) Counsel should be made available at prisons to permit conference with potential petitioners to determine whether federal constitutional issues are presented by their cases and, where such issues exist, to prepare habeas corpus petitions;
>
> (e) Absent earlier availability of counsel, the federal district judge should appoint counsel under the Criminal Justice Act to prepare complete, factually and legally documented habeas corpus petitions, or to amend petitions filed *pro se*. Counsel should be assigned if any non-frivolous constitutional issue is presented and unless it is established beyond doubt that there has been no exhaustion;

(f) Compensation of counsel for the representation of habeas corpus petitioners should be made at a fair rate of payment;

(g) A system of monitoring both assigned and retained counsel to assure competency of performance should be instituted.

More recently, the ABA has recognized the problem relating to the availability of defense counsel in postconviction death penalty cases. In an effort to address the problem in a comprehensive manner, the ABA sponsored the American Bar Association Postconviction Death Penalty Representation Project. The Project now has a staff and a group of consultants prepared to assist in addressing the crisis regarding access to counsel in postconviction death penalty cases around the country.

310. Corcoran, "ABA Establishes Death Row Representation Project," 10 *Litigation News* 1, 8 (Spring 1985).

311. James Rinaman, "Special Committee on Representation of Death Sentenced Inmates in Collateral Proceedings," 60 *Florida Bar Journal* 36, 36–37 (June 1986).

312. Minutes, Florida State-Federal Judicial Council Meeting, Florida Bar Convention, Innisbrook, Florida (June 23, 1984).

313. William Henry, "Representation of Death Sentenced Inmates," 59 *Florida Bar Journal* 53, 53–56 (Dec. 1985); Elvin, "Florida Death Penalty Appeals Office Opens," 7 *National Prison Project Journal* 1, 5 (Spring 1986).

314. Letter from James C. Rinaman, Jr., to Members of Special Committee on Representation of Death Sentenced Inmates in Collateral Proceedings (June 8, 1984) [hereinafter Rinaman Letter].

315. Henry, *supra* n. 313.

316. *Id.* at 53.

317. Letter from Dean Talbot D'Alemberte, Florida State University College of Law, to James C. Rinaman, Jr. (July 6, 1984).

318. Letter from Dean Talbot D'Alemberte, Florida State University College of Law, to James C. Rinaman, Jr. (October 4, 1984).

319. Henry, *supra* n. 313 at 55.

320. Brian Dickerson, "Legal Aid for Death Row," *Miami Herald,* June 3, 1984.

321. Memorandum from William O. Henry, President, Florida Bar, to Special Committee on Representation of Death Sentenced Inmates in Collateral Proceedings, June 1, 1984.

322. Interim Report from James C. Rinaman, Jr., to Gerald F. Richman, Florida Bar President (Sept. 19, 1984).

323. *Id.*

324. *Id.*

325. Letter from C. W. Abbott to James C. Rinaman, Jr. (Aug. 16, 1984). Letter from Michael P. McMahon to James C. Rinaman, Jr. (Aug. 15, 1984) [hereinafter McMahon Letter].

326. These facts are taken from the McMahon Letter, *supra* n. 325.

327. *Id.*

328. *Id.*

329. *Id.*

330. Letters from James C. Rinaman, Jr., to 30 Potential Criminal Defense Attorney Recruits (Feb. 14, 1985).

331. These facts are taken from the series of response letters to the Rinaman recruitment letter, *supra* n. 330.

332. Letter from James C. Rinaman, Jr., to the Special Committee on Representation of Death Sentenced Inmates in Collateral Proceedings (March 8, 1985).

333. *Id.*

334. Interim Report from James C. Rinaman, Jr., to Officers and Board of Governors of the Florida Bar (May 23, 1985).

335. *Id.*

336. *Id.*

337. Volunteer Lawyer's Resource Center Progress Report from Mark Olive, Director, to Special Committee Members (June 11, 1985).

338. CCR commenced operations on October 1, 1985.

339. Henry, *supra* n. 313 at 56; see also Elvin, *supra* n. 313 at 6 (noting that bill to establish CCR had support of Florida attorney general).

340. Florida Senate, "SB 616 Staff Analysis and Economic Impact Statement" 3 (July 15, 1985) [hereinafter "Staff Analysis"].

341. *Id.* The limitations period subsequently was extended to two years and did not become effective until January 1, 1987.

342. Cotterell, "Groups Unable to Find Lawyers for State's Death Row Inmates," *Tampa Tribune,* March 12, 1985.

343. State v. Green, No. 66,724 (Fla. March 18, 1985); State v. Beach, No. 66,725 (Fla. March 18, 1985).

344. Elvin, *supra* n. 313 at 6.

345. "Staff Analysis," *supra* n. 340.

346. Unofficial Transcript of Proceedings Before Florida Senate Judiciary Committee (Criminal Commission) on SB 616 (April 24, 1985) [hereinafter Unofficial Transcript]. See also Transcripts of Proceedings Before the Florida Senate Committee on the Judiciary and Criminal Justice during the 1985 Legislative Session and the Senate Staff Analysis and Economic Impact Statement on CS/SB 616; Laurie Hollman, *St. Petersburg Times,* Aug. 18, 1985; Mary Anne Rhyne, *Gainesville Sun,* Dec. 4, 1985; Daniel Berger, *Tampa Tribune,* March 2, 1986; Jan Elvin *ACLU Journal,* Spring 1986, Jon Nordheimer, *New York Times,* March 31, 1986; Larry King, *St. Petersburg Times,* Nov. 15, 1987; Amy Singer, *American Lawyer,* Jan.–Feb. 1988; Barbara Stewart, *Florida Magazine,* April 23, 1989; Mike Williams, *Atlanta Journal & Constitution,* Aug. 13, 1989; Dudley Clendinin, *New York Times,* Aug. 23, 1982; David Finkel, *St. Petersburg Times/Floridian Magazine,* Nov. 7, 1982; Brian Dickerson, *Miami Herald,* June 3, 1984; *St. Petersburg Times,* June 4, 1984; Judson H. Orrick, *Florida Bar News,* Aug. 15, 1984; Paul Anderson, *Miami Herald,* Dec. 13, 1984; *The Economist,* May 4, 1985; Michael A. Millemann, *Maryland Bar Journal,* Sept. 1985.

347. This was an apparent reference to the *Agan* and *Waterhouse* cases. State v. Green, No. 66,724 (Fla. March 18, 1985); State v. Beach, No. 66,725 (Fla. March 18, 1985).

348. Unofficial Transcript, *supra* n. 346.

349. *Id.*

350. *Id.*

351. See Elvin, *supra* n. 313 at 6. Although Smith hoped that CCR's creation would help speed up executions, he also believed that death row inmates had a right to counsel during the collateral review process. *Id.*

352. *Id.* The legislation creating CCR provided that the Office

> shall represent . . . any person convicted and sentenced to death in . . . [Florida] who is without counsel and who is unable to secure counsel due to his indigency . . . for the purpose of instituting and prosecuting collateral actions challenging the legality of the judgment and sentence . . . in the state courts, federal courts in this state, the United States Court of Appeals for the Eleventh Circuit, and the United States Supreme Court. . . . Representation by . . . [CCR] shall commence upon termination of direct appellate proceedings in state or federal courts.

Fla. Stat. § 27.702 (1985).

353. Memorandum from Larry Helm Spalding to Florida State–Federal Judicial Council (June 17, 1986).

354. Elvin, *supra* n. 313 at 8.

355. CCR Presentation to Senate Appropriations Subcommittee, Florida Senate (Jan. 8, 1987) [hereinafter CCR Presentation].

356. Letter from James C. Rinaman, Jr., to Florida State-Federal Judicial Council (Sept. 5, 1985).

357. Goldner, "Death Row Appeals: Hard Cases To Sell," 61 *Miami Review,* Oct. 15, 1986.

358. Judson H. Orrick, "ABA Studies Cost of Death Sentence Appeals," *Florida Bar News,* March 15, 1987, at 8 ("Florida lawyers who accepted pro bono death penalty cases are withdrawing from those cases, turning them over to CCR, at a rate of one per month").

359. CCR Presentation, *supra* n. 355.

360. That is, CCR represented all unrepresented Florida inmates who had been condemned by a Florida trial court, whose cases had been affirmed by the Florida Supreme Court, denied certiorari review by the U.S. Supreme Court, and (explicitly or implicitly) denied executive clemency by the governor and executive cabinet. The statute creating CCR is codified at Fla. Stat. Ann. § 27.702 (Harrison Supp. 1993).

361. *Id.* at 4. Table 3 represents the cases in which CCR participated during its first eight months of existence, either as sole counsel or as co-counsel with volunteer lawyers, between October 1, 1985, and June 30, 1986.

Table 3   CCR caseload, October 1, 1985–June 30, 1986

A. Executions		3
B. Active Death Warrants		25
C. Prisoners under Sentence of Death		246
D. CCR Caseload		
1. Circuit Trial Court of Florida: State Postconviction Motions		32
Pending	15	
Closed	17	

2. Supreme Court of Florida: State Postconviction Appeals	27
Pending	11
Closed	16
3. Supreme Court of Florida: State Habeas (Original Proceedings)	14
Pending	6
Closed	8
4. Supreme Court of the United States: Petitions for Writ of Certiorari to Supreme Court of Florida	5
Pending	2
Closed	3
5. U.S. District Courts: Habeas Corpus Petitions	16
Pending	4
Closed	12
6. U.S. Court of Appeals Habeas Corpus Appeals	22
Pending	14
Closed	8
7. Supreme Court of the United States: Petitions for Writ of Certiorari to the U.S. Court of Appeals	9
Pending	4
Closed	5
Total Cases	125
E. Clients Currently Represented by CCR	
1. CCR as sole counsel	21
2. CCR as co-counsel with *pro bono* counsel or providing substantial assistance	48
F. New Cases That Must Have State Postconviction Motions Filed by December 31, 1986, Because of Time-Limitation Provision	13
G. New Cases That Must Have State Postconviction Motions filed Between January 1, 1987, and June 30, 1987, Because of Time-Limitation Provision	13

Source: Memorandum from Larry Helm Spalding to Florida State-Federal Judicial Council, at 3–5 (June 17, 1986).

362. "Increase in Death Row Strains Indigent Defense in Florida," 18 *Criminal Justice Newsletter* 3, 4 (May 15, 1987).

363. See Cooper v. Fitzharris, 551 F.2d 1162 (9th Cir. 1977), *modified,* 586 F.2d 1325 (9th Cir. 1978), *cert. denied,* 440 U.S. 974 (1979); State v. Smith, 140 Ariz. 355, 681 P.2d 1374, 1381 (1984); Babb v. Edwards, 412 So. 2d 859, 862 (Fla. 1982); Haggens v. State, 498 So. 2d 953 (Fla. Dist. Ct. App. 1986); Schwartz v. Cianca, 495 So. 2d 1208, 1209 (Fla. Dist. Ct. App. 1986); State v. Behr, 354 So. 2d 974, 975 (Fla. Dist. Ct. App. 1978), *aff'd,* 384 So. 2d 147 (Fla. 1980).

364. Note, "The Right to Counsel and the Indigent Defense System," 14 *New York University Review of Law and Social Change* 221, 222 (1986).

365. In 1984, the year preceding the creation of CCR, eight inmates had been executed in Florida.

366. See Riley v. Wainwright, 517 So. 2d 656 (Fla. 1987); Morgan v. State, 515 So. 2d 975 (Fla. 1987); Margill v. Dugger, 824 F.2d 879 (11th Cir. 1987); Christopher v. Florida, 824 F.2d 836 (11th Cir. 1987); Mann v. Dugger, 817 F.2d

1471 (11th Cir.), *vacated pending rehearing en banc,* 828 F.2d 1498 (11th Cir. 1987); Johnson v. Wainwright, 498 So. 2d 938 (Fla.), *cert. denied,* 107 S. Ct. 1894 (1987).

367. Lee, "Group's Death Row Delay Tactics Lead to Call for Review," *Ocala Star-Banner,* March 11, 1986; "Agency Fights Death Penalty," *Ocala Star-Banner,* March 11, 1986.

368. David Mason, "Cobb's Orchard," *Hudson Review* (Summer 1995), at 191.

369. Judson H. Orrick, "Martinez Speeds Up Death Warrant Signing," *Florida Bar News,* Sept. 1, 1987, at 18.

370. *Id.* Amy Singer, "Enemies Under the Same Roof," *American Lawyer,* Jan.–Feb. 1988.

371. Letter from Commission for the review of Postconviction Representation ("McDonald Commission") to Lawton Chiles, Toni Jennings, and Daniel Webster, Feb. 13, 1997, at 2.

Chapter 6. "On Strike, Shut It Down": An *Apologia* for Conscientious Abstention from the Machinery of Death

1. Michael Mello, "Facing Death Alone," 37 *American University Law Review* 513 (1988).

2. Principally for reasons of squeamishness, I declined the *Albany Law Review*'s invitation to publish my paper along with others presented at the symposium.

3. New York's capital punishment legislation was enacted on March 7, 1995. New York Death Penalty Statute (amending Crim. Pro. Law [1995]); James Dao, *New York Times,* March 8, 1995; "Around the Nation," *Washington Post,* Feb. 17, 1995. For an insightful analysis of New York's new statute, see David Von Drehle, "Cranking Up the Killing Machine," *Washington Post,* Feb. 26, 1995.

4. New York State Defenders Association, *Capital Losses: The Price of the Death Penalty for New York State* 5 (1982).

5. Brief of the New York State Defenders Association, Amicus Curiae, People v. Smith (filed N.Y. Ct. App. Feb. 1, 1994), at 16–68; see also McConeville and Mirsky, "Criminal Defense of the Poor in New York City," 15 *New York University Review of Law and Social Change* 581–964 (1986–87).

6. William Bowers and Margaret Vandiver's Capital Jury Project is a superb example of the sort of social science research I had in mind. See generally "Symposium," 70 *Indiana Law Journal* 1033 (1995).

7. Michael Radelet and George Barnard, "Treating Those Found Incompetent for Execution: Ethical Chaos with Only One Solution," 16 *Bulletin of the American Academy of Psychiatry and Law* 197 (1988); see also Barbara Ward, "Competency for Execution," 14 *Florida State University Law Review* 35 (1986); Note, "Medical Ethics and Competency to Be Executed," 96 *Yale Law Journal* 167 (1986); Richard Bonnie, "Conscientious Abstention, Professional Ethics, and the Needs of the Legal System," 14 *Law and Human Behavior* 67 (1990).

8. Louisiana v. Perry, 610 So. 2d 746 (La. 1992).

9. See William Geimer, "A Decade of Strickland's Tin Horn: Doctrinal and Practical Undermining of the Right to Counsel," 4 *William and Mary Bill of Rights Journal* 1 (1995).

10. Bright and Keenan, "Judges and the Politics of Death," 75 *Boston University Law Review* 759, 762 (1995).

11. 860 F.2d 165, 166 (5th Cir.) (per curiam), *cert. denied,* 109 S. Ct. 332 (1988). Donald Gene Franklin was executed on November 3, 1988.

12. 860 F.2d at 166.

13. 858 F.2d 978, 985–86 (5th Cir.) (Jones, J., concurring), *stay granted,* 109 S. Ct. 254 (1988), *cert. denied,* 109 S. Ct. 3262 (1989), *later proceeding,* 1989 U.S. LEXIS 3489 (Aug. 2, 1989) (suspending denial of certiorari pending disposition for rehearing).

14. David Garrow, "Justice Souter Emerges," *New York Times,* Sept. 25, 1994.

15. 858 F.2d at 985–86 (Jones, J., concurring). See also McFarland v. Collins, 8 F.3d 258, 258–59 (5th Cir. 1993) (Jones, J., dissenting from order granting stay of execution).

16. David Margolick, "Death Row Appeals Are Drawing Sharp Rebukes from Frustrated Federal Judges in the South," *New York Times,* Dec. 2, 1988.

17. See Thomas v. Capital Security Services ("The basic principle governing the choice of sanctions is that the least severe sanction adequate to serve the purpose should be imposed"); Barnard v. Collins, 13 F.3d 870, 879 (5th Cir. 1994) (citation omitted).

Contrast the rantings of the Fifth Circuit's Judge Jones with the 1994 dissenting opinion of the Ninth Circuit's Judge Noonan in Lewis v. Jeffers, 38 F.3d 411 (9th Cir. 1994 (en banc)). Judge John Noonan noted that although 103 persons were sentenced to death in Arizona between 1977 and 1992, only one person was actually executed. Noonan concluded that these facts create an appearance "that the administration of the death penalty in Arizona is so arbitrary as to constitute cruel and unusual punishment in violation of the Eighth Amendment." Although this contention was not advanced by Jeffers, Noonan noted that the Ninth Circuit has the power to address questions of law *sua sponte* when justice so requires and concluded that this is such an instance. Noonan discussed the lengthy delay resulting from the Arizona Supreme Court's close scrutiny of death penalty cases and the high number of reversals in Arizona capital cases. Conceding that the process is extended by the actions of defense lawyers, Noonan argued that

> These lawyers are not to be faulted for their zeal. They are neither pettifoggers nor fanatics. They are either seeking the application of established constitutional principles or presenting fair and reasoned argument for the extension of established principles. They are doing what any good lawyer does for his or her client. They are not obstructing the judicial process but serving it.

Because speed in executing justice has properly been subordinated to assuring accuracy in the judgment and fairness in the procedure, the result has been death sentences carried out at the rate of one in 15 years. "To sentence many and execute almost none is to engage 'in a gruesome charade,' " Noonan argued. "Jeffers is scheduled for execution only because his case was advanced in the process by decisions that bear no rational connection to his special worthiness as a sacrifice; his selection from the pool was arbitrary." Because of the arbitrariness in the administration of Arizona's death penalty law, Noonan would grant Jeffers relief.

More often the judge's contempt for habeas lawyers is framed as hostility toward the habeas writ itself or toward the death row prisoners whom we are trying to represent. Events confirm Bruce Shapiro's view that the habeas corpus debate "goes on, and is likely to continue, no matter what course legislation may take, so long as there are state prisoners and federal courts." The hostility toward allowing a state prisoner broad access to federal habeas corpus remains undiminished. The reasons for this hostility include the perceived waste of judicial resources on stale or frivolous claims; federal review of state court rulings as an affront to the state court system; and the lack of finality. Starting in 1976, the Burger Court began radically to restrict state prisoner access to federal habeas corpus. Proponents of restrictions on access to federal habeas corpus have pressed their cause in Congress for the last 35 years, with little success until 1996.

18. I discuss the conflict between faith in survival and acceptance of death in Chapter 5.

19. William Kloefkorn, "Stealing Melons," 69 *Prairie Schooner* 84, 85 (Fall 1995).

20. 106 S. Ct. 2464 (1986).

21. Straight v. Wainwright, 106 S. Ct. 2004 (1986).

22. *Id.* at 2004 (Powell, J., concurring). Justice White voted to deny the stay but did not join Justice Powell's opinion.

23. *Id.* at 2006 (Brennan, J., dissenting). Justice Stevens voted to grant the stay but did not join Justice Brennan's dissent. See *id.* at 2007 (Stevens, J.).

24. Anthony Amsterdam, "In Favorem Mortis: The Supreme Court and Capital Punishment," 14 *Human Rights,* at 14, 56 (Winter 1987).

25. *Straight,* 106 S. Ct. at 2006 (Brennan, J., dissenting).

26. *Id.* at 2006–7 (Brennan, J., dissenting).

27. *Id.* at 2007 (Brennan, J., dissenting).

28. One commentator stated that the principle rests on the teachings of Aristotle, who "repeatedly defined justice in terms of equality" and stated in *Magna Moralia I:* "The just, then, in relation to one's neighbor is, speaking generally, the equal; . . . since, then, the just is equal, the proportionally equal will be just." Coons, "Consistency," 75 *California Law Review* 59, 59 n. 1 (1987).

29. See United States v. Johnson, 457 U.S. 537, 556 n. 16 (1982) (noting the "potential for unequal treatment" in granting plenary consideration only to one of numerous cases presenting the same question).

Most discussions of this issue concern whether all similarly situated petitioners will "benefit" from the Court's grant. Of course, if the result in the first case is unfavorable to the first petitioner, then no "benefit" will be created. In such a case, clearly the second petitioner will be no worse off than if his case had simply been denied. But, in some circumstances, he will be better off: if the reason the first petitioner loses is unrelated to the merit of the common claims in the two petitions, holding may make it possible for the second petition ultimately to be granted.

30. Straight v. Wainwright, 106 S. Ct. at 2005 n.2 (Powell, J., concurring).
31. *Id.* (citation omitted).
32.   Supreme Court of the United States
Washington, D.C. 20543

Chambers of
Justice Lewis F. Powell, Jr.

May 16, 1986
Straight v. Wainwright, No. 85–6930 (A-889)

MEMORANDUM TO THE CONFERENCE

The history of this case is summarized in my memorandum of May 16, 1986. The Florida Supreme Court has now denied Ronald Straight's petition for postconviction relief, and Straight has filed his cert petition and stay application in this Court. The Florida Court found that Straight is procedurally barred from raising his *Lockett* claim again in state court. That holding is an adequate and independent state ground of decision, and Straight's arguments attacking it have no merit. I accordingly vote to deny both the stay application and cert petition.

Straight has filed a second federal habeas petition, also re-raising his *Lockett* claim. A variant of the same claim was rejected by CAll, 772 F.2d 674 (1985), and we denied cert on March 31, 1986. To the extent that Straight has modified his *Lockett* argument, his petition constitutes an abuse of the writ. Accordingly, as presently advised, I will vote to deny Straight's other cert petition and stay application should the need arise.

/s/

L.F.P., Jr.

Supreme Court of the United States
Washington, D.C. 20543

Chambers of
Justice Lewis F. Powell, Jr.

May 16, 1986
Ronald Straight

MEMORANDUM TO THE CONFERENCE

Ronald Straight is scheduled to be executed in Florida on Tuesday, May 20, 1986. Straight was tried and convicted of one count of first-degree murder in 1977. The evidence at trial showed that Straight and an accomplice had beaten and stabbed the owner of a furniture store, apparently in retaliation for his failure to give the defendants jobs. Straight was sentenced to death. The conviction and sentence were affirmed on direct appeal, 397 So. 2d 903 (Fla. 1981), and this Court denied cert. 454 U.S. 1165 (1981).

Straight then filed his first state habeas petition, claiming, *inter alia,* that the jury instructions at his sentencing proceeding violated the rule of *Lockett v. Ohio,* 438 U.S. 586 (1978). (In conformance with the then-standard practice in Florida, the jury was not told that they could consider nonstatutory mitigating factors.) The TC denied relief, and the Florida Supreme Court affirmed. 422 So. 2d 827 (Fla. 1982). Straight filed his first federal habeas petition, again raising his *Lockett* claim. The DC denied relief, and CA11 affirmed on the ground that the *Lockett* claim was procedurally barred. 772 F.2d 674 (1985).[1] We again denied cert, No. 85–6264 (cert. denied March 31, 1986).

Following the setting of his execution date, Straight sought relief directly from the Florida Supreme Court, once again arguing his *Lockett* claim. Copies of this application have been lodged here. Straight argued that the improper jury instructions prevented him from arguing that (i) the murder was partially a product of his drug dependency, and (ii) the jury should show mercy based on its "non-reasonable" doubts as to Straight's guilt.[2] The Florida Supreme Court denied relief by order on Thursday, May 15.

Straight has now filed another petition for state postconviction relief; that petition is presently pending in a Florida trial court. The Clerk's office informs me that copies of the state habeas petition and a cert petition will be lodged in this Court this evening. Should the TC and Florida Supreme Court then deny relief, Straight plans to file the cert petition and seek a stay in this Court. I will refer any stay application to the Conference, and have requested the Clerk's office to circulate all relevant papers.

/s/
L.F.P., Jr.

cc: Joseph F. Spaniol, Jr.

[1]CA11's position appears to have been erroneous, since the Florida Supreme Court had addressed and decided the *Lockett* claim on state habeas. 422 So. 2d, at 832. See *Ulster County Court v. Allen*, 422 U.S. 140 (1979).

[2]The first part of this argument seems to ignore the fact that the "substantially impaired" capacity of the defendant means he cannot "appreciate the criminality of his conduct or to conform his conduct to the requirements of law." Fla. Stat. Ann. § 921.141(6)(f). Presumably Straight's evidence of drug dependency would have been relevant under this factor. The apparent explanation for defense counsel's failure to so argue is that—as CA11 found—counsel made a strategic choice not to urge any theories of mitigation that might be inconsistent with Straight's innocence. See *Straight v. Wainwright*, 772 F.2d, at 678.

Supreme Court of the United States
Washington, D.C. 20543

Chambers of
Justice Lewis F. Powell, Jr.

May 19, 1986
Ronald Straight

MEMORANDUM TO THE CONFERENCE

Ronald Straight is scheduled to be executed in Florida on Tuesday, May 20, 1986. The history of this case is summarized in my memorandum of May 16, 1986. On Friday, May 16, Straight filed a motion for postconviction relief in state court. The state trial court has denied that motion, and Straight has appealed. The Florida Supreme Court has scheduled a hearing for 10:00 a.m. today on Straight's appeal.

The motion for postconviction relief, an application for a stay, and a petition for certiorari have been lodged in this Court. If the Florida Supreme Court denies relief,

Straight intends to file the stay application and cert petition here—the third time he will have been before this Court.

/s/

L.F.P., Jr.

Supreme Court of the United States
Washington, D.C. 20543

Chambers of
Justice Lewis F. Powell, Jr.

May 20, 1986
85–6947 (A-892) *Straight v. Wainwright*
(Second Application for stay and petition for certiorari)

MEMORANDUM TO THE CONFERENCE:

Four Justices have now voted to stay Straight's execution and hold the cert petition for *Darden v. Wainwright*, 85–5319. I see no justification for holding the cert petition or granting the stay. In my circulating opinion for the Court in *Darden,* I noted that the TC expressly ruled that *any* mitigating evidence could come in. Consequently, the *Lockett* argument made in *Darden* was meritless, and is irrelevant to this case.

There is a cert petition pending in *Hitchcock v. Wainwright,* No. 85–6756 (filed 5/2/86 not yet circulated) that raises the *Lockett* issue more squarely than in *Darden.* In *Hitchcock,* the defendant failed to put on certain mitigating evidence based on his belief that the statute would not permit it. On the basis of a preliminary look, the claim in *Hitchcock* appears to be supported by the record. Moreover, there is no procedural bar in that case.[1]

This case is quite different. Here, the DC—in its opinion that has been circulated—found that all of Straight's claims are barred by Habeas Rule 9, that permits DCs to dismiss successive petitions and petitions that abuse the writ. CAll affirmed the DC decision. We would have to reverse CAll's holding for this Court even to reach the merits of the *Lockett* issue. No basis has been suggested for reversing the procedural rulings of the DC and CAll.

To the extent that Straight is repeating arguments made in his first habeas petition, there have been no changed circumstances that would justify rehearing and deciding those arguments again. (I note that we denied cert on Straight's *Lockett* claim only six weeks ago. No. 85–6264, cert. denied 3/31/86.) And to the extent he is adding new arguments, this is plainly an abuse of the writ. Straight has been relying on various versions of his *Lockett* argument since 1981. He and his lawyers have been fully aware of that argument's significance. The Court has repeatedly stated that it will not tolerate this kind of sandbagging of the judiciary in capital cases. E.g., *Woodard v. Hutchins,* 464 U.S. 377, 378–380 (1984) (POWELL, J., joined by BURGER, C.J., and BLACKMUN, REHNQUIST, and O'CONNOR, JJ., concurring in denial of stay).

For the reasons stated above, this is not a hold for *Darden* or *Hitchcock,* or for any other pending case. My vote therefore is to deny the application for a stay. If the case is held, I will write.

/s/

L.F.P., Jr.

[1]The other cases cited in Bill Brennan's memorandum do not justify holding this case. The petition in *Sireci v. Florida,* No. 84–6895, presently being held for *Darden,* ap-

pears to be an improper hold, as the state habeas court decided the *Lockett* issue on the adequate and independent state-law ground that the issue had been raised and decided on direct appeal. There were only three votes to hold *Sireci*. And *Wainwright v. Songer*, No. 85–567, is being held for *Kuhlmann v. Wilson*, No. 84–1479, not for *Darden*. The issue in both *Songer* and in *Kuhlmann* is whether, and under what circumstances, a federal court abuses its discretion in *choosing to decide* a successive habeas petition on the merits. No one doubts that a DC has some discretion *not* to decide such petitions on the merits. Moreover, there was no finding of abuse of the writ in *Songer*, as there is in this case.

33. Spaziano v. State of Florida, hearing on application for stay of execution, Nov. 25, 1985 (Cir. Ct., Seminole County, Judge Robert McGregor).

34. Von Drehle, *Among Lowest of the Dead, supra* n. 3.

35. This (not terribly original) term was used in the context of Nazi doctors by Robert Jay Lifton, *The Nazi Doctors: Medical Killing and the Psychology of Genocide* 418 (1986). See also Hugh Gallagher, *By Trust Betrayed: Patients, Physicians, and the License to Kill in the Third Reich* (1990). Of more direct interest are Robert Weisberg, *Poethics* 127–75 (1992) (role of lawyers in Vichy France); Ingo Müller, *Hitler's Justice: The Courts of the Third Reich* (1991); Arkadii Vaksberg, *Stalin's Prosecutors* (1991).

36. Samuel Hazo, *The Holy Surprise of Right Now* (1996).

37. E.g., Sullivan v. Wainwright, 464 U.S. 109, 112 (1983) (Burger, C.J., concurring in denial of stay) (accusing death penalty lawyers of turning "the administration of justice into a sporting contest"); Gray v. Lucas, 463 U.S. 1237, 1240 (1983) (Burger, C.J., concurring in denial of certiorari and denial of application for stay) ("This case illustrates a recent pattern of calculated efforts to frustrate valid judgments after painstaking judicial review over a number of years.").

38. Mack Reed, "Dearth of Attorneys," *Los Angeles Times*, April 4, 1996. See also Kathleen Berexa, "A Very Lonely Job," *Pittsburgh Legal Journal*, May 19, 1995.

39. On Florida's jury override generally, see Michael Radelet and Michael Mello, "Death-to-Life Overrides," 20 *Florida State University Law Review* 195 (1992); Michael Mello, "The Jurisdiction to Do Justice: Florida's Jury Override and the State Constitution," 18 *Florida State University Law Review* 923 (1991); Michael Mello, "Taking *Caldwell v. Mississippi* Seriously: The Unconstitutionality of Capital Statutes That Divide Sentencing Responsibility between Judge and Jury," 29 *Boston College Law Review* 233–84 (1989); Michael Mello and Ruthann Robson, "Judge over Jury: Florida's Practice of Imposing Death over Life in Capital Cases," 13 *Florida State University Law Review* 31–75 (1985).

40. Ruthann Robson and Michael Mello, "Ariadne's Provisions: A 'Clue of Thread' to the Intricacies of Procedural Default, Adequate and Independent State Grounds, and Florida's Death Penalty," 76 *California Law Review* 87 (1988); Dugger v. Adams, 489 U.S. 401, 405 (1989).

41. Coleman v. Thompson, 501 U.S. 722, 729 (1991); Wainwright v. Sykes, 433 U.S. 72, 81, 87 (1977).

42. Lori Rosza, "Witness: Don't Kill Convict: My Testimony in '76 Unreliable, He Says," *Miami Herald*, June 11, 1995; Lori Rosza, "A Witness Recants but Electric Chair Looms: Recalling a Story of Sex, Murder," *Miami Herald*, Sept. 6, 1995;

Lori Rosza, " 'Crazy Joe' Trial Witness Told Pastor That He Lied," *Miami Herald,* Sept. 21, 1995; James Kilpatrick, "Florida May Kill the Wrong Man," *Cincinnati Enquirer,* June 15, 1995; Tony Proscio, " 'Memory' of Murder, Mockery of Justice," *Miami Herald,* June 14, 1995; Tony Proscio, "Anatomy of a Lie: The 'Crazy Joe' Story," *Miami Herald,* Sept. 8, 1995; Tom Fiedler, "Taking the Politics Out of Capital Punishment," *Miami Herald,* June 18, 1995; Martin Dyckman, "Call Again for Clemency," *St. Petersburg Times,* June 13, 1995; Tom Blackburn, "The Hypnotist Got What He Wanted," *Palm Beach Post,* June 19, 1995; "The Clemency Factor," *Gainesville Sun,* June 14, 1995; "Too Much Doubt in Spaziano Case," *Tampa Tribune,* June 17, 1995; "Time Is Running out," *St. Petersburg Times,* June 15, 1995; "Chiles Spared Florida from Capital Crime," *Palm Beach Post,* June 16, 1995; "Recover a Little Justice: Give Spaziano a New Trial," *Palm Beach Post,* Sept. 12, 1995.

43. *ABC World News Tonight* (June 30, 1995); Bruce Shapiro, "Not for Burning: Probability of Habeas Corpus Reform," *The Nation,* July 17–24, 1995, at 79; "Notebook," *New Republic,* July 17, 1995, at 8, 9, and July 24, 1995, at 8, 9; William Booth, "Gov. Chiles Halts Execution after Witness Recants; Florida Case of 'Crazy Joe' Spaziano, Which Hinged on Hypnosis, Spurs Death Penalty Debate," *Washington Post,* June 17, 1995; Coleman McCarthy, "The Case of the Hypnotized Witness," *Washington Post,* Aug. 5, 1995; David Von Drehle, "A Hypnotized Witness," *Washington Post,* Sept. 15, 1995; "Change of Heart," *The Economist,* June 24, 1995, at 28.

44. Gene Miller, *Invitation to a Lynching* (1975).

45. Michael Mello, "Innocent Man Faces Execution," *Miami Herald,* June 4, 1995; Michael Mello, "Does This Man Deserve to Die?" *St. Petersburg Times,* June 4, 1995; Michael Mello, "Did Tainted Testimony Doom Man?" *Orlando Sentinel,* June 4, 1995.

46. The Eleventh Circuit's opinion was written by Judge "Ed" Carnes. I opposed Judge Carnes's appointment publicly. See Letter from Mello to Editor, *Rutland Herald,* May 11, 1992. So did many other folks. E.g., Statement of Stephen Bright to Senate Judiciary Committee (April 1, 1992); Statement of Julius Chambers (April 1, 1992); Transcript of Proceedings, Senate Judiciary Committee (April 1, 1992); Press Release, Congressional Black Caucus, July 8, 1992; Nat Hentoff, "The Executioner Who Would Be a Judge," *Village Voice,* July 7, 1992, at 22; Nat Hentoff, "The Dishonoring of Heroic Judge," *Village Voice,* July 17, 1992; Tyrone Brooks, "It's Time for America to End Policy of Racial Exclusion in Federal Judiciary," *Atlanta Journal/Constitution,* July 23, 1992; Nat Hentoff, "Ed Carnes and the Execution of a Retarded Man," *Village Voice,* 1992; Letter from John Conyers to Joseph Biden (May 6, 1992); Lynne Duke, "Black Caucus Fights Judicial Nominee," *Washington Post,* July 30, 1992; Editorial, "Stop Carnes Nomination," *Atlanta Constitution,* July 31, 1992; *Congressional Record*—Senate, S11899 (Aug. 7, 1992); Letter from Mexican American Legal Defense Fund (Aug. 31, 1992); Stan Bailey, "Opponent Built Career Fighting What Carnes Defends—the Death Penalty," *Birmingham Post,* Aug. 30, 1992; Michael Brumas, "Foes, Supporters Lobby as Senate Vote Approaches on Judgeship Next Week," *Birmingham News,* Aug. 30, 1992; Nat Hentoff, "Not the Right Man for a Court of Last Resort," *Washington Post,* Aug 29, 1992; Editorial, "Senate Should Refuse Carnes' Confirmation," *The Tennessean,* Sept. 5, 1992; Editorial, "The Carnes Nomination: Talk

It Down," *New York Times,* Aug. 8, 1992; Editorial, "Keep Ed Carnes off the Bench," *Atlanta Journal,* Sept. 6, 1992; Neil Lewis, "Court Nominee Is Confirmed after Angry Senate Debate," *New York Times,* Sept. 10, 1992; Editorial, "A Shameful Judicial Nomination," *Atlanta Constitution,* Feb. 10, 1992; Editorial, "Another Bad Nomination by Bush," *Dayton Daily News,* April 13, 1992; Anthony Lewis, "Straight and Narrow," *New York Times,* April 16, 1992; Monroe Freedman, "Prosecutor behind the Bench," *Legal Times,* April 20, 1992, at 22; Ronald Smothers, "Court Nominee under Attack over Death Penalty," *New York Times,* March 27, 1992; Statement of NAACP, Senate Judiciary Committee (April 1, 1992); Editorial, "Wrong Man, Wrong Time," *St. Petersburg Times,* June 22, 1992; Editorial, "Tradition Gets Benched," June 18, 1992; Nat Hentoff, "Wrong Judge for the Job," *Washington Post,* June 16, 1992; Letter from Senator Joseph Biden to Colleagues (June 12, 1992); Letter from Concerned Black Clergy, Georgia Civil Rights Network, Clergy and Laity Concerned to Senator Wyche Fowler (June 12, 1992); Editorial, "Color Blindness," *Fayetteville Observer, Times,* June 8, 1992; Editorial, "Where's Sen. Fowler on Carnes?" *Atlanta Constitution,* May 31, 1992; Editorial, "Replacing Judge Johnson: Try Harder," *New York Times,* May 31, 1992; Martin Tolchin, "Court Nominee Splits Advocates of Civil Rights," *New York Times,* June 11, 1992; Editorial, "More Reagan/Bush Hangin' Judges on Way," *Philadelphia Daily News,* May 19, 1992; Editorial, "Nomination by Bush Terrible," *Tallahassee Democrat,* April 23, 1992; Howard Troxler, "A Certain Joyfulness in Pursuit of Death," *St. Petersburg Times,* May 4, 1992; Editorial, "Carnes Comes to Judgment," *Huntsville News,* May 6, 1992; Editorial, "Appellate Nomination Takes a Slap at Justice," *Palm Beach Post,* April 18, 1992; Coleman McCarthy, "Less Than a Thorough Search for Justice," *Washington Post,* April 28, 1992; Marcia Coyle, "Carnes to 11th Circuit?" *National Law Journal,* May 4, 1992, at 1; Editorial, "What's the Rush?" *National Law Journal,* May 4, 1992, at 14; Editorial, "This Death Penalty Advocate Should Not Make Federal Judge," *News Journal* (Wilmington, Del.), April 20, 1992.

47. Cf. Stanley Milgram, *Obedience to Authority* 3–4 (1974).

48. Michael Mello, Draft of Editorial: "Save an Innocent Man, the Courts Refuse" (June 4, 1995) (on file with author). DiLisio's name appears variously as DeLisio, Delisio, and Dilisio in different records.

49. James Kilpatrick, "Facts Undermine Case against Crazy Joe," *Tampa Tribune,* June 9, 1995.

50. Tim Mickins and Lori Rosza, "Chiles Considers Staying Execution of Joe Spaziano," *Miami Herald,* June 15, 1995; Tim Mickins and Lori Rosza, "Governor Chiles Steps In; Execution Called Off," *Miami Herald,* June 16, 1995.

51. "Notebook," *supra* n. 43; Shapiro, *supra* n. 43; Linda Gibson, "Happy Birthday, Mr. Spaziano: Court Gives "Crazy Joe" 11th-Hour Reprieve," *National Law Journal,* Sept. 25, 1995, at A10; Booth, *supra* n. 43; Scott Pendleton, "When Innocence Gets Short Shrift," *Christian Science Monitor,* June 26, 1995, at 1; "Change of Heart," *supra* n. 43; *ABC World News Tonight, supra* n. 43.

52. Letter from Lawton Chiles, Governor of Florida, to James Moore, Commissioner, FDLE 1 (Aug. 17, 1995).

53. Spaziano v. State, 660 So. 2d 1363, cert. denied, 116 S. Ct. 722 (1996). The matter of the sealed report was challenged in Joseph Spaziano's Request to

Enforce Rights. Brief for Joseph Spaziano, Spaziano v. State, 660 So. 2d 1363 (Fla. 1995).

54. Lori Rosza, "Chiles Got a Flawed Report on 'Crazy Joe,' " *Miami Herald,* Sept. 17, 1995.

55. Mike Griffin, "Chiles to OK Spaziano's Death," *Orlando Sentinel,* Aug. 24, 1995. An editorial in the *Orlando Sentinel* supported Chiles' decision. "Justice for Spaziano," *Orlando Sentinel,* Aug. 25, 1995.

56. Memorandum from Michael Mello to Folks, Aug. 27, 1995.

57. Motion for Relief by CCR, *In re* Rule of Criminal Procedure 3.851, No. 82,322 (filed in Florida Supreme Court June 23, 1995); Supplement to Motion for Relief, *supra,* at 2 ("Even before the closing of the Resource Center was announced, CCR had notified this Court of its inability, due to underfunding, to carry out the statutory mandate of representing all its present and potential clients within the time limits established by Rule 3.851"); CCR's Motion for Clarification, *supra* at 3 ("We respectfully reassert that we are not adequately funded due to the confluence of the one-year filing time with the unprecedented rate of direct appeal affirmances"); Pleading Regarding Status of Counsel, *In re* Jerry White, No. 86,706 (filed Oct. 19, 1995), at 1–2 ("Jerry White is currently unrepresented and is therefore without counsel to assist him during his pending death warrant [. CCR] further notifies the Court that [CCR] . . . is presently unable to fulfill its statutory obligation to provide the effective assistance of counsel to Mr. White during this critical warrant period"); *id.* at 8 ("Those warrants have come at a time of great vulnerability and crisis for those attempting to provide counsel to approximately 200 death-sentenced"); *id.* at 10 ("CCR is so swamped it has not assigned counsel to twenty-five clients when such assignment is required. . . . Thus [*sic*] inadequacy of resources for post-conviction counsel has been brought to this court's attention in the recent past. The deteriorating situation was described"); *id.* at 12 ("The stream of new clients likely to be coming to CCR in the ensuing months as volunteer lawyers drop off portends a constant tension between the clients already assigned to CCR and ones which come here from other counsel in various stages of litigation, including those like Jerry White with an active warrant but no lawyer"); *id.* at 14 ("Jerry White has a death warrant and no attorney. CCR cannot give him adequate representation in the time remaining before the execution. Attempting to do so forsakes the interests of some other client or clients. This predicament is a direct result of an unusually large number of affirmed death sentences coupled with the legislature's failure to increase the CCR budget at all"); *id.* at 16 ("CCR cannot render effective representation to Mr. White"); *id.* at 27 ("CCR cannot render effective representation to Mr. White"); Summary of Initial Brief, White v. State, No. 86,900 (filed Dec. 1, 1995), at 72 ("It has become apparent during these past several weeks that Mr. White has not been receiving the effective assistance of counsel"); *id.* at 77 ("Mr. White is not receiving the effective assistance of counsel").

58. An office's caseload raises serious ethical dilemmas, which have led courts and commentators to conclude that such workloads render effective representation impossible. E.g., Cooper v. Fitzharris, 551 F.2d 1162 (9th Cir. 1977), *modified,* 586 F.2d 1325 (9th Cir. 1978); State v. Smith, 140 Ariz. 355, 362, 681 P.2d 1374,

1381 (1984) (en banc); Schwarz v. Cianca, 495 So. 2d 1208, 1209 (Fla. Dist. Ct. App. 1986); State ex rel. Escambia County v. Behr, 354 So. 2d 974, 975 (Fla. Dist. Ct. App. 1978), *aff'd*, 384 So. 2d 147 (Fla. 1980); Note, "The Right to Counsel and the Indigent Defense System," 14 *New York University Review of Law and Social Change* 221, 221–23, 240–41 (1986). For an example of an argument that underfunding might generate systemwide ineffective assistance of counsel, see Samuel Stretton, "Defense of the Indigent Criminal Defendant: When Does the System Become Unethical?" *The Champion*, Sept.–Oct. 1991, at 26.

59. AP, "2nd Killer Dies 22 Hours Later," *St. Petersburg Times*, Dec. 6, 1995. "Atkins' attorneys argued unsuccessfully that the execution should be stopped because the electric chair had malfunctioned in an execution 22 hours earlier. Early Monday afternoon, convicted killer Jerry White uttered a short, muffled scream as he was being put to death. Atkins' attorneys said the scream was evidence that the chair wasn't working properly." *Id.*

60. "The execution marked the first time in Florida history that two inmates were put to death on consecutive days." *Id.*

61. E.g., Letter from Daniel Remeta to Michael Mello (April 18, 1996); Letter from Judith Remeta to Michael Mello (April 16, 1996). Since fall 1995 I have received letters from 16 death row clients of CCR who would drop CCR in a heartbeat if any alternative form of legal aid were available to them. The shotgun marriage between CCR and its clients gives new meaning to the phrase "captive audience."

62. See generally Death Penalty Information Center (DPIC), *With Justice for Few: The Growing Crisis in Death Penalty Representation* (1995); Haftali Remauid, "Death Penalty Centers: RIP?" *Legal Times*, August 7, 1995, at 1; Lis Wiehl, "Program for Death-Row Appeals Facing Its Own Demise," *New York Times*, Aug. 11, 1995; Editorial, "LSC: $278 M; Death Row: 0," *National Law Journal*, July 31, 1995.

63. Letter from Robert Shevin to Chief Justice Stephen Grimes, Feb. 26, 1996.

64. *Id.* at 8.

65. *Id.* at 6.

66. *Id.* at 13.

67. *Id.*

68. Spaziano v. State, 660 So. 2d 1363 (1994 and 1997 *Supp.*).

69. See generally James Liebman and Randy Hertz, *Federal Habeas Corpus Practice and Procedure* (2nd ed. 1995).

70. Attorney General Jim Smith took this position. See Mello, "Facing Death Alone," *supra* n. 1, at 601–3.

71. *Id.* at 567–99.

72. *Id.* at 567–85; see also Amy Singer, "Enemies under the Same Roof," *American Lawyer*, Jan.–Feb. (1988).

73. Mello, "Facing Death Alone," *supra* n. 1.

74. *Id.* at 593–99.

75. *Id.* at 597–99.

76. *Id.* at 600–602.

77. *Id.* at 600–601.

78. Memorandum on Capital Case Representation for Indigents in Florida, from Judge Alacorn to Judge Cox and Judge Cedarbaus.

79. *Id.* at 6.

80. *Id.* at 7.

81. *Id.*

82. *Id.*

83. *Id.*

84. *Id.*

85. DPIC, *With Justice for Few supra* note 62 at 19.

86. So did others. The Georgia office decided as a matter of policy not to file successive habeas petitions: the small chance of success in getting a stay didn't outweigh costs in a time of scarce resources.

87. Spaziano v. State, 660 So. 2d 1363 (Fla. 1995).

88. John McKinnon, "It's Getting Harder to Find Legal Aid for Death Row," *Miami Herald,* June 24, 1995.

89. *Id.*

90. *Id.*

91. Statute § 29, adding a new § 35(b) to the Judiciary Law.

92. 1995 Committee Bill Memorandum at 16 [hereinafter Memo].

93. *Id.* at 17.

94. James Traub, "The Life Preserver," *New Yorker,* April 1996.

95. Memo at 22.

96. Memo filed with SB 2850, at 4.

97. *Id.* at 5.

98. *Id.* at 5.

99. *Id.*

100. *Id.*

101. Ronald J. Tabak et al., 22 *Fordham Urban Law Journal* 597, 611 (1995).

102. Al O'Connor, "New York's Death Penalty Law: An Overview," *Public Defense Backup Center Report* at 8 (March–April 1995).

103. *Id.*

104. E.g., *New York Times* article.

105. Traub, *supra* n. 94 at 47.

106. E.g., Joseph Berger, "A Potential Death Penalty Case in New York Garners a Prime Legal Team," *New York Times,* Nov. 8, 1995; Jan Hoffman, "Lawyers Prepare for New York's Death Penalty," *New York Times,* Aug. 31, 1995.

107. Klein, 68 *Indiana Law Journal* 363 (1993).

108. New York's brand-new capital statute did not get off to a promising start. When the Bronx district attorney—who personally opposes the death penalty—indicated that he would not seek a capital indictment for an accused cop-killer, the governor removed him from the case. E.g., Rachel Swarns, "Prosecutor Resists Pataki on Death Penalty," *New York Times,* March 21, 1996; Rachel Swarns, "Governor Removes Bronx Prosecutor from Murder Case," *New York Times,* March 22, 1996; Rachel Swarns, "District Attorney Sues Pataki over Ouster from Case," *New York Times,* April 19, 1996; Jan Hoffman, "Death Penalty Raises Issues of Obligation of Prosecutor," *New York Times,* March 17, 1996; Derrick

Jackson, "Death Penalty Dissenters," *Boston Globe,* March 29, 1996; Editorial, "A Bronx Cheer," *The Nation,* April 15, 1996, at 5. For an interesting take on the governor's capital prosecutor of choice, see Jan Hoffman, "Lawyers Prepare for New York's Death Penalty," *New York Times,* Aug. 31, 1995, at A1.

Now, does anyone honestly believe that this governor will push (or, indeed, even permit) anything more than the constitutional rock-bottom minimum for defense resources?

109. Robert Cover, "Violence and the Word," *95 Yale Law Journal* 1601, 1601 (1986).

110. Austin Sarat, "Violence, Representation, and Responsibility in Capital Trials," *70 Indiana Law Journal* 1103, 1110 (1995).

111. *Id.* at 1110.

112. Robert Weisberg, "Deregulating Death," *1983 Supreme Court Review* 305, 385.

113. Kevin Cullen, "Nun's Finally Heard," *Boston Globe,* April 11, 1996.

114. For a superb treatment of this shift, see Herbert Haines, *Against Capital Punishment* (1996).

115. David Robertson, "Country Legacy," *9 Witness* 44, 44 (1995).

116. See Fred Marchant's poem "Malebolge" in *Tipping Point* (1993).

117. See generally Isaiah Trunk, *Judenrat* (1972); Ruth Bondy, *Elder of the Jews: Jacob Edelstein of Theresienstadt* (1981).

118. David Lewis Stokes is right that Heidegger "towers as this century's premier philosopher. Like Hegel's before him, Heidegger's heirs span contemporary culture, from that textual whirling dervish, Jacques Derrida, to the luminous critic, George Steiner. Heidegger continues to beckon the wise and stupid, the way Mount Everest used to draw the skilled and the reckless."

Heidegger also was a virulent anti-Semite who embraced National Socialism as a wise career move—on the most charitable reading of the evidence. E.g., *The Heidegger Controversy: A Critical Reader* (Richard Wolin, ed. 1991); *The Heidegger Case: On Philosophy and Politics* (Tom Rockmore, ed. 1992); Gunther Neske and Emil Kettering, *Martin Heidegger and National Socialism* (1990); Victor Farias, *Heidegger and Nazism* (1987); Edith Wyschograd, *Spirit in Ashes* (1985); Tom Rockmore, *On Heidegger's Nazism and Philosophy* (1992); Hugo Ott, *Martin Heidegger: A Political Life* (1993).

The Arendt/Heidegger relationship is examined through their letters in Elzbieta Ettinger, *Hannah Arendt/Martin Heidegger* (1995).

119. E.g., Christopher Browning, *Ordinary Men* (1994); Daniel Goldhagen, *Hitler's Willing Executioners* (1996).

120. The point can be made about Hitler himself. How, for instance, do we deal with Hitler's baby pictures? See Ron Rosenbaum, *New Yorker,* March 24, 1995.

121. Robert Weisberg, *Poethics* 137–58, 167–72 (1992); but see Richard Posner, *Law and Literature* 173–74 (1988). On Vichy France, see Ted Morgan, *An Uncertain Hour: The French, the Germans, the Jews, the Klaus Barbie Trial, and the City of Lyon, 1940–1945* (1990); Judith Miller, *One, By One, By One: Facing the Holocaust* (1990); Henry Rousso, *The Vichy Syndrome: History and Memory*

in France since 1944 (1991); Alain Finkielkraut, *Remembering in Vain: The Klaus Barbie Trial and Crimes against Humanity* (1989); Robert Soucy, *French Fascism: The Second Wave, 1933–1939* (1995); Erhard Dabringhaus, *Klaus Barbie: The Shocking Story of How the U.S. Used This Nazi War Criminal as an Intelligence Agent* (1984); Annette Kahn, *Why My Father Died: A Daughter Confronts Her Family's Past at the Trial of Klaus Barbie* (1991); Alice Kaplan, *French Lessons: A Memoir* (1993); Lawrence D. Kritzman, *Auschwitz and After: Race, Culture, and "the Jewish Question" in France* (1995); Susan Zuccotti, *The Holocaust, the French, and the Jews* (1993).

122. Eugene Genovese, *The Southern Front* (1995).

123. Dr. Miklos Nyiszli, *Auschwitz: A Doctor's Eyewitness Account* (1960); Götz Aly, Peter Chroust, and Christian Pross, *Cleansing the Fatherland: Nazi Medicine and Racial Hygiene* (1994); Hugh Gregory Gallagher, *By Trust Betrayed: Patients, Physicians, and the License to Kill in the Third Reich* (1990); Samuel Drix, M.D., *Witness to Annihilation: Surviving the Holocaust: A Memoir* (1994); Robert Jay Lifton, *The Nazi Doctors: Medical Killing and the Psychology of Genocide* (1986); Benjamin Jacobs, *The Dentist of Auschwitz: A Memoir* (1995).

124. It seems fair to conclude that Heidegger's unworldly philosophy was not of much actual use to the Nazi regime. Still, Heidegger *wanted* to provide the National Socialist revolution with a bona fide philosophical foundation. At least he did in the 1930s.

My point is not that Heidegger did or did not want to be of use to the Nazis. My point is that Heidegger's relationship with the Third Reich is an example of a self-delusion—not uncommon among very smart people—that if only he could find his way to the centers of power, he could turn the revolutionary energies of the regime to philosophical purposes. His rectorate at Freiburg may have seemed important to his attempt to reorganize the faculties of his university so as to protect the various humane disciplines from what he thought was the threat of technology; he may well have thought, and hoped, that he could thereafter mold National Socialism into an instrument of Heideggerian philosophy.

125. Permit me to reply in advance to a possible response to this argument. I am not "burned out." From the time I began doing deathwork in 1983, I have been acutely aware of the dangers of burnout; from early on I've tried to live Susan Cary's admonition that deathwork is a marathon, not a sprint.

So I've paced myself. I quite self-consciously left CCR *before* I became burned out. In the ten years since leaving CCR, I've calibrated my quantity of casework to hold burnout at bay. In fact, I've never felt stronger or more zealous in my desire to fight the system of capital punishment; to paraphrase Richard Nixon, "I'm tanned, rested and ready for the comeback trail."

I love this work; I'll always love this work. Far from burning me out, my recent *Spaziano* experiences have *energized* me: energized me to write and argue and teach. But not to represent condemned people in postconviction proceedings.

The course of action recommended by this chapter flows logically from my own and other scholars' extensively documented critique of capital punishment as a system, if one takes that critique seriously. If that system *really* is as unjust as we say it is—and my experience leaves no doubt in my mind that it is, and that it will continue to be so *regardless* of what we do—we must decide whether the costs of participation outweigh the benefits of saving a few lives here or there.

Not that I deny the pain; far from it, my own anger and frustration and disgust with this lawless monster is one narrative and affective theme of this book.

The fact is that death row demographics are such that more and more people are going to be executed in the years to come. We postconviction attorneys might be able to use litigation to influence the timing of these executions but regardless of what we do, the killing will increase in frequency. The question for us ought to be whether marginal victories justify the aura of legitimacy with which our participation infuses the system. *That* (and, increasingly, not much more than that) *is* within our power to control.

I'm not suggesting that our refusal to participate will shut the system down at once—but that's not the right question, because our continued participation won't shut it down quickly, either. What our conscientious abstention *might* do is shame the system. Shaming uses the infliction of reputational harm to perform an expressive function. A general strike would convey our disgust.

That shaming might push the system toward meaningful change, but I doubt it; and, in any event, such utilitarian interests are not at the core of my proposal. The core intent of my proposal is encapsulated within the lines from Siegfried Sassoon quoted at the beginning of this book: "Possess your soul; that you alone can save."

There is a world of difference between being a quitter and being a realist. I tried to articulate this difference to Joe Spaziano in the summer of 1995:

Spooner, Wisconsin
June 21, 1995

Dear Joe:

I just received your letters today. (My law school secretary express mailed them to me here in Wisconsin.) . . .

Second, I have *some* good news. *Please don't get your hopes up,* but the Florida Supreme Court seems to be taking our motion seriously. The justices go on vacation tomorrow until mid-August, which means that they won't rule on the motion until mid-August. That *probably* means that Chiles won't sign another warrant until mid-August, at the earliest. Between now and August, I'm trying to put together a letter-writing campaign to the Governor. The Sons of Italy are going to get involved in your case. They asked me to write an article for the August 1 issue of their national newspaper—which has a circulation of four million. Lori and ABC are still investigating your case; I speak with them every other day or so. We're all trying to regroup our forces so that, *if* another warrant comes, we'll be ready to mobilize a pretty impressive army of political muscle.

Third, I don't want you to think that I'm quitting the struggle against capital punishment. *No way.* Never. Not until the last dog comes home. I'll *never* give up this fight. *Never.*

What I *am* doing is changing the arena in which I will carry on the fight. When I thought that the place to win this fight was in the courts, then I fought in the courts. I'm a lawyer, and our battleground is in court.

But now I believe that I can do more good outside of court. Sure, I'm a lawyer, but I'm also a writer—and, I have discovered over the past two months, I seem to be a pretty decent writer. What I seem to be able to do is to write about legal issues in a way that non-lawyers can understand.

373

Keep in mind, my friend, that of all the legal briefs I've written in your case over the past twelve years, none of them did the slightest good. The only thing I've ever written in your case that *mattered* was the twelve-page opinion piece I wrote for the *Miami Herald* on June 4.

The only way to get rid of capital punishment, I have become convinced, is to tell the stories of people like you. And not to tell those stories to judges whose principal agenda is to find some legal technicality to permit them to ignore the stories we are trying to tell them. We need to tell these stories to people who will listen to them and who, maybe—if we tell them enough *true* stories—will understand that capital punishment isn't an abstract political thing. Capital punishment is a large collection of stories.

So: I'm not giving up the fight. I am trying to change the battleground, from the court of law to the court of public opinion. I might well be wrong about all of this, and if I am, then I'll go back to being a lawyer and only a lawyer. But I have to try this other way.

In the meantime, I will always be *your* lawyer, until you or your family decide otherwise. I told you in 1985, during the first warrant, that I'm in this with you for the long haul. This is a marathon, not a sprint. You're not in this alone; we're not in it alone. It's a team effort, and we've put together a *hell* of a good team ("the best defense no money can buy"). With the help of God and the *Miami Herald,* we'll cross the finish line together. And alive. And free.

Take care, my friend. And write.

Sincerely,
Crazy Michael

It is a commonplace that human life cannot be assigned a value, because it can never be replaced. My experience leaves me convinced that the criminal justice system decides life and death on the basis of luck, chance warped by racism and poverty, and therefore has no business deciding who lives and who dies.

126. David Cole, "Courting Capital Punishment," *The Nation,* Feb. 26, 1996, at 19. See also Daniel Slocum Hinerfeld, "No Appeal Means No Execution," *Los Angeles Times,* July 5, 1996.

127. The Supreme Court held in Coker v. Georgia, 433 U.S. 72 (1977), that capital punishment is an unconstitutionally disproportionate penalty for the crime of rape of an adult woman. Drawing upon deconstructionist and feminist literary theory, as well as upon critiques of the legal responses to rape, this piece would suggest that the bases of the Court's holding were grounded in misconceptions (1) about the harm of rape, and (2) about the efficacy of using "objective" indicia to identify the United States' understanding of rape. Then, with an appropriate appreciation of the harm actually inflicted by the crime of rape—and *only* then—can one measure that harm against the proportionality standard set out by the Supreme Court. And that proportionality test is no longer *Coker v. Georgia; Coker's* proportionality analysis has been superseded by the proportionality analysis set out in *Tison v. Arizona* and *Stanford v. Kentucky.* The article would then offer an alternative basis for the Court's holding: that capital punishment for rape is unconstitutional because it was (and would be today) applied in a racist manner. However, *McCleskey v. Kemp* suggests that such a challenge would fail.

Index

ABA. *See* American Bar Association

Ables, Alan, 15

Abu-Jamal, Mumia, 295*n82*

abuse: child, 64, 113, 164, 215, 324*n155*; domestic, 285*n25*, 326*n170*. *See also* murder(s); rape

"abuse of the writ" doctrine, 156, 165, 178, 205, 238, 362*n32*, 364*n32*

Acker, James, 201

ACLU, 76, 326*n168*

A.D. (Millett), 86

Adams, (Aubrey) Dennis, 58, 111, 170–73, 317*n111*

Adams, James, 58, 69, 87, 145, 337*n50*

Adams, Randall Dale, 18, 29

Against Our Will (Brownmiller), 118

Agan, James, 191, 249

Alabama: capital sentencing in, 31; chain gangs in, 19; death penalty resource center in, 259; death penalty statute of, 47; inmates in, 155; Mello's work for Judge Vance in, 44–55; number of executions in, 17; as part of "Death Belt," 19, 44, 45; postconviction lawyers not provided by, 91. *See also* Eleventh Circuit Court of Appeals

Albany Law Review, 201

Albany School of Criminal Justice, 201

Albert, Jane, 206–7

alcohol, 76, 85

Alexandria Hospital (Virginia), 81

Alvarez, Nina, 236

Amadeo v. Zant, 163–64

American Academy of Forensic Sciences, 138

American Academy of Psychiatry and the Law, 90

American Bar Association (ABA): on death row inmates, 91, 135, 322*n151;* and Mello, 76, 77; on need for competent postconviction lawyers, 135, 187, 354–55*n309;* Rehnquist's speech before, 91; on resources consumed by capital cases, 158–62, 203

American Bar Association Postconviction Death Penalty Representation Project, 355*n309*

American Jewish Committee, 76

American Jewish Congress, 76

American Psycho (Ellis), 309*n10*

An American Tragedy (Dreiser), 271

Amis, Martin, 50, 259

Amnesty International, 13, 135

Among the Lowest of the Dead (Von Drehle), 88, 92

Amsterdam, Anthony, 68, 129, 343*nn78, 80*

Amtrak Corporation, 57

Anderson, Walter Truett, 39

Angle of Repose (Stegner), 124

Angola State Prison (Louisiana), 7

Antone, Anthony, 58, 69, 175–78, 186, 298*n96*, 340*n63*

Antonio, Walter Jeno, 284*n25*, 327*n180*

Archimedes, 243

Arendt, Hannah, 11, 56, 84, 219, 262–65

Aristotle, 48, 361*n28*

Arizona, 17, 20, 360*n17*

Arkansas, 15–17

Armatrading, Joan, 71

375

379

Index

Index